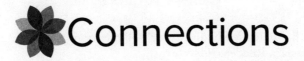Connections

Editorial Board

Connections

A Lectionary Commentary for Preaching and Worship

Joel B. Green

Thomas G. Long

Luke A. Powery

Cynthia L. Rigby

General Editors

WESTMINSTER
JOHN KNOX PRESS
LOUISVILLE · KENTUCKY

2018 Westminster John Knox Press

First edition
Published by Westminster John Knox Press
Louisville, Kentucky

18 19 20 21 22 23 24 25 26 27—10 9 8 7 6 5 4 3 2 1

Unless otherwise indicated, Scripture quotations are from the New Revised Standard Version of the Bible, copyright © 1989 by the Division of Christian Education of the National Council of the Churches of Christ in the U.S.A., and are used by permission. Scripture quotations marked NET are from the NET Bible® copyright ©1996-2006 by Biblical Studies Press, L.L.C. http://bible .org. All rights reserved. Scripture quotations marked NIV are from *The Holy Bible, New International Version*. Copyright © 1973, 1978, 1984, 2011 by Biblica, Inc.® Used by permission. All rights reserved worldwide. Scripture quotations marked NLT are from the Holy Bible, New Living Translation, copyright 1996, 2004. Used by permission of Tyndale House Publishers, Inc., Wheaton, Illinois 60189. All rights reserved.

Excerpt from *Preaching in the Age of Chaucer: Selected Sermons in Translation,* translated by Siegfried Wenzel. Copyright 2008 Catholic University of America Press. Republished with permission of Catholic University of America Press; permission conveyed through Copyright Clearance Center, Inc. Excerpt from *Luther's Works Vol. 12* © 1957 Concordia Publishing House. Used with permission. www.cph.org. Excerpt from pp. 190-91 from *Living under Tension* by Harry Emerson Fosdick. Copyright 1941 by Harper & Brothers. Copyright renewed © 1968 by Harry Emerson Fosdick. Reprinted by permission of HarperCollins Publishers. Excerpt from *Breaking the Fine Rain of Death: African American Health Issues and a Womanist Ethic of Care* by Emilie M. Townes. Copyright 1998 by Emilie M. Townes. Used by permission of Wipf and Stock Publishers. www.wipfandstock.com.

Book and cover design by Allison Taylor

The Library of Congress has cataloged an earlier edition as follows:
Names: Long, Thomas G., 1946- editor.
Title: Connections : a lectionary commentary for preaching and worship / Joel
  B. Green, Thomas G. Long, Luke A. Powery, Cynthia L. Rigby, general
  editors.
Description: Louisville, Kentucky : Westminster John Knox Press, 2018- |
  Includes index. |
Identifiers: LCCN 2018006372 (print) | LCCN 2018012579 (ebook) | ISBN
  9781611648874 (ebk.) | ISBN 9780664262433 (volume 1 : hbk. : alk. paper)
Subjects: LCSH: Lectionary preaching. | Bible--Meditations. | Common
  lectionary (1992) | Lectionaries.
Classification: LCC BV4235.L43 (ebook) | LCC BV4235.L43 C66 2018 (print) |
  DDC 251/.6--dc23
LC record available at https://lccn.loc.gov/2018006372

Connections: Year C, Volume 2
ISBN: 9780664262440 (hardback)
ISBN: 9780664264864 (paperback)
ISBN: 97816116490 (ebook)

PRINTED IN THE UNITED STATES OF AMERICA

♾ The paper used in this publication meets the minimum requirements of the American National Standard for Information Sciences—Permanence of Paper for Printed Library Materials, ANSI Z39.48-1992.

Westminster John Knox Press advocates the responsible use of our natural resources. The text paper of this book is made from 30% postconsumer waste.

Most Westminster John Knox Press books are available at special quantity discounts when purchased in bulk by corporations, organizations, and special-interest groups. For more information, please e-mail SpecialSales@wjkbooks.com.

Contents

LISTING OF SIDEBARS   ix

PUBLISHER'S NOTE   xi

INTRODUCING CONNECTIONS   xiii

INTRODUCING THE REVISED
COMMON LECTIONARY   xv

Ash Wednesday

Isaiah 58:1–12	2
Psalm 51:1–17	7
2 Corinthians 5:20b–6:10	10
Matthew 6:1–6, 16–21	15
Joel 2:1–2, 12–17	19

First Sunday in Lent

Deuteronomy 26:1–11	24
Psalm 91:1–2, 9–16	29
Romans 10:8b–13	31
Luke 4:1–13	35

Second Sunday in Lent

Genesis 15:1–12, 17–18	40
Psalm 27	45
Philippians 3:17–4:1	48
Luke 13:31–35	52
Luke 9:28–36 (37–43)	57

Third Sunday in Lent

Isaiah 55:1–9	61
Psalm 63:1–8	66
1 Corinthians 10:1–13	68
Luke 13:1–9	72

Fourth Sunday in Lent

Joshua 5:9–12	76
Psalm 32	80
2 Corinthians 5:16–21	83
Luke 15:1–3, 11b–32	87

Fifth Sunday in Lent

Isaiah 43:16–21	93
Psalm 126	97
Philippians 3:4b–14	100
John 12:1–8	104

Liturgy of the Palms

Psalm 118:1–2, 19–29	108
Luke 19:28–40	111

Liturgy of the Passion

Isaiah 50:4–9a	115
Psalm 31:9–16	120
Philippians 2:5–11	122
Luke 22:14–23:56	126
Luke 23:1–49	133

Holy Thursday

Exodus 12:1–4 (5–10), 11–14	138
Psalm 116:1–2, 12–19	143
1 Corinthians 11:23–26	146
John 13:1–17, 31b–35	150

Good Friday

Isaiah 52:13–53:12	155
Psalm 22	161
Hebrews 10:16–25 and	
Hebrews 4:14–16; 5:7–9	164
John 18:1–19:42	169

Easter Day/Resurrection of the Lord

Isaiah 65:17–25	176
Psalm 118:1–2, 14–24	181
Acts 10:34–43	183
John 20:1–18	188
1 Corinthians 15:19–26	192
Luke 24:1–12	196

Second Sunday of Easter

Acts 5:27–32 — 200
Psalm 150 and
  Psalm 118:14–29 — 204
Revelation 1:4–8 — 207
John 20:19–31 — 211

Third Sunday of Easter

Acts 9:1–6 (7–20) — 216
Psalm 30 — 221
Revelation 5:11–14 — 224
John 21:1–19 — 228

Fourth Sunday of Easter

Acts 9:36–43 — 233
Psalm 23 — 237
Revelation 7:9–17 — 240
John 10:22–30 — 245

Fifth Sunday of Easter

Acts 11:1–18 — 249
Psalm 148 — 254
Revelation 21:1–6 — 257
John 13:31–35 — 262

Sixth Sunday of Easter

Acts 16:9–15 — 266
Psalm 67 — 271
Revelation 21:10, 22–22:5 — 273
John 14:23–29 — 278
John 5:1–9 — 282

Ascension of the Lord

Acts 1:1–11 — 286
Psalm 47 and Psalm 93 — 291
Ephesians 1:15–23 — 294
Luke 24:44–53 — 298

Seventh Sunday of Easter

Acts 16:16–34 — 302
Psalm 97 — 307
Revelation 22:12–14, 16–17,
  20–21 — 309
John 17:20–26 — 313

Day of Pentecost

Genesis 11:1–9 — 318
Psalm 104:24–34, 35b — 323
Acts 2:1–21 — 326
John 14:8–17 (25–27) — 331
Romans 8:14–17 — 336

CONTRIBUTORS — 341
AUTHOR INDEX — 345
SCRIPTURE INDEX — 347

Sidebars

Imitators of His Patient Endurance 11
Polycarp

A Sign unto This Nation 25
Sojourner Truth

Hallow Thou My Soul 54
Thomas à Kempis

The Fiery Love of God 67
Catherine of Genoa

Conforming Ourselves to
the Will of God 89
Cyril of Alexandria

Give Our Lord Every Sacrifice 98
Teresa of Avila

Old Tyrant Death Disarmed 109
Nicetas/John Dryden

The Goal of the Teacher 144
Origen

Love of God and Pure Desire 157
Bonaventure

Christ Lives in Us If We Love
One Another 184
Thomas Merton

Love So Amazing, So Divine 212
Isaac Watts

The Heat of Charity 218
Thomas Brinton

He and None Other
Is My Shepherd 238
Martin Luther

God Is the Author of Our Love 255
Bernard of Claivaux

Profound Need Met in Christ 268
Harry Emerson Fosdick

Jesus Opened the Eyes
of the Heart 288
Erasmus

On Your Mercy Alone Rests
My Hope 304
Augustine

Printed on My Heart 328
Julia Foote

Publisher's Note

"The preaching of the Word of God is the Word of God," says the Second Helvetic Confession. While that might sound like an exalted estimation of the homiletical task, it comes with an implicit warning: "A lot is riding on this business of preaching. Get it right!"

Believing that much does indeed depend on the church's proclamation, we offer Connections: A Lectionary Commentary for Preaching and Worship. Connections embodies two complementary convictions about the study of Scripture in preparation for preaching and worship. First, to best understand an individual passage of Scripture, we should put it in conversation with the rest of the Bible. Second, since all truth is God's truth, we should bring as many "lenses" as possible to the study of Scripture, drawn from as many sources as we can find. Our prayer is that this unique combination of approaches will illumine your study and preparation, facilitating the weekly task of bringing the Word of God to the people of God.

We at Westminster John Knox Press want to thank the superb editorial team that came together to make Connections possible. At the heart of that team are our general editors: Joel B. Green, Thomas G. Long, Luke A. Powery, and Cynthia L. Rigby. These four gifted scholars and preachers have poured countless hours into brainstorming, planning, reading, editing, and supporting the project. Their passion for authentic preaching and transformative worship shows up on every page. They pushed the writers and their fellow editors, they pushed us at the press, and most especially they pushed themselves to focus always on what you, the users of this resource, genuinely need. We are grateful to Kimberley Bracken Long for her innovative vision of what commentary on the Psalm readings could accomplish and for recruiting a talented group of liturgists and preachers to implement that vision. Bo Adams has shown creativity and insight in exploring an array of sources to provide the sidebars that accompany each worship day's commentaries. At the forefront of the work have been the members of our editorial board, who helped us identify writers, assign passages, and most especially carefully edit each commentary. They have cheerfully allowed the project to intrude on their schedules in order to make possible this contribution to the life of the church. Most especially we thank our writers, drawn from a broad diversity of backgrounds, vocations, and perspectives. The distinctive character of our commentaries required much from our writers. Their passion for the preaching ministry of the church proved them worthy of the challenge.

A project of this size does not come together without the work of excellent support staff. Above all we are indebted to project manager Joan Murchison. Joan's fingerprints are all over the book you hold in your hands; her gentle, yet unconquerable, persistence always kept it moving forward in good shape and on time. Pamela Jarvis skillfully compiled the volume, arranging the hundreds of separate commentaries and Scriptures into a cohesive whole.

Finally, our sincere thanks to the administration, faculty, and staff of Austin Presbyterian Theological Seminary, our institutional partner in producing Connections. President Theodore J. Wardlaw and Dean David H. Jensen have been steadfast friends of the project, enthusiastically agreeing to our partnership, carefully overseeing their faculty and staff's work on it, graciously hosting our meetings, and enthusiastically using their platform to promote Connections among their students, alumni, and friends.

It is with much joy that we commend Connections to you, our readers. May God use this resource to deepen and enrich your ministry of preaching and worship.

WESTMINSTER JOHN KNOX PRESS

Introducing Connections

Connections is a resource designed to help preachers generate sermons that are theologically deeper, liturgically richer, and culturally more pertinent. Based on the Revised Common Lectionary (RCL), which has wide ecumenical use, the hundreds of essays on the full array of biblical passages in the three-year cycle can be used effectively by preachers who follow the RCL, by those who follow other lectionaries, and by nonlectionary preachers alike.

The essential idea of Connections is that biblical texts display their power most fully when they are allowed to interact with a number of contexts, that is, when many connections are made between a biblical text and realities outside that text. Like the two poles of a battery, when the pole of the biblical text is connected to a different pole (another aspect of Scripture or a dimension of life outside Scripture), creative sparks fly and energy surges from pole to pole.

Two major interpretive essays, called Commentary 1 and Commentary 2, address every scriptural reading in the RCL. Commentary 1 explores preaching connections between a lectionary reading and other texts and themes within Scripture, and Commentary 2 makes preaching connections between the lectionary texts and themes in the larger culture outside of Scripture. These essays have been written by pastors, biblical scholars, theologians, and others, all of whom have a commitment to lively biblical preaching.

The writers of Commentary 1 surveyed five possible connections for their texts: the immediate literary context (the passages right around the text), the larger literary context (for example, the cycle of David stories or the passion narrative), the thematic context (such as other feeding stories, other parables, or other passages on the theme of hope), the lectionary context (the other readings for the day in the RCL), and the canonical context (other places in the whole of the Bible that display harmony, or perhaps tension, with the text at hand).

The writers of Commentary 2 surveyed six possible connections for their texts: the liturgical context (such as Advent or Easter), the ecclesial context (the life and mission of the church), the social and ethical context (justice and social responsibility), the cultural context (such as art, music, and literature), the larger expanse of human knowledge (such as science, history, and psychology), and the personal context (the life and faith of individuals).

In each essay, the writers selected from this array of possible connections, emphasizing those connections they saw as most promising for preaching. It is important to note that, even though Commentary 1 makes connections inside the Bible and Commentary 2 makes connections outside the Bible, this does not represent a division between "what the text *meant* in biblical times versus what the text *means* now." *Every* connection made with the text, whether that connection is made within the Bible or out in the larger culture, is seen as generative for preaching, and each author provokes the imagination of the preacher to see in these connections preaching possibilities for today. Connections is not a substitute for traditional scriptural commentaries, concordances, Bible dictionaries, and other interpretive tools. Rather, Connections begins with solid biblical scholarship and then goes on to focus on the act of preaching and on the ultimate goal of allowing the biblical text to come alive in the sermon.

Connections addresses every biblical text in the RCL, and it takes seriously the architecture of the RCL. During the seasons of the Christian year (Advent through Epiphany and Lent through Pentecost), the RCL provides three readings and a psalm for each Sunday and feast day: (1) a first reading, usually from the Old Testament; (2) a psalm, chosen to respond to the first reading; (3) a second reading, usually from one of the New Testament epistles; and (4) a Gospel reading. The first and second readings are chosen as complements to the Gospel reading for the day.

During the time between Pentecost and Advent, however, the RCL includes an additional first reading for every Sunday. There is the usual complementary reading, chosen in relation to the Gospel reading, but there is also a "semicontinuous" reading. These semicontinuous first readings move through the books of the Old Testament more or less continuously in narrative sequence, offering the stories of the patriarchs (Year A), the kings of Israel (Year B), and the prophets (Year C). Connections covers both the complementary and the semicontinuous readings.

The architects of the RCL understand the psalms and canticles to be prayers, and they selected the psalms for each Sunday and feast as prayerful responses to the first reading for the day. Thus the Connections essays on the psalms are different from the other essays, and they have two goals, one homiletical and the other liturgical. First, they comment on ways the psalm might offer insight into preaching the first reading. Second, they describe how the tone and content of the psalm or canticle might inform the day's worship, suggesting ways the psalm or canticle may be read, sung, or prayed.

Preachers will find in Connections many ideas and approaches to sustain lively and provocative preaching for years to come. But beyond the deep reservoir of preaching connections found in these pages, preachers will also find here a habit of mind, a way of thinking about biblical preaching. Being guided by the essays in Connections to see many connections between biblical texts and their various contexts, preachers will be stimulated to make other connections for themselves. Connections is an abundant collection of creative preaching ideas, and it is also a spur to continued creativity.

JOEL B. GREEN
THOMAS G. LONG
LUKE A. POWERY
CYNTHIA L. RIGBY
General Editors

Introducing the Revised Common Lectionary

To derive the greatest benefit from Connections, it will help to understand the structure and purpose of the Revised Common Lectionary (RCL), around which this resource is built. The RCL is a three-year guide to Scripture readings for the Christian Sunday gathering for worship. "Lectionary" simply means a selection of texts for reading and preaching. The RCL is an adaptation of the Roman Lectionary (of 1969, slightly revised in 1981), which itself was a reworking of the medieval Western-church one-year cycle of readings. The RCL resulted from six years of consultations that included representatives from nineteen churches or denominational agencies. Every preacher uses a lectionary—whether it comes from a specific denomination or is the preacher's own choice—but the RCL is unique in that it positions the preacher's homiletical work within a web of specific, ongoing connections.

The RCL has its roots in Jewish lectionary systems and early Christian ways of reading texts to illumine the biblical meaning of a feast day or time in the church calendar. Among our earliest lectionaries are the lists of readings for Holy Week and Easter in fourth-century Jerusalem.

One of the RCL's central connections is intertextuality; multiple texts are listed for each day. This lectionary's way of reading Scripture is based on Scripture's own pattern: texts interpreting texts. In the RCL, every Sunday of the year and each special or festival day is assigned a group of texts, normally three readings and a psalm. For most of the year, the first reading is an Old Testament text, followed by a psalm, a reading from one of the epistles, and a reading from one of the Gospel accounts.

The RCL's three-year cycle centers Year A in Matthew, Year B in Mark, and Year C in Luke. It is less clear how the Gospel according to John fits in, but when preachers learn about the RCL's arrangement of the Gospels, it makes sense. John gets a place of privilege because John's Gospel account, with its high Christology, is assigned for the great feasts. Texts from John's account are also assigned for Lent, Sundays of Easter, and summer Sundays. The second-century bishop Irenaeus's insistence on four Gospels is evident in this lectionary system: John and the Synoptics are in conversation with each other. However, because the RCL pattern contains variations, an extended introduction to the RCL can help the preacher learn the reasons for texts being set next to other texts.

The Gospel reading governs each day's selections. Even though the ancient order of reading texts in the Sunday gathering positions the Gospel reading last, the preacher should know that the RCL receives the Gospel reading as the hermeneutical key.

At certain times in the calendar year, the connections between the texts are less obvious. The RCL offers two tracks for readings in the time after Pentecost (Ordinary Time/standard Sundays): the complementary and the semicontinuous. Complementary texts relate to the church year and its seasons; semicontinuous emphasis is on preaching through a biblical book. Both approaches are historic ways of choosing texts for Sunday. This commentary series includes both the complementary and the semicontinuous readings.

In the complementary track, the Old Testament reading provides an intentional tension, a deeper understanding, or a background reference for another text of the day. The Psalm is the congregation's response to the first reading, following its themes. The Epistle functions as the horizon of the church: we learn about the faith and struggles of early Christian communities. The Gospel tells us where we are in the church's time and is enlivened, as are all the texts, by these intertextual interactions. Because the semicontinuous track prioritizes the narratives of specific books, the intertextual connections are not as apparent. Connections still exist, however. Year A pairs Matthew's account with Old Testament readings from the first five books; Year B pairs Mark's account with stories of anointed kings; Year C pairs Luke's account with the prophetic books.

Historically, lectionaries came into being because they were the church's beloved texts, like the scriptural canon. Choices had to be made regarding readings in the assembly, given the limit of fifty-two Sundays and a handful of festival days. The RCL presupposes that everyone (preachers and congregants) can read these texts—even along with the daily RCL readings that are paired with the Sunday readings.

Another central connection found in the RCL is the connection between text and church seasons or the church's year. The complementary texts make these connections most clear. The intention of the RCL is that the texts of each Sunday or feast day bring biblical meaning to where we are in time. The texts at Christmas announce the incarnation. Texts in Lent renew us to follow Christ, and texts for the fifty days of Easter proclaim God's power over death and sin and our new life in Christ. The entire church's year is a hermeneutical key for using the RCL.

Let it be clear that the connection to the church year is a connection for present-tense proclamation. We read, not to recall history, but to know how those events are true for us today. Now is the time of the Spirit of the risen Christ; now we beseech God in the face of sin and death; now we live baptized into Jesus' life and ministry. To read texts in time does not mean we remind ourselves of Jesus' biography for half of the year and then the mission of the church for the other half. Rather, we follow each Gospel's narrative order to be brought again to the meaning of Jesus' death and resurrection and his risen presence in our midst. The RCL positions the texts as our lens on our life and the life of the world in our time: who we are in Christ now, for the sake of the world.

The RCL intends to be a way of reading texts to bring us again to faith, for these texts to be how we see our lives and our gospel witness in the world. Through these connections, the preacher can find faithful, relevant ways to preach year after year.

JENNIFER L. LORD
Connections Editorial Board Member

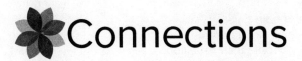Connections

Ash Wednesday

Isaiah 58:1–12
Psalm 51:1–17
2 Corinthians 5:20b–6:10

Matthew 6:1–6, 16–21
Joel 2:1–2, 12–17

Isaiah 58:1–12

¹Shout out, do not hold back!
　　Lift up your voice like a trumpet!
Announce to my people their rebellion,
　　to the house of Jacob their sins.
²Yet day after day they seek me
　　and delight to know my ways,
as if they were a nation that practiced righteousness
　　and did not forsake the ordinance of their God;
they ask of me righteous judgments,
　　they delight to draw near to God.
³"Why do we fast, but you do not see?
　　Why humble ourselves, but you do not notice?"
Look, you serve your own interest on your fast day,
　　and oppress all your workers.
⁴Look, you fast only to quarrel and to fight
　　and to strike with a wicked fist.
Such fasting as you do today
　　will not make your voice heard on high.
⁵Is such the fast that I choose,
　　a day to humble oneself?
Is it to bow down the head like a bulrush,
　　and to lie in sackcloth and ashes?
Will you call this a fast,
　　a day acceptable to the LORD?

⁶Is not this the fast that I choose:
　　to loose the bonds of injustice,
　　to undo the thongs of the yoke,
to let the oppressed go free,
　　and to break every yoke?
⁷Is it not to share your bread with the hungry,
　　and bring the homeless poor into your house;
when you see the naked, to cover them,
　　and not to hide yourself from your own kin?
⁸Then your light shall break forth like the dawn,
　　and your healing shall spring up quickly;
your vindicator shall go before you,
　　the glory of the LORD shall be your rear guard.
⁹Then you shall call, and the LORD will answer;
　　you shall cry for help, and he will say, Here I am.

If you remove the yoke from among you,
    the pointing of the finger, the speaking of evil,
[10]if you offer your food to the hungry
    and satisfy the needs of the afflicted,
then your light shall rise in the darkness
    and your gloom be like the noonday.
[11]The LORD will guide you continually,
    and satisfy your needs in parched places,
    and make your bones strong;
and you shall be like a watered garden,
    like a spring of water,
    whose waters never fail.
[12]Your ancient ruins shall be rebuilt;
    you shall raise up the foundations of many generations;
you shall be called the repairer of the breach,
    the restorer of streets to live in.

Commentary 1: Connecting the Reading with Scripture

In times of heightened conflict, anxiety can degrade the ethical and spiritual foundations on which a community has built its identity. The prophet in such times is called to help believers remember who they are. The prophetic voice must be robust in its rejection of distorted thinking and compelling in its invitation to renewed communal memory. The postexilic traditions in Isaiah 56–66 reflect just such a prophetic sensibility. Isaiah 58:1–12 calls the community back to the care for the vulnerable that had been foundational to Israel's self-understanding in earlier generations.

Verse 1 opens with God's address to a masculine singular subject. The prophet here may stand also for the righteous hearer within the community. In this late Isaianic material we see no biographical details about the prophet, something quite different from the historical realism of the books of Jeremiah and Ezekiel, which brim with names, dates, and locations. Where Isaiah of Jerusalem and all Israel were identified as God's chosen "servant" in earlier Isaiah texts (20:3; 41:8, 9; 42:1, 19; 44:1, 2, 21; 45:4; 49:3; 52:13; 53:11), in later chapters, the Lord speaks of "servants" (54:17; 65:8, 13, 14). Isaiah 58 may be inviting the

faithful to raise their voices in a polyphony of prophetic witness.

The prophet is to decry sin as if with a powerful blast from the ram's horn (*shofar*, NRSV "trumpet"). Mention of this liturgical instrument connects ethics with right worship. The Lord had descended atop Sinai with a supernal blast of the *shofar* (Exod. 19:16, 19; 20:18) to give the Law that would organize Israel's understanding of holiness and justice. The *shofar* was to be sounded on the Day of Atonement in the jubilee year, during which slaves were to receive manumission and leased ancestral land was to be restored to its owners. Here, the transgression of Israel is named with brutal candor: ritual is used to secure self-interest, as if God could be manipulated by those engaged in exploitative economic practices. The venerable Amos of Tekoa had derided liturgy devoid of ethical commitment (Amos 5:21–24). Now Isaiah excoriates believers for seeking the righteousness of God—the Deity's support and vindication of them—without demonstrating their commitment to right behavior in community.

An unjust congregation dares to move blithely toward the altar as if God will disregard their egregious sins? No! Authentic spiritual praxis must be detached from self-interest and the antagonism generated by it (vv. 3–5). Worship should be inseparable from sustained work for justice (vv. 6–7). Mature obedience integrates ritual observance with loving action for the vulnerable.

Sophisticated structuring devices enhance the power of this ancient poetry. First, rhetorical questions hammer at the complacency of the audience. The prophet ventriloquizes his opponents, a tactic of ironic discourse deployed brilliantly by Micah of Moresheth centuries earlier (see Mic. 2:6; 3:11; 6:6–7). The audience hears accusatory questions that transgressors hurl at God: "Why do we fast, but you do not see? Why humble ourselves, but you do not notice?" (v. 3). Those accusations are met by devastating rhetorical responses. God mocks, "Is such the fast that I choose? Is it to bow . . . the head like a bulrush? Such fasting will not make your voice heard on high!" (vv. 4–5). God will not respond to prayers of unrepentant oppressors. The Deity insists on compassion as defining for covenant: "Is not this the fast that I choose: to loose the bonds of injustice . . . to let the oppressed go free?" Does not true piety require that one share bread with the hungry, shelter the homeless, clothe the naked?

A second structuring device consists of key words that repeatedly draw hearers' attention to the heart of the prophetic message. Four motifs are noteworthy in the Hebrew: the verb "to call" (*qr'*); and the nouns "yoke" (*motah*); "appetite, need, self" (*nefesh*); and "righteousness, vindication" (*tsedaqah* and *tsedeq*).

1. The verb "to call" occurs four times in our passage (and a fifth time in v. 13). The prophet's role is to *cry out* about believers' transgressions and callousness toward the poor (v. 1), challenging the deceptive way in which the community calls "fasting" a superficial observance that betrays their lack of knowledge of what God desires (v. 5). When believers show their obedience by caring for the vulnerable, then they will *call* on the Lord and be heard (v. 9). Then the reformed righteous community will see Zion restored, and the congregation—identified in the masculine singular—will be *called* "repairer of the breach" and "restorer of streets" (v. 12).

2. The noun "yoke" occurs three times. In verse 6 it comes up twice: the fast that God ordains is for believers "to loose the thongs of the *yoke*" and to "break every *yoke*." Then in verse 9, the point is reiterated: only when believers have "removed the *yoke*" from their midst will they be guided, protected, and strengthened by God (v. 11).

3. The noun *nefesh* occurs five times. This multivalent term signifies need—mapped along a spectrum from hunger/thirst to desire to greed; thus "appetite," literally or metaphorically—and it signifies the embodied self. In verse 3, *nefesh* occurs in the complaint of unjust worshipers: "When we starved *our bodies*" [NJPS], they ask, Why did the Lord not heed? In verse 5, God repeats the *nefesh* language to rebut the complaint as misguided. In verse 10, *nefesh* occurs twice: two contiguous usages are arranged in a chiasm emphasizing the mutuality that should characterize community. What the NRSV translates as, "if you offer your food [*nafsheka*] to the hungry, and satisfy the needs [*nefesh*] of the afflicted . . ." might also be rendered, "If you offer to the hungry *that which satiates your own need,* and the *need* of the afflicted you satisfy . . ." The final occurrence is in verse 11: the Lord will satisfy the *need* of those who have responded with compassion to the afflicted. The needs of the other are interwoven with believers' own needs in an inescapable mutuality.

4. The motif of righteousness comes up three times. In verse 2, the term signifies the righteousness that the people should demonstrate and the righteous judgments that they expect from God. In verse 8 is an extraordinary image: for those who practice compassion for the downtrodden, their *righteousness* will go before them, and the glory of the Lord will be their rear guard. The image evokes the pillar of cloud/fire that led the Israelites in the exodus and positioned itself between them and the pursuing Egyptian army. A marvelous ambiguity infuses this metaphor: the point may be that the community's own righteousness will direct them in the way they should go, or one may understand this as the Righteous One (NJPS, "your Vindicator"), that is, God, leading and upholding those who do right. Either way, *shalom* obtains only when the community treats the needy with equity.

Care for the vulnerable was at the center of Israel's sacred laws. Israel's ancestors had been enslaved in Egypt, their children born into conditions of grave risk (see Exod. 1). Breaking their chains and escaping under Moses' leadership, Israel struggled through the wilderness to Mount Sinai. There God revealed the mandate of holy rest, Sabbath, as precious gift, not only honoring the cessation of divine work in primordial time (Exod. 20:8–11), but respecting the needs of laborers and slaves (Deut. 5:12–15).

The covenant community must be unfailingly compassionate toward widows, orphans, outsiders, and all who find themselves in conditions of precariousness (Exod. 22:21–24; Lev. 19:9–10, 33–34). Then, and only then, will the believing community be "like a watered garden," fruitful and at peace.

CAROLYN J. SHARP

Commentary 2: Connecting the Reading with the World

The sum of the two tables of the Ten Commandments and—according to Jews and Christians alike—the sum of the Torah/Law, as well as the essence of the gospel of Jesus Christ, is love of God and neighbor. Contrary to trendy affirmations of cultural relativism, proclamation of this form of love is found across the world's classic religious traditions (including, among many others, the Jewish, Hindu, Buddhist, Christian, and Islamic traditions).

The pertinent meaning of "love" must be precisely defined. Its essence can be specified with traditional contrasts among *eros*, *philia*, and *agapē*. *Eros* designates love in the sense of one's desires for oneself. At the other extreme, *agapē*, a power not at all rooted in one's own intentions and desires, designates love by which one is seized for others. *Philia*, commonly referred to as sisterly or brotherly love, is agapaic love for those to whom you are specially connected or whom you personally prefer (e.g., children, comrades, friends, lovers); generally, *philia* designates the area where *eros* and *agapē* overlap.

There is nothing inherently wrong with *eros* or *philia*. However, divine love, kenotic love, the love that is the summary of the Torah, the Ten Commandments, and of the gospel of Jesus Christ, the love to which we are called as faithful children of God, the love of the God who *is* love, is *agapē*.

To be clear, there is nothing wrong with *eros*, with having and fulfilling one's own desires for, say, food, shelter, safety, sex, music, sport, or even social recognition and respect. However, the parameters of *eros* are unremittingly oriented to oneself. Taken alone, *eros* is isolating, solipsistic. So people wholly consumed by *eros*

are not only cut off from all true fellowship, but insofar as they gain social power and influence, they will undercut just and peaceable relations among people as well.

Significantly, the love celebrated above all others in modern Western society—indeed, the only love that is acknowledged by modern Western rationality to be an actual part of the natural world—is *eros*. In modern game theory, individuals' decisions are considered to be rational (e.g., not dictated by misunderstanding, prejudice, or instinct) insofar as they are made in accord with self-interest. In political theory, when it comes to understanding how reasonable people will respond (in contrast, say, to people controlled by propaganda or coercion), it is assumed they will respond in accord with self-interest (at best, enlightened self-interest). Talk of kinship or reciprocal "altruism" in biology is not about *agapē* (or even altruism in the usual sense). For predominant streams of modern rationality, all rational decisions are presumed to be self-interested decisions. In mainstream modern Western ethics and politics, insofar as we are dealing with what is reasonable (again, not coercion or confusion), there is only self-interest (at best, enlightened, but still self-interest). There is no *agapē*, only *eros*.

Accordingly, for mainstream modern Western rationality to act in accord with self-interest is wholly natural. In stark contrast to the world's classic faith traditions, all of which draw a contrast between those who are selfish and those who are loving/generous, modern reason endorses a contrast among those who "understand how the real world really works" and idealistic simpletons. Many people experience the power of *eros* in their work lives, where desires for oneself—for job security, good salary, benefits, and power over others—are presumed to be wholly natural. In this context, one can see, for instance, the value of keeping Sunday (or the Jewish Sabbath, religious holidays, and so forth) as a day when agapaic reality is concretely manifest in this world—perhaps even to the extent that ideally on such days virtually no one, no matter their means, has to work (this in stark contrast to an increasingly economically stratified society in which more and more people must work multiple jobs throughout every day of every week in order to survive).

At an international level, the rule of *eros* is evident in what are now standard, unqualified appeals to national self-interest, or in standard talk of gatherings of "the world's leading economies" (in contrast, for instance, to gatherings of the world's most equitable, loving, or just nations). To be sure, there is no virtue in failing to understand "how the real world really works." There is nothing wrong with attending to one's security and interests. The trick is to be in the world but not of it, to be utterly realistic about "natural" dynamics while striving to live in accord with *agapē*.

The NRSV entitles this passage "False and True Worship." Beyond the significant but obvious distinctions, notice how false worship confusedly treats God as selfishly pleased with otherwise pointless acts meant to direct praise and attention upon God, instead of imagining God as perfect *agapē*, as being consumed with concern over all those suffering on earth. What loving person would want someone to sing praises to them while the singer's suffering was neglected? Here, the essential unity of love of God and love of neighbor becomes visible. The God who *is agapē* rejoices with those who rejoice and cries out with those who cry out, and most urgently wants the needs of those who cry out to be met. So, when we love our neighbor, when we rejoice with those who rejoice and cry out with those who cry out, which includes working urgently to meet the needs of those who cry out, we not only love as God loves and love whom God loves; we address God's greatest

pains and hopes, which is a way of loving God. When we concretely love "the least of these," we concretely love God (Matt. 25).

The "least of these" can carry pejorative connotations that Jesus addresses in his story of the widow's mite, where Jesus says that a penniless widow's giving is greater than the large sums given by the wealthy (Luke 21:1–4; Mark 12:41–44). In this regard, note that Isaiah is speaking not to a mighty nation, but to a recently traumatized and relatively weak and vulnerable people.

This prophetic correction of confused worship and mistaken understanding of God has radical implications for Christian identity. As Jesus makes clear in his parabolic "sheep and goats" reiteration of this proclamation, the *only* factors that distinguish sheep from goats are the kind delineated in Isaiah 58: did you feed the hungry, shelter the homeless, clothe the naked, free the oppressed? Only these factors are included in Jesus' declaration of his own mission when, reading from Isaiah, he publicly initiates his ministry (Luke 4:18–19). According to Isaiah and Jesus, the heart of all true worship is ultimately related to concrete acts of love.

Let's imagine God listening to a church choir. *Confused* theology imagines God enjoying the choir, and enjoying even more the fact that all of the choir's words and thoughts are wholly directed to God. *Discerning* theology imagines God feeling the love experienced by the members of the choir as they revel in their own voices and community, and it imagines God feeling the solace, rest, comfort, communion, or joy experienced in the congregation with whom the choir worships, and it discerns God's joy in all this multifarious loving of neighbor, which is thereby, simultaneously, loving of God. One might imagine too God's delight in the taking of offerings, the passing of the peace, the food bank, the church groups advocating for social justice. According to Isaiah's prophetic word, the true praise and worship in which God delights is primarily a horizontal affair, and the reward is received in the joy givers experience in the giving of gifts.

WILLIAM GREENWAY

Ash Wednesday

Psalm 51:1–17

[1]Have mercy on me, O God,
    according to your steadfast love;
according to your abundant mercy
    blot out my transgressions.
[2]Wash me thoroughly from my iniquity,
    and cleanse me from my sin.

[3]For I know my transgressions,
    and my sin is ever before me.
[4]Against you, you alone, have I sinned,
    and done what is evil in your sight,
so that you are justified in your sentence
    and blameless when you pass judgment.
[5]Indeed, I was born guilty,
    a sinner when my mother conceived me.

[6]You desire truth in the inward being;
    therefore teach me wisdom in my secret heart.
[7]Purge me with hyssop, and I shall be clean;
    wash me, and I shall be whiter than snow.
[8]Let me hear joy and gladness;
    let the bones that you have crushed rejoice.
[9]Hide your face from my sins,
    and blot out all my iniquities.

[10]Create in me a clean heart, O God,
    and put a new and right spirit within me.
[11]Do not cast me away from your presence,
    and do not take your holy spirit from me.
[12]Restore to me the joy of your salvation,
    and sustain in me a willing spirit.

[13]Then I will teach transgressors your ways,
    and sinners will return to you.
[14]Deliver me from bloodshed, O God,
    O God of my salvation,
    and my tongue will sing aloud of your deliverance.

[15]O Lord, open my lips,
    and my mouth will declare your praise.
[16]For you have no delight in sacrifice;
    if I were to give a burnt offering, you would not be pleased.
[17]The sacrifice acceptable to God is a broken spirit;
    a broken and contrite heart, O God, you will not despise.

Connecting the Psalm with Scripture and Worship

Comedian A. Whitney Brown once said, "Any good history book is mainly just a long list of mistakes, complete with names and dates. It's very embarrassing."[1] While the Bible is not exactly a history book, it does narrate the story of the relationship between God and God's people. As far as the people's part is concerned, it is very embarrassing.

While the superscription of the psalm attributing it to David is almost certainly not an accurate historical note, it is instructive to hear Psalm 51 in connection with 2 Samuel 11–12, where the great and heroic King David breaks at least half of the Ten Commandments, including the prohibitions against murder and adultery. It is very embarrassing. Major items of the vocabulary of Psalm 51 also suggest another narrative connection, Exodus 32–34, the golden calf episode (compare especially words describing God's character in Ps. 51:1 with Exod. 34:6, as well as the vocabulary of disobedience in Ps. 51:2–5 with Exod. 34:7). Here, shortly after the people of God have received the Ten Commandments and have promised to obey all that God has spoken (see Exod. 20:1–17; 24:3, 7), they disobey the first two commandments. Again, it is very embarrassing, especially since, as Claus Westermann points out, Exodus 32–34 anticipates the entire subsequent history of Israel.[2]

The lectionary readings for Ash Wednesday provide still another text to place in connection with Psalm 51: Isaiah 58:1–12. Having been forgiven for the history of disobedience that resulted in the Babylonian exile, and having been restored to life in their own land, the people once again disappoint God. The issue is worship: fasting (Isa. 58:2–12) and, later in the chapter, Sabbath observance (vv. 13–14). As it has turned out, worship is not an activity by which the people attempt to put themselves at God's disposal, but rather an activity by which the people attempt to put God at their disposal. In short, as the prophet puts it, "you serve your own interest" (v. 3c; see also v. 13).

It is very embarrassing; but the people, who should have been embarrassed, instead feel entitled (v. 3ab).

To turn worship into a self-serving exercise is a perennial temptation. When our liturgical practices do not facilitate our submission to God's will and do not equip us to obey, God is not pleased. Isaiah 58 clearly communicates God's displeasure, as does Psalm 51, especially verses 16–17, which mention another major liturgical activity, sacrifice (see also Ps. 50:14, 23). Although sacrifice lay at the heart of Israelite worship (see Lev. 1–7), and although Psalm 51 recognizes that there can be "right sacrifices" (v. 19), the danger of self-serving liturgical practice was and is paramount, as both the psalmists and the prophets suggest (see also 1 Sam. 15:22; Isa. 1:10–20; Hos. 6:6; Amos 5:21–24; Mic. 6:6–8). As for us, our worship certainly can be meaningful, faithful, and effective in orienting us to God and God's will; but the danger is that it can also easily devolve into mere entertainment and/or self-congratulation.

When read in connection, Psalm 51 and Isaiah 58 commend the following related postures for faithful worship and discipleship:

Humility, as Opposed to Entitlement. The repetition of "broken" in Psalm 51:17 effectively makes the point, especially in concert with the word "contrite." God invites humility, which is in sharp contrast to the sense of entitlement expressed in Isaiah 58:3ab.

Generosity, as Opposed to Acquisitiveness. The psalmist's prayer for forgiveness and transformation includes, "Sustain in me a willing spirit" (v. 12). While not entirely clear, "willing spirit" may suggest generosity. In any case, the psalmist promises to turn outward (v. 13) and to become a witness to God's "righteousness" (v. 14, my trans.; NRSV "deliverance"). In Isaiah 58, the contrast to the self-interest of the people takes the form of overflowing generosity, involving actions that

1. A. Whitney Brown, *The Big Picture: An American Commentary* (New York: Harper Perennial, 1991), 12.
2. Claus Westermann, *Elements of Old Testament Theology*, trans. D. W. Stott (Atlanta: John Knox, 1982), 50, 54.

the prophets characterize elsewhere as justice and righteousness (see esp. vv. 6–7).

Genuine Praise, as Opposed to Self-assertion or Self-congratulation. Psalm 51:15 is frequently used as a call to worship, but worshipers are seldom aware of its context. The psalmist's promise to praise follows immediately the promise to be a witness to God's "ways" (v. 13) and "righteousness" (v. 14), suggesting that genuine praise involves submission to God's will. In other words, praise is a way of life as well as a liturgical activity. The language of praise is not as explicit in Isaiah 58, but it is clearly implied. When the people live as God intends (vv. 6–7), their "righteousness" will go before them (v. 8, my trans.; NRSV "vindicator"), and they will be followed by the "glory of the LORD" (v. 8). The word "glory" may indicate God's presence, but it also suggests the honor

or praise that is due to God. In both Psalm 51 and Isaiah 58, therefore, submission to God's will—"righteousness" (Ps. 51:14, NRSV "deliverance"; Isa. 58:8, NRSV "vindicator")—will constitute the genuine offering of praise to God. Genuine praise is in sharp contrast to the psalmist's self-assertion (especially if Psalm 51 is read with David's behavior in mind) and to the people's propensity to congratulate themselves in Isaiah 58.

While the embarrassing reality of human sinfulness is amply evident in both Psalm 51 and Isaiah 58, neither text is content to let disobedience be the final word. What is ultimately determinative is God's willingness to forgive (Ps. 51:1; Isa. 58:8–9), as well as God's ability to restore (Ps. 51:10–13; Isa. 58:11–12). The appropriate response, then and now, is humility, generosity, and praise.

J. CLINTON MCCANN JR.

2 Corinthians 5:20b–6:10

20bWe entreat you on behalf of Christ, be reconciled to God. 21For our sake he made him to be sin who knew no sin, so that in him we might become the righteousness of God.

6:1As we work together with him, we urge you also not to accept the grace of God in vain. 2For he says,

"At an acceptable time I have listened to you,
   and on a day of salvation I have helped you."

See, now is the acceptable time; see, now is the day of salvation! 3We are putting no obstacle in anyone's way, so that no fault may be found with our ministry, 4but as servants of God we have commended ourselves in every way: through great endurance, in afflictions, hardships, calamities, 5beatings, imprisonments, riots, labors, sleepless nights, hunger; 6by purity, knowledge, patience, kindness, holiness of spirit, genuine love, 7truthful speech, and the power of God; with the weapons of righteousness for the right hand and for the left; 8in honor and dishonor, in ill repute and good repute. We are treated as impostors, and yet are true; 9as unknown, and yet are well known; as dying, and see—we are alive; as punished, and yet not killed; 10as sorrowful, yet always rejoicing; as poor, yet making many rich; as having nothing, and yet possessing everything.

Commentary 1: Connecting the Reading with Scripture

When a reading begins with verse 20b, it is natural to wonder, "was there something in verse 20a that we were not supposed to hear?" The choice to begin with this half-verse is meant to lead us into chapter 6. If 5:20b announces the theme, we cannot understand this verse in isolation. We need to go back to what Paul said immediately before: "All this is from God, who reconciled us to himself through Christ, and has given us the ministry of reconciliation; that is, in Christ God was reconciling the world to himself, not counting their trespasses against them, and entrusting the message of reconciliation to us" (5:18–19). When Paul says, "Be reconciled to God," he gives an imperative, an urgent command to do this! This reconciliation cannot be done by human effort alone, but only through the power of God in Christ.

We hear several themes from Paul's correspondence with the Corinthians in these verses. God, through Christ, is the source of our reconciliation. Paul made this clear with a beautiful metaphor in 4:7, "but we have this treasure in clay jars, so that it may be made clear that this extraordinary power belongs to God and does not come from us." (The reconciliation Paul talks about is not with only one person or one group of believers, but with "the world.") This is cosmic reconciliation. Yet, Paul brings this reconciliation down to earth, saying that God "has given us the ministry of reconciliation." Such reconciliation is not only between God and the believer, but between one believer and another.

Paul has been deeply concerned about the human realities of reconciliation in Corinth. Paul's first letter pointed out the deep divisions within the community. Some claimed allegiance to Paul, others to Apollos or Cephas, and others to Christ. He asked, "Has Christ been divided?" (1 Cor. 1:12–13a). There were lawsuits among believers, different opinions about sexual morality, divisions at the Lord's table, and arguments over speaking in tongues. Paul had a heavy heart about all these divisions within what he called

Imitators of His Patient Endurance

Let us, then, hold steadfastly and unceasingly to our Hope and to the Pledge of our righteousness, that is, Christ Jesus, who bore our sins in his own body on the tree, who committed no
sin, neither was guile found on his lips but for our sakes he endured everything that we might
live in him. Therefore let us be imitators of his patient endurance, and if we suffer for the sake
of his name, let us glorify him. For he set us this example in his own Person, and this is what
we believed.

Now I exhort all of you to be obedient to the word of righteousness and to exercise all
patient endurance, such as you have seen with your very eyes, not only in the blessed Igna-
tius and Zosimus and Rufus, but also in others who were of your membership, and in Paul
himself and the rest of the apostles; being persuaded that all these "did not run in vain," but in
faith and *righteousness*, and that they are now in their deserved place with the Lord, in whose
suffering they also shared. For they loved not this present world, but Him who died on our
behalf and was raised by God for our sakes.

Stand firm, therefore, in these things and follow the example of the Lord, steadfast and
immovable in the faith, loving the brotherhood, cherishing one another, fellow companions in
the truth, in "the gentleness of the Lord preferring one another and despising no one. Whenever you are able to do a kindness, do not put it off, because almsgiving frees from death."
All of you submit yourselves to one another, having your manner of life above reproach from
the heathen, so that you may receive praise for your good works and the Lord may not be
blasphemed on your account. Woe to them, however, through whom the name of the Lord is
blasphemed. Therefore, all of you teach the sobriety in which you are yourselves living.

"Polycarp to the Philippians," in *Early Christian Fathers*, ed. and trans. Cyril C. Richardson (Philadelphia: Westminster Press, 1953), 134–35.

"the body of Christ" (1 Cor. 12:27). Krister Stendahl said this dissension within the community led Paul to what he wrote in 1 Corinthians 13:

> And then [Paul] ends by saying, so there remain those three: faith, hope, and love, and the greatest of them is faith. Well, that's what he should have said, according to his own thinking. The basic line: He is the apostle of faith, everything depends on faith. But here, suddenly, there is a breakthrough in his thinking, and he says: And the greatest of these is love, agape, esteem of the other, not "insisting on its own way," as the RSV puts it.[1]

Stendahl surprises us when he says, "and the greatest of them is faith." He wants us to be surprised, to see that something happened to Paul in his ministry in Corinth. Paul realized that love was essential to bridge the chasms that divided believers from one another. Paul was writing to people he had come to know well, concerned about their particular questions and conflicts. This was not systematic theology, but a pastor writing to people he cared for deeply.

Paul had received at least one letter from the Corinthians (1 Cor. 7:1) and had written back more than once. Most scholars agree that there are fragments of at least two or three letters within 2 Corinthians. However these fragments were put together, this epistle may not be so different from the way we might write a letter (if anyone still writes letters!). We start with one subject, then remember something that does not quite fit yet should not be forgotten. We may end the letter with a thought we had not expressed before, then add a postscript (P.S.). Paul often had more than one P.S. in his letters. He hinted a warning in a P.S. near the end of his Corinthian letter: "So I write these things while I am away from

1. Krister Stendahl, "Why I Love the Bible," *Harvard Divinity Bulletin* 35 (Winter 2007): https://bulletin.hds.harvard.edu/articles/winter2007/why-i-love-bible.

you, so that when I come, I may not have to be severe in using the authority that the Lord has given me for building up and not for tearing down" (2 Cor. 13:10).

Within the framework of Paul's second letter and with 1 Corinthians ringing in our ears, we return to the half-verse that begins the Ash Wednesday text: "We entreat you on behalf of Christ, be reconciled to God." As the reading moves into chapter 6, there is a sense of urgency. Paul quotes the prophet Isaiah to wake the Corinthians up: "At an acceptable time I have listened to you, and on a day of salvation I have helped you."

Isaiah's words cannot stay in the past. "See, now is the acceptable time, see now is the day of salvation" (2 Cor. 6:2b). Without underlining or italics Paul emphasizes the word "now." Do not wait until I visit you again. "We are putting no obstacle in anyone's way," Paul says, "so that no fault may be found with our ministry" (vv. 3–4a). Paul wants the Corinthians to trust him and his ministry. He knows they have been tempted to follow more showy leaders; "super-apostles" he calls them! (11:3–6).

When Paul says "we" in these verses, he usually means "I." He seems to be bragging that he has endured more than anyone. Such boasting can be very off-putting to contemporary readers; perhaps it was to the Corinthians too. However, for Paul this boasting has a purpose: "If I must boast, I will boast of the things that show my weakness" (11:30). Why? Because he wants all the credit to go to God and not to himself. His credentials involve afflictions, hardships, calamities, beatings, imprisonments, riots, labors,

sleepless nights, and hunger. He puts flesh on this list later on, describing the particular hardships he has endured (vv. 23–27). "And, besides other things," he adds, "I am under daily pressure because of my anxiety for all the churches" (v. 28), which included the Corinthians.

How did Paul survive these hardships? He is not shy. He tells us: "By purity, knowledge, patience, kindness, holiness of spirit, genuine love, truthful speech, and the power of God" (6:6–7a). Depending on how you do the counting, you can see nine hardships and nine gifts, but math is not the main point. Paul's message is clear: I endured only through the power of God. He closes this section with powerful antithetical pairings: "We are treated as imposters, and yet are true; as unknown, and yet are well known; as dying, and see—we are alive; as punished, and yet not killed; as sorrowful, yet always rejoicing; as poor, yet making many rich; as having nothing, and yet possessing everything" (vv. 8b–10).

In many ways this is exactly the right word for Ash Wednesday. The Gospel reading from Matthew 6 tends to draw us into ourselves: give alms secretly, pray inside your room, and do not let anyone know you are fasting. The mood is usually somber as each person receives the sign of ashes in the shape of a cross. One motion downward, another motion across. Most people have probably heard that the vertical line points to our relationship with God while the horizontal line points us toward one another. Paul brings these two lines together in this text. Be reconciled to God. Be reconciled to one another. When? "Now is the acceptable time."

BARBARA K. LUNDBLAD

Commentary 2: Connecting the Reading with the World

Ash Wednesday is a unique day in the church calendar, a day of potent symbol and stark sensory resonance. It marks the beginning of the Lenten season of austerity and preparation, the turn toward Jerusalem and the cross that comes at the bottom of the mountain after the transfiguration. Ash Wednesday is when the Christian journey takes on its darkest and most serious cast. Within the liturgy itself, and within

the readings, we experience the reality of death, the risk of faithful offering, the certainty of the cross on the road to resurrection.

On Ash Wednesday, the church calls her people to repentance and recommitment. The message is harsh, even frightening. You are dust and to dust you shall return. We are reduced to our most elemental components. The ashes—traditionally produced by burning blessed palms from the previous year's Palm Sunday celebration—speak to crushed dreams, a return to essentials, a distillation of our holy stories, the heart of our relationship with our Creator and the creation. We hear the lessons on Ash Wednesday knowing that we will leave marked by our mortality.

This passage from 2 Corinthians, with its insistence on reconciliation and its unflinching description of the sacrifices of Christian life, draws us into the struggles of the early church. There is no easy triumphalism here, no glorious crowds who hear the story but once and fling themselves into Christian life. The introductory chapters of Paul's Second Letter to the Corinthians speak to broken relationship, disappointment, missed connection. Paul has forgone a visit to the Corinthians out of some combination of his own pain and theirs. He counsels reconciliation not as a joyous or easy step, but as the only Christian way forward in a context of real brokenness. Paul and his companions are deep into the hard work of following and proclaiming Jesus. They find themselves called to recommitment, to remembering who they are and why this journey is worth the effort and the pain.

In the passage immediately preceding this one, Paul restates his credentials as an ambassador for Christ. This message of reconciliation is Paul's best translation of God's call to God's people, his best interpretation of the meaning of Christ's sacrifice. His message crosses boundaries of culture and experience; he inhabits the struggling world of his listeners, yet owes allegiance to another world, another set of laws, another sort of economy.

The contradictory and counterintuitive nature of the divine economy as expressed through Christ comes to us through Paul's pairings of opposites in 6:4b–10. The follower of Christ expects and accepts "afflictions, hardships, calamities, beatings, imprisonments, riots, labors, sleepless nights, [and] hunger," but not with long-suffering resignation. Rather, "purity, knowledge, patience, kindness, holiness of spirit, genuine love, truthful speech, and the power of God" provide a vital counterweight, allowing for a life of dignity and even joy under the grimmest of conditions.

The heart of the gospel, in Paul's view, is that the balance always weighs in God's favor, and thus in the favor of the faithful: "We are treated as impostors, and yet are true; as unknown, and yet are well known; as dying, and see—we are alive; as punished, and yet not killed; as sorrowful, yet always rejoicing; as poor, yet making many rich; as having nothing, yet possessing everything." The homiletical challenge here is to convey the underlying hope without romanticizing the very real suffering. Paul does not offer the divine economy as an escape from the cruelty of the world, but rather as an inversion of the expected effects.

Most of the historic liturgical churches in which Ash Wednesday is celebrated are struggling to adapt to changing times and shifting community context. Paul's context of conflict, hurt feelings, church fragility, and exhausted leadership will resonate easily with many congregations, especially in places where the Ash Wednesday services are small gatherings of the most committed members of the congregation. These words from the early church offer a helpful reminder that the faithful church has not always been large and flush. The itinerant preachers of 2 Corinthians appear to aspire to neither for the churches they have planted. They insist on faithfulness as the measure, under the most trying circumstances and in the face of both the open hostility of the world and the intransigence of relationships among the faithful.

In other places, especially in large immigrant Latino communities, Ash Wednesday may draw a larger crowd than usual, filling the churches with people who seek the comfort of a long-remembered ritual, one with ancestral resonance that may well predate any encounter with a Christian church. That group will require a somewhat different homiletical approach, one which considers the possibility that this will be one of the few Christian proclamations that listeners will hear this year, one that honors the humble request for the gift of ashes with a larger context, one that speaks not only to brokenness but also to deep and enduring hope.

Paul's words about grace speak well to this second context. We turn in repentance not because we are dirty or unworthy, but because we are dust. We are made of the substance of creation. We come from God and will return to God. We are of the same substance as one another, inseparable from the world God has made. None of us is left out of the promise or exempt from the love. Christ's sacrifice frames our repentance. We can give the grace that is necessary for reconciliation because that grace was first extended freely to us.

The descriptions of Paul and his companions' suffering beg a connection with the struggles of the day. Is this a multiethnic community struggling to find unity, a community of individuals who live on the edge of economic survival or fear deportation? What are the justice issues with which the congregation has or might engage? Where is the need for reconciliation most pressing? How might this congregation, gathered in a particular time and place, model and invite the larger community into the sacrificial work of reconciliation?

Connections to the personal struggles of the gathered congregation abound as well. Are there those among your listeners who suffer from bullying, exclusion, a sense that the world has no place for them? Someone surely is grieving. Someone is wondering why the material blessings of life offer so little depth of satisfaction.

Increasingly, Ash Wednesday is a time when churches venture outside their walls and sanctuaries. Many clergy and congregations spend time on the streets on Ash Wednesday, offering the gift of ashes with little or no liturgical context. While "ashes to go" is unlikely to offer a conventional homiletical opportunity, the experience of being out and about with ashes is almost certain to offer homiletical connection to this particular passage. For those who went out, what did you see? What were the struggles? Where did you find humility, inspiration, or the urgency of reconciliation? For those who did not share the "going out" experience, how might the stories of the day inspire?

This reading invites a closing connection with the season of Lent ahead. Living into the hopeful contradictions of the divine economy provides a fruitful avenue for contemplative experience as we set our experiences of suffering and persecution alongside our experiences of blessing and transformation. The call to find healing and reconciliation in the midst of broken relationship will offer a practical challenge to the lives of most hearers. The call not to "accept the grace of God in vain," but rather to offer ourselves fully for both death and resurrection, is as good a guide as any for forty days spent moving closer to Christ.

ANNA B. OLSON

Matthew 6:1–6, 16–21

[1]"Beware of practicing your piety before others in order to be seen by them; for then you have no reward from your Father in heaven.

[2]"So whenever you give alms, do not sound a trumpet before you, as the hypocrites do in the synagogues and in the streets, so that they may be praised by others. Truly I tell you, they have received their reward. [3]But when you give alms, do not let your left hand know what your right hand is doing, [4]so that your alms may be done in secret; and your Father who sees in secret will reward you.

[5]"And whenever you pray, do not be like the hypocrites; for they love to stand and pray in the synagogues and at the street corners, so that they may be seen by others. Truly I tell you, they have received their reward. [6]But whenever you pray, go into your room and shut the door and pray to your Father who is in secret; and your Father who sees in secret will reward you. . . .

[16]"And whenever you fast, do not look dismal, like the hypocrites, for they disfigure their faces so as to show others that they are fasting. Truly I tell you, they have received their reward. [17]But when you fast, put oil on your head and wash your face, [18]so that your fasting may be seen not by others but by your Father who is in secret; and your Father who sees in secret will reward you.

[19]"Do not store up for yourselves treasures on earth, where moth and rust consume and where thieves break in and steal; [20]but store up for yourselves treasures in heaven, where neither moth nor rust consumes and where thieves do not break in and steal. [21]For where your treasure is, there your heart will be also."

Commentary 1: Connecting the Reading with Scripture

Ash Wednesday is noteworthy among Christian holy days for several reasons. First, it is one of the few days in the Christian year where believers all over the world wear a visible sign of their faith for others to see. The practice of imposing ashes on the foreheads of worshipers started in the seventh and eighth centuries. In the Roman Catholic Church, the ashes come from burning the leftover leaves from Palm Sunday the previous year. The ashes are placed or "imposed" on the heads of the worshipers with the words, "Remember, man, that thou art dust and to dust shalt thou return."[1] Although the Protestant reformers abolished the practice in the sixteenth and seventeenth centuries, many Protestant churches today have found renewed purpose in observing Ash Wednesday and the practice of imposing ashes as a sign of collective penance and mourning. Ash Wednesday is also important because it is the inaugural day of the Christian Lenten season, the fourth season in the Christian year. Lent is the forty-day period before Easter (six and a half weeks, not counting Sundays), which is dedicated to reflection, penitence, and self-denial. The temptation story of Jesus and his forty-day fast is the biblical rationale for the period of Lent in the lives of believers (Mark 1:13; Matt. 4:2; Luke 4:2).[2]

Today's lection, however, does not launch the Lenten season by reflecting on the story of Jesus' temptation. It revisits Jesus' teaching discourse in Matthew 6 and focuses on three practices: almsgiving, prayer, and fasting. Matthew 6 is part of a larger section in the Gospel known

1. Peter S. Dawes, "Ash Wednesday," in *New International Dictionary of the Christian Church*, paragraph 1220, accord://read/NIDCC#1220.
2. Howard Sainsbury, "Lent," in *NIDCC*, paragraph 7333. accord://read/NIDCC#7333.

widely as the Sermon on the Mount (Matt. 5–7). Here the Gospel carefully and intentionally portrays Jesus doing something he has yet to do in Matthew—namely, sitting down and speaking (5:1–2). Up to this point in the story, the Gospel portrays Jesus on the move, traveling all over Galilee (3:13; 4:12, 13, 23) and teaching as he goes (4:23).

The lectionary for Ash Wednesday can be divided into three smaller, contiguous sections in which the issue of alms is addressed first (6:2–4), the issue of prayer second (vv. 5–6), and the issue of fasting last (vv. 16–18). The Lord's Prayer appears in the middle of these sections, immediately following the warnings against improper approaches to prayer (vv. 7–15). Although this omission is a blaring silence in today's Scripture lesson, it is exceptionally helpful for reconsidering the meaning of the Lord's Prayer. By focusing on Jesus' words before and after he models prayer, readers are reminded that prayer alone—especially public prayer—is not a sufficient indicator of rightness when benevolence for others, private prayer, and voluntary moderation are lacking.

In Jesus' day, the custom of benevolence or almsgiving was a common practice of both the Jewish tradition and the larger Roman world. According to the Old Testament, almsgiving is about offering relief and resources to impoverished members of the Israelite community to ensure their well-being and survival. On one hand, benevolence is an act of obedience in which God's people follow the divine commands to attend to the lower orders of society by caring for the community's orphans, widows, and immigrants (Deut. 24:17–18; 10:18–20; 27:19; Exod. 22:21–27). On other hand, almsgiving is a faithful act of imitation in which believers reenact the precedent God set by providing for the destitute Israelites in the wilderness (Exod. 15:24–26; 16:3–4; cf. Exod. 22:21–24).

The practice of almsgiving is also an important topic for later noncanonical writings from Diaspora Judaism in the early Second Temple era (515 BCE–70 CE). Writings such as the books of Tobit and Sirach in the Apocrypha use the Greek term for almsgiving and benevolence

present in Matthew 6 (*eleēmosynē*) and explain its merits. For example, Tobit 4:6b–8 says, "And to all who do righteousness give alms from your possessions, and do not let your eye be envious when you give alms. Do not turn your face away from any poor person, and the face of God shall not be turned away from you. If you have abundant possessions, give alms from them accordingly; if you have a little, do not be afraid to give alms according to that little" (see also Tob. 1:3, 16; 4:16–17; 14:10–11 *A New English Translation of the Septuagint*). The book of Sirach specifies charitable deeds as not only what God commands, but also as a representation of the finest understanding of what it means to be human: "There is no good for him who persists in evil and for him who does not willingly offer charity" (Sir. 12:3; 35:3; 40:17, 24 *NETS*).

According to Jesus' Jewish tradition, everyone, irrespective of wealth and status, can be charitable. The Roman world made a similar point about the purpose and practice of benevolence in the broader society. Seneca, a first-century Roman philosopher and senator living at the time of Jesus, states that benevolence is "the art of doing a kindness which both bestows pleasure and gains by bestowing it. . . . It is not, therefore, the thing which is done or given, but the spirit in which it is done or given, that must be considered" (Seneca, *On Benefits* 1.6). Similarly, Jesus puts more emphasis on the ulterior motives and spirit of the almsgiver than the actual gift itself. The language of almsgiving (*eleēmosynē*) does not occur in the Gospels of Mark and John. It occurs only in Matthew and Luke, albeit for different purposes. In Luke, the language of almsgiving is positive, encouraging Jesus' disciples to do it as a marker of their identity and loyalty (Luke 11:41; 12:33). In Matthew, however, the term appears only three times and all instances are in chapter 6. In this case, the term is used to censure the Pharisees for doing the right thing for the wrong reasons (Matt. 6:2, 3, 4).[3]

Strikingly, today's lectionary entwines individual authentic acts of charity with communal practices of prayer and fasting. A central issue is

---

3. Kyoung-Jin Kim, "Alms, Almsgiving," in *The New Interpreter's Dictionary of the Bible* (Nashville: Abingdon Press, 2006), 1:106.

about who sees what. In the case of the synagogue leaders, whom Jesus pejoratively labels "hypocrites," the purpose of benevolence, prayer, and fasting is to be seen by others to legitimate one's authority and status in the community. It is an issue of influencing human perception and praise through deceit (Matt. 6:2; 5, 16). In contrast, Jesus names the art of secrecy as a more faithful testament of piety and character (vv. 3–4, 6, 18).

On Ash Wednesday, this passage reminds Christians that true faithfulness is not public spectacle, but quiet and decisive action. The task is to realign one's priorities. Instead of focusing on the accouterments of life that bolster personal reputations and prominence, Jesus challenges listeners to do three things: (1) help others, out of one's means, with little exhibition, (2) align

and realign oneself consistently to God (v. 6), and (3) disengage from a life of consumerism (*aphanizō*, vv. 16, 19–20). Consequently, the ashy mark believers wear on their heads today is pointless if Jesus' challenge is not accepted. Today, Jesus does not call believers to the work of the prophetic trumpeter sounding a warning of danger (Matt. 6:2; Joel 2:1–2; Isa. 58:1–2). Rather, Ash Wednesday is about "commending" oneself to the service of others and to be content with anonymity. Today is about looking inward and reckoning with our own selfish wishes and biases, while willingly looking outward to a world we may not be accustomed to seeing and serving (2 Cor. 5:20b–6:10; Joel 2:12–17).

SHIVELY T. J. SMITH

Commentary 2: Connecting the Reading with the World

How curious is it that on Ash Wednesday, when we are marked with a blackish cross on the forehead, which is visible when we go back to work or the neighborhood, we hear Jesus say, "Beware of practicing your piety before others in order to be seen by them"? Not leaving well enough alone, Jesus warns us not to be "like the hypocrites," who "disfigure their faces to show others that they are fasting."

Ash Wednesday is the one day when what we do in worship lingers visibly through the day. The worship is dark and somber. The truth about each one of us is exposed: you are mortal; you need forgiveness. It is true every day, of course, but the weight of this knowledge might crush us if we carried it daily. So on this day we carry the ashes, whose weight is real but negligible. Most of us forget we have ashes on our heads until someone stares quizzically. Maybe someone asks, or a friend offers you a cloth. Do you rub it off right away? Or carry on with a glimmer of the healthiest possible spiritual pride, in defiance of Jesus' admonition, "When you fast . . . wash your face"?

Way back in Genesis 4, Cain was marked on his forehead as a sign of his guilt, but also of divine protection. Yes, he had killed Abel; but then the Lord, motivated by nothing but mercy,

marked him so he would live safely in Nod, east of Eden. Can we carry this sense of our mortal guilt and yet also the lightness of mercy when we are not sporting the ashes? Maybe when you wash your face in the mornings, you might trace a cross on your forehead with your finger. Or when you rinse away the makeup at day's end, you imagine God's mercy washing away the grime of the day's sin, before bedtime on Ash Wednesday, but maybe also on all the other days. No one will see—except God and you.

The liturgy invites us to create our own liturgies in daily life outside the church. After washing in the morning, you get dressed. The King James Version of our text reads "Enter into thy closet, and . . . pray to thy Father." The result? "Thy Father which seeth in secret shall reward thee." What if every time you enter your closet, you simply pray? If you do, you know you are doing God's will, since Jesus asked us to do just this, and there will be a reward. What might that be?

Spellbound capitalists that we (i.e., North Americans) are, our hopeful hunch is that a reward from God will be monetary, or at least some tangible blessing. Almost as if to clarify things before we traipse off in the wrong direction out of the closet, Jesus presses on to say, "Do not store up for yourselves treasures on earth." It would be hard to pinpoint any biblical commandment more frequently ignored. John Wesley pinpointed the general Christian response to Jesus' command: "They never designed to obey it. From their youth up, it never entered into their thoughts. They were bred up by their Christian parents . . . to break it as soon and as much as they could, and to continue breaking it to their lives' end."[4]

Mind you, this is not the sort of thing a sensitive, pastoral preacher would bring up in an Ash Wednesday homily. Most churches do not even collect an offering on Ash Wednesday. Exegetical experts may have an opinion on how Jesus' thoughts about praying in secret came to be redacted right next to his warnings about laying up treasure on earth. Theologically, the pairing makes all the sense in the world. When we come forward for the imposition of ashes, we are told, "Repent, and believe in the gospel." Repentance, in a spiritual culture where "sin" is a diminished category, is not about this or that peccadillo, but rather who is God and what is not.

Clearly, the greatest of the pseudogods who clamor for our devotion is money. So mighty is the high god of money that we cling to it, and are stingy in giving it to the church where we receive our ashes. Just as Jesus tells his listeners not to make a show of their piety on the one day we do exhibit our ashes, Jesus warns us not to "sound the trumpet when you give alms" so as to elicit the adulation of people in a church where we quite carefully observe anonymous giving. What Christians give to their churches is a closely held secret, but not because of holy devotion to Jesus' words in Matthew 6. Anonymity relieves donors of the competitive spirit that prompts generous giving to universities and nonprofits—but simultaneously relieves donors of the responsibility to give as they are able.

When Mike King, the father of Martin Luther King Jr., arrived at Ebenezer Baptist Church in Atlanta, finances were in disarray. After surveying the situation, he concluded that the problem was anonymous giving, which led to anonymous nongiving. So he placed a ledger at the entry to the sanctuary, detailing each person's contributions for all to see. Feelings were ruffled, but donations soared; the budget crisis was alleviated. Jesus worried about giving to attract attention—which is really no different from his hidden worry about not giving because there is no attention. What do we give in secret?

Cain's fury against his brother was incited because of his sense that God was pleased with Abel's offerings. Then he was marked, for his guilt, but also as a sure sign that the terribly guilty one was also embraced by holy mercy. On Ash Wednesday, and during Lent, should we not raise the question of whether our offerings, of money and passion and self, are pleasing to God? Does the mark of the ashes at the beginning of Lent declare to the world, I am someone who has laid up treasure on earth—and with reckless abandon? This would not be practicing piety to be seen by others; this would be the confession of sorrow and complicity in a world alienated from God.

Matthew raises key questions about the business of giving up something for Lent. Do we choose a trifle, like a donut or coffee or a TV show? Do we dare to go for the gauntlet and think about giving up treasure we may be laying up for ourselves on earth? Could that happen secretly? What goes on in secret anyhow? Sometimes we give up something for Lent, maybe chocolate or alcohol, and we in effect "look dismal" and "disfigure our faces"—to ourselves, pitying or congratulating ourselves for such a noble sacrifice. Could it be cheerful, so we wash our face and look joyful, or actually know the joy of getting unattached or less attached to those treasures on earth?

Lent can begin with good intentions but then fritter away into nothing at all. A season of investment in the treasury of heaven can happen, evidently, only as we withdraw from the treasure we have been banking on earth. This is a hard lesson, won only in prayer, solitude, and humility. Perhaps the best lines in T. S. Eliot's grand poem "Ash Wednesday" form just such a petition: "Teach us to sit still / Even among these rocks, / Our peace in His will."

JAMES C. HOWELL

4. Theodore Jennings, *Good News to the Poor* (Nashville: Abingdon Press, 1990), 31.

Ash Wednesday

Joel 2:1–2, 12–17

[1]Blow the trumpet in Zion;
    sound the alarm on my holy mountain!
Let all the inhabitants of the land tremble,
    for the day of the LORD is coming, it is near—
[2]a day of darkness and gloom,
    a day of clouds and thick darkness!
Like blackness spread upon the mountains
    a great and powerful army comes;
their like has never been from of old,
    nor will be again after them
    in ages to come.
. . . .
[12]Yet even now, says the LORD,
    return to me with all your heart,
with fasting, with weeping, and with mourning;
    [13]rend your hearts and not your clothing.
Return to the LORD, your God,
    for he is gracious and merciful,
slow to anger, and abounding in steadfast love,
    and relents from punishing.
[14]Who knows whether he will not turn and relent,
    and leave a blessing behind him,
a grain offering and a drink offering
    for the LORD, your God?

[15]Blow the trumpet in Zion;
    sanctify a fast;
call a solemn assembly;
    [16]gather the people.
Sanctify the congregation;
    assemble the aged;
gather the children,
    even infants at the breast.
Let the bridegroom leave his room,
    and the bride her canopy.

[17]Between the vestibule and the altar
    let the priests, the ministers of the LORD, weep.
Let them say, "Spare your people, O LORD,
    and do not make your heritage a mockery,
    a byword among the nations.
Why should it be said among the peoples,
    'Where is their God?'"

Commentary 1: Connecting the Reading with Scripture

This Ash Wednesday–appointed passage calls people to repent in anticipation of the "day of the Lord" (2:1). The call follows Joel's vivid depiction of a locust plague that had destroyed the land (1:1–20), a disaster that signified God's judgment on the people. Priests are called to lament (1:13) and to announce a fast. In the opening verses of chapter 2, the prophet shifts to address the Day of the Lord. Now, the locust plague portends larger apocalyptic destruction, with invading army, fire, and signs in the heavens. Verse 12 then invites the people to repent, so that the destruction may be averted. Immediately following the call to repentance in this passage, the Lord has pity and reassures the people that the "northern army" will be removed (2:18–27).

The theme of judgment pervades Joel: starting with the locust plague, expanding to anticipate the Day of the Lord, and here reassuring the people of their salvation from that destruction. Chapter 3 then goes on to describe the Day of the Lord in relation to all nations (not just Judah), leading to holy war between the Lord's warriors and the surrounding nations. The final vision portrays blessings for the Lord's people following the destruction of their enemies (3:17–21). This passage therefore acts as a hinge, turning from the judgment on the people of Israel, toward the judgment on the nations who have scattered the people to other lands. The call to repentance is critical to interrupt the preceding and following destruction, and to connect the wrongdoing of the people of Israel with the wrongdoing of the nations, which has affected them. To neglect either of these—the real guilt of the people or the real oppression that they have faced at the hands of others—would be dangerous.

Judgment and repentance echo throughout the prophetic books, from Isaiah to Malachi. The prophetic section of the Old Testament begins, "Ah, sinful nation, people laden with iniquity, offspring who do evil, children who deal corruptly, who have forsaken the Lord. . . . Why do you seek further beatings? Why do you continue to rebel? . . . Wash yourselves; make yourselves clean; remove the evil of your doings from before my eyes" (Isa. 1:4, 5, 16). The Hebrew canon concludes with Malachi proclaiming, "Lo, I will send you the prophet Elijah before the great and terrible day of the Lord comes. He will turn the hearts of parents to their children and the hearts of children to their parents, so that I will not come and strike the land with a curse" (Mal. 4:5–6). The themes offered here in Joel resonate with the chorus of prophets who call for the people to change their ways before the coming of God's righteous judgment.

The depiction of the Lord as "gracious and merciful, slow to anger, and abounding in steadfast love" (v. 13) is identical to other Old Testament descriptions of God, especially in the Psalms (see Pss. 86:15; 103:8; and 145:8). This same affirmation appears ironically in Jonah 4:2–3, where the antiprophet complains, "I knew that you are a gracious God and merciful, slow to anger and abounding in steadfast love, and ready to relent from punishing. And now, O Lord, please take my life from me." It was obviously a common description of the God of Israel. Joel is not telling the people something they do not already know.

The lectionary pairs this passage from Joel with Scriptures that both echo and challenge the prophet's words. The epistle reading, 2 Corinthians 5:20b–6:10, issues an urgent call to "be reconciled to God," because "now is the day of salvation!" The urgency to repent resonates with Joel's call to return to God. Paul offers a christological claim that stands in some tension with Joel: "For our sake [God] made [Jesus] to be sin who knew no sin, so that in him we might become the righteousness of God" (2 Cor. 5:21). That is, Jesus Christ, who is "without sin," serves as a substitute for our sin, so that we may become righteous in him.

Many classical Christian theological claims are implied here: substitutionary atonement, justification, and a pervasive understanding of sin from which we need to be rescued by God's gracious intervention. The question that arises in juxtaposing these texts is, what is the relationship between our repentance and God's forgiveness? Joel makes it sound as though God may relent *if* we return "with fasting, with weeping, and with mourning" (Joel 2:12). Yet Paul calls people to be reconciled to God *because* of Christ, in whom God has already reconciled the world to God's self (2 Cor. 5:19). Is the logic if/then, or because/therefore? These two affirmations are not necessarily opposed, but they do present an important tension that a preacher may wish to address.

Finally, the Gospel, Matthew 6:1–6, 16–21, presents another fruitful tension with Joel. Together the evangelist and the prophet call their listeners to fasting, prayer, and repentance, traditionally associated with the season of Lent. While Joel instructs us to blow the trumpet to call people together for solemn assembly, Jesus in Matthew's Gospel cautions his followers, "Beware of practicing your piety before others in order to be seen by them. . . . whenever you pray, go into your room and shut the door and pray to your Father who is in secret; and your Father who sees in secret will reward you" (Matt. 6:1, 6). Are solemn assemblies themselves salvific, or can they devolve into displays of pseudo-piety? This is an important caution from Jesus. At the same time, are we only called to individual, private acts of repentance, or are there important occasions when we need to gather as a community, to offer public corporate prayers of confession and repentance? This is the word that Joel might helpfully offer us today.

Beyond the lectionary, and beyond the prophetic themes of judgment and repentance already mentioned, Joel also has important connections to earlier portions of the Hebrew Scriptures, especially descriptions of the priesthood. According to the book of Numbers, blowing the trumpet was the sign appointed to call the people together for a solemn occasion. In Numbers 10, the Lord instructs Moses to make two silver trumpets to be used for this purpose (Num. 10:8; cf. Num. 29:1 and Ps. 81:3). Joel appears to be unique among the prophetic books in calling for a solemn assembly using trumpets, and giving an explicit positive role to the ritual priesthood. This suggests that for Joel more than many other prophets, the priesthood has a vital role in leading the people to repentance (see 2:17).

In the New Testament, John the Baptist and Jesus both echo Joel's call to repentance. So, for instance, John's first words in Matthew are "Repent, for the kingdom of heaven has come near" (Matt. 3:2), and Jesus repeats these words at the beginning of his own ministry (Matt. 4:17). Like Joel, John and Jesus warn of an impending day of judgment, for which people need to prepare by changing their ways. Like Joel also, Jesus (unlike John) emphasizes that God is not only just but also merciful. This is a good opportunity to notice the continuity between Jesus' own teaching and the call of prophets like Joel; rather than portraying Jesus as a break with the teachings of the Old Testament, this is one place where we can see deep resonance.

MARTHA L. MOORE-KEISH

Commentary 2: Connecting the Reading with the World

Amid the devastating experience of mass destruction inflicted on the Jewish people by a scourge of locusts and its residue of famine, drought, and severe heat, the prophet Joel set forth a vision of hope by declaring the possibility for a new life. The restoration of hope in a time of seeming hopelessness is what all suffering people desire most of all, and Joel's listeners were no exception. Both they and the prophet shared a common worldview based on a covenant that their God, YHWH, had initiated with their ancestral father Moses on Mount Sinai. In that agreement, the people promised to remain faithful to God, who in turn promised to protect them from all harm. Alas, the environmental crisis that Joel addressed clearly evidenced their failure to honor the agreement they had made. Yet Joel reminded the people that their God was willing to forgive them if they truly repented of their wrongdoing. That constituted the basis of their renewed hope.

Unlike the OT Jewish nation, the United States is not a theocracy. While not inimical to religion, this nation chose to keep religious institutions and the state separate, so that neither could interfere with the internal life of the other. Nonetheless, that constitutional arrangement has not diminished the importance of religion in the private lives of American citizens.

Certainly much violence accompanied the founding of our nation, beginning with the many wars of conquest with the country's native peoples, wars that greatly diminished their numbers and dispossessed them of their land and pride of sovereignty. Being reduced to vassals must have been the greatest of all indignities for them and their progeny, some of whom live today on reservations, without any hope of having their fortunes restored. Living now as a captive people they can only strive vigilantly to protect the limited territorial rights granted them in the many treaties they made with their conquerors. Thus the extent to which they are hopeful about a new life is a subject worthy of serious inquiry.

Another example of this nation's violent treatment of peoples is seen in the horrific system of chattel slavery, whereby millions of innocent Africans were imported to this country to serve as forced laborers. That brutal system endured for two and a half centuries. Following a bitter civil war it gave way to a similar system of oppression called sharecropping, which lasted for another century. Moreover, the system denied full citizenship rights to former slaves.

Unlike the Native Americans, enslaved Africans eventually discovered in their masters' Bible religious themes and stories that spoke about freedom. In fact, the story of Moses, raised as a slave in the pharaoh's palace, called by God to lead his people out of slavery, brought joy to the hearts and minds of all Africans who heard it. Accordingly, they soon made the story the subject of what has become one of America's most cherished songs, "Go down Moses." In time they organized what black scholars have named "the invisible church." Hidden from their masters in the brush arbors, they would meet to sing, pray, testify, and do what was necessary to encourage and strengthen one another in their suffering by pointing them to the divine source of their hope. Those clandestine meetings became the incubator for the African American religious experience, because in those spaces countless numbers of so-called Negro spirituals were created from tidbits of Scripture and melodies drawn from hybrid African musical rhythms that had survived the experience of slavery. In addition, those spaces nurtured leadership, communal support, and a steadfast hope for a better day.

A further example of the theological meaning of freedom and hope for these oppressed Africans is seen in the practice they instituted of bestowing the name Moses on their cherished leaders, the most prominent of whom was the courageous Harriet Tubman, who led countless numbers of enslaved people to freedom through what came to be called the Underground Railroad.[1] Further still, the hope of seeing the promised land as instilled in them by their leader Moses was invoked by Dr. Martin Luther King Jr. in the sermon he delivered the night before he was assassinated. On that occasion he spoke about having been to the mountaintop, where he saw the promised land. He declared that though he might not live to get there himself, they would certainly get there. That hope envisioned in a dream has sustained African Americans throughout their history in this land.

Alvin Ailey's creative dance "Revelations," one of America's greatest treasures, has inspired generations of peoples round the world in the celebration of that hope. Sorrowful, jubilant, and hopeful, that suite of spirituals, gospel songs, and blues movingly choreographed portrays the deepest grief and greatest joy of the human soul that can be felt by all peoples.

Unlike Native Americans and African Americans, the vast majority of Americans have had little or no experience of mass suffering during the past century and a quarter. Thus, after it became clear on September 11, 2001, that the United States was under attack, the entire nation was surprised, traumatized, and perplexed. Having long assumed that America was a good nation and loved by everyone round

---

1. Readers might be interested in the fine novel that was published recently and which received the National Book Award for Fiction: Colson Whitehead, *The Underground Railroad* (New York: Doubleday, 2016).

the world, many exclaimed, "Why us?" Others asked, "Why do they hate us so?" Needless to say, the 9/11 terrorist attack dispelled the illusion of universal love for our nation.

With the absence of a national religion, spontaneous shrines soon emerged at the working sites where many first responders lost their lives, and photos of lost relatives were posted all over the city. Everyone was in deep mourning. The nearby Trinity Church opened its doors and became a staging site for all the volunteers who very soon began their work of searching through the rubble for possible survivors or remains. Both civic leaders and ordinary citizens seemed to be motivated by the impulse to maintain the normal routines of daily life as a way of signaling to the enemy that their terror had failed to break the spirit of Americans. Thus the collective resolve to return to the normality of daily life as quickly as possible provided the necessary motivation to do something other than watch the repetitive streaming of the event on television news channels.

The citizenry was comforted by the extraordinary outpouring of sympathy and material assistance from around the world. The relatively rapid actions of clearing the site known as Ground Zero, the establishment of the Department of Homeland Security, deliberations about designing a memorial, rebuilding the towers, and devising a method to administer the Victims Compensation Fund all combined in building hope for the future.

Individuals and communities that have experienced little or no hardship take good fortune for granted. Consequently, when they face suffering, they have virtually no coping resources on which to rely. They then must turn for comfort and hope to those who have experienced similar life-and-death struggles. Those resources may be selected parts of sacred literature, music, or the personal visitations, prayers, and testimonies of compassionate souls. All such ministries of grace help the process of enabling hope when and where it is most needed.

PETER J. PARIS

First Sunday in Lent

Deuteronomy 26:1–11
Psalm 91:1–2, 9–16

Romans 10:8b–13
Luke 4:1–13

Deuteronomy 26:1–11

¹When you have come into the land that the LORD your God is giving you as an inheritance to possess, and you possess it, and settle in it, ²you shall take some of the first of all the fruit of the ground, which you harvest from the land that the LORD your God is giving you, and you shall put it in a basket and go to the place that the LORD your God will choose as a dwelling for his name. ³You shall go to the priest who is in office at that time, and say to him, "Today I declare to the LORD your God that I have come into the land that the LORD swore to our ancestors to give us." ⁴When the priest takes the basket from your hand and sets it down before the altar of the LORD your God, ⁵you shall make this response before the LORD your God: "A wandering Aramean was my ancestor; he went down into Egypt and lived there as an alien, few in number, and there he became a great nation, mighty and populous. ⁶When the Egyptians treated us harshly and afflicted us, by imposing hard labor on us, ⁷we cried to the LORD, the God of our ancestors; the LORD heard our voice and saw our affliction, our toil, and our oppression. ⁸The LORD brought us out of Egypt with a mighty hand and an outstretched arm, with a terrifying display of power, and with signs and wonders; ⁹and he brought us into this place and gave us this land, a land flowing with milk and honey. ¹⁰So now I bring the first of the fruit of the ground that you, O LORD, have given me." You shall set it down before the LORD your God and bow down before the LORD your God. ¹¹Then you, together with the Levites and the aliens who reside among you, shall celebrate with all the bounty that the LORD your God has given to you and to your house.

Commentary 1: Connecting the Reading with Scripture

Throughout the Pentateuch, sacred story and law are closely interwoven. After the primordial havoc of the flood, Noah emerges from the ark to build an altar; his ritual offering secures a commitment from God never again to destroy every living creature (Gen. 8:20–22). When the Israelites struggle their way through the wilderness to Sinai, they consecrate themselves (Exod. 19:10–15) to meet a dangerous Lawgiver who descends upon the mountain in thunder and lightning, smoke and fire, with "a blast of a trumpet so loud that all the people who were in the camp trembled" (vv. 16–25). The magnificent remembrance literature of Deuteronomy offers a theological "history" of ancient Israel rich with ritual and juridical practices, forming a people whose polity and cultic observance are narrated as the core of covenantal relation.

In Deuteronomy 26, the offering of first-fruits is grounded in a larger narrative that claims God has ordained the conquest of Canaan by Israel. The territory on the far side of the Jordan is described not as the home of the Hittites, Girgashites, Amorites, Canaanites, Perizzites, Hivites, and Jebusites (Deut. 7:1; cf. 20:17), but as "the land that the LORD your God is giving you" (26:1–3). The Israelites are to become sovereign over this territory through extermination or subjugation of the indigenous inhabitants—the project, literally and rhetorically, of the book of Joshua. The Christian preacher should be mindful of the three verses preceding our passage.

24

Anomalous in a context of case laws about internecine disputes and economic equity, these verses just prior to our lection (25:17–19) serve to fan enmity against a hated antagonist of Israel. Israel is exhorted never to forget the savage attack they suffered at the hands of the Amalekites, indigenes portrayed as scurrilous ("undeterred by the fear of God," v. 18 NJPS) in their assault on Israelites "famished and weary." The image of Amalek ruthlessly picking off the weak and those "who lagged behind" (v. 18) may be meant to evoke the predatory Arabian wolf or lion, a rhetorical move that would surely have catalyzed a fearful and aggressive response in the implied audience. While rhetoric about obliterating Canaanites is not foregrounded in our passage as such, the larger conquest narrative in which 26:1–11 is embedded must be handled with care by the preacher.

The Talmud tractate dealing with firstfruits, *Bikkurim*, discusses legal classifications of various "seed" offerings, who may bring the offering, and who should say the declaration. From other citations in rabbinic literature, we may surmise that the ritual of offering firstfruits was richly resonant for ancient Jewish worshipers. Jeffrey Tigay notes that the Dead Sea scroll known as the Temple Scroll (11QT) "prescribes that the first barley, wheat, wine, and oil be brought on different dates, at fifty-day intervals," and that, according to *Bikkurim*, "in the late Second Temple period farmers . . . would come in groups made up of people from towns in the same region. They traveled in a festive procession, led by a flute player and an ox with gilded horns and an olive wreath, and were welcomed by officials outside Jerusalem."[1]

A Sign unto This Nation

The Lord has made me a sign unto this nation, an' I go round a'testifyin', an' showin' their sins agin my people. My name was Isabella; but when I left the house of bondage, I left everything behind. I wa'n't goin' to keep nothin' of Egypt on me, an' so I went to the Lord an' asked him to give me a new name. An' the Lord gave me Sojourner, because I was to travel up an' down the land, showin' the people their sins, an' bein' a sign unto them. Afterword I told the Lord I wanted another name, 'cause everybody else had two names; and the Lord gave me Truth, because I was to declare the Truth to the people. . . . I journeys round to camp meetin's, an' wherever folks is, an' I sets up my banner, an' then I sings, an' then folks always come up round me, an' then I preaches to 'em. I tells 'em about Jesus, an' I tells 'em about the sins of this people.

Sojourner Truth, "The Lord Has Made Me a Sign," in *The Atlantic Monthly*, vol. 11 (April 1863), 473, 478.

In Deuteronomy 26:5, the unusual way of describing Israel's origin, "My father was a wandering Aramean" (*'arammi 'oved 'avi*), has drawn scholarly attention for many centuries. Both the Pentateuch and the book of Joshua narrate "Israel" as a group that came as landless outsiders to the territory on which they settle. The ritual declaration in the firstfruits ceremony inscribes that foreignness via the demonym "Aramean," one from the region of Aram[2] in what has become modern-day Syria and southeastern Turkey. The modifier *'oved* may be translated as "wandering," but we should not imagine a purposeless traversing of terrain. The term could signify a journey or, alternatively, the nomadic or seminomadic movement of agriculturalists pasturing herds over great distances. Other meanings using that Hebrew root include losing one's way, going astray, and being a fugitive. Thus the semantic possibilities range from the traditional NRSV version to the striking formulation of Louis Stulman: "My father was a Syrian refugee." As Stulman observes, "The confession . . . refuses to suppress language of loss, trauma,

---

1. Jeffrey Tigay, *Deuteronomy*, JPS Torah Commentary (Philadelphia: Jewish Publication Society, 1996), 239.
2. The Arameans were not a unified people but, rather, a diverse group of tribes and states spread across the Levant and southern Mesopotamia. See K. Lawson Younger Jr., "Aram and the Arameans," in *The World around the Old Testament: The People and Places of the Ancient Near East*, ed. Bill T. Arnold and Brent A. Strawn (Grand Rapids: Baker Academic Press, 2016), 229–65.

and marginality. Instead it makes the nation's hardships part of its public narrative."[3]

Who, then, is meant by "my father" (*'avi*)? Abraham could be the referent, as the originary ancestor of Israel; he is said to have come from Aram-naharaim, a region of Haran (see Gen. 11:31; 24:4, 10), and upon arriving in Canaan, he goes immediately down into Egypt (Gen. 12:10–20). Jacob is also a strong possibility, especially if we read "Jacob" as signifying both the patriarch and his kinship group. Conflict with his brother Esau drives Jacob away from the family to his maternal uncle Laban Paddan-aram (Gen. 28–31); see the NJPS translation, "My father was a fugitive Aramean," and Hosea 12:12, "Jacob fled to the land of Aram; there Israel served for a wife, and for a wife he guarded sheep." Many years later, Jacob's son Joseph is betrayed by his brothers, taken by force to Egypt, and imprisoned, later growing politically powerful. The household of Jacob eventually joins Joseph in Egypt; the descriptor "few in number" (*bimte ma'at*, Deut. 26:5) is congruent with an earlier note that seventy persons from the household of Jacob went down to Egypt (Gen. 46:27).

The liturgical recital continues with the narrative thread of the Joseph story: "he became a great nation, mighty and populous," then Egyptian oppression intensified against the Israelites, and "the LORD brought us out of Egypt with a mighty hand and an outstretched arm" (Deut. 26:8). The description of the land of Canaan as a "land flowing with milk and honey" (v. 9) underlines the debt that Israel owes to their redeeming God, not only for their rescue from slavery, but for blessing them with agricultural bounty. Four occurrences of the phrase "land flowing with milk and honey" in Exodus are explicitly connected to the list of Canaanite indigenes whom Israel has been commanded to displace (see Exod. 3:8, 17; 13:5; 33:2–3). Thus even the trope of abundant land cannot be separated from slaughter. Again, the contemporary preacher must consider this liturgical recital with attentiveness to the dark undertones of that larger narrative.

Our passage offers a notable turn to direct address of God in verse 10: "So now I bring the first of the fruit of the ground that you, O LORD, have given me." In continuity with ancestral tradition, the prayerful worshiper makes an offering to God from the abundance that God has graciously bestowed. Rejoicing is the appropriate response of the whole community to God's goodness (v. 11). The landless Levite and stranger (*ger*) are to be included in the jubilant celebration, something that demonstrates care for those who remain vulnerable in this community. Israel thus claims its identity ritually as a people sustained by God's goodness long ago, aware of God's continuing blessings, and mandated by covenant obligation to continue to care for those in need.

CAROLYN J. SHARP

Commentary 2: Connecting the Reading with the World

First, for a reality check about the distance between us and Deuteronomy, see Deuteronomy 25:5–12. The insistence about "firstfruits" in today's lectionary reading may feel more familiar than repulsive verses that dictate merciless cutting off of women's hands, and in sharp contrast to those verses, it is a teaching to be affirmed. But the "firstfruits" call is also profoundly distant from predominant modern Western understanding. For today it is natural to think it reasonable and responsible to give not the firstfruits of our labor—which we think of without qualification as *ours*—but to give from the excess of our wealth (see in this regard Jesus' evaluation of giving from excess in the story of the widow's mite: Mark 12:41–44; Luke 21:1–4). For predominant understanding, giving is admirable because we are going above and beyond any reasonable norm insofar as we are willing to give to others what is, after all, rightly *ours*, from *our* land, *our* labor, *our* talents. To give not from abundance but from

3. See Louis Stulman, "My Father Was a Syrian Refugee," *Journal for Preachers* 40 (2016): 9–14.

firstfruits, by contrast, marks a radically contrary orientation, for it concretely acknowledges all we possess belongs first of all to God. Nothing is first of all *ours*. We give or possess only what we have already been given (Deut. 26:10).

We can think that what is ours is ours, privately, exclusively, firstly ours, because modern Western thought understands the relationship between self and world very differently from Deuteronomy. The modern Western self is conceived as existing first as the discrete, atomistic "I," whose natural, foremost concerns are for personal survival, security, power, and flourishing in a war of all against all. The modern Western ethical and political emphasis upon "rights" is anchored in this picture of self and world, and modern ethics and politics are wholly anchored in the natural rights of individual I's. Smart individuals will pursue their *enlightened* self-interest, but modern thought never escapes the horizon of self-interest. Enlightened self-interest leads people to organize themselves into civil orders (e.g., families, tribes, city-states, nation-states, transnational legal structures) in order to secure degrees of power that far outstrip the potential of any individual. Of course, the selfish motivational structure remains intact, so there is ceaseless struggle both among individuals within each collective and also among collectives in the war of all against all.

Times of greed, when one individual or collective concludes they possess or can successfully seize disproportionate power over others, are ripe for tyrants, tyranny, and oppression. Times of scarcity, when fearful, desperate individuals or collectives conclude there is, for instance, not enough food, water, or treasure to allow for the flourishing or survival of all, are ripe for sectarian intolerance and ethnic cleansing. Dynamics of greed and of scarcity can be mutually reinforcing—most obviously when tyrants leverage others' fear about survival in order to motivate sectarian intolerance and violence (all to the advantage of the tyranny).

Modern ethical and political understanding is extraordinarily vulnerable to these dynamics, for tyrants or sectarians have typically concluded their actions are indeed wholly consistent with their own enlightened self-interest; so for modern rationality the only counter to

greed and tyranny is martial resistance by the oppressed. Notably, in a modern understanding, the oppressed never resist out of commitment to what is loving, just, or good, but out of commitment to their own self-interest (in stark contrast to Amos or Isaiah, or modern prophets like Mahatma Gandhi, Martin Luther King Jr., or Gustavo Gutiérrez). The modern picture is abetted by unqualified Darwinian accounts of motivational dynamics, where the self-interest/enlightened self-interest either/or is described in terms of selfish and cooperative genes (more accurately, parasitic and symbiotic interactions), with all dynamics ultimately subservient to the rule of survival of the fittest (I wholly affirm evolutionary theory delimited within the sphere of science, but not, as in this case, when asserted as an unqualified metaphysic/religion).

What drops out entirely in modern Western understanding is conceptual space for any affirmation of the loving, good, or just. This trivializes the protest of the oppressed by stripping it of any moral dimension (for they too are understood to be wholly motivated by self-interest). It also serves as a salve to the dominant who are acting to preserve their privilege, for on this account they are, after all, only doing what is natural, what anyone in their position would do. Of course, insofar as this understanding of reality holds sway, the oppressed themselves are terribly well prepared to replicate the oppression they have experienced insofar as they gain power; so the vicious wheel of history rolls on in an unending war of all against all (this is precisely the dynamic described and repeatedly decried in the Deuteronomistic History).

The reality of the power of self-centered human motivation has been recognized for millennia. New in modernity is the contention that this story is not only true, but that it is exhaustively true, that all appeals to the call of God, to the call of love and justice, are confused. This passage, by contrast, is not only exquisitely sensitive to all the self-interested dynamics that modernity baptizes as "natural." It proclaims that we are not first of all isolated selves with individual rights; we are first of all children of God, brothers and sisters who have only what we have first received, and who in turn should desire to give as we have been given (in accord with standard triage protocols, with paramount concern/effort for those in the greatest need).

Today's text is exquisitely sensitive to the power of the natural in the modern, selfish sense. Ideas of possessing the "promised land" and of being God's "chosen people," combined with memories of having been oppressed in Egypt and also "natural" tendencies to self-aggrandizement and self-centeredness, threatened to lead (and, as the prophets lamented, did lead) the Israelites to see themselves as specially favored, to forget other peoples who already lived on the "promised land," to nativist intolerance of ethnic diversity, to sectarian ritual purity, and to forget the poor and vulnerable (it may be worth adding Deuteronomy 26:12 to the reading with regard to this last concern).

The text struggles against these diverse threats by anchoring Israelite identity in an immigrant, a "wandering Aramean"; by reminding the Israelites that they were themselves poor, marginalized, oppressed strangers in a strange land; and by urging them to share their bounty "together with the Levites and the aliens who reside among you" (so, no ritual or ethnic sectarianism; all

attend to the basic needs of and break bread with all). This vision is not unrealistically utopian. This is not a classless society. It is built upon and so inescapably embodies the scars of strife (e.g., it includes "aliens"). However, it is a society whose people remember their own forced migration and slavery, a society where diverse peoples are affirmed in their diversity but where all are called to recognize a shared indebtedness to God; and so it is a society in which both diverse identities and common responsibilities to one another are affirmed. In accord with this recognition that firstfruits belong to God, Deuteronomy is saying that Israelite society (and any society) is good and faithful insofar as it is dedicated first and foremost to ensuring a basic standard of living for all, regardless of religious, racial, or ethnic identity. It means that good people and good societies will struggle to ensure *first and foremost, before any toleration of personal excess*, that national and international laws will be structured so that the basic needs of all—education, health care, food, clothing, and personal/familial security—will be met.

WILLIAM GREENWAY

Psalm 91:1–2, 9–16

[1]You who live in the shelter of the Most High,
  who abide in the shadow of the Almighty,
[2]will say to the LORD, "My refuge and my fortress;
  my God, in whom I trust."
. . . .
[9]Because you have made the LORD your refuge,
  the Most High your dwelling place,
[10]no evil shall befall you,
  no scourge come near your tent.

[11]For he will command his angels concerning you
  to guard you in all your ways.
[12]On their hands they will bear you up,
  so that you will not dash your foot against a stone.
[13]You will tread on the lion and the adder,
  the young lion and the serpent you will trample under foot.

[14]Those who love me, I will deliver;
  I will protect those who know my name.
[15]When they call to me, I will answer them;
  I will be with them in trouble,
  I will rescue them and honor them.
[16]With long life I will satisfy them,
  and show them my salvation.

Connecting the Psalm with Scripture and Worship

The Revised Common Lectionary is designed in such a way that the lesson from the Psalter is normally to be understood as a response to the Old Testament lesson; however, this principle of construction is not immediately obvious in the case of Psalm 91:1–2, 9–16 and its relationship with Deuteronomy 26:1–11. Rather, the more obvious connection is between Psalm 91:1–2, 9–16 and the Gospel lesson, Luke 4:1–13, in which verses 10–11 contains a quotation of Psalm 91:11–12. His quotation is puzzling, because it is the devil who is quoting Psalm 91! On the one hand, as a career-long Psalms scholar, I am pleased to see that the Psalms have such wide currency that even the devil can quote them. On the other hand, when the devil quotes the Psalms, it should alert us to the fact

that Scripture in general can be misinterpreted; more particularly, the assurance that the Psalms offer their readers can be misconstrued.

From a form-critical perspective, Psalm 91 is universally categorized as a psalm of confidence/trust/assurance; and it contains a threefold occurrence of one of the Psalter's key words in the vocabulary of the faithful: "refuge" (vv. 2, 4, 9; see Pss. 2:12; 5:11; 7:1; 11:1; and often). Furthermore, the assurance that the psalmist articulates and claims in the midst of overwhelming danger and opposition (see vv. 3–7, 13) is given unique emphasis by the fact that Psalm 91 concludes with a divine speech in verses 14–16. The speech contains seven first-person verbs; and because seven is the biblical number of wholeness or completeness, this syntactical construction reinforces the comprehensiveness of the promise of divine help and protection. Plus, in the midst of the seven verbs there is a verbless clause that stands out by way of its position and differing syntax: "I will be with them in trouble" (v. 15).

Why does Jesus reject the promise of divine protection and deliverance, interpreting the quotation of Psalm 91:11–12 by the devil as a test (Luke 4:12)? As always, context is crucial. For Jesus to claim the assurance of Psalm 91:11–12 in this context would have been self-serving. In another context, later in the Gospel of Luke, Jesus will claim and embrace the assurance that the Psalms offer. This latter context is a cross, from which Jesus says, "Father, into your hands I commend my spirit" (Luke 23:46; see Ps. 31:5).

This complex of connections provides timely and important instruction for the First Sunday in Lent. In particular, Jesus' rejection of the assurance of Psalm 91:11–12 at the beginning of Luke is a reminder that the cross is the destination of Jesus' journey throughout the Gospel. Jesus' journey will not be devoid of opposition and suffering, as the devil suggests might be possible. Rather, Jesus will claim divine deliverance and protection "in trouble" (Ps. 91:15). Herein may lie instruction for our own Lenten journeys. It is entirely possible for our Lenten disciplines, for instance, to become self-serving rather than cross-bearing (see Isa. 58:1–12, the Old Testament lesson for Ash Wednesday).

As Albert Camus once suggested, it seems that some Christians are willing to ascend a cross, only to be seen from a greater distance! The things we give up for Lent can become sources of pride that call attention to ourselves, rather than practices of penitence and humility. As demonstrated in Luke 4, it might even be possible to claim the assurance of Psalm 91 in an attempt to avoid suffering, rather than embracing the suffering that derives from serving God faithfully and enacting God's love in the world, as Jesus did. This is a temptation to be avoided, as Jesus avoided it.

If there is a connection between Psalm 91:1–2, 9–16 and Deuteronomy 26:1–11, the clue may be the Hebrew word translated "dwelling place" (Ps. 91:9). It also occurs in the first verse of Psalm 90, which opens Book IV of the Psalter; this verse seems to offer a response to the crisis of exile that is articulated in the conclusion of Psalm 89. The exile represented a sort of renewed landlessness, and Psalms 90–91 respond by suggesting that the true home of the people of God is not the land; rather, it is God's own self. The true assurance is to make "the Most High your dwelling place" (Ps. 91:9).

While Deuteronomy 26 anticipates entry into the land, the final chapter of the Pentateuch severs this anticipation from the narrative account of entry into the land in the book of Joshua. The canonical effect is to conclude the Pentateuch—the Torah, the first and most authoritative division of the Jewish canon—with the people of God still outside the land. This seems odd, but it almost certainly reflects the crisis of exile and the enduring situation of the people of God in the postexilic era; that is, they would never fully possess and control their land again. That was the bad news, but the good news was that God would be their "dwelling place in all generations" (Ps. 90:1; see 91:9).

That assurance is still good news. It does not promise an easy or carefree existence, but it offers the assurance that empowered Jesus, and empowers us, to bear the cross as we follow Jesus (see Luke 9:23).

J. CLINTON MCCANN JR.

Romans 10:8b–13

8b"The word is near you,
    on your lips and in your heart"

(that is, the word of faith that we proclaim); 9because if you confess with your lips that Jesus is Lord and believe in your heart that God raised him from the dead, you will be saved. 10For one believes with the heart and so is justified, and one confesses with the mouth and so is saved. 11The scripture says, "No one who believes in him will be put to shame." 12For there is no distinction between Jew and Greek; the same Lord is Lord of all and is generous to all who call on him. 13For, "Everyone who calls on the name of the Lord shall be saved."

Commentary 1: Connecting the Reading with Scripture

Paul is writing to people he has never met. When he wrote to the Thessalonians, Philippians, Corinthians, and Galatians, he knew people in those communities and called some of them by name. He had been to those cities and regions, but he has never been to Rome. In the first chapter he voiced his fervent hope to "at last succeed in coming to you" (Rom. 1:10). He repeats that hope near the end of his letter, planning to stop in Rome on his way to Spain (15:23–24). In this letter Paul does not address the kinds of divisions that plagued the community in Corinth, but he is concerned about relationships between Gentiles and Jews. "For there is no distinction between Jew and Greek," he proclaims, "the same Lord is Lord of all and is generous to all who call on him" (10:12). Paul had written similar words in his Letter to the Galatians (Gal. 3:28). In Romans, Paul is working out what that bold proclamation means—not only for the Romans, but also for him. While affirming that Gentiles have a place within the "body of Christ," he is equally passionate to show that God's promise to Israel has not been revoked.

The reading for this First Sunday in Lent is part of Paul's program to affirm God's promise and generosity to *both* Gentiles and Jews. In verse 8b, Paul is quoting the conclusion of a text from Deuteronomy 30: "'The word is near you, on your lips and in your heart' (that is, the word of faith that we proclaim)." He wants his readers to trust God's closeness, but we do not get the full impact of this conclusion unless we know what it is concluding! Beginning in 10:6 Paul quotes the questions that the conclusion answers. He paraphrases Deuteronomy 30:12–13, bringing Christ into the text: "'Who will ascend into heaven?' (that is, to bring Christ down) or 'Who will descend into the abyss?' (that is, to bring Christ up from the dead)." Paul makes a common Jewish exegetical move, using "that is" to bring Christ into the text. He also makes an interpretive turn when he writes, "Who will descend *into the abyss*?" (italics added). The Deuteronomy text asks, "Who will cross to the other side of the sea for us?" (Deut. 30:13). Paul changes the geographical image of crossing the sea to give a picture of Christ rising from the abyss of death.

Is Paul writing primarily to Jews? We might assume so because half of the verses in today's passage are from Hebrew Scriptures (Deut. 30:14 in 10:8b; Isa. 28:16 in 10:11; and Joel 2:32 in 10:13). If he is not writing to Jews, why quote Hebrew Scripture? In the salutation to his letter Paul seems to be writing primarily to Gentiles (Rom. 1:5–6, 13). Paul is a devoted follower of Christ, a believer in the crucified and risen Son of God. Yet Paul remains a Jew:

> Paul saw himself wholly within Judaism, as one who was assigned a special role in the restoration of Israel and the nations (Rom 11.1–15; Gal 1.13–16). He was a reformer, one who sought to redress what he believed to be an oversight (his own, formerly, and that of his fellow Jews, still); he was not the founder of a new religion, even if things later turned out otherwise.[1]

When Paul quotes verses from Hebrew Scripture in today's reading, he is writing as someone shaped by those texts. These words are in his body and in his bones. For Paul, this Scripture is fulfilled in Jesus Christ.

The text appointed for this Sunday comes right in the middle of chapters 9 to 11. These three chapters form a little book within the larger book of Romans. Paul begins this book-within-a-book declaring, "I am speaking the truth in Christ—I am not lying . . ." (9:1a), and ends this section with what sounds like a conclusion: "For from him and through him and to him are all things. To him be the glory forever. Amen" (11:36). In the verses between 9:1 and 11:36, Paul struggles with the reality that some Israelites (his usual word for the Jews) have not come to believe in Christ. This is painful for Paul, for as he says, they are "my own people, my kindred according to the flesh" (9:3b). Paul is a Jew who has come to believe that Jesus Christ is the closeness of God.

Deuteronomy 30 provides the foundation for what he says next. Paul picks up two key phrases in the Deuteronomy text: "on your lips" and "in your heart." The next two verses emphasize these two words: "if you confess with your lips that Jesus is Lord and believe in your heart that God raised him from the dead, you will be saved" (10:9). This is a powerful—and dangerous—proclamation to the believers in Rome. To say Jesus is Lord was treason, for the emperor

of Rome was lord. It would be one thing to speak that confession in a far-flung corner of the empire, but to make that confession in the city of Rome was a different matter. (Hopefully, Paul's letter would not fall into the wrong hands.) In the following verse Paul continues to play on the Deuteronomy text in a slightly different way: "For one believes with the heart and so is justified, and one confesses with the mouth and so is saved" (10:10). Heart (*kardia*) and lips/mouth (*stoma*) are connected. Heart is internal; lips and mouth are external.[2] There must be congruence between the two. What we say with our lips should come from what we believe in our hearts.

There is a connection here with the Gospel reading for this Sunday. In Luke's temptation story Jesus does what Paul does in Romans; he quotes Deuteronomy. In Jesus' case the words of Deuteronomy provide his defense against every temptation of the devil (Luke 4:1–12). Jesus says nothing on his own, but trusts that God's word is near him, in his heart and on his lips. It is as though Jesus reaches up and touches an invisible *mezuzah* with the text of Deuteronomy inside. The devil also quotes Scripture. He quotes verses from Psalm 91 to tempt Jesus to jump from the temple spire (Luke 4:10–11), but the devil's lips do not match what is in his heart. Jesus and Paul, both Jews, trust that God's word is near, in their hearts and on their lips.

In Romans, the lectionary reading closes with a quote from Joel: "Everyone who calls on the name of the Lord shall be saved" (10:13). For Joel, "the Lord" in that sentence was not Jesus, but Paul sees Jesus there. He longs for all his Jewish kin to see Jesus there too, and to confess Jesus as Lord. However, if that does not happen, Paul wants believers in Rome to know that God's promise to Israel remains: "God has not rejected his people whom he foreknew" (11:2). Paul wants those of us who read his letter now to know that too.

BARBARA K. LUNDBLAD

---

1. Mark D. Nanos, "Paul and Judaism," in Amy-Jill Levine and Marc Zvi Brettler, eds., *The Jewish Annotated New Testament* (New York: Oxford University Press, 2011), 552.

2. Audrey West, "Commentary on Romans 10:8b–3," in Working Preacher—Preaching This Week. http://www.workingpreacher.org/preachings.aspx?commentary_id=2774.

Commentary 2: Connecting the Reading with the World

This passage from Romans comes to us on the First Sunday in Lent. For those who did not attend Ash Wednesday services, today's lessons serve as the invitation to the observance of Lent, when repentance and reconciliation, approached through spiritual discipline and austerity, take center stage in Christian life.

We enter the middle of a conversation in Romans, or at least, a discourse by Paul that presumes knowledge of some of the fledgling church's challenges in Rome. Rome is a multi-ethnic, religiously diverse population center. Followers of Christ in Rome include those born into both Jewish and Greco-Roman religious traditions. Having grappled with the question of how Greek and Jewish believers can share in Christian community in previous letters, Paul jumps in with both feet, offering a full-fledged defense of the possibility of an ethnically diverse church and approaches to following Christ that draw on the strengths of multiple religious traditions. Jews and Greeks are religiously distinctive, but also are ethnic, cultural peoples with different histories, social locations, and relationships to empire. Paul affirms that God's generosity is not limited by a particular way of expressing faith. God is large enough to span our ways of expressing our allegiance and the varying shapes of our hearts.

The resonances will be many for US churches that find themselves in diverse or changing communities. As fewer churches find themselves easily recruiting new members of the same ethnic, denominational, and linguistic background as longtime members, increasing numbers of congregations must ask the question of how diverse practices and customs can come together in one church. Especially in the historic denominations, many congregations struggle to see beyond the way things have always been done. This reading invites longtime members to imagine that new people from outside their cultural and religious worlds might bring new gifts, express faith in new ways. Paul points to the unity of Christ and the generosity of God as starting points for this project. This lesson suggests that the tests of what unite us

will be simple ones, ones that will have little to do with liturgical colors, or the ordering of prayers, or the placement of candles. We may sing in different languages, to different familiar melodies, but we will offer what is on our lips and on our hearts.

The reading begins with the word: "The word is near you, on your lips and in your heart" (Rom. 10:8b). The word of faith, in Paul's view, has power to unite a diversity of practice and background. It is not complicated or far off (the rather complex theological argument Paul has undertaken in the Letter to the Romans thus far notwithstanding). The reference to the nearness of the word suggests both a connection to Jewish tradition and accessibility to those with no prior experience of the God of Israel. For those versed in Hebrew Scripture, a word that is near, written on the lips and the heart, calls to mind Deuteronomy 11:18 and Jeremiah 31:33. For those unfamiliar with God's promises through the covenant with Israel, a word that is near and accessible invites fullness of participation. Depth of knowledge and tradition enriches faith, but is not a prerequisite.

The preacher calling her or his congregation to the observance of a holy Lent might well make good use of both "insider" and "outsider" aspects of this claim about the word of faith. It is a chance to root Christian belief in the covenant at Sinai, while at the same time inviting those who are new to the faith into a life of practice and proclamation, equally solid on the ground of their own relationship with the Holy One as those who have more years of faith to their credit.

Paul calls upon the church in Rome to "confess with your lips and believe in your heart." Just as there are insiders and outsiders to the history of God's relationship with Israel, there are internal and external aspects to the faith. In Paul's view, both are required. It is not enough to pay lip service, but neither is the sort of private and personal faith that never reaches the point of public confession adequate to the challenge of following Christ.

So what must we confess and believe? Paul here identifies Jesus' lordship and resurrection as the centers of the gospel narrative. In keeping with Paul's consistent emphasis on the centrality of the cross, this suggests that the hearer must both believe and show forth a willingness to sacrifice everything. Paul emphasizes humility, even humiliation. We must be willing to give up our pride and our good standing in the eyes of others when we are called into the service of Christ. The power to risk humiliation comes in the news of the resurrection. To confess resurrection is to see beyond the visible end of the story, to believe in the triumph of love, and to embrace a life beyond fear (even when we are terrified). Naming collective and personal fears—such as loss of power, status, safety, or identity—that might hold back the confessions of Christians in your particular context may help to make this connection for the listener.

To confess Jesus as Lord is to give up dreams of a worldly and powerful king as our Messiah. Paul uses language that sets Christ in parallel with Caesar and then firmly establishes Christ's precedence. To confess Jesus as Lord is to accept that God has chosen an impoverished Southwest Asian man from a backwater of the Roman Empire to be our savior. This passage begs us to imagine that God might be doing something equally unexpected, even deeply countercultural, in our own day. When we claim a Lord who is not Caesar, what do we risk? What do we give up? Which principalities and powers have a claim on our allegiance? What will happen to that allegiance if we have only one Lord, one leader who is worthy of following? If we are called to public expression of the humiliation of the cross, with whom must

we stand? How will our respectability—often so dear to faithful church folk—be challenged? What might we lose?

In a time of political polarization, this reading from Romans offers a way beyond partisan politics. Whatever our ideal political leader may look like, the call to confess one Lord takes Christians beyond the political divides of the moment, serving as a powerful reminder that no political leader can be our Messiah. This frees the church to speak directly to love for God and neighbor, to forgiveness and to the belovedness of all God's people, values with the potential to unite us when politics divides us.

The reading ends with the affirmation of God's generosity and the universality of the gospel promise. There is hope for all of our hearts of stone. Our willingness to risk all, to take up the cross for love, to publicly offer our lives as an offering and sacrifice to God will make us one church, one community of believers. The creative preacher may start with the gathered community as a safe setting in which to hone the practice of love and forgiveness, then point the faithful out the doors and into their families, neighborhoods, schools, workplaces, and communities to put those basic Christian gifts to work. Paul's extravagant claim on universality is large enough to push Christ's followers into relationships beyond the walls of the church and beyond the bounds of denomination. This reading frames the Lenten invitation to turn toward the cross as one of freedom—freedom to love fearlessly and to live beyond the boundaries we and the world around us so often impose.

ANNA B. OLSON

Luke 4:1–13

¹Jesus, full of the Holy Spirit, returned from the Jordan and was led by the Spirit in the wilderness, ²where for forty days he was tempted by the devil. He ate nothing at all during those days, and when they were over, he was famished. ³The devil said to him, "If you are the Son of God, command this stone to become a loaf of bread." ⁴Jesus answered him, "It is written, 'One does not live by bread alone.'"

⁵Then the devil led him up and showed him in an instant all the kingdoms of the world. ⁶And the devil said to him, "To you I will give their glory and all this authority; for it has been given over to me, and I give it to anyone I please. ⁷If you, then, will worship me, it will all be yours." ⁸Jesus answered him, "It is written,

'Worship the Lord your God,
    and serve only him.'"

⁹Then the devil took him to Jerusalem, and placed him on the pinnacle of the temple, saying to him, "If you are the Son of God, throw yourself down from here, ¹⁰for it is written,

'He will command his angels concerning you,
    to protect you,'

¹¹and

'On their hands they will bear you up,
    so that you will not dash your foot against a stone.'"

¹²Jesus answered him, "It is said, 'Do not put the Lord your God to the test.'" ¹³When the devil had finished every test, he departed from him until an opportune time.

Commentary 1: Connecting the Reading with Scripture

The temptation story of Jesus appears only in the Synoptic Gospels (Mark 1:12–13; Matt. 4:1–11; Luke 4:1–13), not in the Gospel of John. Yet each Synoptic version is unique in its own way. Mark's account is the shortest, providing only a two-verse summary of the story. Although many Christians associate the dialogue between Jesus and the devil with the temptation account, it is present only in the Gospels of Matthew and Luke. Furthermore, while the devil's three challenges to Jesus are essentially the same in Matthew and Luke, their order and the language used are different.

In terms of Lent, Jesus' temptation functions as the basic biblical story and rationale for the forty days leading up to Easter (six and a half weeks, not counting Sundays). This First Sunday in Lent is an invitation for Christians willingly to follow Jesus into the wilderness. Followers subject themselves to the kind of self-scrutiny and testing that unveils each person's deepest hopes as well as the darkest and most self-serving outcomes of their greatest capacities, gifts, and callings. Consequently, Luke's opening scene is particularly striking, since Luke is the only Gospel to portray Jesus in the wilderness being "led by the Spirit." Mark and Matthew's accounts depict the Spirit driving or leading Jesus into wilderness, but not accompanying him during his adventures there (Luke 4:1; Mark 1:12; Matt. 4:1). From Luke's perspective, Jesus is escorted through the wilderness and is not alone during his period of encounter, testing, and moderation.

The description of being led by God's spirit "in the wilderness" echoes the story of Israel's divinely orchestrated wilderness venture after their liberation from Egypt: "So God led the people by the roundabout way of the wilderness toward the Red Sea. The Israelites went up out of the land of Egypt" (Exod. 13:18). God chooses the wilderness setting in which to reconstitute Israel as the people of God. It is the place of God's assured and responsive presence (Exod. 16:9–10) as well as undeserved provision (Exod. 16:11–17). Moreover, the wilderness is the space in which God establishes new ordinances, like Sabbath, that summon Israel to reflect on who God is for the community and who the community is to God (Exod. 16:23, 25–26, 29–30; 20:8–11; 31:13–17).

In the book of Exodus, the wilderness is not just the place of salvation and confirmation of Israel's status as God's people; it is also a venue that generates worry and doubt. Here the community faces its mortality and finitude. Israel experiences collective misgivings about its fate and confronts the uncertainty that often accompanies a new and untold future (Exod. 14:11–12; 16:1–3). Moreover, the wilderness is the place where Israel waits for the manifestation of Moses' prophetic and law-giving work. Moses fasted for forty days while in the presence of God, awaiting God's commandments (Exod. 24:18–25:1; cf. 34:28). In similar fashion, the Gospel of Luke describes Jesus' stint in the wilderness as forty days without food, in which he rehearses the commandments of God as a counter to the devil's enticements. Jesus replies to the devil's lures by restating three Torah pronouncements: (1) "One does not live by bread alone" (Luke 4:4; Deut. 8:3b); (2) "worship the Lord your God and serve God only" (Luke 4:8; Deut. 6:13); (3) and "do not put the Lord your God to the test" (Luke 4:12; Deut. 6:16; Isa. 7:12). In so doing, Luke depicts Jesus as both a teacher of the Law and observant practitioner who can reinterpret it in light of the current challenge confronting him. As such, the wilderness in Luke becomes a place of responsive and contextual theological discourse.

Up until Luke 4:1, the wilderness location in the Gospel of Luke represented the work of John the Baptist. The wilderness is named as the site of John's prophetic preparation and witness (Luke 1:80; 3:2, 4; cf. 7:24). After the temptation, however, the wilderness becomes a space that Jesus traverses; and it is not the site of witness and prophecy. Rather, the wilderness becomes the site of Jesus' prayerful reprieves: "But he would withdraw to deserted places and pray" (Luke 5:16; cf. 4:42). The wilderness becomes a sanctuary for God's agent, providing an escape for rejuvenation and assurance. In Psalm 91:9–11, the psalmist remarks, "Because you have made the LORD your refuge, the Most High your dwelling place, no evil shall befall you, no scourge come near your tent." Even the psalmist's confidence about the work of angels in protecting and providing for God's agent (Ps. 91:11–12) is reminiscent of Luke 4 when Jesus responds to the devil's second challenge (Luke 4:9–11).

Perhaps most striking is the difference between Luke and Matthew's versions of the dialogue between Jesus and the devil. The order of temptations in Matthew is (1) turn stones to bread, (2) throw oneself down from the pinnacle of the temple in "the holy city" (4:5), and (3) worship the devil in exchange for imperial rule. In contrast, Luke's order and language are different. The Lukan order is (1) turn this stone to a loaf of bread, (2) worship the devil in exchange for his sovereign authority, and (3) throw oneself down from the pinnacle of the temple in Jerusalem.

Reading Luke's account against Matthew's alone could suggest that the explicit reference to "Jerusalem," as opposed to the alias "holy city," is an incidental variant. Within the larger storyline of the Gospel of Luke (and even the book of Acts), however, the image of Jerusalem is weighty. After all, the opening scene of the Gospel of Luke places readers in the temple with Zechariah, who receives the prophecy of John the Baptist's birth (Luke 1:8). In Luke 2, baby Jesus is presented in the temple, and the prophets Simeon and Anna proclaim his messianic work publicly (Luke 2:22–38). In fact, the Gospel of Luke is so obsessed with

Jerusalem's role in Jesus' story that it spends an entire ten chapters narrating his journey from Galilee to Jerusalem (Luke 9:51–19:28). This travel narrative is unique to the Gospel of Luke because it expands a journey that occurs in one verse in the Gospel of Mark (Mark 10:1; cf. 9:33). Not only does Luke open with a series of prophetic moments in the Jerusalem temple and spend a large part of its story building anticipation for what will happen in Jerusalem at Jesus' death. The Gospel also closes with readers watching the disciples return to Jerusalem to celebrate Christ's resurrection and ascension (Luke 24:52–53).

Together, the images of the wilderness and Jerusalem in Luke's temptation story provide a rich backdrop for reflection during the Lenten season. Lent is the time Christians purposely give our faith permission to "work on us." We willingly subject ourselves to the pain of fitting into a daily mold or way of being we do not routinely live out, in order to encounter ourselves in new ways and wrestle with our sense of authority and insignificance, no matter how misguided. We deny ourselves the luxuries and conveniences of our surroundings, so we can remember God's provision, protection, and sanctuary for others and ourselves. In addition, we remember that just as Jerusalem is a magnetic landmark in Luke, our confession that Jesus is the Christ who has come to bring justice and salvation is our magnetic landmark of faith. It compels us to take seriously this time of penance so that we can become more patient, equitable, and altruistic in a world obsessed with instant remedies, dominance, and self-glorification.

SHIVELY T. J. SMITH

Commentary 2: Connecting the Reading with the World

Lent commences with combat between Jesus and the devil. Is this devil real? Baudelaire coined the idea that "the devil's greatest wile is to convince you he does not exist." Thomas Merton, taking the opposite approach, noticed Christians who attribute all manner of things to Satan and concluded that what Satan wants mostly is attention. We should not imagine a red guy with horns and a pitchfork. Painters like Titian and Tintoretto captured the sense of it when they portrayed the devil as a strikingly handsome, innocent-looking young man. C. S. Lewis's *Screwtape Letters* helps us understand that what is not of God tries so very hard to undo us. There is evil, and it is intensely personal.

Consider the terrain: from Jericho, tourists lift their gaze westward and see the Mount of Temptation. An ancient monastery, to mark the memory of Jesus' forty-day trial, is carved into the cliffs. It is one thing for Christians to build a church where a healing miracle or the resurrection happened; but why venture out to the place Satan chose to assault Jesus?

This wilderness is not a vast expanse of sand with the occasional cactus or tumbleweed. Instead, we see a rocky, daunting zone of cliffs and caves, the haunt of wild beasts. People avoided the place, believing demons and evil spirits ranged there, knowing that predators and brigands lurked there.

Jesus chose to go there—or, as Luke strangely tells us, was led there by the Spirit. How silly are we to think that if the Spirit leads, it will be to a smooth, comfortable, pleasant place. The Spirit that leads us led Jesus into peril.

In Nikos Kazantzakis's *The Last Temptation of Christ*, every time young Jesus reached out for pleasure, "ten claws nailed themselves into his head and two frenzied wings beat above him, tightly covering his temples. He shrieked and fell down on his face." His mother pleaded with a rabbi (who knew how to drive out demons) to help. The rabbi shook his head. "Mary, your boy isn't being tormented by a devil; it's not a devil, it's God—so what can I do?" "Is there no cure?" the wretched mother asked. "It's God, I tell you. No, there is no cure." "Why does he torment him?" The old exorcist sighed but did not answer. "Why does he torment him?" the mother asked again.

"Because he loves him," the old rabbi finally replied.[1]

If this story is somehow about the love between Jesus and God, we might want to rethink the rationale for reading this passage as the kickoff to Lent. A bevy of predictable sermons will be preached with the plot of "Here is how Jesus overcame temptation; go thou and do likewise." However, the early church's theologians, and the other good ones through the Middle Ages and Reformation, shuddered over their inability to elude the claws of the devil. It is not that we can resist just as Jesus did. No; he is our Savior precisely because he accomplished what we could never do on even our best, holiest days. Martin Luther, whose hymns frequently deal with "the prince of darkness grim," suggested that when we are tempted by the devil, we can be encouraged by the fact that we know and are loved by the One who conquered the devil. It is not about technique, but a relationship.

Relationships are important. John Chrysostom, Luther, and many others pointed out that the devil attacks those who are lonely. So we need to surround ourselves with other Christians. Actually, if this text is not so much about us resisting temptation, but Jesus doing so in our stead, then we have to ask, how then do we, as the body of Christ, find ourselves in this story? Does the church, postmodern and increasingly isolated, find itself in a strange wilderness? What are the temptations, the tests we must undergo? Unlike Christ, we the body of Christ fail so often. In Dostoevsky's *The Brothers Karamazov*, the Son of God who rejected Satan's offer of power is then judged by his own church, which thinks his demands are too high.

How does the church in the world cope with the tests that are about our love for God and God's for us? We do not know how to pull off the stones-into-bread trick. We actually give a lot of bread, through food collections and soup kitchens. Jesus refused bread, preferring that metaphorical bread, God's Word. Do we give bread without attaching the Word—God's Word, or the words of established friendship?

Do we assuage our guilt or pad our spiritual resume by dropping off food, while never building a relationship with the hungry, who are just as lonely as we, who have plenty of food, are?

Jesus' refusal of power might give the church pause when we think about politics in America. Do we try the Moral Majority approach and seize whatever power we can to pursue holy ends? Is there something intrinsically perverse in the very grasping for power? J. R. R. Tolkien must have had this story in the back of his mind when he conceived of that ring of power in *The Lord of the Rings*. How desperately everyone wanted the ring, including those with noble intentions—but the ring would destroy anyone who kept it, even Gandalf the wise wizard, even Frodo the humblest of the hobbits. Power is not to be pursued, but shunned and destroyed. So the church's calling is to be as kenotic as Jesus, emptying ourselves of power, taking the form of a servant (Phil. 2).

Richard Rohr found something profound here: "This second temptation is to doubt that the kingdom of God is here, because we are overwhelmed by the apparent kingdoms of business, money, the media, etc. We 'worship' their influence and thus give them even more. We're so overwhelmed by the sense of evil, so overwhelmed by the kingdom of this world, it is difficult to look beyond it and see the presence of God and the power of the Spirit."[2]

Luke, we may recall, switches the order of the three tests, and his order makes the most theological sense. For him, the final test, the most daunting one, is the thing we have been trying all our faith-lives to do: to trust God. The devil even cites Scripture to buttress his point, reminding us of Shakespeare's wry comment: "What damned error, but some sober brow will bless it and approve it with a text, hiding the grossness with fair ornament?" (*Merchant of Venice*, act 3, scene 2). Just because the church reads and quotes Scripture, and just because the church jabbers away about trusting God, does not mean we are in sync with what God is asking us to do in the world.

1. Nikos Kazantzakis, *The Last Temptation of Christ* (New York: Scribner, 1998), 30.
2. Richard Rohr, *The Good News according to Luke* (New York: Crossroad, 1997), 100.

Luke adds his footnote: that the devil slinked away, but began right away to look for a more opportune time to pounce again. Medieval cathedrals featured gargoyles, those comical yet scary monsters, grotesque apes and pigs. Why? Were they a bit of comic relief in such serious architecture? Were they foils to highlight by contrast the beauty of God? Did they in some way represent that persistent truth that once you have survived the harrowing cleansing of worship, your troubles are only beginning as you cross the threshold back into the world?

So Lent is no time for heroic resilience. We tremble and trust that "one little word shall fell him."

JAMES C. HOWELL

Second Sunday in Lent

Genesis 15:1–12, 17–18
Psalm 27
Philippians 3:17–4:1

Luke 13:31–35
Luke 9:28–36 (37–43)

Genesis 15:1–12, 17–18

¹After these things the word of the LORD came to Abram in a vision, "Do not be afraid, Abram, I am your shield; your reward shall be very great." ²But Abram said, "O Lord GOD, what will you give me, for I continue childless, and the heir of my house is Eliezer of Damascus?" ³And Abram said, "You have given me no offspring, and so a slave born in my house is to be my heir." ⁴But the word of the LORD came to him, "This man shall not be your heir; no one but your very own issue shall be your heir." ⁵He brought him outside and said, "Look toward heaven and count the stars, if you are able to count them." Then he said to him, "So shall your descendants be." ⁶And he believed the LORD; and the LORD reckoned it to him as righteousness.

⁷Then he said to him, "I am the LORD who brought you from Ur of the Chaldeans, to give you this land to possess." ⁸But he said, "O Lord GOD, how am I to know that I shall possess it?" ⁹He said to him, "Bring me a heifer three years old, a female goat three years old, a ram three years old, a turtledove, and a young pigeon." ¹⁰He brought him all these and cut them in two, laying each half over against the other; but he did not cut the birds in two. ¹¹And when birds of prey came down on the carcasses, Abram drove them away.

¹²As the sun was going down, a deep sleep fell upon Abram, and a deep and terrifying darkness descended upon him. . . .

¹⁷When the sun had gone down and it was dark, a smoking fire pot and a flaming torch passed between these pieces. ¹⁸On that day the LORD made a covenant with Abram, saying, "To your descendants I give this land, from the river of Egypt to the great river, the river Euphrates."

Commentary 1: Connecting the Reading with Scripture

This mysterious passage dramatizes a rearticulation of the divine promise to Abram, migrant from Mesopotamia. Much had happened since the Lord commanded Abram to leave his home. Upon arrival in Canaan, Abram and Sarai had been driven by famine to Egypt. There they had experienced a profound threat to Sarai's well-being, the integrity of their kinship group, and the covenantal promise. The anxious Abram had masked his spousal responsibility for Sarai, hoping to forestall violence he imagined might be directed at him as her husband. That episode is the first of three stories (with Gen. 20 and 26) that progressively elaborate a motif of

foreign rulers showing themselves to be more morally responsible than the patriarchs. Sarai had been taken into the Egyptian royal harem (Gen. 12:10–20), and as a result (v. 16) Abram had grown exceedingly wealthy "in livestock, in silver, and in gold" (13:2). Abram had subsequently become embroiled in clashes with kin (chap. 13) and Canaanite antagonists (chap. 14). It is "after these things" that the Lord appears to Abram in a vision.

The Lord assures Abram of divine protection: "Do not be afraid, Abram; I am your shield" (15:1). Indeed, Abram has survived migration, famine, social vulnerability as a refugee

40

in Egypt, and armed conflict with Canaanite indigenes; he now enjoys considerable power and material security. Certainly the Lord has been his shield. But what of Abram's legacy? How will he become a "great nation" (12:2) when he and Sarai continue childless? Note that advanced age (17:17; 18:11) will not suffice as the reason for childlessness throughout the entire marriage. Narrative silence on that point invites reflection on what the relationship between Abram and Sarai could have been, after Abram had voluntarily offered Sarai for the sexual service of an Egyptian potentate. The Lord's "do not be afraid" may be evoking that sordid scene from the past; the biblical narrator has depicted Abram's failings without flinching, and that is the only prior moment in which Abram had been characterized as fearful.

Thus the preacher will avoid romanticizing Abram as a scrappy nomadic wanderer with an unwavering faith. This powerful chieftain has a dark blot on his past: the anxious surrender of his wife preemptively to protect himself, doubtless appalling to an ancient audience that understood males' guarding of the sexual integrity of female kin as a central obligation for the honor of the family group. Abram will display his astonishing capacity for moral weakness in the future too, when he allows Sarai to banish the pregnant Hagar to the desert (chap. 16) and later expels Hagar and the toddler Ishmael immediately after Ishmael's weaning celebration (21:8–14). Preachers in ecclesial traditions that tend to lionize Abraham have rich soil to till here. The literary context of our passage makes clear that this patriarch is a morally compromised leader who enjoys blessing through no merit of his own but only through the grace of God. With homiletical guidance, hearers may be helped to see how disreputable lives can be the sites of God's redeeming work (cf. Matt. 1).

How can Abram be sure he will have the offspring promised by the Lord? For Abram, the matter concerns control of his vast holdings; a foreigner in his household stands to inherit (15:2), via the status of designated heir attested in ancient Near Eastern legal documents, as remedy for the lack of biological offspring (cf. Prov. 17:2). In response, the Lord draws the patriarch's attention to the night sky, radiant with innumerable stars: just as Abram cannot hope to master the glorious details of creation ("count the stars, if you are able to count them," 15:5), so Abram cannot fathom the power of this Creator who promised blessing and offspring to him so long ago. The Lord is able to fulfill the divine promise, no matter how morally reprehensible the patriarch has been, and no matter how hopeless the circumstance may appear.

Abram believes the Lord, "and he reckoned it to him as righteousness" (v. 6). The Hebrew syntax of the second clause is famously ambiguous, because the subject of the verb is not expressed. Divergent readings have been expounded in intertestamental literature and rabbinic tradition. The reading familiar to most Christians is that the Lord accounts Abram as righteous because of his belief. That line is taken up in Romans 4, where God's imputing of righteousness to Abram is characterized as a gift of divine grace, and Galatians 3, where Paul inscribes Gentiles in the lineage of Abraham through a filiation based on faith rather than halakic observance. One implication might be that the patriarch's trust in God eclipses the indisputable lack of righteousness that Abram had shown in his treatment of Sarai, Hagar, and Ishmael. The Hebrew syntax also allows for a reading followed by other interpreters, namely, that here Abram considers the Lord to be righteous in the (metaphorically) legal sense of justification, because the Lord is standing by the obligation incurred in the covenantal promise (cf. Heb. 11:11, God being accounted faithful by Sarah).

The reading of Genesis 15:6 as underlining the Lord's righteousness makes excellent sense in light of what follows. First, the Lord affirms the divine identity precisely as an efficacious covenant partner: "I am the Lord who brought you from Ur of the Chaldeans, to give you this land to possess" (v. 7). Next, Abram counters with a request for additional proof (v. 8). Following is a fascinating narration of a ritual, apparently offered as evidence of the divine resolve. Sacrificial animals are cut in pieces, and a "deep and terrifying darkness" falls upon Abram, who has fallen into a state of supernaturally induced torpor (v. 12).

Here we must pause to note an unfortunate decision of the lectionary framers: the heart of this passage is omitted. Missing are verses 13–16, in which the Lord pronounces a new articulation of divine deliverance that is surely heavy with irony when heard as a response to Abram's query: Abram will have offspring, to be sure, but they will live as aliens in unfamiliar terrain, oppressed for four hundred years. Abram's lineage will enjoy abundant wealth and security, but only after they have escaped from a servitude that will crush their spirits for four generations (this latter calculation is an independent tradition about a shorter captivity). The preacher may consider the thunderous silence caused by this excision at the heart of the narrative, perhaps inviting the congregation to mull the prophetic mystery that the Israelites will endure much before the fulfillment of the divine promise.

The covenant is confirmed by the sign of a "smoking fire pot and a flaming torch" passing between the cut pieces of the animals. This detail may signal that the same condition—dismemberment—would be the fate of the Lord in the unthinkable case of default (see Jer. 34:18–20). If the fire pot and torch gesture proleptically toward the divine Presence guiding Israel via pillar of cloud by day and fiery pillar by night (Exod. 13:21), the allusion is subtle, with vocalic assonance in the Hebrew but no shared vocabulary except "fire." The Law will not be given until much later, at Sinai, but the Priestly material throughout Genesis is animated by the understanding that the One who is covenantally bound to Israel will protect and bless the faithful. Astute readers will notice that the content of the rearticulated promise, then, has to do with the gift of Canaanite territories more than with Abram's future progeny. Here, as often in Genesis, Priestly and non-Priestly materials have been interwoven into a rich tapestry. Diverse motifs and shifts of emphasis will challenge and delight the preacher who appreciates biblical narrative art.

CAROLYN J. SHARP

Commentary 2: Connecting the Reading with the World

The meaning of some verses of Scripture clearly runs contrary to the overarching message of the prophets, Jesus, and mainstream Jewish and Christian confessions. This passage is riddled with problematic verses—a number of which our lectionary readings from Isaiah and Deuteronomy in the last two weeks overtly resist.

First, there is the unqualified reference to the "slave born in" Abram's house. Slavery/servitude, most especially multigenerational servitude—whether anchored in race, as in seventeenth-to-nineteenth-century America, or in gross economic disparity, as in ancient Greece and, increasingly, across our twenty-first-century world—must be named and condemned as contrary to the overwhelming witness of Scripture and of the Jewish and Christian traditions.

Second, there is the bloody confusion of animal sacrifice. The idea that God is pleased by the ritual slaughter of God's beloved creatures—God who delights in every creature at creation, who remembers every creature at the flood, who attends to the fall of every sparrow—is obscene. Multiple prophets inveigh against animal sacrifice. Isaiah 1 is typical when it says that God does not delight in the blood of animals (Isa. 1:11), when it says God turns away because the people's hands are drenched in the blood of sacrifices, when it calls people to worship truly pleasing to God: "do good . . . rescue the oppressed, defend the orphan, plead for the widow" (1:17). Of course, this prophetic concern can apply to any mistreatment of animals (e.g., "factory farms").

Third, there is the "reward" of verse 1, which provides a dangerous opening to self-centered perversions of faith (e.g., the prosperity "gospel"). In part to counter this threat, I would recommend inclusion of Genesis 15:13–16, which anticipates four centuries of servitude in Egypt as another part of God's direct plan for Abraham's descendants.

Notably, these verses—which alert congregants will read anyway—also make a fourth problematic claim: that in some cases God directly intends slavery and oppression for the faithful and violent vengeance for oppressors.

Fifth, there is Abram's lament that he has no biological heir. It is understandable and unobjectionable to celebrate the distinctive traits of biological children—for instance, to enjoy and learn, sometimes to one's chagrin, from seeing oneself in them. It is appropriate on such grounds to lament fertility incapacities. It is vital, however, to be clear one is lamenting distinctive wonders of biological children, not suggesting biological children are better or more beloved than adopted children, whom we may celebrate for different, equally distinctive reasons (e.g., the new and diverse traits that they, like spouses, bring into our families).

Problems with biological favoritism are heightened if one adds in favoritism for one's family as an enduring people. It is unobjectionable to celebrate and be invested in the distinct traditions and traits of one's extended family, and to strive to leave some provision for one's family—as long as one simultaneously appreciates and celebrates the distinct traditions and traits of other families and is equally concerned for their provision. To step from appropriate celebration and responsibility to sectarian preference for "one's own" is easy, so it is vital to guard against sectarian bias and obsession with racial/ethnic purity.

Finally, the threat of sectarian interpretation and of unjust action is potentially realized in what can easily be read as an imperialist version of the "promised land" motif at the end of today's reading. In stark contrast, notably, to the inclusive, all-loving God portrayed in our previous lectionary readings in Isaiah and Deuteronomy, the God pictured here can easily be appropriated for sectarian ends. God appears simply to have given other people's lands to Abram's descendants. The "aliens" whom Deuteronomy 26:11 tells the Israelites to care for and break bread with are named here only as defeated others: the Kenites, Kenizzites, Kadmonites, Hittites, Perizzites, Rephaim, Amorites, Canaanites, Girgashites, and Jebusites.

We find a reminder that Abram is himself an alien in this land, an immigrant from Ur. Nevertheless, taken alone, these verses appear to harness God for imperialist ends (an ever-looming threat with the "promised land" motif). Deuteronomy and the prophets strive against this threat. Moreover, resistance is powerfully manifest in the opening of the Abraham cycle, where the Lord says Abram will be made into a great nation so that he will "be a blessing," so that through him "all the families of the earth shall be blessed" (Gen. 12:1–3). It is hard to imagine a clearer rejection of sectarian understandings of what it is to be a "chosen people" to whom God has bequeathed a promised land. Moreover, the way the Torah and prophets overtly resist sectarian dynamics represents a remarkably insightful blending of realism (acknowledging the power of what is natural/self-interested in the modern sense) and idealism (acknowledging the reality of what is godly/good/loving in the moral realist/faith sense).

People invariably *will* organize themselves into family, kinship, racial, ethnic, and state/nation groups. Moreover, to repeat, it is not only natural but also good to celebrate the distinctive traits and traditions of discrete families, ethnicities, and nations—as long as the celebration of diversity is not sectarian. This is an ever more vital concern as the world shrinks into a global community. Whether thinking of ethnically diverse countries such as the United States or ethnically diverse regions such as the European Union or sub-Saharan Africa, or thinking globally (e.g., the UN), the question of how to celebrate diversity in community without empowering sectarianism is vital. God's call to Abram addresses the dilemma by linking the blessing/affirmation of the particular to the benefit of all. That is, we rightly celebrate our families insofar as they are a blessing to all families, rightly celebrate our nation insofar as it is a blessing to all nations, and rightly celebrate our faith insofar as it is a blessing to people of all faiths.

Genesis 15:6—"And he believed the LORD; and the LORD reckoned it to him as righteousness"—is the most famous verse in Genesis 15 because Paul cites it in Romans 4:9, where he strives to distill the essence of saving faith by identifying what is common to the faith of Jesus (Rom. 3) and the faith of Abraham (Rom. 4). Paul, a "Hebrew born of Hebrews," circumcised, a Pharisee expert in and faithful to the Law (Phil. 3:5), is the consummate insider, perfectly positioned to benefit from a sectarian reading of Genesis 15. Knowingly lifting this verse completely out of its problematic context, Paul famously highlights *only* Abraham's faith. Paul—famed apostle to outsiders, to the Gentiles—specifies that Abraham's ethnicity and circumcision are significant but not essential. In Ephesians (1:5) and Galatians (4:5), Paul refers to the faithful as the "adopted" children of God (an unqualifiedly positive reference to adoption), even as in Romans he specifies that Abraham is "the father *of all of us*," for "as it is written" concerning Abraham, Paul says, "I have made you the father *of many nations*" (Rom. 4:16–17, my emphasis). While he does not address the slaughter of animals (which, notably, he nowhere recommends or celebrates), Paul in all these ways directly counters the sectarian threats of the "chosen people" and "promised land" motifs manifest in Genesis 15.

Paul discerns the subtle, self-deconstructing genius of Genesis 15. The passage itself tempts us with all the sectarian problems I have noted, while pointedly and exactly specifying that Abraham was reckoned righteous through faith alone. What does faith amount to? What is faithful orientation to God and others? In what does God delight? What is true worship? The Prophets and the Law proclaim an answer: aid, rescue, defend, plead, and walk humbly with God.

WILLIAM GREENWAY

Psalm 27

¹The LORD is my light and my salvation;
   whom shall I fear?
The LORD is the stronghold of my life;
   of whom shall I be afraid?

²When evildoers assail me
   to devour my flesh—
my adversaries and foes—
   they shall stumble and fall.

³Though an army encamp against me,
   my heart shall not fear;
though war rise up against me,
   yet I will be confident.

⁴One thing I asked of the LORD,
   that will I seek after:
to live in the house of the LORD
   all the days of my life,
to behold the beauty of the LORD,
   and to inquire in his temple.

⁵For he will hide me in his shelter
   in the day of trouble;
he will conceal me under the cover of his tent;
   he will set me high on a rock.

⁶Now my head is lifted up
   above my enemies all around me,
and I will offer in his tent
   sacrifices with shouts of joy;
I will sing and make melody to the LORD.

⁷Hear, O LORD, when I cry aloud,
   be gracious to me and answer me!
⁸"Come," my heart says, "seek his face!"
   Your face, LORD, do I seek.
⁹Do not hide your face from me.

Do not turn your servant away in anger,
   you who have been my help.
Do not cast me off, do not forsake me,
   O God of my salvation!
¹⁰If my father and mother forsake me,
   the LORD will take me up.

¹¹Teach me your way, O LORD,
  and lead me on a level path
  because of my enemies.
¹²Do not give me up to the will of my adversaries,
  for false witnesses have risen against me,
  and they are breathing out violence.

¹³I believe that I shall see the goodness of the LORD
  in the land of the living.
¹⁴Wait for the LORD;
  be strong, and let your heart take courage;
  wait for the LORD!

Connecting the Psalm with Scripture and Worship

Abraham is often considered to be the exemplar of faith in the Old Testament, and with good reason. Genesis 15 is one of several episodes in which Abraham demonstrates his faith. At the very beginning of the Abraham cycle of narratives, Abraham immediately went when God told him to go (Gen. 12:1–4a); and toward the conclusion of the cycle, Abraham refused to withhold his only son, thus passing what is clearly meant to be understood as the culminating test of his faith in God (Gen. 22:1–18). Between these two episodes lies Genesis 15. In response to what must have sounded like a very unlikely divine promise of progeny, Abraham "believed the LORD; and the LORD reckoned it to him as righteousness" (Gen. 15:6; see Rom 4:3, 21; Gal. 3:6; Jas. 3:23).

The Hebrew root translated "believed" in Genesis 15:6 occurs also in Psalm 27:13, where immediately following the description of a terribly threatening situation, the psalmist affirms, "I believe that I shall see the goodness of the LORD in the land of the living." Despite lack of evidence, or perhaps even with evidence to the contrary, both Abraham and the psalmist entrust life and future to God.

The linguistic link between Genesis 15:6 and Psalm 27:13 is the most obvious connection between the two lessons; however, there are other aspects of the psalm that help us appreciate what faith involved for Abraham, and perhaps what faith involves for us as well. Psalm 27 begins by paralleling two affirmations about God with two questions, "whom shall I fear?" and "of whom shall I be afraid?" In this case, the two questions serve rhetorically to strengthen the two affirmations; that is, the psalmist will be afraid of no one. This posture is reinforced in verse 3a with the occurrence of the phrase "not fear," and verse 3b elaborates with the affirmation "yet I will be confident." While the NRSV translation is not wrong at this point, it frequently translates this same Hebrew verb as "trust." That translation would better reinforce the connection between Abraham and the psalmist; that is, both have entrusted life and future to God.

In any case, the trust that banishes fear is another connection between Genesis 15 and Psalm 27. The first words spoken to Abraham by the Lord in Genesis 15:1 are "Do not be afraid." Both Genesis 15 and Psalm 27 invite us at this point to consider that the opposite of faith is not simply doubt. Rather, it is fear. This may remind us of another connection that is not part of the lectionary readings for the day, namely, the story of the healing of Jairus's daughter. Recall Jesus' words to Jairus: "Do not fear, only believe" (Mark 5:36).

The admonition "do not fear" or "do not be afraid" is generally identified by form critics as a key component of what is usually called an oracle of salvation (see Isa. 41:10, 13–14; Luke 1:30; 2:10). In biblical terms, salvation means life as God intends it. Not coincidentally, God is addressed in the opening line of Psalm 27 as "my salvation," and the phrase occurs again in verse 9. It anticipates the psalmist's affirmation in verse 13: amid deadly threats, the psalmist trusts that he or she will live. The content of the promise to Abraham in Genesis 15 is similar. Abraham and his descendants are promised land (Gen. 15:18–19); in the ancient agrarian context, land means precisely the opportunity to eat and thus to live, which is what God intends.

The final verse of Psalm 27 also helps us to appreciate the dynamics of faith, for it makes clear that faith does not immediately or magically remove all threats and opposition. The double invitation, "wait for the LORD," encompasses the admonitions, "be strong, and let your heart take courage" (Ps. 27:14; see also Ps. 31:24). Apparently, the psalmist continues to experience threat and opposition (see vv. 2–3, 6, 11–12), but his or her faith offers courage and strength to endure and to proceed toward the abundant life that God intends (v. 13). As for Abraham, the land that is promised is for his descendants (Gen. 15:18). Abraham will certainly be part of the movement toward the fulfillment of the promise, but in a real sense, he will always be waiting, as the psalmist must wait. Such waiting is not passive, nor is it devoid of meaning. Rather, grounded in trust, this waiting activates and energizes the courage to move toward the life/land that God intends.

As Hebrews 11:1 puts it, "Now faith is the assurance of things hoped for, the conviction of things not seen." The psalmist knows this, and Abraham knows this (see Heb. 11:8–12). As for us, we too will always be waiting, entrusting our lives and futures to God as we move actively toward the life that God intends. Trusting God, we need not fear; and the good news is that along the way, we shall certainly joyfully experience "the already" amid "the not yet."

J. CLINTON MCCANN JR.

Philippians 3:17–4:1

[17]Brothers and sisters, join in imitating me, and observe those who live according to the example you have in us. [18]For many live as enemies of the cross of Christ; I have often told you of them, and now I tell you even with tears. [19]Their end is destruction; their god is the belly; and their glory is in their shame; their minds are set on earthly things. [20]But our citizenship is in heaven, and it is from there that we are expecting a Savior, the Lord Jesus Christ. [21]He will transform the body of our humiliation that it may be conformed to the body of his glory, by the power that also enables him to make all things subject to himself. [4:1]Therefore, my brothers and sisters, whom I love and long for, my joy and crown, stand firm in the Lord in this way, my beloved.

Commentary 1: Connecting the Reading with Scripture

"Therefore, my brothers and sisters, whom I love and long for, my joy and crown, stand firm in the Lord" (Phil. 4:1a). It is abundantly clear that Paul loves the believers in Philippi. They are a source of deep support for him, especially at this difficult time while he is in prison. Scholars remain uncertain where this prison is. Some assume he is in Rome, because he refers to "the imperial guard" (1:13), but there would have been imperial guards in other cities of the empire, including Ephesus. Wherever he is, Paul has enough freedom to spread the gospel even in prison. The text for this Second Sunday in Lent echoes several themes that Paul lifts up throughout this letter: join in imitating me, beware of those who live as "enemies of the cross," trust that our citizenship is in heaven, count on the return of our Savior Jesus Christ, and stand firm in the Lord. Each of these themes needs further attention to understand why Paul emphasizes these particular things from his prison cell.

Is Paul being arrogant when he says, "Join in imitating me" (3:17)? He can sound arrogant at times, not only in this letter but in others as well. Earlier in this chapter he boasted about his credentials as an authentic "Hebrew born of Hebrews." (3:5–6) In other letters, he boasts about the sufferings he has endured (2 Cor. 6:4–5; 11:23–28). When Paul urges the Philippians to imitate him, such imitation must

be measured by what it means to imitate Jesus Christ. Several times in this letter, Paul urges the Philippians to "be of the same mind" (1:27; 2:2, 5; 3:15; 4:2). This means more than agreeing with each other. Paul turns to a hymn that already existed to describe what he means: "Let the same mind be in you that was in Christ Jesus, who, though he was in the form of God, did not regard equality with God as something to be exploited, but emptied himself, taking the form of a slave" (2:5–7). For Paul, imitation means emptying himself as much as possible in the image of Jesus Christ. Paul does not claim that he has arrived at this point, but he presses on toward the goal of being of one mind with Christ (3:12).

Not everyone is of one mind. Paul warns the Philippians to stay clear of those who are "enemies of the cross of Christ" (3:18). It is not clear exactly who these enemies are. They seem to be gluttons (their god is the belly) or at least those who focus on earthly pleasures. They do not seem to be the ones he spoke about in the first chapter who proclaim Christ "from envy and rivalry" (1:15). He does not seem too angry with those preachers. Indeed, he rejoices that Christ is proclaimed, "whether out of false motives or true" (1:18b). However, Paul is adamantly opposed to those he calls "dogs" and "evil workers" at the beginning of chapter 3. It is not clear if those enemies are already part of the community or if they are rival missionaries traveling the same roads as Paul. They pose a special danger now that he is in prison and cannot be present to refute them. These dogs and evil workers practice something abhorrent to Paul: "Beware of those who mutilate the flesh" (3:2).

Why such a graphic, negative picture of circumcision? Paul himself was "circumcised on the eighth day" (3:5), but he objects to those who insist that Gentile believers must be circumcised. In most cases, this would not happen to infants eight days old, but to adults (of course, only to adult men!). Paul turns circumcision into a metaphor, claiming that those who worship Christ in the Spirit of God are the circumcision (3:3). This circumcision is not imposed or earned but is a gift that comes "through faith in Christ, the righteousness from God based on faith" (3:9)—and this circumcision is available to all, not only to men! In contrast to those who live as enemies of the cross, Paul urges the Philippians to trust in the power of the cross.

Then in today's text he makes a very bold claim: "But our citizenship is in heaven, and it is from there that we are expecting a Savior, the Lord Jesus Christ" (3:20). So much is packed in this one sentence. Obviously, Paul is contrasting those who "set their minds on earthly things" with those whose minds are set on heaven. Paul's language is not only about life after death. How do we understand the Greek term *politeuma*? This is the only place this Greek word is used in the New Testament. *Politeuma* has roots in *polis*, meaning town or city (as in my city Minne-*apolis*!). "Politics," "politician," and "polity" come from this same Greek word. In some biblical translations, *politeuma* is "commonwealth." In the NRSV, it is "citizenship." Richard Horsley translates the word in a rather surprising way: "But our *government* is in heaven."[1] Horsley wants readers to see that this word is not only personal but also political: "Translations and interpretations of the passage have attempted to tone down the implications through devices of

individualization ('citizenship') and spiritualization ('heavenly'), but the meaning is abundantly clear once considered in the imperial context."[2]

Many interpretations of Philippians and Paul's other letters have focused on personal meanings; however, recent scholarship has uncovered more political ramifications of Paul's language. After claiming that our citizenship is from heaven, Paul goes on to say, "It is from there that we are expecting a Savior, the Lord Jesus Christ." That can sound very personal (as in "Jesus Christ is my personal Lord and Savior"), but that word "Savior" also has political dimensions. Again, Richard Horsley:

> Whatever the other connotations (and biblical roots) of "salvation" in Paul, his use of *soteria* . . . would have been understood as an alternative to that supposedly already effected by Augustus and his successors. . . . Precisely because he does not elsewhere use the corresponding term *soter* = savior, the pointed employment of the term in an unmistakably political context at the climax of the argument in Philippians 3 (vv. 20–21) sharply opposes Jesus Christ as Lord to the imperial savior.[3]

Paul wants the Philippians to do more than wait for heaven or pray for personal salvation. Instead Paul urges them to live now as though heaven is shaping their lives on earth. The Roman emperor is not the source of their salvation. Jesus Christ, the one who emptied himself, is the true Savior: "He will transform the body of our humiliation that it may be conformed to the body of his glory, by the power that also enables him to make all things subject to himself" (3:21). The Philippians may live in a Roman colony, often humiliated by imperial powers, but that is not their primary identity. They carry a different passport.

What passport do people carry on this Lenten journey? The journey to the cross is often portrayed as a journey of personal piety and prayer. Paul's Letter to the Philippians is a

---

1. Richard Horsley, ed., *Paul and Empire: Religion and Power in Roman Imperial Society* (Harrisburg, PA: Trinity Press Int., 1997), 140.
2. Horsley, 141.
3. Horsley, 141.

powerful reminder that following Jesus Christ is also a political journey. Our pledge of allegiance is to Christ above all earthly rulers. "Therefore, my brothers and sisters, . . . stand firm in the Lord" (4:1).

BARBARA K. LUNDBLAD

Commentary 2: Connecting the Reading with the World

This passage from Paul's Letter to the Philippian church begins with a renewed salutation. It is shorter than the more formal salutation at the outset of the letter, but calls the attention once again with an emphasis on relationship. "Brothers and sisters," Paul begins, at least in the NRSV version, which has chosen to render the Greek in its most inclusive interpretation. This is a horizontal greeting, a greeting that emphasizes the equality between the greeter and the greeted; it invites horizontal, collegial preaching.

Paul at times runs through lists of credentials for his ministry, boosting his status when he believes it will strengthen his message. This message, however, seems best served by the generational parity inherent in siblinghood. Paul speaks follower to follower, apprentice to apprentice, fellow traveler on the road of faith to fellow traveler. He places himself solidly on the mortal side of the divide between us and Christ. The horizontal greeting lends warmth to the invitation that follows: "Join in imitating me, and observe those who live according to the example you have in us" (3:17). Paul paints a chain of followers, urging one another to greater faithfulness through a life lived in the light of Christ.

The call to imitation suggests a connection to the science of human development. Imitation is the first and most basic way we learn. From birth, babies are able to perceive and imitate human expression. I have a treasured picture of my two daughters lying opposite one another on my bed. The older one is six, and is making a wide-mouth face. Her sister, just days after her birth, offers an exact mirror of the expression. I remember my kids, well before they could follow adult conversations, joining in with the laughter of the adults in the room. We learn to be human by imitating the trusted humans in our lives, watching their faces, hearing their voices, laughing when they laugh, matching our caution to their sense of danger. We learn language and social skills and safe practices and cultural preferences, all by imitating more experienced members of our families and communities.

Paul's invitation to imitation calls out to the church during the Lenten season of repentance, reminding us who we are called to be for one another. We are meant to identify and imitate the most faithful among us; we are meant to be examples worthy of imitation. We often fill our church calendars with content-driven classes and instructions on spiritual practice, but imitation remains the surest way that new believers "join" the culture of our congregations, for good or for ill. This passage invites consideration of the particular challenges facing the church community and the wider community in which the church is situated. Who is showing grace? Who excels in compassion? Who is brave in the face of fear? How does the church community as a whole set a public example, even for neighbors who may never consider joining the church? Conversely, what habits have we developed as a congregation that we might *not* want to pass on to newer believers? How might the call to be worthy of imitation shape the choices of our lives together? How might that call shape us differently than the call to be popular or financially stable?

Paul speaks to the urgency of discipleship in juxtaposition with the prevalence of those who "live as enemies of the cross of Christ" (3:18). This description does not seem to refer to enemies of the followers of Christ; indeed, those living as enemies might more likely be woven in among the faithful as beloved fellow members of families and churches. They might, in fact, be the very same people who are also capable of living as followers, those who might be worthy of imitation. "Living as" an enemy is perhaps not quite the same as *being* an enemy. Paul identifies characteristics of this life in opposition to the cross: "destruction" in opposition to salvation, "the belly" in contrast to sacrifice, "shame" as opposed to honor, and "minds set on earthly things" as a distraction from the unceasing call to focus on God's vision and God's salvific offering in Christ.

A pastoral approach to identifying and calling out these behaviors will of course be a bit more of a homiletical challenge than praising imitation-worthy expressions of faith. A collegial approach, coupled with Paul's distinction between actual sworn enemies and those whose path has strayed into enemy territory, will soften the hearts of listeners to hear. The preacher may want to point back to the address at the beginning of the passage: "Brothers and sisters . . ." We are all in this together.

For Paul, the cross is real and central to the Christian story. For many modern Christians, the cross is a symbol, seen mostly in refined decorative context: on a gold chain or in stained glass. Paul "glories" in the cross, and not the decorative version. Paul means sacrifice, blood, defeat, humiliation, shame. In particular, the humiliation, shame, and criminality of the cross call out for interpretive connection to the lives of modern listeners. Mass incarceration in the United States, which has 5 percent of the world's population and nearly a quarter of the world's prisoners, might be a lens to explore, as might undocumented immigration status or opiate addiction. Being a follower of Jesus in Paul's time was both hard and countercultural, because the cross was a source of shame, not a natural source of glory. The path to Christian glory lies through humiliation; it is not possible to preach the Pauline letters faithfully without reference to this central truth.

"But our citizenship is in heaven" (3:20). The reward of embracing humiliation is belonging in the only sphere that ultimately matters. In a moment when the question of national citizenship is highly politicized, this claim demands attention. For a congregation with members whose immigration status is insecure, Paul's claim holds out hope. The same Roman citizenship that confers privilege on Paul is unavailable to many of his listeners. He speaks with a deep understanding of the power of belonging to the reign of one more powerful than Caesar. In a preaching context where the privilege and security of citizenship is taken for granted—even claimed as a source of pride—the connection will be one of caution. Paul does not concede uncritical national pride as compatible with heavenly belonging. National belonging is among the sacrifices that may be demanded at the foot of the cross. The Lenten turn of repentance will look different in contexts of insecurity and privilege, but the turn will always be toward God.

Paul closes this passage with an outpouring of love. He explicitly links the call to humiliation with the power of God's love: "[The Lord Jesus Christ] will transform the body of our humiliation that it may be conformed to the body of his glory" (3:21). We submit to humiliation, and God transforms our offering into glory. It is this love and promise that grounds faith. Paul reaches out to the Philippians with strong words: "my brothers and sisters, whom I love and long for, my joy and my crown." Although the church is founded on the triumph of love, loving relationships can easily take second seat to a thousand other concerns for satisfaction and self-preservation. Paul's lavish expression of love provides an opportunity for the preacher to express love and to invite the gathered faithful into the extravagant expression of love. The Lenten call to repentance is inherently challenging. It is our grounding in God's love and the love of one another that provides freedom and safety for a life that must travel through and embrace humiliation.

ANNA B. OLSON

Luke 13:31–35

³¹At that very hour some Pharisees came and said to him, "Get away from here, for Herod wants to kill you." ³²He said to them, "Go and tell that fox for me, 'Listen, I am casting out demons and performing cures today and tomorrow, and on the third day I finish my work. ³³Yet today, tomorrow, and the next day I must be on my way, because it is impossible for a prophet to be killed outside of Jerusalem.' ³⁴Jerusalem, Jerusalem, the city that kills the prophets and stones those who are sent to it! How often have I desired to gather your children together as a hen gathers her brood under her wings, and you were not willing! ³⁵See, your house is left to you. And I tell you, you will not see me until the time comes when you say, 'Blessed is the one who comes in the name of the Lord.'"

Commentary 1: Connecting the Reading with Scripture

Today's lectionary reading puts us on the road with Jesus headed to Jerusalem. Since Luke 9:51, we have watched Jesus journey to Jerusalem as he collects new prospective followers (Luke 9:58–62), commissions seventy people to carry his message to others (10:1–12, 17–20), visits old friends (10:38–42), and performs exorcisms (11:14–23) and healings (13:10–17). Throughout his travel, Jesus has also provided instruction in the form of parables (10:25–37; 13:18–21), directives (11:2–4), warnings (10:13–15; 11:42–44; 12:2–12), and now lament (13:31–35).

These few verses of lament in Luke 13 are saturated with metaphors relating Herod to a fox (v. 32), connecting Jesus' care for Jerusalem to a mother hen (v. 34), and likening the city of Jerusalem to a house (v. 35). Such a concentration of metaphorical pictures brings into focus one of the tasks for this Christian season. Lent is not simply about mourning loss, injustice, and error; it is also about using the imagery and symbols of our everyday world to communicate our frustrations, fears, and hopes. Lent is a time for Christians to exercise their theological imaginations, making connections that draw them closer to a prophetic work that shakes people out of their stupor. Lent should strengthen believers' commitment to God's justice and mercy in the

world (v. 35), as well as alert them to opposition against such prophetic action (v. 34).

The literary function of lament in the cultic life of Israel was to voice the perils of the current world and to request divine intervention within it (Ps. 13). It also describes the circumstances that endanger God's people and the loss of life that may have occurred (Jer. 4:23–26). Within the OT, there are at least four major types of lament: funeral (2 Sam. 3:33–34; Jer. 38:22), city (Ps. 137), individual (Pss. 3; 13; 22; 28), and communal (Pss. 42–44).[1] Laments, regardless of type, include statements that reaffirm trust in God's actions, confessions of violations against God, or assertions of innocence (Ps. 51). So lament is a liturgical and communal means of coming to terms with grief, disappointment, and need through expressions of complaint and petition.

Jesus was likely familiar with the role of lament in Israel's liturgical life, given Luke's portrayal of Jesus as an observant Jew who is practiced in its traditions, teachings, and ordinances (Luke 2:21–24; 4:15–17; 13:10). His speech in Luke 13:34–35 represents a city lament of sorts, deviating from the form in some intriguing ways. Typically, city laments rehearse how the city was abandoned or ignored by God because

---

1. F. W. Dobbs-Allsopp, "Lament," in *Eerdmans Dictionary of the Bible*, 785. accord://read/Eerdmans_Dictionary#15196.

of the people's infidelity or faithlessness (Amos 5:1–3, 16–20; Mic. 1:2–16). Jesus, however, reverses that form and discusses how he desires to draw closer to the city and its people, as "a hen gathers her brood under her wings" (Deut. 32:11). Jesus' longing to protect Jerusalem from itself echoes the prophetic words of Isaiah 31:5, which expresses God's eagerness to deliver Jerusalem from its attackers: "Like birds hovering overhead, so the LORD of hosts will protect Jerusalem; he will protect and deliver it, he will spare and rescue it." From Jesus' statement, it is the city, not God, who has done the abandoning, through its unwillingness to receive Jesus' prophetic witness and messianic work.

The city of Jerusalem plays a theological role in the Gospel of Luke in a way distinct from the other Gospels. It is a ubiquitous symbol, appearing as the site of the opening scene in the Gospel, when Zechariah enters the temple (Luke 1:8–9). It appears in the Gospel's conclusion as the destination for Jesus' followers, who are rejoicing over his resurrection and ascension (24:52). Furthermore, the image of Jerusalem looms large in the middle section of the Gospel, known as the travel narrative (9:51–19:28), which includes chapter 13. Although much of the material within this section can be found in Matthew and Mark, only Luke shapes the material into a ten-chapter excursion, which continuously reminds readers that Jerusalem is Jesus' final destination (13:22; 17:11).

While the city of Jerusalem is the chief focus of the lament, Jesus' explicit reference to the fates of former prophets serves as a subtle link to his approaching death and the complicity of Jerusalem's authorities in its outcome. On one hand, Jesus is mourning the deterioration of the city of Jerusalem. On the other hand, the decline Jesus describes is not physical destruction but depravity. Jesus grieves Jerusalem's propensity toward violence against God's prophets (Neh. 9:26). Although Jesus' statement in Luke 13:34 appears to rehearse a common tradition, there is no direct reference in the OT from which Jesus is quoting. Rather, Jesus' sentiment appears to be part of Israel's oral rationale for its troubled history, which may have been circulating in

the air, so to speak, at the time Luke's Gospel was written after the destruction of the Second Temple in 70 CE.

Jesus' lament over Jerusalem's actions comes in response to a confrontation between him and the Pharisees. The hostility that characterizes Jesus' relationship to the Pharisees in Matthew's Gospel (Matt. 3:7; 23:26, 27) does not feature so prominently in Luke. Although Jesus has conflicts with the Pharisees, in Luke he dines with Pharisees three times. They represent a group with whom Jesus shares table fellowship and conversation (Luke 7:36; 11:37; 14:1; 17:20) as well as conflict (5:17; 11:53; 13:31; 16:14; 18:10–14). Luke's depiction of the complicated relationship between Jesus and the Pharisees renders their warning to Jesus all the more significant. They are the first in the Gospel to tell Jesus that Herod is anticipating his arrival to kill him (13:31–32; cf. 9:9). Consequently, they state Herod's antagonism toward Jesus outright and, in turn, echo the earlier conflict between John the Baptist and Herod (3:1–20; cf. 9:7–9).

Taken together—the words of the Pharisees, the threat of Herod's wrath, and the history of Jerusalem's dismissal of its own prophets—it is no wonder Jesus responds with not just a word of lament, but also a word of hostility by calling Herod a "fox" (13:32). In the Greco-Roman world, "fox" could symbolize deceit and maliciousness as well as intelligence and strength. Within rabbinic literature, foxes are regarded as unclean pests that should be avoided.[2] In addition to insulting Herod, Jesus confirms the inevitable. Jesus' ministry is prophetic because he not only performs miracles of exorcisms and healings, but also he will suffer in Jerusalem the ultimate prophetic consequence, execution. Accordingly, his language of the "third day" in verse 32 has a double meaning, alluding to both his death and resurrection (9:22; 18:33).

Jesus' hostile response to the Pharisees and lament over Jerusalem represent a critique of Roman authority and Hellenistic cultural influences. In terms of the Lenten season, today's lection models another task of this season. In addition to practicing self-restraint, spiritual

---

2. Donald Fowler, "Fox," in *Eerdmans Dictionary of the Bible*, 470–71. accord://read/Eerdmans_Dictionary#9460

Hallow Thou My Soul

Lord, what is the trust that I have in this life? Or what is my greatest solace of all things under heaven? Is it not Thou, my Lord God, Whose mercy is without measure? Where hath it been well with me without Thee? Or when hath it not been well with me, Thou being present? I had liefer be poor with Thee, than rich without Thee. I had liefer be with Thee as a pilgrim in this world, than without Thee to be in heaven; for where Thou art, there is heaven, and where Thou art not, there is both death and hell. Thou art to me all that I desire, and therefore it behooveth me to sigh to Thee, to cry to Thee, and heartily to pray to Thee. I have no one to trust in, that may help me in my necessities, but only Thee. Thou art my hope, Thou art my trust, Thou art my comfort, and Thou art my faithful helper in every need.

Man seeketh what is his; but Thou seekest my health and profit, and turnest all things unto the best for me; for if Thou sendest temptations and other adversities Thou ordainest all to my profit, for Thou art wont by a thousand ways to prove Thy chosen people. In which proof Thou art no less to be lauded and praised than if Thou hadst fulfilled them with heavenly comforts.

In Thee, Lord, therefore I put my trust, and in Thee I bear patiently all my adversities; for I find nothing without Thee but unstableness and folly. For the multitude of worldly friends profiteth not, nor may strong helpers anything avail, nor wise counsellors give profitable counsel, nor the cunning of doctors give consolation, nor riches deliver in time of need, nor a secret place defend; if Thou, Lord, do not assist, help, comfort, counsel, inform, and defend.

All things that seem to be ordained to man's solace in this world, if Thou be absent, be nought worth, and may not bring to man any true felicity. For Thou art the end, Lord, of all good things, the highness of life, and the profound wisdom of all things that are in heaven and in earth. Wherefore to trust in Thee above all things is the greatest comfort to all Thy servants.

To Thee, therefore, I lift mine eyes, and in Thee only I put my trust, my Lord, my God, the Father of Mercy. Bless Thou and hallow Thou my soul with Thy heavenly blessings, that it may be Thy dwelling-place, and the seat of Thy eternal glory; so that nothing be found in me at any time that may offend the eye of Thy Majesty.

Behold me, Lord, after the greatness of Thy goodness and of Thy manifold mercies, and graciously hear the prayer of me, Thy poorest servant outlawed and far exiled into the country of the shadow of death. Defend and keep me amidst the manifold dangers of this corruptible life; and through Thy grace direct me by the way of peace into the country of everlasting clearness. Amen.

Thomas à Kempis, "That all our hope and trust is to be put in God alone," in chapter 59, *Of the Imitation of Christ by Thomas à Kempis, as Translated out of Latin by Richard Whytford,* ed. Wilfrid Raynal (New York: Duffield, 1909), 214–16.

---

discipline, and moderation, Christians should seek opportunities to challenge the segments of society that harm innocent people who lobby for the justice and welfare of everyone. Luke 13:31–35 is a siren, compelling believers to unveil political maneuvers and acts of violence that eliminate the voices and bodies of those representing the historic failures, prejudices, and fears of this society and, in turn, who call that same society to improvement and transformation.

SHIVELY T. J. SMITH

Commentary 2: Connecting the Reading with the World

We can be sure that the Herod Jesus was warned to flee was tougher than the comedic portrayals we have grown accustomed to in movies or in shows like *Jesus Christ Superstar*, where he is cast as a sniveling, sleazy buffoon. Jesus, with what feels like a touch of ridicule, disregarded him as if he were laughable, calling him "that fox." Readers might confuse this Herod (called

Antipas) with his father, Herod the Great. Actually, there are six Herods in the Bible, and each one is pretty much the same guy: a petty tyrant with a touch of megalomania, paranoid, callous, in cahoots with the Romans, religious but in a conniving way, rich, and often cruel.

Jesus was courageous—not that he thought he could defeat Herod in battle, but he did not retract from his business, even when his life was threatened. In our post-9/11 culture, courage has many definitions. As Scott Bader-Saye explains, security is our great idolatry today, and so we wind up leading timid lives: "Instead of being courageous, we are content to be safe. . . . We fear excessively when we allow the avoidance of evil to trump the pursuit of the good. . . . Our overwhelming fears need themselves to be overwhelmed by bigger and better things."[3] If Jesus felt terror when he heard Herod was coming for him, it was swiftly overwhelmed by the better things with which he was occupied: "Listen, I am casting out demons and performing cures."

He had plans to steer a course toward Jerusalem, which he knew would set him on a collision course with Herod and the other powers. He had been to Jerusalem as a child and as an adult pilgrim. His family and friends must have harbored mixed emotions about the Holy City, adoring its wonders and hoping in the fulfillment of its dream—yet puzzled by the opulence and chagrined by the corruption. Now that Jesus stopped to weigh Herod's threat, and to ponder the plot of the rest of his life, his mind drifted, and he mused to himself and to anybody who overheard him about what was the center of the universe for all Jews: "Jerusalem, Jerusalem"—repeating the name, perhaps out of affection, perhaps with the tender grief of a parent whose child has gotten into trouble again.

What was Jesus' tone of voice? We never know from the mere letters on a page of a Bible. He might seem angry or grumpy, with a stern "I told you so" tone, but this is surely wrong. Our passage is a very close sibling to Luke 19:41–44, when, during the last week of his life, Jesus not only spoke words of gloom and bereavement

over the city but simultaneously wept over the place. Were tears already welling up in him in chapter 13?

If Jesus had been able to gaze into a crystal ball and witness the centuries of history we know about, he would have shuddered and bawled his eyes out. Of course, the agonies of his own crucifixion were unspeakably gruesome. Before long, his friends Stephen and James had been executed. While many who had known Jesus were still alive, the Romans besieged the city and burned and leveled the place, crucifying five hundred Jews each day.

In the year 1099, Godfrey, Raymond, Tancred, and thousands of Crusaders broke into the Arab-controlled city and slaughtered the population. Ninety years later, Saladin took it back for the Muslims. General Allenby took over the city for the British in 1917, and one thing led to another, including vicious firefights in 1948 and a barrage of wars and terrorist attacks that show no sign of abating. This beautiful city, the center of the hopes of three beautiful religions, is racked by violence and endless sorrow. Its best known pilgrim route is the Via Dolorosa, the "way of sorrows," marking Jesus' path to the cross, appropriately drenched with his own tears, his mother's, and the sympathetic sorrow of countless pilgrims over the centuries.

If we stick close to Jesus, we too will be deeply distressed and racked with grief over the Holy City of Jerusalem and all the other cities where God's will is left undone. Bob Pierce, the founder of World Vision, has memorably said, "Let my heart be broken by the things that break the heart of God." Solidarity with Jesus does not prop you up in a cheerful mood. We want to know, and to feel, the sorrows God feels. Even as we labor for good in the world, we should pause to grieve. Miroslav Volf, suggesting ways Christians might transform political life in America, has written, "Christian communities must learn how to work vigorously for the limited change that is possible, to mourn over persistent and seemingly ineradicable evils, and to celebrate the good wherever it happens."[4] It is the mourning we are most likely to miss.

3. Scott Bader-Saye, *Following Jesus in a Culture of Fear* (Grand Rapids: Brazos, 2007), 31, 60.
4. Miroslav Volf, *A Public Faith: How Followers of Christ Should Serve the Public Good* (Grand Rapids: Brazos Press, 2011), 83.

Perhaps we become like May, the young woman in *The Secret Life of Bees* whose twin sister died. They had been "like one soul sharing two bodies. If April got a toothache, May's gum would plump up red and swollen." After April's death, "it seemed like the world itself became May's twin sister."[5] Any word of anyone suffering struck agony into May's heart. All her family could do was to build a "wailing wall" in the back yard; May would write down the hurts of the world and people she knew on scraps of paper and press them into the wall.

Jesus' bereavement over Jerusalem was not merely that it had lost its way. Jerusalem had proven to be the place that rejected and killed the very people who could have pioneered the way to the recovery of its holy destiny. In every age, reformers are endangered. A roll call of God's messengers who have been shunned, treated brutally, and put to death makes us shudder—and also realize how determined God is to rescue lost people.

Jesus' tone surely was not harsh. Instead of threatening to call down thunderbolts, Jesus plaintively says to anyone listening, to the city far away, and even to us, "How often have I desired to gather your children together as a hen gathers her brood under her wings!" How often had Jesus desired this? The wording implies he had dwelled on this lovely, evocative image, quite a number of times. Had he observed a hen spreading her wings over her chicks and thought, God my Father is like that? Did he ever think, God my Father is like a mother? In a culture replete with masculine images of God, Jesus looked to the hen. Did his mother Mary come to mind? Or one of Mary's hens back home in Nazareth? Richard Rohr suggested that "somewhere in Jesus' life he was in good relationship with a woman or he could not have been that comfortable with feminine perspectives or feminine imagery."[6]

This is striking. Artists have painted everything conceivable that appears in the Bible, but the only artistic representation I have ever seen of Jesus' picturesque longing, the hen gathering her brood, is in a modern mosaic in the Dominus Flevit Church on the Mount of Olives. Luke 13:31–35 closes with Jesus anticipating his upcoming journey on a donkey, down the slope of the Mount of Olives, through the Kidron valley, and into the city over which he had wept. Did he by chance see a hen that day?

JAMES C. HOWELL

---

5. Sue Monk Kidd, *The Secret Life of Bees* (New York: Penguin, 2003), 96.
6. Richard Rohr, *The Good News according to Luke* (New York: Crossroad, 1997), 159.

Luke 9:28–36 (37–43)

²⁸Now about eight days after these sayings Jesus took with him Peter and John and James, and went up on the mountain to pray. ²⁹And while he was praying, the appearance of his face changed, and his clothes became dazzling white. ³⁰Suddenly they saw two men, Moses and Elijah, talking to him. ³¹They appeared in glory and were speaking of his departure, which he was about to accomplish at Jerusalem. ³²Now Peter and his companions were weighed down with sleep; but since they had stayed awake, they saw his glory and the two men who stood with him. ³³Just as they were leaving him, Peter said to Jesus, "Master, it is good for us to be here; let us make three dwellings, one for you, one for Moses, and one for Elijah"—not knowing what he said. ³⁴While he was saying this, a cloud came and overshadowed them; and they were terrified as they entered the cloud. ³⁵Then from the cloud came a voice that said, "This is my Son, my Chosen; listen to him!" ³⁶When the voice had spoken, Jesus was found alone. And they kept silent and in those days told no one any of the things they had seen.

³⁷On the next day, when they had come down from the mountain, a great crowd met him. ³⁸Just then a man from the crowd shouted, "Teacher, I beg you to look at my son; he is my only child. ³⁹Suddenly a spirit seizes him, and all at once he shrieks. It convulses him until he foams at the mouth; it mauls him and will scarcely leave him. ⁴⁰I begged your disciples to cast it out, but they could not." ⁴¹Jesus answered, "You faithless and perverse generation, how much longer must I be with you and bear with you? Bring your son here." ⁴²While he was coming, the demon dashed him to the ground in convulsions. But Jesus rebuked the unclean spirit, healed the boy, and gave him back to his father. ⁴³And all were astounded at the greatness of God.

Commentary 1: Connecting the Reading with Scripture

This story of the transfiguration in Luke immediately follows an exchange between Jesus and his disciples about his true identity, warning about his impending suffering and death, and the teaching that all who wish to follow him must take up their cross and follow (Luke 9:18–23), Following this story come a healing narrative and then another warning that the "Son of Man is going to be betrayed into human hands" (v. 44). Just a few verses later, Luke explicitly turns the corner into the second half of the Gospel story: "When the days drew near for him to be taken up, he set his face to go to Jerusalem" (v. 51). Transfiguration thus sits between two texts that anticipate what is to come: Jesus' coming trials. This moment literally rises above the surrounding narrative, making clear to the audience of readers (if not to Jesus' own perpetually perplexed disciples) who this is who is about to die.

This narrative, with its revelation of Jesus' glory and its voice from heaven, clearly recalls the story of Jesus' baptism in Luke 3. There the voice from heaven declares, "You are my Son, the Beloved; with you I am well pleased" (3:22). Here the voice says, "This is my Son, my Chosen; listen to him!" (9:35). Other ancient sources say "my beloved" rather than "my chosen," which makes the parallel even clearer. These are the only two places in Luke's Gospel where the voice of God speaks directly, both times identifying Jesus as "my Son." In the birth narrative, the angel Gabriel also identifies Jesus as "Son of God," even before he is conceived

(1:35). Such Father/Son language, from the beginning, evokes Jesus' unparalleled relation to the God of the heavens.

Even as this passage looks back to Jesus' baptism, it also anticipates his resurrection at the end of the Gospel. The dazzling clothes of Jesus here anticipate the dazzling clothes of the angels at the tomb (24:4), and the disciples here, like the women at the tomb, are terrified (24:5). This story, then, offers an advance hint of the resurrection, a visual clue of the identity of Jesus, even now, as a participant in heaven.

The appearance of Moses and Elijah with Jesus at this point reveals Jesus' continuity with key representatives of Israel's history. Moses is named eight other times in the Gospel, three times in connection with a particular law, four times as part of the stock phrase "Moses and the prophets" (16:29, 31; 24:27; and 24:44), and once in reference to the story of the burning bush (20:37). Elijah is mentioned five other times outside of this passage: once in connection with John the Baptist, twice in reference to the story of the widow of Zarephath, and twice in speculations about the possible identity of Jesus himself. In the tradition of Jesus' time, Elijah was the forerunner of the Messiah; his appearance signaled the coming of the anointed one. Together, the appearance of Moses and Elijah represent the paradigmatic "law and prophets" being fulfilled in Jesus. In other words, the God who here transfigures Jesus is the same God who gave the Law and spoke through the prophets. Jesus continues and crowns that tradition of God's covenant with Israel.

In the context of the whole Gospel, Jesus Christ is not only the Son of God shining in glory on the mountain. He is also the Son of Man crucified on Good Friday. The disciples are granted the glimpse of glory, but then Christ cautions them not to talk about it until after the crucifixion and resurrection. Right before this story, Peter confesses Jesus as "the Messiah of God," and Jesus "sternly order[s] and command[s] them not to tell anyone" (9:20–21). Then he proceeds to instruct the crowd: "If any want to become my followers, let them deny themselves and take up their cross daily and follow me. For those who want to save their life will lose it, and those who lose their life for my sake will save it" (vv. 23–24). The point is, you may confess Jesus as the Messiah, but the fullness of that confession includes his death and resurrection. Until Peter walks through Good Friday and arrives at Easter morning, he cannot truly know what it means to say, "You are the Messiah of God."

This is the heart of the gospel: in Jesus Christ, glory and suffering are inseparable. We cannot understand the glory until we pass through the suffering. In Christ, love has chosen to be present in the midst of the darkness and suffering of our world. In the transfiguration, we are shown a glorified form of that love, but it is not fully comprehended as love until it is seen broken on the cross.

In the context of the lectionary, this is the alternative Gospel reading to Luke 13:31–35, for those who opt to read the transfiguration story on this day rather than right before Lent. Of the accompanying lectionary texts, Psalm 27 offers the most intriguing resonances for a creative preacher, especially if imagined in the voice of Jesus himself. "The Lord is my light and my salvation," begins the psalm, and it goes on to portray the Lord as the one who will preserve the life of the speaker, even "when evildoers assail me to devour my flesh" (Ps. 27:2). The tone of the whole psalm is reassurance in the face of times of struggle.

The psalm also offers an ironic contrast to Luke 9, when it says, "For [God] will hide me in his shelter in the day of trouble; he will conceal me under the cover of his tent; he will set me high on a rock" (Ps. 27:5). When read against Peter's offer in the Luke passage to build three dwellings (sometimes translated "tents") for Jesus, Moses, and Elijah, this verse of the psalm sounds oddly out of place. Jesus is literally "high on a rock," but no tent will hide or protect him. He is exposed for all to see, and he goes down the mountain to face suffering and death.

The final verse of the psalm sounds a particularly poignant note, particularly if one hears it in the voice of Jesus descending the mountain: "I believe that I shall see the goodness of the Lord in the land of the living. Wait for the Lord; be strong, and let your heart take courage; wait for the Lord!" (27:13–14). Can we imagine Jesus repeating this to himself, under his breath, in the days to come? Might he have said it to his disciples? Might he say it even now to us?

Finally, if we consider this passage in the context of the whole canon, it clearly recalls the exodus narrative, and particularly Moses on Mount Sinai. There too the cloud signifies the mysterious presence and power of God—which later came to be known as the Shekinah. Exodus 13 says, "The LORD went in front of them in a pillar of cloud by day, to lead them along the way, and in a pillar of fire by night, to give them light, so that they might travel by day and by night" (Exod. 13:21). Once the people reach Sinai, "the LORD said to Moses, 'I am going to come to you in a dense cloud, in order that the people may hear when I speak with you and so trust you ever after'" (Exod. 19:9). The transfiguration shows Jesus as a kind of new Moses, similarly intimate with the living God, similarly illuminated by God's presence, similarly leading bewildered people into a new land of promise.

MARTHA L. MOORE-KEISH

Commentary 2: Connecting the Reading with the World

There was a time in recent memory when Jews were discriminated against in America, and many people, including Christians, were largely anti-Semitic. In May 1939, the German transatlantic liner *St. Louis* sailed from Hamburg to Cuba carrying over nine hundred Jews fleeing Nazi Germany. Not allowed to enter Cuba, they sought permission to enter the United States on humanitarian grounds. They were denied permission; it was argued that doing so would have exceeded the country's annual quota for German immigrants. Thus the passengers were forced to return to Europe, where many of them later perished in the Holocaust. Needless to say, that incident left a memorable stain on the character of the United States.

The nation gradually became more welcoming of Jews, due largely to their rapid rise to the middle class and the influential power of their numerous civic, social, religious, and lobbying organizations. As the nation's attitudes toward Jews slowly changed, similar changes gradually occurred in the way theologians and preachers began interpreting the Old Testament. Rather than understanding the New Testament and Jesus of Nazareth as radically disconnected from the Jewish heritage, many came to view the two as integrally related. As a consequence, they began viewing the Christian gospel as the fulfillment of the Hebrew/Jewish Scriptures rather than a substitute for it, as evidenced by the countless small New Testaments that were regularly distributed by Bible societies and others.

In recent decades, both Roman Catholics and Protestants were prepared to embrace the spirit of Pope John Paul II, who in the first Lenten season of the new millennium apologized for the church's many historic sins against various groups, including its sins against the Jewish people. Though he did not mention the Holocaust, its implied reference was apparent to all. Nonetheless, many Jewish leaders responded by saying that though the papal apology told the truth in part, it failed to tell the whole truth about the abiding role of the church's anti-Semitic teaching on the crucifixion of Christ. Rather than following the pope's advice for Christians to treat Jews as "our older brothers" in the faith, many Protestant denominations still sponsor proselytizing missions among Jews.

Nonetheless, it is important to note that during the past decades the World Council of Churches has devoted considerable attention to the issue of Christian-Jewish relations in particular and to the wider concern about Christian identity in a multireligious world. During the same period, the subject has been receiving much attention from many academicians in Christian seminaries and religious studies departments in the United States and around the world.

Both in antiquity and the present time, the discussion about Jesus' relation to Judaism has drawn much of value from the pericope of the transfiguration. Here Jesus' unique status was declared by YHWH in the presence of three of his disciples: Peter, John, and James. In his company on the mountain they witnessed an astounding radiance on his countenance as he was joined by ancestral patriarchs Moses and

Elijah, who respectively personified the Judaic law and the prophets The transfiguration presented the three united in divine glory.

The incalculable significance of that story for Christians was immortalized in the last painting by the great sixteenth-century Italian artist Raphael. His work depicts the three figures united in a triangular format ascending in glory in the midst of a cloud, with Jesus in the center high above the other two. At the bottom of the scene the disciples lie in differing states of slumber, obviously startled. Below them and possibly the earth itself, a variety of people wander about in seeming confusion, with their focus elsewhere. In sum, it is not surprising that the painting has captivated the attention of countless spectators and worshipers over the centuries, probably because it depicts the transfiguration, which is a celebrated story of Jesus' messianic identity in the Eastern Orthodox, Roman Catholic, and Protestant churches.

It should be noticed that the story of the transfiguration is followed immediately by Jesus' healing a boy brought to him presumably in an epileptic seizure. Since he was frothing at the mouth, his father believed he was possessed by a demon. In that day, such a condition would have been a very serious matter. Indeed, the failure to cure the boy would have prevented him from marrying, which, in turn, would have terminated the paternal lineage, since he was the man's only son. When Jesus was told that his disciples had tried to cure the boy and failed, Jesus rebuked them for their lack of faith. Then he, alone, healed the boy, amazing all the onlookers.

Jesus' sensitivity to the well-being of children is of paramount importance, because children comprise the future for all human beings. Thus their health and nurture should be the primary concern for us all, even as it was for the boy's father. In our day, the work of Marian Wright Edelman in founding the Children's Defense Fund in 1973 is worthy of our highest praise for all the above reasons, including the love that Jesus manifested toward them. The purpose of the organization is enabling every child to have a fair chance in life, with none left behind.

In June 2000, The Church of the Transfiguration was dedicated on the shores of Cape Cod Bay after many years of careful work and planning. It is a beautiful contemporary expression of ancient Christian architecture that stands at the center of The Community of Jesus, an ecumenical monastery in the Benedictine tradition. The Eucharist is celebrated daily, and the church is a significant tourist attraction. Further, one discovers in the church numerous artistic renditions of scenes from the life and heritage of Jesus, depicted in various media by a diverse number of international ecumenical artists.

In addition to its function of helping to bridge the Jewish and Christian traditions, the transfiguration event has also been employed artistically and theologically in the process of Africanizing the gospel so as to make it hospitable to African peoples. Such a process is rooted in the notion that if the gospel is not enculturated, it will remain alien and incapable of being fully embraced by its devotees.

Accordingly, in 2014 the Society of African Missions (SMA) opened an art exhibition entitled "Africanizing Christian Art"[1] in its American headquarters in Tenafly, New Jersey. The exhibit introduced the work of Father Kevin Carroll, who had served as an Irish Catholic missionary in Nigeria for over fifty years. He had gone there to manage the Oke-Ekiti Workshop (1947–54) with the purpose of developing a new Yoruba Christian style of art as an alternative to Western colonial art.

Along with many other pieces of art by prominent African artists, the exhibit contained a wood panel by Lamidi Fakeye that depicted the transfiguration of Christ. In that work, Christ stands in the center as King, with Shango (the deity of thunder and lightning) on one side and Osanyin (the deity of healing) on the other. Similar to the New Testament vision, Christ is presented as the one who fulfills the traditional Yoruba belief system that is centered on the human desire for the basic conditions of security and healing. Clearly, that which fulfills can never be an opponent.

PETER J. PARIS

---

1. For further information and pictures of the art works in the exhibition, google "Africanizing Christian Art" exhibition in Tenafly, NJ, 2014.

Third Sunday in Lent

Isaiah 55:1–9
Psalm 63:1–8

1 Corinthians 10:1–13
Luke 13:1–9

Isaiah 55:1–9

¹Ho, everyone who thirsts,
    come to the waters;
and you that have no money,
    come, buy and eat!
Come, buy wine and milk
    without money and without price.
²Why do you spend your money for that which is not bread,
    and your labor for that which does not satisfy?
Listen carefully to me, and eat what is good,
    and delight yourselves in rich food.
³Incline your ear, and come to me;
    listen, so that you may live.
I will make with you an everlasting covenant,
    my steadfast, sure love for David.
⁴See, I made him a witness to the peoples,
    a leader and commander for the peoples.
⁵See, you shall call nations that you do not know,
    and nations that do not know you shall run to you,
because of the LORD your God, the Holy One of Israel,
    for he has glorified you.

⁶Seek the LORD while he may be found,
    call upon him while he is near;
⁷let the wicked forsake their way,
    and the unrighteous their thoughts;
let them return to the LORD, that he may have mercy on them,
    and to our God, for he will abundantly pardon.
⁸For my thoughts are not your thoughts,
    nor are your ways my ways, says the LORD.
⁹For as the heavens are higher than the earth,
    so are my ways higher than your ways
    and my thoughts than your thoughts.

Commentary 1: Connecting the Reading with Scripture

Scholars speak of Isaiah's primary divisions as First Isaiah (chaps. 1–39), Second Isaiah (chaps. 40–55), and Third Isaiah (chaps. 56–66). Second Isaiah is associated with the end of Babylonian control in the mid-sixth century BCE. In view of the new Persian Empire's less restrictive policies, Second Isaiah expresses hope that Judeans whose families were removed from Jerusalem more than a generation before would now return and resettle. Isaiah 55:1–9 comprises most of the final hymn of this exilic portion of Isaiah. Poetry such as this passage, calling for geographical return, served also to describe the spiritual journey of believers reuniting with their God.

Throughout Second Isaiah, water had powerfully symbolized God's provision (Isa. 41:17–18; 43:20; 44:3; 48:21; 49:10). In this final chapter's opening words, God's bounty—imagined not only as water but as wine, milk, and fine food—is extended to all who will come and take. The image of Judah's land as "flowing with milk and honey" (Deut. 26:9) underlies this invitation.

Against the backdrop of the book of Lamentations, to which Second Isaiah often refers, this invitation to feast shines even more brightly. The five lament poems that comprise that little book were most likely composed and used liturgically by Jerusalemites left in the land after its destruction. In Lamentations 5:4 the people complained about the high cost of necessities that had once been free: "We must pay with money for the water we drink; the wood we get must be bought" (literally: "they bring our wood for a price"). Second Isaiah, by contrast, announces free access first to water and then, more extravagantly, to wine and milk, reutilizing several terms found in the lament, notably "water," "money," and "price." Instead of overspending for basics, as they were forced to do during Babylonian rule, the audience is invited to reinvest themselves in a land where, thanks to welcome political changes, they may once again enjoy necessities and more.

A similar passage about Woman Wisdom in Proverbs points toward this banquet's metaphorical resonance. Wisdom describes preparing a meal, setting her table, and sending her servant girls to fetch the ignorant, saying, "Come, eat of my bread and drink of the wine I have mixed. Lay aside immaturity, and live, and walk in the way of insight" (Prov. 9:5–6). Like Woman Wisdom, the prophet beckons toward a new possibility: in a fertile homeland, the choice to rebuild Judean life before God. The bold exhortation embedded in verse 1's thrice-repeated imperative "come . . . come . . . come" is to choose well. Come to the water; come to the banquet; come and buy without money. Do not settle for costly things that provide little;

take only what is good. This applies to water and food in a land of their own, but as the passage unfolds from one metaphor to another, we quickly see that it applies to more: to the decision, by rebuilding Jerusalem, to renew Judah's national covenant with God.

A new image emerges in verses 3–4: Israel as the collective heir of God's promise to David. Second Isaiah's early chapters portrayed God identifying Israel as "my servant" (42:1, 19; 44:21; 45:4; 48:20; 49:3, 6), "my chosen" (42:1; 45:4), and even "my servant whom I have chosen" (43:10). These two designations had been used before in Scripture only in relation to King David. They appear most strikingly in Psalm 89:3 (see also vv. 19–20), in which the king reminds God: "You said, 'I have made a covenant with my chosen one, I have sworn to my servant David.'" According to royal understanding reflected in the psalm, the king's faithfulness to God's rule would guarantee his descendants' reign in a safe Jerusalem. Confidence in this relationship had been overturned by Babylon's destruction of both the city and the kingship. Here in Isaiah 55:3–4, the prophet nominates the collective "chosen servant," Israel, as David's new heir.

Further language from Psalm 89 confirms this allusion. In the last several verses of the celebrative section of the psalm, God's support of David is described as steadfast love and faithfulness (Ps. 89:33). The psalm takes an unexpected turn in verse 38, where an evident addition reflecting upon Jerusalem's destruction upends everything that was avowed before. Verse 49 asks, "Where is your steadfast love of old, which by your faithfulness you swore to David?"

Second Isaiah now responds to this raw question. Remembering both God's covenant with David and the breaking of that covenant first by Judah's leaders and then by God, the prophet confers these graces of steadfast love and faithfulness on all who stand as God's chosen servants, saying, "I will make with you an everlasting covenant, my steadfast, sure [or faithful] love for David" (Isa. 55:3). This covenant is bestowed no longer on the king alone. The promise will pass no longer to David's descendants (who were, in fact, accused of having led Jerusalem to destruction), but rather to the people as a whole, living as a restored nation under Persian rule. Continuity with Judah's royal past is thus reaffirmed in a form acceptable to both disaffected citizens and Persian rulers. (For other exilic expressions of God's "everlasting covenant," see Isa. 61:8; Jer. 32:40; 50:5; Ezek. 16:60; 37:26; Ps. 105:10.)

A third image of promise emerges in verse 5: "You shall call nations that you do not know, and nations that do not know you shall run to you." Second Isaiah has already characterized Israel as God's "covenant to the people" (42:6) and "light to the nations" (49:6). Later portions of Isaiah will likewise express hope that "nations shall come to your light, and kings to the brightness of your dawn" (60:3). This theme coheres with the well-known "swords into plowshares" imagery in Isaiah 2:2–4, in which the nations stream toward Zion to be taught God's ways of peace. It also stands out to Christian readers who, as citizens of Gentile nations, find ourselves included in this prophet's expansive imagination.

Verses 6–9 correlate physical return with theological repentance. In the prophets' imagination, Jerusalem's destruction signaled divine punishment for human rebellion. In the abstract, such an explanation may be morally objectionable. But historically it offered the nation order and hope, since it suggested that the catastrophe was neither random nor caused by outside forces, but instead represented a damaged relationship that could be healed—and thus offered hope that a broken nation might find divine help to survive. Second Isaiah has repeatedly mentioned Israel's sins, only to affirm God's forgiveness (40:2; 43:25; 44:22). According to the prophet, it is God who extends love and help, this time as a proffered do-over for all who respond. Because God's ways are so radically different from human ways, because God's thoughts are not human thoughts, Second Isaiah suggests, they need not make intellectual sense, but can be discovered through the Godward journey the prophet recommends.

The chapter's final four verses, though standing outside the lectionary reading, conclude the passage by returning to the theme of nutrition. God's words are compared to rain and snow that bring forth grain from the ground. Strong trees in a restored habitat are imagined celebrating as the exiles return in procession to their homeland.

Isaiah 55 beckons its audience to position themselves as recipients of God's bounty, both material and spiritual: the necessities and luxuries of daily living, the grace of a renewed history and cultic relationship, a meaningful role on the world stage, and an exuberant reconnection with both past and future.

PATRICIA K. TULL

Commentary 2: Connecting the Reading with the World

Isaiah's opening invitation to delight in abundance seems counterliturgical in the season of Lent. Typically, tradition and practice in Lent call for less, not more. Spiritual disciplines focus on shedding, not adding. The guiding symbolic action in Lent is fasting, not feasting. So on this Third Sunday in Lent the prophet's call to attention, "Ho" (55:1), is appropriately jarring to the listener's ear. It is an exclamation mark at the beginning of the sentence, highlighting the prophet's call to bask in God's abundance: eat, drink, and be satisfied beyond measure. A wonderful invitation. Only, at first blush it does not sound much like Lent.

The most meaningful and fulfilling Lenten journeys, however, include an encounter with God's abundant mercy, grace, and forgiveness. After the prophet strikes the vision of God's bounty so beautifully, the proclamation to follow turns to repentance, restoration, and life. The people in exile are called to turn away from the lure of a secure material future in Babylon and to seek after the lush spiritual reality offered in the sure and steadfast love of God. Isaiah's banquet of food and drink becomes a table overflowing with mercy and pardon for those who return to the Lord. Return, restoration, repentance: familiar themes of Lent.

The promise of hope and restoration to a people in exile transcends any liturgical season. Isaiah provides insight into the subtle spiritual threat posed by the Israelites' life in exile. The Israelites are integrated into Babylonian society and have jobs and money to spend. Yet they are spending their money on that which is not bread, and laboring for that which does not satisfy (v. 2). They are caught up in a transactional, materialist economy foreign to the ways of God. The "captives" participate in a culture that binds them, even as it appears to free them with an invitation to be part of Babylonian society. As a result, wickedness and unrighteousness abound among those whom God calls (v. 7). The state of exile is not primarily a state of physical dislocation, and it does not depend upon physical captivity. The depth of exile comes in a resounding dissonance of spirit. Such dissonance is magnified as the faithful are lured away from service to God by the powers and principalities of darkness. The lure of wealth and accumulation creates distance from the kingdom of light and eats away at notions of justice and righteousness. Exile then is a metaphor for people of God who do not live the life of faith, precisely because they have accepted belonging in a materialistic world. Isaiah urges these people, people living wholly in self-determined spiritual exile, to incline an ear, to listen, and to truly flourish (v. 3).

Traditional spiritual practices of Lent are never the ends themselves. Sacrifice, fasting, penitence, and prayer are pathways to true abundance, spiritual abundance, God's abundance. God's abundance is found in a turn away from desire for worldly abundance. Rather than contemplating the individual's journey in the wilderness of sin and distance from God, the opportunity exists for all eyes to focus first on God's grace. Instead of focusing within in a solitary way, members of the congregation can be encouraged to ponder together God's unending and never-failing forgiveness. Lent and a theology of abundance may not seem like a match for worldly abundance, but prophetic wisdom points to abundance that comes with no price and satisfaction that transforms the soul.

Isaiah's testimony to the overflowing bounty of godly flourishing should shape our understanding of the wondrous goal of the Lenten journey of spiritual lament. Some liturgical traditions avoid singing and saying "Alleluia" during Lent, but it is not clear how one can read and preach Isaiah's vision of God's bountiful blessings and then hold back on joy when it comes to praise and worship. A season of confession and repentance should not be characterized by forgiveness delayed. The fruit of redemption, reconciliation, and new life bursts forth contemporaneously with the promise of God and the power of the Holy Spirit. Isaiah invites the congregation to pray, sing, and shout "Alleluias" and "Amens" smack in the middle of Lent.

The prophet's voice speaks to the congregation gathered before the Word this Sunday in Lent: "Come to the water. Buy wine and milk without price. Listen carefully to me. Incline your ear. Seek the Lord. Call upon the Lord. Return to the Lord. For in Jesus Christ, God is near. In Christ, God can be found. In Christ, God has abundantly pardoned. Hope and restoration abound." It is the promise that rests at the very core of the gospel, God's promise proclaimed by Isaiah and fulfilled in a people restored from exile, God's promise fulfilled in the life, death, and resurrection of Christ. Christ's promise. God's promise.

Do not wait until Easter to shout "Alleluia." Every Sunday the preacher stands before a people in exile, and Isaiah's call to turn and shout "Alleluia" is precisely for people in exile. This hopeful word for lost souls should fill the preacher's mind and heart, should fuel the conviction that some listening need to be reminded that God loves them, that God embraces them just as they are, that God welcomes them, no matter how far they have wandered, that God invites them home. In the context of Lent, with the community gathered for worship, in the spirit of confession and forgiveness, the prophet's words should be heard as a promise: "For my thoughts are not your thoughts, nor are your ways my ways, says the LORD" (v. 8).

Most preachers know that almost paralyzing experience of standing on the Lord's Day before the gathered flock with profound and diverse pastoral needs, standing before folks who are struggling to catch their breath amid daunting personal, social, work, family, financial, and physical challenges. Followers of Jesus are called by God to salvation that comes in a turn away from a culture foreign to the ways of God, a turn away from self-destructive spending on that which will never fill and laboring for that which will never satisfy. Faith-filled people thirst and long to eat what is good. The children of God, even as they live amid those who remain in exile, crave and receive rich food of the spirit.

The preacher bears witness to the prophet's call to seek the Lord. For when in exile, surrounded by all the world offers, it is still true that repentance, confession, and prayer lead to God's mercy, God's pardon, and God's steadfast, sure love. The unending grace of God forever stands in contrast to the world's thirst for wrath, guilt, and punishment. God's unmerited grace defines true abundance. God has made an everlasting covenant that leads to truly abundant and eternal life.

As Isaiah spoke to the ancient Israelites, the Word still speaks, still speaks today. "For as the heavens are higher than the earth, so are my ways higher than your ways and my thoughts than your thoughts" (v. 9). The appropriate prayerful response comes sometimes in silence, sometimes as a sigh, sometimes as a cry, sometimes as a shout, but it is in every case the same response. The collective response of the people of God, even in Lent, even as they live in the midst of others who are still, tragically, captive to spiritual exile, the response of people who have turned from exile and received God's grace is a thankful and joyous "Alleluia."

DAVID A. DAVIS

Psalm 63:1–8

¹O God, you are my God, I seek you,
    my soul thirsts for you;
my flesh faints for you,
    as in a dry and weary land where there is no water.
²So I have looked upon you in the sanctuary,
    beholding your power and glory.
³Because your steadfast love is better than life,
    my lips will praise you.
⁴So I will bless you as long as I live;
    I will lift up my hands and call on your name.

⁵My soul is satisfied as with a rich feast,
    and my mouth praises you with joyful lips
⁶when I think of you on my bed,
    and meditate on you in the watches of the night;
⁷for you have been my help,
    and in the shadow of your wings I sing for joy.
⁸My soul clings to you;
    your right hand upholds me.

Connecting the Psalm with Scripture and Worship

A connection between Psalm 63:1–8 and Isaiah 55:1–9 is evident in the first verse of both texts. In Psalm 63:1, the psalmist "thirsts" as if in a location "where there is no water." In Isaiah 55:1, the invitation is extended to "everyone who thirsts" that they may "come to the waters." What the psalmist needs and longs for is readily available, according to Isaiah 55.

The imagery of physical need and sustenance is extended in both texts beyond thirst to eating. The psalmist affirms that he or she "is satisfied as with a rich feast" (Ps. 63:5). The word "satisfy" also occurs in Isaiah 55:2. Although verse 2 is framed as a question, its rhetorical effect is to affirm that satisfying food is readily available, so that it is possible to "eat what is good, and delight yourselves in rich food" (the same Hebrew word rendered as "rich feast" in Ps. 63:5).

The centrality of this imagery of drinking and eating is reinforced in Psalm 63 by the repetition of "my soul" in verses 1, 5, and 8. The NRSV regularly translates the Hebrew word involved as "soul," but the word originally meant "throat" or "neck" (see Ps. 69:1, where the NRSV translates it as "neck"). Apparently because everything necessary for the sustenance of life—water, food, air—passes through the throat or neck, the word came to mean something like "vitality, life," even "appetite." In short, the issue is life, and what truly sustains life. Not surprisingly, given the food and drink imagery in Isaiah 55 as well, the Hebrew word involved shows up twice: in verse 2, where it is translated "yourselves," and in verse 3, where it is rendered simply by the pronoun "you."

Both texts, of course, make it clear that the imagery of drinking, eating, and satisfaction is functioning metaphorically. What is *truly* necessary for life as God intends it is God's own self. Actually, this is quite clear in the opening line of the psalm: "O God, you are my God, I seek you, my soul thirsts for you." As the psalm unfolds, it is evident that the psalmist has in effect heeded the advice of Isaiah 55:3, "come to me; listen, so that you may live," as well as Isaiah 55:6, "Seek the LORD while he may be found; call upon him while he is near." Psalm 63:2 suggests that the psalmist has sought God by visiting the temple, at least in spirit; and Psalm 63:4 communicates the psalmist's submission to God in prayer. In essence, the psalmist prays to live; and because God is a powerful and loving presence, the psalmist also lives to praise (see Ps. 63:3, 7).

Life is also at issue in Psalm 63:3, which contains one of the most striking affirmations in all of Scripture: "Your steadfast love is better than life." In a real sense, "steadfast love" is something like a one-word summary of the character of God (see Exod. 34:6–7); not surprisingly, it occurs frequently in all types of psalms (see Pss. 5:7; 13:5; 33:5; 36:5; 100:5; 118:1–4; and many more). Its occurrence in the affirmation of Psalm 63:3 is an invitation to consider as well how the character of God may also be featured in Isaiah 55:1–9; and it is.

The phrase "steadfast, sure love" in Isaiah 55:3 contains a form of the word translated "steadfast love" in Psalm 63:3; the invitation to seek, call upon, and "return to the LORD" (Isa. 55:6–7) is predicated upon the affirmation that God will "have mercy" (which could also be translated "show compassion" or even "show motherly compassion," since the noun form of this root means "womb") and "will abundantly pardon." Both of these Hebrew roots—"mercy/compassion" and "pardon"—show up in or near God's self-revelatory speech to Moses in Exodus 34:6–7 to fill out the meaning of "steadfast love" (see "merciful" in Exod. 34:6 and "pardon" in Exod. 34:9). In both Psalm 63 and Isaiah 55, God's

The Fiery Love of God

All that I have said is as nothing compared to what I feel within, the witnessed correspondence of love between God and the Soul; for when God sees the Soul pure as it was in its origins, He tugs at it with a glance, draws it and binds it to Himself with a fiery love that by itself could annihilate the immortal soul. In so acting, God so transforms the soul in Him that it knows nothing other than God; and He continues to draw it up to His fiery love until He restores it to that pure state from which it first issued. As it is being drawn upwards, the soul feels itself melting in the fire of that love of its sweet God, for He will not cease until He has brought the soul to its perfection. That is why the soul seeks to cast off any and all impediments, so that it can be lifted up to God.

Catherine of Genoa, *Purgation and Purgatory, The Spiritual Dialogue*, trans. and notes Serge Hughes (New York: Paulist Press, 1979), 78–79.

love, mercy/compassion, and willingness to forgive are the life-giving realities that the faithful are eagerly to seek and will be able to find.

It is especially important to attend to the focus on God's character in Isaiah 55:7, given the following two verses. Isaiah 55:8–9 are familiar verses, and they are often cited to support the conclusion that God's ways and thoughts are not fully comprehensible, because God's transcendent greatness is more than we human beings can grasp. This may be true; but *in this context*, what sets God's thoughts and ways apart from human thoughts and ways is precisely God's unfailing commitment to be merciful and forgiving. In short, what it means to be God is to be fundamentally, essentially, unfailingly gracious (see also Hos. 11:9, where what sets God apart from mortals is God's willingness to forgive). What the psalmist fervently seeks and finds, and what Isaiah 55 invites its readers to seek, is the powerful, protecting, life-giving presence of a quintessentially loving, compassionate, gracious God.

J. CLINTON MCCANN JR.

1 Corinthians 10:1–13

¹I do not want you to be unaware, brothers and sisters, that our ancestors were all under the cloud, and all passed through the sea, ²and all were baptized into Moses in the cloud and in the sea, ³and all ate the same spiritual food, ⁴and all drank the same spiritual drink. For they drank from the spiritual rock that followed them, and the rock was Christ. ⁵Nevertheless, God was not pleased with most of them, and they were struck down in the wilderness.

⁶Now these things occurred as examples for us, so that we might not desire evil as they did. ⁷Do not become idolaters as some of them did; as it is written, "The people sat down to eat and drink, and they rose up to play." ⁸We must not indulge in sexual immorality as some of them did, and twenty-three thousand fell in a single day. ⁹We must not put Christ to the test, as some of them did, and were destroyed by serpents. ¹⁰And do not complain as some of them did, and were destroyed by the destroyer. ¹¹These things happened to them to serve as an example, and they were written down to instruct us, on whom the ends of the ages have come. ¹²So if you think you are standing, watch out that you do not fall. ¹³No testing has overtaken you that is not common to everyone. God is faithful, and he will not let you be tested beyond your strength, but with the testing he will also provide the way out so that you may be able to endure it.

Commentary 1: Connecting the Reading with Scripture

When we read Paul's famous love poem in 1 Corinthians 13, our hearts warm with affirmation. When we read Paul's words of warning in 1 Corinthians 10:1–13, however, or any of today's lectionary readings (Isa. 55:1–9; Ps. 63:1–8; Luke 13:1–9), we are likely brought up short. First Corinthians 10:8 was horrifically appropriated by some during the HIV/AIDS crisis in the 1980s to proclaim that the awful suffering and death were God's judgment upon gays and lesbians. Most Christians rightly condemned the hateful rhetoric as inconsistent with the overarching biblical witness (including, notably, 1 Cor. 13), but it is true that an unfortunate picture of a vindictive God and a self-centered logic—do not do these things or God is going to hurt you—easily flows from a plain reading of 1 Corinthians 10:5–12. Such a reading can also reinforce a fear among those enduring hardship that God is angry with them and punishing them. First Corinthians 10:13 (God brings no testing not common to everyone, nothing you cannot handle), though

intended as a source of comfort, also harbors harmful potential, for it can appear, first, that God consciously allows the tests we suffer and, second, that those who are overcome by grief, despair, pain, or depression are failing to live up to their full strength.

Sensitivity to the harmful potential of such texts has long led even conservative Christians to speak of Scripture correcting Scripture. In this vein, it is notable that another of today's lectionary texts, Luke 13:1–9, makes clear that Jesus presumes it is mistaken to think people suffer because they are "worse sinners." This is a redemptive word for the suffering that is worthy of emphasis. Still, when Jesus urges people to repent or they will perish (Luke 13:5), he too can be (mis)understood to be appealing to a self-interested rationale.

We must also consider Paul's banner allusion to the famous but complicated story of the golden calf: "the people sat down to eat . . . rose up to play" (1 Cor. 10:7; Exod. 32:6). The Israelites offer sacrifices to idols while Moses is

68

high on Mount Sinai. An angry God tells Moses to step aside so God can "consume" Israel and make *of Moses* a great nation. Moses dares to plead for Israel, changing God's mind and saving the Israelites. When Moses returns to camp, he is so enraged by what he sees that he initiates the distinctive religious role of the tribe of Levi by instructing them to kill their sons, brothers, friends, and neighbors (!). The next day, however, he reascends Mount Sinai and again begs God to forgive the people, going so far as to say that, if necessary, God should blot Moses himself out of God's book. God partially relents, but promises ultimate judgment and sends a plague, "because they made the calf" (Exod. 32:35).

In the face of such complexity and realism, we should be overcome with overwhelming respect for Scripture. These are complex texts. While the dangers of plain readings should be noted, such readings do not give these texts their full due. Above all, it is vital to remember the gospel's signal declaration that while God remains a righteous judge, God is, above all, a God of grace, a God who, while we are yet sinners, first loves us (Rom. 5:8; 1 John 4:10). When one confronts texts of Paul susceptible to problematic interpretation, it is not only fair to Paul but vital to good theology that we remember we are reading the author of 1 Corinthians 13, the man who penned and lived to his own martyrdom the *kenōsis* hymn of Philippians (2:6–11). In the light of Paul's overall life and witness, there is no reason to doubt Paul is offering words of warning about real dangers out of sincere concern for the Corinthians. These "warning" verses are reminiscent of a loving, worried parent who abandons concerns over intrinsic motivation and tries to scare their beloved child out of risky behavior by naming fearful, realistic, real-world consequences. We should guard against harmful misreading, while making clear how Paul's love for the Corinthians shines through in his warnings.

Note the gritty realism of today's lectionary passages. We confront idolatry; deaths in the tens of thousands from plagues/natural disasters and wild animals (snakebite); state-sanctioned torture and executions (the "mingled blood" of the Galileans); construction accidents (tower of Siloam); and sexual immorality (think in terms of child and spousal abuse, incest, and human "spoils of war"). With no sugar-coated escapism here, these texts admirably take on our real world. Paul will not forget those who have been wronged by evildoers, will not compromise on God's enduring condemnation of those evils and God's judgment of political, corporate, social, or family tyrants, and while some victims are clearly innocent, Paul is also concerned for the many evildoers who are suffering from the predictable worldly effects of their own evil. In this latter vein Paul is seriously cautioning the Corinthians because he sees them already as, or in imminent danger of becoming, evildoers, and so suffering from the effects of their actions.

Paul is not writing righteous compatriots a diatribe against mutually despised evildoers. Paul has no patience with self-righteousness. He is against condemnation mixed with hate. He is against any graceless perspective wherein one happily sees people receive their due. This distinguishes Paul from the readily recognizable dynamic among many of today's conservative and progressive activists, religious and secular alike, who often appear to see themselves as blameless, while despising and wishing ill upon their opponents. Paul, by contrast, is *passionately pleading with and concerned for evildoers*. In this respect, Paul is the faithful, grace-filled follower of Jesus, who was himself notorious for eating with tax collectors, prostitutes, and other sinners.

In this respect, Paul is similar to Moses when he offered his life for those whose idolatry he despised. That is, Paul's uncompromising condemnation of evildoers does not displace love for evildoers. What we witness in this text is a high-stakes (literally life-and-death for Paul and early Christians), real-world performance of Paul's theology of law *and* grace. What we hear in 10:13 is Paul's confidence in the ultimate triumph of grace, Paul's conviction that God would never test us beyond what we can bear, that nothing (including execution), not "hardship, or distress, or persecution, or famine, or nakedness, or peril, or sword . . . will be able to separate us from the love of God in Jesus Christ our Lord" (Rom. 8:35–39).

Finally, in retrospect it is clear how Paul's affirmation of both law *and* grace (not grace replacing law, and never legalistic/self-righteous law forgetful of grace) is visible in his startling introductory affirmation that all the generations of the Israelites drank from the same "spiritual rock . . . Christ" (1 Cor. 10:4). This affirmation of the eternal efficacy of God's gracious work through Christ is also stressed by John Wesley and famously developed by twentieth-century theologian Karl Rahner in terms of "anonymous Christianity." The ancient Jews, says Paul, were in true communion with God through Christ. This directly and decisively rebuts anti-Semitism and intolerance toward other faiths (though it still presumes the Christ event is essential).

Paul's treatment of law and grace is complex ("Nevertheless . . . they were struck down," 1 Cor. 10:5). Paul never attempts precisely to coordinate the incommensurable realities of law and grace. At the same time, neither does he abjure the reality either of law (with its often awful, real-world consequences) or of grace. Instead, he insists we acknowledge the presently enduring, incommensurable realities/dynamics of law *and* of grace, even as he performs, affirms, and celebrates grace as primary and ultimate (*simul iustus et peccator*).

WILLIAM GREENWAY

Commentary 2: Connecting the Reading with the World

Consider this. A member of your church comes to sit in your office and speaks to you of some difficulty in her life. She has been doing her best to work through it. She says she has been praying, reading her Bible, and confiding to close friends and seeking their counsel and support. Still, some doubts about her faith have surfaced. Finally, she asks, "Is this what they call a 'test of faith,' pastor?" It is a good question. Does God send things our way to test us? If so, for what purpose?

Some people believe that setting tests in their path is one way God works with God's covenant people to fashion them into becoming agents of grace. In fact, such people can point to several places in the Bible to back up that conviction. First Corinthians 10:1–13 is one such place. If they stop at verse 13, the "tests" they imagine are confined to the arena of personal morality. To pass the tests, one need only steer away from sexual immorality, blasphemy, or even complaining over one's lot in life, that is, what must be done in order to avoid God's wrath. If you add verse 14 to the passage, however, the range of concern widens into a clearer picture of one thing that is testing Paul's faith in the Corinthian church's capacity to embody the gospel: "therefore, my dear friends, flee from the worship of idols."

We speak with admiration of those we idolize. We bring a beloved pastor, teacher, or colleague to mind, and we say, "That one is my idol." The person in question is a paragon of what we value and aspire to be in our own lives, some virtue we want to cultivate or some achievement we want to work toward. Mindful of those we idolize, we put ourselves to the test, especially at Lent, and ask ourselves, "How am I doing at becoming the best person I can be?" We lay our efforts like that before God and pray for strength and courage to develop the ability, integrity, and character embodied by our "idols."

In Corinth idolatry meant something quite different. Imagine yourself taking a stroll with one of the Gentile Christians in Corinth, and you would soon understand why idolatry was such a troubling issue for them. Along the streets of that commercial center you would see the "many gods and many lords" Paul speaks of in 1 Corinthians 8:5. Here and there one would walk by magnificent statues, temples, and shrines dedicated to the worship of those deities. As you walked together through the city, you could discuss how some in the Corinthian church were choosing to live within their own pluralistic religious culture as a small minority. You learn that some of their number saw no problem with attending the meals and festivals in the temples you just passed. "It is just part of what it means to be, well, Corinthian!" they explain. Then there were others who would argue that since they had been baptized and regularly celebrated the Lord's Supper, they were somehow immune to the power of a meal celebrated in a shrine that a close friend attended.

"What was so wrong with accepting hospitality like that?" your companion wondered. For many, it seemed that sharing a meal with others in temples devoted to other gods and lords was hardly a test of their resolve to live "in Christ."

So what was the problem in Corinth? You begin to see the issue in a new light when you and your companion arrive at the *agora,* the marketplace, and behold the majestic statue of Athena at its center. After all the questions that you and your companion have raised on your stroll, the statue stands like an exclamation point. It does indeed have a certain power and presence. In fact, it could inspire reverence, or even devotion to that which the image represents. "Here I am surrounded by powerful images like this," mutters your companion. "That is why it is so difficult to wrap my head around the idea that there is but one God who deserves worship, much less devoted and undivided loyalty."

It would be too easy for us to go around idolatry as a test of contemporary Christian faith and to avoid its implications. The preacher can remind the congregation of what is all too evident in our culture: that we too are under the spell of idolatry. We too live in the presence of powerful, artfully crafted images. Some are chiseled from stone, others forged from iron or bronze; some are painted on walls or canvas, many are digitalized. Images like these command our attention. Those that inspire or haunt are powerful enough to draw us to a way of life or a way of seeing the world in a particular light. Entire industries exist that are devoted to the production of images that test one's convictions about everything from sexuality to consumption of goods to the blind acquisition of personal wealth. They can even obscure the path toward empathy and solidarity with those who simply cannot afford the way of life that many of these images represent. This is the contemporary experience of being enthralled to the "many gods and many lords" present in the marketplace. Though the forms of idolatry may be different from those at Corinth, the challenge to live faithfully in Christ still makes its claim on the church.

We are now ready to hear from Paul. He is going to address these matters with force to sharpen our thinking. He begins the way that many preachers do, by interweaving our dilemmas with the experiences of our spiritual ancestors. There is no way to soften the impact of his warning. He needs to be clear with those Gentiles, recently baptized into Christ and therefore grafted into the story of Israel, that catastrophe awaits those who flirt with idolatry. We would do well to heed the warnings. Idolatry presents itself as statues and shrines to other "gods and lords," as seductive digital images or as a glorification of a way of life that competes with the way of the Christ. Paul understands the way of Christ as being a part of the body of Christ in the world. As that body, the community is empowered to be a base camp for God's new age. In that base camp, differences and boundaries put in place by the old age are overcome as Jews and Gentiles, slave and free, male and female participate in the saving work of a powerful God who raised Jesus up from the dead. It is a deity, Paul warns, with whom you do not want to trifle.

Paul also calls attention to the power of communal spiritual practice. We often think of the season of Lent as a time when we test the level of our understanding and devotion by adopting practices of prayer, fasting, study, and service. We do not do this in order to become immune to the lures of other ways of being in the world, or even to assuage the wrath of a distant tribal god. Rather, think of these practices as rehearsals for the coming age, an age that has dawned in the resurrection of Christ and will be consummated in God's own time.

RICHARD F. WARD

Luke 13:1–9

¹At that very time there were some present who told him about the Galileans whose blood Pilate had mingled with their sacrifices. ²He asked them, "Do you think that because these Galileans suffered in this way they were worse sinners than all other Galileans? ³No, I tell you; but unless you repent, you will all perish as they did. ⁴Or those eighteen who were killed when the tower of Siloam fell on them—do you think that they were worse offenders than all the others living in Jerusalem? ⁵No, I tell you; but unless you repent, you will all perish just as they did."

⁶Then he told this parable: "A man had a fig tree planted in his vineyard; and he came looking for fruit on it and found none. ⁷So he said to the gardener, 'See here! For three years I have come looking for fruit on this fig tree, and still I find none. Cut it down! Why should it be wasting the soil?' ⁸He replied, 'Sir, let it alone for one more year, until I dig around it and put manure on it. ⁹If it bears fruit next year, well and good; but if not, you can cut it down.'"

Commentary 1: Connecting the Reading with Scripture

This text begins with reference to two tragic recent events. The first is an act of government oppression, the kind of imperial violence that happened (and still happens) on a regular basis. The second is a natural disaster, which today might be compared with hurricanes, earthquakes, drought, or floods (Luke 13:1–5). The question is, why do bad things happen to some people? Is it because they were evil? "No," Jesus says in this reading. Yet in 1 Corinthians 10:1–13, another lection this week, Paul recounts several instances in which the Israelites suffered for their evil ways, an interpretation that appears to contradict Luke 13. Nevertheless, what the two texts have in common is that neither invites the reader to participate in pronouncing the judgment of God upon others. Rather, in both cases, the specified tragedies are recounted as a warning for readers to repent (or, "do not desire evil as they did," 1 Cor. 10:6), so that we will not perish (Luke 13:5).

Repentance is a vital theme in Luke. Terms for repentance occur in Luke and Acts more than twice as often as in all the other Gospels combined. The Greek *metanoia* means "to change one's mind." This is more than an intellectual change or passive concept. It signifies changing the focus of one's life, changing one's moral direction, a dynamic change in one's way of living. To repent is to live in a distinct and different way. Luke elucidates the full ramifications of repentance in Acts 26:20: "repent and turn to God and do deeds consistent with repentance."

The text continues with the parable of the Fig Tree (vv. 6–9), which expands Luke's teaching on repentance. The purpose of the fig tree is to bear figs. When the owner finds none after three years, he demands it be cut down. He is stopped by the gardener, who says to give him another year. If it still does not bear fruit, then it can be cut down. The implication is that the one who truly repents will bear fruit, so that the dynamic, transformational character of true repentance is emphasized. In a similar saying earlier in Luke, Jesus says, "No good tree bears bad fruit, nor again does a bad tree bear good fruit; for each tree is known by its own fruit. . . . The good person out of the good treasure of the heart produces good, and the evil person out of evil treasure produces evil" (6:43–45). Luke 13:1–9 then functions as a meditation on the transformational character of true repentance.

It is important to caution that the words of the gardener have been applied another way. In Luke, the interval for repentance has often been applied primarily to the Jewish people in an unfortunate form of anti-Judaism (see, e.g., 16:27–31). This undoes the text's universal power and turns it into an anti-Semitic tool of Christian triumphalism rather than a challenge to all believers.

In order to rightly understand Luke's teaching about repentance and "deeds consistent with repentance," it is vital to read this passage in the light of the whole of Luke's Gospel. Two themes dominate Luke's teachings on discipleship. The first is emphasis on preference for the poor. From the very beginning, Jesus' ministry focuses on the poor. His first sermon, in the synagogue in Nazareth, presents a mission statement derived from Isaiah 61:1: "The Spirit of the Lord is upon me, because he has anointed me to bring good news to the poor" (Luke 4:18). In Luke's version of the Beatitudes, "Blessed are you who are poor" is juxtaposed with "Woe to you who are rich" (6:20, 24). In 18:18–25, when a rich young ruler asks Jesus about the law and assures him he has kept it faithfully, Jesus replies: "Sell all that you own and distribute the money to the poor, and you will have treasure in heaven; then come, follow me." This was a bridge too far: "But when he heard this, he became sad; for he was very rich" (vv. 22–23).

The rich young ruler's fate may be similar to what is described in the parable of the Rich Man and Lazarus (16:19–31). The opening is sparse and tragic: "There was a rich man . . . who feasted sumptuously every day. And at his gate lay a poor man named Lazarus . . . who longed to satisfy his hunger with what fell from the rich man's table" (vv. 19–23). In the afterlife, their fates are reversed. Whereas the rich man had dined luxuriously while the poor man longed for crumbs from his table, in the afterlife the poor man ends up reclining next to Abraham at the banquet of God (the Greek phrase "in the bosom of Abraham" signifies reclining in a position of honor next to Abraham, vv. 22–23), while the rich man longs for a drop of water. This can a difficult saying for many to hear in our age, where conspicuous consumption and stark divisions between rich and poor are commonplace, but it gives concrete contour to one dimension of the transformational character of true Christian repentance. The prophetic imperative should not be interpreted simplistically. The faithful response may be focused upon direct giving of food, clothing, and money, but pastors may also want to urge those with power and influence also to address social and political initiatives that address structural sources of poverty and exploitation.

The parable of the Rich Man and Lazarus also highlights the second dominant theme in Luke's teachings about discipleship, namely, the theme of radical inclusion, symbolized especially by meal practices. The key text concerns Jesus dining with tax collectors and sinners at Levi's house (5:29–32). Here the phrase "tax collectors and sinners" functions as a catchall term for outcasts, a category that includes the poor (as in 7:22, 34). When the Pharisees criticize Jesus for this meal practice, he responds that he came to invite just such people to his banquet, making this meal a symbol for the kingdom of God. In Luke 14, while dining at a Pharisee's house, Jesus expands on this theme. One of the diners refers to the banquet in the afterlife ("eat bread in the kingdom of God," 14:15). Jesus responds with the parable of the Great Banquet (vv. 16–24), in which the host, after being turned down by the first selection of invitees, extends the invitation to "the poor, the crippled, the blind, and the lame" (v. 21). Earlier in the same chapter, the diners are urged to invite the same kind of outcasts to their parties: "when you give a banquet, invite the poor, the crippled, the lame, and the blind" (v. 13).

The story of Zacchaeus is pivotal to the development of these themes (19:1–10). Zacchaeus, a wealthy tax collector who receives Jesus' approval by selling half of his goods and giving them to the poor, becomes the model for the patron hosts in Acts who provide homes for the meal gatherings of the community (typified by Lydia, Acts 16:14–15, 40), the sort of faithful community that is characterized by selling their goods and distributing to any who had need (Acts 2:44–47).

Repent and bear fruit worthy of repentance. More precisely, engage in the sort of spiritual, transformational sort of repentance that quite automatically results in a new way of living, in new eyes to see; engage in the sort of true transformational repentance that quite automatically leads to sensitivity to and loving action on behalf of those who are outcast, despised, needy: this is the essence of discipleship in Luke–Acts.

DENNIS E. SMITH

Commentary 2: Connecting the Reading with the World

Initially, it is difficult to see how this passage fits together. Each few verses almost read like a dislocated thought oddly flowing to the next. What has death by falling tower or murderous Roman authorities to do with repentance? Even if that connection is somehow made, next comes the story of a fig tree and manure. These are not random images, however; together they subtly suggest themes of urgency and the true import of one's decisions. Yet that urgency is mixed with an allowance of patience. Though death itself may be imminent—for people and fig trees—the gospel paradoxically calls for both urgent repentance and patient reprieve.

In many of our congregations, death comes up every Sunday. We speak of it informally in announcements. We share the date for an upcoming funeral. We receive prayer requests for ill members. We acknowledge flowers given in remembrance of the deceased. Yet we rarely stop to consider death more deeply. We certainly do not connect the death of a church member with an urgent call to repentance. In most congregational cultures, discussion of death and dying is not for polite company. Even we whose savior died and rose from the dead rarely pause to consider our own mortality.

The audience before Jesus was wrestling, quite directly, with questions of mortality and justice. They did not ask, "Why do bad things happen to good people?" but their questions surely suggest that great imponderable. Jesus assures those present that the Galileans who died by Pilate's orders had not been made to suffer more greatly because they were worse sinners than other Galileans. However, this assurance quickly shifts to what seems to be Jesus' real concern: "But unless you repent, you will all perish as they did" (v. 3).

Similarly, those eighteen who perished as the tower of Siloam fell were no worse offenders than those who survived, but Jesus pushes again, "Unless you repent, you will all perish just as they did" (v. 5). What should we make of Jesus' warning? Surely, he does not mean that, barring repentance, his hearers will die either at the hands of Pilate or in a tower incident. In what sense will we die "just as they did"? How are these tragedies connected to Jesus' call to repentance?

Jesus is using the real concerns of his audience to emphasize the importance of repentance—"meeting them where they are," we might say. Jesus listens to the concerns of the crowds, comforts briefly, and then quickly pivots to his greater concern: their need to repent.

Repentance is often underplayed in the contemporary church. We may monotonously repeat a confession of sin in each Sunday's liturgy, but Jesus' insistence upon repentance seems to suggest an investment far greater than is common in our typical weekly confessions. This is no mere, "I'm sorry," but a full repentance of sin, a full acknowledgment of the brokenness from which we cannot escape, and a personal accounting for the mess we create, continue, or countenance. Jesus indicates to his audience that, short of a full repentance in light of his teaching, their death will mirror the others. The bar has been raised for those listening to Jesus' teaching. Following him calls for true, soul-felt repentance that shifts actions and frees for new ways of living—and soon, for death is real.

Engaging the realities of death, dying, and repentance is particularly appropriate during Lent. For many, Lent is a season of giving up something or perhaps taking on a spiritual practice. In these focused acts, believers seek to grow in their faith and prepare themselves for life beneath the cross and beyond the tomb. In our culture, frank speech about death and dying can be considered morbid. We are more likely to give up chocolate than reflect on Jesus' response to those gathered: "Unless you repent, you will all perish just as they did" (vv. 3, 5). When can the church take up such realities if not in Lent?

A pediatrician I know specializes in palliative care. That means a significant portion of her work includes helping children with terminal diseases die well, and supporting their families in the process. It is grueling, sad work. After each patient's death, the palliative care team brings together all the medical staff who cared for the patient. Especially for those workers unaccustomed to the death of their young patients, this meeting seems scary. They arrive with their defenses high, but after a few minutes the medical teammates realize the gathering is for sharing stories, acknowledging pain, and providing an opportunity to "be real" about what they are feeling. Tears flow. Hugs are given and received.

What strikes my friend about these meetings is the shift that occurs in the short duration of the gathering. Initially, the room is full of anxiety, perhaps expecting the agenda to be about laying blame. After a few short minutes of good leadership, it becomes clear to everyone that the purpose is acknowledging hurt and sadness. The care team must pause and be honest about our human realities before moving forward to continue to give appropriate care, concern, and emotional openness to other patients. When led appropriately, discussing death and dying can focus our awareness on life's ultimate concerns. To the audience around Jesus, he made clear that the pressing, unaddressed ultimate concern was that they repent.

Cut—however awkwardly—to the parable of the Unfruitful Fig Tree. The tree has had three years to produce, and so the landowner orders the gardener to cut it down. The logic here is sound and in keeping with good stewardship teaching. If the tree is not producing, "Why should it be wasting the soil?" (v. 7). Something fruitful could be planted in its place. Surely the time has come and reality must be faced. The gardener suggests a plan involving digging and manure. Is the tree given a reprieve? Though the text does not say it, one gets the impression that the gardener's words convince the landowner to wait another year.

The landowner's initial instinct is to use his resources in a manner that yields the most fruit (and profits). If the tree is not performing, it must be cut out. He approaches the problem with a sense of urgency. Though he will lose his investment, it is not producing and must be killed. Such an approach seems perfectly sensible. Note that the gardener appreciates the landowner's motives. The gardener too wants the land producing. The gardener and landowner agree on the ideal outcome—a tree producing figs—but they differ on the time horizon and tactics for success.

Many congregations employ the nonprofit leadership approach of using mission and/or vision statements to guide the direction of their ministry. These statements, on the whole, are appropriate, delightful, sometimes even inspiring descriptions of the call of the congregation. They often emphasize welcome, love, evangelism, and mission. Implementing the statements, however, can cause quite the uproar. Like the landowner and the gardener, we can share a common goal—fresh figs!—but differ on the speed and particulars of how to arrive there. One member's urgent call for justice is another member's cry for patience. The lection offers the preacher a paradox of urgency. In the face of death, time for repentance is already here, but the time to tear out the fig tree is not yet. The spirit of patience remains full of a sense of urgency. Repentance, after all, is as much about this life as the next.

ADAM J. COPELAND

Fourth Sunday in Lent

Joshua 5:9–12
Psalm 32

2 Corinthians 5:16–21
Luke 15:1–3, 11b–32

Joshua 5:9–12

⁹The LORD said to Joshua, "Today I have rolled away from you the disgrace of Egypt." And so that place is called Gilgal to this day.
¹⁰While the Israelites were camped in Gilgal they kept the passover in the evening on the fourteenth day of the month in the plains of Jericho. ¹¹On the day after the passover, on that very day, they ate the produce of the land, unleavened cakes and parched grain. ¹²The manna ceased on the day they ate the produce of the land, and the Israelites no longer had manna; they ate the crops of the land of Canaan that year.

Commentary 1: Connecting the Reading with Scripture

Joshua 5:9–12 signals Israel's new era in the land in three different ways. First, God announces that the disgrace of Egypt has been removed. Second, the people celebrate the Passover, reaffirming God's mighty act of rescue forty years before. Third, as foreshadowed in Exodus 16:35, the manna they had eaten forty years in the wilderness ceases, and they taste the promised land's own food.

Throughout Joshua up to this point, episode after episode has emphasized that the Israelite nation is now in new and different territory, both figuratively and literally. Moses, who led them through the past four books (Exodus, Leviticus, Numbers, Deuteronomy) and forty years, is dead, and Joshua is now in charge. From being a people wandering through territory they do not possess, they have become a people treading on land portrayed as promised to them by God. They have crossed the Jordan River into the land, reenacting their exit from Egypt over the Red Sea, and circumcised all the males according to the command given just as they left Egypt (Exod. 12:48).

Finally, having been ritually purified through circumcision, the company keeps the Passover, the first in the promised land. What they eat is not detailed. The story does not say whether they slaughtered lambs and smeared blood on the entrances of their tents, as the Passover law directed. It is a symbolic event, and our curiosity about its details must remain unsatisfied.

According to the Passover tradition, the people were to eat unleavened bread for a week in remembrance of the haste with which the slaves left Egypt, with no time for dough to rise before baking. Verse 11 details that they eat unleavened cakes and parched grain. Now what they eat comes from the new land. Readers may wonder how the newly arriving Israelites procured this new local food. The passage does not say whether they bought, gleaned, or stole it. Instead, it emphasizes one way that they did not obtain it. Having crossed several thresholds—from outside the land to inside it, from uncircumcised to circumcised, from a people lacking rituals to one that celebrates holy days—now they cross from gathering what falls from heaven to enjoying what springs up from the ground. The manna ceases that day; the umbilical cord of the wilderness is finally severed.

The moment is larger than this brief and undramatic narrative may betray. It marks the people's passage from being habituated by circumstantial boundaries that circumscribed their behavior, boundaries they could not transgress, to becoming a people whose behavioral boundaries are prescribed by the ethical laws about

76

land use received at Mount Sinai and preserved for forty years. In this sense, the laws about food represent their graduation into a people voluntarily participating in a community ethic seen as a gift from God.

This community ethic has everything to do with the social conditions from which they came. When the exodus story began, Israelite slaves were building food storage cities—hoarding cities—for a hard-hearted king in a stratified society. Whatever we think about the historicity of the exodus narrative, the nature of ancient Egypt as an unequal society seems to have been accurately portrayed. Figurines and drawings found in Egyptian royal tombs depict spinners, weavers, and farmers laboring under watchful supervision, their toil enriching their rulers.

The economic system instituted by God in the wilderness could hardly have contrasted more. When the people complained of hunger, God told Moses, "I am going to rain bread from heaven for you" (Exod. 16:4). This heavenly food came generously from the Giver of all that is good. The details surrounding its introduction in Exodus 16 illustrate principles that are well worth noticing.

First, in a beautiful line that all who care about food justice should memorize, "those who gathered much had nothing over, and those who gathered little had no shortage" (v. 18). Everyone had enough. The greedy—or, rather, the go-getters, depending on your viewpoint—do not get more; and the lazy—or, rather, the considerate—do not get less.

Second, the manna spoiled after one day, so people could no more hoard it than they could the air they breathed. They could enjoy their daily bread without thought of economic gain and without worry of loss. In the wilderness food served its basic purpose of nutrition, not a side purpose of enriching some at others' expense.

Third, the manna kept Sabbath, allowing its gatherers to do the same. All were expected to rest and to allow others to rest. No more slavery, not even for the animals.

In these three ways, the strange behavior of the manna limited the ways people could play around with their food. They could use it only to serve its basic purpose of sustenance, strength

for the day. Just as children are socialized into certain habits by the boundaries set by parents, the nation had been trained to practice—and to begin seeing the advantages of—certain social ethics that they will now be expected to carry out voluntarily.

When the Israelites had arrived at Mount Sinai, they had been taught these ethics. They learned that food would abound when they reached the land flowing with milk and honey. The physical constraints would vanish with the manna. Instead, the people would be asked to adhere to moral boundaries. They were given a multitude of rules that governed land possession, farming, food choices, food sharing, and the treatment, killing, and eating of animals.

These various rules followed the same moral principles as the manna. First, just as the manna belonged to God and came as a gift to the people, so acreage in the new land would also belong to God, and would come to the people only as a loan. They could not lose it permanently through misfortune, because the jubilee law dictated that it would revert to the original owner every half century, narrowing the gap between rich and poor (Lev. 25:10).

Concern for fairness remained in the laws for the land. Equitable food distribution would become a basic right that no longer came miraculously, but through the voluntary self-control of farmers who left gleanings for the poor and immigrants (Lev. 19:9–10; Deut. 24:19–22).

Like the manna's weekly schedule, the Sinai food rules restricted labor. The Sabbath reappeared in the Ten Commandments as a rest for family, employees, and livestock (Exod. 20:8–11; 23:12; Deut. 5:12–15). Sabbath rest also occurred on the scale of years: for the sake of fields themselves, for the poor, and even for wild animals, the land was periodically left fallow (Exod. 23:10–11; Lev. 25:4).

The manna seemed to work well in the wilderness, and the people's only complaint was that the same meal for forty years became tiresome. The promised land in which Joshua's troops crossing the Jordan eat their first local meal promises more dietary choices than manna. However, Sinai's rules still impose limits on those choices: no longer physical barriers cultivating forced habits, but rather moral boundaries socializing the nation into dependence on God, equity, generosity, and rest.

Even for those of us who do not observe such specific laws regarding land ownership, gleaning, and Sabbath, such principles cohere with environmentally and socially healthy practices. Our

food and all good that comes to us still come as a gift for which to return thanks. We still hold a responsibility to share the earth's wealth equitably. Laborers, animals, and the land all prosper best when provided rest and restoration.

PATRICIA K. TULL

Commentary 2: Connecting the Reading with the World

As the events described in these few verses of Joshua unfold, the people of Israel are just a step or two back inside the promised land. The wilderness wanderings are over. God's promise of deliverance and return is fulfilled, albeit forty years later and with the next generation. The span of time, however, is brought together with covenant ritual: circumcision and Passover. The text tells of the most significant of transitions for God's people, yet that transition is marked by the lasting practices that point spiritually to God's steadfast faithfulness. The preacher ought to push back against the quick movement of the narrative and invite listeners to appreciate the magnitude of the moment in salvation history.

The passage begins with a puzzling word from the Lord: "Today I have rolled away from you the disgrace of Egypt" (v. 9). Not surprisingly, there is a lack of clarity when it comes to "the disgrace of Egypt." The KJV translates it as the "reproach of Egypt." Initial thoughts turn to the ugly reality of the Egyptian captivity. The Lord is removing the stain of disrespect and mistreatment at the hands of the Egyptians that has accompanied God's people for the last forty years. Still on the threshold of the promised land, God is erasing the marks of enslavement. A pastoral approach to such "disgrace" could point to the posttraumatic stress from enslavement, oppression, or abuse that certainly lasts for decades. However, one can also argue that the wilderness cries, the disobedience, and the idolatrous behavior all became part of the "disgrace." In effect, Egypt's reproach has tainted the Israelites as well; after forty years they are far from free when it comes to incurring God's judgment. The Lord's "rolling away" is a necessary cleansing and part of what makes the entrance into the promised land a bigger

deal. The naming of the place as Gilgal and the Hebrew meaning "to roll" is an exclamation point on God's liberating, cleansing action.

The narrator's account of the experience for the people of Israel in Gilgal is crisp and clear. The focus is on celebrating the Passover meal, eating the produce of the land, and the cessation of manna from heaven. The chapters yet to come in Joshua tell of battles and destruction and death. Such violent depictions of the ancient history foreshadow the seemingly endless reality of suffering, occupation, bitterness, and hatred that plagues the region to this day. The preacher should not shy away from the complexity and challenge of the narrative, which never goes away. Here in just these few verses, it is life in Gilgal that provides the theological foundation to the movement toward the promised land.

In Gilgal the people of Israel immediately share in the celebration of Passover. The fathers, mothers, and grandparents who fled Egypt forty years ago would now be few and far between, but remembering God's saving action is passed from generation to generation. The urgency of keeping the feast right there in Gilgal inaugurates new life in the land with an act of worship. It is a rite of remembering all that God has done and offering gratitude for the fulfillment of God's once and future promise. The day after the Passover meal, the people "ate the produce of the land, unleavened cakes and parched grain" (v. 11). Arrival in the promised land comes with an abundant harvest of God's blessings.

The crossing of the river Jordan from wilderness to the land that God has promised is marked by remembering, gratitude, and worship. This seminal transition for God's people marks this historic and distinctive experience of

God's covenantal nature, but the Passover celebration in Gilgal serves as a warrant for God's people in all times of movement and transition. The seasons of life in a congregation come with all kinds of movement: birth, baptism, confirmation, graduations, marriage, pastoral transitions, death. The effective generativity of faith requires that those collective movements of life be marked by remembering, gratitude, and worship. In a similar way, an individual's life of faith inevitably comes with momentous occasions of transition and change. The preacher's opportunity here is to encourage hearers to live into and cling to God's faithfulness in every move and change. Remembering and celebrating what God has done brings assurance, joy, and strength.

Few in the congregation will remember the time here in Joshua when the manna stopped. "The manna ceased on the day they ate the produce of the land" (v. 12). After decades of that daily bread coming from heaven and sustaining God's people in the wilderness, their nourishment was once again to come from the earth. Eating "the crops of the land of Canaan" (v. 12) implies a return to the rhythm and work of being stewards of the earth. As the manna ceases, God's people again share in the responsibilities of community, care, daily living. Other miracles of God will surely come, but once the people are inside the land of Canaan, the manna stops.

Manna was literally a gift from heaven. The word "manna" translated in Hebrew confirms the people had no earthly idea what it was. The word means "what is it?" The daily provision that came with the morning also required a strict adherence to sharing and the avoidance of selfish hoarding. Moses' instructions regarding manna spoon-fed the people on the discipline of community and preparation (Exod. 16). Though it is counterintuitive, with their arrival in the promised land the people of Israel appear to be more on their own. The land now bears fruit, but the building and care of community will require more attention and care. Life in the barren wilderness has a way of defining roles and requirements that sustain life. When the bounty comes and life is flush, responsibilities shift and commitments to faithfulness, justice, and compassion must rise.

It is as if the move to the new land beyond the Jordan comes with the expectation of a deeper maturity among God's people. At the very least, "eating the crops of the land of Canaan" requires a more nuanced understanding and expression of gratitude for the nourishment God provides. Thanksgiving to God comes with the call to righteousness. To feast on the promise of God is to grow ever deeper in the life of discipleship and service in the kingdom of God. As the church often prays during the liturgy of the Lord's Supper: "as this bread is Christ's body for us, send us out to be the body of Christ in the world."

God has to weep when there are so many hungry people in the world in the twenty-first century. Some may pray for a miracle to feed those who suffer. Some will settle for the poor always being with us. Some may think an act of God will reverse the devastating trends of climate change. The church of Jesus Christ ought to point to the day the manna stopped and rise up like the prophets, calling God's people to roll up their sleeves and work for a kingdom where the least are served first and where those who want to be great again are servants of all. Tending to and living off the crops of Canaan can never be separated from God's call to the life of discipleship, nor from our communal life in relationship to the God of the covenant, marked by remembering, gratitude, worship, and a yearning for righteousness.

DAVID A. DAVIS

Fourth Sunday in Lent

Psalm 32

¹Happy are those whose transgression is forgiven,
    whose sin is covered.
²Happy are those to whom the LORD imputes no iniquity,
    and in whose spirit there is no deceit.

³While I kept silence, my body wasted away
    through my groaning all day long.
⁴For day and night your hand was heavy upon me;
    my strength was dried up as by the heat of summer.

⁵Then I acknowledged my sin to you,
    and I did not hide my iniquity;
I said, "I will confess my transgressions to the LORD,"
    and you forgave the guilt of my sin.

⁶Therefore let all who are faithful
    offer prayer to you;
at a time of distress, the rush of mighty waters
    shall not reach them.
⁷You are a hiding place for me;
    you preserve me from trouble;
    you surround me with glad cries of deliverance.

⁸I will instruct you and teach you the way you should go;
    I will counsel you with my eye upon you.
⁹Do not be like a horse or a mule, without understanding,
    whose temper must be curbed with bit and bridle,
    else it will not stay near you.

¹⁰Many are the torments of the wicked,
    but steadfast love surrounds those who trust in the LORD.
¹¹Be glad in the LORD and rejoice, O righteous,
    and shout for joy, all you upright in heart.

Connecting the Psalm with Scripture and Worship

"Happy" is not a word that leaps to mind in Lent. This psalm, with its happy beginning and happy ending, may therefore have all the more power during this penitential season. Its focus on the blessedness of living in right relationship with God makes it a useful companion to today's other lections.

A pair of beatitudes (Ps. 32:1–2) opens the psalm, repeatedly identifying forgiven sinners as "happy" (also translated "blessed"). This happy state is purely a result of God's grace; no human agency is mentioned.

In verse 3, things change. Here there is human agency: instead of having a spirit free of deceit (v. 2), there is now the sinful decision to keep silent before God. People in our pews know what it is to live without acknowledging God, to imagine that we do not need God, to hide our sin from

God. Even if we have not articulated it, we know the debilitated feeling the psalmist describes in verses 3–4. We also recognize the relief implicit at the end of verse 5.

This three-verse exploration of the need for repentance does not require us to think of God as punishing our silence by crushing us until we apologize. Rather, verses 3–5 are an evocative description of how we feel when we strive to live without God. Lent is a season designed for those who seek to repent of this tendency and receive God's healing for sin-sick souls.

Following the blessed relief of God's forgiveness (v. 5c), thankful praise is expressed (vv. 6–7). Then, starting in verse 8, the forgiven psalmist lives out this praise by suddenly speaking as one transformed into a teacher of God's ways. This instruction culminates with heartening vocabulary—"steadfast love" and "trust in the LORD" (v. 10b)—and concludes with the happiest verse of the entire psalm: "Be glad in the LORD and rejoice, O righteous, and shout for joy, all you upright in heart" (v. 11).

Here we sense an exhilarating new way of living life in God's presence. The psalmist, once silent before God, has been forgiven and now actively shares that blessed state by teaching and inspiring us. This theme of new life via God's grace appears in each of today's lections.

Connections with the Joshua text are subtle, but can be found and amplified. The passage opens with God declaring a happy milestone in the exodus saga: God has "rolled away from [the Israelites] the disgrace of Egypt" (Josh. 5:9). Sandwiched between two overtly dramatic episodes—the famous crossing of the Jordan River (chap. 4) and the famous battle of Jericho (chap. 6)—this scene plays out as an almost domestic scene in which the Israelites celebrate the first Passover in the promised land (5:10). Then, on the very next day, they are weaned off the manna that has sustained them throughout their epic journey; God's people finally feast upon the long-promised bounty "of the land of Canaan" (vv. 11–12). This is their first taste of their new way of living in God's care. It is a new way of being what the psalmist terms "happy." It is a fulfillment of the psalm's promise that "steadfast love surrounds those who trust in the LORD" (Ps. 32:10b). The wilderness is behind

them, much as the metaphorical wilderness of the psalmist's silence before God is also a thing of the past.

Another preachable connection between these two Hebrew Bible texts would be noticing how the psalmist's warning against being "like a horse or a mule, without understanding, whose temper must be curbed with bit and bridle, else it will not stay near you" (Ps. 32:9), so aptly describes the balky behavior often exhibited by the Israelites during the exodus. More relevantly, it also sounds like most of us on most days of our lives!

Connections to the two NT texts are more obvious. The psalm aligns so readily with the Gospel lesson that, in reading Luke's beloved parable, you could imagine that the young man we know as the prodigal son comes to his senses after reading Psalm 32. Perhaps a sermon could explore the psalm as a catalyst for how the prodigal "came to himself" (Luke 15:17) and how we might do the same.

Today's epistle lesson also seems sympathetic with Psalm 32's message. It could be fruitful for a preacher to imagine this psalm standing out within the scriptural backstory of Paul's theology. Like the psalmist, the apostle has been transformed into a passionate teacher, and both writers urge us all toward God's mission of reconciliation and the newness of life it creates.

Well-known hymns that complement these texts include "Come, Ye Sinners, Poor and Needy," "Forgive Our Sins as We Forgive," "Rock of Ages, Cleft for Me," and "There Is a Balm in Gilead." To emphasize the "happy" idea, you might also try "Rejoice, Ye Pure in Heart."

Liturgically, the psalm might yield a simple scriptural call to worship, such as this:

| One: | Happy are those whose transgression is forgiven, whose sin is covered. |
| All: | Therefore, let all who are faithful offer prayer to God. |

Building blocks for a confession sequence are also available in Psalm 32. One might say, as a call to confession, "In Psalm 32, the psalmist confesses to God, saying: 'While I kept silence, my body wasted away through my groaning all day long. . . . Then I acknowledged my sin to You. . . . I did not hide my iniquity . . . and You forgave the guilt of my sin.' Confident that we too may rely on God's steadfast love and forgiveness, let us now confess our sin before God and neighbor."

A declaration of forgiveness might include these words: "Be glad in the Lord. Rejoice, O righteous, and shout for joy, all you upright in heart. Know that you are forgiven, and be at peace."

There is not a more faithful way to be happy, during Lent or in any other season.

LEIGH CAMPBELL-TAYLOR

2 Corinthians 5:16–21

[16]From now on, therefore, we regard no one from a human point of view; even though we once knew Christ from a human point of view, we know him no longer in that way. [17]So if anyone is in Christ, there is a new creation: everything old has passed away; see, everything has become new! [18]All this is from God, who reconciled us to himself through Christ, and has given us the ministry of reconciliation; [19]that is, in Christ God was reconciling the world to himself, not counting their trespasses against them, and entrusting the message of reconciliation to us. [20]So we are ambassadors for Christ, since God is making his appeal through us; we entreat you on behalf of Christ, be reconciled to God. [21]For our sake he made him to be sin who knew no sin, so that in him we might become the righteousness of God.

Commentary 1: Connecting the Reading with Scripture

Lent is not usually seen as a season of celebration, but this Lenten text commemorates the divine sacrifice that delivers new life. Thus this passage calls us to celebrate in the same sense that we celebrate the Lord's Supper. We celebrate Jesus' faithfulness to divine righteousness amid horror and injustice, fidelity even unto death on a cross (Phil. 2:8). In Jesus' unjust execution, Paul proclaims, we see the triumph of faith over worldly domination, and we see the grace that ensures our own redemption. This spirit of celebration suffuses today's reading, as a jubilant Paul urges us to embrace and celebrate the new life Jesus' fidelity opens to us.

This lectionary reading begins, "From now on, therefore, we regard no one from a human point of view." The meaning of "a human point of view" (or "according to the flesh," NRSV note) receives a pithy summation in the verse immediately preceding today's reading: "he died for all, so that those who live might live no longer for themselves, but for him who died and was raised for them" (2 Cor. 5:15). Those who operate from a human point of view live for themselves—precisely opposite the way of Jesus Christ.

Why "therefore"? The preceding verses (vv. 14–15) provide Paul's answer: because "the love of Christ urges us on," we live no longer for ourselves but for Christ. In some ways, the call not

to be selfish but, imitating Jesus, to look toward the good of others (Phil. 2:4–5) is stunningly familiar, a common refrain in your average day care. Recently the news carried the story of a mother who objected when her daughter was chastened at day care for being selfish, because being selfish is how the real world works. This mother has a point about our contemporary "greed is good" world, a world that regularly rewards selfishness and celebrates radically inequitable accumulation of wealth and power. In this respect, the world of Paul and his Corinthian readers is very similar to our own. Both then and today, to abandon "the human point of view," and instead to live for Jesus Christ, is radically countercultural, and it is how, Paul says, we live as "ambassadors for Christ" (v. 20)

At the heart of today's reading comes Paul's ringing declaration, "[I]f anyone is in Christ, there is a new creation: everything old has passed away; see, everything has become new!" (v. 17). Paul's declaration echoes the famous hope-filled declaration of Isaiah 65 that God is "about to create new heavens and a new earth." Isaiah 65 famously pictures a world free from disease and premature death, free from economic exploitation ("they shall not build and another inhabit . . . plant and another eat," Isa. 65:22), free even from the strife and violence of natural predation ("wolf and the lamb shall feed together," v. 25). Isaiah's prophetic themes are familiar. Distinctive in Paul is the present tense: for those living in Christ there *is* a new creation. This is startling, for in this vale of tears Isaiah's vision is definitively *not yet* realized.

Paul is not rejecting Isaiah's eschatological hope for some future time. Paul, persecuted and soon to be executed, knows that in many ways all is definitely not wondrously new. Equally obvious, Paul is proclaiming that in some vital way all things *are* new. This dual affirmation leads theologians to talk about Paul's "realized eschatology," an "already/not yet" dynamic in Paul's thought. In our world of strife and injustice, it is easy to name the "not yet"; it is more challenging to name and inhabit the "already."

It may be helpful to remember Saul/Paul as portrayed in Acts. When reading Paul's condemnation of evildoers, it is critical to remember that Paul carries memories of his own evildoing. We are dealing with Paul who was Saul, who approved the stoning of Stephen; Acts venerates Stephen as full of grace, power, faith, and the Holy Spirit (Acts 6:5–8). We are dealing with Saul, who was then "ravaging the church by entering house after house; dragging off both men and women" (Acts 8:3); who heard Stephen cry out, "Lord, do not hold this sin against them" (Acts 7:60). We are dealing with a man who carries concrete memories of participating in state-sanctioned murder, of crashing into people's homes and dragging mothers and fathers off to prison. Saul viscerally knows his awful guilt. In a far more momentous way, eventually Saul is seized by Stephen's gracious God, who—indeed and behold!—does *not* hold Saul's sins against him, who frees him from guilt and shame. Saul becomes a "new creation." Saul is what is "old and has passed away." Paul himself *is* a new creation.

All this is vital to hear as Paul moves from 5:14–15, where new being in Christ is manifest in our love for others, to 5:16–21, where new being in Christ means we know ourselves as all forgiven (by God) and reconciled (to one another). Paul does not explain how God's making Christ "to be sin" makes us righteous, for Paul is not theorizing. Paul is testifying to the gracious reality by which he is seized when he gazes upon the cross (v. 21). One can imagine

him on that Damascus road joyfully, thankfully marveling to himself what he later exclaims in 5:17: "there is a new creation: . . . everything has become new!"

There is an especially powerful, hopeful word here for those who are overwhelmed by their own transgressions, who cannot forgive themselves, who cannot believe God could possibly forgive them. Popular "civil" discourse is often caught in graceless dynamics of self-righteousness, unqualified condemnation of others, strident denials of wrongdoing, and abhorrence of any sense/accusation of guilt. So the idea of original sin or "all have fallen short" (Rom. 3:23) is anathema to mainstream modern Western thought. Saul/Paul's awakening to grace, by contrast, engenders the subtle and profound stereoscopic, already/not yet dynamics of guilt, confession, forgiveness, and reconciliation. All these complex dynamics lie behind Jesus' call to love one's enemies (Matt. 5:43–44; Luke 6:27).

It is critical to note that Jesus calls upon us to love not only those who *were* our enemies, but to love those who *are* our enemies, those whom we may still speak and struggle against, those who may still persecute us. Jesus' call to love one's enemies is incomprehensible to mainstream modern Western rationality. It is wholly comprehensible (if still hard to live) to those seized by grace. Not even saints fully shed the human point of view, but we can all rest confident in a love that loves even enemies.

Fidelity to the radical grace Jesus calls for is manifest in extremis when Jesus from the cross and Stephen, as stones begin breaking his body, call for forgiveness for those killing them. Saul witnessed Stephen's proclamation in all its gritty, intense, awful, mind-bending, wondrous lived reality. I suspect the triumph of grace in extremis that was manifest in Stephen—the grace-pierced irruption of the gospel breaking through the "human point of view" amid the brutal, merciless, deadly reality—was the mustard seed that blossomed on that Damascus road, the spark that finally awakened Saul, so he came to see a triumph of grace on the cross.

The character and complexity of these already/not yet, grace-infused dynamics are unfolded in two other lections for today: first, the parable of the Prodigal Son (Luke 15:1–3, 11b–32); second, Psalm 32, where essentially the same dynamics of sin, confession, forgiveness, and, be sure to note, grace (see esp. Ps. 32:1, 5, 10) are unfolded in a wholly Jewish context. Notably, along a related but distinct trajectory, the lection from Joshua (Josh. 5:9–12) focuses upon release not from guilt but from shame.

WILLIAM GREENWAY

Commentary 2: Connecting the Reading with the World

A pastor just out of seminary was facing his first challenge in his new church. Two brothers, both active, prominent members, were feuding with each other. They lived on neighboring farms, each farm left to them by their parents, and were in dispute over the boundary line between their properties. Those properties were across the road from the church. One day a long-simmering sibling rivalry finally exploded into a pitched argument over the property line. A chilly and enduring silence descended. Neither brother let the feud inhibit his churchgoing. One brother remained active in a Sunday school class. The other sang bass in the choir. Each maintained a good relationship with other members and the pastor.

In trying to establish an effective preaching ministry for the whole church, the young pastor had tried "preaching around" the conflict between the brothers, but the effort was wearing thin. In seminary, the pastor had learned that he was conflict-averse, but he had deflected taking immediate steps to address the warning in that assessment, resolving to "work on that" in his first call. Now was that time. The toxins flowing from the feud began to affect the overall health of the congregation. It was past time to pay some pastoral visits to each of the brothers. Sometimes the situations like those that so troubled the apostle Paul in his churches also live in the churches we are a part of.

Can you see yourself preparing for visits to those two brothers? What advice would you give this pastor? What do you think should be said to each brother? What wisdom from our faith tradition would you draw from? It is hard not to put ourselves in this pastor's place and take that long walk with him up to each brother's home, trying to remember something, anything from personal experience, Bible study, or seminary training that might help bring healing to the situation. How would the bearer of God's word to the brothers be received? The young pastor was welcomed into each brother's home. In each case, the brother gave a tearful account of how the conflict developed and the emotional toll it was taking on his family. Both were deeply grateful for the generous inheritance left to them by their parents. They admitted that their lives were deeply entwined. The children from each family rode the school bus together, and the brothers' wives would visit with one another at church or at the small market in town. Each meeting with the pastor would end with a brother's conviction that this was not how it should be and a prayer that something could be worked out. Despite the pastor's "entreating them on behalf of Christ, be reconciled to God" (5:20), neither seemed willing to take the first step in the other's direction.

It is a small snapshot within the multitude of images that present the tragic predicament of human estrangement and alienation. Each day we bear witness to another honor killing or hear of a young man who murders participants in a Bible study to honor his racial heritage. What of those who await in paralyzing anxiety as a dysfunctional political system debates their immigration status? International leaders refuse to talk to one another, preferring to trade boasts about the capacities of life-destroying weaponry. Where does one begin a ministry of reconciliation, however the opportunity presents itself?

We can turn to Paul's ministry to the Corinthian church for guidance. His Corinthian correspondence gives a glimpse of a cauldron where Paul worked out some of his most durable theological ideas. Apparently, the formative years of the Corinthian church featured periods of chaos, alienation, and estrangement. The empire would flex its muscles and aggravate racial and ethnic tensions. "What," Paul must have wondered, "has God done in Christ that would speak to the brokenness in the church at Corinth?"

Paul places incidences of human brokenness into the context of a much larger drama, a drama where God is the central actor. For Paul, the relationship between God and humanity is littered with broken covenants, fractured resolutions, distortion, and misunderstanding of God's purpose to bring about a new creation. One place where misunderstanding appears was the way a "worldly standard" for judging a person's value could easily be confused with God's standards. Then, as now, prejudices blind humanity to the redemptive purposes God is working out. In fact, from a human point of view the ministry of Jesus misses the mark and is put down as irrelevant, even a failure. That point of view is characteristic of the old order that has a grip on human consciousness and too often governs human behavior. God "through Christ" has dismantled old orders of rank between Jews and Gentiles, male and female, slave and free.

Dawning is a new creation: not simply the creation of a converted individual with a new outlook on life, but something new breaking into the world, a sphere of existence where participants "in Christ" experience the fullness of God's new creation, the anticipated renewal of the world. This is how, says Paul, God has brought about reconciliation, a new alignment between the redemptive purposes of God and humanity. Paul seems to think of the communities he helped establish as outposts of this new creation. Ideally, they would be communities with their spiritual roots set deep in the hope that God in Christ has established new norms and values for relationships, both human and divine.

Paul understands himself to be an ambassador of this good news of God's plan for renewing creation. Why should the community live as if it were still a part of the old order, or relate to one another "according to the flesh," or understand themselves in terms of the worldly standards that they had come out from through their baptism? Why not appropriate and extend the gift of reconciliation that had been extended to them in the drama of God's redemption? In fact, Paul urges, why do you not become ambassadors and become reconciled among yourselves? The good news is that, by virtue of Jesus on the cross having suffered the most severe effects of human estrangement and alienation imaginable, God entered "sin" and through death and resurrection broke asunder its grip on humanity. If Holiness ever did look askance at human suffering or ever did look without grace upon human sin, it does so no longer, because suffering and sin have been taken unto God's very self.

The flesh, that is, the way of the world, still has stubborn power. Though the human community longs for it, the new creation is not here yet, and at times yearning for it can seem like a fading hope. Even so, the call to be ambassadors for Christ persists, some outposts fulfill their missions and die, while others rise up and bear witness to God's reconciling power. Not every effort, no matter how faithful, is successful.

Many years later, in retirement, that young pastor returned to that church to serve as its interim pastor. One of the brothers' farms was still there across from the church. The other had been sold long ago. Death had claimed each brother. They had never reconciled. That pastor had served in ministry long enough to learn what Paul had learned: there are no guaranteed successes in ministry. What endures, though, is a grace-infused call to persist in the ministry of reconciliation with eyes turned toward God's new creation.

RICHARD F. WARD

Luke 15:1–3, 11b–32

¹Now all the tax collectors and sinners were coming near to listen to him. ²And the Pharisees and the scribes were grumbling and saying, "This fellow welcomes sinners and eats with them."

³So he told them this parable. . . . ¹¹"There was a man who had two sons. ¹²The younger of them said to his father, 'Father, give me the share of the property that will belong to me.' So he divided his property between them. ¹³A few days later the younger son gathered all he had and traveled to a distant country, and there he squandered his property in dissolute living. ¹⁴When he had spent everything, a severe famine took place throughout that country, and he began to be in need. ¹⁵So he went and hired himself out to one of the citizens of that country, who sent him to his fields to feed the pigs. ¹⁶He would gladly have filled himself with the pods that the pigs were eating; and no one gave him anything. ¹⁷But when he came to himself he said, 'How many of my father's hired hands have bread enough and to spare, but here I am dying of hunger! ¹⁸I will get up and go to my father, and I will say to him, "Father, I have sinned against heaven and before you; ¹⁹I am no longer worthy to be called your son; treat me like one of your hired hands."' ²⁰So he set off and went to his father. But while he was still far off, his father saw him and was filled with compassion; he ran and put his arms around him and kissed him. ²¹Then the son said to him, 'Father, I have sinned against heaven and before you; I am no longer worthy to be called your son.' ²²But the father said to his slaves, 'Quickly, bring out a robe—the best one—and put it on him; put a ring on his finger and sandals on his feet. ²³And get the fatted calf and kill it, and let us eat and celebrate; ²⁴for this son of mine was dead and is alive again; he was lost and is found!' And they began to celebrate.

²⁵"Now his elder son was in the field; and when he came and approached the house, he heard music and dancing. ²⁶He called one of the slaves and asked what was going on. ²⁷He replied, 'Your brother has come, and your father has killed the fatted calf, because he has got him back safe and sound.' ²⁸Then he became angry and refused to go in. His father came out and began to plead with him. ²⁹But he answered his father, 'Listen! For all these years I have been working like a slave for you, and I have never disobeyed your command; yet you have never given me even a young goat so that I might celebrate with my friends. ³⁰But when this son of yours came back, who has devoured your property with prostitutes, you killed the fatted calf for him!' ³¹Then the father said to him, 'Son, you are always with me, and all that is mine is yours. ³²But we had to celebrate and rejoice, because this brother of yours was dead and has come to life; he was lost and has been found.'"

Commentary 1: Connecting the Reading with Scripture

The three parables of Luke 15 unfold Luke's response to the dynamics revealed in verses 1–3. They spell out how Jesus was attracting a community of people who were at best on the fringe, and more likely outside of the religiously approved social order. They also succinctly describe the adverse reaction of prominent guardians of that order—the Pharisees and scribes—who criticized Jesus for his "open arms" response to these sinners as he shared table fellowship with them.

This criticism represents a well-established foil for the proclamation of the gospel to sinners, but preachers may want to take time carefully to consider and address the legitimacy of the criticism, for then (as the older brother will illustrate) and now (as contemporary norms of faithfulness often imply), the critics might have a point. To be embraced in and by the community of faith is to enter on a way that has patterns of responsive behavior that can scarcely be considered trivial. How do we (and how did Jesus) embrace prodigals without indirectly minimizing or even encouraging prodigal behavior that harms so many members of our communities?

The parable of the Prodigal Son or Loving Father, in tandem with the parables of the Lost Sheep and the Lost Coin, responds to the opening controversy and criticism. The point all three parables drive home with crescendo effect is the profound joy filling the heart of God when those who are alienated from God ("lost") are reconciled to God ("found"). Its fullest expression for human experience comes to light in the concluding parable. There we find the story that well accomplishes what C. H. Dodd famously summarized as the effect of a parable on the human mind, to "tease it into active thought."[1]

The poignant account of the younger son, whose inability to delay gratification leads to a foolish and consequential wasting of his inheritance, resulting in a humiliating and abject poverty that left him teetering on the brink of starvation, is well known. In this slough of despond he "came to himself," realizing that having forfeited the proper privileges of sonship, he nevertheless could enter his father's household in the diminished role of a day laborer. A preacher might well focus here on the contours of genuine repentance that arise from the anguish in which this younger son finds himself—how the particular downward arc of his life is remorsefully acknowledged as constituting sin against heaven and earth (*mea culpa, mea maxima culpa*)—a repentance that is not only met with, but preceded by, a surpassing

forgiveness. For the father saw him while he was far off, and ran to embrace him before the son uttered a mumbling word. Psalm 32, the Psalter reading associated with this Gospel reading in the lectionary, furnishes a compelling portrait of such repentance and its renewing effects in the face of God's steadfast love.

There is more to ponder in this rich text than the gracious, prevenient forgiveness of God. The overwhelming joy that is found at the culmination of the two preceding parables has an especially vibrant expression in the spontaneous celebration to which the father was moved (the best robe on his back, the ring on a finger, sandals on his feet, and the feast with a fatted calf), because one who was dead is alive, the one who was lost has been found! Deep joy is given festive expression in this last of the triptych of parables.

Exploring the joy in the heart of God, joy that arises when what has been cut off from divine blessing has been restored, brings us close to the center of this parable. Such great joy implies the resolution of deep anguish and excruciating heartbreak in God's self. Here the parable (in concert with the two immediately preceding parables) "teases" our minds into the realization of how diminished God is by all that is alienated from the divine life. Sometimes the alienation follows from our own misguided and self-interested decisions, and sometimes the "lostness" simply befalls us; but in every case God intends to salvage what is lost. So, whatever the specific case of someone or something being separated from the God who made all things well—whether it be the lostness embodied in children bereft of family structure and social support, in cultures beguiled into believing that their values and vision must override those of all others, in individuals gripped by physical or psychological addictions that cut them off from supportive human associations, or among victims of natural disasters that destroy every bit of living space for all creatures great and small—these parables assert that God is determined to reach into these situations of loss to bring restoration. When that happens, there is abounding joy in the halls of heaven.

---

1. C. H. Dodd, *The Parables of the Kingdom* (New York: Charles Scribner's Sons, 1961), 16.

Conforming Ourselves to the Will of God

For we also sometimes experience something of this sort. For some there are who live a perfectly honourable and consistent life, practicing every kind of virtuous action, and abstaining from every thing disapproved by the law of God, and crowning themselves with perfect praises in the sight of God and of men: while another is perhaps weak and trodden down, and humbled unto every kind of wickedness, guilty of base deeds, living impurity, given to covetousness, and stained with all evil. And yet such a one often in old age turns unto God, and asks the forgiveness of his former offences: he prays for mercy, and putting away from him his readiness to fall into sin, sets his affection on virtuous deeds. Or even perhaps when about to close his mortal life, he is admitted to divine baptism, and puts away his offences, God being merciful unto him. And perhaps sometimes persons are indignant at this, and even say, "This man, who has been guilty of such and such actions, and has spoken such and such words, has not paid unto the judge the retribution of his conduct, but has been counted worthy of a grace thus noble and admirable: he has been inscribed among the sons of God, and honoured with the glory of the saints." Such complaints men sometime give utterance to from an empty narrowness of mind, not conforming to the purpose of the universal Father. For He greatly rejoices when He sees those who were lost obtaining salvation, and raises them up again to that which they were in the beginning, giving them the dress of freedom, and adorning them with the chief robe, and putting a ring upon their hand, even the orderly behavior which is pleasing to God and suitable to the free.

It is our duty, therefore, to conform ourselves to that which God wills: for He heals those who are sick; He raises those who are fallen; He gives a helping hand to those who have stumbled; He brings back him who has wandered; He forms anew unto a praiseworthy and blameless life those who were wallowing in the mire of sin; He seeks those who were lost; He raises as from the dead those who had suffered the spiritual death. Let us also rejoice: let us, in company with the holy angels, praise Him as being good, and loving unto men; as gentle and not remembering evil. For if such is our state of mind, Christ will receive us, by Whom and with Whom, to God the Father be praise and dominion with the Holy Ghost, for ever and ever, Amen.

Cyril of Alexandria, Sermon 107, in *A Commentary upon the Gospel of St. Luke*, trans. and ed. R. Payne Smith (Oxford: Oxford University Press, 1859), 2.504–5.

The older brother breaks into the parable at this point and leads us to revisit the place where this reflection started. He looks on the celebration of the father and younger son from the outside—just as Pharisees and scribes looked on Jesus' welcoming inclusion of tax collectors and sinners from the outside. The older brother reprises their criticism of open-armed embrace of one who has been away. In his aggrieved conversation with the father, the older brother can speak of the younger only dismissively as "your son." For the older son, the younger may have "returned," but he has certainly not been "found."

His father urgently wants to help the older son see why the occasion is one of deep joy and to invite him into its reality. Gently the father offers a vocabulary different from the one the older brother had employed in describing the younger son. This "*brother of yours*," the father urges, was as good as dead, but is now among us and alive! He was lost but is found, so we "celebrate and rejoice."

The parable does not tell us how successful the father was in his attempt to usher the older brother into the divine joy of the occasion. By rekindling the familial bond in referring to the vagabond at the center of the celebration as "your brother," perhaps some headway was made. The question turns to those of us who now sit in front of the text. We may find ourselves at least mildly peeved by all the attention and even celebration that the parable implies God gives to those outside the recognized community of faith. Pharisees, older brothers, and solid church people like us need to be reminded that all those outsiders are not only God's children, but our sisters and brothers. When they are restored to the family, when they are found, a joyous celebration breaks out in the heart of God. Do we likewise rejoice?

The epistle reading that the lectionary associates with this Gospel text (2 Cor. 5:16–21) speaks to this point, reminding us that because of the life, death, and destiny of Jesus Christ, we no longer regard anyone from a merely human point of view. Insider/outsider, clean/unclean, initiated/uninitiated: such categories no longer work. God's work is for a new creation in which all are reconciled to God, and God has entrusted precisely this ministry of reconciliation to the church. We are summoned to see that when those who are lost are found, the work of reconciliation has at least provisionally been done. We are summoned to the work of reconciliation, and above all we are encouraged to enter into its deep joy.

D. CAMERON MURCHISON

Commentary 2: Connecting the Reading with the World

"Prodigal" is one of those biblical words rarely used in casual conversation. In fact, many people do not know its meaning and search for it using Google. When one types "prodigal" into a Google search, the algorithm both defines the word and surfaces the Prodigal Son passage itself. Paradoxically, though the word "prodigal" may have fallen into disuse—or narrowed use to this passage—the word aptly describes our culture.

Indeed, "prodigal" may be just the word for a time when credit-card debt remains high and just 37 percent of American households have savings to pay for an unexpected $500–$1,000 expense.[2] For years, financial experts have warned us about Americans' low retirement-savings rates. The rich run for office and often succeed, leading to a Congress consisting of mostly millionaires. The prosperity gospel, once in decline, is now resurging. Indeed, while the word "prodigal" is no longer in fashion, spend-thrift, reckless, often wastefully extravagant spending certainly is.

Perhaps it is not unexpected, then, that many Bibles printed for the American market label this passage the parable of the Prodigal Son. Such framing fits our context. Certainly a reading that focuses on the prodigal, self-centered approach of the younger son emphasizes the contrast of the unmerited grace he receives from his father. Coming in Lent, this reading may be particularly fitting, considering the prodigal's missteps and eventual return. While working as a laborer feeding the pigs, he experienced moments of contemplation. Lent too is a time to consider one's current position, mistakes and all, and repent and turn from these ways.

Alternatively, a focus on the father reveals different cultural connections. The father's attitude serves as a model—an inviting one for us, even if we cannot fully attain it. Note that after the son's confession, the father does not hesitate. He says, "Quickly, bring out a robe—the best one," indicating immediate openness (v. 22). Such reflexive, generous response should be affirmed and practiced.

Recent social-science research has found that generosity is a virtue that can be learned and developed. Christian Smith and Hilary Davidson, who define generosity as "the virtue of giving good things to others freely and abundantly," argue that generosity "is a learned character trait that involves both attitudes and actions . . . both a disposition to give liberally and an actual practice of giving liberally." In their view, "generosity is not a random idea or a haphazard behavior, but rather, in its mature form at least, a basic, personal, moral orientation to life."[3]

2. Sheyna Steiner, "Survey: How Do You Pay for Unexpected Expenses?," *Bankrate.com*, January 6, 2016, http://www.bankrate.com/finance/consumer-index/money-pulse-1215.aspx.

3. Christian Smith and Hilary Davidson, *The Paradox of Generosity: Giving We Receive, Grasping We Lose* (New York: Oxford University Press, 2014), 4

This way of conceiving generosity is particularly compelling for Christians for two reasons. First, it suggests generosity is a virtue we can develop further, leaning on the community to teach us how. Even for those who grew up in problematic situations, or for whom generosity is now a struggle, research shows the capacity for generosity can be grown through practice. Second, in our culture, "generosity" is often narrowed in philanthropic settings to concern only money. While financial generosity is important, Smith and Davidson's work paints a fuller picture of generosity, ranging from one's wallet to how often one shares yard tools with neighbors.

Shifting focus to the older son makes manifest another set of challenges the parable poses for audiences who value a sense of equity and justice. Much of the public narrative in the United States emphasizes the value of hard work and honest living. Those who fail to keep up these standards are looked upon with suspicion. Certainly part of the American story also values the granting of second chances, but such chances are never to undermine those who played by the rules. That would be unjust, according to our unofficial social contract. Given this reality, readers may find the older son's exasperation perfectly reasonable. He, after all, has done everything right, and his father never threw him a party! Yet, the father tries to explain, the rules are not quite logical. In fact, they can even seem unfair (perhaps because they are by ordinary standards). The father errs on the side of generous welcome, even if such a welcome unnerves his older son.

For the sake of fairness to the elder son, let us honestly admit that he has a point: the father's lavish welcome of his younger brother makes little sense. How many times do we encounter opportunities to welcome that do not make sense according to America's logic of hard work and honest living? After all, do refugees *deserve* a welcome? Do drug offenders *deserve* to have their records wiped clean so they can gain employment? Do family members *deserve* forgiveness after their poor choices and time away? The story suggests another way to judge fairness

and who deserves what, based not on accomplishments but God's radical welcome. Such a response can be off-putting.

The story may also discomfort congregations due to its focus on a taboo topic: money. Many pastors admit in their congregations they would rather discuss sex or politics than money—and many church members feel the same way. Yet Jesus discussed money often. As much as it may be more comfortable not to mention it, the tension in the parable centers upon the brothers' financial inheritance.

Much has changed since Jesus' time, but the pull of money remains constant. Money concerns haunt many congregations, and money disputes cause rifts in families. Wise pastors take up opportunities to address money when *not* asking for it. Lent is an ideal time to discuss money in a sermon, precisely because usually it is not stewardship season. In this passage, where the motivations of the sons all pivot around money, the actions of the father disregard the power of money. When he welcomes back his son—and throws a lavish, expensive party— the father indicates that his decisions depend upon love for his family. Indeed, the father seems the exact opposite of a smart financial advisor. He does not show "tough love," lecture his son about his poor business decisions, or begin a squabble about his questionable spending habits. Instead, the father's welcome uncovers a love for human persons, not money and possessions.

In the church, we often pigeonhole conversations about money as having to do mainly with giving money to support the congregation's mission. Ultimately, however, stewardship concerns our relationship with money and with God, from whom all blessings flow. Henri Nouwen once put it this way: "Those of us who ask for money need to look carefully at ourselves. The question is not how to get money. Rather, the question is about our relationship with money. We will never be able to ask for money if we do not know how we ourselves relate to money."[4] Such reasoning takes us back to the story's beginning. Perhaps when the father granted

---

4. Henri J. M. Nouwen, *A Spirituality of Fundraising*, The Henri Nouwen Spirituality Series (Nashville: Upper Room Books, 2010), 27.

his younger son's wish and gave him the inheritance, the father had an inkling that his son's priorities were off-base, that his love of money had become greater than his love for God and others. If so, when the son returns, the father's celebration may take on multiple layers: his son has returned and, with any luck, he has grown in his faith. Maybe his prodigal spending has been overtaken by prodigal loving.

ADAM J. COPELAND

Fifth Sunday in Lent

Isaiah 43:16–21
Psalm 126

Philippians 3:4b–14
John 12:1–8

Isaiah 43:16–21

¹⁶Thus says the LORD,
   who makes a way in the sea,
   a path in the mighty waters,
¹⁷who brings out chariot and horse,
   army and warrior;
they lie down, they cannot rise,
   they are extinguished, quenched like a wick:
¹⁸Do not remember the former things,
   or consider the things of old.
¹⁹I am about to do a new thing;
   now it springs forth, do you not perceive it?
I will make a way in the wilderness
   and rivers in the desert.
²⁰The wild animals will honor me,
   the jackals and the ostriches;
for I give water in the wilderness,
   rivers in the desert,
to give drink to my chosen people,
   ²¹the people whom I formed for myself
so that they might declare my praise.

Commentary 1: Connecting the Reading with Scripture

As explained on page 61 above, the book of Isaiah falls into three sections, each reflecting the separate historical setting in the life of Judah during which it was composed. The second of these sections (Isaiah 40–55) came about during the transition from Babylonian to Persian rule, a time when the descendants of those carried into Babylonian exile saw reason to expect the coming fulfillment of their hopes for a return to Jerusalem.

Isaiah 43:16–21 occurs almost midway through Second Isaiah's first half as part of a much longer rolling discourse about what the prophet perceives God doing for the Israelites, both those exiled outside the land and those still subsisting in the destroyed country. The audience has already been told that their Creator intends to restore them by the agency of a new deliverer, and to gather them to their homeland. They have been identified with their ancestor Abraham and promised divine help. This passage emphasizes the dramatic magnitude of what the prophet believes will happen.

Although a few commentators and the lectionary present Isaiah 43:16–21 as a unit, most scholars include verses 14–15 as well. These two verses look both backward and forward. Following God's self-description as the one whose work none can hinder, from whose hand no one can deliver (v. 13), verse 14b narrates the coming defeat of Babylon, surrounding this description with two series of divine titles piled one on another in verses 14a and 15. These verses anticipate what will follow in verses 16–21: explicit reference to a treasured story that the prophet offers as a precedent for what is to happen now.

With verse 16, the prophet discloses a theme underlying the prophet's work throughout: a dialogical call both to remember the past and to forget it—more precisely, to remember the grace of God's mighty deeds in the past while recognizing that new contexts call for the story line to take new forms. Second Isaiah's arguments throughout have creatively recombined elements of earlier Judean traditions. Under the prophet's hand the terms shift—sometimes subtly, sometimes abruptly—so that while the words sound familiar, they are being adapted for a new audience in new circumstances. God is doing a new thing, but what God is doing is continuous with all that has come before. Here, and further on in chapter 46, the prophet's program of remembering with a difference is announced explicitly by means of two contradictory divine commands.

The call to remember is clear in verses 16–17, which present an explicit reminder of the day, recounted in Exodus 14 and celebrated in Exodus 15, when God created Israel as a nation under divine rule by rescuing them from slavery in Egypt. These verses are syntactically complex, first introducing a divine speech with "thus says the LORD," but then delaying the speech with an extended subordinate clause that details the prior deeds of the God who will, momentarily, speak: "who makes a way in the sea, a path in the mighty waters, who brings out chariot and horse, army and warrior; they lie down, they cannot rise, they are extinguished, quenched like a wick." Isaiah 40:26 had claimed YHWH as the one who brings out the starry "host," or army, "calling them all by name." Here it is an earthly army that is remembered as having been brought out by YHWH. Even their coming to pursue the Israelites is considered an act prompted not by Pharaoh but by God.

Verse 17 echoes terms found repeatedly in Exodus 14, especially "chariot," "horse," and "army." Whereas in Isaiah 42:3 God's servant was envisioned refusing to quench a dimly burning wick, here the felled enemy is "quenched like a wick"—a description of defeat as final and graphic as that in Exodus 14:30, when "Israel saw the Egyptians dead on the shore of the sea" (NET). With this evocation, the prophet places the violence of the prior story firmly in the audience's mind.

What God has to say about this explicit recollection of Israel's formative tradition—a recollection that powerfully explodes its parenthetical setting, piling description upon description—is finally offered in verse 18: a thundering, paradoxical "do not remember," reinforced by the parallel "do not consider." Nowhere else in Scripture are people called thus to forget. In fact, Deuteronomy portrays Moses repeatedly calling the Israelites to remember this very event (5:15; 7:18–19; 15:15; 16:3). Most strikingly, the Song of Moses in Deuteronomy 32 uses both of the verbs found in Isaiah 43 when instructing those born in the wilderness not to forget their past: "Remember the days of old, consider the years long past." That is the only other place in Scripture to employ these two verbs in parallel, and its message is exactly the opposite of Second Isaiah's.

Who is this prophet to contradict Moses? Especially to say this to people divided from one another, each suffering over memory: some in a ravaged land, believing themselves forgotten by God (Lam. 5:20–22), and some in a foreign land, resolving never to forget their home (Ps. 137:5–6).

This word is, however, difficult to take at face value. Second Isaiah's forceful order to forget is ironically hedged about with remembrance so powerful that it defies amnesia, perhaps even awakens many from it. In fact, when the subject returns again in chapter 46, the divine word will indeed be its reverse, in line with Deuteronomy: "Remember this and consider, recall it to mind, you transgressors, remember the former things of old" (Isa. 46:8–9). Thus this order to forget the past turns out to be a hyperbolic introduction to an event the prophet expects to be so world-changing that it actually displaces their founding story.

What does the prophet propose that could possibly overshadow the signs and wonders of the exodus? It is a new thing: not a way in the sea, but a way in wilderness; not dry ground in the waters, but waters in the desert. Jeremiah had predicted that one day the return from exile would surpass the exodus from Egypt in import (Jer. 16:14–15; 23:7–8). Second Isaiah now draws analogies between the two events that indeed magnify the present claim, since it reenacts in one event both the ancient sea crossing and God's subsequent provision of water in the wilderness: not a way in the sea but a way in the wilderness and rivers in the desert. In other words, the prophet seems to say that what is new is not really new after all. It was implicit all along for those who, in the passage's terms, could perceive it. The new situation, a desert rather than a sea, has brought forth the old story in new ways. "Do not remember" becomes a call to loosen Israel's grip on things as they were, and to expect something new, but nevertheless recognizable in terms of the past.

What is more, the extravagant wilderness waters will quench the thirst not only of the chosen people, but also of the wild animals, outsiders as the Judeans themselves had become, desert denizens such as jackals and ostriches. Israel's salvation, coupled with that of other creatures who likewise benefit from God's beneficence, reflects a divine deed more comprehensive than the ancient one. In this new act of God, the land itself is restored; the people are saved; the nation is set back on its path to salvation.

PATRICIA K. TULL

Commentary 2: Connecting the Reading to the World

The text begins with the prophetic formula "Thus says the LORD" (v. 16). What immediately follows is a clear description of the Lord's saving activity of the people of Israel in the exodus. The description of the trailing army, warriors, and horses drowning in the sea is specific and vivid. The reference from the history shared between God and God's people comes with such detail that the reader/listener is invited to relive that journey along "a path in the mighty waters" (v. 16). It is a reliving, a remembering, that packs a wallop. Isaiah's history is more than a pious reference to God's miraculous parting of the sea. The pathway in the sea is strewn with death. Like a writer describing the aftermath of battle, Isaiah portrays the reality and the magnitude of death that lies in the wake of deliverance from oppression and suffering.

Notice that God's action is described in the present. The enemies who perish are "extinguished" and "quenched," but the Lord "makes a way in the sea" (v. 16). The invocation of God's past action brings home the reality of and ongoing potential for God's present action. The God who made a way is the God who makes a way. Some moments in salvation history have life and breath for God's people in every generation. It is a sacred remembering that comes in the present. The kind of remembering that undergirds the celebrating and the giving of thanks for the unchanging attributes of the living God.

"Remembering with all of your being," or anamnesis, is what happens when a remembering is a reliving. It is the "I am experiencing it happening now" that is felt, for instance, when those who were part of the civil rights struggle remember the moment they found out Dr. Martin Luther King was assassinated. Taken up in the past made present of remembering with all their being, they find themselves reinvigorated with King's passion for just and loving relations among all people. For Jews remembering the Holocaust, it is remembering filled with resolve: never forget and never again. For Jews and Christians, provoking this kind of fully embodied remembering is the point of proclaiming all God has done and instilling conviction now that the One who acted and who saved is right now acting and saving.

Isaiah's striking image of God is proclamation striving after anamnesis. Isaiah offers an invitation for God's people to experience the ongoing saving action of God. With the prophet's broader message, the people are called to participate in that action, to participate in God's work in the world. Isaiah's call is to bear witness to and further the mission of God in the here and now.

This emphasis upon remembering is a familiar theme in the Scriptures: "Remember that you were a slave in the land of Egypt, and the LORD your God brought you out" (Deut. 5:15); "Remember the wonderful works [the Lord] has done, [the Lord's] miracles, and the judgments [the Lord] uttered" (1 Chr. 16:12); "Remember the former things of old; for I am God, and there is no other" (Isa. 46:9). When the Israelites in exile hear those prophetic words about the Lord "who makes a way in the sea," they know how to remember. When Isaiah is read today in Sunday worship, almost everyone is ready to and expects to remember. We are actually pretty good at remembering with our whole selves what God has done.

Then, however, right at the center of the reading, between the Lord "who makes a way in the sea" (v. 16) and the Lord who "will make a way" (v. 19), comes Isaiah's stunning reversal, "Do not remember the former things, or consider the things of old" (v. 18). Just when remembering is taking shape in the bones of God's people, in seemingly stark contradiction to this recurrent theme in Scripture, Isaiah's imperative stops all right in their tracks. "Do *not* remember," says the Lord.

Biblical scholar Paul Hanson ponders the context in which Israel might not want to be a remembering people. He suggests Isaiah knew the people needed to be shocked out of an exile-induced comfort and lethargy. They might not be home, but things were going along pretty well. They may have been struggling to sing the Lord's song there in the foreign land, but then again, maybe they were getting a bit too used to it. They might have been in exile, but the relationship with God was safely within the bounds of a comfort zone of memory where expectation and anticipation and creativity had long since been lost. When should they not remember? Hanson answers, "At the point where a nostalgic relation to tradition threatens to tie the people to their past and to stultify alertness to present realities, responsiveness to new opportunities, and the potential for growth into yet-unrealized possibilities."[1]

Remembering becomes problematic and stifling when God's people cease to perceive or believe God can do a new thing (v. 19). When it comes to the church, such unhelpful remembering comes in nostalgic longing for church life of bygone years. Survey after survey, statistic after statistic, unwittingly but harmfully boosts that stultifying looking back with what might be called a "death of the church" mentality. Maybe pastors with nostalgic congregations ought to invoke Isaiah's message with passion: "Stop remembering the glory years of the 1950s." Effective pastoral leaders informed by sociological analysis cannot be naive about metrics and finances, but God's promise of a new thing should instill the passion and impetus of a transcendent resurrection hope.

Of course, the mistake of accepting and propounding the faithless narrative of the inevitable collapse of the church is not just lack of imagination. The prophet tells of God making a way again through the wilderness and the desert (v. 19). There will be a need to rely upon God, for the way may be difficult. Part of what it means to journey with God then is journeying on, even when discerning the way and seeing a harvest will not be clear or easy. The promise is not for material prosperity or even institutional survival, but that God will make a way. It is one thing to lack perception when it comes to seeing God at work doing a new thing. It is quite another to fail to believe that God can and is doing that new thing. Remembering becomes idolatry when the followers of Jesus come to believe they have no future together as the body of Christ. The church will look different in coming decades— but it will still be Christ's church. What it looks like, how it functions, its future days? That will be God's new thing, the body of Christ formed and shaped to work toward a kingdom of righteousness, justice, mercy, and compassion.

In verse 21 Isaiah gives the preacher a final word. God makes a way for God's people for a reason. God's new thing has a purpose. God makes a way for us through the deserts and wilderness places of our lives so that we may declare God's praise. The children of God are created, created in God's image, to join in Isaiah's song of praise. That song of praise includes serving the poor, caring for the widow, working for justice, and beating swords into plowshares.

DAVID A. DAVIS

---

1. Paul D. Hanson, *Isaiah 40–66* (Louisville, KY: John Knox Press, 1995), 73.

Fifth Sunday in Lent

Psalm 126

¹When the LORD restored the fortunes of Zion,
  we were like those who dream.
²Then our mouth was filled with laughter,
  and our tongue with shouts of joy;
then it was said among the nations,
  "The LORD has done great things for them."
³The LORD has done great things for us,
  and we rejoiced.

⁴Restore our fortunes, O LORD,
  like the watercourses in the Negeb.
⁵May those who sow in tears
  reap with shouts of joy.
⁶Those who go out weeping,
  bearing the seed for sowing,
shall come home with shouts of joy,
  carrying their sheaves.

Connecting the Psalm with Scripture and Worship

As one of the Psalter's Songs of Ascent, Psalm 126 was probably composed for use by pilgrims on their way up to Jerusalem. That fact is more than a bit of Bible trivia. That designation underscores the perspective of this psalm: pilgrims to Jerusalem, which is the "Zion" named in verse 1, knew something of the history of the city's relationship with God, of how Zion and its people had served God and also failed God, of how Zion and its temple had been built and also destroyed, of how God's promises had been fulfilled there and were still to be fulfilled there. That complex relationship is woven into Psalm 126, which acknowledges the changes in fortune that people—whether ancient Israelites or modern Christians—have experienced even in the midst of God's steadfast love. Psalm 126 was used during the pilgrim journey to Jerusalem and is useful during our Lenten journey to Easter, because it is about journeying with God.

The psalm is built in two segments: verses 1–3 and verses 4–6. As translated in the NRSV and most other commonly used translations, the first three verses look to the past, and the final three verses look to the future. Each segment begins with a line involving the phrase "restore the fortunes," which is a Hebrew idiom suggesting a return to a previous condition. However, the psalm's ending joins today's other lections in pursuing, instead, a new and transformed condition: not simply restoration, but renewal, even resurrection.

Before hurrying to the psalm's ending, let us consider the psalm's initial image: "we were like those who dream" (v. 1). Although some interpreters are tempted to dismiss this dream state as a condition of drowsiness or grogginess, it is the same word used for famous dreams like those of Joseph (Gen. 37 and following) and is also part of God's promise shared in the book of Joel: "Then afterward I will pour out my spirit on all flesh; your sons and your daughters shall prophesy, your old men shall dream dreams, and your young men shall see visions" (Joel 2:28). That is not some sort of hazy lightheadedness. No, that is powerful God-blessed dreaming. Making use of that concept, one's approach to preaching today's Isaiah text would

97

Give Our Lord Every Sacrifice

This, my sisters, is what I would have us strive for—to offer our petitions and to practise prayer, not for our own enjoyment but to gain strength to serve God. Let us seek no fresh path; we should lose ourselves in ways of ease. It would be a strange thing to fancy we should gain these graces by any other road than that by which Jesus and all His saints have gone before. Let us not dream of such a thing: believe me, both Martha and Mary must entertain our Lord and keep Him as their Guest, nor must they be so inhospitable as to offer Him no food. How can Mary do this while she sits at His feet, if her sister does not help her?

His food is that in every possible way we should draw souls to Him so that they may be saved and may praise Him for ever. . . . You may say that you have neither the power nor the means to lead souls to God; though you would willingly do so, you do not know how, as you can neither teach nor preach as did the Apostles. . . . I told you elsewhere how the devil frequently fills our thoughts with great schemes, so that instead of putting our hands to what work we can do to serve our Lord, we may rest satisfied with wishing to perform impossibilities.

You can do much by prayer; and then, do not try to help the whole world, but principally your companions; this work will be all the better because you are the more bound to it. Do you think it is a trifling matter that your humility and mortification, your readiness to serve your sisters, your fervent charity towards them, and your love of God, should be as a fire to enkindle their zeal, and that you should constantly incite them to practise the other virtues? This would be a great work and one most pleasing to our Lord. . . .

In short, my sisters, I will conclude with this advice; do not build towers without a foundation, for our Lord does not care so much for the importance of our works as for the love with which they are done. When we do all we can, His Majesty will enable us to do more every day. If we do not grow weary, but during the brief time this life lasts (and perhaps it will be shorter than any of you think) we give our Lord every sacrifice we can, both interior and exterior, His Majesty will unite them with that He offered to His Father for us on the Cross so that they may be worth the value given them by our love, however mean the works themselves may be.

May it please His Majesty, my sisters and my daughters, that we may all meet together where we may praise Him for ever, and may He give me grace to practice something of what I have taught you, by the merits of His Son, Who liveth and reigneth for ever! Amen.

Teresa of Avila, "The Seventh Mansion," chap. 4, "Mary and Martha," in *The Interior Castle, or The Mansions*, trans. the Benedictines of Stanbrook, rev. the Very Ref. Fr. Benedict Zimmerman (London: Thomas Baker, 1921), 293–97.

be to ponder how faithful people can "perceive" the "new thing" God is doing (Isa. 43:19). What could predispose us to notice this new and extravagant thing God is undertaking in our midst? Could the answer lie in being "like those who dream" (Ps. 126:1)?

The psalm's second verse introduces the emotional vocabulary that the psalmist plays with throughout the psalm: "laughter," the opposite of which is explored in verses 5 and 6, and "shouts of joy," a phrase that appears three times (vv. 2, 5, 6) in just six verses. A sermon might focus on the closing verse of the Isaiah passage, exploring what it means to be "the people whom [God] formed . . . so that they might declare [God's] praise" (Isa. 43:21). There

could be a fruitful connection with this psalm as it points us toward living with shouts of joy, responding to God's goodness by rejoicing and declaring that God "has done great things for us" (Ps. 126:3).

In the latter half of the psalm, there is water imagery that echoes—and yet diverges from—the water imagery in the Isaiah passage. You might intersperse these related OT images in your liturgy, as demonstrated in this call to worship:

> God will make a way in the wilderness
> and rivers in the desert. (Isa. 43:19)
>
> *Restore us, O Lord, like watercourses in a desert.* (Ps. 126:4)

God will give water in the wilderness, rivers in the desert to give drink to God's people. (Isa. 43:20)

O Lord, may those who go out weeping, come home with shouts of joy. (Ps. 126:6)

God will make a way in the sea, a path in the mighty waters. (Isa. 43:16)

Let us worship God.

In each of today's lections, the writer tightly links past, present, and future. In Isaiah, there is mention of "the former things . . . the things of old" (Isa. 43:18), which are not to be dwelt upon here in the exhilarating now wherein "a new thing . . . springs forth" (Isa. 43:19) in preparation for a flourishing future of "rivers in the desert" (Isa. 43:19, 20). Then for Paul, the impeccable pedigree of his Pharisee past (Phil. 3:5–6) means nothing in his faithful now as he declares, "This one thing I do: forgetting what lies behind and straining forward to what lies ahead, I press on toward the goal for the prize of the heavenly call of God in Christ Jesus" (Phil. 3:13–14). In the Gospel passage, the formerly dead Lazarus is at a dinner party with Jesus (John 12:1–2) when Mary anoints Jesus (John 12:3), unknowingly anticipating his impending death. Here on the last regular Sunday in Lent, your sermon might challenge your congregation to recognize their own present moment as linked closely to their past and their future. What of their past do they need to let go of in order to be open to God's future? How do they need to be made different by their present Lenten journey, which is nearing its future conclusion?

As alluded to earlier, this welcoming of something new may be the most valuable insight offered by connecting Psalm 126 with Isaiah 43:16–21 and today's other texts. Although the psalmist does yearn for restoration to a prior way of being, the psalm concludes with transformation: weeping becomes joy (Ps. 126:5–6). In this, the psalmist stands with Isaiah, not looking to the past in hope of restoration to some old way of life, but living into God's new way of life. In our journey with God, we, with all the complexity of our history, are now being readied by Lent for Easter, which is the ultimate proof that God can be relied upon to do a glorious new thing.

LEIGH CAMPBELL-TAYLOR

Philippians 3:4b–14

^{4b}If anyone else has reason to be confident in the flesh, I have more: ⁵circumcised on the eighth day, a member of the people of Israel, of the tribe of Benjamin, a Hebrew born of Hebrews; as to the law, a Pharisee; ⁶as to zeal, a persecutor of the church; as to righteousness under the law, blameless.

⁷Yet whatever gains I had, these I have come to regard as loss because of Christ. ⁸More than that, I regard everything as loss because of the surpassing value of knowing Christ Jesus my Lord. For his sake I have suffered the loss of all things, and I regard them as rubbish, in order that I may gain Christ ⁹and be found in him, not having a righteousness of my own that comes from the law, but one that comes through faith in Christ, the righteousness from God based on faith. ¹⁰I want to know Christ and the power of his resurrection and the sharing of his sufferings by becoming like him in his death, ¹¹if somehow I may attain the resurrection from the dead.

¹²Not that I have already obtained this or have already reached the goal; but I press on to make it my own, because Christ Jesus has made me his own. ¹³Beloved, I do not consider that I have made it my own; but this one thing I do: forgetting what lies behind and straining forward to what lies ahead, ¹⁴I press on toward the goal for the prize of the heavenly call of God in Christ Jesus.

Commentary 1: Connecting the Reading with Scripture

Paul is writing to the Philippians from captivity, under imminent threat of execution. Bearing in mind Paul's extreme circumstance as he writes is vital for apt hearing and proclamation. Our lectionary reading comes just beyond one of the most famous passages in Scripture, the *kenōsis* hymn of Philippians ("Christ Jesus, who, though he was in the form of God . . . emptied himself" 2:5–11). Shortly after the *kenōsis* hymn Paul pauses his theological proclamation and addresses several housekeeping items concerning Timothy and Epaphroditus and their anticipated travel to Philippi (2:19–30). Then he explicitly marks a return to proclamation with the line that introduces our lection for today, "Finally, my brothers and sisters, rejoice in the Lord" (3:1).

Since Paul explicitly uses "rejoice in the Lord" to frame today's reading, pastors should seriously consider beginning their reading at Philippians 3:1 instead of 3:4b. The significance, power, and complexity of Paul's "rejoice in the Lord" is manifest when one remembers

Paul is writing from captivity, facing execution. This is not an easy "rejoice," said smilingly in happy circumstances. From the perspective of "the flesh," it is irrational for Paul to speak of rejoicing. So Paul's exhortation to rejoice is tightly bound up with his contrast between the old, worldly ways of understanding, and new ways of understanding life through Jesus Christ. Notably, Paul's context is similar to the authors of today's lectionary readings from Isaiah and Psalm 126, for both texts speak from a context of exploitation and powerlessness but declare hope and confidence in divine vindication.

The complexity of Paul's "rejoice" is discerned as, in loving sensitivity, we do not lightly expect or demand from others or ourselves a spirit of rejoicing when captive to violence, disease, poverty (for our afflictions may overwhelm any spirit of rejoicing). Pastoral sensitivity is vital because, if it is interpreted as a test of faith, this call to rejoice can become a harmful word to those suffering. In this context, as is illustrated in 3:8, it is important to stress that Paul consistently refers to his sufferings *as sufferings*. That is, Paul's thought is not reductionist but complex. Those who see with the eyes of faith do not forget or fail to take seriously worldly suffering, nor do they take lightly their own suffering, even though they do not face that suffering only with worldly eyes. We might consider, for instance, how the sufferings of the heroes of faith in Hebrews 11 is remembered and lamented, even as confidence in God's ultimate fidelity to and love for them is proclaimed (see esp. Heb. 11:32–40). Moreover, even as Paul is calling us to the "upward call of God in Christ Jesus" (Phil. 3:14), which includes the minds of those who see through the eyes of faith, who rejoice in all circumstances, Paul takes care to say explicitly that he himself has not obtained this goal (Phil. 3:12).

If we begin with 3:1 we should name and rebut the dangers of 3:2, where Paul labels as "dogs" and "evil workers" those who contend that *physical* circumcision is decisive. Unfortunately, this passage has been appropriated to fuel anti-Semitism. It is important to recall that all the heroes of faith in Hebrews 11 are Jewish, that Paul is and always sees himself as a Jew (like Jesus), a "Hebrew of Hebrews," and a Pharisee (Phil. 3:5). While Paul sees these as insufficient apart from faith, he is always careful to celebrate the Jews as God's chosen people.

Paul's talk of "dogs" and "evil workers" brings home the gritty realism of this letter from prison and Paul's passion. However, especially insofar as we have not achieved the mind of those who live "the heavenly call of God in Christ Jesus," such rhetoric can encourage hatred of and unnecessary violence toward opponents. With regard to Paul, note that a few verses later, when Paul speaks of "enemies of the cross," he says he speaks of them "*with tears*" (in his eyes) precisely because "their end is destruction," their "god is the belly," and their "minds are set on earthly things." Paul then mourns the lost, the "dogs," the "evil workers." Paul loves his enemies, even as he remembers and names them as enemies of what is loving and faithful, loves them even as they persecute him, loves them even as he resists them.

At Philippians 3:3, where Paul speaks of "we who *are* the circumcision," he picks up a theme from Romans 2:29: "real circumcision is

a matter of the heart." The surrounding verses in Romans (2:17–3:31), all of which are centered upon the relation of grace/faith and the law, should be kept in mind in relation to Paul's contrast between a "righteousness of my own that comes from the law" and the righteousness "that comes through faith in Christ" (v. 9). The question of the relation between grace and law has been for millennia and remains, to put it mildly, a central and lively topic of theological debate. No matter how one details the relationship of law and grace, two extremes are clearly excluded by Paul, namely, any account that affirms grace but forgets or disparages law, and any account that affirms law but forgets or disparages grace. In other words, precisely how to relate grace and law is an enduringly difficult question that not even Paul answers clearly. Whatever one's answer, Paul clearly thinks it must include affirmation of both law and grace.

A telling danger lurks in the closing verse of today's reading (v. 14), for it is easy to understand Paul to be saying that he presses on in order to receive heaven as his reward. This is a telling danger, for to fall prey to this danger is to understand Paul in accord with the flesh, where self-interest reigns supreme, and so pressing on and enduring for the prize of eternal life in heaven makes sense. This instrumental (i.e., faith as a means to a desired end for oneself) way of reading Paul would thereby participate in and advance a self-centered pseudospirituality that runs contrary to Paul's exhortation to do "nothing from selfish ambition or conceit" (Phil. 2:3), but to "let the same mind be in you that was in Christ Jesus" (Phil. 2:5) by looking "not to your own interests, but to the interests of others" (v. 4). Not only would this reading contradict Paul's repeated warnings not to live in accord with the flesh, but it does not attend to what Paul actually says, which is that he presses on not "for the prize of heaven," but rather "for the prize of *the heavenly call of God in Jesus Christ*" (3:14). This is, quite consistently, the "goal" of knowing *now*, in our daily lives, "the power of his resurrection."

This is Paul's realized eschatology, which is not about a future state in heaven, but about the power to see with eyes of faith in the present, even as, like Jesus, one lives directly in the face of death (v. 10). Paul believes in and celebrates a literal heaven, but he does not let his conviction over the reality of heaven subvert his grace-centered, other-centered, Christlike (Christian) spirituality. In other words, while Christians may believe in and celebrate heaven, the goal of Christian spirituality is never heaven. The goal of Christian spirituality is one's own imitation/realization of *the spirit of Christ* celebrated in the *kenōsis* hymn, a spirit of compassion and sympathy, a spirit which leads to a life that remains faithful to loving action for others, even unto death.

WILLIAM GREENWAY

Commentary 2: Connecting the Reading with the World

Letter writing is becoming a lost art in a world where Twitter feeds and social-media posts swirl about. Letter writers in previous generations practiced their craft not only to inform their readers about their lives, but also to encourage, advise, or comfort them in grief. Sometimes it became necessary to defend one's reputation when the writer's credibility was called into question and trust needed rebuilding. Letter writing was often soul-wrenching work, and receiving letters could be painful. Sometimes reading a letter would take you on an emotional roller-coaster ride—through joy at the reception of news, through the pain for a writer's struggles, through desire for the company of the intimate who held the pen.

Those researching family history are delighted to find a cache of letters hidden away in a trunk or antique desk in an attic. Such things are portals into the past and reveal details forgotten, never known, or never even suspected. One might even find them to be a source of wisdom as well as knowledge, a treasure that has stood the test of time and is ready to be passed along when the family gathers to read them aloud to one another.

It would be unfortunate if letter writing were to be completely eclipsed by the widening array of electronic substitutes. For all their speed and convenience, they stand to displace the concreteness offered by writing, for thoughtful, deliberate correspondence often catches the murmurs of the human soul. Fortunately, we need look no further than the New Testament to find passionate, carefully considered letters, like this one from Paul to the Philippians.

It is too easy in our time to think of Philippians as just another book in the Bible, and forget that it is a personal letter written to a beloved community. It is important for the preacher to take the listener back a couple of verses and in between the lines to catch a glimpse of the unfolding drama in that community. Paul is under attack by a group of missionaries who are competing for the allegiance of the Philippian community. Look carefully at the letter to see how he responds.

At the heart of any drama is conflict, and there is plenty of it here. The challenge of course is to put your ear to the ground and listen for resonances of that conflict in faith communities today. At issue was whether non-Jewish male believers in Christ must become part of the covenant that God made with Abraham through the rite of circumcision. Only then, some said, could such persons be full participants in Christ's body. That is precisely the teaching some were bringing into the Philippian community to undermine Paul's authority and undercut his message of full inclusion of Gentiles.

This is what really makes Paul angry. He calls these teachers "dogs," "evil workers," and mutilators of the flesh (earlier, Phil. 3:2). What is at stake is not only a distortion of God's revelation through Christ, but also the integrity of the Jewish faith. Circumcision was not a badge earned for righteous behavior but signified the gift of relationship between the faithful Jew and the God of Abraham. Motivated by grace, God took the initiative in forging that relationship. It was never intended to be a relationship that would close itself off from the world, but a relationship that would bear witness to a God of grace and justice who was intent on drawing creation unto God's self. Now, through the faith *in* and faithfulness *of* Christ, God has taken a new grace-filled initiative to forge a relationship with Gentiles. Human attempts to earn righteousness quickly reach a dead end; God's initiative of grace moves toward an eternal embrace.

To dramatize that point, Paul walks the Philippians through his resume and then throws it in the trash. Born, raised, formed, educated, even zealous in maintaining synagogue discipline, Paul stacks up his credentials as a teacher of Judaism against those who would distort it. By saying, "None of that stuff matters anymore," he is not denigrating Judaism. He is not saying he regrets having been born into Judaism or that he regrets following its precepts with rigor. By living faithfully to the law, Jews bear witness to the righteousness and grace of the God of Israel. There is nothing wrong with that!

Paul is saying that in his zeal he lost sight of what *else* God was up to in the world. He had first looked at "Christ from a human point of view" (2 Cor. 5:16) and was therefore blind to how God was working through the ministry of Jesus. Now he sees that, through the agency of Christ, God has fulfilled long-standing promises to welcome the Gentiles into the covenantal relationship. This act of God is what counts for Paul, and it is to this message that Paul is devoting his life. Devotion, in Paul's understanding, looks like sharing in the kind of suffering, self-emptying, and passion that Christ Jesus knew. It also means having a share in resurrection hope, the hope that one's salvation begins in this life but reaches completion after death. It is this hope that gives shape to Paul's life journey: "I do not consider that I have made it [the hope of resurrection] my own; but this one thing I do: forgetting what lies behind [my own pursuit of righteousness in the eyes of God] and straining forward to what lies ahead, I press on toward the goal" (Phil. 3:13–14).

How would we cast ourselves and those that will listen to us in the drama that has unfolded through this letter? What religious establishments are we aware of? What boundary lines have those establishments drawn in our communities? Where are the renegade Christians who have apparently found their spiritual identities in Christ but in ways that look suspicious and strange to establishment Christians? Paul looks at all the ferment in the Philippian church and tries to discern God's trajectory through it all. To do that, he must look past his own pedigree and record of religious achievements. What lies ahead is a cross, the symbol for how God has turned human wisdom upside down. Christ shares in our death in order to break the power that death has over us, and through resurrection we share in his risen life.

Elsewhere Paul puts it this way: "For the message about the cross is foolishness to those who are perishing, but to us who are being saved it is the power of God" (1 Cor. 1:18). The phrase "being saved" jumps off the page and shines like a diamond in the rough of all that archaic language about "the law" and "circumcision" and "being like Christ in his death." It catches the ear of all concerned to learn what it means to be in right relationship with God and with our neighbors. "Being saved" is such a potent term that preachers, teachers, and interpreters of all stripes draw fences around it, trying to make it an additional category of human achievement.

For Paul the mystic, "being saved" meant "knowing Christ" and being "found in him." What is there to know? That it is *God* who does the saving. Salvation is not the result of any effort arising from humanity to achieve its own version of righteousness, no matter how earnestly we try. God has acted through Israel and through Christ Jesus, and continues to act even outside the boundaries of our understanding, in order to bring a new creation into being, despite our attempts to contain it.

RICHARD F. WARD

John 12:1–8

¹Six days before the Passover Jesus came to Bethany, the home of Lazarus, whom he had raised from the dead. ²There they gave a dinner for him. Martha served, and Lazarus was one of those at the table with him. ³Mary took a pound of costly perfume made of pure nard, anointed Jesus' feet, and wiped them with her hair. The house was filled with the fragrance of the perfume. ⁴But Judas Iscariot, one of his disciples (the one who was about to betray him), said, ⁵"Why was this perfume not sold for three hundred denarii and the money given to the poor?" ⁶(He said this not because he cared about the poor, but because he was a thief; he kept the common purse and used to steal what was put into it.) ⁷Jesus said, "Leave her alone. She bought it so that she might keep it for the day of my burial. ⁸You always have the poor with you, but you do not always have me."

Commentary 1: Connecting the Reading with Scripture

"Leave her alone," says Jesus to Judas, "because what she has done is important." While this is not an *exact* translation of verse 7, it is an effective paraphrase. Like other stories in John, this story is rich with dramatic action and symbolism. Mary, who does the anointing, does not have a speaking role, yet her deliberate action somehow communicates on another level, perhaps revealing a profound depth of insight into the character of Jesus' ministry, in particular his outspoken condemnation of exploitation and advocacy for the oppressed and a sense of the probable end of such a ministry in occupied first-century Israel, where there was a vast and mostly unbridgeable separation between the rich and the poor.

The earliest version of the story is probably found in Mark (14:3–9). In Mark, an anointing at a meal at the house of Simon the leper in Bethany is the first major event of Passion Week. The woman who anoints Jesus remains unnamed, and an unidentified "some" criticize the woman for wasting expensive perfume on Jesus when it could have been sold and the money given to the poor. John's story includes different characters—Lazarus, Martha, Mary, and Judas—consistent with his theological emphases. The presence of Lazarus, Martha, and Mary hearkens back to John 11, where Lazarus is raised from the dead

and Martha professes profound faith in Jesus. As is the pattern in John, a sign—John says "sign" where other Gospels say "miracle"—is followed by a discourse on its christological meaning. Thus the multiplication of the loaves is followed by a discourse on the bread of life (6:1–15, 22–59), the healing of a blind man is a sign that Jesus is light of the world (9:5), and the raising of Lazarus culminates in Martha's confession of Jesus as the resurrection and the life (11:25–26). Like Mary, Lazarus does not get a speaking role. Unlike Mary, he does nothing symbolic. It is his sisters who become exemplars of faith, Martha with her dramatic confession and Mary with her symbolic action.

As John sets up the scene, Lazarus is the host and is specifically identified as the one "whom he [Jesus] had raised from the dead." The resuscitation of Lazarus—the Greek distinguishes resuscitation from resurrection, reflecting John's sensitivity to the difference between Lazarus's resuscitation from the dead and Jesus' resurrection to new life—foreshadows the ultimate resurrection of Jesus, and John wants us to keep that theme in mind.

The meal itself—like all of the meals of Jesus in the Gospels—is a reclining banquet; the Greek literally says, "Lazarus was one of those reclining with him" (12:2). The roles of Martha and Mary appear to parallel their roles in Luke 10:38–42, where, on an occasion at the house of Martha and Mary, Martha serves while Mary "sat at the feet of Jesus." The picture evoked by this scene is of a Jesus who reclines and a Mary who sits in the position of a respectable woman of the day (a common scene on funerary monuments in the Greco-Roman world). Mary is clearly listening and learning from Jesus, so the discernment revealed in her dramatic anointing is indicated.

As in Luke, Mary takes the initiative in John's anointing story. What she does, however, is rather odd. In Mark's story, Jesus' head is anointed, in keeping with the meal customs of the day (as noted in Luke 7:46) and in service of Mark's symbolic meaning. In John's story, Jesus' feet are anointed. That detail appears to derive from Luke, who radically revises Mark's anointing story and moves it from the passion narrative to an earlier location (7:36–50). Luke's version takes place at the home of Simon, a Pharisee. The unnamed woman who anoints him is described as a "sinner" who washes his feet with her tears and dries them with her hair, thus mimicking the custom of foot washing prior to a meal, as noted in the comments of Jesus (Luke 7:44), and then anoints his feet with the expensive perfume. In Luke, there is no reference to the death of Jesus. The emphasis is on the woman's penitence and presumes awareness that women in Jesus' day typically lacked wealth, power, and even legal standing compared to men. In this sense her anonymity allows her to represent all who are likewise marginalized repentant sinners, even as she performs the central role in the story of Jesus' anointing.

In John's version Mary anoints the feet of Jesus and then wipes them with her hair. We should pause to picture the intimacy and passion of Mary's culturally surprising and celebratory action ("celebratory" in the sense of exceptionality with which we "celebrate" the Eucharist), which enhances our sense for the intimacy and passion of Jesus' surprising washing of the disciples' feet at John 13:1–11 and also for the connection between Jesus' execution and the selfless character of his ministry. Mary enacts the selfless discipleship foot washing represents

(13:14–16), while celebrating Jesus as specially anointed by God as he remains faithful even unto death on a cross.

Judas questions the extravagance of the anointing oil, saying it could have been sold and the money given to the poor. The contrast between the needs of the poor and the extravagance of the ointment is a central theme of the story, and John is sensitive to this concern, even as it is misplaced in this exceptional context. John makes clear that in contrast to Mary, who clearly discerns the exceptional, suffering servant character of the moment, Judas does not even truly believe the significant concern he voices but just wants the money for himself.

Jesus' response has two parts, one referencing his death, the other containing the rejoinder derived from Mark, "You always have the poor with you, but you do not always have me." This saying affirms Mary's discernment of the exceptional character of Jesus' identity and her discernment of the exceptional character of the moment, and should not be taken to imply that selfless care for the poor is not typically a high priority, especially since all the Gospels connect the death of Jesus to his solidarity with the poor and outcast (e.g., Mark 10:43–44).

In Mark, the only anointing is for Jesus' burial (Mark 15:46; 16:1). In John, this parallels an extravagant anointing before Jesus' burial (John 19:39–40), and this distinguishes the anointing by Mary from the anointing by the unnamed woman in Mark. Mary's anointing is a proleptic anointing of Jesus as king, a role he takes on after the anointing during his triumphant entry into Jerusalem (John 12:12–19). His death is defined as the death of a king (John 18:33–38). Of course, Jesus is a very particular kind of king, a king whose feet are anointed, a king who washes feet, a king who is servant to all, a king whose triumph is the cross, a king whose kingdom is not of this world (John 18:36).

The lections for this week emphasize expectation and longing for the "new thing" that God has promised (Isa. 43:19). Psalm 126 expresses a hope that "those who sow in tears may reap with shouts of joy" (Ps. 126:5). In Philippians 3, Paul places his hope in "know[ing] Christ and the power of his resurrection." The hope and longing expressed in these readings are encapsulated in the anointing story in John, in which Mary—in a simple but discerning and deeply spiritually symbolic, profoundly intimate and passionate action—proclaims the meaning and exceptional significance of Jesus' ministry and death.

DENNIS E. SMITH

Commentary 2: Connecting the Reading with the World

If Lent is a season for contemplation, curiosity, and confession, then this story about a dinner for Jesus in the home of Lazarus is a fitting Lenten text, because it evokes them all. Surely, any gathering at the home of Lazarus must have brought delight. After all, they were dining with someone who had been raised from the dead. Even his friends and family would never fully get used to that miracle. Alongside this joy, however, Mary's actions evoke a range of responses: awe concerning the sweet smell of wafting perfume, nagging questions regarding the line between appropriate gift and extravagance, and despair over the mention of Jesus' burial. What other emotions might we allow into Lent if given the opportunity?

Invitation to Wonder. This passage provokes many questions. Judas questions whether such costly perfume has been used wisely, and, honestly, so does every reader of the story. We also wonder where Mary got that perfume. What is Jesus really feeling as his feet are wiped clean with Mary's hair? What would those present have felt at the time—about Mary, about the events to come? We wonder about all of this, and perhaps that is the point: the story provokes us through our wondering about these questions to the place where we experience wonder and awe in a deeper sense.

The experience of sheer wonder is an urgent need for us today. Christianity in the United States is often characterized not in terms of wonder but in terms of belief. The fancy word for this is "orthodoxy," which means "sound doctrine" or "right belief." The history of many Protestant denominations includes fights and divisions over what is orthodox. In the public sphere especially, religious leaders are asked to justify their beliefs about the issues of the day. Many of us long for the clear answers and settled neatness of orthodoxy. The emotion of wonder, however, does not align well with doctrine and orthodoxy. Instead, wonder has more to do with one's state of being. Wonder might cause us to act, but it often discombobulates beliefs, causing us to focus on experience itself, rather than thinking the exactly right thing about it. In this sense, the passage's invitation to wonder cuts against many notions of contemporary Christianity. Mary's actions cannot be easily classified into theological categories. Like all good stories, this story calls us to wonder anew, to embrace the questions and remain unsettled for a time.

Another Sense of Time. The Greek word *kairos* means "time," not time as the mere ticking of a clock, but time as a pivotal, fulsome, transforming moment. This account of Mary washing Jesus' feet is part of a curious mashup of time in the Gospel of John—one in which past, present, and future keep shifting—that suggests we are dealing with just such a *kairos* moment. A chapter earlier, John has described Mary as "the one who anointed the Lord with perfume and wiped his feet with her hair" (John 11:2). In other words, John prefigures our story in the previous story about the raising of Lazarus. Then, in our story, Lazarus is introduced as "Lazarus, whom he had raised from the dead," causing our memory of that past event to hover in the present. Not only that, but John also described in the previous chapter how the raising of Lazarus precipitated the plan of the council to put Jesus to death (John 11:45–53). Thus the presence of Lazarus also foreshadows an event yet in the future: the crucifixion of Jesus.

Past, present, and future have merged in this moment; therefore, dinner at Lazarus's house must have had a particular *kairos* feel. Lazarus, the man who had been dead for four days, has been raised from the dead by Jesus, and now he is hosting Jesus at his house for dinner. Memory of the reality of death is in the air, but also present is the knowledge that on this day death has not prevailed. The stench of Lazarus—dead for four days—is overtaken by the sweet smell of expensive perfume. Even Jesus' response, with its puzzling syntax, recalls interesting play with time, "Leave her alone. She bought it so that she might keep it for the day of my burial" (v. 7). So the smell of perfume wafts about while Jesus anticipates his own burial in the presence of a man previously raised from the dead. Strange time. Godly time.

So much of modern life is a slave to *chronos*, the time on our watch. I once read an article chronicling the hectic lives of working mothers. One of the women described a time-saving habit she had developed when using the microwave. Rather than taking the extra second to press two buttons, she figured she could save time by pressing one twice. So, she microwaved things for thirty-three seconds, one minute eleven seconds, two minutes twenty-two seconds, and so on. Ways to "save time" have become valuable commodities in our culture, fraught with calendar alarms, over-full schedules, and multiple screens calling for our attention. As folk singer David LaMotte puts it, "There's no time like the present, and there's no present like time."

The *kairos* time suggested by the passage also causes confusion for us, and we must acknowledge the unfortunate use of one aspect of the passage's approach to time. Jesus' response to Judas includes the phrase "You always have the poor with you, but you do not always have me" (v. 8). In some circles this line has been employed to justify a lackadaisical approach to loving one's neighbor, or the embrace of economic systems in which the rich get richer and the poor become poorer. In fact, there is no time like the present to live out Jesus' commands to love God and neighbor, *all* our neighbors.

Instead of living under the oppression of *chronos*, trying to squeeze a few extra seconds out of a relentless schedule, people of faith are invited to live in *kairos* time, God's time. Instead of asking, "How can I save some time?" we are allowed to ask, "What is the saving God doing in this moment, and how can I be a part of it?" Mary discerned that the *kairos* of this moment was that Jesus was approaching his death, and her anointing of Jesus was how she participated in that moment.

This attention to *kairos* is also the true meaning of Jesus' word to Judas, "You always have the poor with you, but you do not always have me." Some have seen this as a justification to ignore the poor because, after all, they are always around. Instead, Jesus is saying that God is always at work saving the poor. Every moment of compassion toward the poor is a *kairos* moment.

Life together in Christian community calls for an embrace of *kairos*, a reorienting of our lives to God's time. In fact, Lent itself is a kind of *kairos* time during which the church invites us to ponder anew the mystery of faith. One way many do so is by taking up Lenten practices such as prayer, study of Scripture, fasting, and recommitment to loving our neighbor. With Mary and Lazarus, let us also delve into the complex emotions, questions, and wonder that the Christian faith evokes.

ADAM J. COPELAND

Liturgy of the Palms

Psalm 118:1–2, 19–29   Luke 19:28–40

Psalm 118:1–2, 19–29

¹O give thanks to the LORD, for he is good;
    his steadfast love endures forever!
²Let Israel say,
    "His steadfast love endures forever."
. . . .
¹⁹Open to me the gates of righteousness,
    that I may enter through them
    and give thanks to the LORD.

²⁰This is the gate of the LORD;
    the righteous shall enter through it.

²¹I thank you that you have answered me
    and have become my salvation.
²²The stone that the builders rejected
    has become the chief cornerstone.
²³This is the LORD's doing;
    it is marvelous in our eyes.
²⁴This is the day that the LORD has made;
    let us rejoice and be glad in it.
²⁵Save us, we beseech you, O LORD!
    O LORD, we beseech you, give us success!

²⁶Blessed is the one who comes in the name of the LORD.
    We bless you from the house of the LORD.
²⁷The LORD is God,
    and he has given us light.
Bind the festal procession with branches,
    up to the horns of the altar.

²⁸You are my God, and I will give thanks to you;
    you are my God, I will extol you.

²⁹O give thanks to the LORD, for he is good,
    for his steadfast love endures forever.

Connecting the Psalm with Scripture and Worship

Psalm 118 is the last in the series of Egyptian Hallel psalms. Together, they help retell the exodus narrative, in language of praise and thanksgiving (*hallel*, "praise").[1] Psalm 118 is a call to that praise, an invitation to worship in language so vivid that we can imagine the scene

1. James Limburg, *Psalms,* Westminster Bible Companion (Louisville, KY: Westminster John Knox Press, 2000), 387, 402.

before us. This psalm is public, evoking the spaces and voices of assembly. The psalmist not only speaks to the community but also invites its response: "Let Israel say . . ." We are in an arena of praise and prayer. The gathering is poised at the entrance of worship, and as the psalmist bids the gates to be opened in verses 19 and 20, we envision the people passing through. It is not just a summons *to* worship; it is an arc *of* worship as well. Some of liturgy's greatest hits are found in this psalm: verses 1, 24, and 26 particularly. Congregations may say or sing them reflexively without knowing the psalm number. The people enter into worship (v. 20); they give thanks (v. 21); they declare an affirmation (v. 22); they implore God in prayer (v. 25). Praise is bright-eyed and ecstatic: *it is marvelous, let us rejoice.*

Even supplication is a song and shout: *save us!* We say and sing it in worship as *Hosanna*; the cry for help is also a cry of jubilation.

This Hallel psalm comes, perhaps ironically, at a point in Lent, the threshold of Holy Week, when our *hallelujahs/alleluias* may have been silent for five weeks and will be silent a week longer. Holy Week is the "chief cornerstone" of the Christian year, when the central story is most fully recalled and enacted. At the beginning of this week, our Palm Sunday worship is often grand and glorious, evoking the parade of branches and crowds, a mighty acclamation. In fact, Palm Sunday worship can be strikingly and questionably similar to Easter worship in spirit, expression, and volume. Who does not love a parade?

Old Tyrant Death Disarmed

Thee, Sovereign God, our grateful accents praise;
We own Thee Lord, and bless Thy wondrous ways;
To Thee, eternal Father, earth's whole frame,
With loudest trumpets sounds immortal fame.
Lord God of Hosts! For Thee the heavenly powers
With sounding anthems fill the vaulted towers.
Thy Cherubim thrice, Holy, Holy, Holy, cry;
Thrice, Holy, all the Seraphim reply,
And thrice returning echoes endless songs supply.
Both heaven and earth Thy majesty display;
They owe their beauty to Thy glorious ray.
Thy praises fill the loud Apostles' choir;
The train of prophets in the song conspire.
Legions of martyrs in the chorus shine,
And vocal blood with vocal music join.
By these Thy church, inspired by heavenly art,
Around the world maintains a second part;
And turns her sweetest notes, O God, to Thee,
The Father of unbounded majesty;
The Son adored co-partner of Thy seat,
And equal everlasting Paraclete.
Thou King of Glory, Christ of the Most-High,

Thou co-eternal filial Deity;
Thou who to save the world's impending doom
Vouchsaf'st to dwell within a Virgin's womb.
Old tyrant death disarmed, before Thee flew
The bolts of heaven, and back the foldings drew,
To give access, and make Thy faithful way,
From God's right hand Thy filial beams display.
Thou art to judge the living and the dead;
Then spare those souls for whom Thy veins have bled.
O take us up among Thy blessed above,
To share with them Thy everlasting love.
Preserve, O Lord, Thy people and enhance
Thy blessing on Thine own inheritance.
Forever raise their hearts, and rule their ways;
Each day we bless Thee and proclaim Thy praise;
No age shall fail to celebrate Thy name,
No hour neglect Thy everlasting fame.
Preserve our souls, O Lord, this day from ill;
Have mercy, Lord, have mercy still;
As we have hoped, do Thou reward our pain;
We've hoped in Thee—let not our hope be vain.

Nicetas, "Te Deum," trans. John Dryden, *in The Poetical Works of John Dryden* (New York: Houghton Mifflin, 1908).919.

However, this parade does not lead straight to Easter; it leads to sorrow, betrayal, and death. Along the way will be the washing of feet and the covenant of love. In the clamor of palm and psalm, we might strain to see this one who comes in God's name; our cry for salvation might also be plaintive, weak, or whispered. Other verses of Psalm 118 appear on Easter Sunday, when the fullness and redemption of the preceding week is celebrated; but at the beginning of Holy Week, these particular verses, for all their vitality, keep us *here* in the story, not *there* on Easter. These verses contain space; they make room for a story that is still unfolding. Specific acts of praise are named and invited, to be sure: *give thanks, open the gates, this is the Lord's doing, save us, blessed is the one.* But there is space in the language and in the images for what is to come. The open gates invite us through, and beyond will be both death and life. A rejected stone will become our firm foundation, though we may not know how. What is to come will indeed be the Lord's doing; we cannot always imagine just how marvelous it will be.

This very public, exuberant psalm is in conversation with very personal verses from Isaiah, who, with a face set like flint, recalls what has been demanded and what awaits. Both texts affirm momentous deeds at hand and God's presence and work in the midst of them. The psalm's great congregation seems to affirm the path ahead, of which Isaiah speaks. Though it is customary to hear or sing the psalm as a response to the OT, on this day the reverse order is also fascinating. If Isaiah follows the psalm, it may be a somber yet resolute echo of the massive song of praise. The psalmist bids the gates to open and the people to go through; for Isaiah, it is the ear that God opens, and there is no turning back. The psalmist's crowds beseech God: "Save us!" Isaiah knows that God saves and vindicates. The psalmist sings of the rejected cornerstone as foundation; Isaiah is defiant towards adversaries. When the throngs have passed by and the shouts of praise have faded, Isaiah's words, no less than the psalmist's, make this affirmation: blessed is the one who comes in the name of the Lord. Isaiah reminds us of what that will be like in the week ahead.

How might this psalm be used in worship? Psalms live in being sounded, and that invites us to consider how both speech and music help bring a psalm to life. Psalm 118's well-known liturgical phrases may find their way into a call to worship, prayers, or a communion liturgy, and in those cases they might be spoken or sung. The full pericope for the day may place the psalm alongside other readings. If spoken, whether by individual voices or responsively between one voice and many, it may have a certain solemnity. Musical settings may offer richer and more expressive possibilities. The psalm might be sung in a metrical, hymn-like version. It might also be sung responsively, which would match the inherent call-and-response nature of the text itself. It is important that imaginative care be taken in choosing a musical setting, so that the character of music—the songful utterance—to which we invite a congregation's voice is true to the conversation of texts and preaching that is being prepared for worship.

ERIC WALL

Luke 19:28–40

²⁸After he had said this, he went on ahead, going up to Jerusalem.

²⁹When he had come near Bethphage and Bethany, at the place called the Mount of Olives, he sent two of the disciples, ³⁰saying, "Go into the village ahead of you, and as you enter it you will find tied there a colt that has never been ridden. Untie it and bring it here. ³¹If anyone asks you, 'Why are you untying it?' just say this, 'The Lord needs it.'" ³²So those who were sent departed and found it as he had told them. ³³As they were untying the colt, its owners asked them, "Why are you untying the colt?" ³⁴They said, "The Lord needs it." ³⁵Then they brought it to Jesus; and after throwing their cloaks on the colt, they set Jesus on it. ³⁶As he rode along, people kept spreading their cloaks on the road. ³⁷As he was now approaching the path down from the Mount of Olives, the whole multitude of the disciples began to praise God joyfully with a loud voice for all the deeds of power that they had seen, ³⁸saying,

"Blessed is the king
    who comes in the name of the Lord!
Peace in heaven,
    and glory in the highest heaven!"

³⁹Some of the Pharisees in the crowd said to him, "Teacher, order your disciples to stop." ⁴⁰He answered, "I tell you, if these were silent, the stones would shout out."

Commentary 1: Connecting the Reading to Scripture

When Jesus' parents first took him to Jerusalem as a child, his future was foretold by two faithful prophets. Simeon declared, "This child is destined for the falling and rising of many in Israel, and to be a sign that will be opposed" (Luke 2:34), and in thanksgiving Anna praised God on behalf of all who are "looking for the redemption of Jerusalem" (Luke 2:38). Now, as Jesus arrives at Jerusalem again on his way to the cross, the destiny Simeon foretold is being fulfilled. It is not destiny in the sense of impersonal fate, but of God's loving purpose and appointment. It is not destiny that obliterates human will, but destiny that invites active participation and obedience to God's will. Thus, in this story of Jesus' triumphal entry Luke is at pains to show us that this arrival both fulfills God's long-foretold promise and is a journey of Jesus' own choosing. It is both his destiny and the outworking of his determined fidelity.

The journey to Jerusalem in Luke, often called the travel narrative (Luke 9:51–19:27), opens with this pivotal description: "when the days drew near for him to be taken up, he set his face to go to Jerusalem." The language echoes the Suffering Servant of Isaiah, who declares, "I have set my face like flint" (Isa. 50:7). Jesus is firmly resolved to go to Jerusalem, to proclaim the kingdom of God on the way, even if it brings conflict, and to be obedient to God's will, even if it leads to death.

Just before entering the city, Jesus stops at the Mount of Olives and sends two of the disciples ahead on an errand. He tells them to go into the village and find a colt tied there that has never been ridden; they are to bring it to him. If anyone asks why, Jesus tells them, "Say, 'The Lord needs it.'" In this final part of Luke's Gospel, we encounter a Jesus who is firmly in control of the events around him and infused with divine knowledge. He will soon cleanse the temple with authority, silence the scribes into amazement, foretell calamity on a cosmic scale, and silently offer himself up to suffering and crucifixion. Now he summons a colt that has never been ridden.

What is the significance of the colt? At one level it is a miracle for a person to ride an unbroken colt in a crowd, and that in itself signifies the divinity and control of Jesus in this moment. It may echo the story in 1 Samuel 6 of the cows who had never borne a yoke but could miraculously and willingly pull the ark of the Lord. Many Palm Sunday sermons have imagined the comic mayhem of riding an unbroken colt, but the point of the symbol is that the absence of mayhem bears witness to the identity of the rider. Gabriel said to Mary at Jesus' conception, "The Lord God will give to him the throne of his ancestor David" (Luke 1:32). So, like Solomon who rode to his royal anointing on David's own mule (1 Kgs. 1:28–40), Jesus enters Jerusalem on the back of a colt who is wondrously obedient.

After the disciples throw their cloaks on the colt, they put Jesus on it, and as he rode, "people kept spreading their cloaks on the road." Cloaks are yet another symbol of welcoming a king of Israel. When Jehu announced in a panic to Ahab's officers that the prophet had just anointed him king, "then hurriedly they all took their cloaks and spread them for him on the bare steps" and blew the trumpet for their new king (2 Kgs. 9:13). Unlike Matthew, Mark, and John, Luke has no interest in leafy or palm branches. For Luke, the cloaks are enough to say that a king of Israel is coming. As Jesus began to ride the colt down the Mount of Olives, "the whole multitude of the disciples began to praise God joyfully with a loud voice for all the deeds of power that they had seen" (Luke 19:37). Unlike Matthew, Luke makes no reference to Zechariah's prophecy, but it is nearly impossible to miss the connection. It is as if Zechariah wrote the script, and Jesus directed the scene: "Rejoice greatly, O daughter Zion! Shout aloud, O daughter Jerusalem! Lo, your king comes to you; triumphant and victorious is he, humble and riding on a donkey, on a colt, the foal of a donkey" (Zech. 9:9).

The praises of the crowd are the words of Psalm 118, assigned as the only other lectionary reading with this text. The song is a plea for help, and a welcome for pilgrims to Jerusalem: "Blessed is the one who comes in the name of the LORD!" the psalm reads. In case we have missed Luke's point, he substitutes "one" and puts the word "king" on the lips of the people. They continue to praise him with echoes of the angels' song to the shepherds that announced Jesus' birth: "Peace in heaven, and glory in the highest heaven." Notice, though, that the angels declared peace on earth, and the crowds declare peace in heaven. It is the destiny of Jesus to fulfill both of these promises, but to do so in ways that mystify and offend crowds both then and now.

Triumphal parades are meant to celebrate past triumphs and imply promised conquests. The cheering parade-goers expect their hopes for peace to be fulfilled through the *use* of power, not the abdication of it. King Jesus, however, does not use his power to drive out an oppressive government or to establish a triumphant nation. Rather, Jesus surrenders his power to a will of God that only he truly understands and to a destiny that Anna and Simeon only dimly foresaw. For this destiny he resisted the temptation in the wilderness to abuse his power, and for this destiny he resolutely made his way toward Jerusalem. Now this destiny requires going to the temple once more; it requires a confrontation with power and an unmasking of corruption that ultimately will lead to the cross. The cross is Jesus' embodied obedience to the will of God, an obedience that mysteriously accomplishes both the longing of the crowds and the proclamation of the angels: peace in heaven and on earth.

As the multitudes are shouting their praises, the confrontation with power begins. Some of the Pharisees say, "Teacher, order your disciples to stop." Jesus answers that even if they fell silent, the stones would cry out. In Habakkuk 2:11 the prophet writes that the stones will cry out against the corruption of the wicked. In this royal entry, the cries of praise that welcome the son of David simultaneously bear witness to the brokenness that the king comes to redeem. If the people are silent, the stones will cry out in praise for God's promised redemption.

As we envision this scene, the colt, the cloaks, and the crowds capture our imaginations; but they are only the symbols that bear witness to the identity of Jesus. Astride the colt is the king who comes in the name of the Lord, who is fiercely determined to be obedient to the will of God even at the cost of his own life. Throughout his journey to Jerusalem, Jesus has invited us to follow him and to find our destiny in his, but only if we will share his obedience and match our own determination to his determined fidelity.

PATRICK W. T. JOHNSON

Commentary 2: Connecting the Reading with the World

The Final Journey Begins. On Palm Sunday the church begins its observance of Holy Week by proclaiming the story of Jesus' entrance into Jerusalem. Many congregations join the procession, waving palm branches and singing hymns that declare, "Thou art the king of Israel, thou David's royal Son, who in the Lord's Name comest, the King and Blessed One" (Theodulph of Orleans, eighth–ninth cent.).

Many people attending Palm Sunday worship will not attend any other Holy Week services, so they will not hear the passion narrative that is at the center of our faith before they return to sing the Easter alleluias. An important question, therefore, is whether or not to read and preach only on the entry into Jerusalem. For this reason, many denominations identify this as Passion/Palm Sunday and include the reading of the passion narrative.

Even if you include the passion narrative, the service begins with joyful acclamations of the multitude following Jesus. Why do we join in with palm branches and joyful acclamations? We must take care not to misunderstand the kingship of Jesus. If our procession is too joyful and triumphant, we may miss the point, but with compassionate pastoral guidance, such processions can help the congregation realize that they are a part of the crowd that waves their branches but later also shouts, "Crucify him."

The procession usually pauses to hear the story of Jesus' ride into Jerusalem; then the service continues with singing and the waving of greens until all are once again in their places and, if one includes the passion narrative, the service takes a dramatic turn, and the sweet hosannas are replaced with the proclamation of the passion narrative.

Blessed Is the King. As we move into Holy Week, we will answer the question that is at the heart of Luke's Gospel, "Are you the one who is to come?" (Luke 7:19). What kind of king is coming in the name of the Lord? A challenge for us is that we approach Holy Week through the lens of the resurrection. We know and declare weekly that Jesus is the Messiah, the Son of the living God. Can we, on this Palm Sunday, and during the days ahead, set aside that certainty? Can we listen to each moment unfold as though we do not truly know who this man is? What then are we to make of this man who rides a donkey into the Holy City?

Why is this so crucial? Because we live and move among people who have not yet met Jesus. Even many who are sitting in our pews do not fully understand the story of Jesus. They do not understand how this odd story of Jesus riding on a colt introduces us to the man who will shortly be carrying a cross through the streets of Jerusalem.

Who is this man? That is a question we do well to ponder every day. Is he a prophet? A dedicated teacher? A storyteller? Whether we have spent a lifetime in the church, or are new to the faith, Jesus is always asking us, as he asked his disciples, "Who do you say that I am?" (Luke 9:20). We may declare he is the Messiah, our Lord and Savior, the Son of God; but do we know what that means? Peter was quick to declare Jesus the Messiah. When Peter heard the Messiah would be rejected, suffer, and be killed, he was equally quick to reject that reality. Through this odd and vivid story of a man celebrated in a spontaneous procession who ends the week on a cross, we help people discern who Jesus is and what difference he makes in our lives, and we can raise the challenging question, Do we, like Peter, want only to follow the Jesus who rides triumphantly surrounded by an adoring, cheering crowd?

The Lord Needs It. Jesus sent his followers into a village with instructions. He told them what they would see: a colt. What they were to do: untie the colt. What they were to say when challenged: "The Lord needs it." We will see similar instructions as Jesus prepares his followers for the meal they are to share (22:8–13).

Luke offers us the portrait of a man in control. Unlike so many other moments in the past years when he avoided attention, now Jesus is calling attention to himself. He is not slipping into Jerusalem. He is claiming his authority and kingship. However, in other respects Luke presents us with a very different and surprising portrait of a king, because it is very clear that Jesus has not come to be the earthly ruler of an earthly kingdom. He is not here to overthrow the Romans. He does not want the crowd to see him as the conquering hero.

Luke's listeners quite possibly had experienced other royal processions. Their community may have been conquered. They would have watched as the conqueror moved into the city to hymns and shouts. We too watch political parades and processions, and the point of all the pageantry and displays of power is to stress the importance and power of this new leader. Luke's king is a different kind of leader. Jesus rides not on a horse, a symbol of authority. Rather, he mounts a donkey, a symbol of humility. He comes in peace and in the name of the God who has sent him to live among people and to show people the loving face of God. When Pope Francis arrived in Washington for a tour of the United States, he did not step into a big black limousine. Instead, following in the footsteps of our humble king, he got in a small Fiat.

This is not just any crowd. It is "the whole multitude of the disciples" proclaiming to all that this is "the king who comes in the name of the Lord" (19:38). He is a king like none other, and they are cheering this unusual king. We are cheering for a shepherd, not a sovereign. Francis helps us to understand that this is a Savior, a Messiah, who moves among the people. What does that look like today? Over and over again Francis tells his clergy that they must, like Jesus our shepherd, smell like the sheep. They must spend their days out in the world, caring for all people, the rich and the poor alike. This is a shepherd who is willing to lay down his life for the sheep.

We too cheer this kind of king. Will we also be like those who demanded Jesus be crucified? It is important to remember that we stand with both crowds, as we turn to and then reject Jesus. Are we ready to follow the king who arrives on a humble donkey? Do we long for the earthly king/queen who will trample our earthly enemies? We are watching a world marked by violence and conflict, both internationally and at home. Our political landscape is seen through the lens of "us" and "them." Who, in this conflicted context, is Jesus calling us to be? Are we true followers if we reject those not like us, if we celebrate sovereigns who fight for our own worldly power and prosperity?

The passion narrative is filled with those who reject and betray Jesus, so we must be challenged to think carefully about whom and what we worship. We may be willing to shout with joy at this ironic procession, but will we also follow when Jesus carries his cross?

LUCY LIND HOGAN

Liturgy of the Passion

Isaiah 50:4–9a
Psalm 31:9–16
Philippians 2:5–11

Luke 22:14–23:56
Luke 23:1–49

Isaiah 50:4–9a

⁴The Lord GOD has given me
    the tongue of a teacher,
that I may know how to sustain
    the weary with a word.
Morning by morning he wakens—
    wakens my ear
    to listen as those who are taught.
⁵The Lord GOD has opened my ear,
    and I was not rebellious,
    I did not turn backward.
⁶I gave my back to those who struck me,
    and my cheeks to those who pulled out the beard;
I did not hide my face
    from insult and spitting.

⁷The Lord GOD helps me;
    therefore I have not been disgraced;
therefore I have set my face like flint,
    and I know that I shall not be put to shame;
    ⁸he who vindicates me is near.
Who will contend with me?
    Let us stand up together.
Who are my adversaries?
    Let them confront me.
⁹It is the Lord GOD who helps me;
    who will declare me guilty?

Commentary 1: Connecting the Reading with Scripture

Creativity and fidelity! The poet writes eloquently about his vital mission, his cruel opposition, and his trusting determination. Those reading Isaiah in Hebrew wince in frustration because a few of the poet's points do not translate clearly. He has some connection to God because he listens each day for inspiration, but the translators do not know exactly what he does for the weary. Does he sustain them, answer them, or help them? Does he have the tongue of a teacher, or the tongue of those who are taught (see NRSV footnote)? In either case, he believes himself a conduit between the Lord God and the people. The reader knows the poet has an important ministry to the weary, to those spiritually and emotionally exhausted from the burdens of the exile. Because of his ministry he must endure suffering and perhaps even torture. He chooses to endure his ordeal because his ministry matters. He willingly displays his back to those who strike him and yank out his beard. He does not choose suffering out of

115

self-abnegation, but because the weary need his ministry. He can endure the suffering because he trusts that the Lord God will vindicate and help him. He displays his determination and fidelity by setting his face "like flint."

The dramatic movement of thought and emotion that marks the abrupt transition from verse 3 to verse 4 creates a powerful effect. The poem in verses 1–3 scolds the people for their lack of faith. It uses the recurring metaphor of marriage, with the Lord as the husband to Jerusalem and the people as the children. Although the Lord has seemed to act like an absentee husband and father, the poem declares that no actual divorce happened. The absenteeism came because of the people's sins. The poem assumes that despite the absenteeism, the people should have continued to trust because of the Lord's power, as demonstrated in the exodus from Egypt. When the absentee father/husband returned, he should have found a waiting family ("he" in this sentence refers to the prophet's metaphor, not to a contemporary theological understanding of God). Such an image of God cries out for critique. Contemporary readers would almost certainly have a negative reaction to a portrayal of God as a husband who abandons his wife, only to return expecting joyous welcome. Nevertheless, the essential message remains valid: the people should never give up hope.

The Servant writes in verses 4–9 about his ministry to address the needs of the weary. The Servant has tried to keep up the hopes of the people, despite opposition. The verses following the Servant poem admonish the people to continue to trust in God despite the darkness of exile. Instead of trusting amid the darkness, they try to light their own fires. Verses 10 and 11a seem to come from the prophet, addressed to the people in the second person. Verse 11b likely represents the Lord speaking directly to the people, as in the early part of the chapter. The whole chapter represents a conversation, with the prophet and the Lord admonishing the people, while the Servant remains among them, seeking to ease their weariness.

Preachers and church leaders typically look at each individual Servant Song as preparation for preaching or teaching. The four songs together give a comprehensive look at the role of the Servant within this part of Isaiah. The first Servant poem, in 42:1–4, portrays a powerful, authoritative figure, anointed by the divine spirit. With fortitude and energy the Servant will "establish justice in the earth." In the second poem, in chapter 49, the Servant displays power with allusions to weapons of war. Nevertheless, the Servant expresses doubt about accomplishments in the cry "I have labored in vain; I have spent my strength for nothing and vanity" (49:4). Although the exact identity of the Servant remains in question among scholars, Isaiah 49:3 seems to suggest that the Servant is Israel, one of the usual options, along with the prophet himself, or some other individual. Even though verse 3 suggests that the Servant is Israel, in verses 5–6 the Servant seems to have a ministry to Israel and Judah, so the Servant's exact identity remains unclear. The poem clearly expands the ministry of the Servant beyond Israel and Judah, so that the Servant becomes a "light to the nations."

The fourth Servant poem in chapters 52–53 introduces the understanding of vicarious suffering. The Servant has suffered on behalf of the people in fidelity to God, so the Servant's wounds and bruises offer redemption and healing. The exact identity of the Servant may not matter as much as the theology expressed in the four poems: God has called the Servant and poured out the divine spirit; the Servant ministers within the community of the displaced exiles; the Servant accepts the suffering caused by this ministry; the Servant reveals the divine will for justice among all nations.

The eloquence and theological insight of Second Isaiah (chaps. 40–55) is stunning. The prophet seeks to persuade the exiles to recognize God's hand in political changes. The key verse in this block of material comes in 43:19: "I am about to do a new thing." God's new thing brings both promise and responsibility. The people can start anew, but the people also have to rebuild from rubble. Using such rhetorical/poetic strategies as tenderness (40:1–5), admonition (44:9–20), sarcasm (46:1–7), and invitation (55:1–9), the prophet interprets God's presence in the new circumstances. The Servant poems add their theology of redemptive suffering, divine call, global justice, and endurance.

The OT knows other characters who face tribulation as a consequence of their obedience. Those called by God often had to endure hardship for the sake of faithful ministry. Moses first resisted his call (Exod. 4:13) and later felt such anguish he wanted to give up (Exod. 33:15). Jeremiah wanted to postpone his call (Jer. 1:6) and later bitterly complained to God about all he endured because he followed God's instructions (Jer. 20:7–18). Jeremiah decided he had to follow and speak God's word (Jer. 20:9). Daniel called the wise to endure persecution and martyrdom, because death was preferable to apostasy (Dan. 11:33–35). The reward for endurance would come by resurrection (Dan. 12:2).

The experience of the prophet intersects well with today's epistle reading. Philippians 2:5–11 contains the *kenōsis* hymn about Christ. The prophet chose to set his face to fulfill his ministry despite his suffering. Christ chose to empty himself and endure death on a cross. In the two poems, both Christ and the prophet humbly accept their missions for the benefit of a community. In both cases the suffering was redemptive. The Christ hymn, of course, talks about the salvation of all (Phil. 2:10). The prophet trusted the Lord for vindication. God exalts Christ because of his humility.

The Gospel reading contains Luke's version of the Lord's Supper, the prediction of Peter's denial, Jesus on the Mount of Olives, Jesus' passion, Peter's denial, and Jesus before the council. Within the passion narrative, the concrete shared experience comes in the insults (Isa. 50:6; Luke 22:65) and the beating (Luke 22:63). Just as the prophet shows strength in choosing to endure the suffering and shows determination by setting the face, so Luke's portrayal of the passion and crucifixion portrays Jesus as one who demonstrates a certain power, even while hanging on the cross (see also Luke 9:51). Jesus is in enough control of himself to engage in dialogue with the repentant criminal, and Jesus displays salvific and eschatological power by opening paradise to him. The texts do not glorify suffering or call for unnecessary suffering. They teach faithfulness in suffering and the redemption of suffering.

CHARLES L. AARON JR.

Commentary 2: Connecting the Reading with the World

Who is the Servant in Isaiah 50:4–9? Christians traditionally identify this passage (along with 42:1–9; 49:1–13; and 52:13–53:12) as a poetic collection of Suffering Servant Songs that foreshadow Jesus' own suffering. Not surprisingly, Isaiah 50:4–9 is a primary text for the Liturgy for the Passion. Other identities of the Servant have been proposed. Some think the Servant is a prophet speaking to an exilic audience prior to the return of some Jews from exile in the late 540s BCE. Many Jewish interpreters suggest the Servant represents the whole community of Israel—at that point among the weakest and most politically insignificant of nations—as the people through whom God works to redeem the world. These alternate identities of the Servant open up many connections that relate to, but move beyond, the traditional Christian association of this text with Christ's prophetic ministry, suffering, and death.

The connections between Isaiah 50:4–9 and other texts within the Liturgy for the Passion are fairly clear. The other texts "fill out" the character of the defiant Servant in subtle ways. In Isaiah 50:4–9, the Servant stands resolute in faith in God as the vindicator and source of his strength, despite the ridicule he experiences. Unlike the laments of Jeremiah or the Psalms, however, the poet in 50:4–9 states his oppression as a fact, not in the mode of complaint. The liturgy pairs this text with Psalm 31:9–16, perhaps as a way of acknowledging an inner voice of doubt or despair that tempers the bravado of the Servant in Isaiah 50:4–9. If Isaiah 50 represents the Servant's public face, then Psalm 31:9–16 might convey the inner struggle. The psalmist honestly testifies to his or her plight, a suffering that is at once emotional, spiritual, and physical: "my eye wastes away from grief, my soul and body also" (Ps. 31:9). The psalmist confesses the fear of adversaries all around and the complete abandonment of the community (v. 11). Although these enemies terrify the psalmist (v. 13), as in many lament psalms, the verse ends with a word of confident assurance: "But I trust in you, O LORD; I say, 'You are my God.' My times are in your hand; deliver me from the hand of my enemies and persecutors. Let your face shine upon your servant; save me in your steadfast love" (vv. 14–16). The confident assurance points us back to the Servant's own confidence in God: "he who vindicates me is near. Who will contend with me?" (Isa. 50:8).

In the passion narrative in Luke 22:14–23:56, Jesus exhibits both the boldness of Isaiah's Servant and the vulnerability of Psalm 31's poet. Luke 22:41–46 tells of Jesus' anguish in Gethsemane as Jesus asks God to "remove this cup from me" (v. 42). Despite the reassurances of an angel, Jesus' spiritual anguish displays itself physically with sweat that "became like great drops of blood falling down on the ground" (v. 44). While Jesus looks to God for a release from suffering in this scene, he encounters the disciples who are "sleeping because of grief" (v. 45). The passion narrative in Luke, paired with the psalm of lament, permits believers also to voice our concerns to God, even as we boldly continue to engage our tasks of prophetic ministry.

In light of the Lukan narrative of the passion, the charge of Philippians 2:5, "Let the same mind be in you that was in Christ Jesus," is daunting. The Letter to the Philippians calls Christians to empty themselves as both Christ and the Servant of Isaiah do, trusting in God to sustain us in our prophetic tasks. This challenge propels individuals and the church to look both backward into the text for instruction and sustenance and forward into the world that thirsts for a prophetic word.

When we look back at Isaiah 50 in the light of the passion narrative and the Philippian challenge, we gain some insight into what Christian prophetic ministry could be. The NRSV translates Isaiah 50:4 as, "the Lord GOD has given me the tongue of a teacher, that I may know how to sustain the weary with a word." The Jewish Publication Society's Tanakh translates "tongue of a teacher" as "trained tongue." The implication of both translations is that the Servant was first a pupil, a disciple who attended to the teachings of God and the tradition's memory as prerequisites to prophetic ministry. What does it mean to have a trained tongue? If this song refers originally to a prophet, perhaps this speaks to the need for prophetic discipleship. The prophets were masters of rhetoric. They could often paint masterpieces with their words, using their sharp vocabulary and acerbic wit to slice through the façade of their opponents' indignant self-righteousness. The prophets were also acutely aware of local and national interests that cast their shadow across society. God awakens the prophet and opens the prophet's ear to an awareness of the suffering around them (Isa. 50:4). To borrow a phrase from the African American community that refers to someone who has become aware of our society's injustices, the prophet was literally "woke." If the church is to have the mind of Christ and the spirit of the Servant, it must also awaken to contemporary social injustices, while equipping itself to speak the truth about these injustices effectively.

The newly awakened state, however, also means that the Christian prophetic community must be ready for the backlash of a culture that wants to sustain the status quo. The Servant has the courage to stand in the face of opposition and ridicule. The prophetic Christian community must be willing to expose its face to the potential mocking, physical abuse, and spittle of a stubborn culture that refuses to change (Isa. 50:6).

The church is not without role models in this regard. The Servant in this text foreshadows, for example, the women and men of the civil rights movement who marched, sat in, and spoke out in the face of the culture's grotesque racial violence, in order to lead the United States toward a dream of true unity. The resolve of the Servant shows itself in current advocates for Black Lives Matter, those who champion the full humanity of members of the LGBTQ community, and those who offer sanctuary to the immigrant in politically turbulent times. These prophetic voices do not violate, they do not lash out in retaliation, but they take a stand—sometimes by kneeling—even in the face of economic pressure, cultural ridicule, and physical violence.

Perhaps the greater Christian community can "train its tongue" by opening its ears to them.

It might be easier to stick solely with the traditional understanding of the Servant with Christ, especially as a precursor to Holy Week, but what may seem like an identity crisis can redirect the church to a plurality of holy possibilities: the traditional Christian identification of the Servant with Jesus drives us forward into the passion narrative of Luke and the ecclesial challenge of Philippians to seek to emulate the mind of Christ; the identification of the Servant with the prophet reminds us there is a time to stand defiantly against the wicked and to confess our anguish to God; the communal identification of the Servant with Israel presses the Christian community to consider its actions in the face of societal pressure to maintain the status quo.

DAVID G. GARBER JR.

Psalm 31:9–16

[9]Be gracious to me, O LORD, for I am in distress;
    my eye wastes away from grief,
    my soul and body also.
[10]For my life is spent with sorrow,
    and my years with sighing;
my strength fails because of my misery,
    and my bones waste away.

[11]I am the scorn of all my adversaries,
    a horror to my neighbors,
an object of dread to my acquaintances;
    those who see me in the street flee from me.
[12]I have passed out of mind like one who is dead;
    I have become like a broken vessel.
[13]For I hear the whispering of many—
    terror all around!—
as they scheme together against me,
    as they plot to take my life.

[14]But I trust in you, O LORD;
    I say, "You are my God."
[15]My times are in your hand;
    deliver me from the hand of my enemies and persecutors.
[16]Let your face shine upon your servant;
    save me in your steadfast love.

Connecting the Psalm with Scripture and Worship

Psalm 31:9–16 is paired, for the Liturgy of the Passion, with Isaiah 50:4–9a. In some ways, they share the voice of one who is scorned, shamed, and assaulted. They are like soliloquies, where the story pauses and the Servant of God steps downstage to unfold for us deep inner questions and fears. Isaiah is more public, offering testimony and calling on the community's solidarity: "Who will contend with me? Let us stand up together." In the psalm, though, we overhear a private prayer of greater anguish. God is still trusted (vv. 9 and 14), but this prayer is made by one who is both surrounded and abandoned; we can imagine furtive glances, whispers, and the fear in footsteps and shadows. The recollection of what God has done before helps enable our prayer and hope when they seem least sure, but these psalm verses do not recount God's deeds. They are a prayer for God's presence in a time of isolation.

The only community described here is a community of foes. Both alone and hunted, the psalmist is too weary to hold things back from God. Five rapid verses (vv. 9–13) are a relentless pouring out and piling up of fear, exhaustion, and peril. The psalmist has come to feel invisible, as though already dead (v. 12).[1] *Terror all around!* Many of us have privilege and security that may insulate us from those words, but there are all too many people and places where this

---

1. James Limburg, *Psalms*, Westminster Bible Companion (Louisville, KY: Westminster John Knox Press, 2000), 101.

phrase is lived experience. Isaiah's resolve seems far away; the psalmist can only pray and trust, leaving all to God's hands and God's time.

We might ask why this psalm is heard on this Sunday, when the narrative of Jesus' suffering and death awaits us in five days on Good Friday. It is Friday's narrative, but it is the whole week's story. At the beginning of Holy Week, we are offered two liturgies: Palms and Passion. Both tell the story at the outset of this climactic week, but one of them is easier. The ebullient songs and magisterial processions of Palm Sunday are reassuring, inspiring, and doable. The Liturgy of the Passion is a different tone altogether, but it shares storytelling space with the Palms. These two liturgies are held together because "triumphal entry" is not simple. The psalmist-as-disciple seems to say, "This is what discipleship and the world will sometimes look like." The psalmist-as-liturgist seems to say, "Faithful worship cannot just rest in the easy parts of the story."

We may ask how we attend to a double liturgy, given the realities of worship time and space. Two psalms in worship (Ps. 118 for Palms, Ps. 31 for Passion) might seem like "too much"—until we remember that psalms come to life in sound and utterance. If both psalms are sung in contrasting ways—one as a hymn, another responsorially—then they emerge as distinct voices of storytelling. Alternatively, Psalm 118 might be sung, so that music highlights its fervent praise, but Psalm 31 spoken, so that music's absence underlines its poignancy. The reverse could work as well: a reading of Psalm 118, then a singing of Psalm 31, so that music intensifies the weight of anguish, even in the face of glorious exultation. These two psalms might also be interwoven, spoken by two voices in alternation:

Reader 1: O give thanks to the Lord, for he is good; his steadfast love endures forever!
Reader 2: Be gracious to me, O Lord, for I am in distress; my eye wastes away from grief, my soul and body also.
Reader 1: Open to me the gates of righteousness, that I may enter through them and give thanks to the Lord. This is the gate of the Lord; the righteous shall enter through it.

Reader 2: I am the scorn of all my adversaries, a horror to my neighbors, an object of dread to my acquaintances; those who see me in the street flee from me.
Reader 1: I thank you that you have answered me and have become my salvation.
Reader 2: I have passed out of mind like one who is dead; I have become like a broken vessel.
Reader 1: The stone that the builders rejected has become the chief cornerstone. This is the day that the Lord has made; let us rejoice and be glad in it.
Reader 2: For I hear the whispering of many— terror all around!— as they scheme together against me, as they plot to take my life.
Reader 1: Save us, we beseech you, O Lord!
Reader 2: But I trust in you, O Lord; I say, "You are my God."
Reader 1: Blessed is the one who comes in the name of the Lord. We bless you from the house of the Lord.
Reader 2: My times are in your hand; deliver me from the hand of my enemies and persecutors.
Reader 1: The Lord is God, and he has given us light.
Reader 2: Let your face shine upon your servant; save me in your steadfast love.

The contrasts make an ironic and even heartbreaking conversation, but they show that contrast is not contradiction, that these two psalms are in a single story.

Another verse of Psalm 31 will be on Jesus' lips at the moment of his death: "Father, into your hands I commend my spirit" (v. 5). Are these Palm-Passion Sunday verses also on Jesus' lips, or at least in his mind and heart and soul, as he enters Jerusalem, riding into this Holy Week? Amid donkey steps, waving branches, and public acclamation, does Jesus step downstage to say, "I hear the whispering of many as they plot to take my life"? When disciples flee and deny on Thursday, does Jesus echo the psalmist: "Those who see me in the street flee from me"? Throughout the week, throughout his life, and at his death, does Jesus offer to God the psalmist's prayer: "My times are in your hand"?

ERIC WALL

Philippians 2:5–11

⁵Let the same mind be in you that was in Christ Jesus,

⁶who, though he was in the form of God,
　　did not regard equality with God
　　as something to be exploited,
⁷but emptied himself,
　　taking the form of a slave,
　　being born in human likeness.
And being found in human form,
　　⁸he humbled himself
　　and became obedient to the point of death—
　　even death on a cross.

⁹Therefore God also highly exalted him
　　and gave him the name
　　that is above every name,
¹⁰so that at the name of Jesus
　　every knee should bend,
　　in heaven and on earth and under the earth,
¹¹and every tongue should confess
　　that Jesus Christ is Lord,
　　to the glory of God the Father.

Commentary 1: Connecting the Reading with Scripture

"If not for the grace of God. . . ." This is a resounding theme found in the texts for the Liturgy of the Passion. Isaiah 50 speaks of relying on God, listening to God's voice, and trusting in God's vindication despite the trials we experience. Psalm 31 highlights one's trust in God because God shows us grace in times of distress. Luke 22–23 posits Jesus as the epitome of one who trusts God and obeys God's will no matter what. Jesus, deeply troubled by his impending and undeserved persecution and execution, nonetheless says, "Father, if you are willing, remove this cup from me; yet, not my will but yours be done." During Lent, the church reflects upon and mourns Jesus' suffering and death upon a cross while maintaining hope and assurance that, as with Jesus, God will also be faithful to us. God freely gives us unmerited grace despite our sinful selves. Thus

we should be compelled to be faithful to God and walk humbly before God. As we reflect on God's gift to us through the sacrifice of God's only Son, let us also reflect on, and learn from, Jesus' humility.

Philippians 2:5–11, known as the christological or *kenōsis* hymn, is the quintessential passage illustrating Jesus' humility, namely, his disregard of his divine status, and his self-sacrifice. Jesus "emptied himself" (2:7), "did not regard equality with God as something to be exploited" (2:6), and "humbled himself and became obedient to the point of death—even death on a cross" (2:8). Paul pens this letter of encouragement while imprisoned, in order to tell the church he founded in the city of Philippi that they are to "be of the same mind" that was found in Christ.

What does it mean to "be of the same mind" as Christ? As evident within the literary context of Philippians 2, Paul's message is not one of self-sacrifice as in the manner of Jesus, but in the likeness of his humility. "Do nothing from selfish ambition or conceit, but in humility regard others as better than yourselves" (2:3). It is about how to "shine like stars in the world" (2:15), not in the self-glorifying "shine like a star" way typical in our society, by working together ("without murmuring or arguing," 2:14), putting others' needs before your own, and remaining humble in the midst of your work for God: "For it is God who is at work in you, enabling you both to will and to work for his good pleasure" (2:13). It also refers to mutual appreciation and acknowledgment; Paul prays for them (1:3–4) just as they pray for him (1:19).

． The relationship that Paul and the Philippian community model for us is reciprocity rooted in love and based on faith in Jesus Christ. This form of mutual respect and concern runs counter to the quid-pro-quo model that unfortunately many persons—even persons of faith—follow. Unfortunately, there are persons who only do "something for something" in return (the literal translation of "quid pro quo"). This is not what Jesus teaches. Paul and the Philippian community get Jesus' teaching right. Their mutual relationship is the way it is *because of* their love of Jesus and each other, not *contingent upon* what they can gain from each other.

"Emptying" in Philippians 2:7 refers to humility, not depletion. A common misreading of Jesus' humility in this text, however, is the description that he took the form of a slave (2:7). The text does not say that Jesus *became* a slave, but rather that he *took the form* of one. In other words, Jesus takes on a mind-set. However, this is not a calling to suffer, to regard ourselves as nobodies, or to a form of martyrdom for ministry "to the point of death" (2:8). Sometimes the language of suffering and emptying can be misunderstood. Christians are not called to endure the merciless suffering of abuse under the idea that we are called to be obedient and to suffer. This passage is about finding ways to love ourselves and others in generous and merciful ways, not about self-denigration or having our capacity to love destroyed by the cruelty of an oppressor. This is not Jesus' message to us. Further sacrifice is no longer needed.

In verses 9–11, Paul reminds the Philippians that Jesus was exalted because of his humility. Because of Jesus' obedience he shall be praised. It should be noted that because of Jesus' "emptying" (2:7), God exalted him (2:9). Our being humble, being in right relationship with God and with others, should not be for selfish reasons. Praise from others is not the purpose of being humble. God is the arbiter of our actions. Verse 9 begins, "*Therefore* God . . ." God weighs our actions and our motivations for what we do. As the people of God, the driving force of the mission of the church and our calling as individuals should be our love for God.

We are to be of the same mind as Christ when we do our "work" in both ecclesial and secular settings. At the outset of Philippians, Paul mentions their "sharing in the gospel" (1:5), which leads to "produc[ing] the harvest of righteousness" (1:11). Some translations call it the "fruits of justice." Paul's instruction to the Philippian congregation—a message that is still relevant for us—includes a command to do acts of justice, maintaining fairness and integrity for others. Reminiscent of Micah 6:8, Paul's instruction is to "do justice, and to love kindness, and to walk humbly with your God." The life and mission of the church are based on this teaching.

In the chapter that follows, Paul expands his teaching on humility and works by insisting that they have "no confidence in the flesh" (3:3). While the "flesh" normally referred to circumcision, Paul expands this view to include an obedience to Jewish law. Paul does not negate the law, but rather encourages his community to strive for "righteousness that comes from God on the basis of faith" (3:9 NIV).

Paul offers himself as an example for the community to follow (3:17). This may appear to be contrary to Paul's teaching on humility, but it is more generous and consistent to understand Paul to be presenting himself as a flawed human example who continues to strive to be like Jesus despite his imperfections, and to understand that Paul is doing this in order to encourage readers who may see themselves as hopelessly inadequate. Mitigating fearful expectations that what is demanded is perfection, Paul writes, "I do not consider myself yet to have taken hold of it. But one thing I do: Forgetting what is behind and straining toward what is ahead, I press on" (3:13–14 NIV).

Philippians 2:5–11, as a stand-alone text, and also within the literary context of all of Philippians, reminds us that during the Lenten season we should set our hearts and minds to be humble like Jesus Christ. Jesus espoused this way of thinking and being when he sacrificed himself for our sins so that we might be reconciled to God. This passage encourages Christians to be of the same accord as they work on relationships with others. This may not be an easy task, especially when engaging people who make being like Jesus extraordinarily difficult; however, this is why Paul reminds us to strive, to strain, and to press on.

SHANELL T. SMITH

Commentary 2: Connecting the Reading with the World

This early Christian hymn tells the story of the Christ event and our relation to it in a way that is consistent with the rhythm of baptism. Entering obediently into the water, we are emptied, with Christ Jesus; emerging from the water we are exalted to new life, joining hands with all people everywhere who confess Jesus Christ as Lord.

Read at the start of Passion Week, the hymn connects what is happening in the current liturgical seasons of Lent and Easter to the seasons of Advent and Christmas that have come before. It accomplishes this by way of its focus on the life and history of Jesus Christ, characterized specifically by his "self-emptying," "humility," and "obedience." The nonresistant posture Jesus will take in relation to Pontius Pilate and again on the road to Golgotha is not to be understood as exceptional behavior, but characteristic of who God decided to be in Jesus Christ from the very beginning. The preacher might note, along these lines, that the God who self-empties in order to be "with us" during the happiest and most hopeful moments of Christmas is also the self-emptying God who is with us during the hardest moments of Passiontide, entering deeply into the turmoil of betrayal, despair, agony, and death. This same one will leave no one behind even after he is "exalted . . . above all names" in the resurrection: "*every* knee will bend," the hymn tells us, and "*every* tongue" confess him as Lord—the Lord who does not lord over or engage from a distance, but who himself bows to meet us.

This text raises three controversial issues of concern to contemporary people of faith. First, it suggests a way of understanding the place and importance of the cross in the context of Jesus' entire life and person, correcting our tendency to isolate the crucifixion as the exclusive moment when Jesus' work of atonement is accomplished. Second, in portraying "every knee bending" and "every tongue confessing," it insists on the ultimate inclusion, in some way, of everyone. Does this argue for some form of universal salvation? Does it buttress imperialistic understandings of Christendom? Third, in an era when we are profoundly aware of the ways in which "servanthood" translates into "oppression," when, if at all, is it acceptable to "empty ourselves" in our relationship to one another? Is this a self-denial that devalues ourselves? Does it encourage passivity in the face of oppression? Furthermore, can we have the "same mind that was in Christ Jesus" without opening ourselves to the possibility of death? I will now briefly reflect upon these three vital areas of concern.

Atonement, the Cross, and the Entire Life and Ministry of Jesus Christ. Many Christians think of the cross as the singular site where the work of atonement was achieved through Jesus dying for our sins. Often this is coupled with the assumption that the Father somehow needed the Son to die in order to be able to forgive us. Serious questions about this assumption are today being raised both by those who identify as members of Christian communities and by those who have left the church because they are "done" with church teachings they find nonsensical, even abusive. Why, they are asking, would a sovereign God need Christ's death to remedy God's honor (as in substitution theory) or to pay a ransom to the devil?

The hymn of Philippians 2 helps us think in a different way about the significance of the cross, reminding us that the earliest Christians understood it in the context of Jesus' entire life of obedience rather than as a singular transaction necessary for delivering salvation. This idea that "the secret of the cross" is the "secret of the incarnation in all of its fullness"[1] might go a long way toward addressing the disillusionment and despair of those who are concerned that understanding the cross as payment for sins has distorted the central message of the Gospel: that God loves us freely, forgiving us without qualification or need for recompense.

On Palm/Passion Sunday the preacher might ponder with amazement the truth that the one who humbled himself at Christmas surrounded by wondrous cries of "Gloria!" is not only the one who today rides a borrowed donkey into Jerusalem to the sound of our glad cries of "Hosanna!" but also the one who will, in the week just ahead, refuse to abandon us when we yell, "Crucify him!" The cross, seen alongside the manger and the donkey, is a symbol of the divine steadfastness. Christ Jesus is "God with us" all along and for all eternity—with no qualification, holding nothing in reserve.

Universalism and Imperialism. The picture of a day when all will finally bow before Christ Jesus and confess him as Lord has a broad range of interpretations. Many Christians share Rob Bell's hope and conviction that the invitation to salvation has no expiration date; that God will wait until all have come to faith.[2] Others understand the scene more as a time of reckoning, when all will come to knowledge of the truth, even if it means recognizing they are rightly damned for not having accepted sooner. Some register concern that this scene promotes a kind of Christian hegemony. What about people of other religions? Does confession of Jesus as Lord require wholesale rejection of every other faith? In this era when we are having serious debate about the possibilities and limits of interfaith

dialogue, this text might well create an opportunity for the preacher to reflect on how difficult it is for Christian believers to be at once both inclusive and humble, truly manifesting "the mind of Christ" (2:5) in the ways that we converse with those outside of our immediate faith communities.

Self-emptying and Exaltation. In our cultural milieu, important questions are being raised about advocating "humility" and "obedience" across the board and equally for all, without taking particular contexts and systems driven by oppressive power dynamics into consideration. It is one thing to ask someone with a great deal of power to be self-emptying; it is another to ask one who has less power to give up what little they have. It was not so long ago that some preachers recommended "humility" and "obedience" to slaves. Similarly, too many women, convinced self-negating submission is a Christian virtue, have not fully developed and shared their own God-given talents, even allowing themselves to be used up by others. The popularity of books and talks that counter such abuses is a hopeful sign; bestsellers by Brené Brown, Maya Angelou, and Toni Morrison offer wisdom about how every person can be the self they were born to be.

Given these concerns and interests, preachers of Philippians 2 might attend as much to the exaltation of Christ as to his self-emptying. Similarly, pastoral caretakers and liturgists writing prayers of confession will want to be sensitive to multiple spiritual needs. For example, to have the "same mind" as Christ, some should be challenged to be more self-giving, repenting of their pride. However, others need be encouraged to live with greater cognizance of how precious they are, resisting shame and self-denigration as those who have been exalted in Christ. Any disciple who has been disempowered by the mishandled rhetoric of "submission" will surely find healing in the good news that Christ is lifted up—and we with him.

CYNTHIA L. RIGBY

1. Karl Barth, *Church Dogmatics*, IV/2 (Edinburgh: T. & T. Clark, 1958), 293.
2. Rob Bell, *Love Wins* (New York: HarperCollins, 2012).

Luke 22:14–23:56

[14]When the hour came, he took his place at the table, and the apostles with him. [15]He said to them, "I have eagerly desired to eat this Passover with you before I suffer; [16]for I tell you, I will not eat it until it is fulfilled in the kingdom of God." [17]Then he took a cup, and after giving thanks he said, "Take this and divide it among yourselves; [18]for I tell you that from now on I will not drink of the fruit of the vine until the kingdom of God comes." [19]Then he took a loaf of bread, and when he had given thanks, he broke it and gave it to them, saying, "This is my body, which is given for you. Do this in remembrance of me." [20]And he did the same with the cup after supper, saying, "This cup that is poured out for you is the new covenant in my blood. [21]But see, the one who betrays me is with me, and his hand is on the table. [22]For the Son of Man is going as it has been determined, but woe to that one by whom he is betrayed!" [23]Then they began to ask one another which one of them it could be who would do this.

[24]A dispute also arose among them as to which one of them was to be regarded as the greatest. [25]But he said to them, "The kings of the Gentiles lord it over them; and those in authority over them are called benefactors. [26]But not so with you; rather the greatest among you must become like the youngest, and the leader like one who serves. [27]For who is greater, the one who is at the table or the one who serves? Is it not the one at the table? But I am among you as one who serves.

[28]"You are those who have stood by me in my trials; [29]and I confer on you, just as my Father has conferred on me, a kingdom, [30]so that you may eat and drink at my table in my kingdom, and you will sit on thrones judging the twelve tribes of Israel.

[31]"Simon, Simon, listen! Satan has demanded to sift all of you like wheat, [32]but I have prayed for you that your own faith may not fail; and you, when once you have turned back, strengthen your brothers." [33]And he said to him, "Lord, I am ready to go with you to prison and to death!" [34]Jesus said, "I tell you, Peter, the cock will not crow this day, until you have denied three times that you know me."

[35]He said to them, "When I sent you out without a purse, bag, or sandals, did you lack anything?" They said, "No, not a thing." [36]He said to them, "But now, the one who has a purse must take it, and likewise a bag. And the one who has no sword must sell his cloak and buy one. [37]For I tell you, this scripture must be fulfilled in me, 'And he was counted among the lawless'; and indeed what is written about me is being fulfilled." [38]They said, "Lord, look, here are two swords." He replied, "It is enough."

[39]He came out and went, as was his custom, to the Mount of Olives; and the disciples followed him. [40]When he reached the place, he said to them, "Pray that you may not come into the time of trial." [41]Then he withdrew from them about a stone's throw, knelt down, and prayed, [42]"Father, if you are willing, remove this cup from me; yet, not my will but yours be done." [[43]Then an angel from heaven appeared to him and gave him strength. [44]In his anguish he prayed more earnestly, and his sweat became like great drops of blood falling down on the ground.] [45]When he got up from prayer, he came to the disciples and found them sleeping because of grief, [46]and he said to them, "Why are you sleeping? Get up and pray that you may not come into the time of trial."

[47]While he was still speaking, suddenly a crowd came, and the one called Judas, one of the twelve, was leading them. He approached Jesus to kiss him;

⁴⁸but Jesus said to him, "Judas, is it with a kiss that you are betraying the Son of Man?" ⁴⁹When those who were around him saw what was coming, they asked, "Lord, should we strike with the sword?" ⁵⁰Then one of them struck the slave of the high priest and cut off his right ear. ⁵¹But Jesus said, "No more of this!" And he touched his ear and healed him. ⁵²Then Jesus said to the chief priests, the officers of the temple police, and the elders who had come for him, "Have you come out with swords and clubs as if I were a bandit? ⁵³When I was with you day after day in the temple, you did not lay hands on me. But this is your hour, and the power of darkness!"

⁵⁴Then they seized him and led him away, bringing him into the high priest's house. But Peter was following at a distance. ⁵⁵ When they had kindled a fire in the middle of the courtyard and sat down together, Peter sat among them. ⁵⁶Then a servant-girl, seeing him in the firelight, stared at him and said, "This man also was with him." ⁵⁷But he denied it, saying, "Woman, I do not know him." ⁵⁸A little later someone else, on seeing him, said, "You also are one of them." But Peter said, "Man, I am not!" ⁵⁹Then about an hour later still another kept insisting, "Surely this man also was with him; for he is a Galilean." ⁶⁰But Peter said, "Man, I do not know what you are talking about!" At that moment, while he was still speaking, the cock crowed. ⁶¹The Lord turned and looked at Peter. Then Peter remembered the word of the Lord, how he had said to him, "Before the cock crows today, you will deny me three times." ⁶²And he went out and wept bitterly.

⁶³Now the men who were holding Jesus began to mock him and beat him; ⁶⁴they also blindfolded him and kept asking him, "Prophesy! Who is it that struck you?" ⁶⁵They kept heaping many other insults on him.

⁶⁶When day came, the assembly of the elders of the people, both chief priests and scribes, gathered together, and they brought him to their council. ⁶⁷They said, "If you are the Messiah, tell us." He replied, "If I tell you, you will not believe; ⁶⁸and if I question you, you will not answer. ⁶⁹But from now on the Son of Man will be seated at the right hand of the power of God." ⁷⁰All of them asked, "Are you, then, the Son of God?" He said to them, "You say that I am." ⁷¹Then they said, "What further testimony do we need? We have heard it ourselves from his own lips!"

²³:¹Then the assembly rose as a body and brought Jesus before Pilate. ²They began to accuse him, saying, "We found this man perverting our nation, forbidding us to pay taxes to the emperor, and saying that he himself is the Messiah, a king." ³Then Pilate asked him, "Are you the king of the Jews?" He answered, "You say so." ⁴Then Pilate said to the chief priests and the crowds, "I find no basis for an accusation against this man." ⁵But they were insistent and said, "He stirs up the people by teaching throughout all Judea, from Galilee where he began even to this place."

⁶When Pilate heard this, he asked whether the man was a Galilean. ⁷And when he learned that he was under Herod's jurisdiction, he sent him off to Herod, who was himself in Jerusalem at that time. ⁸When Herod saw Jesus, he was very glad, for he had been wanting to see him for a long time, because he had heard about him and was hoping to see him perform some sign. ⁹He questioned him at some length, but Jesus gave him no answer. ¹⁰The chief priests and the scribes stood by, vehemently accusing him. ¹¹Even Herod with his soldiers treated him with contempt and mocked him; then he put an elegant robe on him, and sent him back to Pilate. ¹²That same day Herod and Pilate became friends with each other; before this they had been enemies.

¹³Pilate then called together the chief priests, the leaders, and the people, ¹⁴and said to them, "You brought me this man as one who was perverting the people; and here I have examined him in your presence and have not found this

man guilty of any of your charges against him. [15]Neither has Herod, for he sent him back to us. Indeed, he has done nothing to deserve death. [16]I will therefore have him flogged and release him."

[18] Then they all shouted out together, "Away with this fellow! Release Barabbas for us!" [19](This was a man who had been put in prison for an insurrection that had taken place in the city, and for murder.) [20]Pilate, wanting to release Jesus, addressed them again; [21]but they kept shouting, "Crucify, crucify him!" [22]A third time he said to them, "Why, what evil has he done? I have found in him no ground for the sentence of death; I will therefore have him flogged and then release him." [23]But they kept urgently demanding with loud shouts that he should be crucified; and their voices prevailed. [24]So Pilate gave his verdict that their demand should be granted. [25]He released the man they asked for, the one who had been put in prison for insurrection and murder, and he handed Jesus over as they wished.

[26]As they led him away, they seized a man, Simon of Cyrene, who was coming from the country, and they laid the cross on him, and made him carry it behind Jesus. [27]A great number of the people followed him, and among them were women who were beating their breasts and wailing for him. [28]But Jesus turned to them and said, "Daughters of Jerusalem, do not weep for me, but weep for yourselves and for your children. [29]For the days are surely coming when they will say, 'Blessed are the barren, and the wombs that never bore, and the breasts that never nursed.' [30]Then they will begin to say to the mountains, 'Fall on us'; and to the hills, 'Cover us.' [31]For if they do this when the wood is green, what will happen when it is dry?"

[32]Two others also, who were criminals, were led away to be put to death with him. [33]When they came to the place that is called The Skull, they crucified Jesus there with the criminals, one on his right and one on his left. [[34]Then Jesus said, "Father, forgive them; for they do not know what they are doing."] And they cast lots to divide his clothing. [35]And the people stood by, watching; but the leaders scoffed at him, saying, "He saved others; let him save himself if he is the Messiah of God, his chosen one!" [36]The soldiers also mocked him, coming up and offering him sour wine, [37]and saying, "If you are the King of the Jews, save yourself!" [38]There was also an inscription over him, "This is the King of the Jews."

[39]One of the criminals who were hanged there kept deriding him and saying, "Are you not the Messiah? Save yourself and us!" [40]But the other rebuked him, saying, "Do you not fear God, since you are under the same sentence of condemnation? [41]And we indeed have been condemned justly, for we are getting what we deserve for our deeds, but this man has done nothing wrong." [42]Then he said, "Jesus, remember me when you come into your kingdom." [43]He replied, "Truly I tell you, today you will be with me in Paradise."

[44]It was now about noon, and darkness came over the whole land until three in the afternoon, [45]while the sun's light failed; and the curtain of the temple was torn in two. [46]Then Jesus, crying with a loud voice, said, "Father, into your hands I commend my spirit." Having said this, he breathed his last. [47]When the centurion saw what had taken place, he praised God and said, "Certainly this man was innocent." [48]And when all the crowds who had gathered there for this spectacle saw what had taken place, they returned home, beating their breasts. [49]But all his acquaintances, including the women who had followed him from Galilee, stood at a distance, watching these things.

[50]Now there was a good and righteous man named Joseph, who, though a member of the council, [51]had not agreed to their plan and action. He came from the Jewish town of Arimathea, and he was waiting expectantly for the kingdom of God. [52]This man went to Pilate and asked for the body of Jesus. [53]Then he

took it down, wrapped it in a linen cloth, and laid it in a rock-hewn tomb where no one had ever been laid. [54]It was the day of Preparation, and the sabbath was beginning. [55]The women who had come with him from Galilee followed, and they saw the tomb and how his body was laid. [56]Then they returned, and prepared spices and ointments.

On the sabbath they rested according to the commandment.

Commentary 1: Connecting the Reading with Scripture

The longer Liturgy of the Passion encompasses nearly two chapters of Luke's Gospel, while the shorter version tightens the focus to the trials, crucifixion, and death. Though Luke's telling is similar to Matthew and Mark and shares some features with John, the physician tells the story in his own way. Many of the important connections found in this reading are in the form of distinctions, as Luke underlines and highlights certain aspects of the passion through his telling.

We begin when "the hour" has come, signifying both the beginning of the Passover feast and the full weight of appointed time in the history of salvation. As in the other Synoptics, Jesus and the disciples are eating the meal that commemorates Israel's escape from Egypt, except Jesus reinterprets the supper as a meal at which his disciples will remember him as they anticipate the Passover's fulfillment in the kingdom of God. In Luke, this is the climactic meal in a series of dinners that have foreshadowed this supper, both narratively and theologically.

As in John, but unlike Matthew and Mark, Jesus now teaches the disciples through a conversation at the table. He first foretells his betrayal, and Luke uniquely places this *after* the meal, thus heightening both the grace of the supper and the betrayal by a friend. After this prediction, in a somewhat odd sequence, Luke inserts the disciples' dispute about greatness, but Jesus redirects their concerns by pointing to himself as their example. He is among them as one who serves, a statement which may recall for us Jesus washing the disciples' feet at the Last Supper in John.

As the conversation continues, Jesus warns Simon Peter and the others that their faith will be tested. "Satan," says Jesus, "has demanded to sift all of you like wheat" (Luke 22:31). Though

Peter objects, Jesus assures him his faith will indeed be tested and, moreover, that none of Peter's virtues will restore him to faith. Only Jesus' prayer for him will bring him back, and once he has returned, he will strengthen his brothers. While "brothers" indicates the other disciples, in Acts Luke uses *adelphoi* for Christians generally (Acts 1:15; 15:23, 32), and thus this conversation foreshadows Peter's role in the early Christian mission.

The last part of the after-dinner conversation presents a dramatic reversal of the instructions Jesus has given earlier in Luke. When he sent out the twelve (Luke 9:1–3) and the seventy others (Luke 10:1–12), he instructed them to carry nothing with them: no staff, no bag, no money. Now he tells them to gather the very things they left behind earlier: a purse, a bag, and a sword. There is a coming crisis for which they must now prepare, and these are the symbols of their preparation. Jesus is not speaking literally, but figuratively, about their spiritual readiness and resources to face opposition. The opposition that he now faces they will face later, when they set out in his name (Acts 8:1–3; 12:1–5). The literal-minded disciples, however, point to two swords, prompting Jesus to exclaim an exasperated, "Enough!" (Luke 22:38).

He then goes out to the Mount of Olives, and the disciples follow. Unlike Matthew and Mark, who recount a longer scene with multiple visits to sleeping disciples, Luke focuses on Jesus' prayer to the Father. In Luke 9, the Lord had set his face toward Jerusalem (Luke 9:51, 53), and this is the climax of that journey, as he decisively chooses ultimate faithfulness to God. Jesus prays that the Father would remove this "cup," recalling the cup of wrath that is reserved for the wicked in Isaiah, Lamentations, and the Psalms. Yet, he concludes, "not my will but yours be done" (Luke 22:42). The arrest, trials, and crucifixion are a consequence of this decisive moment on the Mount of Olives. Perhaps here more than anywhere else, Jesus' humanity and divinity are revealed in equal measure: he agonizes over his destiny, yet chooses God's will above his own.

After his prayer, Judas betrays him with a kiss. Those around him were ready to defend the Lord with violence, and one cut off a slave's right ear. Luke alone tells us that Jesus healed the servant's ear before handing himself over to the temple police. They could have arrested him earlier, in the daylight, but it was not yet time. Now is the "hour," and this hour is given to the power of darkness—a darkness that will cover creation when Jesus commends his spirit.

The temple police then take the Lord to the house of the high priest, where the prophecy of Peter's denial will be fulfilled and where Jesus will be beaten and mocked. Jesus' prophetic identity, a constant theme in Luke, is now underlined with betrayal and cruelty. He is brought before the council and asked if he is the Messiah. Earlier in Luke's Gospel this title might have had more political connotations, but here Luke intends it with full messianic force. Jesus responds, "From now on the Son of Man will be seated at the right hand of the power of God." The image of the right hand echoes Psalm 110:1, and the vision of the "Human One" coming to rule recalls Daniel 7:13. This was enough for them to take Jesus to Pilate.

At this point, the shorter Liturgy of the Passion continues through the four trials (unique to Luke), the sentencing, crucifixion, and death. Connections to those parts of the narrative are made in the commentary on that liturgy. The longer liturgy then concludes with the burial. Joseph, a member of the same council that handed Jesus over, asks Pilate to release the body

to him. Unlike Matthew, Luke does not tell us that Joseph is a disciple, only that he is a "good and righteous man." Like Anna and Simeon at the beginning of Luke's Gospel, Joseph was "waiting expectantly for the kingdom of God" (Luke 23:51). Joseph wraps the body and places it in a new tomb. The women, who would soon proclaim the resurrection, follow to see how the body was laid, presumably with insufficient washing and anointing, and then they return to prepare spices and ointments.

Today's other lectionary readings give prophetic and theological shape to the Lukan narrative. The reading from Isaiah 50 foreshadows much of the passion: Jesus "setting his face like a flint" (Isa. 50:7), which is the driving force of his journey to Jerusalem in Luke; his faithfulness to God on the Mount of Olives; Pilate's refusal to find him guilty; the insults and abuse he endures; and the peace with which he commends his spirit to the Father, trusting that "he who vindicates me is near" (Isa. 50:8). The hymn from Philippians 2 gives theological and cosmic shape to the passion, moving from Jesus' preexistence to incarnation, through the passion, to his exaltation and glorification.

The challenge in this liturgy for the preacher is how to handle such a long reading in worship and in the sermon. We often use the word "liturgy" to describe the printed words of a worship service, but at its deepest level "liturgy" means the work of the people of God, a work that is done in service to the wider world. If you choose to use the longer Liturgy of the Passion, perhaps it can become the primary and participatory work of the people on this day, with its proclamation contextualized through song and prayer. Performing this liturgy is a work in service to the world, for this reading tells the story of the long-awaited *hour* that proved to be the turn of the ages.

PATRICK W. T. JOHNSON

Commentary 2: Connecting the Reading with the World

We begin the journey from the table to the cross, the journey at the heart of our faith. It is the journey of Jesus and of the disciples, and

it is our journey. I learned an important lesson from a rabbi friend of mine, who helped me understand that when Jews tell the story of the

Passover, they are telling more than the story of what happened to people long ago. They are also telling the story of what they have experienced. They themselves have eaten the meal with staffs in hand. They have walked through the sea on dry land. I came to understand how important it is for us to enter into the passion narrative this way. We are the ones who sit at the table with Jesus. We are the ones who fall asleep in the garden. We declare, when questioned, "We do not know the man."

It is a journey filled with confusion, fear, and failure. It is also a journey in which we come to know fully this man Jesus. We recline at the table and are given the gift of bread and cup, the gift of his body and blood. We pray with Jesus in the garden and hear not only his anguish, but also his firm resolve. God has called him to this moment for us, that we will have life eternal, and he is willing to journey to the cross. We stand with the faithful disciples at the foot of that cross, with those who walked with Jesus to what they thought would be the end. This commentary cannot cover everything in the passion narrative, so I will highlight several landmarks along the journey to the cross.

This Is My Body. We are on a journey to open our eyes, our hearts, and our minds. Our journey begins with a meal. This was not the first time Jesus had taken bread, blessed and shared it (Luke 9:16). On that faraway hillside, with only five loaves and two fish, Jesus fed five thousand. The disciples had seen the signs and wonders Jesus could do. However, as they gathered in an upper room to share the Passover meal, it was only Jesus and the persons he had called.

We have entered into this most intimate holy moment to listen and watch as the Passover meal of freedom from slavery and death into new life is fulfilled. That night, as they told the story of their escape from Egypt and recalled their fear when they felt the army of Pharaoh approaching, they recognized that they were once again gathered in fear. The forces of the chief priests, scribes, and Pharisees were gathering. They were living through Passover once again.

God told Moses, "I have observed the misery of my people who are in Egypt. . . . Indeed, I know their sufferings. . . . I will be with you"

(Exod. 3:7, 12). The Passover is about God's liberating presence in the lives of the children of Israel. On this night it begins the final chapter of God's liberating presence through the life, death, resurrection, and ascension of Jesus. God is with us, the bread come down from heaven (John 6:51). Jesus takes bread, gives thanks, breaks it, and declares to them that on this night Jesus is giving them the gift of himself. This cup and this bread are, this night, his body and his blood given for the disciples, for us.

Luke assumed his reader had some understanding of the Passover meal. We cannot always assume that of our listeners. It may be important, if the sermon will focus on the Last Supper, to explore the history and meaning of that meal. It is this meal that we continue to share with one another in the Eucharist. It is the foretaste of the meal we will share in God's kingdom, and in that meal we declare Jesus was God with us, who came to reconcile us and bring us the gift of everlasting life.

As we walk with Jesus on the way to the cross, he is the incarnation of the Passover. It is a journey through the agony in the garden, the trial before the powerful, and the torture of the cross. It is a journey of faithfulness to God and to the children of God.

Are We Willing? The passion narrative tells the story of the last hours of Jesus' life. It also tells of the testing of Peter and the disciples. The time of trial for the Messiah and his followers has begun. What does it mean to declare to our savior, "I am ready to go with you to prison and to death" (Luke 22:33)? Are we willing to join the walk to the cross?

Throughout Luke's Gospel we witness the complicated relationship between Jesus and Peter. While Peter was willing to put down his net when called by Jesus, his response to the miraculous catch was one of fear: "Go away from me, Lord, for I am a sinful man!" (Luke 5:8). It was Peter who was able to declare that Jesus was the Messiah. When confronted with the reality of the journey that lay before the anointed one of God, Peter refused to listen (Mark 8:31–32).

As the disciples gather with Jesus at the meal lifting up God's love and the life of freedom, their table is also marked by human frailty.

Events will now unfold fulfilling all that has been ordained. Jesus knows that he will share no more meals with his disciples on this side of God's reign. He also looks into the future actions of his disciples. At the table reclining with Jesus are the man who will betray him and the man who will deny him. As the disciples eat with Jesus, no doubt trying to decide what he meant by his baffling comments about his body and blood, Jesus confronts them with uncomfortable accusations. One, who is left unnamed, will betray Jesus. Jesus also confronts Peter with the knowledge that he will deny his relationship with Jesus—not once, but three times.

In these final hours the disciples betray and deny. They argue who will be the greatest. Like the disciples on the Mount of the Transfiguration, they fall asleep in the garden while Jesus prays. They strike out at those who come to arrest Jesus, thinking that theirs will be a battle of swords, not of love. But Jesus declares to them and to us, what it means to walk the way of the cross. Like Jesus, they are to become like the youngest, like the least, like one who serves. Yes, he declares, they will betray and abandon him, but they will also turn back to him; and when they do, it will be their mission to strengthen their sisters and brothers. When they turn back, he wants them to know that they will "eat and drink at my table in my kingdom" (Luke 22:30).

Are we willing to journey to the cross, to pick up our cross daily? We pick up the cross through the myriad decisions we make, decisions that seek for justice and mercy. We pick up our cross when we confront the powers of violence and evil. We pick up our cross when we bring comfort and joy. May we pray for strength that we are able to make the walk as true disciples of the one who gave his life that we might have life abundantly.

LUCY LIND HOGAN

Luke 23:1–49

[1]Then the assembly rose as a body and brought Jesus before Pilate. [2]They began to accuse him, saying, "We found this man perverting our nation, forbidding us to pay taxes to the emperor, and saying that he himself is the Messiah, a king." [3]Then Pilate asked him, "Are you the king of the Jews?" He answered, "You say so." [4]Then Pilate said to the chief priests and the crowds, "I find no basis for an accusation against this man." [5]But they were insistent and said, "He stirs up the people by teaching throughout all Judea, from Galilee where he began even to this place."

[6]When Pilate heard this, he asked whether the man was a Galilean. [7]And when he learned that he was under Herod's jurisdiction, he sent him off to Herod, who was himself in Jerusalem at that time. [8]When Herod saw Jesus, he was very glad, for he had been wanting to see him for a long time, because he had heard about him and was hoping to see him perform some sign. [9]He questioned him at some length, but Jesus gave him no answer. [10]The chief priests and the scribes stood by, vehemently accusing him. [11]Even Herod with his soldiers treated him with contempt and mocked him; then he put an elegant robe on him, and sent him back to Pilate. [12]That same day Herod and Pilate became friends with each other; before this they had been enemies.

[13]Pilate then called together the chief priests, the leaders, and the people, [14]and said to them, "You brought me this man as one who was perverting the people; and here I have examined him in your presence and have not found this man guilty of any of your charges against him. [15]Neither has Herod, for he sent him back to us. Indeed, he has done nothing to deserve death. [16]I will therefore have him flogged and release him."

[18]Then they all shouted out together, "Away with this fellow! Release Barabbas for us!" [19](This was a man who had been put in prison for an insurrection that had taken place in the city, and for murder.) [20]Pilate, wanting to release Jesus, addressed them again; [21]but they kept shouting, "Crucify, crucify him!" [22]A third time he said to them, "Why, what evil has he done? I have found in him no ground for the sentence of death; I will therefore have him flogged and then release him." [23]But they kept urgently demanding with loud shouts that he should be crucified; and their voices prevailed. [24]So Pilate gave his verdict that their demand should be granted. [25]He released the man they asked for, the one who had been put in prison for insurrection and murder, and he handed Jesus over as they wished.

[26]As they led him away, they seized a man, Simon of Cyrene, who was coming from the country, and they laid the cross on him, and made him carry it behind Jesus. [27]A great number of the people followed him, and among them were women who were beating their breasts and wailing for him. [28]But Jesus turned to them and said, "Daughters of Jerusalem, do not weep for me, but weep for yourselves and for your children. [29]For the days are surely coming when they will say, 'Blessed are the barren, and the wombs that never bore, and the breasts that never nursed.' [30]Then they will begin to say to the mountains, 'Fall on us'; and to the hills, 'Cover us.' [31]For if they do this when the wood is green, what will happen when it is dry?"

[32]Two others also, who were criminals, were led away to be put to death with him. [33]When they came to the place that is called The Skull, they crucified Jesus there with the criminals, one on his right and one on his left. [[34]Then Jesus said,

"Father, forgive them; for they do not know what they are doing."] And they cast lots to divide his clothing. [35]And the people stood by, watching; but the leaders scoffed at him, saying, "He saved others; let him save himself if he is the Messiah of God, his chosen one!" [36]The soldiers also mocked him, coming up and offering him sour wine, [37]and saying, "If you are the King of the Jews, save yourself!" [38]There was also an inscription over him, "This is the King of the Jews."

[39]One of the criminals who were hanged there kept deriding him and saying, "Are you not the Messiah? Save yourself and us!" [40]But the other rebuked him, saying, "Do you not fear God, since you are under the same sentence of condemnation? [41]And we indeed have been condemned justly, for we are getting what we deserve for our deeds, but this man has done nothing wrong." [42]Then he said, "Jesus, remember me when you come into your kingdom." [43]He replied, "Truly I tell you, today you will be with me in Paradise."

[44]It was now about noon, and darkness came over the whole land until three in the afternoon, [45]while the sun's light failed; and the curtain of the temple was torn in two. [46]Then Jesus, crying with a loud voice, said, "Father, into your hands I commend my spirit." Having said this, he breathed his last. [47]When the centurion saw what had taken place, he praised God and said, "Certainly this man was innocent." [48]And when all the crowds who had gathered there for this spectacle saw what had taken place, they returned home, beating their breasts. [49]But all his acquaintances, including the women who had followed him from Galilee, stood at a distance, watching these things.

Commentary 1: Connecting the Reading with Scripture

In the shorter reading of the passion liturgy, our attention is focused on the trial, sentencing, and crucifixion of Jesus. We start in the middle of the story, when Jesus has been arrested by chief priests, elders, and officers of the temple police. The morning after his arrest, he is brought to the "assembly of elders of the people, both chief priests and scribes," who present him before their council (Luke 22:66ff.). They first ask Jesus if he is the Messiah, and he answers cryptically. Then they ask, "Are you the Son of God?" Jesus cannot honestly deny the charge, yet he cannot affirm it either. His accusers are seeking to define his identity with labels they misunderstand and distort. He is the Son of God, but not in the way they think. So he replies, "You say so." Jesus' nonanswer is enough for the assembly to rise "as a body" and bring Jesus before Pilate.

Luke has already introduced us to Pontius Pilate. Pilate was the Roman governor of Judah (3:1), and a story was circulated that Pilate had mingled the blood of some Galileans with their sacrifices (13:1). Pilate has no interest in religious charges of blasphemy, so the accusers appeal to his core concerns: Jesus is agitating the people by forbidding them to pay taxes to the emperor and claiming to be a king. Their charges seem ill-founded to Pilate, but when he hears that Jesus is a Galilean, he sends him to see Herod, governor of Galilee.

Luke is the only evangelist who includes this trial before Herod. Herod had imprisoned and beheaded John the Baptist (9:9), and Joanna, the wife of Herod's steward, Chuza, followed Jesus from early days (8:3). On his way to Jerusalem, when Jesus hears Herod has decided to kill him, he sends word back to "that fox" that if he is going to die, it will be in Jerusalem (13:31–33). So now they meet in Jerusalem. Like others of the "evil generation" who ask for a sign (11:29), Herod hopes Jesus will dazzle him with a miracle. He gets neither sign nor answer, only silence. Surely disappointed, Herod contents himself with mocking the man, dressing him up, and sending him back to Pilate.

Again, in this fourth trial, Pilate finds no evidence that Jesus is guilty of the charges. Nevertheless the "chief priests, the leaders, and the people" shout that they want Jesus taken away and Barabbas released instead. Pilate tries again, but the crowd still shouts, "Crucify, crucify him!" A third time Pilate tries, but the condemnation of the crowd prevails. This scene is somewhat baffling in Luke, as the evangelist depicts Pilate as an innocent and relatively weak magistrate who pleads with the crowds three times. By all accounts, both within the New Testament and in Josephus, Pilate is a man known for authoritarian violence and a shrewd politician. Rather than bowing to the will of the crowd, it seems more likely that Pilate makes a calculated decision to let one person die, though unjustly, and keep the peace. His reasoning is no different from that of Caiaphas in John 11, or that of anyone who sacrifices justice on the altar of the "greater good."

So "they" led him away. Who are "they"? Luke does not introduce Roman soldiers here. In the way he tells the story, the ones who lead Jesus away are the ones to whom Pilate has handed Jesus over, "as they wished" (23:25). In the narrative, "they" are the chief priests, the leaders, and the people who have clamored for Jesus' crucifixion. Yet, "they" may also provide a doorway through which to bring the congregation into the story. A danger in Luke's narrative, as in the other Gospels, is for us blithely to lay blame for Jesus' crucifixion at the feet of the Jewish leaders and Jewish people. The preacher could use Luke's ambiguous "they" to bring *us* into the shouting crowd and to place *us* with those who lead Jesus away. If we think this whole tragic scene is about the sins of *other* people, we have missed the point.

As they lead Jesus to be crucified, Simon the Cyrene is drafted to carry the cross. Luke does not tell us why he was pressed into service, yet it is hard to miss the significance of the image. It is one of three portraits of discipleship in this crucifixion scene. Simon embodies Jesus' own definition of discipleship, "carrying the cross" and following him daily in a path of self-denial, even if that path leads to the ultimate self-denial of martyrdom (cf. 9:23; 14:27). In this sense, Simon the Cyrene dramatizes the basic posture of following Jesus. The emphasis is not on his opinion of Jesus, or even his belief in Jesus. Rather, he is pressed into Jesus' service, taking up the cross and following in this way.

Once they arrive at the place called The Skull, which is Luke's translation of the Aramaic "Golgotha," Jesus is crucified between two criminals. Here we find echoes of Isaiah 53:12, "he poured out himself to death, and was numbered with the transgressors." With Jesus on the cross, "they" (Luke still has no soldiers in the narrative) gambled for Jesus' clothing, and the leaders mocked him. Just as Simon dramatizes Jesus' understanding of discipleship, so Jesus dramatizes the tragedy of the psalmist's lament in Psalm 22, both in the division of clothes (Ps. 22:17–18) and in the mockery of "all who see me" (Ps. 22:7).

Amid the taunts of the gathered people, we come to the climax of the crucifixion scene in Luke, a scene only Luke portrays. One of the criminals begins to taunt Jesus, but the other comes to Jesus' defense. The theme of innocence is struck again, as he too declares Jesus unjustly condemned. He then asks Jesus to "remember me when you come into your kingdom." The sign "King of the Jews" was placed over Jesus' head in mockery, but the criminal sees truth behind the taunt. He gives us yet another portrait of discipleship, and this scene encapsulates the saving nature of Jesus' death in Luke.

Throughout the Gospel, Jesus has been described as a Savior. When he began his ministry, in Luke 4, he read promises of salvation from the scroll of Isaiah. When he rolled up the scroll, he declared, "*Today* this scripture has been fulfilled in your hearing" (4:21). Now, responding to this fellow prisoner, Jesus says, "*Today* you will be with me in Paradise" (23:43). At his death, Jesus thus accomplishes the saving promise of his ministry to suffering people, even those of us who are "getting what we deserve" (23:41). Jesus extends mercy to all who turn to him, and welcomes them to be with him in paradise.

Finally, we come to Jesus' death. Just before he dies, darkness covers the land and the veil of the temple is torn in two. When Jesus submitted himself to arrest, he told those who came for him, "This is your hour, and the power of darkness" (22:53). Now the power of darkness is at its peak. Jesus, however, is at peace. Luke gives us no cry of dereliction, but draws on Psalm 31 as Jesus entrusts himself to God.

Following his death, we hear a final declaration of innocence, this time from a Roman centurion who thereby "glorifies God." Luke concludes the scene at the cross with the women from Galilee looking on. Unlike the crowds, who beat their breasts, they are not gawking. They are *bearing witness*, painting a third portrait of discipleship, as those who follow Jesus attend to him with love.

PATRICK W. T. JOHNSON

Commentary 2: Connecting the Reading with the World

The journey that began at the river Jordan draws to a close. As he came up out of the water, Jesus heard the assurance of God's love and faithfulness: "You are my Son, the Beloved; with you I am well pleased" (Luke 3:22). It is a journey that will end with his faithfulness, "Not my will but yours be done" (22:42). As the church moves into the days of Holy Week, we will walk the journey that helps us to understand what it means to live a life following God's will.

At Christmas we tell the story of a baby laid in a manger (2:7). On Good Friday we tell of a man laid in a rock-hewn tomb (23:53). On Easter we shout for joy that the tomb was empty, "Why do you look for the living among the dead? He is not here, but has risen" (24:5). An important part of our faith journey is also telling the story of the trial and execution of that man at the hand of oppressors. Paul correctly observed, "the message of the cross is foolishness to those who are perishing" (1 Cor. 1:18). We must continue to proclaim not only the birth and resurrection, but also Jesus' death on the cross. Jesus proclaimed, "If any want to become my followers, let them deny themselves and take up their cross daily and follow me" (Luke 9:23). We must daily be reminded, "Whoever does not carry the cross and follow me cannot be my disciple" (14:27). We walk the way of the cross with Jesus to know what it means to be his disciples, to take up the cross, and to follow in his faithful footsteps.

The Time of Trial. Immediately after his baptism, the Spirit led Jesus into the time of trial in the wilderness. There the devil tested Jesus, urging him to forsake his call from God and follow the way of the world. When Jesus did not succumb to the devil, the devil "departed from him until an opportune time" (4:13). That time has now come. The devil has returned. Judas will betray Jesus (22:3). Peter will deny Jesus. Jesus will enter into his final time of trial. What does it mean to follow God's will?

While this text, Luke 23:1–49, begins with Jesus' appearance before Pilate, one might argue that Jesus' time of trial began in the Garden of Gethsemane. What choices lay before Jesus? Would he follow toward safety, away from those who were seeking to arrest him and possibly have him killed? Was that his will? Is that the path we, so often, want to follow? Jesus prayed that God would "remove the cup from me" (22: 42). This journey, this time of trial is not about following our own path, but the narrow path of God, "not my will but yours be done" (22:42).

As the journey continues, Jesus appears before the council of chief priests and scribes. The council wants to know the answer to only one question, the question that has been central to Luke's Gospel: is Jesus the Messiah? Again we hear the titles voiced on the lips of the council: Messiah and Son of God.

In this first trial scene the focus is on Jesus' blasphemy. Then, having decided that Jesus claimed to be the Messiah, as one they hand Jesus over to the Roman authorities. However, when presented to Pilate, Jesus now is accused of political crimes, urging people not to pay their taxes and claiming to be a king. Back and forth the scenes then change: from Pilate to Herod and back to Pilate.

Jesus has told his disciples what it means to be the Messiah. He has come not to be a king of this world. He is not going to free them from the Roman oppressors as so many have hoped. He enters Jerusalem on a donkey, not on the horse of a king. To be the beloved Son of God, to be God's chosen one, means that he "must undergo great suffering, and be rejected by the elders, chief priests, and scribes, and be killed"

(9:22). How does Jesus answer his accusers? He tells the council that he will not answer them, because they will not believe. Likewise Jesus answers Pilate's question, "Are you the king of the Jews?" with the simple declaration, "You say so" (23:3).

As we take this final walk with Jesus, we learn what the time of trial is like. It is to be faithful to the God who created us, who loves us. It is to be willing to be handed over to those who "hate you, . . . revile you, and defame you" (6:22). In those times we keep our eyes on Jesus, who is faithful to the end. We are upheld by the stories of the saints who went before us, those who were faithful in their time of trial. Christians today who suffer for their faith also surround us. We do well to lift up their stories. We draw strength from their examples.

Release Barabbas. An important question that needed to be answered by the Gospel writers and by Christians in the centuries following was, Who was responsible for the death of Jesus? Did the blame fall on the Jewish officials, the crowd, or the Roman occupiers?

Luke wrote his story for a particular people at a particular time. Given the relationship between the followers of Jesus and the Jewish leaders, it is understandable that the early church wanted to place the blame solely on the Jewish authorities. It was Jewish leaders and a Jewish crowd calling for Pilate to crucify Jesus. The Jewish leaders brought Jesus before Pilate. They certainly bear responsibility. The crucifixion was, according to Roman law, the punishment for a civil offense. They too bear responsibility. Is this a question we must also explore today?

We have witnessed horrific retribution against the Jewish people, even to the past century, for having been held responsible for Jesus' death. This question is still relevant in a world marked by religious violence and persecution: Who is responsible? If we walk to the cross with Jesus, we want to place ourselves alongside the cheering crowd entering Jerusalem. We want to be with the faithful women at the foot of the cross. Should we not also stand in the crowd calling for Pilate to demand the release of Barabbas and the crucifixion of Jesus? In the end, might we all bear the responsibility for the death of Jesus?

Jesus reminded us that when we ignore the poor, the hungry, and the oppressed, we are ignoring him. When we remain silent as the innocent suffer persecution and death, are we responsible? We betray and deny Jesus when we ignore the pain of our world. We reject all that he has done for us. Even from the cross, the one who was obedient even to death proclaimed a message of love and acceptance: "Father, forgive them; for they do not know what they are doing" (23:34). We do not always know what we are doing, but year after year we, the followers of Jesus, walk the way of the cross so that we can learn what we must do. We make the walk so that we will be able to pick up our cross and be faithful to the God who loves us into eternal life.

LUCY LIND HOGAN

Holy Thursday

Exodus 12:1–4 (5–10), 11–14   1 Corinthians 11:23–26
Psalm 116:1–2, 12–19   John 13:1–17, 31b–35

Exodus 12:1–4 (5–10), 11–14

¹The LORD said to Moses and Aaron in the land of Egypt: ²This month shall mark for you the beginning of months; it shall be the first month of the year for you. ³Tell the whole congregation of Israel that on the tenth of this month they are to take a lamb for each family, a lamb for each household. ⁴If a household is too small for a whole lamb, it shall join its closest neighbor in obtaining one; the lamb shall be divided in proportion to the number of people who eat of it. ⁵Your lamb shall be without blemish, a year-old male; you may take it from the sheep or from the goats. ⁶You shall keep it until the fourteenth day of this month; then the whole assembled congregation of Israel shall slaughter it at twilight. ⁷They shall take some of the blood and put it on the two doorposts and the lintel of the houses in which they eat it. ⁸They shall eat the lamb that same night; they shall eat it roasted over the fire with unleavened bread and bitter herbs. ⁹Do not eat any of it raw or boiled in water, but roasted over the fire, with its head, legs, and inner organs. ¹⁰You shall let none of it remain until the morning; anything that remains until the morning you shall burn. ¹¹This is how you shall eat it: your loins girded, your sandals on your feet, and your staff in your hand; and you shall eat it hurriedly. It is the passover of the LORD. ¹²For I will pass through the land of Egypt that night, and I will strike down every firstborn in the land of Egypt, both human beings and animals; on all the gods of Egypt I will execute judgments: I am the LORD. ¹³The blood shall be a sign for you on the houses where you live: when I see the blood, I will pass over you, and no plague shall destroy you when I strike the land of Egypt.

¹⁴This day shall be a day of remembrance for you. You shall celebrate it as a festival to the LORD; throughout your generations you shall observe it as a perpetual ordinance.

Commentary 1: Connecting the Reading with Scripture

Sobering. Troubling. Powerful. What adjective best describes the narrative that unfolds around Exodus 12? Within the book of Exodus itself, this chapter summarizes the experiences of the people to this point in the overall story. The people cry out to God because they suffer under the cruel oppression of Pharaoh (2:23–25). God sends Moses to confront Pharaoh. God and Pharaoh engage in a battle, with God using the tools of creation as weapons. Through Moses, the Lord describes a ritual that will remind the people of Israel how they gained their freedom, identity, and mission (19:1–6). The ritual

contains the haunting reminder that Israel's formation involved the death of children. Such a reminder would puncture any temptation toward arrogance. How could God's people not feel troubled by the death of children who had not caused either the stubbornness of Pharaoh or their suffering? At a minimum, the people would look back on the event with powerful emotions as they reflected on how God propelled them into the wilderness.

In multiple ways, the ritual of the Passover influences the Hebrew slaves who become God's people, Israel. The ritual reorients their perspective on time. The month of Passover (Nisan) becomes the beginning of months. The people celebrate their new identity at the start of the year. Passover occurs within the family, a basic unit of society. Economic necessity may bring two families together. The family divides the lamb in an equitable manner. Because the families choose a lamb without blemish, the ritual reflects the respect toward God of offering the best. The family does not sacrifice the lamb to God as in a burnt offering, but the principle of offering an animal without blemish still applies. The required dress and instruction to eat hurriedly physically link the ritual to the worshipers' own bodies, as does the taste of the bitter herbs. When enacted, the comprehensive ritual serves to connect the worshiper to the body, the family, the community, time, the mystery of freedom, and to God.

The word of the Lord coming through Moses initiates a ritual to commemorate the escape from Egypt and the new identity. God establishes the ritual before the actual departure. The ritual enables the people to maintain the memory of their identity. Exodus 12:21–28 contains a second account of the ritual (likely from a source different from verses 1–14). That second account emphasizes more clearly that the purpose of the ritual is to instruct children in its meaning.

A significant theological conflict emerges when this passage is placed in the context of the Pentateuch, including the rest of the book of Exodus. The image of a caring God who hears the cries of the people and wants to bless all of humanity is difficult to reconcile with the violence involved in the escape from Egypt and the conquest of the promised land. Jewish and Christian interpreters struggle with the narrative of the death of the firstborn Egyptians. Throughout the ages, readers have lamented the death of the Egyptian children, though Egyptian history contains no record of such an event. The contemporary emphasis on the Old Testament narratives as story instead of history reassures us that no children actually died. Nevertheless, this narrative plays a defining role in the identity of God's people, who escaped from Egyptian bondage. The narrative speaks to an understanding of God, not an historical event. The image of God in the narrative should cause

contemporary interpreters much discomfort. However stubborn Pharaoh comes across in the narrative, the children who died bore no responsibility for his obstinacy. As with the Noah story (Gen. 6–8), the image of God strikes the reader as unnecessarily punitive.

Although the reader recoils at the violence of the Passover event (see 12:29–32), the whole book of Exodus and the Pentateuch bring balance to the image of God in this narrative. A verse that stands in tension with the violent images of the Passover appears in Genesis 12:3, which declares to Abraham that "in you all the families of the earth shall be blessed." Abraham's descendants had the mission of becoming a universal means of blessing. Within the book of Exodus, the role of the people of Israel includes becoming a "priestly kingdom" (Exod. 19:6). Part of the role of a priest involves mediating God's presence to the people. A priestly kingdom would mediate God's presence to the world. Even the escape from Egypt itself had as one of its purposes the revelation of YHWH's presence to the Egyptians (Exod. 7:5).

Some of the commands of God within the Pentateuch toward the inhabitants of the promised land further complicate the picture of Israel's mission. Deuteronomy affirms the exodus experience as God's act on behalf of the people: "He brought you out of Egypt with his own presence, by his great power" (Deut. 4:37b). This image of God's acts on behalf of Israel stands in tension with the treatment of the people of Canaan. Deuteronomy 7:2 contains the instruction to "utterly destroy" the people already living in the land. The Deuteronomistic History (Joshua–2 Kings) reinforces this commandment (see Josh. 3:10). Taken together, the two sides of the theological tension are, on the one hand, God's care for the oppressed Israelites and their universal mission and, on the other, the deaths of the Egyptian children and the people living in Canaan. God intends Israel as a blessing to all people, and a priestly entity; yet that identity involves much death and violence. Jewish and Christian readers cannot easily resolve this tension and must live with it. The church and synagogue can affirm that God's call to Abraham to become the parent of those who will bring a universal blessing represents the most basic understanding of God's purposes. One interprets the exodus and the Passover in light of that call. Israel is God's chosen people, but at a terrible cost.

Reading this passage from Exodus in the context of the lectionary passages for Holy Thursday moves the church from one violent event, the death of the Egyptian children, to preparation for another violent event, the cross. The readings from John 13 and 1 Corinthians 11 give the two versions of what happened at the Last Supper. John's foot washing forms part of the farewell discourse, and Paul's teaching describes the institution of the sacrament. Both passages presuppose Jesus' crucifixion. Both John and Paul interpret Jesus' violent death as an event through which God intentionally worked (1 Cor. 1:18; John 12:27–34).

In both Testaments the act of violence resulted in healing, redemption, and blessing. No passage of Scripture explains the violence necessary for salvation in a way that resolves all of the tension and answers the agonizing questions. The reader can only affirm that God's ultimate purpose was reconciliation and salvation. As part of the preparation for Passover, the people of Israel receive the instruction to share a lamb with neighboring families who cannot afford a lamb themselves. The act of securing a lamb leads to sharing. Jesus' new commandment to the disciples is to love one another. As part of the preparation for a barbaric act of crucifixion, Jesus establishes the defining characteristic of the church as love. Paul interprets the sacrament, commemorating a great act of violence, as a unifying event in the life of the church. Just as sharing the lamb brought unity to the people of Israel, so the sacrament should foster unity in the church. The sacrament brings together persons who normally experience separation over socioeconomic stratification (1 Cor. 11:18–22). The church and synagogue do not use violence for their purposes, recognizing the conciliatory purpose underlying the violence of the Passover and the cross.

CHARLES L. AARON JR.

Commentary 2: Connecting the Reading with the World

As with many of the texts in Holy Week that we reflect on yearly, interpreting the text of Passover can become stale. The connections in the history of Christian interpretation of lamb and blood symbolism with Christ and Christ's blood can become so dominant in our interpretations that we lose sight of the original context of the Exodus narrative. Our tendency in Christian circles to focus on redemption and salvation through Christ, while appropriate to the tradition, might preclude us from making connections with other biblical traditions. The inclusion of this text for Maundy Thursday in the lectionary potentially narrows our perspective, as does the parenthetical inclusion of verses 5–10, which seems to indicate that these verses are less important to the Christian community than verses 1–4 or 11–14. When we, however, take the narrative context of the exodus event itself into consideration, we might find that there are even more palpable connections in Scripture and beyond that impact our understanding of Passover and remind us of its social significance.

The Passover story is a liminal and disturbing text that describes the gateway from slavery to liberation. Within the narrative context of the exodus, the Passover text serves as a pause for the community to gain strength for the journey. The pause, however, is an urgent pause—not a time of rest, but a mustering of faith. The parenthetical inclusion of verses 5–10 indicates secondary importance for the Christian liturgy, a neglect that might stem from the Christian, and often Protestant, tendency to shun priestly matters associated with Judaism and Catholicism. Verses 5–6 begin by articulating the type of lamb for the sacrifice and the precise date of the ritual. Verse 6 also emphasizes the unity of an entire community on the precipice of its flight from captivity. Everyone in the community will slaughter the same type of unblemished, male lamb. This will occur at twilight, a liminal time signifying the end of one day and the beginning of the next, when read in context with the pattern of evening and morning in the Genesis 1 creation narrative. The application of the blood in verse 7 serves as a sign of protection as God passes through the land that marks each obedient Hebrew household for omission during the final plague. Verses 8–10 illustrate the urgency of the meal, with the Hebrews roasting and eating the lamb the same night, incinerating any leftovers. Verse 11 explains the urgency: events the following morning will move quickly, and the Hebrews must be ready to embark with their loins girded, shoes on, and staff at the ready.

In the narrative context of this passage, the Hebrews had already witnessed God's destructive plagues, and verse 12 tells them they will witness the final and most bloody of God's judgment upon their oppressors: the death of every firstborn human and animal. The prospect of the Hebrews' liberation will come at a high cost of human and animal life, highlighting God's sovereignty and judgment over the empire that holds them captive. The blood of the lamb serves as a sign of protection, but is also an ominous foreshadowing of the blood of the Egyptians spilt in the night.

The liminal setting between slavery and liberation echoes itself throughout the history of Israel. As Terence E. Fretheim notes, in the annual celebration of this ritual, "every generation of Israelites was the recipient of God's exodus-shaped redemption."[1] The Passover represents the birth of the nation of Israel out of captivity, as well as the marriage between Israel and God in later traditions. Jewish tradition, for example, reads the Song of Songs at Passover as an expression of the love between God and Israel.

The book of Ezekiel embellishes the tradition and turns its dangerous nature back upon the people of Israel. In one of Ezekiel's visions, God calls a man clothed in linen to pass through Jerusalem placing a mark on the foreheads of everyone who mourns the abominations committed inside the temple (Ezek. 9:4). The term for "pass through" is the same verb in Hebrew used in Exodus 12:12 describing God's passing through Egypt. God then instructs executioners to follow behind the man clothed in linen

and kill everyone who does not bear the mark. Like those who have the mark on their doorpost (Exod. 12:13), only those who have the mark will survive. Utilizing the trope of the reversal of expectations, the text employs the Passover motif—usually associated with liberation from Egypt—to depict the calamity of Israel itself. One can also see the travel urgency of Exodus 12:8–11 in a symbolic action Ezekiel later performs in Ezekiel 12. In this chapter, God instructs Ezekiel to pack gear for travel to symbolize the coming exile of the people of Israel. Ezekiel complies, preparing for the journey during the day and breaking through the wall in the evening, carrying his travel gear precisely as God instructed (Ezek. 12:7).

When read in the fullness of the tradition the Passover certainly recalls liberation, but even the exodus tradition of liberation leads to a forty-year exile in the wilderness. The exodus tradition and its later prophetic appropriation in Ezekiel emphasize that while the trajectory of the tradition is freedom, the freedom comes only toward the end of an arduous journey. The Passover symbolizes the trek's beginning, not its conclusion. When read in this light, perhaps we might find other connections with the long-suffering path toward liberation to which this passage summons us. As we remember the plight of the earliest Hebrew slaves, who had witnessed the shock and awe of God's destructive plagues and who long for a new start, we might look toward other communities of suffering, perhaps even our own, and empathize with the struggles of refugee groups who have witnessed the shock and awe of modern warfare, terrorism, economic disparities, and other natural and human-caused traumas with a new sense of urgency. How do we reflect on Passover and the possibilities of the long and wearying process of liberation, even as we reflect on the activity of a dangerous God in the world?

The final verse in the lection. Exodus 12:14, establishes the yearly ritual of remembrance that also serves as the model for the Last Supper in the Synoptic Gospel traditions (Matt. 26:17–30; Mark 14:12–25; Luke 22:14–23) and the text from 1 Corinthians 11:23–26 listed as a reading

---

1. Terence E. Fretheim, *Exodus*, Interpretation (Louisville, KY: John Knox Press, 1991), 135.

for Maundy Thursday during Holy Week. Placing the Passover festival in its narrative context of the liberation from Egypt reminds us during Holy Week to place our commemoration of the Last Supper itself in the narrative context of the Gospels. Just as the Passover feast preceded the Israelites' difficult transition from a group of slaves to a free people, the Last Supper, celebrated on the most liminal of evenings in the Christian tradition, precedes both Christ's suffering in the days ahead and the long and difficult transition from a group of disciples to the early church.

In times of plenty, the reading of Passover and the Last Supper reminds us of God's dangerous judgment of oppression, lest we abuse our own privilege. In times of transition, our taking into account all of the solemn details of the tradition gives us energy for what lies ahead, tempered by the realism that we may have many miles to go. In times of exile, the yearly observance may give us pause as we muster our faith to continue the journey, reminding us of our beginnings with God, as well as our trajectory toward freedom.

DAVID G. GARBER JR.

Psalm 116:1–2, 12–19

¹I love the LORD, because he has heard
    my voice and my supplications.
²Because he inclined his ear to me,
    therefore I will call on him as long as I live.
. . . .
¹²What shall I return to the LORD
    for all his bounty to me?
¹³I will lift up the cup of salvation
    and call on the name of the LORD,
¹⁴I will pay my vows to the LORD
    in the presence of all his people.
¹⁵Precious in the sight of the LORD
    is the death of his faithful ones.
¹⁶O LORD, I am your servant;
    I am your servant, the child of your serving girl.
    You have loosed my bonds.
¹⁷I will offer to you a thanksgiving sacrifice
    and call on the name of the LORD.
¹⁸I will pay my vows to the LORD
    in the presence of all his people,
¹⁹in the courts of the house of the LORD,
    in your midst, O Jerusalem.
Praise the LORD!

Connecting the Psalm with Scripture and Worship

This night is rich with symbolism. The cries of an oppressed people suffering under cruel Egyptian subjugators have reached the merciful ears of God, and God has decided to release the people from the burdens that shackle them. In compassion God declares what God will do. Passover tells the story of how God acts, of what God will do, of how God continues to act to protect innocence and preserve the lives of those whom, by no merit of their own, God has chosen.

Worship on Holy Thursday is rooted in Israel's keeping of Passover. What we do as Christians, and the meaning we discover, are in the context of the Passover Seder, or meal. Passover is a defining, constituting moment for Israel. For Christians, Passover provides a context of thanksgiving, praise, and celebration of deliverance, even in the face of Jesus' suffering. What Jesus does with his disciples, and will do on Calvary, foreshadows what will become ritualized in our celebrations on Holy Thursday. In prayer and deeds of mercy, in hope and trust in the Lord's command to love, in actions of offering the "lamb of God" who was slain, we see in Jesus God's offering of God's self. In the Christian community, what we do on Holy Thursday reflects our attempt at appropriating what God has done and is doing in the life, death, and resurrection of Jesus. What we do on this night is to be perpetually remembered and lifted up. When we call on the name of the Lord, celebrating the "feast of unleavened bread," we bear witness to God's saving activity and liberating grace.

The Goal of the Teacher

It is likely that those who perceived the magnitude of Jesus' power, and understood what he had done when he washed the disciples' feet, that is, that by washing their most extreme and ordinary parts, even the bodies mingled with earth, he might cleanse [their inner bodies] of which those bodies were a symbol, were amazed and would not have dared also to perform so great a deed themselves in the washing. They would have thought themselves to be too insignificant to wash the feet of the inner and secret man of those who embrace the same teachings of God, unless Jesus had assumed the form of the host and urged them to do this through the words we are expounding, when he was about to teach them the words spoken after they had eaten. . . .

Jesus, therefore, washed the feet of the disciples insofar as he was their teacher, and the feet of the servants insofar as he was their Lord. For the dust from the earth and from worldly things is cleared away by teaching, since it reaches nothing else than the extremities and lower parts of the disciples. But those things that defile the feet are also removed by the lordship of the ruler, since he has authority over those who still receive common defilement because they still have the spirit of bondage.

Someone not thinking clearly might say that Jesus washes the feet of the disciples and servants insofar as he is door, or shepherd, or physician. I think, however, that the disciples' feet need to be washed by the teacher insofar as they have not yet reached the sufficiency, but still lack that sufficiency referred to in the statement, "It is sufficient for the disciple that he be as his teacher." And this is the goal of the teacher, qua teacher, for the disciple: to make the disciple as himself, that he may no longer need the teacher, qua teacher, although he will need him in other respects. For as the goal of the physician, whom the sick need, but the well have no need of a physician, is to stop the sick from being sick so that they no longer need him, so the goal of the teacher is to achieve for his disciple what is called "sufficient" in the statement, "It is sufficient for the disciple that he be as his teacher.

Origen, *Commentary on the Gospel according to John, Books 13–32*, trans. Ronald E. Heine, in Fathers of the Church 89 (Washington: The Catholic University of America Press, 1989), 363–65.

Psalm 116 is a psalm of thanksgiving and deliverance.[1] A lay person comes to the temple in Jerusalem to offer a sacrifice of thanksgiving for deliverance from some extremely grievous danger. The psalmist expresses a joyful sense of liberation because the Lord "has heard my voice and my supplications" (Ps. 116:1). Because the Lord hears and acts, the psalm overflows with expressions of trust and devotion: "I love the Lord." Why? Because God rescues us, even when "the snares of death encompass [us]," even when "distress and anguish" are all around (116:3).

The experience of one person becomes the shared experience of the whole community. Whenever Israel called, the Lord God heard and answered. Our pleas for mercy are heeded; God hears. God makes and keeps the promises of covenant, even as Jesus gives a new commandment and calls for new actions—the washing of feet, the sharing of a eucharistic meal. By sharing in a sacramental meal, Jesus indicates his participation in our afflictions. This is no insignificant matter, for "the untimely death of God's beloved is not a matter of indifference."[2]

The servants of the servant of God, we are released from trials and the grave injustices of sin, death, and evil by the one who bore our infirmities. What happens on this night once again reconnects Passover's paschal lamb with the "Lamb of God," Jesus. As we remember Jesus' washing the disciples' feet—and as we wash one another's feet—we remember his deep love and great sacrifice. This simple act is an

1. A. A. Andersen, *The New Century Bible Commentary: Psalms (73–150)* (Grand Rapids: Eerdmans, 1972), 2:790.
2. Andersen, 794.

act of hospitality that a host would provide for those who have traveled some distance to celebrate Passover. Normally, a host would have had a servant see to the washing of the feet of the guests, but now the host becomes the servant, and Jesus declares to us the enormity of God's compassion.

What Jesus does to prepare the disciples for what is to come, we now do, remembering that the actions of Jesus are oft accompanied this night with the declaration: "Love one another. As I have loved you, so also you must love one another" (e.g., John 13:34; 15:12). The last hours of captivity yield to a new way of being, but this does not happen without anguish, without lament.

Betrayal and denial, echoes of which are heard in those portions of Psalm 116 not included in the lectionary reading, are very much in the foreground as Christian communities recall that for Jesus, this night culminates in experiences of humiliation and desertion. Those who are closest to him act out of fear. And we who claim closeness to him, fear how we might behave, how we do behave, when we must face those whose ears are deaf to God's cry for mercy. Faced with the world's difficulties, will we remain faithful, or will we desert the one who would not leave us as orphans? Silence unfolds as we strip altars, remove paraments, and in stillness ponder so great a love.

JOSEPH A. DONNELLA II

Holy Thursday

1 Corinthians 11:23–26

²³For I received from the Lord what I also handed on to you, that the Lord Jesus on the night when he was betrayed took a loaf of bread, ²⁴and when he had given thanks, he broke it and said, "This is my body that is for you. Do this in remembrance of me." ²⁵In the same way he took the cup also, after supper, saying, "This cup is the new covenant in my blood. Do this, as often as you drink it, in remembrance of me." ²⁶For as often as you eat this bread and drink the cup, you proclaim the Lord's death until he comes.

Commentary 1: Connecting the Reading with Scripture

On Holy Thursday, also known as Maundy Thursday, we encounter an emphasis on remembrance with the institution of rituals that mark God's faithfulness to us. The lectionary texts for this day are evidence of this. Exodus 12 describes the first Passover, when God struck the land of Egypt but protected the people of Israel from multiple plagues, including the death of their firstborn children. God also established it as a Jewish tradition: "This day shall be a day of remembrance for you. You shall celebrate it as a festival to the LORD; throughout your generations you shall observe it as a perpetual ordinance" (Exod. 12:14). Psalm 116:1–2, 12–19 speaks of offering a thanksgiving sacrifice and publicly declaring one's faith in God (Ps. 116:17) as a response to God "for all his bounty" (Ps. 116:12). In John 13, Jesus washes his disciples' feet, illustrating the importance of humility and servanthood (John 13:1–7). He gives them a "new commandment" (John 13:31b–35): "that you love one another. Just as I have loved you, "you also should love one another." The washing of each other's feet, prayers of thanksgiving, and reflecting on the saving grace of God are all practices we celebrate and reenact on Holy Thursday. At the center of these practices is the celebration of the Lord's Supper.

First Corinthians 11:23–26 recounts the Last Supper Jesus had with his disciples on the night he was betrayed. In the midst of his disciples, Jesus broke a loaf of bread, representing his body, and took the cup, representing "the new covenant in [his] blood" (1 Cor. 11:24–25). He instructs his disciples to partake of these elements "in remembrance of me" (1 Cor. 11:24, 25). When Jesus says, "For as often as you eat this bread and drink the cup, you proclaim the Lord's death until he comes" (1 Cor. 11:26), he institutes a ritual: the Lord's Supper.

Before describing Jesus' Last Supper with his disciples, Paul gives instructions on the proper way the community should share a meal together. This is because during this time, the celebration of the Lord's Supper was held during the common meal. The problem is that there is evidence of class discrimination, contradicting the idea that every member of the community be included. "For when the time comes to eat," Paul points out, "each of you goes ahead with your own supper, and one goes hungry and another becomes drunk" (1 Cor. 11:21). There are divisions between the rich and the poor. Paul asks, "Do you show contempt for the church of God and humiliate those who have nothing?" (1 Cor. 11:22).

Paul continues his instruction concerning common-meal etiquette about ten verses later by stating that when disciples come together for this meal, they are to show solidarity by waiting for each other (1 Cor. 11:33); the poor who prepare and serve the meal should not be left out. In addition, if they are hungry, they are to eat at home so that they can practice discipline during the meal, and so they can focus on the meal's occasion: remembering Jesus' sacrifice on our behalf (1 Cor. 11:34).

The behavior of the Corinthian community at the common meal reflects the practices of Greco-Roman culture, in which it is customary for the rich, not only to be fed first, but also to get the best portion of the meal and to overindulge. The lower class ate at a later time, consuming whatever remained.

The Corinthian disciples' motives for gathering at the meal, Paul implies, seem to be based on self-gratification, and their actions compromise the integrity of the community by perpetuating the divisions among them. It is important that they learn the proper way of eating the common meal, because if they behave this way when the Lord's Supper is served, there will be grave consequences. These consequences are explicitly stated in the passage following Jesus' Last Supper with his disciples: "Whoever, therefore, eats the bread or drinks the cup of the Lord in an unworthy manner will be answerable for the body and blood of the Lord" (1 Cor. 11:27). Before partaking in the Lord's Supper, Paul tells them to "examine themselves," or they will incur judgment in the form of weakness, illness, and death (1 Cor. 11:28–30).

What might the early church have thought it meant to "examine themselves"? Consistent with what Paul writes in Galatians 6:4, before they come to the "table," they must "test their own work." Paul's emphasis on building a Christian community in this text suggests that they must reflect on their *in-Christ-ness*, that is, how much Christ is in them (Rom. 8:10). This self-reflection would lead to a confession of sins, a petition for forgiveness, and a reorienting of one's focus to the Christ-centered community. This process of self-examination would serve to guard partakers of the Lord's Supper against misconduct, strengthening community.

Paul's teaching regarding the Lord's Supper is consistent with his overall message in 1 Corinthians, namely, how to live together as the body of Christ. At the outset, Paul mentions that he has heard about the divisions within the community (1 Cor. 1:11). Not only is there competing leadership (1 Cor. 1:11–17), but there are issues pertaining to worship practices (such as prophecy over speaking in tongues; 1 Cor. 14:1–25) and, as indicated with the common meal, the division of social class.

Paul seeks to remind the community at Corinth that Jesus' death on the cross is not just for the rich, but for everyone. Nevertheless, one wonders whether Paul's own privileged position causes his message to be misinterpreted. A well-known teacher of the law as a Pharisee who professes that his authority to proclaim the gospel was granted by a direct revelation from Jesus Christ (Gal. 1:12) writes that Jesus says, "This is my body that is for *you*" (11:24). To whom does "you" refer? We know that Paul founded this church and that his teachings are delivered orally. It is fair to assume that perhaps the affluent members of the community thought Paul was speaking directly to them, or once Paul left they resumed common practices that reflected the class distinctions of that time. So conceivably this letter is a correction, a more detailed explanation of what it means to truly be a community of believers in Jesus, a savior who died for *everyone*.

The nondiscriminatory ethic of the cross that Paul posits should be reflected in the nondiscriminatory ethic of the community. This teaching of Paul to the church in Corinth remains relevant today. In addition to class divisions, the church is divided in terms of race, gender, sexual orientation, and political affiliations, among other things. We would do well to ask ourselves Paul's most pressing question: "Has Christ been divided?" (1 Cor. 1:13). The answer is no, but the victimizing, categorizing, and prejudicial tendencies of those of us who make up the body of Christ suggest that we must continue to "examine ourselves." Following Jesus' example, we are to celebrate difference, counter dissonance, and promote unity within the church.

On Holy Thursday, as we partake of the Lord's Supper in remembrance of Jesus' death on the cross, and as we wash each other's feet to reflect on Jesus' humility and servanthood, let us first examine ourselves, making sure our motives for partaking in these sacred rituals are rooted in faith in Jesus Christ, and let us continue the work of Jesus Christ "until he comes" again (1 Cor. 11:26).

SHANELL T. SMITH

Commentary 2: Connecting the Reading with the World

Jesus' "words of institution," here recounted by Paul to the Corinthian church, are rehearsed and cherished by Christians in every time and place. Spoken in the context of a shared meal, they draw Christ's disciples back into his life, death, and resurrection even as they invite them to watch for his second coming. The purpose of the words and the meal is to "remember" Christ and his death so well that we are joined, in our lives, to our Lord and his life—not only to the life he once had, but to the life we now have in him; not only to the saving events that happened in the past, but also to the promised completion of redemption in the future.

I explore here how the particular "remembering" Paul sees as essential to the life of the church resonates with discussions about "memory" and experiences of time and place in our contemporary culture. Considering the context in which Paul writes, I will also propose there is a connection between sharing the meal in an orderly fashion and doing justice in the world.

Memory and Re-membering. In a culture in which it is possible to ask Siri, Alexa, and Google for all manner of information, there is arguably less incentive to remember things— not only general facts, but even personal data such as bank account passwords, weight-loss goals, and dates of family members' birthdays. Surveys done over the last decade show we have trouble remembering what we once knew (in our schooldays) about how our government functions. One-quarter to one-third of Americans cannot name the US vice president. In the sphere of education, students are less likely to be required to memorize than they used to be—the concern being that memorizing and regurgitating can impede creative thinking. Similarly, many mainline churches no longer encourage learning Bible verses by heart, as they did a generation ago. The preacher might want to reflect on how, in a culture less concerned about committing things to memory, people hear and respond to Jesus' instruction "Do this in remembrance of me."

If people think of remembering merely as a cognitive exercise, they might wonder how the eating of the bread and drinking of the cup facilitates it. Psychological and sociological studies show that remembering often correlates with certain smells, tastes, places, and music. Consistent with this, Paul's words suggest Jesus wants us to remember him not only with our minds, but with all of our faculties, all of our selves. Further, Jesus wants us to remember him not only periodically but habitually, which is why he insists on associating the giving of his body with our everyday practices of eating and sharing meals.

What exactly does Jesus want us to remember by way of this shared meal? Certainly he wants us to remember his death on our behalf. However, the preacher might note that Jesus says, "Do this in remembrance *of me*," not "Do this, so you will not forget what I have done for you." Could it be that Jesus wants us to remember not only *what he did* for us but, also, *that he is* for us?

Pressing this a bit further: when looking at displays in museums featuring the histories of oppressed peoples, I have noticed that the goal of their creators is not simply that we learn "the facts" and hear the stories, but that we also come to know the people that the facts and stories are about. In the Holocaust Memorial Museum in Washington, DC, for example, there is a roomful of shoes that immediately humanizes the Jews who were sent to the gas chambers. You might walk into that particular room already caught up in and appalled by all the information you have been absorbing about the concentration camps, but as you stand among the assorted shoes of those who were brutally exterminated, you somehow know also the people who wore the shoes. This is one illustration, and preachers will find others, of how the end of our remembering is, finally, to so thoroughly recognize our connection to the subjects of histories that we are formed by our ongoing relationship to them.

Related to this, hearers of this text might want to reflect on how, in their experience, partaking of the bread and the cup provides an occasion to connect to the person of their Lord. Testimonies to meaningful and/or disappointing spiritual experiences related to gathering around the Table may be in order, and might encourage more wholehearted participation. Pastors should be ready to answer questions about different ways various traditions understand the eating and drinking of the elements to join us to the body and blood of Christ, emphasizing that Christians of all persuasions share the conviction that the eucharistic rite is, in part, a mystical experience through which the Holy Spirit works to re-member us, or "put us back together," as members of Christ's body (1 Cor. 12).

Holy Thursday and Time. When this text is opened in a Holy Thursday worship service, where people are gathered to ponder the final days of their Savior's life, the preacher has a special opportunity to make connections between the sacrament of the Lord's Supper and the events of Jesus' betrayal and death. Knowing what is about to transpire, congregants will wonder why Judas acted as he did or how Jesus was able to serve him the bread and the wine. The preacher might speak to how commonly we experience betrayal in this world, which sees no one as irreplaceable. Listeners might imagine the shock of the disciples when they hear Jesus relate the bread to his body, the cup to his blood. Given our cultural emphasis on honoring the boundaries between bodies, the hazards associated with Jesus' unbounded analogies might be named and pondered.

When this text is read on Holy Thursday, curious things happen to an attentive listener's sense of space and time. Whether the community is gathered in first-century Corinth or twenty-first-century Austin, worshipers hear the preacher directing them to Paul, who in turn directs them to Christ. From Jesus to Paul, from Paul to preacher, from preacher to hearer: the text itself marks a succession of the faithful, a series of witnesses who gather to remember Jesus' broken body and shed blood by looking forward to the dreadful, suffering days that are at once behind him and just ahead. The serendipitous swirl of past and future experienced in text and at Table distills clearly in the present: Christ pleads with us to remember "as often as we eat and drink"—*today* and *every day.* At the Table of remembrance, eternity is, most poignantly, now.

Institutions and Justice. Americans enjoy questioning authorities, structures, and rules. Indeed, it is one of the great things about the United States that we are free to rethink the way we order civil society. These days, the growing number of religiously nonaffiliated, suspicious that institutions are unjust, may not be moved by Paul's insistence that the Lord's Supper be celebrated because it originated with Jesus himself. Attending to this, the preacher might note Paul's concern: the Corinthians who have plenty of food have been withholding it from those who do not (1 Cor. 11:21). To follow the institution of Christ, Paul believes, would mean that all are included and none are hungry.

In our world today, where institutional processes too often perpetuate injustice, how can adhering to Christ's words of institution create a space where all are included and fed?

CYNTHIA L. RIGBY

Holy Thursday

John 13:1–17, 31b–35

[1]Now before the festival of the Passover, Jesus knew that his hour had come to depart from this world and go to the Father. Having loved his own who were in the world, he loved them to the end. [2]The devil had already put it into the heart of Judas son of Simon Iscariot to betray him. And during supper [3]Jesus, knowing that the Father had given all things into his hands, and that he had come from God and was going to God, [4]got up from the table, took off his outer robe, and tied a towel around himself. [5]Then he poured water into a basin and began to wash the disciples' feet and to wipe them with the towel that was tied around him. [6]He came to Simon Peter, who said to him, "Lord, are you going to wash my feet?" [7]Jesus answered, "You do not know now what I am doing, but later you will understand." [8]Peter said to him, "You will never wash my feet." Jesus answered, "Unless I wash you, you have no share with me." [9]Simon Peter said to him, "Lord, not my feet only but also my hands and my head!" [10]Jesus said to him, "One who has bathed does not need to wash, except for the feet, but is entirely clean. And you are clean, though not all of you." [11]For he knew who was to betray him; for this reason he said, "Not all of you are clean."

[12]After he had washed their feet, had put on his robe, and had returned to the table, he said to them, "Do you know what I have done to you? [13]You call me Teacher and Lord—and you are right, for that is what I am. [14]So if I, your Lord and Teacher, have washed your feet, you also ought to wash one another's feet. [15]For I have set you an example, that you also should do as I have done to you. [16]Very truly, I tell you, servants are not greater than their master, nor are messengers greater than the one who sent them. [17]If you know these things, you are blessed if you do them." . . .

[31]When [Judas] had gone out, Jesus said, "Now the Son of Man has been glorified, and God has been glorified in him. [32]If God has been glorified in him, God will also glorify him in himself and will glorify him at once. [33]Little children, I am with you only a little longer. You will look for me; and as I said to the Jews so now I say to you, 'Where I am going, you cannot come.' [34]I give you a new commandment, that you love one another. Just as I have loved you, you also should love one another. [35]By this everyone will know that you are my disciples, if you have love for one another."

Commentary 1: Connecting the Reading with Scripture

The glaring dissonance between the two pending events mentioned in the introduction to John 13 is as captivating as it is disconcerting. The sense of joy and anticipation for the Festival of the Passover when the Jewish people celebrate their liberation from slavery in Egypt is subdued by the revelation that the hour for Jesus to depart from this world has come. This is immediately followed by what, in most stories, would really be the ending: Jesus, "having loved his own who were in the world, he loved them to the end." Truly, as introductions come, this one leaves us a bit baffled. Why has the author begun his introduction to the account with what clearly seems to be the ending? What does he mean when he writes that Jesus, "having loved his own who were in the world, loved them to the end"? Does this mean that Jesus loved them despite the fact that perhaps they merited another response? Moreover, what is this "end" to which the writer refers? Given the Gospel's overall concern for avowing the full divinity and humanity of Christ, might John be creating a hermeneutical bridge between Jesus' abiding, faithful love and God's "steadfast love that endures forever"? God's steadfast and enduring love would have been a central theme especially reiterated at the Passover (e.g., Pss. 117, 118). How is Jesus' love the same as God's? If opening the account of the preparation for the Passover with the ending is a writer's hook, it worked to get our attention.

Exploring the context may respond to some of these questions. There were at least two major issues in the Johannine community that John felt compelled to address. They centered on strong disagreement among the members (1 John 2:11, 19) over the question of the full humanity and divinity of Christ, which meant also questioning his saving work (1 John 2:26; 4:1–6) and led to disunity in the church engendered by this disagreement. Hate and apathy replaced care for their mutual well-being, breaching the bond of love that true children of the loving God ought to have and display (1 John 3:17). Too many were professing to know the truth but lived as though they did not (1 John 2:9–11, 29; 1 John 3; 2 John 6).

Thus, while John wanted to help the community assert the full divinity and humanity of Christ, his concern went beyond a mere intellectual exercise. To know the Son is to know God (John 1:1, 14, 18). This is not an "acquired" knowledge; it is a gift of God to be received, believed. Indeed, only true God gives us true God (John 1:1, 18). In Jesus' own words, it is only when we believe that we truly understand (John 8:43)! But what is it that we understand?

If Jesus' signs express his divinity, the *kinds* of signs—healings and feeding of the five thousand—express his great care and love for others. It is the passionate, self-giving love behind the signs that John wants to underscore for the community. This lesson, here expressed through the only foot washing account in the Gospels, takes up the majority of John 13 and is, therefore, telling.

Jesus' washing of the disciples' feet emphasizes the Johannine penchant for the kind of discourse that is conveyed best through example rather than words. What Jesus does is shocking; it is so out of character with social conventions about hierarchy—the master does not wash the servants' feet—that Peter will have none of it (John 13:8)! Reference to Jesus' titles as Lord and Teacher underscores the weight of Jesus' provocation. Explanation follows action here. To commit to being followers of the one they call Lord and Teacher means being open to the kind of holy provocation that dares to break with social mores for the sake of the gospel. This kind of unruly, defiant love for one another is the difference that will allow "everyone" to "know that you are my disciples" (John 13:35; Matt. 5:13–16; Eph. 5:7–14). True love is love incarnate; it speaks best through care of the most basic, even paltry physical needs of the other (washing dirty, smelly feet!). Only this kind of unpretentious, unassuming, Godlike love comes with the promise of blessing (see the beatitude in John 13:17; see also 12:25–26 and compare to 13:2). In congruence with the divine order of things, all who imitate their Lord and Teacher move from being novices to being disciples—or as Jesus' actions portray, true slaves (*douloi*) of the Master (John 13:16; 2 Cor. 4:5). It is no paradox that later Jesus will call "friend" only those who do what he commands and are thus made worthy of knowing "what the master is doing" (John 15:14, 15).

John shares little of Jesus' internal struggle over the pending crucifixion so powerfully illustrated in the Synoptic Gospels (cf. John 12 and 13:21 with Matt. 26:37, 38; Mark 14:34; Luke 22:41–45). According to the other Gospels, Jesus is more than "troubled in Spirit" (John 13:21); he is "consumed with sorrow to the point of death" (Matt. 26:38; Mark 14:34; Luke 22:44). This seeming minimization of Jesus' inner struggle is second only to the importance of reaffirming Jesus' resolve to fulfill his purpose. The suffering to come does not overtake Jesus; he knows he has come for this hour, when the Father will be glorified in the Son, and the Son in the Father. John wants to dwell, not on the crucifixion of Jesus (as compared to emphases in 1 Cor. 11:23–26 and the other Gospels), but on the personal, corporate, and eternal significance of his descent, death, resurrection, and return to the Father. This may explain why John leads into the pain of betrayal (John 12; 13:21–30) only after triumphalist imagery about "the kind of death he was to die" (John 12:33).

Unlike the other Gospels, John does not mention Jesus' blood or his body being shed or broken for them. By being "lifted up" through his crucifixion and ascension, Jesus is casting out the "ruler of this world" and drawing all to himself (John 12:31, 32). The light of the "father's only son" is shining in the darkness; death is giving way to life for all people (John 1:4, 14). The present-future triumph of "his hour" is juxtaposed with the present knowledge that victory and the judgment of this world (John 12:31) is already a present event in the eschatological "here not yet" (note three references to John's proleptical "now" in John 12:27 and 31). The Father, who has glorified Christ and is glorified in Christ (John 12:28; 13:32), has already given all things to him (John 13:3).

As noted above, John 13:1 heightens the relationship of the Passover to the approaching "hour," mentioned in John 12:23, 27, by personalizing it now as "*his* hour" (John 13:1). Jewish disciples familiar with God's depiction of the Passover event as "the passover of the LORD" in Exodus 12:11, and with Jesus' own unequivocal affirmation of his identity as "Lord" (John 13:13 et al.), later resonate with the significance of these words confirmed through Jesus' death, resurrection, and ascension. "The passover of the LORD" and "his hour" converge on Jesus, the Passover lamb, who "takes away the sin of the world" (John 1:29). Christ, the Lamb of God, is the promised Messiah (John 4:26). Rejection, betrayal, and suffering do not keep him from loving to the end.

That "end" is now really the beginning, the introduction of a new "hour" when, in imitation of our Lord, we are empowered to witness to God's grace and truth through our love for each other . . . to the end (John 13:34, 35).

ZAIDA MALDONADO PÉREZ

Commentary 2: Connecting the Reading with the World

In much of the English-speaking world, the Thursday before Easter is known as Maundy Thursday. The name derives from the text of this lesson, which tells what Jesus said and did that day, including his words in verse 34: "I give you a new commandment." The word for "commandment" used in the Latin translation of this verse is *mandatum*. So Maundy Thursday is the Thursday of the new commandment, which is "that you love one another." The theme is obviously crucial for Jesus: "By this everyone will know that you are my disciples, if you have love for one another" (John 13:35), and it is picked up in the Johannine Epistles, which refer explicitly to this commandment (1 John 3:23). Moreover, the message seems to have had a concrete impact on the early church, for in the third century Tertullian reports that in his North African context

Christians have become notorious for their love, which, he says, "lead[s] many to put a brand upon us: 'See, they say, how they love one another'—for themselves are animated by mutual hatred—'how they are ready even to die for one another'—for they themselves will sooner put to death."[1]

Tertullian explains what the love that Jesus commands looks like in practice by correlating Christians' love with their willingness to die for one another. It is certainly easy to connect this with Jesus' description of himself as the good shepherd who "lays down his life for the sheep" (John 10:11), not to mention his declaration a couple of chapters later in the Gospel that "no one has greater love than this, to lay down one's life for one's friends" (15:13). So when Jesus explains his new commandment with the words, "Just as I have loved you, you also should

---

1. Tertullian, *Apology*, 39 (http://www.ccel.org/ccel/schaff/anf03.iv.iii.xxxix.html).

love one another" (13:34), it may seem obvious that he has dying on his mind.

Many contemporary theologians resist identifying "love" with "sacrifice." Feminist theologians are among those who note that this connection has all too often been used as a means of subjugation and control: if to love means sacrificing one's life, it becomes all too easy for those in power to encourage those who are not in power to be content with and, indeed, to celebrate their powerlessness as the manifestation of a Christlike act of loving self-surrender. According to this line of reasoning, to love is to sacrifice, so that the greatest love is proved by the ultimate sacrifice, namely, giving up one's very life. Yet it seems odd that the same Jesus who came to bring his followers "life abundant" (10:10) would then tell them, on the eve of his departure, that they should give up their lives.

A still more immediate problem with the idea that the love Jesus commands in this passage takes the form of dying for others is the simple fact that at the time Jesus instructs his disciples, "Just as I have loved you, you also should love one another," he has *not* yet died for them. His death may be imminent (as we are reminded at the very beginning of the chapter, and again in v. 33), but at the point he gives his "new commandment," his love for the disciples has not taken the form of dying for them and so cannot be invoked as the model for Christian love that Jesus has in mind. A different line of approach therefore seems called for.

One possible way forward involves going back to the first part of the reading and the story of Jesus' washing his disciples' feet. Here John's account of Jesus' final evening with his disciples deviates from the Synoptic Gospels, where the focus is on the meal: a Passover Seder (itself redolent of the theme of sacrifice) in which Jesus distributes bread and wine he shares as tokens of his forthcoming death. By contrast, in John there is no mention of broken bodies or blood outpoured, and the supper (which is not a Passover meal) is mentioned only in passing, as the context for Jesus' washing the disciples feet. Moreover, because it is this act (rather than the Synoptic sharing of bread and wine) that Jesus specifically describes as an example for

his disciples to follow (13:15), it makes sense to conclude that this episode models the way in which Jesus has loved his disciples, and expects his disciples to love one another: "So if I, your Lord and Teacher, have washed your feet, you also ought to wash one another's feet" (13:14).

The model of love illustrated here is rather different from one that commends self-sacrifice. To be sure, Jesus identifies precisely his position of power—his status as "Teacher and Lord" (13:13)—as important for understanding his action; but the point is not simply that Jesus as the "master" (13:16) undertakes an act of servitude. Clearly, that example too could easily be appropriated to promote a generalized demand to give up status—and then be used as a model to exacerbate the degradation of the lowly, rather than to humble the exalted. It is arguably better to think of Jesus' love here as an act of promoting another's well-being that does not require any permanent loss or surrender of self. For it is certainly true that Jesus "got up from the table, took off his outer robe, and tied a towel around himself. Then he poured water into a basin and began to wash his disciples' feet" (13:4–5); but when he was finished, he "put on his robe, and . . . returned to the table" (13:12). Jesus comes so that his followers could have life, and in performing an action that enhances their lives, he shows them love; but this does not involve any permanent position of abasement: after he finishes washing their feet, he resumes his previous position at the table.

By this act, Jesus shows that love need not be conceived in zero-sum terms, as though it were defined by a kind of double-entry accounting, in which any gain on one side must be matched by equal loss on the other. On such an understanding, love is a finite, limited resource—like a reserve of oil or apples or cookies or dollar bills—such that once it is used, it is gone. Thinking of love on a zero-sum model, we might imagine a mother showing love by pushing her child out of the way of an onrushing car and taking the impact herself. A very different vision is suggested by the much more typical example of a mother showing love in the act of giving birth. Within this framework the act of love is neither a one-off event that precludes any further opportunities of showing love nor a matter of self-subjugation. Quite the contrary, giving birth is normally just the first in a series of loving acts that extends through infancy, childhood, adolescence, and even into adulthood, throughout which it is precisely as mother, and thus as someone with a particular kind of authority, that the woman serves her child—in part by providing an example of love that the child can imitate in his or her own life. So when Jesus reminds his followers in this passage of their duty to do as he has done (13:17, 34–35), it is this kind of love that he arguably has in mind: not giving *up* life, but giving life *to* others.

IAN A. MCFARLAND

Good Friday

Isaiah 52:13–53:12
Psalm 22

Hebrews 10:16–25 and Hebrews
4:14–16; 5:7–9
John 18:1–19:42

Isaiah 52:13–53:12

[13]See, my servant shall prosper;
    he shall be exalted and lifted up,
    and shall be very high.
[14]Just as there were many who were astonished at him
    —so marred was his appearance, beyond human semblance,
    and his form beyond that of mortals—
[15]so he shall startle many nations;
    kings shall shut their mouths because of him;
for that which had not been told them they shall see,
    and that which they had not heard they shall contemplate.
[53:1]Who has believed what we have heard?
    And to whom has the arm of the LORD been revealed?
[2]For he grew up before him like a young plant,
    and like a root out of dry ground;
he had no form or majesty that we should look at him,
    nothing in his appearance that we should desire him.
[3]He was despised and rejected by others;
    a man of suffering and acquainted with infirmity;
and as one from whom others hide their faces
    he was despised, and we held him of no account.

[4]Surely he has borne our infirmities
    and carried our diseases;
yet we accounted him stricken,
    struck down by God, and afflicted.
[5]But he was wounded for our transgressions,
    crushed for our iniquities;
upon him was the punishment that made us whole,
    and by his bruises we are healed.
[6]All we like sheep have gone astray;
    we have all turned to our own way,
and the LORD has laid on him
    the iniquity of us all.

[7]He was oppressed, and he was afflicted,
    yet he did not open his mouth;
like a lamb that is led to the slaughter,
    and like a sheep that before its shearers is silent,
    so he did not open his mouth.
[8]By a perversion of justice he was taken away.
    Who could have imagined his future?

For he was cut off from the land of the living,
    stricken for the transgression of my people.
⁹They made his grave with the wicked
    and his tomb with the rich,
although he had done no violence,
    and there was no deceit in his mouth.

¹⁰Yet it was the will of the LORD to crush him with pain.
When you make his life an offering for sin,
    he shall see his offspring, and shall prolong his days;
through him the will of the LORD shall prosper.
¹¹   Out of his anguish he shall see light;
he shall find satisfaction through his knowledge.
    The righteous one, my servant, shall make many righteous,
    and he shall bear their iniquities.
¹²Therefore I will allot him a portion with the great,
    and he shall divide the spoil with the strong;
because he poured out himself to death,
    and was numbered with the transgressors;
yet he bore the sin of many,
    and made intercession for the transgressors.

Commentary 1: Connecting the Reading with Scripture

Starting in the nineteenth century, Old Testament scholars identified Isaiah 42:1–4; 49:1–6; 50:4–9; and this text as the Servant Songs that deserve special attention because of the importance of the character of the servant that they introduce. As the last of these poems, this text helps in interpreting the first three. This fourth Servant Song from Isaiah can fit into one of three contexts. It fills in the last piece of the puzzle of the other three songs, giving a fuller understanding of the servant. This passage interrupts, yet also complements, the rest of chapter 52, while offering theology in creative tension with chapter 54. Finally, it appears abruptly and stands on its own. Each of the three contexts provides insight for the interpreter.

The brilliant, but inscrutable songs introduce a character into the consciousness of the dispirited Judean exiles. Whether that character represents Israel, or the prophet, a third entity, or a mysterious intertwining conflation of different characters, the songs present a powerful message. God will work through a human agent to "bring forth justice to the nations" (42:1). In the first song (42:1–4), the character appears

resolute and fearless. The song does not describe the details of that justice among nations. The prophets considered justice a key component of the response of Israel and Judah to the call of God. That justice, at a minimum, entailed fairness, access to goods, defense of the vulnerable, and a sense of solidarity within the community. The second Servant Song (49:1–6) presents the character with military images, and introduces a sense of frustration at the lack of progress toward the mission of the servant (49:4). The song ends with an assurance that the servant's mission will encompass the whole earth. Although the servant often bears the title of the Suffering Servant, the motif of suffering begins only in the third song (50:4–9). Here the servant chooses suffering, or at least does not shrink back from it. Because of the mission, the servant declares the intention to "set my face like flint," showing determination (50:7). This willingness to endure suffering derives from deep trust in God's help (50:9).

Chapter 52 issues an invitation to prepare for the departure from Babylonia and the journey back home. That journey merits a change

Love of God and Pure Desire

Lord, thy death upon the tree
Brings uplifting thoughts to me,
Calm of mind and holy fire,
Love of God and pure desire.

O to bear in memory
All thy grief and obloquy,
Holy Christ, thy thorny wreath,
Spear and nails and crucial death!

All these blessed wounds of thine,
Witness of thy love divine,
Cruel scourging and distress,
O the mortal bitterness!

Lord, the thought is of such dole,
So intoxicates the soul,
That we bow in tearful prayers;
But what glorious fruit it bears!

Low, before thee, Crucified,
Sink all selfishness and pride;
Loud to thee, dear Christ, we cry;
Join us with thy saint on high.

Honor, praise and glory bring
Unto Jesus, heavenly King,
Who, all pure and faultless, gave
His sweet life our lives to save.

Bonaventure, "The Passion of Our Lord," in Daniel Joseph Donahoe, *Early Christian Hymns: Translations of the Verses of the Most Notable Latin Writers of the Early and Middle Ages* (New York: The Grafton Press, 1908), 179.

of clothes, singing, and joy. The Servant Song interrupts the rejoicing over the journey, but also offers a new dimension. The servant will experience exaltation and prosperity. That sense of triumph comes despite the ordeal of the servant. The servant has experienced rejection, shame, and suffering. The servant's affliction has played a part in the new freedom and celebration of the people. The people experience real joy, yet they should feel a sense of gratitude and humility as well. The chapter immediately following the song presents an interesting, even daring image for God. In Isaiah 54 God appears as a husband who has abandoned his wife, Judah (54:7). The husband now comes back, ready to renew the relationship. The prophets and biblical theologians often interpreted the exile as a deserved punishment for the sins of the people (2 Kgs. 17:20). In Isaiah 54, God assumes some of the blame. In an important way, chapter 54 presents the broken "marriage" between God and the people as mutual. Each must work to repair the relationship. The people acknowledge their sins, but God will work to earn back the trust that once marked the bond between them (54:4).

Chapters 52–54 depict the situation of the exiles on the verge of returning home in complex ways. The people rejoice, wake up, and put on new clothes for their new situation. Isaiah 52:3 uses the imagery of being sold into slavery and then redeemed or freed. The Servant Song in the middle reminds the people that another has endured suffering on their behalf. They have committed transgressions, for which another has experienced wounds (53:5). God will also use their suffering in redemptive ways. God has acted like a husband who has deserted a wife, but has now come back (chap. 54). These complicated and somewhat conflicting images give the people multiple ways to understand what happened to them in the Babylonian exile. The experiences evoked include joy, gratitude, humility, and the tender effort to reestablish a broken relationship.

Apart from any context, this passage in its own internal movement startles the reader with its profound message of redemptive suffering and exaltation. The song begins with language of exaltation. The accumulation of adjectives in 52:13 implies success, dignity, honor, and even the kind of exaltation typically associated with God. The reader might expect a movement from suffering to exaltation, yet the poem begins with exaltation, moving to degradation and then ending with exaltation again. Perhaps the movement of the poem reflects the experience of Israel, who went from being God's treasured possession

(Exod. 19:5), to vanquished exiles, and now back to a time of renewal. The servant becomes an instrument both for gaining the attention of foreign rulers and for effecting atonement between the people and God. Just as God chose Israel, despite its small size and lack of power (Deut. 7:7–11), so God chose the unattractive, lowly servant to silence foreign rulers.

The poem does not describe exactly how the suffering of the servant benefits the people. The work of the servant brought physical healing (53:4), forgiveness of transgressions and iniquities (53:5), and wholeness (the familiar word *shalom* in 53:5b). The poem does not explain, but affirms that one person's suffering can offer healing, forgiveness, and atonement for others. The poem may draw on the practice of placing the sins of the people on an animal (see Lev. 16). The psalmist understood that God does not require any sacrifice to offer forgiveness (Ps. 51). Yet the experience of the servant grabs the attention of the reader to note that God uses suffering in a salvific way. Verses 8 and 12 suggest that the servant died. His exaltation and prosperity remain a mystery, but the verse may have influenced the writers of Daniel, who affirmed resurrection for those who remained faithful (Dan. 12:2).

The lectionary suggests two possible readings from Hebrews for this Sunday (Heb. 10:16–25; and Heb. 4:14–16; 5:7–9). Both present Jesus as the high priest, who has suffered on behalf of the church. Essential to the Christology of Hebrews is the idea of Jesus as the priest who has made himself the sacrifice. This theology of vicarious suffering is common to both the Isaiah text and the two Hebrews readings. Hebrews 4:15 asserts Jesus' lack of sin, consistent with the description of the servant, "he had done no violence, and there was no deceit in his mouth" (Isa. 53:9).

The reader can see a number of ways in which the account of Jesus' passion and crucifixion in John 18 and 19 draws upon the ideas of Isaiah. The servant was "despised and rejected by others" (Isa. 53:3), consistent with Jesus' rejection by his own disciples. The servant was taken away "by a perversion of justice" (53:8), consistent with Pilate finding no case against Jesus. The reader should not assume that the prophet "predicted" these consistencies. The prophet speaks to his own time, and introduces insights about God's use of vicarious suffering. The writers of Hebrews and John recognize the insights of the prophet into God's ways, and shape their depiction of Jesus' ministry and death in light of the insights of the prophet. Hebrews and John portray Jesus' passion and death as vicarious suffering that leads to healing, wholeness, and righteousness, in ways consistent with what the prophet writing in Isaiah teaches his community about the mysterious servant.

CHARLES L. AARON JR.

Commentary 2: Connecting the Reading with the World

The liturgical connection of Isaiah 52:13–53:12 to Good Friday in all three lectionary cycles reveals a history of Christian identification of Isaiah's Suffering Servant with Christ, who suffered indignities and physical beating before an ironic exaltation on the cross. While this may continue to be the servant's primary identification for many Christians, the other identifications of Isaiah's servant in the history of tradition may open alternative associations that allow God to speak to the church in unlikely ways.

Alternative identities of the servant include the exilic prophet who composed the Servant Songs (including 42:1–9; 49:1–13; and 50:4–9a); the nation of Israel, which suffers as the least among many nations while in exile; and a select group from the nation of Israel that embodies God's favor and suffers the greater community's contempt. These various identities of the servant within the text's reception history offer many homiletical possibilities that might breathe new life into the bones of overworked or oversimplified readings. Perhaps, as the text suggests, some of these new identities of the Suffering Servant may shock us out of a complacent reading of both the Isaiah text and its appropriation in the New Testament.

The rhythmic use of this passage in the Christian year might have numbed us to the shock and awe of its poetry. Even attempts in our culture to reclaim the gory details of the Messiah's suffering have capitulated to the oversaturation of violence in mainstream media. Mel Gibson's movie *The Passion of the Christ* opens with a truncated quote of Isaiah 53:5: "He was wounded for our transgressions, crushed for our iniquities; by his wounds we are healed." Gibson's use of this verse to frame his version of the passion highlights the brutal nature of the text, transforming the humble Suffering Servant into a modern superhero capable of sustaining great physical pain on his way to a sacrificial death.

Gibson's problematic interpretation of Jesus as a suffering hero figure has also influenced other manifestations of the Christ figure in popular culture. Many contemporary superhero narratives mimic the pain and anguish displayed in Isaiah 52–53 and the passion narratives. Both of the most recent Hollywood versions of the Superman myth (*Superman Returns* and *Man of Steel*) portray a battered but strong man who saves the world much as Gibson's Christ does—by overcoming suffering through pure mental and physical will. In *Batman vs. Superman*, the creators continued the motif with the death of Superman, anticipating Superman's resurrection in a future feature. Similar depictions of self-sacrifice typically follow the same pattern: a powerful figure, typically a European male, sacrifices himself to physical and mental anguish. The movie and television versions of Bruce Wayne, Oliver Queen, and Tony Stark (all millionaire white messiahs turned superhero: Batman, Green Arrow, and Iron Man, respectively), as well as Thor (European god and prince), all "sacrifice" themselves in order to save their love interest, city, world, or even galaxy. Moreover, these hero narratives often reinforce a violent redemptive process with battles occurring before and/or after the sacrifice. In a predominately patriarchal Eurocentric society, the image of Christ giving up his divinity in order to save humankind often reinforces the stereotypical messiah complex. We know the story. We

find comfort in the pattern. We lose the text's element of surprise. Moreover, because of the triumphalism of resurrection in these interpretations—real or anticipated—we lose the focus on the suffering itself.

In contrast, Isaiah 52–53 treats the servant as a shock, an anomaly, rather than a hero or a strongman: "Just as there were many who were astonished at him—so marred was his appearance, beyond human semblance, and his form beyond that of mortals—so he shall startle many nations; kings shall shut their mouths because of him" (Isa. 52:14–15a). Using an agricultural metaphor, the text announces that this servant is like a stump out of dry ground that we otherwise would ignore (53:2). Moreover, the servant's grotesque nature would repel our view (53:3). If we set aside the christological approach for a moment, this servant poem asks us poignant questions: Who might God be using that would shock us? Whom would we ignore, either actively or passively, as we carry out our work? Who might be currently bearing the iniquities of our culture?

Phyllis Trible, in her classic work *Texts of Terror*, suggests two alternative identities of the Suffering Servant—women characters in the patriarchal tradition of the Bible. For two women in her book, Trible places an epitaph from this Servant Song. For Hagar, she writes, "She was wounded for our transgressions; she was bruised for our iniquities" (Isa. 53:5); for Tamar (of 2 Sam. 13:1–22), she writes, "A woman of sorrows and acquainted with grief" (Isa. 53:3).[1] Trible's identification of these women as the Suffering Servant is a prophetic response to her encounters with oppression in the world, particularly because of misogyny, but also because of poverty and racism.[2] By reading the tragic stories of these two women, Trible models a new way of reframing the Suffering Servant Songs by looking toward those in our society and tradition whom we typically ignore, but whose suffering is poignant.

Trible's reframing begs us to ask whom our culture continues to treat with the contempt of the servant. Is Christian culture perpetuating suffering upon our neighbors and forcing

---

1. Phyllis Trible, *Texts of Terror: Literary-Feminist Readings of Biblical Narratives* (Philadelphia: Fortress Press, 1984), 8 and 36.
2. Trible, 1–2.

them to bear our transgressions? Does the current oppression of the poor, the immigrant, and the outsider reflect the brutality of the Suffering Servant in Isaiah 52–53? In what ways do we continue to inflict pain on the servant? Might we ask if the individual victims of police brutality are women and men "of suffering acquainted with infirmity" (53:3)? Are the refugee children from predominately Muslim countries for whom the European, historically Christian, nations in the West are denying sanctuary bearing the infirmities of our xenophobic tendencies (53:4)? Are the minority, impoverished, and silent voices occupying our prison systems the silent lambs our society is currently leading to the slaughter (53:7)? While these are questions we might ask on a national and global scale, individual ministers might also seek to identify the ignored suffering on local and congregational levels. This work requires us not only to pay attention to this passage's history of interpretation, but also to develop an awareness of the suffering of others as we interpret.

Discovering current individual and communal connections with the Suffering Servant by bracketing the traditional christocentric reading does not have to be anti-Christian. In fact, it can be a decidedly Christian hermeneutical move when we make another connection with a text outside the liturgical calendar for Good Friday, Matthew 25:31–46. Matthew portrays both positive and negative examples of how we might respond to the Suffering Servants in our midst by feeding the hungry, giving drink to the thirsty, clothing the naked, caring for the sick, and visiting the incarcerated. Reading the servant poem in this light challenges the Christian audience to face the ways we may perpetuate suffering in the world while also encouraging us to persevere in works of reconciliation and justice, despite social and cultural pressure to acquiesce. By suffering alongside the least of these, the church can participate in Christ's work. Instead of perpetuating suffering and alienation, we might read Isaiah 52:13–53:12 as a call to stand in solidarity with the least of these in our own era. Reading this passage on Good Friday might also remind us that by attending to the plight of the downtrodden in this world, we are attending to Christ.

DAVID G. GARBER JR.

Psalm 22

¹My God, my God, why have you forsaken me?
   Why are you so far from helping me, from the words of my groaning?
²O my God, I cry by day, but you do not answer;
   and by night, but find no rest.

³Yet you are holy,
   enthroned on the praises of Israel.
⁴In you our ancestors trusted;
   they trusted, and you delivered them.
⁵To you they cried, and were saved;
   in you they trusted, and were not put to shame.

⁶But I am a worm, and not human;
   scorned by others, and despised by the people.
⁷All who see me mock at me;
   they make mouths at me, they shake their heads;
⁸"Commit your cause to the LORD; let him deliver—
   let him rescue the one in whom he delights!"

⁹Yet it was you who took me from the womb;
   you kept me safe on my mother's breast.
¹⁰On you I was cast from my birth,
   and since my mother bore me you have been my God.
¹¹Do not be far from me,
   for trouble is near
   and there is no one to help.

¹²Many bulls encircle me,
   strong bulls of Bashan surround me;
¹³they open wide their mouths at me,
   like a ravening and roaring lion.

¹⁴I am poured out like water,
   and all my bones are out of joint;
my heart is like wax;
   it is melted within my breast;
¹⁵my mouth is dried up like a potsherd,
   and my tongue sticks to my jaws;
   you lay me in the dust of death.

¹⁶For dogs are all around me;
   a company of evildoers encircles me.
My hands and feet have shriveled;
¹⁷I can count all my bones.
They stare and gloat over me;
¹⁸they divide my clothes among themselves,
   and for my clothing they cast lots.

¹⁹But you, O LORD, do not be far away!
O my help, come quickly to my aid!
²⁰Deliver my soul from the sword,
my life from the power of the dog!
²¹Save me from the mouth of the lion!

From the horns of the wild oxen you have rescued me.
²²I will tell of your name to my brothers and sisters;
in the midst of the congregation I will praise you:
²³You who fear the LORD, praise him!
All you offspring of Jacob, glorify him;
stand in awe of him, all you offspring of Israel!
²⁴For he did not despise or abhor
the affliction of the afflicted;
he did not hide his face from me,
but heard when I cried to him.

²⁵From you comes my praise in the great congregation;
my vows I will pay before those who fear him.
²⁶The poor shall eat and be satisfied;
those who seek him shall praise the LORD.
May your hearts live forever!

²⁷All the ends of the earth shall remember
and turn to the LORD;
and all the families of the nations
shall worship before him.
²⁸For dominion belongs to the LORD,
and he rules over the nations.

²⁹To him, indeed, shall all who sleep in the earth bow down;
before him shall bow all who go down to the dust,
and I shall live for him.
³⁰Posterity will serve him;
future generations will be told about the Lord,
³¹and proclaim his deliverance to a people yet unborn,
saying that he has done it.

Connecting the Psalm with Scripture and Worship

An injustice has been done. An innocent has been betrayed, taken away from the community of those who cherish him, falsely accused and convicted, then executed in ignominious fashion. The situation on that Good Friday bears striking similarity to the world in which we dwell. Innocents are "taken away": children of lowly birth—orphans, immigrants, the foreigners in our midst—often find themselves targeted, easy prey for political machinations by us who "turn our own way." We neglect the ordinances of the Divine, while we lay afflictions and illnesses on the innocent.

The innocent suffer the torments and punishments that come by way of society's collective sin. They are stricken by the calamities of injustice, and God uses (God does not require) the innocent self-offering of the slain who are "cut off from the land on the living" (Isa. 53:8) to bring about a better future. Salvation will come—through the self-offering of the righteous (just) one (Isa. 53:11).

Seeing that God thwarts the designs of the wicked by using what was meant for evil to bring about goodness and mercy and grace, Christians draw a connection between the song of the Suffering Servant in the Isaiah reading and the words of Psalm 22, spoken by a crucified Jesus. As innocence is betrayed, a cry is heard: "My God, my God, why?" Jesus laments the dehumanization set in motion by enemies and subjugators, by those who abandon him, and by those who unwittingly comply with the evil acts of denial and betrayal. We watch these acts mushroom into concentric cyclones, ever more intense, filled with mockery and torture, pain and death.

Left to the jeers and devices of the predatory, the psalmist feels abandoned and is scathed by the cruelty of his persecutors: "I am a worm, and not human; scorned by others, and despised by the people" (Ps. 22:6). Describing sensations of emptiness, shame, and humiliation, the innocent one reveals: "All who see me mock at me, they make mouths at me, they shake their heads"(v. 7).

Good Friday puts in plain sight the violent death of Jesus. What do we make of this? How is God at work in this moment shadowed with loneliness, pain, and rejection? Are we able to sense God's presence even when we feel anxious, utterly helpless, or stricken with a sickness near unto death?

The pall of death shrouds this day. The lamenter pleads to the only one who can help, as we are reminded of the innocent Christ who was slain and "marred . . . beyond human semblance" (Isa. 52:14). This very one shall "startle many nations" (Isa. 52:15). For this one who was so cruelly treated and disfigured is God's instrument, "like the lamb of the Passover" who will open God's way, a way for new life to continue and death to be vanquished by love.

At Good Friday services where the passion of our Lord Jesus Christ is recalled and these Suffering Servant passages from the prophet Isaiah are heard—where those assembled prayerfully bid, asking God for the advance of God's realm—we mindfully contemplate the mystery of the crucified One and adoringly and sometimes physically embrace the feet of Jesus on the cross. In silence, we are transported to witness in the presence of Jesus, that here, in this moment, "there can be no greater love."[1]

Psalm 22 and Isaiah 52:13–53:12 invite us to imagine how Jesus may have felt. The emotions that accompany sheer and utter abandonment can shake us to the core. Yet the tone of suffering is disrupted as the sufferer moves beyond lament to thanksgiving. The psalmist testifies to misery and wretchedness (Ps. 22:1–11), to what happens when evil is allowed free rein.[2] What is sacrificial in this regard is the giving of one's self in pursuit of a better, godlier, more human way of being. The witness of the innocent sufferer challenges all orientations governed by and limited to evil and violence. There is something redemptive in the suffering of the innocent. Freedom is given when the afflicted are not bound by suffering but released in hope.

Use of this psalm, especially on this day, revolves around our claims about Jesus. The psalm raises the question of theodicy, as the one who suffers and dies is the one who trusts in God. For Christians, the one who pleads is our intercessor, our Messiah. The anguish we feel as we witness his suffering innocence leads us to ask, "Where is God amidst such affliction? Does God will the affliction of the afflicted?"[3]

Jesus' life bears witness to God's willingness to suffer "affliction with the afflicted." By dying, Jesus destroys death. By rising, Jesus restores life. Even in the seeming despair of Good Friday, we wait in hope. We watch for the consummation of God's kingdom, when Jesus returns and the fullness of God's realm is, at last, all in all.

JOSEPH A. DONNELLA II

---

1. "There Can Be No Greater Love" / Grande es ta bonté, in *Taizé: Songs for Prayer* (Chicago: GIA Publications, Inc., 1998).
2. James L. Mays, *Psalms*, Interpretation (Louisville, KY: John Knox Press, 1994), 108.
3. Mays, 114.

Hebrews 10:16–25

¹⁶"This is the covenant that I will make with them
>   after those days, says the Lord:
> I will put my laws in their hearts,
>   and I will write them on their minds,"

¹⁷he also adds,

> "I will remember their sins and their lawless deeds no more."

¹⁸Where there is forgiveness of these, there is no longer any offering for sin. ¹⁹Therefore, my friends, since we have confidence to enter the sanctuary by the blood of Jesus, ²⁰by the new and living way that he opened for us through the curtain (that is, through his flesh), ²¹and since we have a great priest over the house of God, ²²let us approach with a true heart in full assurance of faith, with our hearts sprinkled clean from an evil conscience and our bodies washed with pure water. ²³Let us hold fast to the confession of our hope without wavering, for he who has promised is faithful. ²⁴And let us consider how to provoke one another to love and good deeds, ²⁵not neglecting to meet together, as is the habit of some, but encouraging one another, and all the more as you see the Day approaching.

Hebrews 4:14–16; 5:7–9

¹⁴Since, then, we have a great high priest who has passed through the heavens, Jesus, the Son of God, let us hold fast to our confession. ¹⁵For we do not have a high priest who is unable to sympathize with our weaknesses, but we have one who in every respect has been tested as we are, yet without sin. ¹⁶Let us therefore approach the throne of grace with boldness, so that we may receive mercy and find grace to help in time of need. . . .

^{5:7}In the days of his flesh, Jesus offered up prayers and supplications, with loud cries and tears, to the one who was able to save him from death, and he was heard because of his reverent submission. ⁸Although he was a Son, he learned obedience through what he suffered; ⁹and having been made perfect, he became the source of eternal salvation for all who obey him.

Commentary 1: Connecting the Reading with Scripture

The lectionary texts for Good Friday, the day in which Christians commemorate Jesus' death on the cross, have a thematic focus on suffering. In Isaiah 52:13–53:12, the prophet speaks of the Suffering Servant—the one whom people despised and rejected (53:3) and deemed afflicted by God, despite the fact that his infirmities were theirs alone (53:4). Psalm 22 captures a believer's practice of questioning God's disappearance in his times of struggle: "My God, my God, why have you forsaken me?" (Ps. 22:1), and a desperate plea for deliverance. The

Gospel of John 18:1–19:42 recounts in detailed fashion Jesus' passion from his betrayal to his burial. Suffering is at the center of each of these texts. The theme of suffering is also found in the book of Hebrews; however, in Hebrews the emphasis is less on suffering and more on the significance of the position of the one who suffers. Jesus is the chief religious leader who makes a sacrifice on behalf of those who believe in him. Jesus is the high priest, offering himself to God for the forgiveness of sins.

The book of Hebrews, a Jewish Christian homily, has a central theme of Jesus as the heavenly high priest. It is first expressed in Hebrews 2:17: "Therefore he had to become like his brothers and sisters in every respect, so that he might be a merciful and faithful high priest in the service of God, to make a sacrifice of atonement for the sins of the people." The understanding of Jesus as a divine high priest has been associated with a passage in Genesis that tells of a man, King Melchizedek of Salem, referred to as "priest of God Most High," who blesses Abram and, in return, is gifted a tenth of Abram's possessions (Gen. 14:17–24). Thus Melchizedek has been referred to as a type of precursor of Jesus in this regard, a unique high priest who comes from God.

The high priest, a hereditary position of the descendants of Aaron (Moses' brother), was the highest religious office in Judaism. High priests had many tasks, such as supervising the priests, overseeing temple worship, collecting tithes, and performing purification rites; but their most important duty was to make a sin offering. On the Day of Atonement, the high priest would sacrifice an animal and sprinkle the blood on the mercy seat in the Holy of Holies, to atone for the sins that he and the people of Israel committed during the year just ended (Lev. 16).

Hebrews 4:14–16; 5:7–9 not only identifies Jesus as the heavenly high priest, but also states that because of his role, Christians have a two-fold assurance. First, Jesus understands human suffering: "For we do not have a high priest who is unable to sympathize with our weaknesses, but we have one who in every respect has been tested as we are, yet without sin" (Heb. 4:15). Second, Christians can be confident in requesting mercy (4:16) as long as they are obedient

and have faith in Jesus (5:8). Jesus' prayers were heard because of his "reverent submission" (5:7).

The understanding of Jesus as a divine high priest is one that requires spiritual maturity. This is evident in the remainder of chapter 5. "About this we have much to say that is hard to explain, since you have become dull in understanding" (v. 11). The author states that his readers should have been able to grasp this knowledge by now; instead, they "need someone to teach [them] again the basic elements of the oracles of God. [They] need milk, not solid food" (v. 12). The hearers of this message do not understand the true meaning of Jesus' priesthood. Those who are "mature," however, "have been trained by practice to distinguish good from evil" (v. 14). This is what Jesus did when he walked the earth, distinguishing good from evil (5:7).

Because of Jesus' sinless nature and sacrifice, he is able to bring about a new type of covenant about which Hebrews 10:16–25 speaks. Not only is Jesus the final blood sacrifice required for the atonement of sins, but the law is described in terms of faith and conscience: "I will put my laws in their hearts, and I will write them on their minds" (v. 16). Because of Jesus' death on the cross, God will forget and forgive our sins (v. 17). "Where there is forgiveness of these, there is no longer any offering for sin" (v. 18). Like the high priests before Jesus who entered the Holy of Holies, Christians can "have confidence to enter the sanctuary" (v. 19), but unlike the high priests before Jesus, Christians do not need to bring a blood sacrifice. "By the blood of Jesus" (v. 19), "by the new and living way that he opened for us through the curtain (that is, through his flesh)" (v. 20), we have been made clean (v. 22). Therefore, we can boldly enter the sanctuary—the place of worship—with faith and assurance (v. 22).

Chapter 10 also includes a call to endurance and encouragement. In the midst of suffering, Christians are to remain confident in their faith "without wavering," because God is faithful (v. 23). They are to inspire and impel each other to "love and good deeds" (v. 24). They are not to distance themselves from one another, but rather make the practice of gathering together to maintain and enhance their relationship with each other and their faith in God (v. 25).

There is a seamless transition to chapter 11, which defines the faith the author mentions earlier (4:2; 6:1, 12) and offers numerous examples of people in the Hebrew Bible who express it. "Now faith is the assurance of things hoped for, the conviction of things not seen" (11:1). After illustrating the faith of Abel, Enoch, and Noah (vv. 4–7), Abraham (vv. 8–22), Moses (vv. 23–28), and other Israelites (vv. 29–38), we are reminded that although they had faith, they did not receive what God had promised them while they were living. "Yet all these, though they were commended for their faith, did not receive what was promised" (v. 39). This supports the writer's call to endurance and encouragement. In the midst of one's suffering, we should have unwavering faith, trusting that God will deliver us.

The book of Hebrews, the only New Testament book that describes Jesus' ministry in terms of priesthood, is a text of choice during the Lenten season. This is not only because it highlights Jesus' sacrifice for us and the mercy and grace we are freely given because of it, but also because it defines and exemplifies faith, understood as the proper response of the believer to Jesus' actions.

A word of caution is in order, however. While Christians may celebrate the message in Hebrews of Jesus being the unique and sufficient sacrifice needed for mercy and the forgiveness of sins, they should be wary of using the letter to support anti-Judaism. Too often themes such as new covenant, Jesus as the heavenly high priest, and the writing of the law on our hearts can lead to notions of replacement and correction, also known as Christian supersessionism. Supersessionism suggests that, since the emergence of Christianity, Judaism is no longer needed or valid. The idea is problematic in many ways, clearly forgetting that Jesus himself was a Jew.

Good Friday invites Christians to reflect on Jesus' ministry that includes his unique priesthood and his subsequent death. It argues that Jesus has made a way for Christians to be bold and unwavering in their faith during times of suffering, encouraging believers to take courage from the high priest who gave his life for the world.

SHANELL T. SMITH

Commentary 2: Connecting the Reading with the World

How do we hold faith in the face of suffering, sin, and despair? These texts, heard on Good Friday, reply: Jesus represents us, forgiveness frees us, and life in covenantal community forms us in hope.

Jesus Represents Us. Throughout the book of Hebrews Jesus is associated with the great high priest in the order of Melchizedek (Heb. 7:13–17). While this analogy was likely powerful and connotative for the Jewish Christians to whom the letter was first written, it may be unfamiliar to contemporary hearers. Preachers might consider introducing Melchizedek, because knowing something about him helps us better understand who Jesus is and how Jesus saves us. According to Genesis 14, Melchizedek was a king and priest of "God Most High" who blessed Abram, and to whom Abram therefore paid a tithe. The association of Jesus with Melchizedek conveys Jesus as a priest who stands apart from the proscribed order of things. While it has been required since the days of Moses that priests be descendants of Aaron, Jesus is not. Like Melchizedek, who lived before Moses, Aaron, and Miriam and worshiped God by a different name, Jesus does not meet the standards for priesthood upheld by his contemporaries. Preachers might ask those listening to this text: Do we respect Jesus' priesthood, laying aside the "rules," even as Abram paid Melchizedek homage?

Attending to Jesus' nonconformity lends insight into how Jesus is able to "sympathize with our weaknesses" (4:15). He is not a brocaded priest with the proper pedigree who appears to hover above the sufferings of the world, but an ordinary person who participates fully in our trials and temptations. It is tenable, therefore, that he represents us effectively before God, offering up heartfelt "prayers and supplications" (5:7) and obeying on our behalf (5:8). Preachers might want to highlight how the association between Jesus and Melchizedek resonates with the rising numbers of those who have experienced organized religion as hypocritical and legalistic; those who often identify themselves as religiously unaffiliated, "spiritual, but not religious," or "nones."

A related theme that may be taken up, consistent with Hebrews's more Abelardian take on the atonement, is representation (Abélard argued, in the twelfth century, that the example of Jesus saves us by compelling us to respond to God's love). True representation is hard to come by in contemporary American culture. Those who claim to represent the people—politicians, salespeople, lawyers, doctors—are often distrusted, suspected of making false promises for the sake of votes or money. In contrast, Jesus the great high priest in the order of Melchizedek is the real deal according to Hebrews. He does not simply pretend to understand and advocate for our circumstances; he shares deeply in our struggles with sin (4:15), despair (5:7), and suffering (5:8), working obediently on our behalf to keep these things from becoming barriers to hope (10:23), community (10:24–25), and salvation (5:9). He does this by becoming a "new and living way" (10:20) through whom we experience forgiveness (10:18), mercy, and grace (4:16).

Engagers of these texts might further reflect that the Jesus who shares in the suffering and struggles of all creatures is not limited to representing those who address him as Lord. His association with Melchizedek suggests he identifies with and acts on behalf of those who seek God outside the Judeo-Christian tradition. In our global, pluralistic world, in which leaders are often asked, "What about people of other faiths?" the inclusive character of Jesus' high priesthood, as it is born witness to here, might open us to productive interreligious dialogue.

Forgiveness Frees Us. Brené Brown is a popular speaker and writer who has helped

millions of people find a path out of debilitating shame and to living a more "courageous" life.[1] The preacher might want to note the widespread experience people have of feeling defective, suggesting that Good Friday offers special opportunity to remember Jesus has entered as deeply into the experience of creaturely brokenness as it is possible to go. The beginning of courage, from a Christian perspective, comes when we witness Jesus praying "with loud cries and tears" (5:7); when we look at the cross and recognize that we are not alone in our suffering and struggle and need not, therefore, feel isolated and ashamed. A "new and living way" is "opened . . . by the blood of Jesus" and we are able to "enter the sanctuary" (10:19), to hold "without wavering" to hope (10:23), and to "approach the throne of grace with boldness" (4:16).

Could the assertion that "our hearts [are] sprinkled clean from an evil conscience" mean precisely that we are somehow released, by way of Jesus' blood, from our bondage to shame? It is clear that 10:22 associates Jesus' sacrifice on the cross with the animal sacrifices hitherto made as sin offerings, where blood was sprinkled as part of the ritual. The preacher or educator might choose to ponder the significance of this, given that 10:18 states that sacrifices are no longer needed where there is "forgiveness." Worship leaders might attend to the hymn "There Is Power in the Blood"—a hymn highly valued by many Christians but often omitted from mainline hymnals, a hymn that is very true to today's texts insofar as it celebrates our being "freed from the burden of sin" that incapacitates us.[2] (I do, however, suggest adding a stanza: "Would you be free from your shame and disgrace? . . . Filled with Christ's courage our new life to face? There's wonderful pow'r in the blood!")

Covenantal Community Forms Us. As those represented by the Jesus who understands our trials, as those forgiven by way of his "reverent submission" and "obedience" (5:7–8), Hebrews suggests we have a direct relationship with God. We live in holy spaces once off

1. Brené Brown, "The Power of Vulnerability," at ted.com.
2. Lewis E. Jones (1899). Public domain. http://library.timelesstruths.org/music/There_Is_Power_in_the_Blood/.

limits, as members of Christian community. No longer must we offer sin offerings (10:18); Jesus, operating in the order of Melchizedek, changed the system of blood sacrifice by way of his faithfulness, which led to the shedding of blood, even as he resisted suffering and death. Just as sacrifices no longer mediate our relationship to God, so the laws of God now have no place as external rules to which we are subject. They are, rather, manifestations of our identity, as those who live before God. We know them in our "hearts" and "minds" (10:16), engaging one another with the "love and good deeds" that follow from them. Teachers might explore, along these lines, Calvin's understanding that Christians are free from the law to obey it voluntarily,[3] noting how countercultural it is to imagine adherence to God's law as an expression of freedom.

The very idea of "covenant" challenges cultural values. Global capitalism trains us to think in terms of contracts and transactions, rather than covenants. We might reflect on how this has affected our relationships, spiritualities, and theologies. On this Good Friday, how does our radical transactionalism control how we think about Jesus' suffering and death? If we understand the cross as one side of a transaction that somehow purchases forgiveness, we have missed the message of Hebrews. Our high priest, Jesus, did not trade his blood for the gift of salvation he then extended to us. It is Jesus himself who is the gift, Jesus himself who is given. He tears the curtain away, and we enter the house of God, where transactions are unneeded because God's presence to us, and ours to one another, is immediate. This is our hope (10:23).

CYNTHIA L. RIGBY

3. John Calvin, *Institutes of the Christian Religion*, ed. John T. McNeill (Philadelphia: Westminster Press, 1960), 3.19.

Good Friday

John 18:1–19:42

[1]After Jesus had spoken these words, he went out with his disciples across the Kidron valley to a place where there was a garden, which he and his disciples entered. [2]Now Judas, who betrayed him, also knew the place, because Jesus often met there with his disciples. [3]So Judas brought a detachment of soldiers together with police from the chief priests and the Pharisees, and they came there with lanterns and torches and weapons. [4]Then Jesus, knowing all that was to happen to him, came forward and asked them, "Whom are you looking for?" [5]They answered, "Jesus of Nazareth." Jesus replied, "I am he." Judas, who betrayed him, was standing with them. [6]When Jesus said to them, "I am he," they stepped back and fell to the ground. [7]Again he asked them, "Whom are you looking for?" And they said, "Jesus of Nazareth." [8]Jesus answered, "I told you that I am he. So if you are looking for me, let these men go." [9]This was to fulfill the word that he had spoken, "I did not lose a single one of those whom you gave me." [10]Then Simon Peter, who had a sword, drew it, struck the high priest's slave, and cut off his right ear. The slave's name was Malchus. [11]Jesus said to Peter, "Put your sword back into its sheath. Am I not to drink the cup that the Father has given me?"

[12]So the soldiers, their officer, and the Jewish police arrested Jesus and bound him. [13]First they took him to Annas, who was the father-in-law of Caiaphas, the high priest that year. [14]Caiaphas was the one who had advised the Jews that it was better to have one person die for the people.

[15]Simon Peter and another disciple followed Jesus. Since that disciple was known to the high priest, he went with Jesus into the courtyard of the high priest, [16]but Peter was standing outside at the gate. So the other disciple, who was known to the high priest, went out, spoke to the woman who guarded the gate, and brought Peter in. [17]The woman said to Peter, "You are not also one of this man's disciples, are you?" He said, "I am not." [18]Now the slaves and the police had made a charcoal fire because it was cold, and they were standing around it and warming themselves. Peter also was standing with them and warming himself.

[19]Then the high priest questioned Jesus about his disciples and about his teaching. [20]Jesus answered, "I have spoken openly to the world; I have always taught in synagogues and in the temple, where all the Jews come together. I have said nothing in secret. [21]Why do you ask me? Ask those who heard what I said to them; they know what I said." [22]When he had said this, one of the police standing nearby struck Jesus on the face, saying, "Is that how you answer the high priest?" [23]Jesus answered, "If I have spoken wrongly, testify to the wrong. But if I have spoken rightly, why do you strike me?" [24]Then Annas sent him bound to Caiaphas the high priest.

[25]Now Simon Peter was standing and warming himself. They asked him, "You are not also one of his disciples, are you?" He denied it and said, "I am not." [26]One of the slaves of the high priest, a relative of the man whose ear Peter had cut off, asked, "Did I not see you in the garden with him?" [27]Again Peter denied it, and at that moment the cock crowed.

[28]Then they took Jesus from Caiaphas to Pilate's headquarters. It was early in the morning. They themselves did not enter the headquarters, so as to avoid ritual defilement and to be able to eat the Passover. [29]So Pilate went out to them and said, "What accusation do you bring against this man?" [30]They answered, "If

this man were not a criminal, we would not have handed him over to you." [31]Pilate said to them, "Take him yourselves and judge him according to your law." The Jews replied, "We are not permitted to put anyone to death." [32](This was to fulfill what Jesus had said when he indicated the kind of death he was to die.)

[33]Then Pilate entered the headquarters again, summoned Jesus, and asked him, "Are you the King of the Jews?" [34]Jesus answered, "Do you ask this on your own, or did others tell you about me?" [35]Pilate replied, "I am not a Jew, am I? Your own nation and the chief priests have handed you over to me. What have you done?" [36]Jesus answered, "My kingdom is not from this world. If my kingdom were from this world, my followers would be fighting to keep me from being handed over to the Jews. But as it is, my kingdom is not from here." [37]Pilate asked him, "So you are a king?" Jesus answered, "You say that I am a king. For this I was born, and for this I came into the world, to testify to the truth. Everyone who belongs to the truth listens to my voice." [38]Pilate asked him, "What is truth?"

After he had said this, he went out to the Jews again and told them, "I find no case against him. [39]But you have a custom that I release someone for you at the Passover. Do you want me to release for you the King of the Jews?" [40]They shouted in reply, "Not this man, but Barabbas!" Now Barabbas was a bandit.

[19:1]Then Pilate took Jesus and had him flogged. [2]And the soldiers wove a crown of thorns and put it on his head, and they dressed him in a purple robe. [3]They kept coming up to him, saying, "Hail, King of the Jews!" and striking him on the face. [4]Pilate went out again and said to them, "Look, I am bringing him out to you to let you know that I find no case against him." [5]So Jesus came out, wearing the crown of thorns and the purple robe. Pilate said to them, "Here is the man!" [6]When the chief priests and the police saw him, they shouted, "Crucify him! Crucify him!" Pilate said to them, "Take him yourselves and crucify him; I find no case against him." [7]The Jews answered him, "We have a law, and according to that law he ought to die because he has claimed to be the Son of God."

[8]Now when Pilate heard this, he was more afraid than ever. [9]He entered his headquarters again and asked Jesus, "Where are you from?" But Jesus gave him no answer. [10]Pilate therefore said to him, "Do you refuse to speak to me? Do you not know that I have power to release you, and power to crucify you?" [11]Jesus answered him, "You would have no power over me unless it had been given you from above; therefore the one who handed me over to you is guilty of a greater sin." [12]From then on Pilate tried to release him, but the Jews cried out, "If you release this man, you are no friend of the emperor. Everyone who claims to be a king sets himself against the emperor."

[13]When Pilate heard these words, he brought Jesus outside and sat on the judge's bench at a place called The Stone Pavement, or in Hebrew Gabbatha. [14]Now it was the day of Preparation for the Passover; and it was about noon. He said to the Jews, "Here is your King!" [15]They cried out, "Away with him! Away with him! Crucify him!" Pilate asked them, "Shall I crucify your King?" The chief priests answered, "We have no king but the emperor." [16]Then he handed him over to them to be crucified.

So they took Jesus; [17]and carrying the cross by himself, he went out to what is called The Place of the Skull, which in Hebrew is called Golgotha. [18]There they crucified him, and with him two others, one on either side, with Jesus between them. [19]Pilate also had an inscription written and put on the cross. It read, "Jesus of Nazareth, the King of the Jews." [20]Many of the Jews read this inscription, because the place where Jesus was crucified was near the city; and it was written in Hebrew, in Latin, and in Greek. [21]Then the chief priests of the Jews said to Pilate, "Do not write, 'The King of the Jews,' but, 'This man said, I am King of the Jews.'" ²²Pilate answered, "What I have written I have written." ²³When the soldiers had crucified Jesus, they took his clothes and divided them into four parts, one for each soldier. They also took his tunic; now the tunic was seamless, woven in one piece from the top. ²⁴So they said to one another, "Let us not tear it, but cast lots for it to see who will get it." This was to fulfill what the scripture says,

"They divided my clothes among themselves,
   and for my clothing they cast lots."

²⁵And that is what the soldiers did.

Meanwhile, standing near the cross of Jesus were his mother, and his mother's sister, Mary the wife of Clopas, and Mary Magdalene. ²⁶When Jesus saw his mother and the disciple whom he loved standing beside her, he said to his mother, "Woman, here is your son." ²⁷Then he said to the disciple, "Here is your mother." And from that hour the disciple took her into his own home.

²⁸After this, when Jesus knew that all was now finished, he said (in order to fulfill the scripture), "I am thirsty." ²⁹A jar full of sour wine was standing there. So they put a sponge full of the wine on a branch of hyssop and held it to his mouth. ³⁰When Jesus had received the wine, he said, "It is finished." Then he bowed his head and gave up his spirit.

³¹Since it was the day of Preparation, the Jews did not want the bodies left on the cross during the sabbath, especially because that sabbath was a day of great solemnity. So they asked Pilate to have the legs of the crucified men broken and the bodies removed. ³²Then the soldiers came and broke the legs of the first and of the other who had been crucified with him. ³³But when they came to Jesus and saw that he was already dead, they did not break his legs. ³⁴Instead, one of the soldiers pierced his side with a spear, and at once blood and water came out. ³⁵(He who saw this has testified so that you also may believe. His testimony is true, and he knows that he tells the truth.) ³⁶These things occurred so that the scripture might be fulfilled, "None of his bones shall be broken." ³⁷And again another passage of scripture says, "They will look on the one whom they have pierced."

³⁸After these things, Joseph of Arimathea, who was a disciple of Jesus, though a secret one because of his fear of the Jews, asked Pilate to let him take away the body of Jesus. Pilate gave him permission; so he came and removed his body. ³⁹Nicodemus, who had at first come to Jesus by night, also came, bringing a mixture of myrrh and aloes, weighing about a hundred pounds. ⁴⁰They took the body of Jesus and wrapped it with the spices in linen cloths, according to the burial custom of the Jews. ⁴¹Now there was a garden in the place where he was crucified, and in the garden there was a new tomb in which no one had ever been laid. ⁴²And so, because it was the Jewish day of Preparation, and the tomb was nearby, they laid Jesus there.

Commentary 1: Connecting the Reading with Scripture

John's prefatory words in 18:1 do more than provide an easy segue from Jesus' farewell discourse (John 13–17) to Jesus' arrest, trial, crucifixion, and burial. By referencing what Jesus "had spoken," John creates a transition marked by passionate dissonance between what has just been revealed—Jesus' steadfast love for his disciples and those "who will believe in me"—and the betrayal and hatred to be unleashed against him. Note that John sets the tone for such binary oppositions early on in the prologue. Hence, Jesus is "the *light* [or life] that shines in the *darkness*"; he is the One who "*came to what was his own*, and *his own people did not accept him*" (1:11); we become "children of God" by being "born *not of* blood or the will of the flesh, or of man, *but of* God" (1:13, italics mine, see also vv. 15 and 17). We also find this contrast when comparing the quiet intimacy of the garden wherein Jesus and his disciples went to find respite before the Passover, with the violent mob-like encounter about to betray that intimacy and transform their peace into sorrow (18:3, 10). The scene is set. The hour to which Jesus has alluded over and over again has come.

Allusions to the Hebrew Scriptures about the meaning of the "the hour" throughout John create a prophetic and theological link meant to inform and strengthen the Johannine community's faith in Jesus as the expected Messiah come to redeem his people (20:31). Thus, in John's Gospel, Jesus is the obedient servant of God (14:31), the "righteous one" (18:38b; 19:6b) that Isaiah prophesied would be "lifted up," making "many righteous" by "bearing their iniquities" (Isa. 52:13; 53:6, 11; John 12:32).

In John, Jesus does not ask the Father about the possibility of passing "this cup from me"; he does not waver over his pending sacrifice (cf. Matt. 26:39; Luke 22:42; Mark 14:36). As Messiah, he requires no sympathy (Ps. 22 evokes the anguish Jesus would have experienced during his crucifixion). He has come for this very reason, to face and defeat the ruler of this world (John 12:27, 31; 14:30; 16:11; 18:11). Thus it is significant that Jesus is not betrayed by Judas's kiss. Rather, "knowing all that was to happen," Jesus preempts Judas, the chief priests, Pharisees, soldiers, and the police who come to arrest him by going out to meet them (18:4). Jesus lays down his life of his own accord; the incarnation and crucifixion were not forced upon him (1:14; 10:18; 19:30). As the Son of God, Creator, and true ruler of this world, Jesus, not his circumstances, is in control.

The religious authorities looking for Jesus of Nazareth are met with Jesus' "I am [he]" or *egō eimi* (18:5, 6, 8). The direct allusion to God's identity in Exodus in Jesus' response here is not merely coincidental. God tells Moses to tell the Israelites that "I AM" has sent him (Exod. 3:13, 14). Jesus' reply indicates that he has not only

been *sent* by the "I AM," he *is* the "I AM." He is also the Jesus of Nazareth, the one born in the flesh to Mary. He is the "I AM" incarnate in history. Unknowingly, Pilate will affirm Jesus' human-divine natures with the inscription on the cross, "Jesus of Nazareth, the King of the Jews" (John 19:19).

This christological claim is stated clearly in the prologue (1:1, 14) and continues throughout the Gospel. Ironically, the ones in the dark about Jesus' true identity are the supposed religious "authorities." To them, Jesus' claim to be the Son of God is scandalous (5:18; 10:19; 19:7). John gives us the reason: "they loved human glory more than the glory that comes from God" (12:43). Blinded by their own theological conceptions, expectations, and self-preservation, they see only the man Jesus and the danger he poses to their ministerial authority and traditions (12:11, 19). They are spiritually dead.

Finally, Jesus' three "I am [he]" responses to his persecutors serve as a powerful contrast to Peter's three denials, "I am not" (18:17, 25, 27). Jesus' obedience and faithful love tower above all others.

John focuses the bulk of his crucifixion narrative on the arrest and trial of Jesus. We get only what is necessary to reaffirm Jesus' identity as King or Messiah and the nature of his kingdom. His conversation with Pilate is revealing. Jesus' averment about "his kingdom" prompts Pilate to ask Jesus if he is indeed a king. Jesus, who owns this title from the beginning of his ministry, claims it as his purpose for coming into the world (18:37b). His kingdom, however, is "not from this world" (18:33–38); it is not a place. It is a new order that befuddles and challenges the ways of the world. It is the difference between light and darkness—God's expression of truth in Christ through the power of the Spirit. Thus Pilate's question "What is truth?" (18:38) has already been answered. Jesus is "the way, and the truth, and the life" (14:6). He is the key to understanding and experiencing this kingdom wherein we abide in the joy of the Holy Spirit and seek to bear witness to the love of God in us by being grace to one another. It is no wonder then, why Jesus was consternated over Peter's violence against the slave of the high priest who came to arrest him (18:10, 11). Indeed, the contrast between kingdoms is as clear as it is daunting.

What Jesus has proclaimed as truth, others claim is blasphemy. The acrimony that demands his crucifixion, despite his being found innocent of any crime, is heightened only by the guile that convinces Pilate to crucify him. The confession by the religious authorities, "We have no king but Caesar [NRSV "the emperor"] (19:15), belies their true status as subjects of this world and children of darkness. Indeed, the physical experience of the crucifixion expresses with morbid eloquence what Jesus has already experienced through their betrayal (1:11).

John underscores the meaning and purpose of the crucifixion by aligning the events with the will of God recorded in the Scriptures (19:11, 24, 28, 36, et al.). Three times, Jesus speaks from the cross. His limp head bleeding from the crown of thorns, he is able to see the women, his mother, and "the disciple whom he loved" beside his cross. His words to his mother and the disciple— "Woman, here is your son. . . . Here is your mother"—seem to manifest his humanity as her "earthly" son. Jesus graces both of them with a new family. The reference to his next words, "I am thirsty" (19:28–29), provides another connection to the Scriptures through the story of the exodus and the use of hyssop to sprinkle the doorframes with the blood of a Passover lamb (Exod. 12:22). The connection is fitting. His next words, "It is finished" (John 19:30), signal the end of his mission, and he gives up his spirit to the Father who sent him.

Although confirmed dead, one of the soldiers pierces Jesus' side with his spear. The sight of blood and water coming out of Jesus' side so astonishes the author of the Gospel that he goes to great pains to affirm his truthfulness as an eyewitness (19:31–37). As the giver of life, Jesus "becomes in us a spring of water gushing up to eternal life" (4:14), and his blood liberates us to live out that new life through death into eternity (Heb. 5:9).

ZAIDA MALDONADO PÉREZ

Commentary 2: Connecting the Reading with the World

Good Friday is supposed to be sad. It is the day of Jesus' death, and the long Gospel reading for the day is the story of that death: Jesus' arrest, trial, and execution on the cross, collectively referred to as the passion. "Passion" comes from the Latin word for suffering. It is also etymologically related to "passive," suggesting that the final days of Jesus' life are best described in terms of what happens to him, his role as victim. While that is certainly how the story is told in the Synoptic Gospels, things are different in John. Long before Holy Week, the Johannine Jesus makes it clear that he is no victim: "I lay down my life in order to take it up again. No one takes it from me, but I lay it down of my own accord. I have power to lay it down, and I have power to take it up again" (10:17–18). In this way the reader is forewarned that the crucifixion is less something Jesus suffers than something he enacts: it reveals him as the great I AM (8:28), and sets in motion the process through which he draws all people to himself (12:32; cf. 3:14).

So in John's telling of the story Jesus is not a victim: the soldiers who come to arrest him fall to the ground when they hear his voice (18:6) and seemingly are able to complete their task only on Jesus' say-so (18:8). When Jesus is sentenced, he carries the cross himself (19:17—no Simon of Cyrene here!) and from the cross calmly makes arrangements for his mother's care (19:25b–27). In the Synoptics, Jesus' drinking gall on the cross is a testimony to his helplessness: the product of the crowd's misunderstanding of his cry of dereliction (Matt. 27:46–48; Mark 15:34–36). In John, by contrast, Jesus deliberately says, "I am thirsty," in order to fulfill the words of Scripture (19:28), and then brings the drama to an end himself with the words, "It is finished" (19:30; cf. Matt. 27:50; Mark 15:37). None of this makes Jesus' execution any less unjust, but it does ask the reader to reposition herself in relation to it. Realistically, even those who deliberately choose a path that includes suffering as part of their witness to the gospel are not in control of circumstances in the way that John describes Jesus, but there nevertheless is something here that finds an echo in the African American woman who summarized her experience of the Birmingham bus boycott in the words, "My feets is tired, but my soul is rested."

For John, the cross is more a symbol of exaltation than of degradation, and the crucified is far more in charge of the process than Annas, Caiaphas, or Pilate. Indeed, the focus of the drama in John is not really the figure of Jesus at all; he is more like the still point around which other people and events swirl. Since we do not have Jesus' power to lay down and take up our lives, his death—at least as it is portrayed in John—does not provide a particularly useful model for our imitation. We can learn a lot, however, from the way others react to him. Peter, Pilate, and Joseph of Arimathea, for example, are all in different ways cast as disciples of Jesus, yet in each case their discipleship is compromised by fear. Although John gives other examples of how fear compromises individuals' commitment to Jesus (see, e.g., 7:13; 9:22), in these three characters the effects are particularly sharp.

Peter has been a public disciple of Jesus from the very first days of his ministry, and he hardly comes across as fearful at the beginning of the reading, when he seeks to defend Jesus from arrest to the extent of wounding one of the high priest's slaves (18:10). How he manages to avoid arrest himself is not clear (unlike the Synoptics, John makes no mention of the disciples fleeing the scene), but he ends up following Jesus to Annas's house, where his fear becomes manifest, as three times he denies being Jesus' disciple (18:17–18, 25–27).

Pilate is obviously not a disciple like Peter is, but in his own way he bears public witness to Jesus' status by having an inscription reading "Jesus of Nazareth, King of the Jews" put on the cross, defending it against the complaints of the chief priests (19:19–22). Pilate too is motivated by fear: though he is afraid of Jesus (19:8), he is even more afraid of appearing disloyal to the emperor (19:12). So even though he three times declares that Jesus is innocent

(18:38b; 19:4, 6), he nevertheless hands him over to be crucified (19:16).

Joseph of Arimathea is described as "a disciple of Jesus, though a secret one because of his fear of the Jews" (19:38). This is yet another contrast with the Synoptics, where Joseph is simply described as a disciple without qualification (Matt. 27:57), or, with more detail, as "a respected member" of the Sanhedrin who addresses Pilate "boldly" (Mark 15:43), or, more elaborately still, as a "good and righteous man," who, though a Sanhedrin member, "had not agreed to their plan and action" (Luke 23:50–51). John's description of Joseph is much less flattering (all the more so given his association with Nicodemus): one imagines him coming to Pilate in secret and burying Jesus in secret.

Crucially, in none of these three cases is the characters' fear prompted by an immediately life-threatening situation. Peter was physically far more at risk with his sword in the garden than in the high priest's courtyard; Pilate is not going to be convicted of treason against Caesar based on the cries of a Jewish mob. From what we read earlier in the Gospel (9:22), the most Joseph has to fear is expulsion from his synagogue. The immediate object of their fear is thus not death, but social marginalization and loss of prestige. It is here that the story hits close to home: elsewhere in the world being a Christian can be genuinely dangerous; in North America, the only risk likely to accompany public confession of the faith is the kind of social discomfort that Peter, Pilate, and Joseph faced.

We often think of the situation of the earliest Christians as worlds removed from our present context, and in many respects it was. But it is surely interesting that at the climax of the Fourth Gospel the threat highlighted is not martyrdom in the classic sense (i.e., putting one's body on the line), but the much more mundane activity of publicly affirming one's discipleship. As John tells the passion story, Jesus goes about his business quite calmly and deliberately, to the extent that from his perspective there really does not seem to be much either frightening or sad about it (no "agony in the garden" here!). He is the calm center of things. The drama of the story lies in the way other characters interact with him. It is their fear that raises questions about what it means to be a disciple, and if the story remains the spiritual low point of Holy Week, it is less because of what happens to Jesus than for what it threatens to reveal about us. One of the lessons of this reading is that confessing Jesus publicly—not only in the supportive environment of worship on a Sunday morning—is awkward and difficult. If we fail to do so, we will find ourselves with Joseph of Arimathea, burying Jesus.

IAN A. MCFARLAND

Easter Day/Resurrection of the Lord

Isaiah 65:17–25
Psalm 118:1–2, 14–24
Acts 10:34–43

John 20:1–18
1 Corinthians 15:19–26
Luke 24:1–12

Isaiah 65:17–25

¹⁷For I am about to create new heavens
and a new earth;
the former things shall not be remembered
or come to mind.
¹⁸But be glad and rejoice forever
in what I am creating;
for I am about to create Jerusalem as a joy,
and its people as a delight.
¹⁹I will rejoice in Jerusalem,
and delight in my people;
no more shall the sound of weeping be heard in it,
or the cry of distress.
²⁰No more shall there be in it
an infant that lives but a few days,
or an old person who does not live out a lifetime;
for one who dies at a hundred years will be considered a youth,
and one who falls short of a hundred will be considered accursed.
²¹They shall build houses and inhabit them;
they shall plant vineyards and eat their fruit.
²²They shall not build and another inhabit;
they shall not plant and another eat;
for like the days of a tree shall the days of my people be,
and my chosen shall long enjoy the work of their hands.
²³They shall not labor in vain,
or bear children for calamity;
for they shall be offspring blessed by the LORD—
and their descendants as well.
²⁴Before they call I will answer,
while they are yet speaking I will hear.
²⁵The wolf and the lamb shall feed together,
the lion shall eat straw like the ox;
but the serpent—its food shall be dust!
They shall not hurt or destroy
on all my holy mountain,
says the LORD.

Commentary 1: Connecting the Reading with Scripture

The book of Isaiah provides a theological map of the old city of Jerusalem in the experience of ancient Israel, both its failure and its possibility. The first part of the book (chaps. 1–39) narrates the failure of the city all the way from being like Sodom and Gomorrah (1:10), through the one-time miraculous rescue (37:33–38) to its expected demise at the hands of the Babylonians (39:1–8). The second half of the book (40–66), in a surging explosion of new promissory poetry, anticipates the restoration of the city and the return of the deportees to the city. The characterization of the new city includes a welcome to the excluded ("foreigners and eunuchs," 56:3–6), new worship as neighborliness (58:5–9), new commercial prosperity (60:6–11), a new jubilee year ("the year of the LORD's favor," 61:2), and new agricultural flourishing (62:4). Thus the book of Isaiah moves dramatically from *destruction* (chaps. 1–39) to *restoration* (chaps. 40–66). It is as though the anticipation of God-given newness builds until the climactic poetry of our verses in chapter 65.

Our verses are a divine oracle of promise in which God declares a wholly new future for Jerusalem that is not derived from anything old, but is a new free unconditional gift from God. The triad of "new heaven, new earth, new Jerusalem" means "everything new!" The accent is on the city in which there will be new social relationships of justice, security, and well-being, all of which contradict the old Jerusalem, which was, in prophetic view (see Isa. 1), a venue for exploitative oppressive relationship in which the strong devoured the vulnerable. In Isaiah's horizon, "new Jerusalem" is a real urban population with alternative socioeconomic possibilities.

This will be a city in which there will be no more cries of distress over injustice (65:19). There will be adequate health care that results in extravagant longevity, and no more infant mortality (v. 20). There will be economic stability and security so that the vulnerable will not lose their treasured property by confiscation (eminent domain) or by seizure in war (vv. 21–22). The old curse of pain at childbirth (Gen. 3:16) will be relieved by new procedures (Isa. 65:23). At the end of the poem, moreover, it is anticipated that God will be utterly attentive to the city, as a mother attends to her child in the night (v. 24), and a reconciled creation, no more destructive ecology (v. 25). This sweeping promise from God is not unlike Martin Luther King Jr.'s "I have a Dream" speech, a word of poetic imagination that contradicts all present circumstance. It is future grounded in the public goodness of God, but a future that is concretely this-worldly, political, and economic.

The theme of newness from God pervades the lectionary texts. In Psalm 118, a great victory, wrought by God and grounded in God's fidelity, is celebrated. Thus in verses 1–2 and 29, the psalm is framed by God's "steadfast love," to which the only appropriate response is thanks. God's victory permits a new era of well-being grounded in gratitude.

The church's appeal to our text from Isaiah is made possible by an interpretive move that morphs *the destruction and restoration of Jerusalem* into *the crucifixion and resurrection of Jesus*, without losing any of the "this-worldly" socioeconomic political accent of the old text. The "new Jerusalem" becomes, in Christian interpretation, the risen Christ and the new world of well-being that he makes possible and over which he governs. In the Gospel reading the Easter reality of Jesus can no more be explained than can be the new Jerusalem of Isaiah, which defies all conventional political wisdom. In the epistle reading of 1 Corinthians 15, Paul anticipates the defeat of "the last enemy," death (v. 26; see vv. 54–55). This is clearly parallel to the defeat of chaos and the coming of new flourishing creation, so that in both cases, the new triumph and victory of God (defeat of the chaos of empire and defeat of death) make possible a new safe place in which creation and all of its inhabitants can prosper in well-being.

The visionary promise of our Isaiah text is the extreme expression of newness in the Old Testament that is matched in the New Testament by the vision of "new heaven, new earth, new Jerusalem" that pushes beyond the dread exploitative power of the Roman Empire (Rev. 21:1–7). While Isaiah's vision is the extreme expression, it does not live in isolation. The text is commonly dated to the early Persian period of Israel's life after the exile, when Jerusalem was in shambles and the vision of a reconstituted Jerusalem was an urgent necessity. In that same period of the sixth and fifth centuries BCE (550–450), a time of discouragement and disappointment, Judaism witnessed an immense eruption of new poetry of promise of which our text is a part. The circumstance of deportation and an anemic restoration to a dismal economic circumstance in Jerusalem did not lead to despair or retreat into old patterns of conventional society. It led, rather, to a fresh poetic possibility in a rich array of texts. Thus in the same period we get:

- *Isaiah's* declaration that God will do a new deliverance that will cause Israel to forget the exodus (Isa. 43:16–21), a "new song" that sings about "new things" (42:9), "new things" not known before (48:6), and a "new name" (identity, 62:2). The new name will be Married, which means "flourishing," the one in whom God delights (62:4).
- *Jeremiah's* anticipation of newness in which God will "reverse the fortunes" of Israel, a reversal from distress and defeat to prosperity and flourishing (Jer. 30:3, 18; 33:7, 11, 26). Specifically there will be a "restored covenant" ("new covenant") that is in contrast to the old failed covenant of Sinai. The new covenant will be grounded in forgiveness and will yield a readiness to obey Torah and live in sync with God. This text has been appropriated in Hebrews 8:8–12, where it is taken to refer to the "new covenant" effected in Jesus (see 1 Cor. 11:25).
- *Ezekiel's* plethora of images for the newness of God. Thus God is the new shepherd who will displace old exploitative rulers: "I will seek the lost, and I will bring back the strayed, and I will bind up the injured, and I will strengthen the weak, but the fat and the strong I will destroy. I will feed them with justice" (Ezek. 34:16).

A new blessing of prosperity for the land is grounded in God's own self-regard (36:28–32). A return to the land is presented as a resurrection whereby the "dry bones" of Israel are given new life by the spirit of God (37:1–14). A new temple will be an adequate habitat for God abiding presence (chaps. 43–44). In that new temple, there will be streams of the "water of life" coming from the altar (47:1–12, on which see Rev. 22:1–2).

This array of images is mobilized to express the newness of God that outruns every image. The return to Jerusalem, in the Old Testament, is a quintessential newness of God. The news is that God has not quit or been defeated. In the very depth of misery, the power and fidelity of God persist. Both the new city of Isaiah and the risen Christ of the evangelists attest that God is not a prisoner or victim of circumstance. God is free and faithful beyond every disability of death, chaos, or injustice.

WALTER BRUEGGEMANN

Commentary 2: Connecting the Reading with the World

The blessings of our triune God, Creator, Redeemer, and Sustainer, spoken by the prophet Isaiah long before the first Easter morning, resound throughout this passage. As the preacher, it is your privilege to bring these words of comfort, hope, healing, and *challenge* to the congregation.

Isaiah offers a powerful complement to the Easter story, especially if your congregation heard the prophet's words on Christmas Eve or Christmas Day (Isa. 9:2–7, "a child is born to us"; Isa. 52:7–10, "how beautiful upon the mountains"; or Isa. 62:6–12, "see, your salvation comes"). As God creates a new earth on Easter morning, the circle is brought to a holy completion. Remind the worshipers of the promises they heard as they awaited Christ's birth, and invite them to imagine how Christ's resurrection reiterates God's vision for wholeness throughout creation.

"But be glad and rejoice forever in what I am creating" (Isa. 65:18a). On this day, when your church will welcome both those who rarely darken the doors and those for whom this is the holiest day of the year, let this phrase shape your Easter worship. Our God has created, is creating, and will continue to create. Even those with little knowledge of the Bible may be familiar with the story of creation. Begin with what they know, by reminding them of the garden where God first created. Remind them how God visualized a world of diversity and beauty, all living beings dwelling in harmony. At Easter, God brings us back to a garden, so that we may witness God's destruction of death's constraints and may renew our covenantal relationship with God. On this day of resurrection, it is enormously appropriate to incorporate the words of Isaiah, which flesh out the details of the restoration of life in God's "garden." The Isaiah passage is an opportunity to invite the worshipers to look back in time, back into the long arc of God's mercy, while also gazing into the "not yet" of creation's fulfillment. God is not finished designing, restoring, and remaking our world.

The prophet's words are breathtaking. Speaking to a remnant community that has limped home from exile, Isaiah is aware of their disappointments, both corporate and personal. Who does not long for a world in which there is no sorrow, no loss, no one who "falls short of one hundred"? You are deeply aware of the members of your congregation who are experiencing Easter for the first time without a loved one. The resurrection promise, despite its comforts, does not erase the pain of that empty space on the pew.

God cares about individual grief. It is never God's plan for an infant to die, or for a life to be cut short. If your congregation has been experiencing a season of grief, comfort them with the prophet's words. God understands human pain and suffering, grief and loss. God's promises that the suffering will not last, and God's deeper promise is this: "before they call, I will answer." Give your listeners time to consider that idea. Invite church members to share a personal story of how God answered their need before they called out for God's aid. These stories can provide a balm for the soul of those who suffer.

We also can affirm that it is never God's plan for people to suffer under systems of oppression. "They shall build houses and inhabit them. . . . They shall not labor in vain" (vv. 21a, 23a. Depending upon your context, your Easter preaching will employ an affirming, encouraging voice or a voice of challenge, as in "I dare you!" You will know what they need to hear. If your congregants are weary from daily laboring against injustice, they need a reminder that God's promises are true. Celebrate with them the ways that they are feeding, sheltering, laboring with God. If, however, your congregants have been silent in the face of oppression, dare them to begin a new life, a life rooted in Easter's power.

Isaiah spoke to a people who had forgotten the joy of eating the fruit of their own vineyards. They had been sojourners in a strange land, and were only beginning to trust what it meant to be "home," even if that home was, in some ways, unrecognizable. To their broken hearts and discouraged souls, Isaiah spoke words of reassurance. God's vision for God's people is not a lifetime bookmarked with grief. God's vision is not for people to live in fear and despair. "Imagine a just world, a joy-filled world, a realm of peace," God says.

Preachers and congregants alike shout, "Yes! I can imagine that!" Preachers and congregants alike whisper, "Impossible." Lions eat lambs, and so do we. People pay money to shoot rare lions just for sport. Snakes eat more than dust; they eat our pets. People are destroyed by people, emotionally, mentally, physically, spiritually. This is the tension in which we live on Easter.

It is the Christian's catch-22 for the ages. If we do not believe in resurrection, how can we believe in a day when lions will eat straw and no one dies before their hundred years are up? The vision God described through Isaiah is the invitation to participate in resurrection. Death comes in many forms, and tombs come in a variety of shapes and sizes. When we overwork and underpay our neighbors, we promote death instead of life. When we make it impossible for people to afford health care or access to education, we condemn people to a life of suffering that is only a step above death. If these words have not been spoken in your sanctuary, then let Easter be the day when Isaiah's words are translated into contemporary language.

When we do not atone for the wrongs we have done to entire groups of people, we are clinging to paths that isolate rather than unite. When we do not seek new ways of understanding, new ways of hearing another's grief or fear, we bury hope instead of breathing life into it. The faces that look up at you from the pews are longing to know how the words of Isaiah and the implausible story of resurrection matter to them today. Dare those faces to resist the comfortable urge to shove resurrection back in a tomb, and roll an enormous stone across its opening. Challenge them instead to run with the women from the tomb, sharing the freeing news that captivity and death have been overcome by life.

Once that news has been proclaimed, it cannot be "un-proclaimed." Easter is the ultimate creative moment, and creativity is risky and vulnerable. You never know how it will go over. Brainstorm ways your congregation could take a holy risk this Easter. In collaboration with your church's mission team (or evangelism? or worship?), claim the Easter season as an opportunity for rebirth. Isaiah's vision offers multiple suggestions.

Perhaps your congregation could birth a plan to provide space for a community garden, where hungry people could "plant vineyards and eat their fruit." Is activism your community's gift? Look for the food deserts and swamps in your neighborhood, and enlist others to provide alternatives. Every community has housing needs; today could be a day to introduce advocacy for subsidized housing or homeless-shelter improvements or to announce a Habitat for Humanity project.

Whether through words of comfort or challenge, celebrate Easter as a day of empowerment and new beginnings. There is the strong possibility that in the engagement, in the "doing," that "believing" (for even the weariest) will be reborn. Not only is God still creating, but God is creating through your preaching voice. May you "be glad and rejoice forever"!

CATHY CALDWELL HOOP

Psalm 118:1–2, 14–24

¹O give thanks to the LORD, for he is good;
  his steadfast love endures forever!

²Let Israel say,
  "His steadfast love endures forever."
. . . .
¹⁴The LORD is my strength and my might;
  he has become my salvation.

¹⁵There are glad songs of victory in the tents of the righteous:
"The right hand of the LORD does valiantly;
    ¹⁶the right hand of the LORD is exalted;
  the right hand of the LORD does valiantly."
¹⁷I shall not die, but I shall live,
  and recount the deeds of the LORD.
¹⁸The LORD has punished me severely,
  but he did not give me over to death.

¹⁹Open to me the gates of righteousness,
  that I may enter through them
  and give thanks to the LORD.

²⁰This is the gate of the LORD;
  the righteous shall enter through it.

²¹I thank you that you have answered me
  and have become my salvation.
²²The stone that the builders rejected
  has become the chief cornerstone.
²³This is the LORD's doing;
  it is marvelous in our eyes.
²⁴This is the day that the LORD has made;
  let us rejoice and be glad in it.

Connecting the Psalm with Scripture and Worship

Psalm 118 is a thanksgiving hymn of praise. The liturgical formula of (1) a call to praise ("O give thanks to the LORD") and (2) the reason for the praise ("for the LORD is good; God's steadfast love endures forever") constitutes the psalm's introduction. God's goodness is the foundation of our thanksgiving; God bestows mercy and steadfast love on those who willingly rely on God for help, for saving grace.[1]

---

1. James L. Mays, *Psalms*, Interpretation (Louisville, KY: John Knox Press, 1994), 378.

The community celebrating the presence of the risen Christ echoes Israel's exuberant praise (v. 14) and the joyful song sung at the parting of the waters of the sea (Exod. 15:2). God acts and God saves. Death will not have the final word. Those who rejoice in resurrection life acknowledge on this day that our confidence and hope is in Christ with God. "I shall not die, but I shall live, and recount the deeds of the LORD" (v. 17).

Life and death are at issue. Jesus, the one in whom the children of God have placed their hope, has been executed like the vilest of criminals. For days now, we have recalled and reflected on the circumstances leading to this end. The inertia of our days and these times has been focused on the meaning of this life and death. What are we to make of it? What is God doing? What is God up to?

Psalm 118 gives thanks for God's steadfast love, which endures forever. This enduring power of God's steadfast love stands in stark contrast with the deadly concerns of the unfaithful, who perceive life's reality with an entirely this-worldly orientation. Jesus, who seemingly dies in ignominy and disgrace, has been raised. Now, we, who are disciples of Jesus, hear the promise of God being brought to fulfillment: "For I am about to create new heavens and a new earth" (Isa. 65:17).

Do we fear what death has come to mean in our culture? Are we afraid that no one will remember us, or care that we ever existed? Resurrection opens us to see life and death in a different guise, to experience life in a new condition of life with God. We declare that what Jesus experiences, we will experience. Our hoped-for future with God is made possible by what happens to Jesus in life, death, and resurrection.

Hence, the voice of the psalmist is our voice, declaring thanks and joy for God's gift to us, as we remember that "the stone that the builders rejected has become the chief cornerstone" (Ps. 118:22). "This is [God] the LORD's doing; it is marvelous in our eyes" (v. 23). As God's people we proclaim the mystery of the resurrection: though death may look as if it has the final word, God is not defeated. Jesus' resurrection puts death to death, as the increase of God's salvation swells across generations.

Life is more than a steadfast rush toward death's emptiness and nothingness. God rejoices in what God is doing: "Be glad and rejoice forever in what I am creating; for I am about to create Jerusalem as a joy, and its people as a delight" (Isa. 65:18). Can we know redemption when it feels as if we are in the grips of desolation? Can hope endure despite the grave? Easter proclaims, "Yes!" Why? Because Jesus lives. "This is the day that the LORD has made" (Ps. 118:24a). "It is marvelous in our eyes" (v. 23b). "This is the LORD's doing" (v. 23a). "Let us rejoice and be glad in it" (v. 24b).

The shadows of death that have permeated this world we live in are now overshadowed by Easter's glorious light. This feast of feasts, Easter, celebrated as early as the second century, begins on Holy Saturday evening with the great vigil of Easter. A fire is lit and the paschal candle is processed out of twilight's darkness into the community of believers, where the faithful exchange the lumen Christi, the light of Christ, with one another as the sanctuary grows radiant with the presence of Christ. The Easter vigil, the first of the celebrations of this Sunday of Sundays, centers on sharing the great stories of creation, the patriarchs and matriarchs (our ancestors in faith), the exodus, the prophets, and the deliverance from the fiery furnace of Shadrach, Meshach, and Abednego. God's saving action is recounted in narrative after narrative, culminating in what is for Christians the great narrative, in which the body of Jesus is discovered to no longer be in the grave. The treacherous uncertainty of the moment yields to the encounter of Mary Magdalene, apostle to the apostles, with Jesus now risen.[2]

The truth and challenge of Easter are acknowledged in such sharing. Are we, even in life's most dire circumstances, able to trust God, to believe that God acts and will act for us? With such trusting confidence, we may then with the psalmist declare: "I shall not die, but live, and declare the works of the LORD" (Ps. 118:17 KJV). The Lord "did not give [us] over to death" (v. 18b).

JOSEPH A. DONNELLA II

---

2. Joan D. Chittister, "Mary Magdalene: Icon of Ministry," in *A Passion For Life: Fragments of the Face of God* (Maryknoll, NY: Orbis, 2001), 43–46.

Acts 10:34–43

[34]Then Peter began to speak to them: "I truly understand that God shows no partiality, [35]but in every nation anyone who fears him and does what is right is acceptable to him. [36]You know the message he sent to the people of Israel, preaching peace by Jesus Christ—he is Lord of all. [37]That message spread throughout Judea, beginning in Galilee after the baptism that John announced: [38]how God anointed Jesus of Nazareth with the Holy Spirit and with power; how he went about doing good and healing all who were oppressed by the devil, for God was with him. [39]We are witnesses to all that he did both in Judea and in Jerusalem. They put him to death by hanging him on a tree; [40]but God raised him on the third day and allowed him to appear, [41]not to all the people but to us who were chosen by God as witnesses, and who ate and drank with him after he rose from the dead. [42]He commanded us to preach to the people and to testify that he is the one ordained by God as judge of the living and the dead. [43]All the prophets testify about him that everyone who believes in him receives forgiveness of sins through his name."

Commentary 1: Connecting the Reading with Scripture

Acts 10:34–43 is chosen for the Sunday of the Resurrection of the Lord Jesus for a reason: Peter's speech makes it clear that the resurrection of Jesus changes everything that he thought he knew about what God wanted from him. Acts 9 and 10 are twin chapters with a chiastic structure (ABBA). In other words, Luke narrates the conversions of Paul and Peter back to back. As readers, we have barely taken in the significance of Paul's encounter with the risen Lord (A) and his dramatic turn from the persecutor of believers in Jesus to the proclaimer of the gospel he once tried to destroy (B) in chapter 9 of Acts, when we are struck by the equally dramatic story of Peter's conversion on the topic of Gentile inclusion (B), which he attributes to God's action of sending Jesus Christ, "who is Lord of all" (A), in Acts, chapter 10. Luke has given his readers "a double whammy"; we see the lives of two powerful people completely changed by the resurrection of Jesus. We can only wonder: if Jesus' resurrection has had this kind of power already, what will God do next? Suddenly, anything is possible!

If Paul's conversion is an external movement from physical blindness to sight, Peter's conversion is more of an internal movement, from unquestioned assumption to insight. Peter is saying his noonday prayers on the housetop of Simon the tanner in Joppa. Hungry, he falls into a trance and sees a remarkable vision that is repeated in triplicate. Three times a sheet full of ritually unclean animals is lowered from heaven before him and a heavenly voice summons him: "Get up, Peter; kill and eat." Three times he protests that he has never eaten anything profane or unclean. Three times the voice replies: "What God has made clean, you must not call profane." Puzzled, Peter descends to the house, only to be met by three men, evidently Gentiles, asking for him by name. While he is still thinking about that, the Holy Spirit prompts him: "Look, three men are searching for you. . . . Go with them without hesitation; for I have sent them." Finally the penny drops for Peter: the threefold vision, the three Gentiles, and he goes with them to the house of Cornelius, a Gentile centurion, only to discover that Cornelius has had an experience parallel to his own, arranged by the same Holy Spirit that had called him.

Cornelius invites Peter to speak whatever God has commanded him to say. With

Cornelius and his friends, we readers wait to hear what Peter will make of this rather strange set of circumstances that has brought him, an observant Jew, into the house of a Gentile that until now he would have called unclean. Our lesson for the day is the speech Peter gives on that occasion, his newfound realization that the resurrection of Jesus has profound social implications: specifically, the division of the world into Jew and Gentile has been problematized. Jesus Christ is Lord of all.

Peter's insight that the traditional socially constructed division of the world into Jew and Gentile has been called into question by the action of God in Jesus Christ is mirrored in other early Christian writings. Paul writes in Romans 3:21–26. that God's righteousness (justice), which has been attested by the prophets, has now been disclosed through the faithfulness of Jesus Christ. Just as there is no distinction between Jew and Gentile with respect to sin (all have sinned and fallen short of God's glory), so also there is no distinction between Jew and Gentile with respect to salvation: all are put right with God by God's own grace (gift), through the redemption of Christ Jesus, whom God put forward as an atoning sacrifice for sin. Paul appeals to one of the classic texts of Judaism ("Hear, O Israel; the LORD our God is one LORD," Deut. 6:4) as a warrant for his argument in Romans 3:29–30 that God is not only God of Jews but is also the God of Gentiles, because "God is one." So, reasons Paul, God will put right both the circumcised (Jews) and the uncircumcised (Gentiles) on the same basis, the faithfulness of Christ, who was faithful even to death on a cross (Phil. 2:8).

The author of Ephesians frames a similar argument in chapter 2, writing from a Jewish perspective to "you Gentiles by birth, called 'the

Christ Lives in Us If We Love One Another

Christ is risen. Christ lives. Christ is the Lord of the living and the dead. He is the Lord of history.

Christ is the Lord of a history that moves. He not only holds the beginning and the end in his hands, but he is in history with us, walking ahead of us to where we are going. He is not always in the same place.

The cult of the Holy Sepulchre is Christian only in so far as it is the cult of the place where Christ is no longer found. But such a cult can be valid only on one condition: that we are willing to move on, to follow him to where we are not yet, to seek him where he goes before us—"to Galilee."

So we are called not only to believe that Christ once rose from the dead, thereby proving that he was God; we are called to experience the Resurrection in our own lives by entering into this dynamic movement, by following Christ who lives in us. This life, this dynamism, is expressed by the power of love and of encounter: Christ lives in us if we love one another. And our love for one another means involvement in one another's history.

Christ lives in us and leads us, through mutual encounter and commitment, into a new future which we build together for one another. That future is called the Kingdom of God. The Kingdom is already established; the Kingdom is a present reality. But there is still work to be done. Christ calls us to work together in building his Kingdom. We cooperate with him in bringing it to perfection.

Such is the timeless message of the Church not only on Easter Sunday but on every day of the year and every year until the world's end. The dynamism of the Easter mystery is at the heart of the Christian faith. It is the life of the Church. The Resurrection is not a doctrine we try to prove or a problem we argue about: it is the life and action of Christ himself in us by his Holy Spirit.

A Christian bases his entire life on these truths. His entire life is changed by the presence and the action of the Risen Christ.

Thomas Merton, *He is Risen* (Niles, IL: Argus Communications, 1975), 1–2.

uncircumcision' by those who are called 'the circumcision'" (Eph. 2:11), reminding them that once they were "without Christ," alienated from Israel, and strangers to the covenants of promise, "having no hope and without God in the world" (v. 12). Now those Gentiles have been brought near. Ephesians 2:14 describes the work of Christ on the cross as a work of peace: "in his flesh he has made both groups into one and has broken down the dividing wall, that is, the hostility between us." So also 1 Peter 2:9–10, probably taken from an early baptismal homily, addresses Gentiles who are now Christian: "Once you were not a people, but now you are God's people." These newly baptized are "a chosen race, a royal priesthood, a holy nation, God's own people" (as in Exod. 19:6 and Hos. 2:23). Words traditionally spoken to Jews are now also being applied to Gentile converts to Christianity.

While Paul in Romans 3 and the author of Ephesians 2 focus their arguments about the unity of Jews and Gentiles on the atoning work of Jesus Christ on the cross, Peter's speech in Acts 10 takes a larger view. He reminds Cornelius and his friends—and us, as we listen in—that the entire ministry of Jesus Christ was God's way of preaching peace to the people of Israel and the message that Jesus is Lord of all. Peter describes how that message had been spreading from the time of Jesus' baptism by John. Anointed by God's Holy Spirit, Jesus "went about doing good and healing all who were oppressed by the devil" (Acts 10:38).

Although he was put to death, God raised him from the dead. Peter tells how those who were witnesses of his resurrection ate and drank with him after he rose from the dead, and how he commanded them to testify that he is "the one ordained by God as judge of the living and the dead" (v. 42). When Peter adds that "all the prophets testify about him" that whoever believes in him receives forgiveness of sins, he probably has in mind the prophet Joel, in particular. Peter's Pentecost speech in chapter 2 of Acts had included a lengthy quotation from Joel that ended with the words, "Then everyone who calls on the name of the Lord shall be saved" (Acts 2:21, quoting Joel 2:32).

Clearly Luke wants us to understand that the resurrection of Jesus Christ is an event of cosmic significance: the very structures of the universe, as well as the socially constructed "givens," what we have always assumed to be true, are all to be rethought and reimagined in light of the exciting new events triggered by God's work in Christ. The early Christians went back to their Scriptures, God's word spoken through the patriarchs and prophets of Israel, for clues about what God's crucified and risen Messiah would mean for the world. One thing was clear: suspicions about those who were strangers, foreigners, profane, unclean—not part of us—all those would have to be reevaluated in the light of the One Lord of all, the One whom God had raised from the dead.

A. KATHERINE GRIEB

Commentary 2: Connecting the Reading with the World

Peter's sermon in Acts 10:34–43 demonstrates the transformative power of resurrection on how we view the world. Resurrection implies a conflict that is not merely resolved but is somehow transformed to reveal a new paradigm—a new way of being. Similar to Mahatma Gandhi's axiom of being the change you wish to see, so too is the concept of the resurrection of Jesus. In Peter's proclamation, resurrection as exemplified in Jesus is not simply about having a world in which people "get along" and act nice. Rather, it is about becoming someone we cannot imagine

yet. It is also like becoming a community that heretofore lacks any awareness that the concept of communion even exists. By wrapping our heads and hearts around such paradigm shifts we come closer to the kingdom of God.

It is important to explore resurrection in this way because it is a theological concept that is not easily explained, nor should it be. There are no easy answers here, only transformative questions that enable a first-century world to come to grips with how God leads the world to resurrection. Peter proclaims boldly that

"God shows no partiality" (v. 34), and that the message God sent to the people of Israel was "preaching peace by Jesus Christ" and that "he is Lord of all" (v. 37). "God anointed Jesus of Nazareth with the Holy Spirit and with power; . . . he went about doing good and healing all who were oppressed by the devil, for God was with him" (v. 38).

What Peter preaches here is bold and seemingly impossible. After all, how could he be preaching about an impartial God, given Peter's reputation for being prejudiced himself? This was certainly the case before Peter's encounter with Cornelius, who convinced Peter that God loves the Gentiles just as much as the Jews (Acts 10:1–33). In this topsy-turvy world of culture wars, the irony here is in Peter now being the foundation stone for the early church's survival amid difference and socioeconomic disparity. Peter is *petros* or rock—the one that Jesus relied upon.

Being Faithful. The image of a rock does not easily lend itself to being something that can change, and being faithful against insurmountable challenges can seem like pushing against a boulder. We see, however, in Peter, that we too can change, and we believe that which we once thought impossible. In Peter's case, the message he hears is that Gentiles are also loved by God. This was a powerful new story in which old perceptions and norms were challenged and even removed. Ultimately, Jesus' resurrection left all the disciples ready for new paradigms of possibilities. Peter preaches that he witnessed Jesus "hanging on a tree" (v. 39), and yet God raised Jesus from the dead (v. 40).

The retelling of the story of Jesus' resurrection for Peter was profound for several reasons. First, it was the opportunity for Peter to come clean about his own conversion in the face of his previous resistance to preaching to Gentiles. This is one of Peter's finest moments of displaying Jesus' discipleship. In contrast to earlier texts (Luke 9:33; 22:60), Peter was no longer making a fool of himself; on the contrary, he was witnessing Jesus after he rose from the dead (Acts 10:41). Second, Peter helps religious folks with a paradigm shift: how to live in the world

in such a way that it becomes a better place through religious practices. Peter helps us resist the natural pessimism that this world could ever systemically become a better place through religion and diverse religious practices.

Second, Peter has much to teach detractors who think Christians are so heavenly minded that they are of no earthly worth. Karl Marx criticized Christianity as "the sigh of the oppressed creature," and "the opium of the people." For Marx, religion consoles the oppressed by offering them heaven as that which they are denied upon earth, namely, an abstracted good form of human existence. Karl Marx argued that the foundation of social conflict is seen in incessant socioeconomic disparities, and that revolution is necessary and good. Marx believed religion to be essentially functionless and irrelevant for society.

Peter is not a Marxist, but it seems as though Peter understands this dilemma of articulating what the resurrection of our Lord means for a contested world. Like Marx, Peter understands how our earthly life is ontologically violent, that the very nature of life is about struggle and rebellion. Through the resurrection of Jesus, however, Peter understands a different kind of revolution than Marx. Peter's Christianity does not require violent revolution. Because of the resurrection of Jesus, violence is not necessary. For Marx the necessity of violence might be predicated on incommensurate human differences. Marxism shares the content and function of Christianity as an interpretation of human existence, but it fails to offer resurrection.

Peter offers an apologetic for Christianity because in a strong sense the resurrection of Jesus plays a progressive role by giving common people some idea of what a better world order should be. Peter is humble enough to realize that when it becomes possible to realize this better order upon earth, particularly in the form of concrete social structures, then religion must not become reactionary and distract from establishing a new and possible good society on earth. In other words, our need for heaven that Jesus' resurrection makes clear should not make heaven and earth exclusive existential realities.

That Jesus was resurrected on earth rationally implies heaven on earth.[1]

In our twenty-first-century world, we have a lot to learn from this understanding of the resurrection of Jesus. Since revolution still occurs today, we are wise to take resurrection seriously. Peter helps us see that revolution is not the counterforce of religion but provides the telos for Christianity to become essentially vital in how and why to revolt. Those of Christian faith should share Marx's revolutionary end, that there will no longer be an exploiting class of people. We should, however, resist the means of violence. Karl Marx may be correct that there is inherent socioeconomic struggle, but like Peter we believe the unexpected can also happen on communal levels, in which there is conversion and paradigm change. Apartheid can end. Berlin walls crumble.

Third, Peter helps us navigate our specific challenges today. One such challenge is the Black Lives Matter movement. This movement started in the aftermath of the killing of Trayvon Martin on February 26, 2012. It is a movement trying to broaden the conversation around state violence to include all the ways in which black people struggle on this planet. Black lives are often deprived of basic human rights and dignity, a history that can be traced back to the beginnings of the North Atlantic Slave Trade.[2] Despite the affliction of this slavery that still manifests itself in the socioeconomic struggles of African Americans, Peter helps us with this specific challenge when he says God shows no partiality, but in all *ethnoi* or nations, anyone who respects God and does what is good is acceptable to God. The Black Lives Matter movement provokes many in the United States, simply because it challenges democratic hypocrisy. Peter is helpful here in his own conversion and powerful proclamation that Jesus' Life Matters—and even more particularly, Jesus' resurrection.

MICHAEL BATTLE

1. See Michael Battle, *Heaven on Earth: God's Call to Community in the Book of Revelation* (Louisville, KY: Westminster John Knox, 2017).
2. Learn more about the Black Lives Matter Movement by going to blacklivesmatter.com/about.

John 20:1–18

¹Early on the first day of the week, while it was still dark, Mary Magdalene came to the tomb and saw that the stone had been removed from the tomb. ²So she ran and went to Simon Peter and the other disciple, the one whom Jesus loved, and said to them, "They have taken the Lord out of the tomb, and we do not know where they have laid him." ³Then Peter and the other disciple set out and went toward the tomb. ⁴The two were running together, but the other disciple outran Peter and reached the tomb first. ⁵He bent down to look in and saw the linen wrappings lying there, but he did not go in. ⁶Then Simon Peter came, following him, and went into the tomb. He saw the linen wrappings lying there, ⁷and the cloth that had been on Jesus' head, not lying with the linen wrappings but rolled up in a place by itself. ⁸Then the other disciple, who reached the tomb first, also went in, and he saw and believed; ⁹for as yet they did not understand the scripture, that he must rise from the dead. ¹⁰Then the disciples returned to their homes.

¹¹But Mary stood weeping outside the tomb. As she wept, she bent over to look into the tomb; ¹²and she saw two angels in white, sitting where the body of Jesus had been lying, one at the head and the other at the feet. ¹³They said to her, "Woman, why are you weeping?" She said to them, "They have taken away my Lord, and I do not know where they have laid him." ¹⁴When she had said this, she turned around and saw Jesus standing there, but she did not know that it was Jesus. ¹⁵Jesus said to her, "Woman, why are you weeping? Whom are you looking for?" Supposing him to be the gardener, she said to him, "Sir, if you have carried him away, tell me where you have laid him, and I will take him away." ¹⁶Jesus said to her, "Mary!" She turned and said to him in Hebrew, "Rabbouni!" (which means Teacher). ¹⁷Jesus said to her, "Do not hold on to me, because I have not yet ascended to the Father. But go to my brothers and say to them, 'I am ascending to my Father and your Father, to my God and your God.'" ¹⁸Mary Magdalene went and announced to the disciples, "I have seen the Lord"; and she told them that he had said these things to her.

Commentary 1: Connecting the Reading with Scripture

The account of the appearance of the risen Jesus to Mary Magdalene on Easter morning is one of the most poignant of Jesus' resurrection appearances narrated in the Gospels. We see Mary, alone, weeping at the tomb. Having found the tomb empty, she not only laments Jesus' death, but the loss of his body, which she cannot now properly care for. When she does first glimpse Jesus, she does not recognize him: she thinks he is the gardener. Perhaps the gardener has taken Jesus' body; perhaps he will know where the body of her Lord is. There is of course palpable

irony here: Mary is looking for a body, the body of a dead man—but Jesus is not dead. He is alive. Indeed, if Mary could find what she thought she wanted—Jesus' corpse—she would have little reason for her mourning to turn to joy (John 16:20). Jesus would still be dead.

While the silent witness of the empty tomb is that Jesus is not there, it remains a puzzle until Jesus makes himself known. The empty tomb itself means only that Jesus' body is gone. Then Jesus speaks, simply calling the grieving woman's name: "Mary." In that moment, Mary turns to Jesus, recognizing who he is. As John says elsewhere, the good shepherd "calls his own sheep by name"; the sheep follow him because "they know his voice" (10:3–5). When Jesus calls Mary by name, she hears and recognizes his voice. She knows now that this is Jesus standing in front of her. Perhaps surprisingly, when she responds to Jesus, she says simply, "Rabbouni!" (Aramaic for teacher). Here there is no acclamation of Jesus as Messiah, Son of God, Lord, or God, designations used for Jesus elsewhere in the Gospel. Rather, Mary addresses Jesus as teacher, a common designation used by disciples for Jesus in this Gospel (1:38; 11:28; 13:13–14). In the address to Jesus as teacher we simply see the humble response of a disciple to the presence of her teacher and Lord.

Like other narratives in the Gospel, this one reveals that unless Jesus makes himself known, people will remain in darkness or ignorance, misunderstanding who he is (4:25–26; 9:35–38; 11:23–27). People sometimes go looking for the thing that Jesus will supply—water, the bread of life—thinking that they will be given an endless supply of material benefits. Jesus does provide for the material needs of people; but he also redirects their seeking. Like Mary at the empty tomb, people do not always know what they are looking for. Misunderstandings need to be corrected; ignorance needs to be illumined. Throughout the Gospel, Jesus takes the initiative to make known who he is and what he brings: "I am the bread of life." "I am the resurrection and the life." In making himself known, Jesus invites people to see who he is and respond to him with allegiance and trust.

One of the striking features of the Gospel is that a number of key revelations are made to women. To the Samaritan woman Jesus acknowledges that he is the Messiah whom both the Jews and Samaritans have been expecting (4:26). She becomes a witness of his identity to her townspeople. To be sure, she remains somewhat diffident, inviting them to "come and see" Jesus, and wondering, "He cannot be the Messiah, can he?" (4:29). Even her halting witness brings her townspeople to their own encounter with Jesus. Similarly, Jesus tells Martha that he is the resurrection and life, leading her to make the confession of Jesus as Messiah and Son of God, precisely that confession to which the Gospel calls its readers (11:25–27; 20:30–31). Jesus' self-revelation is often not in public, but in private; not to the powerful or elite of society, but to those of lower status. At the tomb in the garden, Jesus makes his first resurrection appearance to one faithful, grieving woman. She in turn bears the news that he is alive to the other disciples (20:18). Even so, the apostle Peter declares that from every nation God has raised up those who are "chosen" to be witnesses (Acts 10:41): these witnesses include the Samaritan woman, Martha, Mary, and every disciple who, with Mary, declares, "We have seen the Lord!"—however differently that happens in our circumstances today.

The narrative of Jesus' encounter with Mary shows the restoration of a relationship that appeared to have been destroyed with his death. John's resurrection appearances tend to focus on individuals: here Mary, later Thomas and then Simon Peter. In each case, Jesus addresses one of his disciples with a command or invitation that aims to restore the relationship that his death had brought to an end. To be sure, memories of loved ones linger after their death, but death puts an end to the ongoing personal relationship.

However, Jesus is not dead. He is alive, and the relationship of teacher and disciple, master and friend, good shepherd and sheep, now continues. Jesus still calls Mary by name (10:3). Yet Jesus has not returned to stay. If Mary had thought that by finding the body of Jesus she could somehow hold on to him, she now discovers that even though Jesus is alive, he has not returned to life as before. Lazarus had been "brought back to life," but Jesus has been raised from the dead in order to return to be with God. Jesus tells Mary that she is to report to the disciples that he is going to "my Father and your Father, to my God and your God" (20:17). This unusual and striking formulation reveals that Jesus shares a relationship to God that his disciples also have: God is the Father of all. Yet there remains a difference since Jesus' sonship is distinctive. Yet, as Paul writes in his Letter to the Corinthians, Jesus is the firstfruits of the resurrection. Not only is Jesus the first to be raised to resurrection life. In and through him, all are raised. In Adam, all die, for all are mortal like Adam; but in Christ all will be made alive (1 Cor. 15:22–23). Here is the family of Jesus: brothers and sisters in the family of the one God.

The one true God is the God of the living, the God who brings life. Isaiah points to the power of the creating and life-giving God who "creates new heavens and earth" (Isa. 65:17). Isaiah's vision of the creator comes to expression in the Gospel's promise that God continues to give life to the world: this is the expression of God's love (John 3:16). God's life-giving work can be seen in the raising of Jesus from the dead and the promise that those in him will also be raised. The promise applies to every

person, every nation (Acts 10:34, 41). Hence, with the psalmist, those who celebrate may say, "I shall not die"—not because of their intrinsic immortality, but because God continually demonstrates his steadfast love, manifested in his life-giving purposes for all the world. Indeed, God's steadfast love endures forever (Ps. 118:1). If Jesus was crucified, the "stone that the builders rejected," he has become the chief cornerstone, the ultimate testimony to the God of all life. For this reason, especially on Easter, the church proclaims, "This is the day that the LORD has made; let us rejoice and be glad in it" (Ps. 118:22–24).

MARIANNE MEYE THOMPSON

Commentary 2: Connecting the Reading with the World

John 20:1–18 is a lectionary text for Easter Sunday in each year of the three-year cycle. Yet there is a noticeable disconnect between the loud and jubilant celebration of a typical Easter Sunday worship service and the bewilderment, grief, and silences of the text. Easter liturgies boldly proclaim the resurrection as God's decisive victory over death, but it was not nearly that clear to the first followers of Jesus who arrived at the tomb. John, always the eccentric among the evangelists, gives us a distinctive vantage point on the shock and confusion of the first Easter morning.

The central figure of John 20:1–18 is Mary Magdalene. Mary Magdalene is a prominent figure in all four Gospels, mentioned more times than many of the male disciples of Jesus. She appears at the tomb on Easter morning in all the resurrection accounts, but John alone gives her a special cameo appearance that is among the most poignant scenes in the New Testament. According to John, Mary arrives at the tomb early, while it is still dark (v. 1), and this darkness is metaphorical as well as literal, a symbol of Mary's grief and lack of understanding. She has come to grieve over the body of a dead friend. In the ordinary world of cause and effect, dead people stay dead. Upon discovering that the tomb is empty, Mary reaches the logical

conclusion that someone has stolen Jesus' body and rushes off to tell the disciples the bad news (v. 2).

The narrative of what happens next is not linear. It zigs and zags, mirroring the confusion and disorientation of Jesus' followers. Following Mary Magdalene's report, Simon Peter and the beloved disciple race off to the tomb. The beloved disciple gets there first, but does not enter the tomb first. Simon Peter arrives second, but is the first to enter the tomb. The beloved disciple "saw and believed" (v. 8), but his faith is still seeking understanding. The shock of Jesus' resurrection will take some time for the disciples to absorb. It is only gradually that they begin to piece together this startling reality with the testimony of Scripture and Jesus' teaching (John 2:17–22; 12:16). For now, the two disciples are silent. They head home together, giving no word of comfort or reassurance to Mary, who is left alone again at the tomb (v. 10).

With the two disciples out of the way, the rest of the passage belongs to Mary. The weeping Mary remains at the tomb without even knowing what she is looking for, until the person she mistakes for the gardener calls her by name. In a scene of startling intimacy, Mary finds her beloved Jesus, and at the same time finds herself. Unlike the risen Jesus' encounters with Simon Peter in chapter 21 of John, here there are no echoes of earlier betrayals. There is instead a reaffirmation of the intimate trust between a disciple and her teacher.

From medieval legends to *The DaVinci Code*, there have been speculations about Mary Magdalene's sexual promiscuity and some secret scandalous relationship with Jesus, but there is no evidence of either in this passage or elsewhere in Scripture. These speculations say more about the preoccupations and preconceptions of male readers than about the biblical text. The temptation to identify Mary Magdalene with the woman described as "a sinner" in Luke 7:37 and to contrast her with an idealized image of the Virgin Mary, the mother of Jesus, should be firmly resisted. In John's Gospel, the two Marys are not opposing caricatures of the sinful and the virtuous woman, but rather fully human people of faith, who follow Jesus all the way to his death on the cross (John 19:25).

Resurrection is a new reality not just for Mary, but also for Jesus. The risen Jesus tells Mary not to hold on to him, because he is still in the process of ascending to be with his Father (v. 17). The exaltation of Jesus seems to be something gradual: not completed once for all on the cross, but still unfolding in Mary's presence. Easter morning is an awkward, in-between time for both Jesus and Mary, in which old patterns and assumptions make way for the new. What is new for Mary is a new vocation. Unlike the beloved disciple and Peter, Mary does not remain silent. Jesus sends her to be an apostle to the apostles, sharing with them the good news that she has seen the Lord (vv. 17–18).

Mary is the first Easter witness: the first to see the risen Jesus, and the first to tell others what she has seen. Female disciples of Jesus in later centuries have appealed to her when they faced resistance from church authorities to their own call to proclaim the gospel. As Jarena Lee, a nineteenth-century member of the African Methodist Episcopal Church, demanded, "And why should it be thought impossible, heterodox, or improper for a woman to preach? . . .

Did not Mary *first* preach the risen Saviour, and is not the doctrine of the resurrection the very climax of Christianity?"[1] According to John, the Easter gospel is an unlikely story brought by an unlikely messenger.

While our Easter celebrations tend to present the resurrection as a triumphant fait accompli, this text from John reminds us that faith in the risen Christ is still a struggle and a risk. It was for the first disciples, and it remains that way for us. People in the modern West live in what has been called "a secular age,"[2] in which belief in God is no longer the default setting in society. Many of the social supports for trusting in a transcendent dimension of reality have fallen away. We spend most of our time living within the immanent frame of a natural order in which disengaged reason is assumed to be the sole path to genuine knowledge. With Mary, we instinctively want a logical explanation for Jesus' empty tomb. Mary leads us to seek the fullness that comes when we remain open to what lies beyond our ordinary frame of thinking and living. Her search to know and be known by God awakens our own spiritual hunger. We too want to encounter the living Stranger who calls each of us by name.

Like Mary returning to the tomb when others went back home, many people come to church on Easter morning not sure what they are looking for. They come weighed down with grief and disappointment, hungry for hope. Even those who come to church confident and joyful are still learning what it means to believe in Jesus' name and claim their identity as children of God (John 1:12). We are all, like Mary, somewhere between grief and joy, somewhere between despair and faith. John's Gospel is a story of encounters, from Nicodemus and the Samaritan woman to Mary and Thomas. The good news of Easter is that these encounters continue. Because of the resurrection, Christ's presence now knows no geographic or temporal boundaries. Christ is risen indeed, and so we come to church hoping to say with Mary, "I have seen the Lord" (v. 18).

AMY PLANTINGA PAUW

1. "Document 10. Jarena Lee: Black Women Wrestle with the 'Call to Preach the Gospel,'" in *In Our Own Voices: Four Centuries of American Women's Religious Writing*, ed. Rosemary S. Keller and Rosemary R. Ruether (San Francisco: HarperSanFrancisco, 1995), 335.

2. Charles Taylor, *A Secular Age* (Cambridge: Harvard University Press, 2007). In this paragraph I use some of Taylor's language to describe the possibilities for faith in our secular age.

1 Corinthians 15:19–26

[19]If for this life only we have hoped in Christ, we are of all people most to be pitied.

[20]But in fact Christ has been raised from the dead, the first fruits of those who have died. [21]For since death came through a human being, the resurrection of the dead has also come through a human being; [22]for as all die in Adam, so all will be made alive in Christ. [23]But each in his own order: Christ the first fruits, then at his coming those who belong to Christ. [24]Then comes the end, when he hands over the kingdom to God the Father, after he has destroyed every ruler and every authority and power. [25]For he must reign until he has put all his enemies under his feet. [26]The last enemy to be destroyed is death.

Commentary 1: Connecting the Reading with Scripture

On Easter morning, Christians around the world will be welcomed to worship with the ancient greeting "Christ is risen!" The response to those words will be an enthusiastic affirmation that "He is risen indeed!" That brief but profound ritual summarizes the essential message of Easter and the core conviction of the Christian faith. It is also the theme of today's epistle text from the First Letter to the Corinthians.

As with most of Paul's letters, the letters to the Corinthians are addressed to a community of faith that Paul knew and loved. He had founded the church and remained concerned with its welfare. He opens his First Letter to the Corinthians with his usual salutation and commendation for the work of the faithful community, but the reason for the letter becomes apparent in the first chapter when he notes the report "by Chloe's people" that there are "quarrels among you" (1:11). As the letter unfolds, we learn that those quarrels have been provoked by disagreements over a variety of issues, as the community struggled to define the boundaries of the Christian life. The issues creating divisions in the church were wide-ranging moral and ethical issues and included practices related to marriage and sexuality, litigation, food offered to idols, worship, and the nature of spiritual gifts.

The final chapter of the letter, from which today's text is drawn, takes a very different turn, as Paul moves from offering advice on dealing with practices creating divisions in the community to a theological and doctrinal excursus on the resurrection of Christ. At first it seems as though this theological capstone to the letter is out of place, but a closer look at the chapter demonstrates the genius of Paul in setting forth the resurrection as the defining event of Christian faith, against which all Christian practices and beliefs should be judged. The first section of the chapter (15:1–11) includes the earliest New Testament account of the resurrection appearances of Jesus and became a creedal statement used by the church. Paul then addresses what is obviously another contentious issue in the Corinthian church: skepticism over the resurrection of the dead, including the resurrection of both Jesus and those who have faith in him (vv. 12–18).

The text for Easter morning begins with verse 19, which, according to most commentators, belongs to the previous pericope. It concludes Paul's argument that if there is no resurrection of the dead, then Christ could not have been raised, rendering Christian faith futile (vv. 13–14). Its inclusion in the lection, however, sets forth the theme of hope that pervades the text and the celebration of Easter Day. We have hope for this life *and* the next because, as Paul affirms in the first verse of the next section, "Christ has been raised from the dead" (v. 20).

To confirm the idea of hope and assure believers that Christ is not the only one to be raised from the dead, Paul invokes the Old Testament image of "first fruits" as related to Jewish sacrificial practice (Lev. 23:9–10). If Christ is the first fruits of those who have died, then there is the promise of more to come. The connections to the Old Testament continue with Paul's argument for what Christ has accomplished by means of a typological argument rooted in the creation story. Just as sin and death came into the world through one human being, Adam (Gen. 3), so new life—resurrected life, life eternal—can come through the work of another human being, the resurrected Christ.

While not a prevalent concept, the idea of resurrection was not unknown in Jewish apocalyptic material. The prophet Isaiah speaks a word of hope to the Babylonian exiles, declaring, "Your dead shall live, their corpses shall rise" (Isa. 26:19). In a similar way, Daniel offers those living under foreign oppression the vision of a future time when "many of those who sleep in the dust of the earth shall awake, some to everlasting life" (Dan. 12:2).

Nevertheless, the Corinthian Christians struggled with the idea of bodily resurrection. Their resistance was due less to the unfamiliarity of the concept than to the Hellenistic worldview that pervaded their culture and regarded the body as transitory at best and evil at worst. Paul challenges the assumptions of the Corinthians by declaring that our bodies are so valued by God as to be redeemed by means of resurrection. In that way, he denies the prevailing ideology of a soul/body dualism and confirms the continuity of our identity and our whole being after death as we are caught up into the life of God through resurrection. This redemptive view of the body also reinforces the appropriate use of our mortal bodies as we live and work for God until we are received into God's presence at death.

The ultimate victory of Christ is over the power of death, the "enemy" (v. 26). That conquest is foreshadowed in Psalm 110:1. The destruction of death itself is the confirmation of the eschatological plan of God who, at "the end" (v. 24) receives all things from Christ, including the powers that continue to resist God's rule, even the power of death. Because of that assertion, this text also has significant liturgical connections. It is heard frequently as part of the funeral liturgy as testimony to the hope we have in the resurrection to eternal life. It also points to our baptismal identity as those who die to sin and rise to new life in Christ in the waters of baptism.

The theme of resurrection resounds through the lectionary texts designated for Easter morning. The first reading of Acts 10 is Peter's speech to the Gentiles at Caesarea, in which he states, "God raised [Jesus] on the third day" (Acts 10:40). It is meant to confirm the centrality of the resurrection for Christian faith. The alternate first reading is the vision of new heavens and a new earth from Isaiah 65, connecting to the apocalyptic dimension of the epistle text. The psalm for the day, Psalm 118, declares God's work in securing the psalmist's salvation, confirming that the Lord "has become my salvation" (Ps. 118:14) and hinting at eternal life ("I shall not die, but I shall live," v. 17). All of this is "the LORD's doing" (v. 23), confirming the omnipotence of God.

The Gospel lesson from Luke 24 is Luke's version of the events of Easter morning, including the discovery of the empty tomb by several women who were followers of Jesus and the declaration by "two men" (Luke 24:4) that Christ "has risen" (v. 5). Thus the connections among the lectionary texts for this day are clear, as the theme of resurrection echoes through them, from Old Testament affirmations of God's salvific power to the ultimate demonstration of that power in the raising of Jesus from the dead and the hope of *our* being raised as well.

On this most grand and glorious day of the Christian year, we affirm the centrality of God's saving work in Jesus Christ by raising him from the dead, as well as the belief that we too shall ultimately be raised with him. Indeed, as Paul contends in the previous section, "If Christ has not been raised, your faith is futile and you are still in your sins" (1 Cor. 15:17). Thus the resurrection remains the defining act of God on our behalf and must resound through our proclamation. In response, we live in the knowledge that, no matter what we encounter in life, God in Christ will have the last word, even victory over "the last enemy" (v. 26), death.

BEVERLY ZINK-SAWYER

Commentary 2: Connecting the Reading with the World

The benefit of lectionaries is qualified by several drawbacks, including the isolation of readings from their context. That limitation is evident in the separation of 1 Corinthians 15:19–26 from Paul's sustained thinking about resurrection, beginning in verse 1 and reaching its climax in verse 57. Especially unfortunate is the uncoupling of the Easter lection from the issue that occasions it: "Now if Christ is proclaimed as raised from the dead, how can some of you say there is no resurrection of the dead?" (v. 12).

Some in the Corinthian community rejoiced in the resurrection of the crucified Christ, but denied the bodily resurrection of the dead. Their view is not unique to first-century Christians. On Easter, twenty-first-century worshipers proclaim, fervently or perfunctorily, "Christ is risen; he is risen indeed!" However, if asked whether they believe that *their* dead bodies will be raised, many would respond with puzzlement, doubt, or denial. Affirming the resurrection of Jesus Christ, truly God and truly human, is not always accompanied by affirming the resurrection of merely *human* bodies.

Many congregations regularly confess the Apostles' Creed, including belief "in the resurrection of the body," without realizing that they are voicing confidence in the resurrection of those who have died, and firm hope that they too will be raised in Christ. The creed confesses that Christ rose from the dead on the third day *and* that humans will be resurrected in him. Christ was embodied for us, and we are embodied in him; Christ's body was raised for us, and our bodies shall be raised in him. Affirmation of Christ's resurrection from the dead and mortals' resurrection from the dead are intimately related in the grace of Christ, the love of God, and the communion of the Holy Spirit.

The intertwining of "Christ is risen" and "the resurrection of the body" is vividly displayed in Orthodox iconography. *Anastasis* (Greek for "resurrection") icons depict the resurrection of Christ in an unexpected way. They do not picture empty tombs or the risen Christ's appearances to disciples. Instead, resurrection is depicted by Christ's descent into hell, the place of the dead! Anastasis icons (viewable online by typing "anastasis icons" into a search engine) often show the raised, glorified, and descended Christ standing with the broken gates of hell beneath his feet. He reaches down to grasp the hands of Adam and Eve, drawing them out of their caskets. Around this central focus, the icons typically picture David and Solomon, Moses and the prophets, John the Baptist, and anonymous representatives of all who have died. Symbols of the disciples represent the living who will also die. At the bottom of the icon, almost concealed in darkness beneath Hades's shattered gates, lies the satanic figure of death, now vanquished by Christ and, in Christ, now conquered by those who have died. "In fact," says Paul, "Christ has been raised from the dead, the first fruits of those who have died" (v. 20). The icon depicts the fullness of the harvest.

Resurrection icons are a window into a deep mystery of faith, vividly displaying Paul's proclamation, "for as all die in Adam, so all will be made alive in Christ" (v. 22). Resurrection is not confined to Christ, nor is it focused on the salvation of individuals. The cosmic sweep of resurrection encompasses *all*, from Adam through Abraham and Sarah and on to their heirs (Gen. 12:2–3; 17:15–16). Resurrection is not for the One, or the few, but for the many who have died and will die.

Easter celebration of Christ's resurrection is oddly constricted apart from its profound social significance. In the resurrection of Christ, every oppressive rule and authority and power that holds people captive is overcome, for "just as Christ was raised from the dead by the glory of the Father, so we too might walk in newness of life" (Rom. 6:4). In human life, as it was in the life of Christ, the last enemy to be destroyed is death. Now, as we hope in "the redemption of our bodies" (Rom. 8:23), human resurrection is prefigured in Christ's victory over all enemies of life's fullness that seek to imprison people (1 Cor. 15:24–27).

Paul's rhetorical question—"How can some of you say there is no resurrection of the dead?" v. 12—is addressed to twenty-first-century Americans who affirm Christ's rising from death, yet ignore, doubt, or deny the resurrection of all who have died and will die. We are not alone in our skepticism and rejection, however. Refusing belief in the resurrection of the body has been a constant throughout the church's life. Although we moderns may think that contemporary science has rendered belief in bodily resurrection implausible, resurrection of the dead was no more credible twenty centuries ago than it is today. Christian resurrection was never thought to be a natural phenomenon, however; it is God's new creation, breathing the Spirit into lifeless bodies (Gen. 2:7; Ezek. 37:1–14).

Something more than scientific skepticism was at work then, however, and remains at work now. A century after Paul, Justin Martyr put the matter starkly in dialogue with a literary partner: "If you have fallen in with some who are called Christians, but . . . who say that there is no resurrection of the dead, and that their souls, when they die are taken to heaven, do not imagine that they are Christians. . . ."[1] Justin's "not-Christian Christians" were inheritors of Greco-Roman philosophies that counseled escape from the limitations of the physical world to the lofty heights of purely spiritual existence. Bodies were thought to be imperfect vessels for the spirit within, and death of the body was thought to set the spirit free. Justin, faithful to Paul's witness, denounces those who scorn the body, prizing instead untainted spirit.

Belief in the "immortality of the soul" is an unchristian idea that will endure, for it is as widespread now as it was then. Bodies die, it is said, but souls do not. Bodies lie molding in the grave or are reduced to ash in the crematorium, but the soul lives for eternity. "Immortality of the soul" promises release from the temptations, evils, pains, and suffering of bodily existence by transcending earthly matter. In contrast, resurrection of the body affirms the conquering of temptations, evils, pain, and suffering through union with the bodily death and resurrection of Christ.

Contemporary American culture is deeply ambiguous about the human body. On one hand we are obsessed with human bodies, while on the other we denigrate them. Bodies, especially female bodies, are routinely sexualized in advertising, movies, magazines, television, and, of course, pornography. Celebration of perfect body types holds ordinary people captive to unattainable ideals, while aging bodies are promised rejuvenating plastic surgery. Gym memberships and diet plans seek to preserve or restore youthful bodies. Cultural glorification of the body is also accompanied by dread of *de*formity, *dis*ability, and *dis*ease. Dissatisfaction with bodies is the flip side of their idealization. Another pernicious effect of body glorification is evident in the racializing of some bodily characteristics, especially skin color, leading to divisions and gradations of human worth.

The inclusive resurrection of Christ and human bodies affirms the goodness of creation. Bodily life is not a lower form of existence, to be disdained or discarded. The obvious question, now as then, is, "How are the dead raised? With what kind of body do they come?" (15:35). A "spiritual body," says Paul. Not a bodiless spirit, but a transformed body. Easter gospel!

JOSEPH D. SMALL

1. Justin Martyr, "Dialogue with Trypho," LXXX, in *The Ante-Nicene Fathers: The Writings of the Fathers Down to A.D. 325*, ed. Alexander Roberts and James Donaldson (New York: Charles Scribner's Sons, 1903), 239.

Luke 24:1–12

¹But on the first day of the week, at early dawn, they came to the tomb, taking the spices that they had prepared. ²They found the stone rolled away from the tomb, ³but when they went in, they did not find the body. ⁴While they were perplexed about this, suddenly two men in dazzling clothes stood beside them. ⁵The women were terrified and bowed their faces to the ground, but the men said to them, "Why do you look for the living among the dead? He is not here, but has risen. ⁶Remember how he told you, while he was still in Galilee, ⁷that the Son of Man must be handed over to sinners, and be crucified, and on the third day rise again." ⁸Then they remembered his words, ⁹and returning from the tomb, they told all this to the eleven and to all the rest. ¹⁰Now it was Mary Magdalene, Joanna, Mary the mother of James, and the other women with them who told this to the apostles. ¹¹But these words seemed to them an idle tale, and they did not believe them. ¹²But Peter got up and ran to the tomb; stooping and looking in, he saw the linen cloths by themselves; then he went home, amazed at what had happened.

Commentary 1: Connecting the Reading with Scripture

The Gospel lesson for this Easter day is Luke's version of the events of the first Easter morning. While the essence of the story echoes the versions found in Matthew, Mark, and John, Luke offers his own unique details in shaping the narrative. The message, however, remains the same as that conveyed by the other Gospel writers: the women who journey to the tomb on the morning after the Sabbath to anoint Jesus' body find the tomb empty and receive the message of his resurrection. They begin the transmission of the good news that inaugurates the faith we celebrate today.

The opening of the twenty-fourth chapter of Luke continues the narrative of Jesus' death and burial reported in the previous chapter. The unnamed "women who had come with [Jesus] from Galilee" (23:55) had watched from afar as Joseph of Arimathea removed Jesus' body from the cross, wrapped it, and placed it in a tomb. That these unnamed women did not leave Jesus as he traveled to the cross and to his place of burial is significant in their role as witnesses to his resurrection. It is important to note that in all four Gospels women were the first to receive and proclaim the good news of Jesus' resurrection, but in Luke, more women are mentioned as being present at the empty tomb (24:10) than are noted in the other Gospels. This is in keeping with Luke's inclusion of women as persons of faith and instruments of God's plan of salvation from the beginning of his Gospel. Women, including Elizabeth, Mary, and Anna, are the bearers and conveyers of the wondrous work of God as recorded in the birth narratives of Luke (chaps. 1–2). Luke also notes many other women whom Jesus encounters during his ministry, such as the widow of Nain, whose son Jesus brings back to life (7:11–17); the woman who anoints Jesus in the Pharisee's house (7:36–50); the women who accompany and provide resources for Jesus and the Twelve (8:1–3); Jairus's daughter, who is restored to life (8:40–42, 49–56); the hemorrhaging woman who is healed (8:43–48); and Martha and Mary (10:38–42). The inclusion of those stories reveals the high regard Jesus has for women, despite the cultural norms of first-century Palestine, as well as the concern for the poor and marginalized that characterizes Luke's Gospel.

The women in the resurrection story journey to Jesus' tomb as soon as they are able, following mandated Sabbath rest. Despite what must have been paralyzing grief, they prepare the requisite "spices and ointments" (23:56) and set out to do what they have to do. Upon seeing the stone rolled away from the tomb and finding the tomb empty, however, the women are "perplexed" (24:4). Their reaction brings to mind many biblical stories of those who find themselves disoriented by the work of God in their midst. From the patriarchs and prophets of the Old Testament to the disciples and apostles of the New Testament to those of us who are part of the Christian community today, perplexity in reaction to the amazing work of God is not uncommon. Indeed, this is a text that reveals a pattern of disorientation (as the women encounter the empty tomb), orientation (as they receive the message of Jesus' resurrection from the two men), and reorientation (as they respond to the good news of the resurrection by sharing the message with others). This pattern reflects the transformative work of God within and among us.

The "two men" who startle the "perplexed" women are described as clothed in "dazzling" garments (v. 4). That description connects the stories of the transfiguration of Jesus (9:28–36) and of his ascension as reported in Luke's second volume (Acts 1:6–11) to the report of his resurrection. In the transfiguration story, Jesus is the one whose "clothes became dazzling white" (Luke 9:29) and the "two men" who appear with him are recognized as Moses and Elijah (v. 30). In the ascension story, "two men in white robes" appear among the gathered apostles as they watch Jesus ascend to heaven (Acts 1:10). Luke appears to be establishing a continuum among these events, purposefully connecting Jesus' resurrection to the confirmation of his identity at his transfiguration and the fulfillment of his mission and commissioning of his followers upon his ascension into heaven. With the inclusion of the two messengers at the tomb, Luke frames his Gospel by means of heavenly figures who appear to interpret significant events. Angels bring the news of the impending births of John and Jesus to Zechariah (Luke 1:11) and Mary (1:26) and announce the birth of Jesus to the shepherds (2:9).

Memory plays an important part in the unfolding of this text and in its connection to the larger Gospel. In the encounter at the tomb, the two messengers challenge the women to "remember" what Jesus told them earlier, thus connecting the event of the resurrection with Jesus' prediction about his death and resurrection (9:22). The Christian faith is built upon recalling the promises of God and the many ways in which those promises have been fulfilled. The promise of a Messiah echoes through the Hebrew Scriptures until we see that promise fulfilled in Jesus Christ. In this text, the women are challenged to recall Jesus' own words about his impending death and resurrection. The recollection of his prediction ("they remembered his words," 24:8) and its obvious fulfillment prompt their belief and inspire them to return from the tomb to proclaim the good news of the resurrection to the other followers of Jesus. Their experience reminds us that remembering God's faithfulness in the past is the best way to generate faith in the future God holds for us. Belief comes when we recall what we have heard; this is a compelling argument for the recitation of creedal statements and the reading of Scripture that we experience in our liturgical practices.

On this highest of holy days, the Gospel text drives the selection of the other lectionary texts. The themes of salvation and victory over death resound loudly and clearly through all the texts, including the appointed psalm. Luke's story of the resurrection is most closely connected, however, to the epistle lesson from 1 Corinthians 15. The testimony of the women who find the empty tomb is the foundation for Paul's declaration of faith in the resurrection of Christ and the promise that we too shall be raised with him. That good news, however, is often met with perplexity and amazement at best and disbelief at worst. When the women return to the other disciples to share what they have experienced, their words are greeted as "an idle tale" (v. 11). Even though we read this story with postresurrection eyes, it is easy for us to succumb to the perplexity of the women who find the empty tomb, as well as to the skepticism of the disciples who hear their story. The idea of resurrection can be as challenging for us as for the women who encountered the empty tomb. We might even be as disbelieving as the Corinthians were. As we remember the promises of God throughout Scripture and in the life, death, and resurrection of Jesus, the hope is that we, like Peter, will be "amazed at what has happened" (v. 12) and come to believe.

The hope is that we, once we believe, will share that good news with others, even as did the faithful women of this Easter story.

BEVERLY ZINK-SAWYER

Commentary 2: Connecting the Reading with the World

The New Testament does not narrate Jesus' resurrection. Gospel accounts of the empty tomb simply attest to the absence of Jesus' crucified, dead, and buried body. Subsequent accounts of the risen Christ's appearances to his disciples affirm the living presence of the crucified Jesus. Neither the empty tomb nor the appearances depict the resurrection itself, nor do they have much to say about its meaning and significance. The Gospels' Easter narratives are sparse accounts that only preface full awareness of the significance of Christ's rising from the dead.

In Luke's Gospel, the empty tomb is met by perplexity, and the strange appearance of two luminous men produces terror. Terror, amazement, and sadness also mark responses to the empty tomb in the other Gospel narratives. The early morning events on that first day of the week are not greeted by joyous cries of "Christ is risen! He is risen indeed!" The first indication of what is happening comes from the men in dazzling clothes: "Why do you look for the living among the dead? He is not here, but has risen." What does his resurrection mean? More explanation is needed, and so the men say, "Remember how he told you, while he was still in Galilee, that the Son of Man must be handed over to sinners, and be crucified, and on the third day rise again" (24:6–7). The women remembered (v. 8).

That the dead and buried Jesus is risen and alive remains perplexing to contemporary congregations, unless it is accompanied by "remembering" all that had gone before in Jesus' acts and words. This consistent message of the Gospels is amplified by what follows in Luke's account, the well-known Emmaus road narrative. Cleopas and his travelling companion had heard the report of the empty tomb, and they remembered that Jesus was "a prophet mighty in deed and word" (v. 19). However,

their memory produced only the wistful "we had hoped that he was the one to redeem Israel" (v. 21). Full remembering occurred only when the still-unrecognized risen Christ "interpreted to them the things about himself in all the scriptures" (v. 27).

Even interpreted remembering was not sufficient to open the full significance of the resurrection, however. That became apparent only when the still unrecognized One stayed with the two travelers and sat at table with them. The risen Christ then "took bread, blessed and broke it, and gave it to them" (v. 30). *Then* they recognized him. The significance of resurrection is not known in the absence of the crucified One, not even in the truth about the crucified and risen One, but in the living presence of Christ with his people.

Much contemporary Easter preaching, together with anthems, hymns, and prayers, gives primary attention to Gospel narratives of the first Easter morning, rather than to the real presence of Christ with his people now. Exclusive focus on the empty tomb and the reaction of followers may serve to confine Jesus' resurrection in the distant past, with the unintended effect of altering the Easter acclamation to "Christ *was* risen! He *was* risen indeed!"

Exclusive meditation on the early morning events at the empty tomb can obscure the dynamic trajectory of those events, a movement forward to Christ's resurrection appearances with his disciples, and on to the presence of Christ with his people now. Luke's account of the empty tomb is not designed to keep us there and then, but to place us on the road to Emmaus, at table with Jesus' traveling companions, in the room where Christ appeared to a group of disciples, then on to ascension, Pentecost, apostolic witness, and the life of the church.

The trajectory of resurrection begins with "the women who had come with [Jesus] from Galilee" (23:55). Disciples were not limited to the Twelve, although that group had obvious symbolic preeminence. From beginning to end, a larger group followed Jesus—including, prominently, women. It was women who formed a procession to the tomb where Jesus was interred, and it was women who went to the tomb at dawn on the third day. It was women—"Mary Magdalene, Joanna, Mary the mother of James, and the other women with them" (24:10)—who told the men about the rolled-away stone, the absence of Jesus' dead body, the strange men, and their remembrance of what Jesus had taught about his death and his rising. Women were the first witnesses; yet they and countless women who followed them in bearing faithful testimony have too often been shunted backstage in the continuing drama of good news for the world.

The response of male apostles to the account of female disciples was blunt: nonsense. Perhaps their response would have been softened if the reporters had been men, but report of a dead person's resurrection was far-fetched then, and remains difficult to imagine now. Even those who believe it to be true have difficulty making sense of it. The resurrection of Jesus Christ makes Christian sense only in the remembering and learning that began with the women, continued with the travelers and the Twelve, and found a wide, inclusive audience through Peter's Pentecost preaching, Paul's missionary travels and letters, and the church's continuous witness.

Making sense of Easter morning resurrection is only prelude to knowing the living presence of Christ in the life of contemporary Christian communities. In the Gospels, deep knowledge of Christ's presence comes through sacrament as well as Word. Eucharistic resonance is clear in the repeated formulation: "took . . . blessed . . . broke . . . gave." At Emmaus as in the upper room (22:14–20), and in Eucharist throughout the church's life (1 Cor. 11:23–26), the presence of the living Lord is known as he gives himself in bread and wine. The Lord's Supper in the church is not a re-creation of the Last Supper, but a celebration of resurrection, a testimony to the living Lord, an awareness of the real presence of Christ in the midst of his people.

There is more. The resurrected Christ is present beyond the confines of his people. The prominent Orthodox icon Christ Pantocrator (all sovereign) pictures the risen Christ as Lord of the cosmos. Regularly painted on the interior of the central dome in Orthodox churches, Christ Pantocrator is shown as head of the church and ruler of the world. In the icon, the risen Lord holds the Gospel book, with his right hand raised in a teaching gesture. Far more vividly than empty Protestant crosses, the icon displays the universal import of Christ's resurrection. The risen One continues to interpret "the things about himself in all the scriptures" to the church and in the world. Both church and world are transformed by Christ's resurrection.

The women at the tomb "remembered his words," and their witness inaugurated recognition of Christ's reign. The witness continues to be handed on as the church proclaims the good news of Christ's resurrection and the reality of Christ's universal lordship. An affirmation of faith in the Presbyterian Church (U.S.A.)'s *Book of Common Worship* paraphrases 1 Corinthians 15:1–6, recognizing the originating witness of the women: "that he was raised on the third day, and that he appeared first to the women, then to Peter, and to the Twelve, and then to many faithful witnesses." The affirmation concludes with faith in the risen Christ's universal reign: "We believe that Jesus is the Christ, the Son of the living God. Jesus Christ is the first and the last, the beginning and the end; he is our Lord and our God."[1] Easter gospel for church *and world*!

JOSEPH D. SMALL

1. Office of Theology and Worship, Presbyterian Church (U.S.A.), *Book of Common Worship* (Louisville, KY: Westminster John Knox Press, 2018), 80–81.

Second Sunday of Easter

Acts 5:27–32
Psalm 150 and Psalm 118:14–29

Revelation 1:4–8
John 20:19–31

Acts 5:27–32

²⁷When they had brought them, they had them stand before the council. The high priest questioned them, ²⁸saying, "We gave you strict orders not to teach in this name, yet here you have filled Jerusalem with your teaching and you are determined to bring this man's blood on us." ²⁹But Peter and the apostles answered, "We must obey God rather than any human authority. ³⁰The God of our ancestors raised up Jesus, whom you had killed by hanging him on a tree. ³¹God exalted him at his right hand as Leader and Savior that he might give repentance to Israel and forgiveness of sins. ³²And we are witnesses to these things, and so is the Holy Spirit whom God has given to those who obey him."

Commentary 1: Connecting the Reading with Scripture

The book of Acts is the story of the earliest Christian movement, an inexplicable happening in the ancient world of the Roman Empire that unsettled conventional establishment Jewish religion. Grounded in the inexplicable claim of the resurrection of Jesus, it was inevitable that this peculiar movement that manifested courage and freedom of a transformative kind would collide with the status quo of the Roman Empire and of the established Jewish leadership that was in cahoots with the empire. Our reading in Acts 5:27–32 narrates a dramatic confrontation between "Peter and the apostles" (who were the carriers of Easter truth) and the high priest in Jerusalem (the point person for status-quo religion that had behind it the authority of Rome).

In our verses the confrontation is quick and terse. The high priest, who is a cipher for established religious power, speaks once. His work is to silence those who disrupt the establishment. The apostles, led by Peter, answer the high priest and also speak only once. The core of their answer to the high priest is the message of Easter: God "raised up Jesus" and "exalted him" in power and honor. No explanation! The claim is not the conclusion of an argument. It is the premise of the Christian movement. The risen

Jesus forgives and so wipes out the leverage of the old systems of control. Peter and his cohorts are witnesses to this countertruth that subverts established power.

As a result, the conclusion is drawn that dominates the book of Acts: the Easter community will obey God, the God exalted in the Easter Christ. Human authority will not be obeyed when it contradicts the claims of Easter. It is difficult to imagine a challenge to the established order that could be more stunning or more wholesale.

These themes dominate our reading and the book of Acts more generally: (a) the countertruth that collides with established order; (b) witness to that countertruth in an embodied community that is unafraid; and (c) alternative obedience performed through the narrative that follows. The apostles are undeterred by the hostility of established order in their proclaiming Easter truth and thus in their readiness to run risks for the sake of the truth entrusted to them.

In the Gospel reading for this Sunday, John 20:19–31, Jesus responds to Thomas by commending "those who have not seen and yet have come to believe" (v. 29). In the book of Acts the preaching of the apostles is aimed at those who have "not seen" but who may "come to believe" on the basis of the apostles' preaching.

The reading in Revelation 1:4–8 is a great doxology to Jesus, "the firstborn of the dead, and the ruler of the kings of the earth" (Rev. 1:5). The language is unabashedly political. The doxology subordinates "kings of the earth"—all of them—to the rule of Christ. That political accent is reinforced by the use of "kingdom," "dominion," and "almighty" (*pantokratōr*) in what follows. The same political accent is reiterated in Psalm 118, the celebration of a great victory, presumably by the Davidic king who is supported "by the right hand of the LORD" (Ps. 118:15–16). The petition "save us" (v. 25) is the phrase "hosanna" and is followed by "blessed is the one who comes in the name of the LORD" (v. 26). This is, of course, the rhetoric of Jesus' "triumphal entry" that the church reiterates in the Eucharist.

Both the doxology in Revelation and the victory psalm are permeated with political rhetoric. These readings, taken together, are an unambiguous affirmation that the rule of Christ is a real rule in the world, and that the apostolic movement is a political enterprise that lives in tension if not contradiction with established order in the world. Thus our brief confrontation in Acts is like a summation of the entire account of the rule of God that impinges upon the world and that evokes the bodied testimony of the faithful. We may indeed wonder how we in the church have learned to so programmatically misread the biblical text that the dangerous subversive claims of the gospel have been trivialized and made impotent as a "religious phenomenon."

The themes of our text are recurring in Scripture:

1. The faithful community of God is characteristically a community with a subversion of reality that aims to subvert. The most dramatic account of "silencing" in ancient Israel that anticipates the silencing by the high priest in our text is the narrative of Amos, who is silenced by the priest at Bethel, the high priest of the kingdom of northern Israel (Amos 7:10–17). In that paradigmatic exchange, the priest banishes Amos from the kingdom and prohibits his prophetic speech there. Kings are always silencing

prophets, on which see Ahab and Elijah, and Zedekiah and Jeremiah.

2. Proclamation of the resurrection concerns the defeat of the power of death. Elisha's restoration of the dead son of a helpless widow is a resurrection to life (2 Kgs. 4:8–37), but no more so than Elisha's restoration of life and future to the bereft widow without food in 2 Kings 4:1–7, and no more so than Elisha's healing of the Syrian leper (2 Kgs. 5:10–14). These are all Easter acts by the power of God. On a more public scale, Jon Levenson, in his *The Death and Resurrection of the Beloved Son*, has seen that the Joseph narrative is a resurrection story through which a lost son of Israel is restored to life and power in the world (Gen. 37–50). This God is everywhere doing Easter!

3. Easter truth that refuses the silencing of established authority is a dominant theme in the Old Testament. Already in the exodus narrative, the emancipatory intent of God, voiced by Moses, contradicts the exploitative rule of Pharaoh, which depended upon silent submission to Pharaoh. At the other end of the Old Testament in very late literature, the narrative of Daniel is replete with Daniel's acts of defiance against the rule of Nebuchadnezzar. His defiance, however, is conducted in a cunning way that is for the most part not confrontational. Daniel refuses to eat the rich food of the empire (Dan. 1). Daniel testifies to the panic-stricken king that "mercy and righteousness" constitute an alternative way to govern (4:27). In 3:16–18, however, defiance of the king is overt and assertive: "We have no need to present a defense to you in this matter. If our God whom we serve is able to deliver us from the furnace of blazing fire and out of your hand, O king, let him deliver us. But if not, be it known to you, O king, that we will not serve your gods and we will not worship the golden statue that you have set up."

It is no wonder that "obey God and not human authority" becomes the final dictum of John Calvin in his *Institutes*. Calvin had clearly seen the deep summons of Easter.

4. The vocation of "witness" is explicit in the poetry of exilic Isaiah. That poetry, addressed to Jewish deportees in sixth-century-BCE

Babylon, offers a sub-version of reality to the dominant version of the empire: God will emancipate the Jews from Babylon, as the Hebrews had departed Pharaoh's Egypt. The poet recruits witnesses to proclaim a historical possibility of restoration that defies the empire: "Do not fear, or be afraid. . . . You are my witnesses!" (Isa. 44:8 see 43:9–10).

This testimony contradicts the claims of empire in the same way in which the apostolic witness in our text contradicted the old order, refusing to be silenced.

WALTER BRUEGGEMANN

Commentary 2: Connecting the Reading with the World

The fifth chapter of Acts has some strange goings on. It kicks off with the unsettling story of Ananias and Sapphira, who both fall down dead for lying about their donation to the church. We also hear about the growing numbers of believers, many of whom are drawn to the prospect of receiving physical healing. God's Spirit is so strong in Peter that the touch of his mere shadow can make someone well. The Sadducees, feeling severely threatened, place the apostles in jail. An angel frees them and urges them to return to their acts of civil disobedience, to return to their preaching. Without resorting to violence, the temple police bring Peter and the apostles to the high priest for questioning, which is where our passage begins.

The apostles are filled with energy and passion, despite the possibility of persecution. What a fabulous text to preach on the Sunday after Easter. If you are a solo pastor, you may be beyond weary from the services of Holy Week. The faithful who turn out on this Sunday, traditionally the lowest attendance Sunday of the year, need to be encouraged to take the Easter miracle to a deeper level of commitment and discipleship. Whether they have returned because they are "every Sunday" people, or they have reappeared because something happened on Easter that drew them back to worship, feed them with the hope and vision of the apostles.

Perhaps you are the associate pastor, who is blessed to preach this text, an affirmation of Christ-inspired civil disobedience. If you have the opportunity to preach only occasionally, then you should have some strong illustrations tucked aside. Where in your congregation have you seen contemporary examples of bold preaching? Your congregants live out their faith in numerous ways: they "preach" through their witness of teaching, service, and outreach. They preach through their experiences of recovery, reconciliation, and resilience. Celebrate this witness of faith. Others in your congregation are searching for opportunities, longing for ways to connect. They do not see themselves as "Peter." So in your preaching suggest a personal reimagining of how they already embody Christ. One of the worst disservices a church can do is to allow someone to believe he or he has nothing to offer. As a way of continually holding the truth before their communities, some churches include this phrase on their staff list: "Every Member a Minister."

Some churches choose this day for Youth Sunday or Confirmation Sunday, a sure way to draw people back to worship on this "low" Sunday. If that is your context, then you have the privilege of partnering with youth to unpack a testimony that holds relevant truth for adolescents. Youth have something to say about the life of faith, and they long to be heard. Set them free from the prison of perceived immaturity, and empower them to proclaim the good news with all of its challenging realities. Their struggles may include sorting through the various ways of being Christian, or how to walk in Christ's way when peers demand an entirely different path. The riskiness of this passage is a holy riskiness that speaks to youth.

Whether you are a solo pastor, the associate who has one Sunday a month, or the youth director entrusted with guiding the teenagers in worship design, be bold. Whatever your situation, there will be someone in those pews who needs to hear this brave word. Today's text, filled with the postresurrection realities, of which we are all too familiar in our daily life, is terribly sobering. A life of faith, the author reminds us, holds the promise of persecution in tension with the promise of eternal life.

There is something that often precedes persecution: the silencing of the voice. In keeping with the theme of the apostles as civilly disobedient, a possible trajectory for preaching includes the voices in your congregation, in your community, in our nation, or in our world that are being silenced. Just as the religious leaders of Peter's day believed they were doing the right thing to attempt to silence Jesus' followers, we often silence voices that disturb us. Stories of oppression and exploitation clamor for our attention.

In 2013, Alicia Garza, Patrisse Cullors, and Opal Tometi launched the Black Lives Matter movement as a means to channel their rage over the injustices directed at people of color. Images of grieving parents of gunned-down sons, of crowds marching and crying out that "Black Lives Matter," filled the news sources. We had the choice of listening for discernment or of silencing the voices that shed light on the racial divide in our nation.

When indigenous peoples seek to protect the land and resources of the earth for all (such as the Standing Rock protectors of 2016), we can listen to their pleas, we can join with them in honoring the sacredness of the earth, or we can turn a deaf ear, refusing to engage the conversation. As Presbyterians, we are people of action, and we have clearly defined ways to make our voices of solidarity heard.

Every generation has its movements and protests, but as Christians and citizens we often wonder how far our faith demands us to go. By the end of this chapter, the apostles will be flogged (Acts 5:40) and again commanded to stop preaching. Considering it an honor to suffer for Jesus' sake, they are barely through the door of the prison when they open their mouths to preach anew. "God," they confess, "is our only authority" (based on v. 29).

You will have to gauge your congregation to decide if this passage is an invitation to explore questions such as, when is it right to break the law? What if breaking the law to help one, puts another at risk? Scripture offers us a variety of stories of those who broke human laws in order to be fully obedient to God, such as the story of Shadrach, Meshach, and Abednego in Daniel 3. Jesus was known to break Sabbath laws, allowing his friends to pick grain when they were hungry and providing healing to those who were ill. On Easter, God broke the natural laws governing life and death, declaring that death is not the final word. Holy disruption is our salvation.

Disruption and silencing happen very close to home as well. If it is inconvenient, or unsettling, we silence the voices of those we consider "other." Perhaps they are on either end of the age time line, or on a minority point on the gender spectrum. A visually impaired person may name a truth about the church that sighted people have never considered. The apostles spoke words of healing in the form of repentance and forgiveness, but they also named the injustice they had witnessed, Jesus' execution. Look for the apostles in your midst whose voices have been muffled, if not silenced. Look for the apostles who name difficult realities. Their perceptive vision may encourage your congregation to practice an even deeper love of neighbor.

When we embrace the Easter miracle, we commit ourselves to embrace all that comes after it: joy and sorrow, clarity and confusion, celebration and persecution. When your faith community gathers in worship, offer them the encouragement to walk in the way of Peter and those first apostles. Encourage them not to fear or simply endure this world but, rather, to work to transform this world in God's name. The apostles got in trouble for doing two things: proclaiming good news and preaching truth. What wonderful, and holy, disruption!

CATHY CALDWELL HOOP

Psalm 150

¹Praise the LORD!
Praise God in his sanctuary;
    praise him in his mighty firmament!
²Praise him for his mighty deeds;
    praise him according to his surpassing greatness!

³Praise him with trumpet sound;
    praise him with lute and harp!
⁴Praise him with tambourine and dance;
    praise him with strings and pipe!
⁵Praise him with clanging cymbals;
    praise him with loud clashing cymbals!
⁶Let everything that breathes praise the LORD!
Praise the LORD!

Psalm 118:14–29

¹⁴The LORD is my strength and my might;
    he has become my salvation.

¹⁵There are glad songs of victory in the tents of the righteous:
"The right hand of the LORD does valiantly;
    ¹⁶the right hand of the LORD is exalted;
    the right hand of the LORD does valiantly."
¹⁷I shall not die, but I shall live,
    and recount the deeds of the LORD.
¹⁸The LORD has punished me severely,
    but he did not give me over to death.

¹⁹Open to me the gates of righteousness,
    that I may enter through them
    and give thanks to the LORD.

²⁰This is the gate of the LORD;
    the righteous shall enter through it.

²¹I thank you that you have answered me
    and have become my salvation.
²²The stone that the builders rejected
    has become the chief cornerstone.
²³This is the LORD's doing;
    it is marvelous in our eyes.
²⁴This is the day that the LORD has made;
    let us rejoice and be glad in it.
²⁵Save us, we beseech you, O LORD!
    O LORD, we beseech you, give us success!

²⁶Blessed is the one who comes in the name of the LORD.
  We bless you from the house of the LORD.
²⁷The LORD is God,
  and he has given us light.
Bind the festal procession with branches,
  up to the horns of the altar.

²⁸You are my God, and I will give thanks to you;
  you are my God, I will extol you.

²⁹O give thanks to the LORD, for he is good,
  for his steadfast love endures forever.

Connecting the Psalm with Scripture and Worship

The book of Psalms is anchored by Psalm 150, which begins and ends with the word *hallelujah,* translated "Praise the LORD" in the NRSV. As we leave Lent, and enter the season of Easter, this psalm reminds us to unbury our hallelujahs and return to a season of praise.

Psalm 150 calls on "everything that breathes" to praise the Lord (v. 6), a reminder that all of God's creatures are called to praise, whether one is a human at worship in the temple, or a wombat, wildebeest, or whale. This is not a collection of writings of relevance only to the people of ancient Israel. The praise and worship of God is a universal instruction. We join our voices to the chorus of creation, singing *hallelujah*, praise to God.

Psalm 150 also echoes a theme that recurs throughout the psalms: since only the living can praise God, it is our job, our vocation, to lift up praise while we live. This theme of the job of the living to lift up praise to God also appears in the other assigned psalm of the day, Psalm 118. In verse 17, the psalmist writes, "I shall not die, but I shall live, and recount the deeds of the LORD." To put it another way, "If I am not going to recount the deeds of the Lord, what is my purpose in living?"

If the human vocation is to praise God while we have breath, what does praise look like in an era when fewer and fewer people are gathering to join their voices in worship? Organized worship is not the only place from which creation praises God, yet it is a common thread connecting us across the years to the people who wrote and sang the psalms in corporate worship. What does praise look like in a postmodern, post-Christendom, postdenominational world?

The passage from Acts 5 shows Peter and the apostles living out their vocation of praise by speaking and teaching about God, even after being instructed to be silent by the authorities. How do we see our vocation of praise play out in our lives? Does it lead us to speak and teach about God? Does it get us brought before the authorities? Is obedience a word we associate with hallelujahs?

Peter and the apostles had been teaching and healing in Jerusalem, with "many signs and wonders done among the people" (Acts 5:12). People were hoping even Peter's shadow might fall on them, so they might be healed (v. 15). The high priest jails the apostles, and in the night the angel of the Lord opens the doors of the prison and sends the apostles back out to continue their teaching. The high priest is not pleased to find them back in the temple preaching, when he expected them to be in prison. It is at this point the passage from Acts 5 begins.

In the face of human demands for obedience, Peter makes it clear that God is their authority and the one they will obey. God's angel had, after all, opened their cell doors, brought them out, and sent them back to the temple to "tell the people the whole message about [Jesus'] life"

(v. 20). What is human authority in the face of such divine instruction?

We might not always think to pair obedience and praise, yet when Peter and the apostles obey God's command to teach, there is a sense of praise and deliverance in their obedience. God, who heals people through their work, and opens the doors of the prison, is a God of salvation. A natural response to salvation is praise.

The assigned Acts reading is followed by the story of the wisdom of Gamaliel, a teacher of the law, who wisely instructs the religious authorities to "keep away from these men and let them alone; because if this plan or this undertaking is of human origin, it will fail; but if it is of God, you will not be able to overthrow them—in that case you may even be found fighting against God!" (vv. 38–39). Gamaliel's obedience to praise looks different from that of Peter and the apostles, yet both reflect praise and belief in the power and goodness of God.

In Psalm 150, we are exhorted to praise God both in God's sanctuary and in God's mighty firmament, or dome. Robert Alter translates "mighty firmament" as "the vault of His power,"[1] reminding God's people that God resides in power both in the temple and in the heavens. Human power is limited in the face of divine power, even for the high priest, who tries to silence Peter and the apostles.

Attention to our physical surroundings is woven throughout both Psalm 150 and Psalm 118, as well as the passage from Acts 5. God's sanctuary and mighty firmament frame Psalm 150, locating our praise and God's presence in both human-built structures like the temple and in the theater of God's creation. In Acts 5, Peter and the apostles are taken from the temple to the prison, sent back to the temple, and brought before the council, transported by both human and divine instruction from one venue to another. Psalm 118, even more than the other readings, is a psalm of architecture and place. This psalm is full of structural imagery—tents where righteous sing glad songs, gates through which people enter to praise God, stones that become the chief cornerstone.

How could this psalm be used in worship to remind people of the way physical location informs worship? One might lead a call to worship from the door to the sanctuary: "Open to me the gates of righteousness, that I may enter through them and give thanks to the Lord!" (v. 19). These words remind us that whether we gather in a Gothic sanctuary, a storefront, a school cafeteria, or at camp, we are entering into God's space, God's architecture, God's building. Whatever the differences of our physical space, whenever the people of God gather, we enter a place where God's *hesed,* or steadfast love, endures forever. Psalm 118 ends as it begins, extolling the steadfast love of God. Steadfast love is a refrain carried throughout the Psalms to ensure that God's people will remember that while human-constructed temples, tents, sanctuaries, and other ventures will collapse and turn to dust, God's steadfast love is what will endure forever. Whatever humans build is subservient to the love and mercy of God.

Either of these psalms is easily adapted for use as a call to worship, using language that will be familiar to many worshipers. The following example may be led from the door to the worship space:

Reader 1: Open to me the gates of righteousness, that I may enter through them and give thanks to the Lord!

Reader 2: Praise the Lord! Praise God in the sanctuary! Praise God in all creation!

Reader 1: The stone that the builders rejected has become the chief cornerstone.

Reader 2: This is the Lord's doing. It is marvelous in our eyes.

Reader 1: Blessed is the one who comes in the name of the Lord!

Reader 2: O give thanks to the Lord, for God is good. God's steadfast love endures forever.

All: Let everything that breathes praise the Lord! Let us worship this day in joy and peace.

MARCI AULD GLASS

---

1. Robert Alter, *The Book of Psalms: A Translation with Commentary* (New York: Norton, 2007), 515.

Revelation 1:4–8

⁴John to the seven churches that are in Asia:

Grace to you and peace from him who is and who was and who is to come, and from the seven spirits who are before his throne, ⁵and from Jesus Christ, the faithful witness, the firstborn of the dead, and the ruler of the kings of the earth.

To him who loves us and freed us from our sins by his blood, ⁶and made us to be a kingdom, priests serving his God and Father, to him be glory and dominion forever and ever. Amen.

⁷Look! He is coming with the clouds;
    every eye will see him,
even those who pierced him;
    and on his account all the tribes of the earth will wail.

So it is to be. Amen.

⁸"I am the Alpha and the Omega," says the Lord God, who is and who was and who is to come, the Almighty.

Commentary 1: Connecting the Reading with Scripture

One of the several challenges of interpreting the book of Revelation is figuring out how the various parts of the book are related to one another. This problem is further complicated by what look like sudden shifts of voice (who is speaking and who is being addressed) and genre (what kind of writing it is and what is expected of the reader/hearer). We see one of these sudden shifts happen right at the beginning of the book, in fact, where our lesson begins (Rev. 1:4).

In order to appreciate the significance of this shift, it is helpful to consider the three verses that precede our lesson (these are sometimes called a prologue or an introduction). Right away we can see that verses 1–3 contain two different kinds of writing: the first two verses function as a kind of title sentence or perhaps a synopsis (summary) of the book as a whole. The third verse stands by itself as the first of seven beatitudes or blessings that are scattered throughout the book. Numbers are significant within this writing, and the number seven is particularly important, for both the structure and the content of the book. Seven is related to the seven days of the week, the six days of creation and the

seventh or Sabbath day on which God rested. For this reason, it is often considered a symbol of wholeness or completion. In addition to the seven churches that are first mentioned in verse 4, there are three series of sevens that structure the plot of Revelation: seven seals, seven trumpets, and seven bowls. Sometimes the number seven is explicitly mentioned, even featured. Other times there are "sevens" that are almost invisible, as in the case of the seven beatitudes. In other words, you would not know there were seven unless you counted them.

Verse 3 also identifies the writing as a prophecy, announcing, "Blessed is the one who reads aloud the words of the prophecy." In light of this, the tone at the start of our lesson (beginning at v. 4) comes as something of a surprise. It does not sound like a prophecy, but like the beginning of a letter in the ancient Greco-Roman world. Ancient letters followed the same convention as a contemporary e-mail or office memo: first the sender was identified, then the recipient was named, then there was some kind of a greeting. In ancient business letters the greeting was usually a brief wish for good health or the favor of the gods upon the recipient. Then the writer moved on to the business of the letter. Early Christian letters (including Paul's, which are the earliest we have) modified the secular greeting to a theological "grace wish" (a greeting that hoped and prayed for God's blessing upon the recipients of the letter). The writer of the Revelation or Apocalypse to John clearly knows this ancient convention and its early Christian modification. "John to the seven churches that are in Asia: Grace to you and peace from [the One] who is and who was and who is to come" would normally be at the beginning of an early Christian writing (see the letters of Paul, Peter, John, James, and Jude). However, here it appears as the fourth verse.

The puzzle continues as we notice that chapters 2 and 3 of Revelation consist of seven highly stylized, almost formulaic, letters written to the angels of the seven churches referred to in 1:4. Each of the letters is addressed to the angel of a church in a major city in Asia Minor. Further research indicates that they are in the order of locations that a messenger carrying such a letter would probably travel. If these chapters were actual letters, intended to be a circular communication where the members of each church would hear what was written to all the churches, it is easy to imagine our passage (1:4–8) as a general introduction to the seven letters. Moreover, if we jump to the very end of the Revelation, to 22:21, we find the kind of closing grace wish that often ends early Christian letters. So the genre of a circular letter to seven churches is not only introduced in our lesson for today, but is carried through deliberately in chapters 2–3 and also at the very end of the writing.

Interposed between our lesson (1:4–8) and chapters 2–3 is a section that sounds more like a prophetic call narrative (such as Isa. 6, Jer. 1:4–10, Ezek. 1–2, or Amos 7:14–17), which fits with the beatitude in 1:3 referring to the writing as a prophecy. It includes what is often called an inaugural vision, in which the seer John is commissioned to "write in a book what you see and send it to the seven churches, to Ephesus, to Smyrna, to Pergamum, to Thyatira, to Sardis, to Philadelphia, and to Laodicea" (1:11). The figure of the risen Christ is described in this vision by phrases that are then carried over to each of the letters (cf., e.g., 1:12; 1:16; and 2:1). So already it is clear that we have a carefully planned and tightly integrated composition, written in a way that feels disjointed and confused, like a dream sequence, where images blend, sights and sounds are interwoven in strange ways, and the plot moves in ways that are clearly patterned, but not necessarily linear.

Turning our attention to the specific content of our lesson for today, what are John's first words to the seven churches that are in Asia? The grace wish describes God as timeless, present, past, and future: "Grace to you and peace from him who is and who was and who is to come, and from the seven spirits who are before his throne" (1:4). Again, the number seven may refer to the entirety or completeness of the Holy Spirit of God, or the seven spirits may be related to the seven golden lampstands, which we are told are the seven churches (v. 20). The wish for grace is also extended to Jesus Christ (note the proto-Trinitarian construction of this blessing), who is described as "the faithful witness" or "the faithful one, the martyr" (either is possible in the Greek), "the firstborn of the dead" (a reference to his resurrection and new life), and "the ruler of the kings of the earth" (v. 5). This is the first clear signal that earthly powers, even imperial Rome, are not immune from God's judgment.

The end of 1:5 and 1:6 form a doxology (a hymn of praise) to the Lord Jesus Christ for his redemptive work on the cross and for his formation of the church, which is described as "a kingdom and priests serving his God and Father" (the language, here, is borrowed from Exod. 19:6 and Isa. 61:6). In verse 7, the author combines the idea that the Son of Man will come on the clouds (Dan. 7:13) with the prophecy about the death of the firstborn (Zech. 12:10) as it is connected to the image of Jesus being pierced in the Johannine passion narrative (John 19:37).

Verse 8 provides a perfect bookend to the description of God as eternal found in verse 4. Alpha and Omega are the first and last letters of the Greek alphabet, so God the all powerful, the Pantocrator, is "the One who is and who was and who is to come."

A. KATHERINE GRIEB

Commentary 2: Connecting the Reading with the World

It seems surreal when John exclaims, "Look! [Jesus Christ] is coming with the clouds; every eye will see him, even those who pierced him" (Rev. 1:7). On one hand, the return of Jesus is like a superhero movie—his hair like wool, eyes like fire, and a voice with the sound of many waters. Upon seeing this warrior holding stars and wielding a two-edge sword, one quickly concludes not much heaven will be brought to earth. This looks more like war. Yet as we move through John's vision, Jesus as warrior becomes a lamb, who ironically leads us to the healing or resurrection of a new heaven and new earth.

John's Apocalypse is controversial. The word "apocalypse" literally means an unveiling of what is already there. This apocalyptic book is a natural lightning rod for affinity groups trying to buttress their own concerns and worldviews. In other words, conservative and progressive religious voices who often quote the book of Revelation usually reveal their own biases and expectations. An example of this is when Pat Robertson claimed that the earthquake in Haiti was caused by its people's "pact with the devil." Robertson and other evangelical ministers often make such claims by blaming disasters on the victims.[1] At the end of the day, however, they display only their self-interested outcomes. Naturally, a conservative political reading of Revelation will end up championing how heroes and heroines in Revelation look like them. Likewise, liberally minded readings rearrange virtues to match liberal agendas. So the numerous commentaries, as well as the thousands of people reading them, are often abiding in self-fulfilling prophecies—preaching to the choir.

Many readers treat Revelation as though it is some kind of oracle in which to find who is in or out of favor with God. Who will go to hell? However, in this passage of John's Apocalypse we catch a glimpse of the paradox of judgment: be careful who we assume is in or out of God's salvation. When John shouts, "Look!" perhaps he is conveying his own surprise at who will see the resurrected Jesus. John says that "every eye will see Jesus, even those who pierced him" (v. 7).

On this basis I think John begs for a patient reading of the text. Progressives, conservatives, and liberals should resist those solipsistic readings of Revelation that perpetuate war, and instead be prepared and ready to unlearn what promotes self-interest alone, and learn afresh from the Word that is near you. "Blessed is the one who reads aloud the words of the prophecy, and blessed are those who hear and who keep what is written in it; for the time is near" (v. 3).

Not many of us really want what I describe as heaven: that state of God's presence in which *all* persons are made wholly complete. Sad to say for some, but heaven is not ultimately about whether you or I get there as individuals. The ultimate reality of heaven is *the joy derived from interdependent persons who adore someone greater than themselves: God.* I argue for this definition of heaven because I cannot imagine being wholly complete unless everyone else is. In other words, how could I be completely happy, and still be conscious of someone else weeping and gnashing their teeth forever in hell? John's own quantum physics also invites us into this reality as he collapses space and time into one person: "'I am the Alpha and the Omega,' says the Lord God, who is and who was and who is to come, the Almighty. I, John, your brother who share with you in Jesus the persecution and the kingdom and the patient endurance, was on the island called Patmos because of the word of God and the testimony of Jesus" (vv. 8–9).

If one did an informal poll, asking Christians whether they personally hoped they would go to heaven, the answer would be a resounding yes. Even in popular culture, outside of Christian circles, one's personal expectation of going to heaven, except for those perpetuating the most heinous crimes, is widespread. In prison ministries, many of the prisoners on death row or who committed violent crimes still have faith that God can forgive them, allowing redemption to enter heaven one day. For many Christians,

---

1. John Hudson, "Pat Robertson Blames Natural Disaster Victims," in *The Atlantic*, January 10, 2010, https://www.theatlantic.com/technology/archive/2010/01/pat-robertson-blames-natural-disaster-victims/341489/.

there is the expectation that we will go to a better place after we die—even if it is not called heaven. This text in John's Revelation encourages us to identify the interpersonal dimension of heaven.

According to most Christian conceptions, God's domicile is in heaven and not on earth. What is cloaked in this dualistic construct is the idea that the transcendent God is beyond the earth. However, God lodging in heaven is an attempt to transform the abstract idea of transcendence into a more concrete space and time. This problem also leads to the confusion of terms like "heaven," "eschatology," and "kingdom of God" or "kingdom of heaven." It may be that we imagine God as being far away because we cannot imagine God being on a suffering earth.

Although we have many questions about heaven and have difficulty talking about it, there is good news. We long so much for a different world from this one because the desire for a perfect world becomes the proper reaction to God's act in the crucified Christ. In other words, through the birth, life, death, and resurrection of Christ, God shows us that there is no once-removed reality between God and this earth. Christian theology does not delude itself into thinking that it is easy to imagine heaven, but it knows how to get there through the special revelation of Jesus.

When heaven becomes a land of Oz (some distant place), believers indulge in an addiction to a delusory world, restricted only to the medium of fantasy, and articulated by those in high socioeconomic positions who are capable of telling the story to those barely making it in life and who desperately need to believe an alternative reality. Whether one is rich or poor, then, it does not matter what happens in this life so long as I personally make it to heaven.

White people, in forging the foundation of the United States, justified the enslavement of Africans by believing they were helping heathens to heaven. There was no worry for many white Christian slaveholders that their behavior contradicted finding God's presence (Matt. 25:34–36). Today Christians move to the suburbs and talk about heaven abstracted from the suffering that we may (inadvertently or not) be causing the rest of the world by ignoring those in the inner cities. Even though it may be overwhelming to imagine heaven for every living soul, it still remains the great commission to which Christians are called.

When preaching this text, preachers must talk about heaven as more than a place for individual selves. Instead, Christians must confess a failure of language around heaven. Whether conservative, liberal, or moderate, individuals' and groups' pursuits of heaven are making this earth even more vulnerable to our destruction. If our concept of heaven is really a subtext or euphemism in which we retreat from a suffering world in order to enjoy our own spoils of war, then we are not following Jesus.

MICHAEL BATTLE

John 20:19–31

¹⁹When it was evening on that day, the first day of the week, and the doors of the house where the disciples had met were locked for fear of the Jews, Jesus came and stood among them and said, "Peace be with you." ²⁰After he said this, he showed them his hands and his side. Then the disciples rejoiced when they saw the Lord. ²¹Jesus said to them again, "Peace be with you. As the Father has sent me, so I send you." ²²When he had said this, he breathed on them and said to them, "Receive the Holy Spirit. ²³If you forgive the sins of any, they are forgiven them; if you retain the sins of any, they are retained."

²⁴But Thomas (who was called the Twin), one of the twelve, was not with them when Jesus came. ²⁵So the other disciples told him, "We have seen the Lord." But he said to them, "Unless I see the mark of the nails in his hands, and put my finger in the mark of the nails and my hand in his side, I will not believe."

²⁶A week later his disciples were again in the house, and Thomas was with them. Although the doors were shut, Jesus came and stood among them and said, "Peace be with you." ²⁷Then he said to Thomas, "Put your finger here and see my hands. Reach out your hand and put it in my side. Do not doubt but believe." ²⁸Thomas answered him, "My Lord and my God!" ²⁹Jesus said to him, "Have you believed because you have seen me? Blessed are those who have not seen and yet have come to believe."

³⁰Now Jesus did many other signs in the presence of his disciples, which are not written in this book. ³¹But these are written so that you may come to believe that Jesus is the Messiah, the Son of God, and that through believing you may have life in his name.

Commentary 1: Connecting the Reading with Scripture

The Gospel texts in today's lectionary narrate two appearances of Jesus to his disciples: first, an appearance apparently to ten of them (without Thomas or Judas), and a second appearance to the disciples with Thomas present. Together Jesus' appearances show in narrative form what he offers and what he asks of his disciples in the future, when he will no longer be with them in body. Simply put, he offers them peace (John 20:21, 26), evokes joy (v. 20), calls them to trust in him (v. 27), and appoints them as witnesses in the world (v. 27). The encounter with Thomas crystalizes the invitation to believe, or trust in Jesus. Earlier in the Gospel, Thomas had expressed his willingness to follow Jesus, even though the path would lead to death, but he lacked the understanding that Jesus' death

would not mark the end of his life (11:16; 14:5). Now, upon seeing the risen Lord, Thomas confesses his full allegiance to Jesus, the living Lord.

Jesus appears to his disciples, speaking the traditional greeting, "Peace," to them (20:19), even as he had promised them that he would give them his peace upon his departure (14:27; 16:33). Peace is the assurance of Jesus' ongoing, life-giving presence, now made real through the Holy Spirit. If earlier John the Baptist had promised Jesus would baptize with Spirit, and Jesus himself had promised his disciples to send the Holy Spirit to them (14:17, 26; 15:26; 16:13), he now fulfills that promise by breathing it on them. The scene is reminiscent of the story of the creation of humankind in Genesis, where, having "formed man from the dust of

211

Love So Amazing, So Divine

When I survey the wondrous cross
On which the Prince of glory died,
My richest gain I count but loss,
And pour contempt on all my pride.

Forbid it, Lord, that I should boast,
Save in the death of Christ my God!
All the vain things that charm me most,
I sacrifice them to His blood.

See from His head, His hands, His feet,
Sorrow and love flow mingled down!
Did e'er such love and sorrow meet,
Or thorns compose so rich a crown?

Were the whole realm of nature mine,
That were a present far too small;
Love so amazing, so divine,
Demands my soul, my life, my all.

Isaac Watts, "When I Survey the Wondrous Cross," in *The Psalms, Hymns, and Spiritual Songs of Isaac Watts*, ed. Samuel Worcester (Boston: Crocker & Brewster, 1860), 478.

the ground," God breathed "the breath of life" into his nostrils, so that he became a living being (Gen. 2:7).

Now Jesus breathes the life-giving Spirit on his disciples. Having received the new life of the Spirit, they themselves are commissioned to be agents of extending that new life to others in the task of forgiving sins. They can do so because Jesus is the Lamb of God, who takes away the sin of the world (John 1:29) and, by so doing, gives life. Because of his life-giving work through his death, and his gift of the life-giving Spirit, the disciples may serve as agents of Jesus' forgiveness.

The disciples then report to Thomas, who had not been with them, "We have seen the Lord." Interestingly, in the Gospel of John, various disciples formulate the announcement that Jesus has risen, not with the familiar Easter greeting "He is risen!" but with the first person declaration "I (or we) have seen the Lord." This is what the disciples report to Thomas upon having seen Jesus (20:25). They have seen what Thomas has not. While there is an emphasis on sight, on what the eyes see, it is clear in John that sight

is not always insight. Many see Jesus' signs, but they do not necessarily believe the witness of the signs that Jesus is the life-giving Son of God. Now who would believe the testimony of Jesus' followers that they had seen Jesus alive?

Apparently not Thomas! He protests that unless he too can see what the others saw, he will not believe. Thomas does not ask for more than they received, but he does ask to see what they saw. Mary has seen the risen Lord; the other disciples have seen the risen Lord. Thomas too wants to see the risen Jesus. Then he does. When Jesus appears among his disciples, he shows Thomas the evidence of the torture and abuse he experienced at the hands of the Romans as they crucified him. Jesus does not show Thomas his wounds because Thomas had doubted that Jesus had really died. What Thomas did not believe was that Jesus, who was so brutally killed, was now living—that the other disciples had seen the Lord, as they said they had. So Jesus shows Thomas his wounds, and then invites him to believe, that is, to believe that although Jesus was crucified, he is indeed now living.

Jesus does not ask Thomas simply to believe a fact, as it were, about him. Although Thomas is frequently called a doubter, Jesus does not invite him to stop doubting. Rather, Jesus invites Thomas to turn from being unbelieving (Greek *apistos*) to believing (*pistos*), that is, to put his trust in Jesus. This invitation to trust Jesus as the living Lord is the same invitation given to everyone who reads the pages of the Gospel in other places or subsequent centuries. They may yearn to see Jesus, as Thomas did, but they will not see him as Thomas did. They have the witness of those who did see him, though, borne through the pages of the Gospel, and they are invited by means of it to "see" the work of Jesus, to "see" the crucified Jesus, to "see" the risen Lord, and so to believe or to trust him (20:30–31). Thomas does not err by doubting, but by failing to believe in the living Jesus by accepting the testimony of Mary and the other disciples to the resurrection of Jesus. He thus shows that although he did come to believe by seeing, others will come to believe without seeing (v. 29).

Thomas's encounter with Jesus leads him to confess Jesus in exalted terms, "My Lord and My God!" (v. 28). Thomas thus echoes the opening verses of the Gospel, where "the Word" who was with God and was God took on flesh (1:1, 14). Flesh is frail and mortal, and so dies. The man who stands before Thomas is the Word incarnate, whose flesh was subject to humiliation and death. Thus Thomas's confession not only echoes the opening lines of the Gospel, where the Word is acknowledged as God; but as the climactic confession in the Gospel, it also includes within its witness to Jesus as "Lord and God" the entire narrative of Jesus' human life, death, and resurrection. It is this man, the incarnate Word of God, who gave his life and now lives, who is properly acknowledged by Thomas as "my Lord and my God." All who read the Gospel are invited to stand with Thomas in this confession of Jesus.

A narrative in the book of Acts portrays the emboldened disciples as bearing witness to the risen Jesus. Having healed in Jesus' name, the disciples are forbidden by the Jewish authorities to teach in his name. They continue to do so anyway, explaining their persistence by appeal to their role and that of the Holy Spirit as witnesses to Jesus and the resurrection. They must speak of what they know. Jesus himself is described in the book of Revelation as "the faithful witness" (Rev. 1:5). Revelation, like the Gospel of John, joins together that picture of Jesus in his earthly life as a "faithful witness," with the announcement of his great power as "ruler of the kings of the earth." Disciples who, in spite of the efforts of the authorities to silence them, bear witness to the work of God, follow in the footsteps of Jesus, who bore his faithful witness even unto death. In Scripture, God's people and God's world are invited to "see" and to "bear witness" to the salvation that they have come to know. Even though that witness, like the cornerstone, like Jesus himself, is sometimes rejected (Ps. 118:22), the narratives in John testify that God has given the Spirit so that such witness may continue, and may be agents of God's life-giving work in the world.

MARIANNE MEYE THOMPSON

Commentary 2: Connecting the Reading with the World

This text appears the Second Sunday of Easter in all three years of the lectionary. The Sunday after Easter often feels like a bit of a letdown. After all the crowds and excitement of the week before, the service can seem tame and disappointing by comparison. Regular preachers often take that week off. The temptation for everyone is to go back to life as usual, leaving the drama of Easter behind.

Even Jesus' disciples seem to have returned to their old fears and routines. It did not take them long. On Easter morning, they heard the witness of Mary Magdalene that she had seen the risen Lord (John 20:18), but by that evening they are hiding behind locked doors "for fear of the Jews" (v. 19). John's Gospel reflects the hostility between the followers of Jesus and the synagogue at the time it was written, and that antagonistic relationship colors John's account of the resurrection. Even after the resurrection, old alienations remain. This needs to change in contemporary tellings of the Easter story. Christians believe that the resurrection is the inauguration of God's new reign of justice and joy for the whole world, and the fear and contempt of Jews that has lived on for centuries in Christian communities of faith is a denial of this resurrection hope.

The good news of this text is that human weakness and failure do not keep Christ from being present in power and grace. Darkness, alienation, even locked doors do not prevent Jesus from suddenly appearing among the disciples (v. 19). His first act is to give them peace, the peace that he promised them before his crucifixion (14:27) and that they desperately need. Next, Jesus removes all doubt about his identity by showing them his wounded hands and side (v. 20). In this gesture, Jesus also shows the disciples that their betrayal and abandonment of him do not have the last word on their relationship to him. Their response to Jesus' presence is joy (v. 20). Just as Jesus promised them beforehand (16:22), this is a joy that not even their own fear and failure can take away from them.

Just as in the prior story of Mary Magdalene (20:1–18), connection with the risen Jesus leads to commissioning. Filled with Jesus' peace, the disciples are sent to witness to others to the peace of Jesus. Jesus taught them that to see him is to see the Father (14:9). Now the lives of the disciples are to be so transparent to Jesus that to see them is to see Jesus. This is a daunting assignment for this cowardly and unreliable group, hiding in the dark behind locked doors. Only the gift of the Spirit (20:22) makes it possible for them to overcome their doubt and fear and respond to their commission.

Their fellow disciple Thomas, who missed all the drama of Jesus' initial appearance to them, is the first recipient of their witness. Thomas demands more tangible proof, declaring that he will not be convinced that it is Jesus who appeared to them until he can see and touch Jesus' wounds. A week later, in same place, the door still shut, Thomas gets his proof. Jesus appears and invites Thomas to touch the wounds of his hands and side (v. 27). In a flash of Johannine irony, the disciple who becomes known in later Christian tradition as "doubting Thomas" responds with the highest expression of faith in Jesus uttered in any Gospel: "My Lord and my God" (v. 28).

We might wish that Jesus' resurrection would erase the troubles of our past and catapult us into a wholly new future. In this fantasy, the Easter crowds at church would keep coming back week after week, and our own faith and witness would be fearless and exemplary, bearing none of the scars of our past failings and enmities. Instead, we look more like the disciples,

our lives a mixture of fear and joy, doubt and faith. It is to people like us that what seems like the natural ending of John's Gospel (vv. 30–31) speaks: John has written his Gospel, he tells us, so that we might go on believing, and through believing have life in Jesus' name.

John emphasizes that Jesus' resurrected body carries the wounds of his earthly life (see a similar emphasis in Luke 24:38–40). Resurrection transforms but does not erase Jesus' prior suffering. In Caravaggio's painting *The Incredulity of St. Thomas*, as Thomas inserts his finger into Jesus' side, his eyes and the eyes of the other disciples are on the open wound. Caravaggio directs us to look where they are looking. The risen Jesus encounters his followers, both then and now, as the one who has been wounded.

Contemporary theologians who engage human trauma and disability have picked up on this detail of John's resurrection account. They reject the idea that Jesus' invitation to Thomas is merely a visual aid—a sensory accommodation to Thomas's weak faith. Instead, they interpret Jesus' challenge to believe (v. 27) as a test of faith in a different sense. Jesus is challenging Thomas and the other disciples to confront the wounds of their personal and collective life, instead of trying to deny or hide them. As Shelly Rambo insists, "Jesus is directing them to the collective work of healing by reorienting their sense, pointing them to truths that rarely come to light."[1] Rambo likens this focus on Jesus' wounds to healing circles for veteran groups, in which wounds are the very purpose for gathering.[2]

For the disciples, these wounds will include their betrayal of Jesus and their broken relationship with the Jewish community. For Jesus' disciples today, these wounds may be the result of war, serious illness, or abuse. The healing and hope that the risen Jesus offers do not reverse the passage of time and bring back our life exactly as it once was. New life in Jesus' name (v. 31) arises amid the dislocation and lasting wounds that traumatic suffering inflicts. For North American Christians, this new life cannot avoid the wounds of our racial history. Our collective

1. Shelly Rambo, *Resurrecting Wounds: Living in the Afterlife of Trauma* (Waco: Baylor University Press, 2017), 136.
2. Rambo, 115.

healing requires the faith to look honestly at the racial traumas of our past and present.

The wounds of the risen Jesus are also an invitation to reshape our hopes for eternal life with God. In a book prompted by having a brother with Down syndrome, Amos Yong suggests that our own resurrection life will still bear the marks of our earthly disabilities. The eschatological redemption of disability does not mean its erasure, but rather the end of the physical and social suffering associated with it. Yong imagines the deaf anticipating that "when we get to heaven, the signing will be tremendous!" In the

new creation, disability will no longer be a cause of alienation and exclusion, and Yong declares that this eschatological hope should shape "how we organize, structure, and arrange our present life in this world."[3]

John 20:19–31 is a guide for being an Easter community where the wounds of crucifixion are not denied, where the continuing reality of death and failure and trauma is not covered up, where our lament finds a communal home alongside our joy. Resurrection faith means having the courage to look at our wounds.

AMY PLANTINGA PAUW

---

3. Amos Yong, *Theology and Down Syndrome: Reimagining Disability in Late Modernity* (Waco: Baylor University Press, 2007), 291.

Third Sunday of Easter

Acts 9:1–6 (7–20)
Psalm 30

Revelation 5:11–14
John 21:1–19

Acts 9:1–6 (7–20)

[1]Meanwhile Saul, still breathing threats and murder against the disciples of the Lord, went to the high priest [2]and asked him for letters to the synagogues at Damascus, so that if he found any who belonged to the Way, men or women, he might bring them bound to Jerusalem. [3]Now as he was going along and approaching Damascus, suddenly a light from heaven flashed around him. [4]He fell to the ground and heard a voice saying to him, "Saul, Saul, why do you persecute me?" [5]He asked, "Who are you, Lord?" The reply came, "I am Jesus, whom you are persecuting. [6]But get up and enter the city, and you will be told what you are to do." [7]The men who were traveling with him stood speechless because they heard the voice but saw no one. [8]Saul got up from the ground, and though his eyes were open, he could see nothing; so they led him by the hand and brought him into Damascus. [9]For three days he was without sight, and neither ate nor drank.

[10]Now there was a disciple in Damascus named Ananias. The Lord said to him in a vision, "Ananias." He answered, "Here I am, Lord." [11]The Lord said to him, "Get up and go to the street called Straight, and at the house of Judas look for a man of Tarsus named Saul. At this moment he is praying, [12]and he has seen in a vision a man named Ananias come in and lay his hands on him so that he might regain his sight." [13]But Ananias answered, "Lord, I have heard from many about this man, how much evil he has done to your saints in Jerusalem; [14]and here he has authority from the chief priests to bind all who invoke your name." [15]But the Lord said to him, "Go, for he is an instrument whom I have chosen to bring my name before Gentiles and kings and before the people of Israel; [16]I myself will show him how much he must suffer for the sake of my name." [17]So Ananias went and entered the house. He laid his hands on Saul and said, "Brother Saul, the Lord Jesus, who appeared to you on your way here, has sent me so that you may regain your sight and be filled with the Holy Spirit." [18]And immediately something like scales fell from his eyes, and his sight was restored. Then he got up and was baptized, [19]and after taking some food, he regained his strength.

For several days he was with the disciples in Damascus, [20]and immediately he began to proclaim Jesus in the synagogues, saying, "He is the Son of God."

Commentary 1: Connecting the Reading with Scripture

As we approach this text on the conversion of Saul, our beginning point is to acknowledge that this is no ordinary event subject to our psychological analysis. The narrative insists that this is a real encounter that cannot be explained away by appeals to generic religious phenomena or by a psychology of spirituality. Karl Barth

emphasized the centrality of Christ's presence in understanding the scene: "It is Jesus who met him and announced himself: 'I am Jesus' [v. 5]. Jesus himself met him before Damascus. This is the new factor in relation to everything that goes before. This is the decisive element in the story. It was solely and simply in the power of the fact

216

that Jesus met him that the event became that of his conversion."[1]

Before this encounter, Saul is a persecutor, because he correctly took Jesus to be a threat to the "old economy" of tribal Judaism. His change of names signifies his radical transformation, from persecutor to witness. In like manner, the summons to Ananias is an extraordinary event. Jesus' entry into Ananias's life is by the way in which Jesus calls so that Ananias is compelled to respond (v. 11). His response is an act of submission and obedience, for Ananias recognizes Jesus as Lord, thereby acknowledging himself as one summoned to obedience. Thus, with both Saul and Ananias, the direct witness of Jesus' lordly presence occupies the drama of the narrative. It is the presence of Jesus that makes all things new for both men.

The completion of the conversion of Saul requires the ministration of Ananias, something that is essential to the equipment of this new apostle. He has been struck blind when he met Jesus: "He could see nothing" (v. 8). Only through the presence of Ananias does he see and so receive the spirit (v. 17). It is the community that permits him to know and embrace his new vocation and identity.

> Whereas in the first [encounter] Saul apparently has to do directly and solely with Jesus, the community now enters into consideration in the person of Ananias. . . . He [Paul] is now to encounter the community in a very different way, with all the initiative on its side rather than his. And it is as he does so, his past done away and his future opened up, that there is revealed to him what was previously hidden, namely, what is to become of him and what he is to do. It is by the community that there is shown to him the only possible way now that he is at the end of his former way.[2]

His new assignment, however, is not just to be a "follower of the Way." Rather, the newly named Paul is to be an "instrument" ("vehicle") for a wholly new enterprise, one that the earliest Jewish church could not have anticipated.

The call of Paul is in fact a subset of the new gospel horizon that will dominate the book of Acts. The explicit command of Jesus via Ananias is to witness the risen Christ to "Gentiles and kings" and "the people of Israel" (v. 15). In this moment Paul's perspective is moved beyond tribalism to reach all of humanity as the sphere of Christ's domain. For Paul it is not an either/or of his own people and "the other"; it is a both/and from the outset.

For this new vocation, Paul "must suffer for the sake of my name" (v. 16). Indeed he does suffer, as the book of Acts narrates, at the hands of the Roman magistrates and at the hands of his fellow Jews. The message of Jesus is unwelcome news in both circles. The challenge to Paul and the congregations he will form and lead is how to hold in one community both Jewish followers who adhere to the Torah of Moses and followers who are not committed to the Torah. This tension dominates Paul's epistles to the Romans and Galatians, and continues to be a primal preoccupation in the church. The famous Jerusalem council of Acts 15 provided a provisional settlement of the tension, but it could not dispose of the issue that has left the inescapable diversity of the movement under negotiation.

The direct intrusion and self-announcement of Jesus summon Saul away from old theological commitments of a reductive Judaism that has strayed away from covenantal vitality. It is also a summons away from the gods of the empire. The summons of Jesus away from both Jewish reductionism and imperial idols is a summons to the specificity of Jesus, whose lordship is evidenced in his self-giving love. Thus the point of our reading is not Paul's experience (for that is derivative) but the self-disclosure of Jesus:

> I am Jesus. (9:5)

> [Paul is] an instrument *I have chosen.* (v. 15)

> I myself will show him. (v. 16)

This focus on Jesus as Lord is at the center of these New Testament lections. In the Gospel

1. Karl Barth, *Church Dogmatics*, IV/3 (Edinburgh: T. & T. Clark, 1961), 1:202.
2. Barth, 206.

The Heat of Charity

We must rise from the night of sin perfectly and without relapse. Just as "Christ rising from the dead dies now no more, death shall no more have dominion over him," so a sinner who has once risen from the death of sin must never want to relapse, as far as it lies in him, and eagerly reflect that in the same flesh in which we live we shall rise again in the end. For as Job says: "I believe that my Redeemer lives, and in the last day I shall rise out of the earth, and in my flesh I will see my God." An example occurs in nature: When the phoenix, who lives for many years, senses that his powers fail, he makes a nest from aromatic twigs. When in summer these twigs are lit by the heat of the sun, he willingly enters his nest and is set on fire and burned to ashes. From these ashes a small worm is born within days, which soon grows feather and takes again the shape of a bird. Spiritually speaking, by this phoenix I understand a just man. When he has lived for many years, he fashions for himself a nest of aromatic twigs, by putting together a bundle made up of the good works he has done in his life, in the firm hope of being saved eternally, as scripture says, "the just man has hope in his death." Without doubt, if the bundle of good works is set afire in his life by the heat of charity, and when then his spirit is in death separated from his body and his flesh turns to decay and decay into ashes, from these ashes the just man will at last rise again in his body and soul to receive his reward from the Lord. And thus his body, which in life was a burden to his soul, will after his resurrection be his glory.

Thomas Brinton, "Easter," in *Preaching in the Age of Chaucer: Selected Sermons in Translation*, trans. Siegfried Wenzel (Washington: The Catholic University of America Press, 2008), 131–32.

reading we get the recognition of the Easter Christ by Peter: "It is the Lord" (John 21:7). In the reading from Revelation we get a doxology to the Lamb who is praised by the myriad company of heaven. All of these readings attest that it is specifically Jesus—the one who met Saul, the one who encountered Peter, the one sung by the angels—who governs. It is he who has in his suffering ("slaughter," Rev. 5:12) come to power, wealth, wisdom, might, honor, and glory (v. 13). In his death and governance Jesus is not translatable to any more convenient religious phenomenon. It is this Jesus and none other who advocates and insists upon Gentiles, kings, and Israel living together in common community in a mode that scandalizes more comfortable arrangements of truth and power.

The psalm for the day celebrates the overnight turn wrought by God from sadness to joy, from distress to well-being, mindful that "joy comes in the morning" (Ps. 30:5). We could imagine this psalm on Paul's lips. He knew about the stressful demands of being a persecutor as he felt compelled to be by his faith. His "joy in the morning" is his entry into a new vocation and identity by his abrupt embrace of the economy of crucifixion and resurrection. For that reason Paul can write, "May the God of hope fill you with all joy" (Rom. 15:13). He himself is filled with joy in his new life, joy in the morning.

We may identify two accents that pervade the Bible, one personal and one public. The personal accent is the truth that the God of the gospel does indeed summon and empower persons to new life, as in the case of Paul. That is evident in the series of prophets, beginning with Moses, who were pressed by the power of God to a new life of daring and demanding obedience. Every pastor, moreover, can attest to the truth that individual persons are called out to a life of joyous obedience that they could not have imagined.

The public accent is the reach of the gospel, always and everywhere, to "the other" who is unlike us, and who feels to us like a threat or at best an inconvenience. This reach to "the other" is of course an urgent matter now in church and in society, as we face a new multiculturalism that jeopardizes old entitlements. That same jeopardy was strongly felt in the life of the early church. Paul's mandate is uncompromising on the matter, a fact evidenced everywhere in his apostolic mission.

WALTER BRUEGGEMANN

Commentary 2: Connecting the Reading with the World

Everyone has a conversion experience, and these experiences range from humorous to life saving. They may be able to tell you when they gave up their PC for a Mac, or discovered that they actually *like* brussels sprouts. Maybe they can tell you the moment when they decided to get married after years of swearing allegiance to the single life, or the hour they found the strength to walk through the door of an Alcoholics Anonymous meeting. In this Third Sunday of Easter, we encounter just how radical a conversion experience can be.

Break down a transformational experience, and you discover that it contains three stages: the unaware or unenlightened phase, the moment of interruption or "aha," and the response. The lectionary for this week offers the preacher an intriguing option. You may choose to stop at verse 6, pausing at the "aha" moment, or you may read through to verse 20 to discover how Saul will answer Jesus' voice. These are two distinct preaching paths, and the choice may depend upon your context. Does the congregation need to stay with Saul in the middle of the road, or do they need to journey on to meet Saul on Straight Street?

Is your church biblically literate? If so, consider the first option, and leave them with a cliffhanger. You will need to walk the congregation back from the edge, ask them to suspend what they know in order to embody the moment of decision. Challenge them to stay in the discomfort of darkness. Truth is waiting there, although we typically associate truth with *light*!

Barbara Brown Taylor, in her book *Learning to Walk in the Dark*, asks the reader to consider the blessing of darkness. She draws attention to the story of Jesus healing a man born blind. After being questioned by the religious authorities, the now-sighted man is eventually thrown out of the temple. Hearing of this painful ending to a day initiated in hope, Jesus returns to the man and says, "I came into this world for judgment so that those who do not see may see, and those who do see may become blind" (John 9:39). Taylor's book is an invitation to wonder if this "judgment" of blindness is a verdict that leads to freedom rather than despair. What we

witness in Saul's adventure is the necessity for blindness.

Hold your congregation in this darkness. Experiment with the lighting or candles in your preaching. Explore the possibility that darkness has other dimensions. Though so often a metaphor for despair and hopelessness, it can also be a metaphor for healing. It is not our natural ability to sit with moments of "blindness," but it is something that the congregation might be able to practice together. In corporate worship we practice forgiveness; we practice the sharing of God's peace, so that we can carry these practices out into the world. Perhaps your congregation, like Saul, needs to practice being at peace with the darkness.

If you dare, challenge your congregation to visualize the church in the role of Saul. While it is easy to point a finger at Saul for his persecution of Christians, we have a short memory when it comes to the life-destroying practices in which we have been engaged. It was not that long ago that Christian churches participated in the lynchings of people of color. Even when the church has progressed beyond discrimination of transgender and nonbinary individuals, there will be a persecuted community in our culture. Is it time for you to suggest that your church needs an atoning conversion experience?

Your congregation may not be ready for that word. They may need the full story of how Saul is pursued by a God who never abandons anyone. They may need to hear the story of a man who is humbled, brought low, and *restored* to fullness of life. This is not the vengeful act of an angry God, but the merciful act of a loving God, much like God sending a fish to rescue Jonah from the depths of the sea. God throws Saul to the ground to get his attention. Not everyone needs to be shaken by the shoulders, but Saul does. He was "breathing threats and murder against the disciples of the Lord" (Acts 9:1).

Of course Jesus is going to love and forgive the bumbling Peter (the companion Gospel text, John 21). Peter made a rather embarrassing mistake, but he was not trying to *kill* anyone! We all stumble on our faith journeys, and are glad for God to forgive Peter. Saul's rescue, on the other hand, is so outrageous that it can only be the work of a foolishly forgiving God. Some, living with the invisible scars of mistakes, have never imagined that God could love them, and Saul's story can bring the Easter promise home for them.

Others will be a little irritated that Saul gets off so easily. Acknowledge that this is an unsettling, even disturbing story. Bring it into contemporary language. Imagine a parent, their child murdered, approaching the perpetrator and offering them an executive position in the family business. It is a theological puzzle that we cannot ignore and that could launch an entire sermon series. If we believe it is God's work to seek out and save the lost, we must ask ourselves if we prefer to worship a God of punishment or a God of mercy.

Regardless of the preaching path you choose, artists' renderings of this dramatic story can bring it to life for your congregants. Those long familiar with the text may discover new insights, while those who hear it with fresh ears will be enhanced in their understanding. Visit Caravaggio's interpretation of a young, muscular Saul laid flat on his back, his powerful horse standing over him. In William Blake's scene, both Saul and Jesus are nude, a theological choice by the artist. Consider Michelangelo's fresco, in which an elderly Saul is knocked from a horse by a column of light extending from the hand of God. For a more contemporary interpretation, explore the artwork of He Qi. Saul is confronted by a pillar of fire, on which is perched a descending dove.

Study Saul's face in each of these depictions, and encourage congregants to find connections with their unique epiphanies. Artists offer us everything from steely calm to bewilderment to awe. In many studies, those around Saul appear terrified, while he remains calm and reverential. In this is another truth you may wish to explore: how do our individual, life-changing holy breakthroughs, our sacred insights, affect the corporate community? Invite congregants to share stories of metaphorical blindness that has opened the door to new life. Share a few stories up to the point of the "blinding," leave space for silent contemplation, then move into the joy of redemption.

As you pick up your pen, or turn on your computer to craft this sermon, picture your congregation capturing God's vision of mercy. God redeemed Saul, gave him a new name, and placed him on a new path. This same mercy is accessible to each of us, and to our corporate communities. The Easter miracle proves that God loves and forgives friends, betrayers, doubters, skeptics . . . even God's own enemies. The God who is Love has no need to be defended by violent means. Love grabs Saul's fist in midpunch and unbalances him, saving him from a life of hatred and violence. What if we could do this for one another? May Easter miracles abound!

CATHY CALDWELL HOOP

Psalm 30

¹I will extol you, O LORD, for you have drawn me up,
 and did not let my foes rejoice over me.
²O LORD my God, I cried to you for help,
 and you have healed me.
³O LORD, you brought up my soul from Sheol,
 restored me to life from among those gone down to the Pit.
⁴Sing praises to the LORD, O you his faithful ones,
 and give thanks to his holy name.
⁵For his anger is but for a moment;
 his favor is for a lifetime.
Weeping may linger for the night,
 but joy comes with the morning.
⁶As for me, I said in my prosperity,
 "I shall never be moved."
⁷By your favor, O LORD,
 you had established me as a strong mountain;
you hid your face;
 I was dismayed.
⁸To you, O LORD, I cried,
 and to the LORD I made supplication:
⁹"What profit is there in my death,
 if I go down to the Pit?
Will the dust praise you?
 Will it tell of your faithfulness?
¹⁰Hear, O LORD, and be gracious to me!
 O LORD, be my helper!"
¹¹You have turned my mourning into dancing;
 you have taken off my sackcloth
 and clothed me with joy,
¹²so that my soul may praise you and not be silent.
 O LORD my God, I will give thanks to you forever.

Connecting the Psalm with Scripture and Worship

While the superscription of Psalm 30 describes it as a psalm sung for the dedication of the temple, the text of the psalm is thanksgiving for personal deliverance, with a call for the worshiping body to join in with hymns of praise (vv. 4–5). In the Psalms, personal prayers are rarely private, reminding us to share our stories of deliverance with the community gathered to worship

and praise. We carry our own stories, but we do not have to carry them alone.

The Hebrew in Psalm 30 reveals some interesting translation possibilities and textual mysteries. The Hebrew verb *daloh* (v. 1) is translated in the NRSV as "drawn up." This is the word used to describe drawing water from a well. The visual imagery and language of wells and of the deep could enhance the worship service.

Verse 7 can be translated in several ways. The Hebrew words themselves are clear, but their sequence is unclear, making translating a challenge. The NRSV reads "By your favor, O LORD, you had established me as a strong mountain." Robert Alter translates it as "LORD, in your pleasure You made me stand mountain-strong."[1] What may seem at first to be some fun with Hebrew actually points to important theological decisions. Is the psalmist saying God has made him a mountain, figuratively at least? Or is the psalmist saying God has helped him stand with strength? If one is a mountain, one would not imagine any more falls in the near geologic future. If one is standing strong, as a mountain, however, one could fall down again.

How does this psalm read for those gathered in worship who have fallen, even if they may have once felt mountain strong? Occasionally the language of the Psalms can make people feel that if they had only been more faithful, God would have established them as a strong mountain, when in fact they feel like crumbled rocks and dust, wallowing in a pit. The NRSV translates *shalu* as "prosperity" instead of "ease" in verse 6, and, depending on one's cultural context, the word "prosperity" may mean financial wealth and flourishing more than security or ease. Attention to translation choices can help one navigate those minefields, and keeps this from being a prosperity-gospel psalm.

In Psalm 30, past deliverance leads to hope and faith in future deliverance. In saying, "O LORD my God, I will give thanks to you forever" (v. 12), the psalmist shows that praise is our permanent way of being, even in the midst of trouble. In claiming that "weeping may linger for the night, but joy comes with the morning" (v. 5), the psalmist is not telling people to get over their grief before their grief is done with them, but reminds them that grief will not be with them forever. God turned the psalmist's "mourning into dancing" (v. 11), and such deliverance is the focus of our prayers and hopes.

Psalm 30 is well paired with the story of Saul's conversion in Acts 9. As a faithful Jew, Saul was practiced in offering praise as the psalmist instructed. He was zealous. In his mind, he heard verse 7, "By your favor, O LORD, you had established me as a strong mountain," and likely thought, "Yep, that's me. A strong mountain for God"—that is, until he found himself brought down to the ground, and Jesus' voice asking, "Saul, Saul, why do you persecute me?" Thus begins Saul's descent into the proverbial pit, where, blinded for three days, he has to ponder the truth that he has been persecuting the God he loves so much. It is a pit nobody would choose to inhabit. Saul might have spoken the psalmist's words: "You hid your face; I was dismayed" (Ps. 30:7b). Saul's three days of blindness and the transformation by God's work through Ananias nicely illustrate the arc of Psalm 30. Deliverance from the pit, mourning turned to dancing, and praise to God for salvation are mirrored in both texts.

Acts 9 is often cited as the moment where God changes the name of Saul to Paul. Unlike Jacob becoming Israel (Gen. 32), Abram and Sarai becoming Abraham and Sarah (Gen. 17), and Simon being named Peter (John 1), Saul does not experience a name change in Acts 9. He is referred to as Saul, his Hebrew name, throughout that passage. It is only in Acts 13:9, as Saul's ministry to the Greek-speaking Gentiles begins, that the writer of Luke–Acts first uses the Greek name of Paul. While name changes in Scripture often signal identity shifts, Saul's multiple monikers locate him in the first-century Roman Empire, where he moved between cultures, religious traditions, and languages. Even as he embraces the new movement of Jesus' followers, the Hebrew traditions and culture of his past continue to inform his identity. In Saul's life, much like Psalm 30, the mourning and the dancing, the Hebrew and Greek identities, exist together, and he offers praise to God through it all.

The following paraphrase of Psalm 30 might be used as a call to worship:

---

1. Robert Alter, *The Book of Psalms: A Translation with Commentary* (New York: Norton, 2007), 103.

Reader 1: We praise you, O Lord, for you have drawn us up out of the depths.

Reader 2: We cried to you for help, O God, and you offered us healing.

Reader 1: We, the faithful, will sing praises to the Lord. We give thanks to God's holy name.

Reader 2: You have turned our mourning into dancing.
You have taken our sackcloth and clothed us, instead, with joy.

Reader 1: Our souls will praise you and will not be silent.

All: To you, O God, we will give our thanks forever.

MARCI AULD GLASS

Revelation 5:11–14

¹¹Then I looked, and I heard the voice of many angels surrounding the throne and the living creatures and the elders; they numbered myriads of myriads and thousands of thousands, ¹²singing with full voice,

> "Worthy is the Lamb that was slaughtered
> to receive power and wealth and wisdom and might
> and honor and glory and blessing!"

¹³Then I heard every creature in heaven and on earth and under the earth and in the sea, and all that is in them, singing,

> "To the one seated on the throne and to the Lamb
> be blessing and honor and glory and might
> forever and ever!"

¹⁴And the four living creatures said, "Amen!" And the elders fell down and worshiped.

Commentary 1: Connecting the Reading with Scripture

Marva Dawn, one of the church's treasures as an interpreter of Scripture and commentator on Christian life, has a book on worship entitled *A Royal Waste of Time.* Her title is already both a critique of our culture, which values only outcomes that can be measured (contrasting this with worship, which does not produce any material thing), and a reminder of God's sovereignty (giving glory to an invisible ruler who cannot be bought or otherwise controlled, but only obediently adored and glorified, makes worship already a countercultural activity).

The seer John punctuates the narrative sequences in the Revelation which bears his name with snapshots of the heavenly throne room where God is always worshiped and adored. This pattern begins in 4:6–11, where we see the four living creatures (borrowed from Ezek. 1 and applied as early as Irenaeus to the four evangelists) who sing day and night without ceasing, "Holy, holy, holy, the Lord God the Almighty, who was and is and is to come." The four living creatures have six wings. That description of them, and the content of their hymn, remind us of the six-winged seraphim from Isaiah 6 who are worshiping God in the temple at Jerusalem, an earthly copy of the one in heaven.

John follows the Jewish practice of honoring the holy name of the Tetragrammaton, the four-lettered YHWH that is not pronounced, by referring to God as the "One" (NRSV does not capitalize "one"). John tells us that whenever the four living creatures sing their hymn to "the One who is seated on the throne," the twenty-four elders match their devotion by falling down before the enthroned One, casting their crowns before God's throne and singing, "You are worthy, our Lord and God, to receive glory and honor and power, for you created all things, and by your will they were created and have their being" (4:11 NIV). Since the four living creatures are always praising God, we are invited to imagine, to whatever extent our human minds can fathom it, an endless cycle of alternating choruses praising the glory of God.

In chapter 5, just before our lesson for today, John reports seeing in his vision an imperial scroll, in the right hand of the One who is seated on the throne. The scroll is "written on the inside and on the back, sealed with seven seals" (5:1). The first recipients of John's Revelation would have immediately understood what that meant. Whenever one of the Roman emperors sent out a decree to the provinces, the content of the decree would have been written on the inside and the name of the governor or other person who was to implement it would have been written on the back. The confidentiality of such decrees would have been protected by the emperor's seal. The claim of John's vision is that God is the real emperor (never mind what Caesar thinks; what does he know?), whose royal decree is about to be published and carried out. The suspense is killing us: what's in it? "No one in heaven or on earth or under the earth" (note John's regular use of triadic formulations) is found worthy to open the scroll, which is to know God's will for the future.

Do not worry, says the angel, "the Lion of the tribe of Judah, the Root of David, has conquered, so that he can open the scroll and its seven seals" (v. 5). Just when we are looking for a lion king or perhaps the boxer Rocky having laid low all opponents, we are shown instead "a Lamb standing as if it had been slaughtered" (v. 6), John's paradoxical description of the crucified and risen Messiah Jesus. He goes and takes the scroll from the right hand of God, the One seated on the throne. At this point the singing becomes even more intense, as the four living creatures and the twenty-four elders sing in unison "a new song," reflecting the new creation brought about by the death and resurrection of Jesus Christ: "You are worthy to take the scroll and to open its seals, for you were slaughtered and by your blood you ransomed for God saints from every tribe and language and people and nation; you have made them to be a kingdom and priests serving our God" (vv. 9–10a).

At this point, where our lesson for today begins, John's vision (and his hearing) is expanded, so that he becomes aware of the many angels surrounding the heavenly throne where the four living creatures and the twenty-four elders are worshiping God (and now also the Lamb!). How many angels are in a myriad? If we go back to Daniel 7:10, which seems to have inspired this part of John's vision, we are told there that "a thousand thousands served him and ten thousand times ten thousand stood attending him." In other words, do not even bother trying to count how many angels are now singing with full voice, "Worthy is the Lamb that was slaughtered to receive power and wealth and wisdom and might and honor and glory and blessing!" (Rev. 5:12). Note another one of the hidden "sevens" in the book of Revelation: the seven traits the Lamb is worthy to receive. Then, as if that were not enough to dazzle us forever, John's vision is expanded once again to see and hear "every creature in heaven and on earth and under the earth and in the sea, and all that is in them" singing joyful praises "to the One seated on the throne and to the Lamb." As the entire universe joins in the victory song, the four living creatures say "Amen!"—which means "that's true!"—and the twenty-four elders continue to fall down before the throne in worship.

Based on these passages from Revelation 4 and 5, the Orthodox churches have reminded the rest of us that the worship of God that takes place in our churches is a tiny fraction of the endless praise and glory offered to God in heaven. Apart from the five books of the Psalter, many of which are songs of praise, the Revelation to John contains much of the biblical material by which God is "enthroned upon the praises of Israel" (Ps. 22:3). Hymn texts and descriptions of heavenly worship like these invite us—almost compel us—to add our own praises to those of the myriads of angels in the heavenly throne room. Whenever we pray, in the prayer Jesus taught us, that God's name will be "hallowed" (kept holy) on earth as it is in heaven, we are reminding ourselves of the great privilege we have of participating in the everlasting heavenly worship of God.

We cannot expect the culture around us to understand why we would engage in such "a royal waste of time," but Christians throughout the centuries have written and sung hymns to the glory of God the Creator, Jesus Christ the Savior, and the Holy Spirit, the Sanctifier. Not many of us have the gifts of great poets, composers, artists, musical performers, arrangers, and others who help us to glorify God. Not many of us have the fervor of Charles Wesley, who wrote more than a thousand hymns and wished for "a thousand tongues" in order to praise God more adequately. Nevertheless each of us can add our note and voice to the most joyful song in the world.

A. KATHERINE GRIEB

Commentary 2: Connecting the Reading with the World

It is important in this passage of Revelation not to miss the blatant contradiction of images in heaven. As if there could be nothing weirder, a strange thing occurs; the most powerful beast, the only one capable of opening the scrolls, is a Lamb, with seven horns and seven eyes, looking as if it has been slaughtered (Rev. 5:6). This passage suggests that the most powerful beast is a Lamb, and that should strike the reader as strange. The angels surrounding the throne and the living creatures (*zōa*) and elders sing like a celestial choir: "Worthy is the Lamb that was slaughtered to receive power and wealth and wisdom and might and honor and glory and blessing!" (v. 12). No one in heaven and earth has power comparable to this Lamb. Ferocious-looking monsters, sing to a Lamb.

John's vision here includes a disconcerting image of the Lamb saving us. What power does a lamb have to save anyone? It cannot even save itself. In many sacrificial rituals, the lamb is the chief victim. How can the victim save the perpetrator? The contradiction of a Lamb with power concedes the need for a sacrificial victim. Here René Girard is important in his brilliant articulation in anthropology for how human beings learn the desire to create victims.[1] What is exciting about Jesus, however, is that he explodes this sacrificial nature of needing a victim.

The Lamb represents nothing less than the redemption of creation, accomplished by one who was altogether worthy. Although Jesus may be compared to the Lion of the tribe of Judah (v. 5), the prevailing metaphor for Jesus' saving power is a Lamb slain. Hence, when in his vision John turned, looking for the powerful Lion able to open the scroll, what he saw was not a Lion, according to the elder's announcement (v. 5), but a Lamb. The Lamb is now seen in the midst of the throne—an embarrassing sight. A Lamb dripping with blood now occupies the place of power, alone entitled to enter and approach the throne, for it alone is "worthy." Of course this discourse is reminiscent of the apocalyptic vision of Matthew in the judgment of the nations (Matt. 25:31–46). The Lamb is the one with power and salvation—not the goat, the wolf, or the lion. Redemption has already occurred, and that is why John assents to a Lamb "slaughtered." The power of the gospel is in how Jesus' sacrifice is the basis of our power (Col. 2:15; Heb. 2:14). This is the theme of the new song; and now the worthiness of the Lamb controls the interpretation of redemption in the book of Revelation. In Jesus there is no longer a need to create victims. This kind of atonement theology is congruent with René Girard's rich insight that humanity needs to relearn desire that no longer needs a victim. Girard provides renewed self -esteem to Christians to see how Jesus explodes the sacrificial, violent nature of human community. Jesus explodes the mechanism in human beings to need another victim. Girardians like James Allison conclude that Jesus offers "an ongoing set of words and acted-out stories which always serve as ways to detect how sacrificial mechanisms operate in any human group, how we must not accept them, and what the consequences are of refusing to accept them."[2]

Many read the book of Revelation as saying that God has bloodlust, wanting to kill his only Son. I think this Girardian voice articulates an important corrective for this. God wants not sacrifice, but redemption. Jesus even says, "Go and learn what this means, 'I desire mercy, not

---

1. For more context, see René Girard, *Violence and the Sacred*, trans. Patrick Gregory (Baltimore: Johns Hopkins University Press, 1977).

2. James Alison, *Faith beyond Resentment: Fragments Catholic and Gay* (New York: Crossroads, 2001), 158. Alison is a Roman Catholic theologian and priest noted for his application of René Girard's anthropological theory to Christian systematic theology and for his work on LGBT issues.

sacrifice'" (Matt. 9:13). Redemption is key to reading Revelation. Those who are entertained or enticed with bloodlust and horror stories are not reading this book correctly. John has the vision of the Lamb with power in order to throw us all off our Pavlovian association of power with blood.

So, how should the resulting power of the Lamb be used? With this question the nightmares and horror movies begin in Revelation. Because the Lamb is not understood by many as having power—which even John initially did not understand as he looked first to the Lion— the paradox of power erodes into a nightmare. Here we enter into John's nightmares and evil monsters who try to wield power they do not rightfully own. The Lamb is the truly powerful one. John's nightmares result because he tries to see the redemption of the Lamb in heaven but struggles to hold the same vision on earth. For example, how does John's vision for redemption work for Israel?

Few Scriptures have suffered more at the hands of Christians than those having to do with Jews, women, sexual orientation, and slaves. The example of the sealing of the 144,000 (Rev. 7:1–8) is no exception. Notwithstanding the fact that many Christians commit the heresy of supersessionism, popular interpretations of Revelation insist on God's wrath on earth smiting everyone except those with the particular socioeconomic and religious perspective doing the smiting. Any system of interpretation that has this for its foundation only makes apocalyptic discourse worse.

Those who misinterpret Revelation, from both the political left and the political right, often fail to feel the gravity of matters that John describes. Even though I am a self-confessed theologian of nonviolence, I understand how many grow impatient with dysfunctional interpretations of the book of Revelation. From the political right, often there is a skewed vision for who is included in heaven, with little regard for who goes to hell. On the left, there is often little belief in God's necessary acts of judgment and justice. We would be wise to pay attention to the parabolic nature of John's visions as we see the description of power given to a Lamb.

This is the same parabolic wisdom of Jesus when he gives us the parable of the Judgment of the Nations (Matt. 25:31–46). Like Jesus in Matthew, John in Revelation tells the same parable: "They will hunger no more, and thirst no more; the sun will not strike them, nor any scorching heat; for the Lamb at the center of the throne will be their shepherd, and he will guide them to springs of the water of life, and God will wipe away every tear from their eyes" (Rev. 7:16–17). How strange! The Lamb will be the shepherd.

In the wisdom of the parables, Christians must realize a humility that comes with a recognition: narratives of Scripture may point to how God first chose Israel, but the blessing of being chosen extends also to the Gentiles. If white slave masters understood this, they would have been more reticent in their white interpretations of God's power. In addition, the tensions in the Holy Land could loosen theologically if the Abrahamic faiths understood the parabolic nature of how God chooses people and leaders. This discussion is especially important as international violence has increased among Muslims, Christians, and Jews. In Holy Scripture, whether it be from the Torah, the Qur'an, or the Christian Bible, we must not literalize the salvation of any people based upon the slaughter of another.

MICHAEL BATTLE

John 21:1–19

¹After these things Jesus showed himself again to the disciples by the Sea of Tiberias; and he showed himself in this way. ²Gathered there together were Simon Peter, Thomas called the Twin, Nathanael of Cana in Galilee, the sons of Zebedee, and two others of his disciples. ³Simon Peter said to them, "I am going fishing." They said to him, "We will go with you." They went out and got into the boat, but that night they caught nothing.

⁴Just after daybreak, Jesus stood on the beach; but the disciples did not know that it was Jesus. ⁵Jesus said to them, "Children, you have no fish, have you?" They answered him, "No." ⁶He said to them, "Cast the net to the right side of the boat, and you will find some." So they cast it, and now they were not able to haul it in because there were so many fish. ⁷That disciple whom Jesus loved said to Peter, "It is the Lord!" When Simon Peter heard that it was the Lord, he put on some clothes, for he was naked, and jumped into the sea. ⁸But the other disciples came in the boat, dragging the net full of fish, for they were not far from the land, only about a hundred yards off.

⁹When they had gone ashore, they saw a charcoal fire there, with fish on it, and bread. ¹⁰Jesus said to them, "Bring some of the fish that you have just caught." ¹¹So Simon Peter went aboard and hauled the net ashore, full of large fish, a hundred fifty-three of them; and though there were so many, the net was not torn. ¹²Jesus said to them, "Come and have breakfast." Now none of the disciples dared to ask him, "Who are you?" because they knew it was the Lord. ¹³Jesus came and took the bread and gave it to them, and did the same with the fish. ¹⁴This was now the third time that Jesus appeared to the disciples after he was raised from the dead.

¹⁵When they had finished breakfast, Jesus said to Simon Peter, "Simon son of John, do you love me more than these?" He said to him, "Yes, Lord; you know that I love you." Jesus said to him, "Feed my lambs." ¹⁶A second time he said to him, "Simon son of John, do you love me?" He said to him, "Yes, Lord; you know that I love you." Jesus said to him, "Tend my sheep." ¹⁷He said to him the third time, "Simon son of John, do you love me?" Peter felt hurt because he said to him the third time, "Do you love me?" And he said to him, "Lord, you know everything; you know that I love you." Jesus said to him, "Feed my sheep. ¹⁸Very truly, I tell you, when you were younger, you used to fasten your own belt and to go wherever you wished. But when you grow old, you will stretch out your hands, and someone else will fasten a belt around you and take you where you do not wish to go." ¹⁹(He said this to indicate the kind of death by which he would glorify God.) After this he said to him, "Follow me."

Commentary 1: Connecting the Reading with Scripture

Jesus' crucifixion at the hand of the Romans crushes the hopes and expectations of his followers that he might be the Messiah, God's anointed one for the salvation of his people. Jesus' resurrection by the power of God demonstrates God's reversal of the Roman sentence of death: the living God raises to life Jesus, the agent of life for the world. He does not allow his faithful one to "go down to the Pit" (Ps. 30:9). The resurrection appearances bear witness to the reality that Jesus is alive. They bear witness to the identity of God as the living God, and the God of the living. In John's Gospel they also have the particular function of bearing witness that Jesus is not only alive but still present with them. In other words, these appearances bear witness to the ongoing presence of Jesus, despite his obvious absence.

That is especially the case with Jesus' appearances to his disciples along the shores of the Sea of Galilee, recounted in John 21. The appearances on Easter, immediately after the crucifixion, and then a week later establish that Jesus is indeed alive. The appearance to the disciples by the lake shows that Jesus, the Good Shepherd, still feeds them and calls them to follow him and to carry on the work that he has given them to do. Those tasks vary: the disciple whom Jesus loved is presented here primarily as a witness to Jesus; Peter is commissioned as a pastor, a shepherd of the sheep. Each has a distinctive role, but each is called to follow Jesus.

In this account, there are seven disciples, five of them named—Peter, Thomas, Nathanael, and the sons of Zebedee—and two unnamed others, who decide to go fishing. The other Gospels tell us that Jesus' disciples were fishermen; the Gospel of John does not. So while they may have been returning to their previous means of livelihood, no reason is given here for their decision to go fishing. In any case, they are unsuccessful in their attempt. At daybreak, someone appears on the shore and, upon learning they have caught nothing, tells them to cast the net to the other side of the boat. When they do as he commands, they catch more fish than they can haul into the boat.

Then the "disciple whom Jesus loved" recognizes that this is Jesus, and bears witness to the others that this is indeed the Lord. Here is a pattern we have seen before in the Gospel: someone bears witness to Jesus, and others hear and act. John the Baptist identifies Jesus as the Lamb of God, and some of his own disciples begin to follow Jesus. The Samaritan woman tells her townspeople about the remarkable man she has met, and they come to acknowledge Jesus as the Savior of the world. In the present account, upon hearing the words of his fellow disciple that "this is the Lord," Peter jumps into the lake and swims to shore. Peter depends upon the witness of others; when he hears that witness, he responds accordingly. He wants to be with Jesus.

Soon all the disciples make it to shore, dragging their catch of "a hundred fifty-three" large fish. Over the years commentators have puzzled whether this number should be read symbolically, and numerous suggestions have been proposed. Perhaps this story, like others in the Gospels, emphasizes the abundance of Jesus' provision: just as the Gospel calls attention to the size and volume of the water jars at the wedding feast of Cana (2:6) and notes the number of baskets of bread gathered after the feeding of the five thousand (6:13), here it calls the reader's attention to both the size and number of the fish. Jesus provides abundantly. In spite of the huge catch, the net does not tear: nothing is lost (cf. 6:12, 39; 17:12; 18:9).

In a particularly touching scene on the shore of the lake, Jesus serves a breakfast of bread and fish to his disciples. The scene is reminiscent of the feeding of the five thousand, where Jesus had fed many with five loaves and two fish. Jesus feeds them again. Then Jesus engages Peter in what is likely a painful conversation, asking him three questions, recalling the three questions that Peter is asked during Jesus' interrogation by the high priest (18:15–18, 25–27). Three times Peter is asked, "Are not you one of Jesus' disciples?" Three times he denies that he is. Now Jesus asks Peter three times, "Peter, do you love me?" When Peter affirms that he does, Jesus gives Peter three commands. The question about love precedes the command. Jesus has demonstrated his commitment to his flock by laying down his life for them, out of his love for them. Peter will demonstrate his commitment to Jesus and to his flock by his love for Jesus and by his tending to the flock. As Jesus told his disciples earlier, love for him will be demonstrated by keeping his commandments (14:15, 21–24). The mere keeping of commandments, without love, is a dry obedience that does not embody the relationship of the good shepherd to his sheep.

To keep Jesus' commands to take care of his sheep is to love Jesus. This text resonates with the lectionary reading from Acts. There we see Paul on the road to Damascus as he persecutes the church. As he journeys, the risen Jesus appears to him and asks, "Saul, why do you persecute *me?*" Jesus is one with his disciples; so, to persecute them is to persecute him. Because of the unity of Jesus and his church, to feed the sheep of Jesus is to show one's love for Jesus.

Peter is now himself entrusted with the role of shepherding the flock. He does not thereby take Jesus' place, but he does carry out work that depends upon and imitates the work that Jesus himself does: he too shepherds the people, tending and feeding them. Peter is an exemplar for all who pastor the flock of Jesus: it is still Jesus' flock, but Jesus' commissioned shepherds take care of them.

The last words that Jesus speaks to Peter—and to any of the disciples—in this Gospel are the invitation "Follow me!" (21:19, 22). These are also among the first words spoken to any of the disciples (1:43). Even though there are obvious differences in the relationship of Jesus to his own after Easter, the character of discipleship

remains fundamentally unchanged: it still consists in following after Jesus, the Good Shepherd. Disciples who follow Jesus in the twenty-first century share something fundamental with those who followed him in the first century: they follow Jesus by loving him and keeping his commandments.

The lectionary text in Revelation portrays Jesus not as the Shepherd, but as the Lamb and, more particularly, as the Lamb who was slain and is therefore worthy to receive all honor and glory (Rev. 5:12–13). The Good Shepherd in John is portrayed as good precisely because he lays down his life for his sheep. Not only is he willing to give his life, but he does so. Jesus' death lies at the heart of John's witness to Jesus; it is not all that Jesus does, but it brings his self-giving work of love to its climax. All that he does is for the good of the world and the life of his sheep, whom he still loves, tends, and feeds.

MARIANNE MEYE THOMPSON

Commentary 2: Connecting the Reading with the World

This text, which appears as a P.S. on John's Gospel, occurs only once in the three-year lectionary cycle, on the Third Sunday of Easter in Year C. It is Jesus' last resurrection appearance in John. The scene shifts abruptly from Jerusalem to Galilee, from indoors (20:19–31) to outdoors. The chief function of this passage is to provide a setting for the official rehabilitation of Simon Peter, who has remained silently on the margins ever since his betrayal of Jesus. The lectionary omits the final coda (21:20–25), but those verses will be important to our interpretation of the first part of the chapter.

Up to this point in John's resurrection narratives, Peter has been present but silent. We do not know exactly what he is thinking or feeling, but he has not come off as the most perceptive or steadfast of Jesus' followers. Mary Magdalene shows more devotion to Jesus (20:1–18). Thomas shows more theological insight (20:28). The beloved disciple shows more alacrity in his faith: he is the first to believe that Jesus has been raised (20:8) and

will be the first to recognize him standing on the shore (21:7).

Indeed, the very way he is repeatedly referred to in John's Gospel—"the disciple whom Jesus loved"—creates an unfavorable comparison with Peter. By contrast, Simon Peter appears impulsive, quick to act, and slow to follow through. In the previous chapter he rushes off to the tomb, enters it, and then returns home without saying a word (20:3–10). In this passage, he abruptly announces that he is going fishing (21:3), and the other disciples volunteer to go with him. When the beloved disciple, not Peter, identifies the stranger on the beach as the risen Jesus, Peter immediately throws on some clothes and jumps into the sea (v. 7), abandoning the boat and his fellow disciples. After the others come ashore, Peter goes aboard the boat again and hauls in the net full of fish (v. 11).

When Jesus invites the disciples to gather around a charcoal fire to have breakfast (v. 12), Peter should know that he is in the hot seat. Before his fishing announcement in verse 3, the last time Peter spoke in John's Gospel was when he was warming himself by a fire in the courtyard of the high priest. There he proceeded to deny Jesus three times (18:15–27). Sure enough, right after breakfast, Peter's discipleship exam begins. When it comes to following Jesus, Peter has not exactly been the rock that his name might imply (Matt. 16:18). Perhaps this is why Jesus addresses him three times as "Simon, son of John" (John 21:15, 16, 17). Three times Jesus asks Peter if he loves him. Three times Peter answers affirmatively. Three times Jesus responds by telling Peter to feed his lambs and tend his sheep. The echo of Peter's threefold denial of Jesus is unmistakable.

By the third round of this, Peter is feeling hurt. "You know all things," he protests to Jesus. "You know that I love you" (v. 17). Yet Jesus has good reason to ask about the depth of Peter's devotion. Before the crucifixion, Peter had extravagantly declared that he would follow Jesus to the end and lay down his life for him (13:37). After all, Jesus had taught that to lay down one's life for one's friends was the greatest sign of love (15:13). Peter had failed miserably. Does he really love Jesus? The risen Jesus forces Peter to confront his past, but he does not leave him there. Instead, he gives Peter another way to make his love manifest: he invites Peter to put his faith into action.

The commission to feed Jesus' sheep certainly involves the care of souls. It also involves the care of bodies. There is no dualism here between spiritual and physical needs. Jesus' own ministry in this passage provides the model: he both teaches the disciples and feeds them breakfast. There are eucharistic echoes in verse 13, as Jesus takes the bread and gives it to his disciples. It suggests that, in being gathered and fed, Jesus' disciples will continue to encounter their risen Lord.

Contemporary readers can be glad for this odd little appendix to John's Gospel. It shows us that it is not enough to see and believe, like the beloved disciple. It is not enough to give verbal testimony, like Mary Magdalene. It is not enough to articulate one's trust in Jesus with deep

theological insight, like Thomas. Peter shows us a practical way of knowing and proclaiming Jesus: responding faithfully in concrete situations to the material and spiritual needs of the world God so loves (3:16). As Rowan Williams notes, Christian life is a material life, a way of conducting public, bodily life in community. "It has to do with gesture, place, sound, habit—not first and foremost with what is supposed to be going on inside."[1] Words are important, but they are not enough. We are creatures whose orientation to the world is mediated first of all through our bodies, and our religious lives are no exception. Everything we do spiritually as Christians has a bodily basis. Our bodies are the sites of our deepest religious knowing. In the work of feeding Jesus' sheep, Peter will discover the true depths of his love for Jesus. Peter's story encourages us to trust that Jesus continues to meet us at his Table, where he feeds us, just as he fed the disciples. He continues to meet us on the road, as we tend to his most vulnerable sheep.

The newly restored Peter is still a bit status-conscious, and cannot resist inquiring about the fate of the favored disciple, the one who did not betray Jesus (21:20–21). Jesus tells him to mind his own business (v. 22). Discipleship is not a competitive sport. Peter has his own work to attend to. So it is with us. Like Peter, we do not know how long our earthly lives will last (vv. 18–19), but we can be grateful for the time God has given us to carry out the particular work we have been called to.

John 21:1–19 is sandwiched between two brief reflections on the importance of written testimony for knowing Jesus (20:30–31; 21:24–25). This written testimony is irreplaceable in the life of the church. Scripture is where, by the power of the Spirit, we meet Jesus again and again. The texts of Scripture stabilize our access to the risen Jesus, assuring future generations that he can be present with them too. Yet, as Marianne Sawicki notes, these texts "are curious stabilizers. What they stabilize is instability: the impossibility of text to fence the space of risen life."[2] The writer of John's Gospel admits

---

1. Rowan Williams, *Faith in the Public Square* (London: Bloomsbury Publishing, 2012), 313.

2. Marianne Sawicki, *Seeing the Lord: Resurrection and Early Christian Practices* (Minneapolis: Fortress Press), 282.

as much: there are "many other things that Jesus did" (21:25) that are not recorded. There are other flocks of sheep (10:16), there are other settings where Jesus' followers continue to gather, be fed, and be sent out. The risen Christ always retains some of the strangeness of the original encounters with him (21:4, 12). Christ's presence is never wholly predictable, never under our control. Yet in Scripture, at the Table, and in the care of the suffering and vulnerable, we meet him still.

AMY PLANTINGA PAUW

Fourth Sunday of Easter

Acts 9:36–43
Psalm 23

Revelation 7:9–17
John 10:22–30

Acts 9:36–43

³⁶Now in Joppa there was a disciple whose name was Tabitha, which in Greek is Dorcas. She was devoted to good works and acts of charity. ³⁷At that time she became ill and died. When they had washed her, they laid her in a room upstairs. ³⁸Since Lydda was near Joppa, the disciples, who heard that Peter was there, sent two men to him with the request, "Please come to us without delay." ³⁹So Peter got up and went with them; and when he arrived, they took him to the room upstairs. All the widows stood beside him, weeping and showing tunics and other clothing that Dorcas had made while she was with them. ⁴⁰Peter put all of them outside, and then he knelt down and prayed. He turned to the body and said, "Tabitha, get up." Then she opened her eyes, and seeing Peter, she sat up. ⁴¹He gave her his hand and helped her up. Then calling the saints and widows, he showed her to be alive. ⁴²This became known throughout Joppa, and many believed in the Lord. ⁴³Meanwhile he stayed in Joppa for some time with a certain Simon, a tanner.

Commentary 1: Connecting the Reading with Scripture

Dorcas is dead. We are told little about Dorcas while she is living and little more when she dies. What Luke tells us is enough to establish her as a remarkable saint. In a patriarchal world and an emerging church led by a male cadre of followers, Luke introduces us to Dorcas/Tabitha/Gazelle. She is a remarkable saint for her acts of benevolence, which are significant, and she also bears the distinction of being the only person in the New Testament specifically designated as a female disciple.

A disciple, for Luke, is a person, male *or* female, who follows Jesus out of the waters of baptism into a life of healing, reconciliation, confrontation with those holding religious and political power, and love. The character of Dorcas's discipleship is one of provision and compassion, tending to the needs of the neediest around her. In the public square, she confronts the prevailing patriarchal understanding of discipleship by modeling discipleship not defined by gender.

Writing about the remarkable discipleship of Dorcas and others, William Willimon contends: "Here in this new community no one stays in his or her place. Common fishermen are preaching to the temple authorities, paralyzed old men are up and walking about and changing lives, and a woman called Gazelle heads a welfare program among the poor at Joppa. In her work Tabitha is busy making a new configuration of power in which God uses what is lowly and despised in the world to bring to naught the things that are (1 Cor. 1:26–31)."[1]

As this story opens, Dorcas is in fact not dead. Early on in the story, she falls ill suddenly, grows seriously ill quickly, and dies. We do not know the nature of her illness, but we do know that her discipleship does not immunize her to human vulnerability, nor will it do so for future disciples, no matter how meritorious their service. It is essential to Luke's theology to note that Dorcas is not critically ill. She is not in hospice care or someone experiencing a "near death"

---

1. William Willimon, *Acts*, Interpretation (Atlanta: John Knox Press, 1988), 84.

233

experience who sees a long hallway, at the end of which is a great bright light. Dorcas is certifiably dead. The rest of the story depends on it.

The death of Dorcas is not simply a personal or family loss; it has significant societal ramifications for the most vulnerable in her town. She has attended to the physical and financial needs of many (Acts 9:36). She has especially addressed the needs of widows, easily among the most vulnerable citizens of her society, as Luke reminds us by adding them specifically to the crowd that celebrates her return to life (v. 41). Dorcas has provided security to those whose status in life rendered them insecure. No doubt her death not only elicited their sorrow, but also heightened their sense of insecurity.

The action begins in this story when Dorcas dies. The disciples in town hear that Peter is in nearby Lydda, and they send for the apostle. They have an implicit confidence in Peter, and in such a time of death and disaster, the disciples in Joppa do not hesitate to summon him. They do not say why they are sending for him with such urgency. Luke does not tell the reader what difference it will make if Peter drops everything and rushes to the upper room in Joppa or if he lingers in a nearby town. Whatever the reason he is summoned, Peter does leave immediately, commands the respect of all present, and quickly moves on to his healing purpose.

Luke, who a large community of scholars believe to be the author of Acts, now brings us into the presence of a new age of God's eschatological purpose dawning. Listen for the phonetic resonance with dead Dorcas, known by Peter as Tabitha in Acts 9; it brings to mind Mark 5, in which Jesus commands the dead daughter of Jairus, "Talitha cum" (Mark 5:41, "little girl, rise up!"). Just as in Mark 5 Jesus sends all but his closest cadre of followers outside, so Peter sends outside everyone in the "death house" in Joppa, so he can get on with his life's work of restoring life. First Mark and now Luke, first Jesus and now Peter, enter dramatically into the eschatological realm of God's new age.

The more immediate context of this dramatic story is the conversion of Saul at the onset of the chapter and then the story of Peter healing Aeneas. Peter tells first a man, Aeneas, and next a woman, Dorcas, to "get up." The command is all the more powerful in the second scenario, for the woman is not a paralytic, nor bedridden. Dorcas is dead.

At first glance, Peter may seem the headliner in this story, the disciple who is summoned and then comes to the rescue of a saintly woman who has died. Look more closely. The true headliner of this story is neither Peter nor Dorcas. It is God, who uses Peter to restore Dorcas to life. Luke assumes that Dorcas has the resources to lead a life of charity. Such a life assumes a level of wealth and privilege not present in the common man or woman. Dorcas uses her privileges not to her own advantage but on behalf of those who had none: widows, the poor, the alien.

The rising of Dorcas brings with it not only the rising of hope of those most downcast in her community, but the rising of hope for anyone in any time who has been isolated, alienated, beaten down, cast out by life or society or family. The rising of Dorcas is a beacon of hope even today for those who are neglected or abused by the most powerful in society. New life in Christ means renewed hope for those deemed by society as hopeless.

At the end of this story, not only is Dorcas alive, but so is hope that the present structures of oppression and death are not nearly as impenetrable as they seem. When the story of the rising of Dorcas is told by the church, "the social system of paralysis and death is rendered null and void. The church comes out and speaks the evangelical and prophetic 'Rise!' and nothing is ever quite the same."[2]

There is no great mystery why Acts 9:36–43 is woven into the lectionary fabric of Easter in Year C. Psalm 23 and John 10 are passages that take the reader into the eschatological realm in which God is shepherd and the people of God are God's sheep, a fascinating prism through which to explore the relationship of God and God's people in the Easter season. In many ways, though, Revelation 7:9–17 and Acts 9:36–43 deal more directly with the inferred and eternal

---

2. Willimon, 86.

consequences of Easter and the promise of the resurrection.

This is a story located in the Easter cycle of the church, not simply because death is defied and God's will for life prevails, but because Dorcas rises and her Easter life leads disciples—female and male—to attend to the ones who are most often neglected or forgotten by society, but never forgotten by God.

Surrounded by a continuing, lingering patriarchal patina to society in the West and across the world, despairing at the obscene number of God's children living in abject poverty, grieving over the premature death of too many of the most vulnerable, this brief story in Luke is a herald call to action for the Easter community who must never tire in proclaiming, "Rise!"

GARY W. CHARLES

Commentary 2: Connecting the Reading with the World

The story of Tabitha continues the post-Easter theme of hope for new life that spreads throughout the world. Today's passages feature Jesus as the Good Shepherd (Ps. 23; John 10; Rev. 7) and the resurrection of the saints, imagined as a great multitude from every nation, people, and language, robed in white (Rev. 7:9). The description of Tabitha indicates she has heard the Good Shepherd's voice and followed him (John 10:11–18; Rev. 7:17; cf. Ps. 23:1), and through her acts of charity, she has been "feeding Jesus' sheep," just as Jesus has exhorted Peter to do (John 21:15–19). Her love and self-sacrifice link her to the saints who have washed their robes in the blood of the Lamb, whom the Shepherd guides by the waters of life (Rev. 7:14–17; cf. Ps. 23:2). Think of the poetic symmetry: Tabitha is a seamstress who clothes others, but whose own robes are washed white in the blood of the Lamb.

Tabitha is called a disciple using the feminine form of the word used of the twelve disciples, including Peter, who was "devoted to good works and acts of charity" (Acts 9:36). Her charity probably was demonstrated most often through her garment making, and the passage hints that she was generous with this clothing. We might hear an echo of Jesus' words in Matthew: "I was naked, and you gave me clothing" (Matt. 25:36). Most churches have one of these "pillars of the church" in their congregation, someone who selflessly involves herself in everything—someone the congregation cannot imagine doing without. Tabitha/Dorcas was remembered as one of these people, a true disciple of Jesus because of her acts of charity. In

artwork and stained-glass windows she often is depicted sewing or giving food to others. In the 1800s many Dorcas societies were established in her name to provide clothing and food for the poor.

Tabitha's story exemplifies resurrection hope not just for one person, but for a whole community. As Tabitha took care of others, she enacted the gift of the Spirit that empowered Christ's followers to boldly proclaim the gospel (Acts 2:1–42). Tabitha's life and death impacted the community so greatly that they asked the apostle Peter to come witness what she had done, and they showed him the garments she stitched, which suggests that Tabitha had given many of these garments to those in need. Tabitha's story exemplifies the scene described in Acts 2:43–47, where believers are awed by the "wonders and signs" being done by the apostles, so they share all things with those who are in need, and the Lord adds to their number. When Peter raises Tabitha from death, he is demonstrating the resurrection hope of a transformed community, described in Acts 2. Again, the Lord adds to their number. The miracle is not merely the restoration of one individual; it is a community event.

Peter was moved—perhaps by the community's grief and Tabitha's charity—to restore Tabitha to her people. To listeners who are grieving, this story can engender hope for a miracle, and if a miracle does not happen, their disappointment will be crushing. In the story, the people who summoned Peter did not actually ask Peter to restore Tabitha to life. On the basis of other biblical stories of people being raised from death, by Elijah (1 Kgs. 17:17–22), Elisha (2 Kgs. 4:32–35), and Jesus (Luke 7:11–15; 8:41–42, 49–55; John 11:1–44), we might conjecture that members of Tabitha's community hope Peter can restore her to life, but the story does not say they specifically ask for a miracle. Their purpose is to call attention to who she was and what she has done for them. Such love needs a witness.

Such a bold confirmation of community love has a tendency to spread outward to touch even more lives, until—like the Holy Spirit moving like wind and fire—it brings hope and sustenance to multitudes. As the popular song says, "They will know we are Christians by our love." What would the world look like if everyone were a Tabitha?

The passage does not tell us much about Tabitha, other than that she was a disciple and beloved seamstress who was devoted to acts of charity. People show Peter Tabitha's handmade garments, suggesting Tabitha's charity was personal; that is, Tabitha knew and cared about those who received the clothing, and that is why they grieve so for her loss. Some commentators think Tabitha was a well-to-do patroness who gave charity out of her wealth. Others imagine that Tabitha was one of the widows in the community, like the ones who gathered to grieve for her. Widows often were among the most poor and vulnerable (Exod. 22:22; Deut. 24:17–21; Job 24:21; Ps. 68:5; Isa. 1:17). If she was poor, Tabitha's charity was sacrificial. She was not merely cleaning out her closet and giving away clothes that were no longer fashionable or that made her look fat. She was sharing from what little she had, like the widow who gave two small coins out of her poverty (Mark 12:42). Perhaps the story does not tell us whether she was rich or poor because, in Luke–Acts, people from all economic strata are inspired to give self-sacrificially.

Tabitha was a maker of garments. This brings to mind modern-day garment workers and other low-wage laborers who provide goods that consumers enjoy and rather take for granted. As consumers shop for clothing—whether low-priced or high-end—they rarely consider the garment workers, the abysmal conditions under which they work, and what tiny portion of the retail price goes to them. A web search of the term "garment workers" reveals that tens of thousands of people today are working ten- to twelve-hour days in horrible conditions for subsistence-level pay. Are there people in our own faith communities with similar employment conditions? As we think about Tabitha, perhaps we could ask, who will come forward to recognize these workers' labor and lives? Who will uplift them to new life?

Tabitha was known by two names, indicating that she was a person of mingled cultures, like many people in our world today. The Aramaic Tabitha identifies her as a Jew, and the Greek name Dorcas indicates that she lived among Gentiles in Greek-speaking Joppa. Thus Tabitha is an example of the recurring theme in Luke–Acts about the spread of the gospel from its origins in Judaism to the inclusion of the Gentiles, from one culture and ethnicity to many others. Tabitha's charitable activities embody the Jewish ideal of "repairing the world" (*tikkun olam*), an ideal that is also foundational to Christianity. Tabitha reminds Christians today that being a follower of Jesus includes selflessly demonstrating one's love and faith through action across cultural divides.

Many Christians, influenced by the notion of *sola fide*, mistakenly believe that Jews do good works to earn God's mercy. In reality, it is in Judaism that the concept of grace originated: the story of Israel repeatedly shows that God redeems humans even though they have done nothing to deserve it. The story of Jesus' self-sacrifice and mercy reinforces this story of grace, but it also demands of Christians that we show our faith by actively caring for others. Tabitha, as a Jewish Christian, did good works not to earn God's love—which cannot be earned—but in grateful response to God's generous love and mercy already given. Tabitha's restoration to life was not a reward for her good deeds; rather, it testified to the community's post-Easter hope in the resurrection, a new heaven, and new earth, when death will be no more (Rev. 21:1–5).

MARIANNE BLICKENSTAFF

Psalm 23

[1]The LORD is my shepherd, I shall not want.
  [2]He makes me lie down in green pastures;
he leads me beside still waters;
  [3]he restores my soul.
He leads me in right paths
  for his name's sake.

[4]Even though I walk through the darkest valley,
  I fear no evil;
for you are with me;
  your rod and your staff—
  they comfort me.

[5]You prepare a table before me
  in the presence of my enemies;
you anoint my head with oil;
  my cup overflows.
[6]Surely goodness and mercy shall follow me
  all the days of my life,
and I shall dwell in the house of the LORD
  my whole life long.

Connecting the Psalm with Scripture and Worship

Psalm 23 is one of the best-known passages of Scripture. People with advanced dementia may not recognize their own children but can often recite this psalm. While it may be a very familiar and comfortable text to longtime churchgoers, it may also be completely new to other people in the pews. Some people did not learn the psalm in Sunday school and may know it better from popular-culture references such as Coolio's song "Gangsta's Paradise," Kanye West's "Jesus Walks," or Clint Eastwood's film *Pale Rider*. Treating language that is so familiar to some and completely new to others is a challenge for worship leaders today.

The beautiful and lyrical poetry of Psalm 23 lends itself well to both spoken and sung liturgy. "Shepherd Me, O God" by Marty Haugen[1] is a lovely arrangement of the psalm and is included in some hymnals. Reading the psalm as a responsive call to worship or singing it can bring comfort to the people who find it a familiar psalm while introducing its refrains to a new audience. Reading a translation less familiar than the KJV or NRSV may also help people hear familiar phrases in a new way.

There are a few translation decisions worth considering, such as the lyrical phrase "he restores my soul" in verse 3. The Hebrew *nefesh* means "life breath," and while it is usually translated as "soul," the phrase is stronger than "restores my soul" suggests. A nice, hot bubble bath restores my soul. Without *nefesh*, humans are not alive. Verse 3 is a description of divine CPR, where God brings us back to life.

The NRSV removed the familiar KJV refrain "though I walk through the valley of the shadow

---

1. https://www.giamusic.com/store/resource/shepherd-me-o-god-print-g5402.

He and None Other Is My Shepherd

This metaphor is one of the most beautiful and comforting and yet most common of all in Scripture, when it compares His Divine Majesty to a pious, faithful, or as Christ says, "good shepherd," and compares us poor, weak, miserable sinners to sheep. One can, however, understand this comforting and beautiful picture best when one goes to nature, from which the Prophets have taken this picture and similar ones, and carefully learns from it the traits and characteristics of a natural sheep and the office, the work, and the care of a pious shepherd. . . .

A sheep must live entirely by its shepherd's help, protection, and care. As soon as it loses him, it is surrounded by all kinds of dangers and must perish, for it is quite unable to help itself. The reason? It is a poor, weak, simple little beast that can neither feed nor rule itself, nor find the right way, nor protect itself against any kind of danger or misfortune. Moreover, it is by nature timid, shy, and likely to go astray. When it does go a bit astray and leaves its shepherd, it is unable to find its way back to him; indeed, it merely runs farther away from him. Though it may find other shepherds and sheep, that does not help it, for it does not know the voices of strange shepherds. Therefore it flees them and strays about until the wolf seizes it or it perishes some other way.

Still, however weak and small an animal a sheep may be, it nevertheless has this trait about it: it is very careful to stay near its shepherd, take comfort in his help and protection, and follow him however and wherever he may lead it. And if it can only so much as be near him, it worries about nothing, fears no one, and is secure and happy; for it lacks absolutely nothing. It also has this virtue—and this is to be marked well, because Christ praises it especially in His sheep—that it very carefully and surely hears and knows its shepherd's voice, is guided by it, does not let itself be turned away from it, but follows it without swerving. On the other hand, it pays no attention at all to the voices of strange shepherds. . . .

Let us therefore conclude freely: as little as a natural sheep can help itself in even the slightest degree but must simply depend on its shepherd for all benefits, just so little—and much less—can a man govern himself and find comfort, help, and counsel in himself in the things that pertain to his salvation. He must depend on God, his Shepherd, for all of that. And God is a thousand times more willing and ready to do everything that is to be done for His sheep than is any faithful human shepherd. . . .

From what has been said until now one can, I hope, easily understand these words, "The Lord is my Shepherd," and indeed the whole psalm. The words "The Lord is my Shepherd" are brief but also very impressive and apt. The world glories and trusts in honor, power, riches, and the favor of men. Our psalm, however, glories in none of these, for they are all uncertain and perishable. It says briefly, "The Lord is my Shepherd." Thus speaks a sure, certain faith, that turns its back on everything temporal and transitory, however noble and precious it may be, and turns its face and heart directly to the Lord, who alone is Lord and is and does everything. "He and none other, be he a king or an emperor, is my Shepherd," the psalmist says.

Martin Luther, "Psalm 23, Expounded One Evening after Grace at the Dinner Table," trans. W. A. Lambert, rev. Harold J. Grimm, in *Luther's Works*, ed. Jaroslav Pelikan (St. Louis, Concordia, 2007), 12:153–57.

of death" in verse 4 and replaced it with "though I walk through the darkest valley." The Hebrew word, *tsalmavet*, comes from two words that mean "shadow" and "death." The concise construction of the NRSV does match the compact Hebrew poetry, but to walk through a "darkest valley," one just needs a good flashlight. To walk through the "valley of death's shadow," one wants God alongside.

In verse 5, the common translation of *dashen* is "anoint," which is a different Hebrew word than the one used for anointing in a sacramental sense. *Dashen* means "to make fat," a sensuous word suggesting a life with enough prosperity and comfort to enjoy oil massaged into one's hair. It evokes the imagery of Psalm 133:1–2: "How very good and pleasant it is when kindred live together in unity! It is like the precious oil on the head, running down upon the beard, on the beard of Aaron, running down over the collar of his robes." Our cup overflows with pleasure, harmony, and abundance.

The generosity of a cup that overflows is a good connection to the Table, as is the image of the feast prepared in the presence of our enemies. Often invitations to the Table sanitize the communion feast, setting aside the truth that it commemorates a meal Jesus shared with Judas on the night he was betrayed. It would be a powerful invitation to proclaim we are invited to God's table, even as we are people whose relationships with others are fractured to the point of having/being enemies. God our shepherd prepares the feast at the Table, where our cup overflows, and where our enemies who betray us are invited to sit next to us.

While the passage from Acts (9:36–43) has no mention of sheep or shepherds, the story of Tabitha (Dorcas) illustrates a life lived in the model of Psalm 23. Tabitha was "devoted to good works and acts of charity" (Acts 9:36). She walked "right paths" in God's name, to use the psalm's language. Peter is brought to her bedside after she dies, where he calls her by name, as a shepherd might call his sheep. "He calls his own sheep by name and leads them out" (John 10:3b). God restores her soul and accompanies her through the valley of death's shadow, bringing her life-spark back. If only

her name meant "lamb" instead of "gazelle," as it does in both the Greek (Dorcas) and Aramaic (Tabitha), the connection to Psalm 23 would be perfect.

One can guess Tabitha was thankful to be named for a graceful wild deer and not for a sheep, an animal not known for its brilliance and good decisions. We, however, are not gazelles. We are the sheep of God's pasture. We, like sheep, have gone astray. The good news is that the Lord is our Shepherd, and we shall dwell in the house of the Lord our whole lives long.

Here is a call to worship that could also be adapted as an invitation to the table for the Lord's Supper.

Reader 1: The Lord is our shepherd; we shall not want.
Reader 2: God is our shepherd, and we are the sheep of God's pasture.
Reader 1: God restores our souls and then leads us down paths of justice and mercy.
Reader 2: Even when those paths take us through dark valleys, we fear no evil.
Reader 1: The Lord prepares a table for us, larger than we can imagine. The welcome is wider than we dare hope. Even in the presence of our enemies, God makes us one and restores us to each other.
Reader 2: The Lord is our shepherd, who provides for our need. Our cups overflow; goodness and mercy will follow us, all the days of our lives.
Reader 1: In goodness and mercy, let us gather in the house of the Lord to worship, where we may dwell our whole lives long.

MARCI AULD GLASS

Revelation 7:9–17

[9]After this I looked, and there was a great multitude that no one could count, from every nation, from all tribes and peoples and languages, standing before the throne and before the Lamb, robed in white, with palm branches in their hands. [10]They cried out in a loud voice, saying,

"Salvation belongs to our God who is seated on the throne, and to the Lamb!"

[11]And all the angels stood around the throne and around the elders and the four living creatures, and they fell on their faces before the throne and worshiped God, [12]singing,

"Amen! Blessing and glory and wisdom
and thanksgiving and honor
and power and might
be to our God forever and ever! Amen."

[13]Then one of the elders addressed me, saying, "Who are these, robed in white, and where have they come from?" [14]I said to him, "Sir, you are the one that knows." Then he said to me, "These are they who have come out of the great ordeal; they have washed their robes and made them white in the blood of the Lamb.

[15]For this reason they are before the throne of God,
    and worship him day and night within his temple,
    and the one who is seated on the throne will shelter them.
[16]They will hunger no more, and thirst no more;
    the sun will not strike them,
    nor any scorching heat;
[17]for the Lamb at the center of the throne will be their shepherd,
    and he will guide them to springs of the water of life,
and God will wipe away every tear from their eyes."

Commentary 1: Connecting the Reading with Scripture

Countless multitudes from every population sing forth praise to God and to the Lamb. The book of Revelation pauses from scenes of devastation, from the wrath of the Lamb (Rev. 6:16), for moments of worship. When history jumps off the tracks and chaos reigns, worship matters.

Revelation 7:9–17 raises tough questions for interpreters that deserve our attention, but in the end, our focus remains clear. Rooted in Israel, God's people include all nationalities and ethnicities. The culmination of all things features their ecumenical solidarity and joyful praise.

Attention to literary context is essential for grappling with this passage in two major respects. First, Revelation 7:9–17 is part of a larger scene, which encompasses 7:1–17. Second, this larger scene provides an interlude after the opening of the sixth seal, which brings cosmic portents so terrifying that even the kings of the earth seek hiding places, preferring death to the Lamb's wrath (6:12–17). Chapter 5 introduces the seven seals, the first major series of judgments executed against the earth and its inhabitants. Immediately after this interlude in 7:1–17, the seventh seal is opened, with silence in heaven for about half an hour (8:1). What follows is another series of judgments, the seven trumpets. The seventh trumpet opens the way for the seven bowls, completing Revelation's three great series of judgments. Revelation 7:1–17 marks a suspension of chaos, a moment of clarity that acknowledges God's people and their worship.

The lectionary's decision to limit our reading to 7:9–17 has one unfortunate consequence. The larger unit echoes Paul's declaration that the gospel accomplishes salvation "to the Jew first and also to the Greek" (Rom. 1:16). Paul took this insight seriously, and Revelation does as well. As the Apocalypse reaches a moment of complete chaos, Revelation 7:1 introduces a respite. Angels hold back the winds of judgment, and John hears the number of those who have been saved: 12,000 from each of Israel's tribes, 144,000 in all. We do not take seriously this number as a fixed census of Jews who will embrace the gospel. Instead, most commentators observe that Revelation deploys the number twelve to indicate a sense of fullness, and thousands lend magnitude to that concept.

The acknowledgment of Israel lays a foundation for the diversity reflected in 7:9–17. John hears of the 144,000 Israelites, and then he sees the countless multitude. Revelation rejoices in the diversity of God's people, "from every nation, from all tribes and peoples and languages" (7:9). We encounter this celebration of diversity on multiple occasions (5:9; 14:6). This is no vague melting-pot diversity. In their unity, the diverse peoples who follow the Lamb and sing hymns of praise retain their distinctive identities. The first identity, the one upon which all the others depend, is Israel. We return to Paul, who recognized the potential that Gentile Christians might spurn our obligation to Israel. In Romans, the root supports the branches, not the other way around (Rom. 11:16–19). Jews and Christians may disagree over Jesus and his significance. We Christians may not take that disagreement as evidence that Israel is somehow inferior. The 144,000 of Israel precede the countless multitude.

The language of diversity—"from every nation, from all tribes and peoples and languages"—applies both to the Lamb's followers and to those who oppose them (10:11; 11:9; 13:7; 17:15). As much as Revelation values diversity, it recognizes that diversity does not guarantee virtue. This needs to be acknowledged. Nevertheless, Revelation imagines an ecumenical people of God in which diversity is valued and named rather than erased. The end of the story involves healing for the nations (22:2).

Revelation does not lump together the 144,000 Israelites and the multitude of Gentiles. John hears of the 144,000 but does not mention seeing them or knowing where they reside. In contrast, John sees the Gentile multitude and describes where they stand, in front of God's throne. Only the 144,000 receive seals on their foreheads, indicating their identity as God's slaves. Unfortunately, this is the metaphor John chooses. Elsewhere in Revelation, however, Israelite and Gentile followers of Jesus share a common status. Physical marks distinguish those who follow the beast (13:16–17; 14:9; 20:4) from all those who follow the Lamb, Jew and Gentile alike (9:4; 14:1; 22:4).

One critical question involving this scene of worship has to do with time. Do the multitude worship in the here and now, or do they worship after the consummation of Christ's reign? This is a difficult question to answer, because the martyrs of 6:9–11 seem to reside under the throne right now, while the references to the great multitude make better sense at the end of history. The martyrs, like the multitude, receive white robes. On the other hand, the countless multitude is said to have escaped the great ordeal (7:14), and their worship occurs before the opening of the seventh seal. This great multitude apparently represents the ingathering of all the Lamb's followers. This suggests that their worship occurs at the consummation of history. Revelation does not always follow ordinary chronological reckoning. From its apocalyptic perspective the book describes the world as we know it, the heavenly realms, and the unfolding of God's future. Some judge this temporal confusion as a sign of clumsy composition. I would suggest that, for Revelation, God's future already impinges upon our present in disorienting ways.

Outbreaks of heavenly worship occur throughout Revelation. John hears singing when he enters the heavenly throne room (4:8–11) and when the Lamb takes the scroll (5:9–13). Singing breaks out not only as we wait for the seventh seal in 7:9–17, but also upon the blowing of the seventh trumpet (11:15–18), and just before the angels receive the seven bowls (15:3–4). Often these songs occur in the midst of horrific judgment, as in 7:9–17, affirming the justice of God's ways (15:3–4; 16:5–7; 19:1–8). It is not always pretty in Revelation.

We should be careful not to think of worship in a generic way. In Revelation worship demonstrates loyalty. Worship is dangerous. Not only do God and the Lamb receive worship, but so does the beast (13:4, 11–18; 14:9–11). Local elites sponsored worship of Rome and its emperors as signs of their allegiance. To reject Rome by offering worship only to the Lamb is to invite criticism, perhaps even suppression. For these reasons John says of the Lamb's followers: "they did not cling to life even in the face of death" (12:11b).

The shouting multitude wears white robes and carries palm branches. White garments indicate purity. Believers who endure faithfully receive white stones (2:17) and white garments (3:4–5, 18). Even the twenty-four heavenly elders wear white (4:4), as do the heavenly armies (19:14). Before we think of purity in terms of narrow piety, let us recall that for Revelation purity has a social, cultural, and even political edge. Revelation calls its audience to "come out" from the unholy city, Babylon, with its idolatry and commercial exploitation (18:4). Followers of the Lamb testify to Jesus and refuse to participate in the cults devoted to Rome and its emperors. This is what it means to wear white.

The white robes acquire added significance when we attend to the worship practices of ancient Rome. White garments and palm branches were frequent features of worshipers in various cults. For the various local festivals that marked civic life, local elites outfitted choirs in precisely such fashion. Revelation confronted an either/or choice concerning who was worthy of worship: the Lamb or the imperial gods. As for the latter, let us return to Paul: Had "the rulers of this age" understood God's wisdom, "they would not have crucified the Lord of glory" (1 Cor. 2:8).

GREG CAREY

Commentary 2: Connecting the Reading with the World

The sounds of music have had the power to inspire people throughout the centuries. Whether classical, country, rock, or contemporary rap, lyrics woven into melodies have the ability to touch the depths of human hearts, transporting us to places of hope when the words alone just do not seem to reach us. This movement of music continues to be central to worshiping communities in our liturgies, reminding those gathered of our corporate identity, reaffirming our call as a people of faith, and encouraging us to rise to the challenges before us. In many ways music allows us to connect the truth of our past with the reality of the present, as we reach in hope for our yet-unknown future.

John's vision in Revelation is framed within this liturgical movement as his vision shifts from the earthly reality of war and destruction to a place in heaven. By weaving together symbols and sounds of his cultural and religious context, he transports us beyond our reality. He engages a liturgical movement familiar to the people of God across salvation history (Ps. 41:13; 106:48; 1 Tim. 1:17; 2 Pet. 3:18) as he describes the sounds of a great multitude singing, "Blessing and glory and wisdom and thanksgiving and honor and power and might be to our God forever and ever! Amen" (Rev. 7:12).

Versions of these words have been repeated over centuries, affirming the belief and hopes of believers wrestling with what it means to be a faithful witness, resisting despair, encouraging the boldness of hope and faith in any given time and place. Consider the Doxology that continues to be sung in churches, bringing us together with Christians from around the world. This moment of heavenly ascent reminded those first-century Christians to whom John writes that the ultimate victory belongs to God. That victory, however, does not deny the war, famine, and injustice that would be experienced by humanity. It instead provides a vision of resurrection hope for the faithful. Claiming this hope is important for us as believers two thousand years later, especially in this Easter season, as we consider how John's melodic vision in Revelation 7:9–17 continues to encourage our witness today.

It is poignant to recall that John describes this vision of heavenly hope from an isolated island, one separating him from the great multitude to which he belongs (v. 9). He witnessed firsthand the life, death, and resurrection of Jesus. He experienced the power of their faith at Pentecost. He watched as both the beloved religious institutions of his formation and the occupying Roman government became uneasy with the growth and faithfulness of Jesus' followers. His incarceration is the result of the collision of his faith with the powers of his time. Yet he hopes. By describing the image of heaven, not only does he carry that hope within him; he is ensuring that his sisters and brothers in the churches in Asia do not surrender the hope of their faith as they confront the pressures around them.

By the time of this letter to the seven churches, "the imperial cult had risen to an impressive social, religious and political height."[1] Its presence in Asia was visible in the many Roman temples built for worship, giving way to an idolatry demanding allegiance to Rome and its emperor. Christianity had also spread throughout the region, calling followers to a countercultural allegiance to God. These two competing allegiances would clash, giving way to the persecution of those ancient Christians. John's letter encourages that ancient community in the midst of their Greco-Roman reality to resist, while reminding them that in spite of the power of the political forces, they will be part of God's final victory.

Although we in the United States do not encounter the kind of persecution the early Christians endured, there are many in the world today for whom this message is invaluable. According to the 2017 World Watch List released by Open Doors, there are some 215 million Christians in the world experiencing persecution for claiming

their faith.[2] It is easy to forget this truth in the United States, as we are not faced with ultimatums demanding our allegiance at the risk of losing our lives. There are, however, many contemporary temples and idols that challenge our faithfulness. Money, status, power, and influence are but a few. They compete for our identity and commitment of time, talent, and treasure. Two connections come to mind as we consider how John's articulation of his heavenly vision can be of encouragement to believers today.

First, John's vision, employing familiar liturgical images and sounds, is an effective way to teach and encourage disciples across human time. The visual triumph of this moment recalls Jesus' triumphant entry into Jerusalem, with palms waving, affirming the identity of the Messiah. The multitude's voices come together in adoration across nations and tribes. One can hear the history of a people, their current challenges, and their hope to create a new reality. Like music across centuries, these melodic images invite a call to action. From the African American spirituals of our early nation to the folk songs of the sixties, we have found our voices in the images and words of song. Today that tradition includes rap. Revelation, not unlike rap, brings together a "dangerous blend of memorable music and recalcitrant rhetoric."[3] Like rap, Revelation identifies societal injustices, calling for action to remedy that injustice, offering hope to many. This once "inner city only" expression has made its way to mainstream culture, debuting on Broadway in the 2016 Tony Award–winning *Hamilton– An American Musical.* The story of our nation's founding is retold through the weaving together of classical Broadway melodies and lyrics with the sounds of contemporary rap, making distant historical challenges intersect with our current realities. Inviting us to rise up, we experience this kind of connection when engaging the words of John in Revelation.

Second, the image of the great multitude reminds us that people of "all tribes and peoples and languages" (7:9, 14) will participate in

1. Brian Blount, *Can I Get a Witness? Reading Revelation through African American Culture* (Louisville, KY: Westminster John Knox Press, 2005), ix.
2. Scott Weber, "'Worst Year Yet': The Top 50 Countries Where It's Hardest to Be a Christian," *Christianity Today* (January 11, 2017). http://www.christianitytoday.com/news/2017/january/top-50-countries-christian-persecution-world-watch-list.html.
3. Blount, 102.

God's ultimate victory. The white-robed multitude of diversity is bound together by their faithful witness while on this earth. In a world of increased polarization and fearmongering of those unlike ourselves, we are tempted to stay within our own individual tribes—safely living within the assumptions of our cultural truths and traditions. Thus we often refuse to step out and get to know brothers and sisters of other cultures and languages, often creating unintentional provincial tribes, even in our places of worship. We forget the prophetic echoes of Isaiah 60:3 and Micah 4:2, reminding believers across time that God's vision has always been inclusive of *the other*. Experiencing the presence of a great multitude, standing together across what humanly divides, offers both encouragement and reassurance about the significance of our global witness together.

We see a heavenly image, composed of a throne, an infinite multitude in white robes, the presence of the Lamb. John's music-like movement engages the intersection of faith and culture in a way that calls upon faithful witnesses across the centuries to be "strong and courageous" (Josh. 1:9), for deliverance is once and for all time of God. We are invited to *rise up* because in the end, "God will wipe away every tear from their eyes" (Rev. 7:17).

RUTH FAITH SANTANA-GRACE

John 10:22–30

²²At that time the festival of the Dedication took place in Jerusalem. It was winter, ²³and Jesus was walking in the temple, in the portico of Solomon. ²⁴So the Jews gathered around him and said to him, "How long will you keep us in suspense? If you are the Messiah, tell us plainly." ²⁵Jesus answered, "I have told you, and you do not believe. The works that I do in my Father's name testify to me; ²⁶but you do not believe, because you do not belong to my sheep. ²⁷My sheep hear my voice. I know them, and they follow me. ²⁸I give them eternal life, and they will never perish. No one will snatch them out of my hand. ²⁹What my Father has given me is greater than all else, and no one can snatch it out of the Father's hand. ³⁰The Father and I are one."

Commentary 1: Connecting the Reading to Scripture

The opening of this text creates a visual image for the reader: the Festival of Dedication is taking place in the city of Jerusalem, and it is winter. The Festival of the Dedication dates back to 164 BCE, after the Maccabean revolt, when the Syrians had attacked the Israelites and besieged the city of Jerusalem (1 Macc. 4:52–59). During the time that the Syrians were in control of the city, they commanded the people to burn offerings for their (Syrian) gods in the temple. When Judas Maccabeus had defeated the army that had control of Jerusalem, he demolished the altar that the Seleucid king Antiochus IV had profaned, replacing it with a new altar and rededicating it to the Lord. In order to remove the abomination from the temple, the old altar had to be removed stone by stone and replaced with new stones that had not been hewn. The Israelites held eight nights of celebration for this dedication, which was henceforth called the Festival of Hanukkah, which means "dedication." The first verse also tells us it is winter, which is somewhat redundant, since the Festival of Dedication took place during the lunar month of Chislev, generally aligning with the month of December. Readers familiar with the Jewish festivals and customs would have a clear picture in their minds of what was going on in Jerusalem at that time: it was cold, and the city of Jerusalem showed signs of the celebration of Hanukkah.

The next verse continues to provide the reader with imagery: Jesus was in the temple, walking in the portico of Solomon. The porticos were courtyards surrounding the temple, with the columns opening toward the temple with walls against the outside. The portico of Solomon, named after the king who built the temple, was the oldest of the porticos, located on the eastern side of the temple. This particular space is later referenced in Acts 3:11 as the place where Peter and John stood following the healing of the man lame from birth. This is where Peter preaches to the Israelites, connecting their history to the story of Jesus as the fulfillment of the promises of God.

This text continues the theme found earlier in chapter 10, that Jesus is the Good Shepherd, a title people would recognize as connected to God who is called "shepherd" in Psalm 23, one of the other lectionary texts for this Sunday. Jesus makes this connection both by identifying himself as the Good Shepherd and by declaring, "The Father and I are one" (John 10:30). By claiming to be one with the Father, Jesus makes explicit the connection between himself as the Good Shepherd and God as the shepherd of Psalm 23. One of the other lectionary texts for this Sunday includes the passage in Revelation 7 in which the "Lamb at the center of the throne will be their shepherd" (Rev. 7:17). Together, these passages link the eschatological vision of Jesus with the image of the Good Shepherd who is also the Lamb who was slain.

The connection between the work of Jesus and the work of God the Father is stated repeatedly in these verses: Jesus gathers all whom God has given to him, and God protects those whom Jesus gathers. Jesus says God will prevent any from being snatched from his hand (John 10:28), which simultaneously means none will be snatched from God's hand (v. 29).

This context sets the stage for yet another confrontation between Jesus and "the Jews," the group of people in John's Gospel who are like Jesus but who are not followers of Jesus. The group referred to in John as "the Jews" does not actually refer to all Jewish persons, since the disciples were Jewish persons who believed in Jesus, and Jesus engaged in conversation with many other Jewish persons. The contrast in John is between those who believe in Jesus and those who do not. John labels generically as "the Jews" all those who do not believe in Jesus, even though this title is not technically accurate.

In interpreting this passage, it is important to consider ways that our depiction of Jesus in John's Gospel can unintentionally convey anti-Jewish sentiments. This interchange represents another example of how the Gospel of John is both "the most Jewish and the most anti-Jewish of the Gospels."[1] John's Gospel contains many references to Jewish culture and customs. The Festival of Dedication is the most recent of a list of festivals mentioned (Sabbath, Passover, and Tabernacles or Booths), describing a specific location within the Jewish temple, which are all things a Jewish audience would readily understand. Yet the Gospel is also anti-Jewish in its repeated insistence that "the Jews" have not heard the voice of Jesus, have not believed in him, because they "do not belong to [Jesus'] sheep" (v. 26).

In order to avoid conveying anti-Jewish messages in interpreting this text, it is helpful to understand the larger context. The story of the Maccabean revolt, told in the books of Maccabees, involved a series of leaders tricking the Jewish people into worshiping false idols and coercing them to burn sacrifices in the temple to idols, blaspheming the name of their God. During the Festival of Dedication, this Maccabean revolt would have been on the minds of persons who were going to the temple. There in the surrounding courtyard of the temple, standing in the portico of Solomon, Jesus proclaims that "the Father and I are one" (v. 30). In the following verse, "the Jews" take up stones to stone Jesus. Thinking about this scene from the perspective of "the Jews" during Jesus' time, this reaction of anger seems righteously motivated. "The Jews" in John's Gospel may be thinking: "Here is someone who is claiming equal status with God, who is claiming to be a good shepherd, when our prophets have spoken of false shepherds (Ezek. 34:1–6; Jer. 23:1–2) who led us astray. We do not want a repeat of Antiochus IV's treachery, profaning the altar of the temple. Just as we tore down the old altar stone by stone, replacing them with new stones, now we lift up stones to resist this one who is trying to lead us to blasphemy."

When we imagine in this way their reaction to Jesus, "the Jews" in this context are zealously protecting the temple that they have been called to preserve for the one true God. "The Jews" ask Jesus in the portico of Solomon during the Festival of Dedication whether he is the Messiah, and Jesus responds by continuing to identify himself with God. This is not the image of the Messiah they anticipate. They look for a military leader, perhaps closer to the figure of Judas Maccabeus, who fought to defend the people from foreign occupation. The Messiah they expect will bring military might and destroy their enemies. No wonder Jesus makes them suspicious. Instead of fighting off the Romans, Jesus is healing the blind man in John 9 and raising Lazarus in John 11. This kind of act does not point to a military revolution. The Jesus of John's Gospel challenges all expectations of redemption through a military revolution. Jesus instead invites hearers to trust in him as a Good Shepherd, even if we do not know where he is leading.

CAROLYN B. HELSEL

---

1. Adele Reinhartz, "The Gospel according to John," in *Jewish Annotated New Testament*, ed. Amy-Jill Levine and Marc Zvi Brettler (Oxford: Oxford University Press, 2011), 152.

Commentary 2: Connecting the Reading to the World

It is important to know when and where Jesus is when speaking in this lectionary text. The last half of Jesus' discourse on the Good Shepherd (John 10:11–21) is an example of why this is so. By the beginning of today's text, Jesus has been speaking since John 9:35, when he runs into the blind man he has recently healed. Jesus goes from speaking of seeing and not seeing, to speaking of hearing and not hearing—alerting his followers to their aptitude for spiritual deafness and blindness. Then, while he has their attention, Jesus speaks about himself: he is the door of the sheep, and those who enter by him are promised abundant life (10:7). He is the Good Shepherd (v. 14), and those who know his voice belong to his fold and are promised eternal life. Midway into this familiar discourse, John abruptly plants this Good Shepherd in a specific place and time: the Festival of Dedication, winter, and the temple in the portico of Solomon.

Suddenly, the context for Jesus' words is Jerusalem (the place), during Hanukkah, the eight-day Feast of Lights (the time). Jesus is in the temple during the winter. More specifically, Jesus is on the temple's eastern side, somewhere in Solomon's porch, and he is speaking while walking. John has purposely established a setting—a where and when—for Jesus' words. John's use of setting in this instance is particularly instructive for those of us who preach and teach Jesus' words throughout the liturgical seasons. Whether we use the Revised Common Lectionary as a guide or follow a thematic scheme of our own devising, we can be especially effective when we present Jesus' words about himself in contexts that amplify the meaning in the texts.

Notice in this week's text that John places Jesus in the temple during a specific liturgical season, the Festival of Dedication, recalling the reconsecration of the altar by Judas Maccabeus in 164 BCE. Moreover, Jesus is not just anywhere in the temple. He is in an area of Herod's temple thought to date back to the time of Solomon's temple, the great temple whose glorious dimensions were recorded in Scripture (see 1 Kgs. 6; 2 Chr. 3). The purification of the temple following its desecration was an act of community renewal. It was a recommitment by God's people to the reality of God's promised presence among them as symbolized in the physical structure of the dwelling place of the Lord. Imagine Jesus stopping by a column, anticipating the question to come. "If you are the Christ, tell us plainly" (John 10:24). What more apt place and time could there be for those first-century Jews to hear Jesus proclaim his identity than in this particular place of worship and during this specific time of worship? We should pose ourselves that very question: when and where in our worship as twenty-first-century Christians might we best hear Jesus "tell us plainly" who he is?

One response to that question is to be intentional in using all the elements of our worship—from printed words to chancel walls—as contextual amplifiers for Jesus' words. Jesus' pronouncement in the temple during the Dedication festival was amplified by the candles of the eight-branched menorah illuminating the altar, burning brightly in the dark of winter, as a light in the darkness, an assurance of renewal. When Jesus declares in verse 30, "The Father and I are one," he says as plainly as possible that God is present through him, just as God has always been present in the temple. The irony is striking (a characteristic of John's Gospel): God in the flesh walks and speaks in the temple, during a temple celebration, recalling a historical temple rededication event. However, those who regularly celebrate God's presence in the temple will not acknowledge it. "The Jews took up stones again to stone him" (v. 31). The temple does not necessarily make an effective hearing aid. Neither does the church for that matter. This is why it is crucial to be clear about the aim of our liturgy and the presentation of our sacred places.

Week after week, season after season, throughout the Christian year, we work to re-create worship space—pulpit, altar, rail, chancel wall, window—and recraft liturgical practice into the shape of the particular word to be proclaimed and sacrament to be observed. Ideally, we operate out of two primary assumptions: (1) the aim of liturgy—the work of the congregation gathered during the Advent season, on Christmas Eve, during the Lenten season, on Good Friday and Easter Sunday, and all the times in between—is to tell people plainly that Jesus is the Christ; and (2) the presentation of sacred places—spaces and structures consecrated as the symbolic locus of God's presence—is to provide a place where people can encounter Jesus plainly, as Bread, as Light, as Gate, as Shepherd, as Lord and Savior, and so on. Translating those assumptions about ecclesial tasks into amplifications of biblical texts calls for intentionality and a little imagination.

So when we teach or preach on this Gospel text on the Fourth Sunday of Eastertide, let us remember that:

- The liturgy should be bright with words—sung and spoken, perhaps even shouted—that Jesus is God incarnate. "The Father and I are one" should be treated as the radical revelation it is.
- The sacred space should be bright with candles (in clusters of eight?), light illuminating every dim space, all celebrating Jesus as the light that shines in the darkness as a living menorah.
- The voice of the Good Shepherd should be heard clearly and often in the words of worship. These words beckon and call. "Follow me" are words that promise and assure. "I know my sheep and they know me" are words that invite attentiveness and response.
- The image of the Christ as the Good Shepherd, one of the earliest and still most

familiar depictions of Christ, should be on display in the worship space, for example, an early Christian catacomb painting of Christ as Shepherd reproduced on the bulletin cover or as an art panel on a wall, or a wooden staff leaning against the entrance door of the sanctuary.

Whenever we teach or preach on a text that seeks to tell plainly who Jesus is—Good Shepherd, King of Kings, Suffering Servant, risen Lord—we should bring to the planning table, along with our Bible, a blank sheet on which to imagine how best to shape the liturgy and design the space. Before us is always the statement: "If [Jesus is] the Christ, tell us plainly" (v. 24).

Jesus says, "The works that I do in my Father's name testify to me" (v. 25). His actions say who he is. Jesus' works, the self-giving acts of God though Christ Jesus on display in the world, confirm and reiterate Jesus' words. When we fully imagine the liturgy and spaces that form our worship, we in turn form ourselves as worshipers. "Think first of the church gathered," says Don Saliers, "as the on-going prayer and word of Jesus Christ—and the on-going self-giving of God in and through Christ's body in the world made alive by the Spirit. . . . [this] on-going prayer of Jesus, and the on-going word and self-giving of Jesus, shapes our existence and brings *us* to expression."[2] Only then can we tell the world plainly that Jesus is the Christ.

MARK PRICE

2. Don E. Saliers, *Worship as Theology: Foretaste of Glory Divine* (Nashville: Abingdon Press, 1994), 28, italics in original.

Fifth Sunday of Easter

Acts 11:1–18
Psalm 148

Revelation 21:1–6
John 13:31–35

Acts 11:1–18

¹Now the apostles and the believers who were in Judea heard that the Gentiles had also accepted the word of God. ²So when Peter went up to Jerusalem, the circumcised believers criticized him, ³saying, "Why did you go to uncircumcised men and eat with them?" ⁴Then Peter began to explain it to them, step by step, saying, ⁵"I was in the city of Joppa praying, and in a trance I saw a vision. There was something like a large sheet coming down from heaven, being lowered by its four corners; and it came close to me. ⁶As I looked at it closely I saw four-footed animals, beasts of prey, reptiles, and birds of the air. ⁷I also heard a voice saying to me, 'Get up, Peter; kill and eat.' ⁸But I replied, 'By no means, Lord; for nothing profane or unclean has ever entered my mouth.' ⁹But a second time the voice answered from heaven, 'What God has made clean, you must not call profane.' ¹⁰This happened three times; then everything was pulled up again to heaven. ¹¹At that very moment three men, sent to me from Caesarea, arrived at the house where we were. ¹²The Spirit told me to go with them and not to make a distinction between them and us. These six brothers also accompanied me, and we entered the man's house. ¹³He told us how he had seen the angel standing in his house and saying, 'Send to Joppa and bring Simon, who is called Peter; ¹⁴he will give you a message by which you and your entire household will be saved.' ¹⁵And as I began to speak, the Holy Spirit fell upon them just as it had upon us at the beginning. ¹⁶And I remembered the word of the Lord, how he had said, 'John baptized with water, but you will be baptized with the Holy Spirit.' ¹⁷If then God gave them the same gift that he gave us when we believed in the Lord Jesus Christ, who was I that I could hinder God?" ¹⁸When they heard this, they were silenced. And they praised God, saying, "Then God has given even to the Gentiles the repentance that leads to life."

Commentary 1: Connecting the Reading with Scripture

Stories of life-changing visions appear with some frequency in the book of Acts. In our text, Peter is summoned to Jerusalem. He is greeted not with a parade to celebrate his faithful discipleship and his amazing acts of healing and hope, having evolved from the flawed and failed disciple who denied Jesus three times until the cock crowed (Luke 22:61). He is greeted with consternation and condemnation for defying the fundamentals of his Jewish tradition by eating with the uncircumcised Cornelius and his household based on a vision he received.

As soon as Peter arrives in town, he is attacked by "the circumcision party," a group of Jewish Christian believers who insisted that Jesus did not come to overrule or diminish Jewish law but to fulfill it. Those holding this view felt that in order for Jews to be true Christians, they must be baptized; but equally important, they must maintain ritual purity, follow the dietary laws, and, if male, be circumcised. This is not a fight between Jewish Christians and Gentile Christians. This is a family feud into which Peter introduces a new vision from God.

This family feud occurs in the heart of Judaism and emerging Christianity, in Jerusalem. It is in Jerusalem that the newly emerging church is sorting through its relationship with its roots in Judaism. Peter's recounting of the conversion of Cornelius and his household (Acts 10) is thus not only a cause for celebration, but also a source of confusion and consternation for those who understand Christian practice as simply a new subset of Jewish tradition.

Peter is charged by the religious leaders in Jerusalem with entering the house of uncircumcised men (Acts 10) and eating with them (11:2). These charges are nearly identical to those leveled at Jesus whenever he shared table fellowship with those considered to be ritually unclean (Luke 5:29–30). Confronted by these serious charges, Peter does not avoid or deny them. He cannot, for they are true. Nor does Peter engage in a philosophical debate to justify such radical, antitradition behavior. Instead, Peter turns to the power of a divine vision as he recounts his vision from God of a shared table: "What God has made clean, you must not call profane" (Acts 10:15). This experience is an indisputable rebuttal of the charges leveled against him. Peter will need to make a similar defense later in Acts (Acts 15).

It is critical to the understanding of this text that Peter's accusers in Jerusalem are not petty religious enthusiasts. After all, Peter shared their same concerns before he received the divine vision (10:14). Those within "the circumcision party" in Jerusalem are respecting years of religious tradition that they feel Peter has set aside. They express deep concern that Peter has lost perspective and ignored the divine imperative not to associate, much less to engage in table fellowship, with those who are unclean. It is one thing for faithful Jews who follow Jesus, like Peter and Paul, to baptize Gentiles; it is quite another for them to defy purity traditions by sitting at table with the uncircumcised.

In Jerusalem, Peter recounts the story of his divine vision that Luke records in Acts 10. In this telling, though, Peter adds a reminder to his critics that Cornelius, a Gentile, also received a vision from an angel from God. His critics are faced with the question of whether they can trust Peter and whether God would speak in a way that overturns a key element of their holiness ritual tradition.

The vision that Peter recounts only intensifies the family feud when he tells of the unclean Roman centurion, Cornelius, and his unclean cohort being visited by the Holy Spirit of God (11:15). Like Peter and all his Jewish Christian family in Jerusalem, the Gentile God-fearer Cornelius also receives the baptism of God's Spirit. This baptism does not differentiate its recipients into "clean" and "unclean," "Jew" and "Gentile," "male or female" (Gal. 3:27–28). Initially an affront to traditional purity traditions, the vision that Peter recounts to the leaders in Jerusalem challenges the newly forming church to expand its vision of who belongs in the family of God, a vision that welcomes not only Gentiles but also women.

To the credit of his strongest critics, after Peter recounts his vision from God in Acts 10 and he tells of the conversion and baptism of Cornelius and his household, not only are his critics silenced, but finally they celebrate: "They praised God, saying, 'Then God has given even to the Gentiles the repentance that leads to life'" (11:18). Peter recounts a vision from God that not only converted his heart but also converted theirs.

Essential to Peter's conversion is the question that he asked the critics in Jerusalem: "Who am I to hinder God?" (11:17). That question assumes that God is at work in the world to bring about God's purposes. Though religious tradition plays an essential role, it does not restrict God from building upon and even moving beyond tradition. Another key assumption in the question is that God is still at work, and God's purpose often extends far beyond the horizon of longstanding tradition.

Beware of those who have had a vision from God. This warning should be issued before the reader begins the long march of the biblical story, because powerful divine visions frequently appear from Genesis to Revelation. Early on in the biblical narrative, this promise from God comes to the first patriarch in a vision: "Do not be afraid, Abram, I am your shield; your reward shall be very great" (Gen. 15:1). Years later, the young, soon-to-be-prophet Samuel is afraid to recount his vision from God in 1 Samuel 3, lest he bear the wrath of Eli. Isaiah opens his prophecy with an ominous vision about the state of the nation: "The vision of Isaiah son of Amoz, which he saw concerning Judah and Jerusalem in the days of Uzziah, Jothan, Ahaz, and Hezekiah, kings of Judah" (Isa. 1:1). An even more terrifying reality is noted by Jeremiah when his colleagues claim falsely to be recounting a vision from God (Jer. 14:14). The most dreaded reality for God's people is when there is no vision from God (Lam. 2:9).

The canon is replete with divine visions, and the spiritual health of God's people is a direct result of how they attend to these visions from God. A text from Revelation accompanies our text from Acts for the Fifth Sunday of Easter. It too is a text in which a vision from God plays a prominent role. It is powerful vision

of God's eschatological promise: "Then I saw a new heaven and a new earth; for the first heaven and the first earth had passed away, and the sea was no more. . . . And I heard a loud voice from the throne saying, 'See, the home of God is among mortals . . . he will wipe every tear from their eyes. Death will be no more'" (Rev. 21:1, 3a, 4a).

Coupled with the eschatological vision from Revelation 21:1–6 on this Fifth Sunday of Easter in Year C is John's vision of the glorification of Jesus and the gift of a new commandment (John 13:34). Surely the church should read each of these visions with caution. Taking these visions from God seriously could shake the church from trying to hinder the movement of God by its obsession with what has always been and open it up to celebrate what it can become by the power of the Holy Spirit.

GARY W. CHARLES

Commentary 2: Connecting the Reading with the World

For the Fifth Sunday of Easter, the lectionary pairs Peter's acceptance of the Gentiles with the jubilant Psalm 148, in which all of heaven and earth, including all creatures of land and sea and all peoples, praises the Lord. The reading from Revelation offers joyful, beautiful images of a new heaven and a new earth, with the new Jerusalem descending like a bride from the heavens (Rev. 21:1–6). The ideal that all nations will be included in God's promise was embedded in God's promise to Abraham that, through his descendants, all nations would be blessed (Gen. 12:3; 22:18). From the beginnings of the covenant people, the plan has been to include all the nations, and the prophets looked forward to the time when people from many nations (the Gentiles) would say, "Come, let us go up to the mountain of the LORD, to the house of Jacob's God. There he will teach us his ways" (Isa. 2:3 NLT; see also Ps. 86:9 and Mic. 4:1–2). The book of Acts demonstrates how the plan is coming to fruition as the doors to the "house of Jacob's God" were opening to all sorts of people hearing the gospel message.

To understand this story, we need to remember that Jesus was a Jew, and his first followers were Jews, all of them steeped in Jewish tradition. Many Jewish followers of Jesus believed that for the Gentiles to become members of the church, they had to be circumcised and keep dietary laws. Apostles like Paul, however, were opening the church to Gentiles without the strictures of the law. There are several accounts of Paul's conflicts with Peter and some of the other apostles who insisted that the Gentiles must be circumcised (Gal. 2:1–14). Why was this a big deal? Keeping these traditions was what had identified them as members of the people of God, and it was going to take some extraordinary persuasion to convince them that people who had always been outside of Israel could now be part of the people of God too, without keeping these covenant laws.

There is a revealing story in the Gospels about Jesus' encounter with a Gentile woman who begged Jesus to heal her daughter. Jesus refused because he said the children of Israel must be fed first. The woman replied that even the dogs eat the crumbs that fall from the table. For this faithful testimony, Jesus did as she requested and healed her daughter (Matt. 15:21–28; Mark 7:24–30). The testimony of a Gentile woman convinced him that there was faith in God outside of Israel. The book of Acts reveals how Jesus' Jewish followers eventually came to understand the width and depth of the gospel's embrace.

As Acts 11 opens, Peter is in Jerusalem, standing before the "apostles and the believers who were in Judea," that is, many of the most respected Jewish leaders of the nascent church. These Jewish Christian leaders criticize Peter for eating with Gentiles, because, by doing so, he was violating kosher law (see Gal. 2:11–14). Peter had crossed a boundary they were not yet ready to cross. Table fellowship is an important way that human beings demonstrate friendship, kinship, and religious community. That Peter was eating with "uncircumcised men" (Acts 11:3) meant that he was breaking one of the most ancient Jewish traditions. Peter explains to the Jewish council that these Gentiles do worship the one true God. Through his visions and encounter with Cornelius and other Gentile converts, Peter has come to understand that God has given the Holy Spirit to these Gentiles, and they can be baptized in the name of Jesus (10:48).

Because Peter was considered by many of Jesus' followers to be the most prominent of the disciples, the Jewish Christians gathered at Jerusalem listened to his testimony. We do not know if Peter was a powerful speaker, or if his words held the power of truth, but his testimony must have been convincing, because his audience was persuaded. By the power of Peter's testimony, these traditional Jews were able to see a tradition-shattering, new way of being faithful. They praised God, saying, "Then God has given even to the Gentiles the repentance that leads to life" (v. 18). The book of Acts reports this event as if the council's approval was unanimous; the author of Acts focuses on the joyful success of the gospel that includes the Gentiles in God's promise.

This story encourages us to remember the times we have experienced testimony so strong that it opened our eyes to new ways of seeing God's work in our midst. We can remember convincing testimony that the Holy Spirit really is at work in our lives, and that God's plan succeeds spectacularly. Congregations might want to name and honor the people whose testimony moved them to renewed faith or helped them through a difficult decision. In Roman Catholic tradition, the saints are reminders of ordinary people who had extraordinary faith and demonstrated extraordinary service and love. Who are our saints?

In reflecting on powerful testimony, we might consider what it is about the testimony that moves us: Is it the speaker's emotion or conviction? Is it the power in the words themselves? Is it the movement of the Holy Spirit? Is it a combination of these things? Reflection on powerful testimony can inspire us to speak faithfully. When we feel intimidated, the author of Luke–Acts continually reminds us that "nothing is impossible with God" (Luke 1:37). Rather than block the Holy Spirit's movement, we can ride the wave of the gospel's success and rejoice when we are given an opportunity to offer new life.

Peter did not come to his new insight about the inclusion of the Gentiles without some necessary convincing, a lot of prayer, and a willingness to change. In fact, the story of Peter's change of mind in regard to the Gentiles is so important that it is told *twice* in the book of Acts (once in chap. 10 and again in chap. 11). In the first story, Peter resists a vision that compels him to eat unclean foods, but when the story is told a second time, he has been transformed. He understands that God has proclaimed the Gentiles holy. Peter came to accept the new path on which the Spirit was calling the church. Can we be so transformed?

Peter had to rethink the importance of certain requirements for holiness that he had held dear all his life, traditions that his ancestors had practiced for centuries, practices that had distinguished Israel as the people of God. The Gentiles were receiving the Holy Spirit quite apart from the traditional ways. We see the same kind of struggle taking place today in the church. The very practices that have distinguished us, that have been so useful in identifying ourselves as a congregation, a denomination, a church, and a religion, can become an impediment. There is a fine balance between remaining true to our roots and at the same time being open to new growth. Peter found that balance and was able to persuade the early church to include the Gentiles.

Congregations might reflect on who the outsiders are today that want to become part of our fellowship but are blocked by traditions or expectations that exclude them. Like the early church, the church today must be open to hearing: "See! I am making all things new!" (Rev. 21:5).

MARIANNE BLICKENSTAFF

Psalm 148

[1]Praise the LORD!
Praise the LORD from the heavens;
    praise him in the heights!
[2]Praise him, all his angels;
    praise him, all his host!

[3]Praise him, sun and moon;
    praise him, all you shining stars!
[4]Praise him, you highest heavens,
    and you waters above the heavens!

[5]Let them praise the name of the LORD,
    for he commanded and they were created.
[6]He established them forever and ever;
    he fixed their bounds, which cannot be passed.

[7]Praise the LORD from the earth,
    you sea monsters and all deeps,
[8]fire and hail, snow and frost,
    stormy wind fulfilling his command!

[9]Mountains and all hills,
    fruit trees and all cedars!
[10]Wild animals and all cattle,
    creeping things and flying birds!

[11]Kings of the earth and all peoples,
    princes and all rulers of the earth!
[12]Young men and women alike,
    old and young together!

[13]Let them praise the name of the LORD,
    for his name alone is exalted;
    his glory is above earth and heaven.
[14]He has raised up a horn for his people,
    praise for all his faithful,
    for the people of Israel who are close to him.
Praise the LORD!

Connecting the Psalm with Scripture and Worship

The story of God's people, as seen in the arc of Scripture, is a story of the particular relationship God has with the people of Israel. It is, at the same time, a story of God's love and concern for the entire cosmos, which God spoke into being at the beginning of the world. There is often a tension between how God's people understood the particularity of God's relationship with

Israel, and how God's people understood God's relationship to the rest of the world.

One can understand how a small tribe of people, seemingly constantly under siege on all sides, might not consider that God may also love the people who were trying to defeat Israel and keep them from their promised land. Plenty of stories in the Hebrew Bible reflect how Israel saw a divine command to vanquish their foes in order to claim their land. Even more stories in Scripture, however, speak of the ever-expanding reach of God's steadfast love and mercy.

Psalm 148 and Acts 11 both live in this tension between the particularity of God's love for Israel and the powerful concern God shows for the entirety of the divine creation—from the minutiae of a blade of grass to the vastness of the heavens. The psalmist instructs the people and the rulers, the young and the old, to praise the Lord (Ps. 148:11–12). At the very end of the psalm, the psalmist mentions Israel in particular: "He has raised up a horn for his people, praise for all his faithful, for the people of Israel who are close to him. Praise the Lord!" (v. 14).

The particularity of God's support of Israel anchors the end of Psalm 148, even as the vastness of God's concern makes up the bulk of the psalm. The people are not called to praise God because God made the heavens. The heavens are called to praise God themselves (v. 4). The sun, moon, stars, and outer reaches of the universe too have their song to sing: "Let them praise the name of the Lord, for he commanded and they were created. He established them for ever and ever; he fixed their bounds, which cannot be passed" (vv. 5–6).

Setting aside the divine telescope, the psalmist also focuses on earthly praise. Sea monsters, wild animals, creeping things, domestic animals, and birds in the air all are called to praise the Lord (vv. 7, 10). Even the weather praises

God Is the Author of Our Love

But for love of neighbor to be entirely right, God must have his part in it; it is not possible to love our neighbor as we ought to do, except in God. He that does not love God can love nothing in him. We must therefore begin by loving God, and thus love our neighbor in him. God is the author, as of all other things, so of our love for him—and more—as he created nature, so he sustains it; for she could neither exist nor subsist without him. That we might thoroughly know this, and not attribute anything to ourselves, God, in the depths of his wisdom and love, made us subject to tribulation. Being feeble and needy, we are forced to turn to God, and being saved by him we give glory to his name. These are his words: "Call upon me in this day of trouble; I will deliver you, and you shall glorify me" (Ps. 50.15). In this way man, by nature carnal, with no love but for himself, is brought through self-love to love God, realizing that all his ability, he has from God, and without him he can do nothing.

Bernard of Clairvaux, *On the Love of God* (London: Burns & Oates, 1884), 10–11.

the Lord: "Fire and hail, snow and frost, stormy wind fulfilling his command!" (v. 8). It is an awesome thought to consider that we humans have a part in singing praise to God, as do the moon, the sea monster, and the stormy wind. At the same time, it is hard to be too full of oneself if creeping things and cedar trees are standing next to you in the heavenly chorus. Humanity is adept at pretending we are kind of a big deal. Perhaps we even forget just who it was that spun the whirling planets and set the stars in their courses. The psalmist does not forget: "Let them praise the name of the Lord, for his name alone is exalted; his glory is above earth and heaven" (v. 13). Only God's name is exalted. Only God's glory is above earth and heaven. Psalm 148 is a corrective to human hubris and self-importance. We matter. We are not all that matters.

Similarly, in Acts 11, Peter has a vision about the inclusion of the Gentiles in the life of the church. God tells Peter, "What God has made clean, you must not call profane" (Acts 11:9). Observant Jews would remember it was God who helped them determine the foods, animals, and practices they were to consider unclean. The moral of Acts 11 is not so much that the

Jews had been wrong in remembering their instructions about how and what to eat. Peter's vision from God is calling them to remember that their ability to follow the rules is subject to God's call to love our neighbor as ourselves. Our understanding of God's call requires a vulnerable listening. It is humbling to have God show us that our love of the law has become stronger than our law of love; this requires us to acknowledge our error. We matter. We are not all that matters. To love one another, to "not make a distinction between them and us" (v. 12), requires compromise. We are called to set aside some of the things that matter to us in order to welcome the other people God has brought into our midst.

Psalm 148 calls us to take our place alongside the creeping things we may call unclean, the fire that burns and destroys, and even the foreign kings and princes, leaving room for the idea that someday God, who alone is exalted, may see fit to welcome the stranger to our table and *the* Table. The ending of the Acts passage shows the believers gathered together in praise, in response to Peter's testimony and vision. The psalmist's drumbeat of praise continues through the ages, to be picked up by the early church and continued by all who still gather to worship.

The following paraphrase may be used as a call to worship:

All:	Praise the Lord! Praise the Lord from the heavens; praise God in the heights!
Reader 1:	Join the heavenly host in praising God!
Reader 2:	Praise the Lord, sun and moon; praise God, all you shining stars!
All:	Let the highest heavens, nebulas, and cosmos praise the Lord!
Reader 1:	For God spoke and they were created, established for ever and ever; their bounds are fixed beyond our reach.
Reader 2:	Praise the Lord, all peoples! Praise the Lord, all rulers of the earth!
All:	Let young and old together praise the name of the Lord.
Reader 1:	God's glory is above earth and heaven.
Reader 2:	Praise the Lord!

MARCI AULD GLASS

Revelation 21:1–6

¹Then I saw a new heaven and a new earth; for the first heaven and the first earth had passed away, and the sea was no more. ²And I saw the holy city, the new Jerusalem, coming down out of heaven from God, prepared as a bride adorned for her husband. ³And I heard a loud voice from the throne saying,

"See, the home of God is among mortals.
He will dwell with them;
they will be his peoples,
and God himself will be with them;
⁴he will wipe every tear from their eyes.
Death will be no more;
mourning and crying and pain will be no more,
for the first things have passed away."

⁵And the one who was seated on the throne said, "See, I am making all things new." Also he said, "Write this, for these words are trustworthy and true." ⁶Then he said to me, "It is done! I am the Alpha and the Omega, the beginning and the end. To the thirsty I will give water as a gift from the spring of the water of life."

Commentary 1: Connecting the Reading with Scripture

Lots of people imagine that Revelation promises a pie-in-the-sky salvation, one that abandons this world for an otherworldly hope. Revelation does not offer escape from this world to a heavenly paradise. Believers do not escape this world for heaven; instead, the new Jerusalem comes down to earth. Salvation comes to those who conquer in the struggle against evil (Rev. 21:7), and it involves a glorious renewal of this present creation.

Revelation promises believers that good things await. The lectionary selection of 21:1–6 does not include one of Revelation's favorite phrases: "Those who conquer" inherit the promises outlined in the book (v. 7). It is easy to understand why the lectionary would avoid conquest imagery and its militaristic connotations, but omitting that imagery skews our appreciation for Revelation's this-worldly outlook. Revelation uses the language of conquest on sixteen separate occasions, thirteen referring to the Lamb and his followers (see esp. 12:11), and three to their oppressors (e.g., 13:7). Revelation calls believers to conquer idolatry and

commercial exploitation, not with violent means but through daily faithfulness.

Rome literally worshiped Victory (Greek: *Nikē*, Latin: *Victoria*). The cult of Nike, reflected in temples, statues, coins, and other representations, was ubiquitous throughout the empire. For the Romans, Nike connoted more than simple victory on the athletic fields. The goddess favored Rome with conquest, the foundation of its imperial rule. Rome governed through intimidation, a capacity it enjoyed due to its military ferocity. In Revelation we encounter this reality when the earth's inhabitants cry, "Who is like the beast, and who can fight against it?" (13:4). No wonder, then, that this beast is "allowed to make war on the saints and to conquer them" (13:7). We modern readers may resist such militaristic language, but for Revelation, one conquers the beast by following Jesus faithfully. Jesus, we remember, is the "faithful witness" (1:5) who died at the hands of Roman authorities. As Jesus conquered through his own faithfulness, so will his followers. Those who conquer will inherit the Holy City.

Revelation 21:1–6 marks a transition from scenes of judgment and destruction to prepare the way for a detailed tour of the new Jerusalem. As the Holy City descends from heaven, heavenly voices announce the new Jerusalem as God's dwelling place. Notice the luxurious, layered language rendered as poetry:

> "See, the home of God is among mortals.
> He will dwell with them;
> they will be his peoples,
> and God himself will be with them;
> he will wipe every tear from their eyes.
> Death will be no more;
> mourning and crying and pain will be no
>   more,
> for the first things have passed away."
>   Revelation 21:3–4

In ancient Judaism Zion represented God's singular dwelling place. It is not that Jews believed God dwelled in *only* one place and could not be present elsewhere. However, if people wanted to gather in the presence of God, Jerusalem and its temple were the place to go. The city's destruction in 586 BCE and again in 70 CE posed crises for Jewish identity and practice for precisely this reason: through the temple God had graciously appointed a place and a process through which Israel could commune with the Divine. From a historical perspective Revelation is one of several literary apocalypses written in the wake of Jerusalem's destruction in 70 CE by the Romans. Revelation shows how apparently powerless believers can conquer Rome through their faithful witness. Now a new Jerusalem descends from heaven to earth.

This passage raises one question that resists resolution: Who gets to dwell in this splendid city? The lectionary selection does not address the question directly, but the following verses do. Only those who conquer receive this inheritance, while sinners suffer the "second death" in the burning lake (21:7–8)—hardly an inviting scenario. But some hints suggest a more inclusive promise. Illuminated by God's glory, the city provides bright paths in which the nations walk. The gates remain open, and the nations bring

their gifts into it. The tree of life bears fruit for the healing of the nations (21:22–22:2). Dare we imagine that the saints' victory accomplishes salvation for all peoples?

Revelation imagines the new Jerusalem "as a bride adorned for her husband" (21:2). Biblical and ancient Mediterranean literature frequently personified cities as women. The bridal imagery derives from Israel's prophets, especially from Isaiah (Isa. 61:10; 62:5) and Jeremiah (Jer. 2:2). Perhaps rooted in Jesus' imagery of the wedding banquet with himself as the bridegroom (Mark 2:19–20; John 3:29), early Christians developed the image of the church as Christ's bride (2 Cor. 11:2; Eph. 5:22–33). The image of the bride is a conventional metaphor. Her adornment, almost surely modest, as Roman brides were expected to be, is intended to represent the purity of her devotion to Christ.[1]

Unfortunately the image of the bride relies on and fosters troubling assumptions about gender in Revelation. Revelation apparently can conceive of women only in terms of their sexual status. Jezebel, a prophet in Thyatira whose teachings conflict with John's, is envisioned as an adulteress who is "thrown" onto a bed and whose children are struck dead (Rev. 2:20–23). The woman clothed with the sun is pregnant and gives birth (12:1–17). Babylon, one of Revelation's two great symbols for Rome, is an opulent prostitute who is burned and devoured by her clients (chaps. 17–18). If we had reservations concerning gendered imagery for the church, further investigation only intensifies our concern.

The bridal imagery certainly has problems. However, the work of Lynn R. Huber demonstrates that if we ignore it, we also lose some of the power this imagery conveys. For one thing, the bride's adornment suggests her preparation for and transition to a new identity. This new identity reveals itself in the faithfulness suggested throughout Revelation: an enduring testimony to Jesus that rejects idolatry and exploitation. The bride's modesty stands in contrast to Babylon's opulence, for Babylon has gained its luxury through trade in luxury items,

---

1. Lynn R. Huber, *Like a Bride Adorned: Reading Metaphor in John's Apocalypse*, Emory Studies in Early Christianity (New York: T. & T. Clark, 2007), 120–22.

even slavery (18:11–13). Moreover, weddings are beginnings, not endings. This wedding creates a new home, a renewed participation in God's creation.[2]

The new Jerusalem and its bridal imagery remind us that our faith is deeply committed to embodiment. Few things are more embodied than a wedding celebration, with its food, drink, dance, and revelry in human pleasure. Rather than clouds and harps—though white robes come included—the new Jerusalem gives us streets to walk, water to drink, and food to enjoy. This is no escape from reality.

The lectionary links Revelation 21:1–6 with Psalm 148 and John 13:31–35. With a sense of wonder Psalm 148 gives voice to the manifold created beings, animate and inanimate, who attest to God's greatness. Angels and heavenly beings, celestial bodies, sea creatures, and even the winds are summoned to praise Israel's God. God "has raised up a horn" for Israel, a very worldly blessing attested even in the realms of heaven. In John 13:31–35 Jesus announces his own glorification and transcendent destiny: "I am with you only a little longer." Jesus then turns his attention to the community of disciples who must make their way on this earth, giving them the new commandment to love one another. Joined to Revelation 21:1–6, these lectionary selections all attest that God's heavenly blessing is effective in the here and now.

GREG CAREY

Commentary 2: Connecting the Reading with the World

Written to first-century believers, John's vision in Revelation serves as an affirmation that Jesus will return, bringing with him the ultimate victory against all that brings persecution and pain upon the earth. Notwithstanding this defining assertion, Christians have not always agreed about when and how this return would take place. Books and movies have been written and produced interpreting end-time scenarios framed by popular religious or scientific theories.

Using digital art, Ron Miller portrays scientific theories of the earth's end time, inclusive of a black hole swallowing the earth, a planet buried under ashes, and a planet submerged under rising seas. Religious scenarios have also provided images. Consider the *Left Behind* series of the late 1990s. These popular-religious end-time "beam me up" scenarios have taken hold in segments of the Christian population who envision the redeemed being lifted up from the earth while the remaining inhabitants are left to perish eternally. Whatever we might think of these interpretations, Christian hope is intimately tied to the promises of Jesus spoken by Paul in 1 Corinthians 11:26: "For as often as you eat this bread and drink the cup,

you proclaim the Lord's death until he comes." Our witness is shaped by the mystery of Jesus' return, along with the belief in God's ultimate victory over evil.

In this climactic moment in Revelation, the God of creation is once again the God of surprises. God takes what has been—the old earth—and transforms it. God does not destroy it. John's vision of the end times threads together the biblical narrative affirming the heart of a God whose goal has always been to redeem a broken relationship. The vision of a new heaven and new earth (Rev. 21:1) descending from heaven reaffirms God's commitment to redeeming creation. It reflects a bringing together of both scientific and popular assumptions when the "evil elements will be removed and the goal will be unified."[3] It is in this transformed place that God will dwell with the creatures (v. 3), thereby inviting us to see ourselves as part of this vision.

The question of God's dwelling place has always been a concern to believers. Where is God in the midst of our journey, especially when it is framed by injustice and inexplicable acts of violence? The verb "dwell" (v. 3) means

---

2. Huber, 183.
3. Louis M. Savary, *Teilhard de Chardin, The Divine Milieu Explained* (Mahwah, NJ: Paulist Press, 2007), 238.

"tabernacle." It recalls God's residing with Israel during postexodus wilderness wandering. God chose to tabernacle with the Israelites in the wilderness. At the time of this letter in John's Revelation, the temple and the city of Jerusalem were but a memory. They had been destroyed, making encouragement critical to believers as they struggled to find hope in the midst of despair. God embodies that hope in this vision, as once again God chooses to tabernacle with humanity in this new Jerusalem, a center free from death, mourning, crying, and pain (v. 4).

Several connections are points of consideration for us today. First, this new heaven and earth are embodied in the form of a holy city. Cities have always been centers of gathered people. The seven cities named in Revelation were economic and cultural centers of the ancient world. Today cities continue to be economic and cultural centers, places of great possibilities and challenges. Many are plagued by violence and poverty, while simultaneously being centers of employment, transportation, art, culture, and diversity. Urban centers provide a synergy of life requiring an interconnectedness of many dimensions. It is this model of life that John sees: God at work in the complexity of human interaction. The words of the song "God of This City" come to mind: *"For greater things have yet to come and greater things are still to be done in this city."*[4] God chooses to redeem the city as the place of new life and resurrection hope. This is a compelling reminder and call to the church today, prompting the church to reinvest our resources in these populated and complex centers of human engagement.

For decades, churches have moved from urban centers to the suburbs, often abandoning the most economically impoverished populations. This abandonment of urban centers has left decaying buildings to the care of populations unable to afford the upkeep of these edifices, a people still faithfully determined to maintain a witness in those spaces. Most of these populations are made up of people of color or new immigrants, many limited in economic resources. This new Jerusalem calls us to be present in the urban centers. We are invited to reclaim our communal witness in these spaces. We are invited to consider the ways in which we might develop covenant relationships with churches inside and outside the urban centers in a mutual effort to help create and sustain cities reflective of the new Jerusalem, as places of justice, peace, and dignity for all residents.

A second point of connection for us today is the vision of a city without a sea. The disappearance of the sea allows John and all believers to reunite, ending his life of exile and isolation on Patmos. For John, the sea represents a separation from those he loves. The sea also represents the chaos separating us from God and one another. At creation God speaks, and the sea is pushed back, bringing about a divine order between land and sea (Gen. 1:9–10). In the Gospel stories, Jesus speaks and tames the sea and storm (Mark 4:35–41). In Revelation the sea is portrayed as the abyss from which the dragon arises to torment the earth (Rev. 4:6; 11:7; 13:1). Affirming the absence of the sea announces "a new creation without separations, without isolations, without exiles."[5] This sea-less city provides a unifying vision, one that compels us to consider the metaphorical seas that separate us from God and one another.

These seas are powerful and prevalent today. The deep seas of race, economics, culture, and language continue to torment us, tempting us to live in isolated islands or ghettos, spiritually and intellectually made up of like-minded people. John's vision rejects that model, instead calling us to heal the chasm. What are those seas that currently keep us isolated from our call to be in covenant life together? In what ways is the church called to close that chasm?

Finally, God's claim and ultimate promise are profound words of reassurance yesterday and today. "It is done!" offers a sense of fulfillment about what has been prophesied for years (Isa. 65:17; 2 Pet. 3:13). It becomes not so much about something being over, but about something that has been re-created. God has been at work since the beginning of time, the Alpha and the Omega, the protagonist on the

---

4. Richard Bleakley, Aaron Boyd, Peter Comfort, Ian Jordan, Peter Kernaghan, and Andrew McCann, "God of This City," recorded by Chris Tomlin on *Hell Love*, sixstepsrecords, 2008.

5. Justo L. González, *Three Months with Revelation* (Nashville: Abingdon Press, 2004), 165.

journey. God's hope and love for all humanity and creation have always been redemption, not destruction.

This climactic moment, this descent of the new heaven and earth, invites us to model the witness of God in this vision, a vision of covenant life in a place that continues to be about the business of the Gospel. We are invited to be a faithful people, a people that "tabernacle" among the complexities of human reality, such as urban centers, working to remove all that separates and isolates us from God and one another.

RUTH FAITH SANTANA-GRACE

John 13:31–35

³¹When he had gone out, Jesus said, "Now the Son of Man has been glorified, and God has been glorified in him. ³²If God has been glorified in him, God will also glorify him in himself and will glorify him at once. ³³Little children, I am with you only a little longer. You will look for me; and as I said to the Jews so now I say to you, 'Where I am going, you cannot come.' ³⁴I give you a new commandment, that you love one another. Just as I have loved you, you also should love one another. ³⁵By this everyone will know that you are my disciples, if you have love for one another."

Commentary 1: Connecting the Reading to Scripture

This passage begins with the words "when he had gone out," referring to the departure of Judas Iscariot. Immediately this text calls our attention to the connections between this text and the verses preceding it: the departure of one who went to betray Jesus to the authorities. The previous scene showed Jesus handing a piece of bread to Judas and instructing him to "do quickly what you are going to do" (John 13:27). Just after Judas leaves, Jesus says, "Now the Son of Man has been glorified" (v. 31). This connection leads us to wonder what Judas's betrayal of Jesus has to do with Jesus' glorification. The final four chapters in John include Jesus' arrest, crucifixion, and resurrection, and Jesus appears to be saying that he is glorified through these events. As Judas leaves to betray Jesus, the chain of events that leads to Jesus' death and glorification is set into motion.

Throughout John, Jesus performs a series of signs that testify to his role as the Son of God. Previously in John, the pattern has been that Jesus gives a sign, and the discussion of that sign's significance follows. Here the order is reversed. The discussion of the significance of the final sign—Jesus' death and resurrection—takes place before the actual events. This lectionary text introduces Jesus' four-chapter discussion on the importance of this final sign.

The four chapters that begin here at 13:31 are known as the Farewell Discourse, a speech in which Jesus speaks about his upcoming death and glorification, consoling his disciples and commanding them to love one another. Chapters 14–17 are described as a Farewell Discourse not simply because they are Jesus' final words to the disciples, but also because this speech matches the pattern of other farewell speeches of the time, a pattern that would have been familiar to the readers of John's Gospel.[1] In the Old Testament, Jacob gives a farewell speech to his children in Genesis 47:29–49:33. The book of Deuteronomy contains Moses' farewell speeches to the people of Israel. David gives farewell speeches in 1 Chronicles 28–29, and in Joshua 22–24 the book's namesake says good-bye to Israel. Additionally, writings during the intertestamental period contained farewell speeches, such as speeches for Noah (Jub. 10), Abraham (Jub. 20–22), and Rebekah and Isaac (Jub. 35–36).

Common characteristics of these farewell speeches include the person gathering those closest to him or her, such as followers or children, announcing his or her imminent departure, and calling upon these followers to obey God's commands, including the command to love one another (see Jub. 20:2 and 36:3–4). Other themes often present within this genre of farewell speeches include unity, peace, the promise of God's presence with the faithful, and picking

---

1. Raymond Brown, *The Gospel according to John XIII–XXI*, Anchor Bible Commentary 30 (New York: Doubleday, 1970), 598.

a successor.[2] Within our lectionary text, the themes that most closely demonstrate the genre of the farewell speech are the announcement of Jesus' imminent departure and his giving a commandment that his disciples love one another.

The first theme that Jesus addresses, however, that of glorification, does not mirror the farewell-speech genre, and Jesus' glorification remains something of a mystery. One of the ways in which it is mysterious is the confusing mix of tenses. Jesus says the Son of Man "has been glorified" (past tense), that "now" the Son of Man has been glorified (present tense), and that God "will" glorify him (future tense). These three tenses point to the mystery of what it means for Jesus to be glorified. Did it already happen because John is writing this account after the fact? Is Jesus announcing that it is currently happening because of the events that Judas precipitated by his departure? Is he alluding to something that is yet to come? The future tense seems to make the most sense. In a few chapters, Jesus will be arrested, crucified, raised from the dead, and revealed to the disciples. The future tense also points the readers to imagine the future return of Christ and the future indwelling of God in Jesus' followers through the Holy Spirit. Yet in these various ways the glorification of Jesus continues to point to the cross, the final mystery that his disciples continue to misunderstand.

The new commandment to love one another is part of the genre of farewell speeches, reminding the children or followers that they must keep the commands of God. There is confusion about what is "new" about this commandment, since the command was already given in Leviticus 19:18 and in extracanonical writings. It has been suggested that this refers to the newness of the covenant that Jesus is making with his disciples, similar to the words spoken at the Lord's Supper ("the new covenant, poured out for you," Luke 22:20 and 1 Cor. 11:25). The author of Hebrews calls Jesus the "mediator of a new covenant" (Heb. 12:24). Connecting the idea of this new commandment with the new covenant, we can see echoes of this newness in the lectionary text from Revelation.

The kind of love that Jesus has demonstrated and is calling his disciples to imitate ("love one another as I have loved you") is also new in the kind of love Jesus has shown to them. The preceding passage in John 13 includes the table meal with his disciples and the washing of their feet, in which Jesus shows them that he loves them. This radical act of hospitality, the washing of his disciples' feet, demonstrates Jesus' profound love for his followers, even for those who would betray him. Jesus waits until after the foot washing to send Judas away, including Judas in the act of love Jesus shows to his disciples.

In John, the love that Jesus commands his disciples to have for one another is specifically a love for other believers. It is a love directed toward those who have believed in Jesus as the Messiah and who follow him. This group of believers includes both Jews and Gentiles, as seen by the different groups of people represented in the narratives in John, such as the Samaritan woman at the well (4:1–42) and Nicodemus the Pharisee (3:1–21). This kind of love extending to believers of all groups is seen also in the lectionary text in Acts 11, in which Peter is criticized for eating with the uncircumcised. In response to these criticisms, Peter shares his testimony of the experience he had with Cornelius, recorded in Acts 10. God showed Peter that God calls people from all groups to believe in Christ.

Our lectionary text also connects with the other lectionary texts from Revelation 21 and Psalm 148 through the use of the word "new" and the context of Jesus' glorification. In Revelation 21, John of Patmos sees "a new heaven and a new earth," and hears the one seated on the throne saying, "See, I am making all things new" (Rev. 21:5). The new commandment that Jesus gives to his disciples is part of the newness of all of creation, ushered in by Christ's glorification. All things are made new by the presence of Christ: a new heaven, a new earth, a new way to love one another through his example. Because of this newness, we can join with the psalmist who calls out for the highest heavens, sun, moon, and stars to praise the one whose "glory is above earth and heaven" (Ps. 148:13).

CAROLYN B. HELSEL

---

2. Brown, 598–601.

Commentary 2: Connecting the Reading with the World

Jesus' love command in 13:34–35 is one of the more challenging Scripture texts for Christians to grasp fully. Part of the reason is self-evident: a commandment whose aim is the giving away of one's life is a hard sell. Like the disciples, we *hear* Jesus' words but do not or cannot always rightly *see* them. Earlier in John 13, Jesus performs what the disciples see as a shocking act of humility. Peter, for one, wants none of it. In spite of their apprehensions, Jesus takes basin and towel and washes the feet of each of his friends. He chooses to preface the shocking words he will tell them by first showing them what those words look like. Yet even with their feet washed, the disciples struggle—as we do—to comprehend what Jesus says.

Jesus' announcement in 13:31–33 of his glorification and departure is similarly difficult to comprehend, certainly for the disciples, since they can hardly imagine Jesus' coming death and resurrection. Why must Jesus leave? Where is he going? Why can no one go with him? The answers lie in the incredible truth of the incarnation. God is in Christ and so is not bound by earthly limits. Indeed God cannot be so bound, in order to bring about the redemption of those limits, chiefly death. Jesus' words about his glorification and departure refer to the same thing: his self-revelation that he is God enfleshed for the redemption of the world. Once the disciples see Jesus on the cross, will they begin to understand what they heard him say around the table? John's Gospel leaves that unspoken question hanging in the air. It remains one of those recurring questions of Christian discipleship.

So how might we help Christians rightly see the hard meaning in Jesus' love command? How might we provide a way to see more clearly God revealed and glorified in the crucified and risen Christ? Teachers and preachers looking for fresh ways to illuminate biblical narratives should be on the lookout, not so much for cinematic retellings of the biblical texts, but for films whose themes and storylines reimagine or illuminate a key meaning in these texts. Consider the following two films.

1. *The Spitfire Grill* (1996) is the story of a small Maine town's struggle to welcome a stranger. The stranger is Percy Talbot, a young girl just released from a nearby prison. When she arrives in Gilead, the townspeople are not as ready to receive her as she is to receive them. The owner of the Spitfire Grill, Hannah, does not trust her right away, even though she hires Percy to help her cook and serve the very people who cannot accept her. For the most part, in spite of all she invests in the people of the town, Percy remains a stranger. In the end, it is the circumstance of her death that becomes a gift to the townspeople, transforming their understanding of Percy and of themselves.

A central aspect of the command Jesus gives his disciples is its focus "specifically on love *within* and *among* members of the faith community."[3] As most members of a faith community well know, that kind of love is not easy. Most of Paul's letters reveal that loving one another was a challenge, even for those earliest communities of believers. The small town depicted in *The Spitfire Grill* seems at first to be a friendly, close-knit group. The arrival of a stranger—a recently released prisoner named Percy—however, reveals the town to be something else: a community unraveling in the wake of long-held resentments, painful secrets, and mutual distrust. Love within and among the townspeople is in short supply. Percy turns out to be the one whose life, and eventual death, invites the community to a renewed love of neighbor and stranger alike.

The film connects with our Gospel reading in the following ways

- In the film, Percy's life is offered in serving others by waiting tables. Her death comes in the act of trying to rescue another, an outsider like herself. In the Gospel, Jesus' life of love is an offering to others, often at table. The foot washing is, in a way, Jesus waiting tables. Jesus' death is an act of rescuing others, all others, especially the outsiders. Jesus' command to love

---

3. Gail O'Day, "The Gospel of John," in *The New Interpreter's Bible* (Nashville: Abingdon Press, 1995), 9:733.

is an extension of his life of love, given away for the sake of others.

- In the film, Percy's death, though accidental, becomes a gift essential to the transformation of the community into a people who love one another. Key characters come to understand the significance of Percy's life only in the aftermath of her death. Though Percy does not preannounce her departure (death), her personal narrative and certain of her relationships foreshadow her coming death. In the Gospel, Jesus' death, though imposed upon him, becomes a gift essential to the transformation of his followers into a community defined by mutual love. Percy's physical departure (by death) from the community is the catalyst for its change of heart and the revelation of what Percy's life and presence meant. Similarly, Jesus' physical departure (in the death, resurrection, and ascension) is the necessary impetus for his disciples to form a new community based on an understanding of what Jesus said in his life and what he did in his death—the embodiment of the love command.

2. *The Mission* (1986) is the story of Father Gabriel, a Spanish Jesuit who goes into the South American jungles to build a mission in the hope of converting the Indians of the region to Christianity. Rodrigo Mendoza, a Spanish slave hunter, is converted and joins the Jesuits in their work in the mission. When Spain relinquishes the mission territories to Portugal, the Guaraní Indians and the Jesuit community are forced to defend themselves against the Portuguese aggressors. Father Gabriel, who believes that God is love, and violence is a direct crime against that love, argues that they should not resort to violence. They should trust God. Mendoza, however, decides on a different course of action. The final scene leaves the viewer wondering whose sacrifice carries the most meaning: that of Gabriel, that of Mendoza, or that of the Guaraní people.

The film connects with our Gospel reading in the following ways:

- In this film the Christian missionary impulse is portrayed as both gracious and tragic, calling into question the radical implications of Jesus' love command in the real world, in this case, European colonization in the mid-eighteenth century. If we interpret Jesus' death as "not the giving *up* of one's life, but the giving *away* of one's life . . . grace not sacrifice,"[4] then the deaths of Gabriel, Mendoza, and the Guaraní are troubling. It is not clear that the deaths of Gabriel or Mendoza are like that of Martin Luther King Jr., whose "death came not because he chose to give up his life, but because he chose to live the love of Jesus fully."[5] Does the converted Guaraní community's love of one another make their eventual slaughter a gracious death like Christ's or something else?
- The death of a priest opens the film, setting the story into motion and announcing the deaths to come of another priest and with him the entire community. Jesus' announcement of his departure signals his glorification by way of his coming death. Whether the sacrificial deaths of the Catholic Christians who serve the Guaraní or of the Guaraní Christians themselves point to or detract from the glory of the crucified and risen Christ is a central question raised by the film.

MARK PRICE

---

4. O'Day, 734. Italics in original.
5. O'Day, 734.

Sixth Sunday of Easter

Acts 16:9–15
Psalm 67
Revelation 21:10, 22–22:5

John 14:23–29
John 5:1–9

Acts 16:9–15

⁹During the night Paul had a vision: there stood a man of Macedonia pleading with him and saying, "Come over to Macedonia and help us." ¹⁰When he had seen the vision, we immediately tried to cross over to Macedonia, being convinced that God had called us to proclaim the good news to them.

¹¹We set sail from Troas and took a straight course to Samothrace, the following day to Neapolis, ¹²and from there to Philippi, which is a leading city of the district of Macedonia and a Roman colony. We remained in this city for some days. ¹³On the sabbath day we went outside the gate by the river, where we supposed there was a place of prayer; and we sat down and spoke to the women who had gathered there. ¹⁴A certain woman named Lydia, a worshiper of God, was listening to us; she was from the city of Thyatira and a dealer in purple cloth. The Lord opened her heart to listen eagerly to what was said by Paul. ¹⁵When she and her household were baptized, she urged us, saying, "If you have judged me to be faithful to the Lord, come and stay at my home." And she prevailed upon us.

Commentary 1: Connecting the Reading with Scripture

Acts 16:9–15 fits within a carefully crafted chapter in which Luke traces the story of the apostle Paul's divinely guided missionary journey. In the verses that precede our text, Paul has left the first church council in Jerusalem (chap. 15) and heads into Asia Minor (present-day Turkey). In his travels, Paul enlists Timothy as a fellow mission worker. He then discovers that his travel itinerary is not the one God has in mind. In the verses that follow our text, Paul and Silas hold a revival in prison. When released, they are welcomed again into the home of Lydia, the pivotal figure in our text. Therefore, the most effective way to preach and teach Acts 16:9–15 requires a lively conversation with the entire chapter.

As our text opens, once again a narrative in Acts is shaped by a transformative vision from God. In Acts 10, while on his way to visit the Gentile centurion Cornelius, Peter has a life-changing vision (10:10). Now, stymied in his travel plans by the Holy Spirit (16:6–7), Paul has a life-changing vision from God in which

an anonymous man calls out to the new apostle and urges him to come to Macedonia (v. 9).

This vision that Paul receives from God is followed by the first use of the "we narrative" in Acts (v. 10). There is broad scholarly speculation about the source of the "we passages" in Acts; possibilities include Luke's first-person narration of what happened; an eyewitness account from someone other than Luke; a classical literary technique for accounting sea passages. In this story, this change of voice (from reporting about Paul to reporting about "us") serves mainly as an additional confirmation that Paul's vision is from God and that Paul and his entire missionary team are convinced that they are to preach the gospel in Macedonia, thus expanding the plans for Paul's second missionary journey and actualizing the prophecy of the risen Jesus in Acts 1:8.

After the nocturnal vision of an unnamed man from Macedonia pleading for Paul to come there, Paul and his companions change their itinerary and set sail for their new destination

266

and soon arrive in the Roman colony of Philippi. The city received this name in 358 BCE from Philip II, father of Alexander the Great. This was not where they had planned to preach the gospel, but by attending to the voice of God, they found a new and fertile ground to share God's good news, just as they had done in the regions of Phrygia and Galatia (16:6). Once more in Acts, Luke reminds his readers that God takes the initiative in calling followers to go where God wills.

The first Sabbath audience for Paul's preaching in Philippi is women (v. 13), not in a public building but by the river. It is not altogether clear why Paul and a company of seekers and believers find a river outside the gate of the city to worship God. What is clear is that a group of those in Philippi who would worship God on Sabbath includes women, including a "God-fearing" woman who is most likely not Jewish. Paul will preach not only to men gathered in a town synagogue, but to women, and not only Jewish women, enacting what he preaches in Galatians 3:27–29.

By the river on the Sabbath, Luke introduces us to a prominent woman in the crowd who identifies as a "worshiper of God" or a "God-fearer" (v. 14; see Acts 18:7, where Luke introduces us to Titius Justus, who is also "a worshiper of God"). J. Bradley Chance argues that "a worshiper of God" or "God-fearer" is a "semi-technical term to denote Gentiles sympathetic with the Jewish faith, but who were not formal converts to Judaism."[1]

The "God-fearer" that Paul encounters in Philippi is Lydia, a prominent merchant from Thyatira (see Rev. 2:18–29). As a businesswoman, Lydia traded in purple cloth, an expensive commodity exchanged primarily by those with considerable wealth. As the story concludes, we learn also that Lydia is a woman of means who has sufficient resources to own a house large enough to accommodate Paul and all his companions, just as Cornelius from Caesarea, another "God-fearer" (Acts 10:2), had earlier provided such accommodation.

For Luke, who frequently emphasizes God's acute care for the poor (Luke 1:53; 6:24–25)

over the already self-satisfied affluent, Lydia serves as a theological reminder that God's grace crosses all economic boundaries. Along with Zacchaeus in Luke 19, the good news of Jesus is for those of "low estate" (Luke 1:48) *and* also for those who are wealthy. It is for anyone whose heart is open to the gospel message from God.

As Paul preaches to a Philippian audience that includes Lydia, Luke expands the audience of the gospel to those with varieties of economic means. The gospel Paul preaches reaches beyond Judaism and gender. This is a gospel not only for Jews and not only for men, but for male and female "God-fearers" who are ready to be washed in the waters of baptism and called to a new way of life. This inclusive gospel reaches beyond economic, religious, and gender boundaries to create a beloved new community of faith.

Lydia is converted to the way of Jesus, says Luke, not because Paul was such a magnificent orator and preacher, but because God opened her heart to God's transforming word (Acts 16:14). Just as the powerful Gentile man, Cornelius, and his household, are baptized in the name of Jesus in Acts 10, so now a powerful Gentile woman, Lydia, and her household are baptized (16:15). These two stories in Acts resist any reductive notion of baptism as simply a singular, individual, and private sacrament. Lydia "and her household" are baptized that Sabbath day. Throughout Acts, baptism transforms everyone, from "God-fearers" like Lydia to persecutors of the church like Paul (9:18), into gracious gospel-bearers.

Lydia quickly realizes that the mark of baptism carries consequences with it. One is not baptized into privilege or into some sort of protective shield against all the ills and travails of life. One is baptized into the often challenging and even confrontational ministry of the one who willingly walked into a hostile Jerusalem and who even pronounced forgiveness from the cross (Luke 23:34). As our text ends, Lydia does more than thank Paul for baptizing her and her household. She extends the gift of hospitality to Paul and also to all his companions. The text says that this hospitality required some

---

1. J. Bradley Chance, *Acts*, Smyth & Helwys Bible Commentary (Macon, GA: Smyth & Helwys Publishing Co.), 167.

Profound Need Met in Christ

Now compulsion is a part of every man's life. One way or another, life coerces all of us and no one of us can escape the word "must." But how vast the difference between those mere creatures of circumstance, pushed and pulled by outward chance and fortune, on one side, and, on the other side, the elect spirits of the race whose compulsion is from within! The great musicians, the Beethovens, Tschaikowskys, Brahmses, must write music. Why must they? No one makes them. But they know the need that only music can supply; they have had an experience of music bringing to them its saving satisfaction; they have a gratitude toward music that no words can express; and so they are under a compulsion strong as steel and ineluctable as destiny. They must give their lives to music. The elect spirits of the race know this compulsion from within.

So Paul said: "I must also see Rome." Why must he? No one made him undertake that risky adventure that ended with his beheading on the Appian Way. . . . Here is the secret of man's greatness and his liberty, to have compulsion not from without but from within. And in quieter lives among our friends or in our families, who of us has not known such characters, who could have said: "O Love that wilt not let me go"?

No need of the modern world is so deep as the need for this kind of character. We could muddle along without much more scientific invention. We could get by with no more sky-scrapers and gadgets. But we cannot get by without more Christian character if by that we mean what we have been talking about. Theologies change; creeds alter; the world views of one generation are incredible to the next; the mental patterns that Paul, Augustine, Calvin used we cannot exactly copy. But when we range up into this experience of profound need met in Christ by a great salvation, that issues in a deep gratitude so that we are inwardly taken possession of by a high compulsion, we not only overpass the differences between our contemporary sects but the differences between the centuries. Paul would understand *that*, and St. Augustine and Luther and Phillips Brooks. In that experience is the real communion of the saints. When one pleads for that one is pleading for the basic structural material without which no decent society can be built. When one pleads for that one is pleading for a quality of character without which man at his best cannot be satisfied. If you lack it, seek it. If you have a little of it, deepen it—a great need, a great salvation, a great gratitude, a great compulsion.

Harry Emerson Fosdick, *Living under Tension* (New York: Harper & Brothers, 1941), 190--91.

insistence on her part: "She prevailed upon us" (v. 15). She will prevail again upon Paul and his companions to accept her hospitality as this chapter ends (v. 40). In the newly baptized Lydia's house, Paul will not only enjoy more hospitality after leaving prison. He will find that her house has become a gathering place for those who would follow Jesus. Baptized households in Acts are not communities of privilege; rather, they have become communities of hospitality, ready through the practice of welcome to extend the good news of the gospel to all who visit and beyond. Lydia's hospitality must not be mistaken as the required response of any woman to male visitors. Her hospitality is insistent and expansive, marks of those who go down into the transforming, healing waters of baptism.

GARY W. CHARLES

Commentary 2: Connecting the Reading with the World

The Sixth Sunday of Easter anticipates the celebration of Pentecost, when the Holy Spirit empowered the apostles to go out into the world to proclaim the good news. Acts 16 continues the theme of Gentiles eagerly accepting the gospel and being baptized. The psalm for today extols God's "saving power among all nations" and exhorts "all the peoples" to praise God (Ps. 67:2b, 3b, 5b), which happens before our eyes in Acts. The reading from Revelation also envisions the nations walking by the light of Jesus (Rev. 21:23–24). In this post-Easter world, the Holy Spirit comforts and teaches Christ's followers (John 14:26) and inspires new converts to accept baptism.

The story of Lydia in Acts 16 illustrates Lukan themes such as the elevation of the lowly, true faith, prayer, and the gospel spreading far beyond the bounds of Judea. As the scene opens, Paul sees a vision of a man from Macedonia, a part of Greece in Gentile territory that included a Roman colony at Philippi. The man begs for their help, and Paul and his cohorts literally "cross over" by boat, into a new part of the world (Acts 16:11–12). The reader participates in the scene as the gospel brings salvation to "the nations" (as in Ps. 67), so that the Gentiles in faraway places can walk by Jesus' light (Rev. 21:24).

On the Sabbath, Paul and his company went outside the city gates of Philippi and down to the river to find a "place of prayer." Paul might have been seeking a synagogue, as was his habit (Acts 17:2), but he finds an unexpected—but no less worthy—place of prayer. The detail that they went "outside the gates" is important. City gates protected the people inside, so that Paul and his company are crossing another boundary into unknown and potentially dangerous territory.

By the river, Paul meets some women gathered there. The old hymns "Shall We Gather at the River?" and "As I Went Down to the River to Pray" remind us of the Israelites' joy as they ended their long journey in the wilderness and crossed the Jordan into the land. Though they do not yet know it, these women at the river are about to cross a boundary into God's kingdom.

One of the women, whose name was Lydia, was a worshiper of God, and God opened her heart to hear the gospel from Paul. She was particularly receptive to the good news and eagerly accepted baptism for herself and her household (16:13–15). The detail that God was the one who opened Lydia's heart is an important reminder that it is God who inspires faith through the workings of the Holy Spirit. Paul and his entourage preach the good news, but the opening of hearts is God's doing. We sometimes need to be reminded of this when we talk about "our" ministry. When we become discouraged, we can remember with gratitude and trust that it is the Holy Spirit's power, not ours, that opens hearts.

Like Tabitha and the widows of Acts 9:36–43, Lydia and the women at the river represent the important place of women in the early church. Lydia's leadership in "a place of prayer" and as head of her household models women's leadership role in the early church, a role that the apostle Paul acknowledges when he commends several women as his coworkers and fellow apostles (Rom. 16:1–16). Awareness of women's leadership from the earliest days of the church can help balance other passages in the NT that have been used to suppress women's voices and leadership.

That Lydia has a "household" (which would include family, servants, and other retainers) has suggested to some interpreters that she was a wealthy and respected woman. However, Acts presents her first and foremost as an outsider. She is a Gentile; she is head of house in a patriarchal society; she is outside the city gates in a liminal space where anything can happen. When Paul approaches Lydia and her people by the river, he is taking a risk. How will they respond? However, Paul does not hesitate. He does not stop to weigh the risks. He approaches Lydia and her people with an open heart, trusting that God will break down the boundaries. God does. Lydia and her people not only welcome Paul but eagerly listen to him. Paul's attitude of welcome and acceptance allows new converts to cross over into salvation.

The story encourages us to examine our own reluctance to approach unknown people in our community—and outside our community— with the gospel message. We often hesitate to approach people because we assume they will not be interested or will resent the intrusion; their response could be anything from indifference to hostility. Luke–Acts asks us to set such worry aside. If the good news is offered in the spirit of love (not coercion, judgment, or for self-serving reasons), the Holy Spirit will reach hearts open to the gospel message. If we deliberately go outside our comfort zone, where we are no longer in control of what happens, and if we allow the Holy Spirit to work, miracles can happen.

Like ancient cities with walls and gates to separate the known from the unknown, our society today is compartmentalized. We have made it very easy to isolate ourselves from those we consider to be "outsiders." Though we may *say* anyone is welcome, there are many ways in which we signal to others that they are unwelcome, or that they will be comfortable among us only if they conform to certain expectations. This passage in Acts encourages us to cross over into unfamiliar and possibly dangerous territory, to open our city gates, to seek new places of prayer, and to do this without hesitation, because success or failure is not our responsibility but God's. Luke–Acts suggests that we need not obsess over how transformation will take place; God is at work opening hearts. We are not the ones who do the work of conversion; we simply need to cross boundaries with open arms.

In Luke–Acts, the good news astonishes readers again and again as it overturns expectations, and it can still do so today. As homeless and refugee persons pray for a safe place to live, where city gates never close in their faces, Acts encourages us to fling wide the gates of our cities, churches, and hearts. Revelation imagines a beautiful, ideal future city with gates that are never shut (Rev. 21:25–26). Luke–Acts offers us a story of a woman who knelt to anoint Jesus' feet (Luke 7:36–50), and Acts tells this story of Lydia, who is eager to believe. Jesus singles out Zacchaeus, a tax collector who is an outsider in his community, and asks to dine with him (Luke 19:1–10), and Paul finds Lydia, who is outside the city gates, and offers her the gospel. Unlikely saints join Lydia in illustrating the Lukan theme that the most unexpected people are often the very ones whose hearts are opened to the good news and who then proclaim what wonders Jesus has done. Sometimes, all they need is someone to cross over the boundary and speak the good news. The church today can follow this example by prayerfully examining what boundaries we have put up. We can also ask God how we might "cross over" into unknown territory to find open hearts waiting for the good news.

MARIANNE BLICKENSTAFF

Psalm 67

¹May God be gracious to us and bless us
 and make his face to shine upon us,
²that your way may be known upon earth,
 your saving power among all nations.
³Let the peoples praise you, O God;
 let all the peoples praise you.

⁴Let the nations be glad and sing for joy,
 for you judge the peoples with equity
 and guide the nations upon earth.
⁵Let the peoples praise you, O God;
 let all the peoples praise you.

⁶The earth has yielded its increase;
 God, our God, has blessed us.
⁷May God continue to bless us;
 let all the ends of the earth revere him.

Connecting the Psalm with Scripture and Worship

In the Gospel according to Luke, the Holy Spirit of God comes to Mary, to Zechariah, to old Simeon, to John the Baptist, and to Jesus at his baptism; then "full of the Holy Spirit," Jesus begins his ministry, promising that the heavenly Father will give the Holy Spirit to those who ask (Luke 11:13). In the author's second volume, the book of Acts, this same Spirit fills and transforms the entire community of believers. Equipped with this divine power, those baptized with the Spirit now preach Christ's resurrection, first in Jerusalem to Jews, as well as to the foreigners visiting in the city, then around the Mediterranean, and finally in Rome, the secular capital of Luke's world. By appointing Acts as the first reading during the weeks of Easter, the lectionary means to say that all the Sundays of Easter celebrate the resurrection of Christ, that the book of Acts is filled with the evidence of Christ's resurrection, and that the Holy Spirit, present at the baptisms of Easter, has transformed and is still transforming the whole world.

The first reading on the Sixth Sunday of Easter exemplifies this recurring theme of Acts. The excerpt speaks of Paul—who was not an eyewitness to the ministry of Jesus but is already one step of the Holy Spirit beyond the original disciples (Acts 9:17)—being sent to Macedonia, a region in northern Greece. Thus this reading testifies that the circle of believers is widening. Then in Philippi the narrative moves beyond a list of men to include a prayer circle of women and the wealthy outsider Lydia, a "worshiper of God." The Holy Spirit has brought the good news of the resurrection from the women at the tomb to a half-convert to Judaism residing in Europe—and also to us.

For an assembly response to this reading, Psalm 67 is an excellent choice.

Psalm 67 relies on the idea of blessing, as happens throughout the Hebrew Scriptures. The ancient Israelite idea of blessing is something like a yo-yo. God blesses the people; that is, God shows divine favor and gives life to humankind. All that we need is sent to us from

God. In grateful response, the people bless God; that is, they assemble to praise the name of the Lord, and their blessing of God is heard by the whole world. We Christians who have inherited use of these ancient Hebrew poems now join in this blessing, by receiving what God gives and by praising God for continuous benevolence.

The psalm echoes the Aaronic blessing in Numbers 6:24–26 and invokes the biblical image of the face of God. In their poetic descriptions of God, the Psalms repeatedly speak of God's face, as if a benevolent God, in looking at us and really seeing us in our need, will send blessing. As Christians, we have seen that face most clearly in the body of the man Jesus. As we are gathered for worship, the body of Christ is around us, and we marvel to recognize in our fellow worshipers the face of a merciful God.

Psalm 67 is a communal thanksgiving for a bountiful harvest: "God, our God, has blessed us" (Ps. 67:6b). On the basis of this past blessing, the people ask God to continue to bless. In the Hebrew Bible, God continually creates. In the biblical worldview, the availability of food for humankind is not a natural condition, an expected result of the cycles of nature. Famine is often the given situation, and the story in Genesis 3 states that humans will have to work for their food. Throughout, the people must look to God as continually creating, so that humans can continue to eat. Historically, Christians did pray for successful harvest, and in the present, we have learned to offer such prayer more fervently each week, since we know that, even if not in our neighborhood, somewhere in the world people suffer from intense hunger and the horror of starvation.

That God continuously creates and provides is a wholesome reminder to contemporary Christians, who are sometimes caught up in quarrels about when in the past God created the world. For believers, God's creation was not a one-time event, but goes on each day. God is the life of the land, of the earth, of our solar system, of the immense unknown beyond, so that daily we rely on God's gracious care.

Benedict of Nursia, the sixth-century founder of Benedictine monasticism, stipulated that every single morning in a monk's life was to include the chanting of Psalm 67. Yet it is especially appropriate on the Sixth Sunday of Easter in Revised Common Lectionary year C that we join in singing this psalm. While the psalm means to praise God for a local harvest, the psalm claims that we are joined in praise by all nations, all the peoples, the nations upon earth, all the ends of the earth. According to this psalm, God's blessing on the chosen people calls out to the whole world, gathering all the nations into praise.

Back to this day's reading from Acts: after the ministry of Jesus comes Paul, preaching in Macedonia and speaking with an association of women. We respond to this Lukan reading of widening circles of grace by joining with ancient Israelites, with centuries of Christian monks and nuns, and now with the baptized from all the nations of the earth, to praise God for showing to us the face of Jesus Christ.

GAIL RAMSHAW

Revelation 21:10, 22–22:5

[10]And in the spirit he carried me away to a great, high mountain and showed me the holy city Jerusalem coming down out of heaven from God. . . .

[22]I saw no temple in the city, for its temple is the Lord God the Almighty and the Lamb. [23]And the city has no need of sun or moon to shine on it, for the glory of God is its light, and its lamp is the Lamb. [24]The nations will walk by its light, and the kings of the earth will bring their glory into it. [25]Its gates will never be shut by day—and there will be no night there. [26]People will bring into it the glory and the honor of the nations. [27]But nothing unclean will enter it, nor anyone who practices abomination or falsehood, but only those who are written in the Lamb's book of life.

[22:1]Then the angel showed me the river of the water of life, bright as crystal, flowing from the throne of God and of the Lamb [2]through the middle of the street of the city. On either side of the river is the tree of life with its twelve kinds of fruit, producing its fruit each month; and the leaves of the tree are for the healing of the nations. [3]Nothing accursed will be found there any more. But the throne of God and of the Lamb will be in it, and his servants will worship him; [4]they will see his face, and his name will be on their foreheads. [5]And there will be no more night; they need no light of lamp or sun, for the Lord God will be their light, and they will reign forever and ever.

Commentary 1: Connecting the Reading with Scripture

As Revelation draws to a conclusion, it allows its audience a tour of the new Jerusalem. Seven seals of judgment and conflict have ravaged the earth, followed by seven trumpets and seven bowls. Readers have trembled before the dragon, the beast (chap. 13), and the prostitute (chaps. 17–18). We have witnessed cosmic conflict between the forces of the Lamb and those of the beast. Throughout this story, we have been promised a blessed new reality. Only at the end does this reality unveil itself.

The term "unveil" calls our attention to two simultaneous realities. First, Revelation calls itself an apocalypse, an unveiling. Literary apocalypses, like Revelation and Daniel, purport to unveil reality. Where life appears chaotic, violent, and hopeless, the apocalypses reveal that things are not as they seem. They acknowledge the violence and disorder, but they also unveil a reality in which God reigns with justice. Many apocalypses, like Revelation and Daniel, also reveal a blessed future.

Second, our passage unveils the bride, the Lamb's holy companion (21:9). This imagery runs closer to the prophets' vision of Zion as the wife of YHWH (Isa. 61:10; 62:5) than to the church as the bride of Christ. Ancient brides veiled themselves, their unveiling occurring at the moment of intimacy. Modern readers recognize how this convention reflects the patriarchy that defined ancient societies. Caution with such imagery is warranted. At the same time, the unveiling of the new Jerusalem portends the intimate ways in which God is present in this new holy city.

Visions of pearly gates and a golden street may impress some readers more than others. Our reactions may reflect the degree to which we expect from Revelation literal descriptions of the new Jerusalem. Some readers find comfort and hope by envisioning a glorious future reality. Revelation surely acknowledges the violence and oppression endemic to this present age, and repeatedly promises to faithful believers eternal blessings beyond this world. The seven letters to the churches in chapters 2–3 all promise blessings "to the one who conquers." Throughout the book we encounter believers participating in heavenly worship. As conflict continues to rage on a cosmic scale, a heavenly voice announces that God's salvation, power, and reign have already arrived and the Lamb's followers have already conquered (12:10–11). Revelation insistently reminds its audience of a hope beyond this life.

The Gospel lesson for this week, John 14:23–29, likewise locates God's blessing for faithful discipleship within a transcendent blessing. Jesus is returning to his Father. He acknowledges his departure as a source of grief for his disciples, but he also promises the Holy Spirit to provide comfort and aid as they live out their vocation.

How do *we* relate to pearly gates and golden streets? Revelation's imagery is best understood as creative and dynamic rather than literal. If Revelation concludes with a detailed architectural model of the new Jerusalem, this picture reminds us that the book of Ezekiel devotes nine chapters (chaps. 40–48) to a tour of the idealized Holy City. The *Temple Scroll,* one of the Dead Sea Scrolls, has a similar description of the Holy City. These specific representations perform a common rhetorical technique: a vivid description meant to place a picture "before the eyes" of its audience. The technique is used to invite the audience to experience this new city through imagination, to walk around in it rather than to describe the literal details of this future city. In this way Revelation, like all apocalyptic literature, works on the boundaries between rhetoric and poetry, creating space for readers to imagine and desire a blessed renewal of creation.

Poetry may not require literal description, but its distinctive way of communicating is no less serious. For Revelation the stakes are enormous: faithfulness versus idolatry, abundance against exploitation, life opposed to death. We cannot simply translate Revelation's poetry into modern dogmatic categories, but we can meditate upon what this vision clearly affirms.

First, the new Jerusalem is resplendent, its luxury beyond literal imagination. A city at once golden and transparent defies the imagination (21:18, 21), as do gates formed from what must be enormous pearls (21:21). Ancient cities often featured high-rise buildings of four to six stories, but who has ever heard of a city built into a perfect cube, standing thousands of feet high (21:16)? Consider a city wall adorned with precious stones at the foundation. Is not this where the stones are most vulnerable to plunder and damage?

The new Jerusalem's splendor does not exist for its own sake. It stands in contrast to Revelation's unholy city, Babylon (meaning Rome). Like the new Jerusalem, Babylon is portrayed as a woman, in this case a prostitute, reflective of the negative gendered assumptions about women found in Revelation. Like the new Jerusalem, Babylon is adorned with "gold and jewels and pearls." Dressed in purple and scarlet, she holds a golden cup. She, like the new Jerusalem, is resplendent. But there is a deeper reality: from that golden cup she drinks the blood of martyrs (17:4–6). When Babylon meets her end, the people who mourn for her are those who exploit other people, including those who trade in luxury items. The list begins with "gold, silver, jewels and pearls" and concludes with slaves (18:12–13). Her violence and exploitation provide a stark contrast to the description of the Bride. The new Jerusalem's wealth carries a sharp criticism of Roman imperial commerce and exploitation.

Second, the new Jerusalem has no temple, and no sun or moon. It is filled with the presence of God and of the Lamb, who provide light in which all the nations walk. This is a vision of confidence and inclusion. God's abiding presence in the new city means the gates never need to be shut (21:22–27).

Revelation is a thoroughly Jewish vision. The book alludes to Israel's Scriptures more intensely than any other New Testament document. Jews would recognize Revelation's language here as an expression of Isaiah: "but the Lord will arise upon you, and his glory will appear over you. Nations shall come to your light, and kings to the brightness of your dawn" (Isa. 60:2b–3). Likewise, the psalm for this Sunday, Psalm 67, invites all the nations and all the peoples to offer praise to God. Interpreters will be careful to avoid supersessionism, the notion that Christianity somehow completes or displaces Judaism. We should emphasize the new Jerusalem's continuity with the glorious Zion envisioned in Isaiah and in the Psalms. In doing so, we remember that John almost surely composed Revelation after Jerusalem's destruction, when no physical temple resided on Zion.

Third, Revelation envisions not an escape to another world but a renewal of this one. We cannot say often enough that the new Jerusalem *comes down from heaven*. New Jerusalem imagery features not only gold and pearls but fresh flowing water and a tree producing diverse fruits. In God's presence the city dwellers enjoy abundance and delight. As in Eden, God dwells personally, nourishing its inhabitants with fresh water and the tree of life (Rev. 22:1–5).

Apocalypses like Revelation indeed imagine "other worlds." These visions conjure a heavenly city come down to earth. They do so not to provide fake road maps of the afterlife but to express fundamental convictions. More than a selfish fantasy, the new Jerusalem's luxury rejects greed and exploitation. Its open gates and perpetual light attest to the fullness of divine presence. Rather than rejecting this world, Revelation exults in the hope of abundant renewal, with fresh water and delicious fruit in abundance.

GREG CAREY

Commentary 2: Connecting the Reading with the World

This final vision in the book of Revelation is rich with imagery pointing beyond itself to John's message that judgment and redemption have been fulfilled. It reveals God's vision for humanity, reaffirming God's hope and love for all creation. Everything in this final reading invites us to focus on the presence of God. John is transported to a high mountain in his vision, so we are invited to join him as together we see beyond what has been and see what will be.

As a writer, John can be viewed as the Rembrandt of the New Testament. Rembrandt uses the light in his paintings to direct our eyes and our attention to the focal point of his work. John uses images and words to direct our attention to the focal point of his message: the presence of God the Almighty and the Lamb. Our hearts and minds are made to understand that something whole and new has come into being. The intersection of this imagery with the reality of the "here and not yet" compel us to explore how John's vision of two thousand years ago provides a vision for us today.

Like John we are called to embody and proclaim the hope of the gospel in the midst of the "here," the broken places and spaces where we find ourselves. The "here" of where we find ourselves is similar to the "here" of John's first-century reality. It is framed by isolation, intolerance, oppression, violence, hate, greed, disregard of humans, and the pursuit of power. John's reality was shaped by the presence of the Roman government, which erected temples, demanding allegiance of its residents. With that allegiance came cultural values that often clashed with the upside-down-kingdom values of Jesus as proclaimed in the Beatitudes in Matthew 5.

It is against this dissonance and backdrop that John reaffirms the "not yet" of God's ultimate victory over all that separates us from God and one another. By allowing ourselves to be spiritually lifted with John to a mountaintop, we become witnesses with John of this ultimate moment of fulfillment in the scriptural narrative. We are reminded that throughout history it has been on the mountain that the holy and the human have met. Moses met God on Mount Sinai (Exod. 19). Elijah encountered God on Mount Horeb (1 Kgs. 19:11–13). Jesus offered the Sermon on the Mount (Matt. 5–7). The transfiguration occurred on a mountain (Matt. 17:1–13). Finally, Jesus offered the great commission to the disciples from a mountain (Matt. 28:16).

This mountaintop view and experience affirm that what John is about to witness is indeed "holy" and "of God." What a picturesque view it is! Like a Rembrandt painting, the images employed by John invite us to consider their relevance for our witness today. While the images of the tree, the river, the plants all invite us into vibrant dimensions of this new Jerusalem, we will focus on two primary images: the temple and light. They provide us with rich insights and connections for our witness and presence in the world today.

First, there is no physical temple in this new Jerusalem that John envisions. Consider the central role that temples and churches have played across human civilization. Great edifices have been built in the centers of cities and towns, representing the heart of a given community. In this vision, we are reminded that physical structures of churches or temples are no longer the center of civilization. There is no need for a temple because in this new Jerusalem "the relationship with God and with the Lamb is direct, immediate, and constant."[1] No longer defined or confined by human constructs, the relationship with God is the center of the community.

The significance and relevance of contemporary temples are being challenged today as many church buildings have become peripheral to the neighborhoods in which they exist, standing as reminders of another time in history. Today many old and decaying buildings have become financial burdens on their communities, forcing a congregation to choose between serving the needs of the building and serving the needs of the community in which the building finds itself. Unfortunately at times congregations have chosen maintenance of a structure instead of sustaining a much-needed witness. This growing reality compels us to consider what to do with unsustainable buildings as we seek to embody a relevant witness of hope and mission. It is an opportunity compelling us to consider options for new and creative spaces in which to welcome believers and nonbelievers alike, places where God, not bricks, is at the center.

Then there is John's image of the light. In this final vision the light as we have known it is no longer determined or controlled by nature or human sources. This new light emanates from the throne, from God and the Lamb, eliminating darkness forever. From the moment of creation, light and darkness have coexisted—with the early reminder that God's spoken and powerful Word separated them. Yet throughout human history, the shadows of darkness have threatened the light and, with that, our ability to see the ways of God with our eyes and hearts. Notwithstanding this truth, darkness could not contain the light that broke into the world in the infant Christ child. The darkness of the tomb could not contain the light that broke forth in the resurrection. God's light has always found ways to offer hope in the midst of what seems like impenetrable darkness.

In response to this conviction, we are encouraged to turn from the shadows and consider where we see God's light breaking into the darkness today. This is our witness as we build and live into the "not yet" before us. We are encouraged to use that conviction to be light bearers in a dark and broken world, pointing to this final vision of hope. We are invited to consider where we see glimpses of light around us. When have you been the recipient of an unexpected word of encouragement while your heart was breaking from loss or grief? That is light breaking through darkness. When have you experienced the gathering of a people speaking on behalf of those without a voice? That is light breaking through darkness. When have you seen the feeding of the hungry, the clothing of the naked, the embrace of "the other"? That is God's light faithfully breaking through the darkness, compromising and ultimately destroying that power over all creation.

This is a significant word for us today. We, like John, understand what it means to live between the here and the not yet. We understand what it means to live with the reality of light and darkness existing side by side. It is precisely in that tension and dissonance that we are called to serve and witness. That witness is

---

1. Justo L. González, *Three Months with Revelation* (Nashville: Abingdon Press, 2004), 170.

not limited to human-created spaces as defined by the physical structures of temples. That witness is God's boundless light reaching across all creation, inviting us to "do justice, love kindness, and walk humbly with our God" (Mic. 6:8). That witness—our witness—proclaims to followers across time, "Be encouraged! The victory belongs to God!" "God is completely on the loose among God's people."[2] We—God's people—have the privilege of being on the loose with God, embracing and embodying God's victory of redemption, hope, and love for all time!

RUTH FAITH SANTANA-GRACE

2. Brian K. Blount, *Revelation: A Commentary*, New Testament Library (Louisville, KY: Westminster John Knox Press, 2009), 393.

John 14:23–29

²³Jesus answered him, "Those who love me will keep my word, and my Father will love them, and we will come to them and make our home with them. ²⁴Whoever does not love me does not keep my words; and the word that you hear is not mine, but is from the Father who sent me.

²⁵"I have said these things to you while I am still with you. ²⁶But the Advocate, the Holy Spirit, whom the Father will send in my name, will teach you everything, and remind you of all that I have said to you. ²⁷Peace I leave with you; my peace I give to you. I do not give to you as the world gives. Do not let your hearts be troubled, and do not let them be afraid. ²⁸You heard me say to you, 'I am going away, and I am coming to you.' If you loved me, you would rejoice that I am going to the Father, because the Father is greater than I. ²⁹And now I have told you this before it occurs, so that when it does occur, you may believe."

Commentary 1: Connecting the Reading with Scripture

The opening verses of this lectionary text invite us to consider its immediate context. Who is Jesus answering? What was the question? The question posed to Jesus comes from Judas (not Iscariot), who is the third questioner within this chapter to ask Jesus about the things he has been saying so far in his Farewell Discourse. Judas (not Iscariot) has asked Jesus why he does not reveal himself to the world but only to them, the disciples. Jesus responds by saying that those who love him will keep his word. Jesus' response is what we read in these verses, though they do not obviously follow from the question. The pattern in John has been that the disciples continue to misunderstand Jesus. It seems as though Jesus responds to his disciples' questions in such a way as to say that even their questions miss the mark.

This text is part of a longer section of the Gospel of John known as the Farewell Discourse. The name comes not only because it is Jesus' final words to his disciples before his arrest and crucifixion, but also because it fits within a pattern of farewell speeches that Jewish writings recorded as coming from famous people who had died. Jesus' farewell words match the pattern of a farewell speech, and his message shares

many of the same elements. In this passage, the similarities we see between Jesus' words and the farewell speeches include appointing a successor, comforting those left behind, and announcing his impending departure or death.[1]

In a way similar to Elijah appointing Elisha or Moses appointing Joshua, Jesus appoints a successor. The successor Jesus appoints in this passage is the Holy Spirit. Of course, the Holy Spirit is different from these other successors, in that the Holy Spirit will remain with the believers for generations to come. The Holy Spirit is the successor who makes known the one who is no longer in their presence.

This is only the third time that the name "Holy Spirit" is used in John, as opposed to the Advocate or Counselor. The first time it occurs is when John the Baptist announces that after him will come someone greater, "one who baptizes with the Holy Spirit" (John 1:33). John witnesses the Spirit descend on Jesus at his baptism (1:32). Now, in the lectionary text for this Sunday, Jesus fulfills those words by promising to send the Holy Spirit. By referring to the Holy Spirit by this name, Jesus reiterates that he, Jesus, is the one whom John the Baptist proclaimed as

---

1. Raymond Brown, *The Gospel according to John XIII–XXI*, Anchor Bible Commentary 30 (New York: Doubleday, 1970), 598.

baptizing with the Holy Spirit. The only other time the name "Holy Spirit" occurs in John is in one of the resurrection appearances, when Jesus breathes on his disciples the Holy Spirit (20:22). This shows Jesus' authority as the one whom John foretold, baptizing with the Holy Spirit, fulfilling the promises he has made to them in his Farewell Discourse.

The Holy Spirit is also the Advocate, the one who reminds the disciples of all that Jesus said and taught, helping them to understand what Jesus meant. Perhaps it is this same Holy Spirit that enables the author of John to write down all these things so that you may believe (see 20:31). The frequent misunderstandings of the disciples in John makes apparent their need for the Advocate. They need someone to help interpret the meaning of Jesus, known as the Word of God (1:1).

This passage also focuses on the idea of God the Father and Jesus as dwelling within believers. While at the beginning of this chapter Jesus has promised that he will prepare a place for them in God's house with many rooms, here that promise is brought closer. Jesus not only brings believers into God's house, but Jesus turns believers into a home for God: "We will come to them [who keep Jesus' word] and make our home with them" (14:23).

Jesus also promises that he will give the disciples his peace. Jesus encourages his disciples to be at peace, to not let their hearts be troubled. This is a mysterious peace, in that Jesus distinguishes it from that of the world. It is not clear what peace the world gives, but Judas (not Iscariot) had just asked why Jesus does not show himself to the world. Perhaps it is the peace of Jesus that makes himself known to believers, a peace that opens the eyes of persons to see Jesus in their midst.

Connecting this passage to the other Gospels, the use of the word "peace" echoes other ways Gospel writers have used the word. In Matthew, the Beatitudes of Jesus include "blessed are the peacemakers" (Matt. 5:9). Also in Matthew, Jesus says "I have not come to bring peace, but a sword" (Matt. 10:34). These various texts suggest that the peace Jesus gives, a peace different from what the world gives, is a peace that may not evoke calm and idyllic moments free of conflict. Perhaps it is the peace in the midst of conflict that Jesus gives, a peace that enters into conflict in order to serve as a peacemaker, or a peace that comes only through division and separation. Jesus' peace is unclear, which cautions us against making too simplistic an idea of "peace" when we hear Jesus' words to the disciples.

At the same time, Jesus, in his Farewell Discourse in John, seeks to comfort those who will be left behind after his death, a message not uncommon in other farewell speeches. Jesus promises his disciples, "I am going away, and am coming to you" (John 14:28). John's Jesus does not lay out an elaborate eschatological vision of apocalyptic imagery, so it is unclear in what sense Jesus means he will be "coming to" the disciples. It could refer to the postresurrection appearances at the end of John, or it could be referring to the Holy Spirit, or even the second coming of Christ, though these ideas are not spelled out clearly in John's Gospel.

This lectionary passage is read during Eastertide, which calls our attention to ways we are to live in light of Christ's resurrection. In his Farewell Discourse, Jesus invites believers to see their spiritual life as beginning now. Now that the resurrection has taken place, we look back on Jesus' words, "when it does occur, you may believe" (v. 29), and we see that the invitation to the spiritual life is present even now, asking us to believe in the resurrected Christ.

One of the other lectionary texts for this Sunday is the dream of Paul in Acts 16, calling to go to Macedonia. Along the way he meets the woman Lydia of Philippi. The text says that God opened her heart to believe, and that she invited Paul and his companions to her home. This text has several resonances with the John 14 lectionary text, in that they both refer indirectly to the idea that God opens the heart of some to believe, suggesting that belief itself is a gift from God. The other echo is that of hospitality. Just as those who will keep Jesus' word will become Jesus' home, so too does the invitation to believe in Jesus empower Lydia to invite Paul and his companions to her home to share in hospitality together. We are invited to do the same.

CAROLYN B. HELSEL

Commentary 2: Connecting the Reading to the World

"Stop being afraid" is one of the Bible's most familiar refrains. "Stop being afraid" is also what Jesus tells his disciples in his farewell speech recorded in John 14–17. Jesus sets the tone in his first sentence (14:1): "Do not let your hearts be troubled." Then, by the time we get to our lection passage (14:23–29), we hear Jesus say the same thing again, adding, "and do not let them be afraid" (v. 27). Why is Jesus concerned about addressing his disciples' fears?

When we consider Jesus' promise of the Paraclete and the implications of its various translations—"Advocate," "Counselor," "Comforter," "Helper"—we should keep in mind its context. Jesus is going to his death; everything he has done and said since he sat down to supper with his disciples has been a sign of that. He has more than once intimated that his time is short. He is leaving his disciples, and whether or not they fully understand what Jesus means, they surely must be fearful. John's Gospel intentionally highlights, through both action (betrayal) and setting (night), a sense of impending doom. At the very least, the disciples must be afraid simply of what they cannot yet know. What they do know is that Jesus has clearly said he is going away, and at the same time he has said, "I am coming to you" (v. 28). Jesus is going *and* coming, leaving *and* staying. Those seemingly contradictory promises are made possible through the Holy Spirit, whose primary function is to "teach you everything, and remind you of all that I have said to you" (v. 26). What Jesus is saying to his disciples—by describing the coming Paraclete, who can bring continual guidance and remembrance, promising the gift of peace, and clarifying the Paraclete's relationship to God the Father—is this: "Stop being afraid. Because of these things I am saying, you can stop being afraid."

One of the more pernicious threats to a thriving Christian faith today is fear. Tune in to any of the always-broadcasting media channels or social-media sites, and you will hear reports, posts, and commentary about the many things

that frighten us, from mosquito-borne viruses to terrorist threats near and far to natural disasters. We are in danger. Be very afraid.

Fear is nothing new. Fear has long been an issue among Christians. Consider the Protestant reformer John Calvin, who in the year 1536 published these words:

> Innumerable are the ills which beset human life, and present death in as many different forms. . . . Go on board a ship, you are but a plank's breadth from death. Mount a horse, the stumbling of a foot endangers your life. Walk along the streets, every tile upon the roofs is a source of danger. . . . It may be said that these things happen seldom, at least not always, or to all, certainly never all at once. I admit it; but since we are reminded by the example of others, that they may also happen to us, and that our life is not an exception any more than theirs, it is impossible not to fear and dread as if they were to befall us.[2]

Scott Bader-Saye, in his recent book, *Following Jesus in a Culture of Fear*, observes that "fear is produced, in part, by our judgment that we are not strong enough to fight off a threat."[3] Fear of the unknown and fear of losing something dear were fears that held sway with Jesus' first disciples. Such fears also belonged to those first believers who made up John's community. Jesus' promise of the Holy Spirit was the response to the fears among both groups. In promising his own presence and his own teachings made real through the mediation of God's own Spirit, Jesus assured those who could not imagine living without him and those who were growing weary of his delayed return, that they had the strength to be faithful followers in the meantime. So, how should we hear this promise today—we who are even further removed from Jesus' living, breathing presence on earth, beset even more by the fears of our time, and perhaps wondering if Jesus will ever return at

---

2. John Calvin, *Institutes of the Christian Religion*, trans. Henry Beveridge (London: Arnold Hatfield for Bonham Norton, 1845), 1.17; https://www.ccel.org/ccel/calvin/institutes.iii.xviii.html.

3. Scott Bader-Saye, *Following Jesus in a Culture of Fear* (Grand Rapids: Brazos Press, 2007), 28.

all? How can Jesus' promise of the Holy Spirit remain a primary and vital assurance to Christians even now?

First consider this. We fear most losing what we love most. What we love most invariably includes the things that make us, and those closest to us, safe and secure, and comfortable and healthy now and in the future. We resist losing control over or letting go of those things we believe will guard against what we fear could happen in the future. When we do that, we tighten our grip and close our hands. As a result we can become uncharitable, inhospitable, even unchristian. The more we allow our lives to be shaped by fear, the easier it becomes to value being safe over being faithful. If, however, we presume that our lives are shaped by the promised presence of the Holy Spirit, then we will be busy fulfilling an earlier promise of Jesus: doing "the works I do and, in fact . . . greater works than these" (John 14:12). If we love Jesus most—even more than those things that make us feel safe and comfortable—then we will keep his commandments (v. 15).

Second, the first disciples were afraid of Jesus' leaving because in part it meant they would be left alone. In truth, though, they were not going to be left alone. "I will not leave you orphaned" (v. 18). Jesus promised the Holy Spirit not as a private companion to each disciple, but as an abiding presence among the believing community. Together, as a gathered community, the disciples would experience Jesus' continuing presence. Together, they would share in the words and works of Jesus. Jesus' description in John 14 of the interrelationship among God the Father, God the Son, and God the Holy Spirit is an exemplar for the disciples' relationships, and the exemplar for those of us who make up the church. The Holy Spirit lives and moves among us. A Spirit-animated community is the gospel's response to our individual fears and anxieties.

Finally, consider this. To those of us who wring our hands watching the evening news or weep for our children's future after they have gone to bed, Jesus reminds us that he is not leaving us alone. God's teaching, guiding, comforting presence will be with us. Even more: "Peace I leave with you," so "do not . . . be afraid" (v. 27). Yes, the peace of Christ is just what we need, and just what we have. The church has known that from the start, which is why it included in its worship the practice of confirming this promise of Jesus. In the *Book of Common Prayer*, the Sunday communion liturgy calls for the celebrant to say, "The peace of the Lord be always with you." The people respond, "And also with you." Perhaps we should consider exchanging those words with one another daily, not as a casual greeting, but as the assurance Jesus meant it to be.

MARK PRICE

John 5:1–9

¹After this there was a festival of the Jews, and Jesus went up to Jerusalem.
²Now in Jerusalem by the Sheep Gate there is a pool, called in Hebrew Beth-zatha, which has five porticoes. ³In these lay many invalids—blind, lame, and paralyzed. ⁵One man was there who had been ill for thirty-eight years. ⁶When Jesus saw him lying there and knew that he had been there a long time, he said to him, "Do you want to be made well?" ⁷The sick man answered him, "Sir, I have no one to put me into the pool when the water is stirred up; and while I am making my way, someone else steps down ahead of me." ⁸Jesus said to him, "Stand up, take your mat and walk." ⁹At once the man was made well, and he took up his mat and began to walk.
Now that day was a sabbath.

Commentary 1: Connecting the Reading with Scripture

John's Gospel calls the miracles of Jesus signs, wondrous deeds that signify God's dynamic glory and gracious desire to mend a broken world. The Gospel's first half features seven signs affecting the natural and human environment (2:1–11; 4:46–54; 5:1–18; 6:1–15; 6:16–21; 9:1–41; 11:1–44). Several of these involve water, life's most basic element (see Gen. 1:1–2, 6–10, 20–23), and result in healing infirm bodies. One of these is the third sign, in John 5:1–9, which portrays Jesus' restoration of a long-term invalid beside the pool of Beth-zatha.

The time and place of this event are critical for understanding its significance. Jesus has come to Jerusalem to celebrate one of the Jewish festivals commemorating God's past salvation and sustenance of Israel (5:1). Here John does not specify the occasion, but festivals of Passover (Pesach), Tabernacles (Sukkot), and Dedication (Hanukkah)—sites of Jesus' activity elsewhere in this Gospel—are possibilities (2:13, 23; 4:45; 6:4; 7:1–14, 37; 10:22; 11:55; 12:1, 12, 20; 13:1, 29; 18:28, 39; 19:14). Jesus' life and work are deeply embedded in Jewish faith and practice, including the weekly Sabbath, which happens to be the day during the festival when he heals the invalid (v. 9). Although some Jews criticize Jesus for doing elective medical work on this sacred holiday, Jesus boldly defends his

action as part of his intimate collaboration with his divine Father: "My Father is still working, and I also am working" (v. 17; for another controversial Sabbath healing, see 9:1–41).

Within Jerusalem, the incident occurs beside a pool proximate to a gate in the city's northern wall. The entrance was known as the Sheep Gate, perhaps because it was close to the sheep market and served as the main portal for bringing in sheep to sacrifice in the temple (see 2:14). Given this Gospel's penchant for symbolic language, an allusive connection seems likely with Jesus' later announcement, "Very truly, I tell you, I am the gate for the sheep"—that is, the way of pastoral care for his cherished "flock" (10:1–9).

In preparation for ritual offering, the sheep could be washed in the nearby large tank of water, surrounded by "five covered porches" (5:2 CEB). The exact name of the pool, beginning with "Beth," meaning "house" in Hebrew, is uncertain. The two best options in early manuscripts are Beth-zatha ("House of Olive") and Bethesda ("House of Mercy"). The latter may seem most suited to Jesus' benevolent action in this scene, but that may be precisely what prompted a later scribe to add this touch of "mercy." In any case, olive oil was also thought to have soothing medicinal properties, as were special springs of water near holy sites. Although the statement about the angel of the Lord's periodic stirring these waters with therapeutic energy (v. 4 KJV) represents a later addition, the paralyzed man clearly believes this whirlpool generates healing power (v. 7). Archaeological evidence supports this holy spa scenario, including a healing cult associated with the pagan deity Asclepius in the second-century CE, when Emperor Hadrian reconstructed Jerusalem and named it Aelia Capitolina.[1]

The narrator describes the needy man as suffering from *astheneia*, a term denoting illness or sickness, with an accent on weakness or impotence (vv. 3, 5, 7). Particular types of afflicted persons who parked beside the pool of Bethzatha were the "blind, lame, and paralyzed" (v. 2). Our focal figure fits the last two categories, with his inability to walk and transport himself into the bubbling waters at the optimal time (v. 7). The term *xēros*, rendered "paralyzed," carries shades of "dried up, withered" (cf. Matt. 12:10; Mark 3:3; Luke 6:6, 8).

The duration of the man's weak, withered condition, together with his isolation, exacerbate his terrible state. He has suffered for thirty-eight years (v. 5), a long stretch by any accounting, but all the more so in an era with average life spans around forty. An intriguing, suggestive parallel may be found in Deuteronomy 2:14 (John's Gospel is full of OT allusions), where the same thirty-eight-year period designates the length of travel time in the wilderness "until the entire generation of [Israelite] warriors had perished from the camp" for not trusting in God's power to overcome the mighty inhabitants of Canaan (see Num. 13–14). Thirty-eight years (just shy of the more complete forty-year unit in biblical numerology) then represents a stage of national paralysis, faithlessness, and failure to cross through troubled waters into the bountiful land of promise.

Though lumped among other invalids amid a bustling center near the temple, especially during festival season, the infirm man remains profoundly alone. He utters the most tragic statement in our passage: "Sir, I have no one to put me into the pool when the water is stirred up" (v. 7). This amounts to a poignant plea for help, reminiscent of the famous call in Acts 16:9, a companion lection. In a vision, Paul hears, "Come over to Macedonia and help us." Instead of asking for aid across interprovincial waters of the Aegean Sea, the disabled man in John 5 ironically requires help to enter healing waters he lies right next to, in the shadow of God's holy house. Would that he had even one helper, to say nothing of four who team up to lower their paralyzed friend through the roof of a Capernaum house to gain access to Jesus (Mark 2:3–4)!

Though the Johannine Jesus regularly uses water as a teaching motif and miracle-working means, including instructing a blind man in another Sabbath healing incident to wash in another pool, Siloam (9:6–7; cf. 2:6–11; 3:5; 4:4–15; 6:16–21; 7:37–39; 13:5–15), in the present case, he bypasses the adjacent pool of Beth-zatha altogether. In straightforward fashion, he succinctly orders the man: "Stand up, take your mat and walk" (v. 8). Jesus himself directly accomplishes what the man expects the whirlpool to do. Jesus is the water of life, reminiscent of Revelation 22:1–2, another lectionary text.

What motivates Jesus' help in the first place? It is important to see that Jesus initiates the encounter with the paralytic, who, after all this while, scarcely expects anyone to give him the time of day. The story stresses that "when Jesus saw him lying there and knew that he had been there a long time," he proceeded to draw the man out by asking if he wanted to be "made well" (v. 6). After the man responds by reporting his helpless condition (no hearty "Yes, I want to be healed!"), Jesus moves to command him to rise and walk, which he is enabled to do "at once" (v. 9). The seeing-knowing Jesus in a weak world of negligence and ignorance is the key to restoration. As the needy woman in another water-springing story in the previous chapter puts it, "Come and see a man [Jesus Messiah] who told me everything I have ever done!" (4:29).

---

1. See James F. Strange, "Beth-zatha," in *Anchor Bible Dictionary*, 1:700–701; John J. Rousseau and Rami Arav, *Jesus and His World: An Archaeological and Cultural Dictionary* (Minneapolis: Fortress Press, 1995), 154–57, 175–79.

Though no magic formula, the words of healing Jesus utters are powerful and purposeful. "Rise" and "take up" are uplifting imperatives, obviously apt for the man's lowly, leaden state, but also for resurrection from death, whether that of the four-day-dead Lazarus (11:39–44) or the three-day-dead Jesus—in the latter case an eternal resurrection guaranteeing eternal life. "Walk" is an outgoing command in biblical language, and especially Johannine-speak for faithful living in the world, for "walking just as Jesus walked" (1 John 2:6; cf. John 8:12; 11:9–10; 12:35). After thirty-eight long years of suffering and going nowhere, this man has not only a new physical lease on life, but also a renewed purpose for living.

F. SCOTT SPENCER

Commentary 2: Connecting the Reading to the World

Jesus breaks the Sabbath taboos by healing at the most sacred time of the week. Part of the power of John's Gospel is that Jesus shows up at unexpected times, creating conditions for healing that come from God's overflowing love. It was difficult for the world to recognize the healing brought by Jesus because it occurred at the wrong time and it involved going to ritually impure places.

In John's time disabled people congregated in public places that would have been deemed ritually impure. The context of the healing matters. By choosing the pool by the Sheep Gate for healing, Jesus built upon the medical wisdom of his day. At Beth-zatha there were several pools associated with the Greek god Asclepius. Jesus did not reject this form of medicine but brought the fullness of his transforming self into this place. The fact that Beth-zatha can mean either "house of grace" or "house of disgrace" suggests that this healing location was stigmatized because of its association with the sick. Because of Jesus' presence, this place that was seen as a house of disgrace becomes a site of grace.

Because John's Gospel highlights the identity of Jesus Christ as salvific, it is important to foreground Jesus' activity. This story occurs in the Gospel's book of signs, a section where God transforms situations of suffering through presence. Since all of the Gospels include healing stories, these are an important part of Jesus' ministry, but it is not immediately evident how we should understand them in a twenty-first-century context. However, it is important to point to rich and multivalent expressions of Jesus' healing ministry, which is a ministry of hope founded on personal engagement.

One connection a preacher might make is with the concept of disability. Because of the length of this man's illness, it is fair to think of him as being disabled. Physical impairments are the limitations placed on a person by their disability. Impairment is not sin but is part of embodied existence. On average, Americans will spend eight years of their lives with some form of impairment. Exclusionary barriers are the limitations placed on a person because of prejudice against the disabled, and also lack of treatment, or its inaccessibility. When people cannot enter a building, fill out tax forms, vote, or use the telephone, they are excluded. Modern disability scholars are challenging our notion of disability as simply physical impairment and critiquing exclusionary barriers. Barriers are sinful and must be removed for the conditions of justice to be met.

Despite the fact that this man faced multiple exclusionary barriers, he continued to hope. The man's response to Jesus' question "Do you want to be made well?" names how he persisted in his hopeful desire for treatment. In conversation with Jesus, the sick man explained the barriers he was facing to getting well. Jesus offered healing rather than a cure because his engagement included a conversation. A cure is a one-time event undertaken by an expert; healing is a negotiation that involves a story. Cure means immediate removal of the condition; healing is a movement toward wholeness that involves psychological dynamics such as acceptance, negotiation, and trust. In an encounter with Jesus, healing is deepened in conversation.

There is an important connection to make with the literature on faith and prayer in memoirs of ministry. In Richard Lischer's memoir of his ministry in a Midwest town, *Open Secrets,* a teenage congregant with muscular dystrophy named Amy wants to visit Kathryn Kuhlman's Crusade of Miracles in a nearby city. Lischer pulls Amy aside to discuss the upcoming event. He wonders whether her faith can survive the disappointment of not being cured. She attends the revival hoping for a cure, but when she is not cured, she states that it was a positive spiritual experience for her and her family. Amy does not lose her faith, and she minimizes Lischer's concerns. Amy was already trying to find Jesus in her experience of illness, regardless of what her pastor thought, and she experienced Jesus at the healing crusade, even if she was not cured. This connection shows how people with illness and disability may have already met God in their experience of illness and thus meet the Gospel narrative with experience in healing.

This Gospel story has provided inspiration for music, which in turn helps us interpret the passage in the present time. The African American spiritual "Wade in the Water" echoes the language of Beth-zatha to promise that God's action will heal, but in a context that also allows room for lament. Fannie Lou Hamer sang a version of this song in 1963 in Greenwood, Alabama, where she interjected verses about the persecution of the African American community under Jim Crow. In this context, a call for healing included the voicing of lament and a cry for justice expressed in song. Note that this song was sung in a protest march: the lyrics expressed reliance on God's action, but human actors were already crying out for justice.

Whereas cure is a total removal of illness, healing is a longer-term negotiation with illness that involves telling a story. On any given Sunday, many in the congregation will struggle with illnesses that might disable them. It is important that ministers avoid the spiritualization of disability. Preachers who spiritualize healing stories may inadvertently contribute to the mistaken notion that disability is sinful. Preachers can work, instead, to point people to Jesus' presence in the midst of illness. It is instructive to consider that God was already present in the man at Beth-zatha's attempts to get into the pool. Jesus did not bring God to this man, but rather met God already present in his story. People who use wheelchairs complain of how frequently Christians want to pray for them to be healed, implying that it is their own fault for being disabled and that disability is something that should be cured. All such responses are paternalistic. A preferable approach is to discuss how the disabled experience God's presence.

One connection that a preacher might make is between the pastoral prayer of the service and the time they spend visiting sick and disabled congregants. Pastoral prayers in the service should avoid metaphors of faith such as opening blind eyes or helping the deaf to hear. Prayers with the sick involve discernment. First, a minister needs to discern whether people expect cure from a pastoral prayer and instead frame the prayer as a conversation with God about illness in which a person might meet Jesus. Second, the minister can wonder how God is already present in a person's attempts to remove barriers. Regardless, pastoral prayer in the midst of illness is one of the most important ways to help people feel that God remembers them.

Today in urban settings homeless people congregate, and many have disabilities. With the lack of social services, many are being forced to seek care in public by going to nonprofit agencies. Conversely, disappearing rural hospitals force people to travel many miles to receive care. At a time of widespread care crises, believers should follow Jesus' example. Since Jesus was not at home worshiping God on the Sabbath, but traveling to where the sick congregated and engaging them in conversation, believers can do the same. Because Jesus knew the man had been there a long time, it is likely that he had visited this place before. It seems likely that he frequented such places. When he did so, he brought his presence, full of mercy, to meet everything hopeful about the human condition.

PHILIP BROWNING HELSEL

Ascension of the Lord

Acts 1:1–11
Psalm 47 and Psalm 93

Ephesians 1:15–23
Luke 24:44–53

Acts 1:1–11

[1]In the first book, Theophilus, I wrote about all that Jesus did and taught from the beginning [2]until the day when he was taken up to heaven, after giving instructions through the Holy Spirit to the apostles whom he had chosen. [3]After his suffering he presented himself alive to them by many convincing proofs, appearing to them during forty days and speaking about the kingdom of God. [4]While staying with them, he ordered them not to leave Jerusalem, but to wait there for the promise of the Father. "This," he said, "is what you have heard from me; [5]for John baptized with water, but you will be baptized with the Holy Spirit not many days from now."

[6]So when they had come together, they asked him, "Lord, is this the time when you will restore the kingdom to Israel?" [7]He replied, "It is not for you to know the times or periods that the Father has set by his own authority. [8]But you will receive power when the Holy Spirit has come upon you; and you will be my witnesses in Jerusalem, in all Judea and Samaria, and to the ends of the earth." [9]When he had said this, as they were watching, he was lifted up, and a cloud took him out of their sight. [10]While he was going and they were gazing up toward heaven, suddenly two men in white robes stood by them. [11]They said, "Men of Galilee, why do you stand looking up toward heaven? This Jesus, who has been taken up from you into heaven, will come in the same way as you saw him go into heaven."

Commentary 1: Connecting the Reading with Scripture

The opening verses of Acts create a narrative bridge between the Gospel and its sequel. As Luke closes, Jesus teaches his disciples before ascending into the heavens. Acts also begins with Jesus' instruction to his followers prior to his ascension. The narrative and theological connections between the Gospel's conclusion and the beginning of Acts are even more complex than these initial parallels: these connections set the theological horizon of Luke's second volume, which is a narrative account of *God's* activity through Jesus and his followers.

Acts 1:1–5 pairs with Luke 1:1–4. These twin prologues calibrate the reader's expectations. In the Gospel, Luke describes his process to validate the reliability of his writing, but he also indicates a sense of purpose: "so that you may know the truth concerning the things about you

have been instructed" (Luke 1:4). Luke writes to believers who already know the story of Jesus. Why retell these stories? It may be because Luke intends to tell these stories in a new light, especially from the perspective of the anxieties and hopes of the community he addresses. That is, these texts are pastoral and theological in their aims. It may be the formation of a particular kind of communal identity rooted in a theological confession that is at the forefront of these texts, rather than the narration of cause-and-effect and historical chronology.

The connections between the Gospel and Acts are made explicit in Acts 1:1 when the text refers back to "the first book" and addresses a certain "Theophilus," who is mentioned in Luke 1:3. Acts summarizes this first book by pointing to "all that Jesus did and taught from the beginning"—or, better, "all that Jesus *began* to do and to teach." After all, the beginning of Acts does not narrate the permanent departure of Jesus from the narrative of Acts but his ascension and glorification (v. 9). Ascension is not absence in Acts. Jesus is an active and living presence in the stories of these early followers. His name is invoked to heal (e.g., Acts 3:6; 4:10; 9:34). He encounters Saul on the road to Damascus (as narrated in chaps. 9, 22, and 26). The Spirit he promises propels the disciples to become witnesses to the very edges of the world (1:8).

Before the disciples join in beginning to do and to teach, they must first wait. As Matthew Skinner has pointed out, the first instruction the risen Jesus gives is rather unexpected.[1] The first command is to "*wait* [in Jerusalem] for the promise of the Father" (1:4). The baptism of the Holy Spirit is an anticipated but not yet realized event in these opening verses.

In the midst of this pregnant waiting, the disciples ask a critical question in verse 6: "Lord, is this the time when you will restore the kingdom to Israel?" Commentators tend to assume misapprehension in this question. The disciples simply do not get it; Jesus is not that kind of Messiah. However, the expectations Luke himself sets in the Gospel are at play here. Remember the opening chapters of the Gospel. Recall the Magnificat's appeal to "the promise [God] made to our ancestors, to Abraham and to his descendants forever" (Luke 1:55).

Perhaps the expectation that Jesus would restore the kingdom is precisely right and consistent with the preaching, healing, and ministry we see in Luke.[2] In that light, we can reread Jesus' response not as a rejection of the question but a potent response for those still waiting for the ultimate fulfillment of God's promises. We cannot and will not know the times God has set, but we can still trust that God's kingdom is at hand. If that is the case, if the kingdom is tangibly present already while we are waiting for it, what should we do? First, the disciples wait, but then they will receive a magnificent gift: the outpouring of the Holy Spirit. That same Spirit

brings a call in its wake, a call to be witnesses near and far.

For many readers, Acts 1:8b serves as a table of contents. It sets geographical signposts, reminding readers on the road down which Acts leads us that God has set the itinerary. We might wonder how verse 8 sets our expectations. First, we learn that the summons is expansive. These Jesus followers are drawn to leave more familiar environs to explore the uncertainty of lands and peoples beyond their quotidian experience. Second, we learn that the call necessarily involves the encounter of cultural and ethnic differences. In the journey to the ends of the earth, the followers of Jesus will encounter the panoply of God's diverse creation. Third, we learn that the call extends beyond the end of the narrative of Acts. Not many would have counted Rome as the "ends of the earth," though we find Paul in prison there in chapter 28. The call is not just to the retinue of followers at the beginning of Acts but to those of us still reading this text all these years later.

Here we can also draw a connection to Psalm 47. The psalmist exhorts "all you peoples" to join in praise of a God who reigns over every empire, every people. Acts thus joins a long chorus of prophets and poets of Israel who envision the reign of God stretching as far as our maps go—and even farther. Last, we learn that the call is to "witness," to give testimony to what God has done in and through us. The narrative of Acts shows these disciples inhabiting, embodying, and modeling what such witness might look like.

Having given these formative instructions, Jesus ascends into the clouds. Stephen will later witness Jesus' position at the right hand of God (Acts 7:56). It is vital to clarify the significance of the ascension in the narrative of Acts. This is not a departure as much as it is an enthroning. It is not exit as much as it is glorification. The ascension confirms the prophetic promises Jesus speaks and lives out in the Gospel. Jesus will continue to accompany the disciples throughout Acts.

The disciples are tempted to follow Jesus' ascension with their eyes, gazing into the heavens

---

1. Matthew L. Skinner, *Intrusive God, Disruptive Gospel: Encountering the Divine in the Book of Acts* (Grand Rapids: Brazos, 2015), 6–7.

2. As noted by Beverly Roberts Gaventa, *Acts* (Nashville: Abingdon Press, 2003), 65.

Jesus Opened the Eyes of the Heart

Since the mystic writings are not understood unless God opens our mind, Jesus opened the eyes of their heart, so that they might read, believe, and understand what was written. For only the believer understands. "It seemed good to my Father," he said, "to restore the human race by means of the course of events, and what he had decided upon was by his inspiration made known in the divine text. I foretold the same thing before it came to pass, and it could not have happened otherwise, because the decrees of God cannot be changed, and Holy Scripture can no more lie than can the Spirit himself by whose inspiration it is made known. The road to glory was through death and the shame of the cross; resurrection on the third day was necessary so that you would know that you have a living Lord and advocate who hereafter will not die. When he returns to heaven he will send you thence the heavenly Spirit.

"Then in the name of Jesus Christ you must preach repentance of former life and remission of all sins without keeping the law of Moses. Remission will be granted to all through the gospel faith alone. I have paid the penalty in the name of all; they need only believe and they will attain to innocence without cost. And you must preach not only to the Jews but to all the nations of the world, though you will take your start from Jerusalem. I was born in Judea, there I performed miracles; I taught in Jerusalem and there I met my death. Among these people you will find hearts in many ways already prepared for faith. For them you will recall what you have seen and heard. You will transmit to them my teaching, which I handed on to you as I received it from my Father. The world will rail against your testimony, as it has always railed against me."

Erasmus, "Paraphrase on Luke 11–24," trans. and annotated Jane E. Phillips, in, *Collected Works of Erasmus 48: New Testament Scholarship*, ed. Robert D. Sider (Toronto: University of Toronto Press, 2003), 277–78.

rather than the diverse world to which they have been called. So intent is their gaze that they do not notice the appearance of "two men in white robes" until they speak to remind the disciples what Jesus commanded. "Go," they say. The road is before you. The way has been laid out. "Go," because, though he has ascended, he is not gone. He is with you, and he will come back.

The opening verses of Acts close with eschatological promise, a future hope that will inspire, guide, and shape the work of these witnesses. The followers of Jesus do not walk the road of testimony under their own power or authority;

instead, the return of Jesus is a guarantee of God's faithfulness.

The beginnings of narratives matter. Whether we hear, "Once upon a time . . . ," or read, "A long time ago in a galaxy far, far away . . . ," a memorable opening sets expectations and shapes how we will remember a story. What if our preaching can introduce our sisters and brothers to such a memorable introduction? Instead of a throat-clearing exercise, Luke here tells us the story of Acts in miniature. God has called us to the very ends of the earth, and God will lead us along the way.

ERIC D. BARRETO

Commentary 2: Connecting the Reading with the World

How do we speak of the present location of our risen Lord? Second, what does it mean for the church that Jesus is no longer with us, at least not in bodily form? How can we speak of Jesus present, for example, in the stranger, or sacramentally in the Eucharist, while at the same time claiming with the Apostles' Creed that he is "seated at the right hand of God the Father"? Finally, why should we celebrate the departure of Jesus from the earth, when we will turn around in Advent, just six months from now, and long for his return?

The liturgical year willingly colludes with this final point of confusion, conveniently landing the ascension story late in the week on a Thursday, exactly forty days after Easter. The annual weekday event gives Lord's-Day-focused Protestants the option of skipping the ascension story altogether. Yet the fact that the lectionary returns to this same story each year demonstrates the church's attachment to its mystery.

Perhaps this places us in good company with the disciples, who themselves seem confused about what Jesus' ascension means for them. Only forty days earlier they rejoiced in an up-from-the-grave resurrection party. Deep grief for an unspeakable loss and fear of crucifying powers hanging over all of their heads were upended by resurrection power. Now they face another departure whose significance is yet unknown. Rather than attempting to explain the confusion, the preacher might find more value in situating the congregation in the midst of it. What does faithfulness look like in the absence of clarity about God's plans and God's presence? How can the church be an effective witness to a God whose activity is unclear even to Jesus' closest followers?

It is useful to notice the verbs Jesus issues to disciples in the midst of their confusion: "do not leave" and "wait for the promise." On first read, both commands sound rather passive, yet they are extraordinarily difficult commands to obey in the presence of mystery, grief, and uncertainty. Entertaining these may be less popular in a hyperactive internet world where more aerobic biblical commands of "depart!" (Gen. 12:1) or "get up and go!" (Acts 8:26) capture the church's attention. Yet every pastor has marveled at the faith of the attentive spouse at the deathbed of her beloved, steeled to stay until the shadows finally lengthen and God relieves her of her post. Still others have testified to congregations that stayed to minister to forgotten people in their decaying neighborhood, knowing it would most likely lead to the death of the congregation. More prophetically, history is replete with people like Rosa Parks, who refused to be moved, trusting that a divine promise is stronger than any human threat.

Faith is too often represented as clarity about God's activity—where God is located and what

God is up to in a confusing world. This story from Acts reminds us that a deeper faith requires trust in God's commitment to us precisely when we are confused about where God is located and uncertain of what God is up to. It is helpful to remember that the church has often faced such crises and that clarity often comes as a result of our decision to stay and wait.

Actually, what Jesus promises on the other side of the staying and the waiting is not clarity but power. Power is an uncomfortable word for church folk shaped by a culture that speaks disparagingly of power that corrupts and of "the power hungry." Though power is a basic necessity not only for life but also for justice, its negative connotations may discourage the preacher from engaging this centerpiece of good news in the text. Power is coming, Jesus tells the church—Holy Spirit power. This is good news to a church called to follow Jesus into the fray. The world does not have a monopoly on power. God traffics in it as well.

Similar to traditional notions of power, Holy Spirit power will enable disciples to act with freedom and consequence in the world, challenging forces that are opposed to their efforts. However, Holy Spirit power is distinct. First, this power is given to, rather than taken by, the church. It is given by God, which implies that it can be revoked. Second, it is given alongside an explicit vocation: to be witnesses. Thus, even as divine power is gifted to human beings, authorization for its use is narrowed by the vocation God attaches to it.

Our vocation is to be witnesses to what God has done in the world through Jesus Christ and what God continues to do in this moment. To be a witness is a tricky term, since it bears formulaic notions of proselytizing. It can be helpful to point away from churchy notions of the word and toward more forensic ones. A witness tells the truth about what she sees. She gives testimony about what she has observed. Others bear responsibility for how to weigh the value of that testimony and even whether it is to be believed. The witness simply tells the truth.

Telling the truth about what God has done through Jesus Christ and where one observes the Spirit at work today may seem weak in a world that often understands power as coercive force applied over and against other human beings. This perceived weakness only demonstrates the difference between power as it is commonly understood and power that is defined by the gospel. When we tell the truth about this different kind of power and testify to the places we see God's power at work, others seek after this God.

These are important points for preachers to make at a time in our country when the exercise of power at the highest levels is being questioned and critiqued, and trust in institutions of every sort (including the church) is at record lows. Preachers may find themselves tempted to shrink from any talk of the church's exercise of power on the one hand, or to collude with partisan forces on the other.

The church is called to tell the truth about where we have seen God in the world through Jesus and the good news that we continue to see God hewing out of suffering, injustice, and fear. Power is given to fulfill that vocation in the face of a world that can be indifferent or hostile to it.

While Christians are not sent to create conflict in the world, we do not shrink from it either. The rest of the book of Acts edifies the church for this challenge.

Christians who honor our calling are given what we need to fulfill it. We know this precisely because the giver of that vocation is now "in heaven." Heaven is not so much a geographic pinpoint on the map of the universe as it is the place where God's reign has come to full fruition. The crucified one now reigns there, which implies that his way of living— crossing boundaries, sharing bread, preaching justice, announcing grace—is vindicated. Holy Spirit power can be trusted. The disciples are discouraged from looking up toward heaven for too long. They have work to do. The ascension, then, is not so much an account of Jesus' departure as it is a confirmation of his power, power that now accompanies the church that witnesses to his name.

ANDREW FOSTER CONNORS

Psalm 47

[1]Clap your hands, all you peoples;
shout to God with loud songs of joy.
[2]For the LORD, the Most High, is awesome,
a great king over all the earth.
[3]He subdued peoples under us,
and nations under our feet.
[4]He chose our heritage for us,
the pride of Jacob whom he loves.

[5]God has gone up with a shout,
the LORD with the sound of a trumpet.
[6]Sing praises to God, sing praises;
sing praises to our King, sing praises.
[7]For God is the king of all the earth;
sing praises with a psalm.

[8]God is king over the nations;
God sits on his holy throne.
[9]The princes of the peoples gather
as the people of the God of Abraham.
For the shields of the earth belong to God;
he is highly exalted.

Psalm 93

[1]The LORD is king, he is robed in majesty;
the LORD is robed, he is girded with strength.
He has established the world; it shall never be moved;
[2]   your throne is established from of old;
you are from everlasting.

[3]The floods have lifted up, O LORD,
the floods have lifted up their voice;
the floods lift up their roaring.
[4]More majestic than the thunders of mighty waters,
more majestic than the waves of the sea,
majestic on high is the LORD!

[5]Your decrees are very sure;
holiness befits your house,
O LORD, forevermore.

Connecting the Psalm with Scripture and Worship

The first reading for Ascension Day gives us an example of the mastery of the author of Luke and Acts: the author conveys a theological statement of faith—that Christ is risen from death and is ruling the universe—using a literalized narrative. According to Acts, after the symbolically significant time period of forty days, Jesus leaves his human companions and resumes his dwelling with God, reclaiming his place as one with God. Given the ancient worldview of a three-tier universe, Jesus must go up, must ascend from the lowest level (the realm of the dead on Good Friday), into the middle level (our earth, for forty days of Easter), and up in a realm above the sky (beyond heaven, on the ascension). Whether or not Luke accepted a three-tier universe as factually accurate, he used this ancient imagery in a memorable way to proclaim his Christology, and Psalm 47 provides Christians with a most appropriate response to the ascension narrative.

The cosmology of the psalm corresponds with that of the Lukan narrative. According to this hierarchical universe, God is up above the earth, the people participating in the ritual are on earth, and other peoples—those who are not worshipers of YHWH—are "under our feet." This unscientific depiction of the earth remains in human imagination and is expressed in our speech, and not only our poetry. Christians readily refer to God and heaven as "up" and the dead or hell as "down." One theory suggests that since the eyes and the brain are on the top of the human body, this naturally leads to speech that considers that what is most important—whether one's cranium, the "head" of state, or God—is up. So in Psalm 47 "God has gone up" and "is highly exalted" (Ps. 47:5a, 9b).

Secondly, both Acts and Psalm 47 rely on the imagery of kingship. The ascension narrative depicts the disciples looking up—albeit erroneously—while awaiting the manifestation of the king of Israel. The psalm also assumes that at the very top of everything is a male monarch. In verses 2 and 5, God, who is above all, is named YHWH (LORD in NRSV), the Most High (a title appropriated from the pre-Israelite Semitic deity *El'Elyon*), and is pictured sitting above the

heavens on a throne as king over all. The Old Testament commonly uses the depiction of God as king. Thus hope for the salvation of the people awaited the arrival of a messiah, an anointed king. God is king, and God will save through a king.

The last fifty years have witnessed considerable uneasiness among some Christians with the predominance of male, monarchial imagery for God and the centrality of this image in the Psalms. In both past and present, literalizing this imagery has led to the defense of male sovereignty in all things: thus, the divine right of kings and the husband's authority to beat his wife. Our liturgical speech is filled with the metaphor of God as king, especially in English-language hymnody, in which "king" conveniently rhymes with "sing."

In recent decades, the metaphor of divine kingship has indeed been moderated, surrounded by other metaphors, but it is here on Ascension Day, when we praise Christ enthroned as the sovereign power of our lives. Americans claim the populace as sovereign; popular culture claims the self to be sovereign; Christians proclaim Christ as sovereign. Christians apply the imagery of a male monarch to Jesus, who, although a male, was certainly not a king. Thus the ancient imagery of kingship comes to be recognized as supreme metaphor: the wrong way to speak that is, surprisingly, discovered to be in an important way the best expression of truth. So, on Ascension Day, Christians sing an ancient praise to God as enthroned above Israel, by which they laud Jesus Christ, risen from death and enthroned above all as the sovereign power of all. Although Christ is not king, Christ is king.

Scholars debate the original ritual use of Psalm 47. Did ancient Israel conduct an annual enthronement festival, praising YHWH as the king of the nation? Was there some religious festival that focused perhaps on the ark of the covenant, a complement to national tributes of obeisance to the Israelite kings? Was this psalm meant eschatologically, the trumpet (shofar) of verse 5 blown in Zion to signify the end of estrangement from God while pleading for a new year of grace? As with those lament psalms that current scholars say influenced how the evangelists described a crucifixion scene at which they were not present, maybe the enthronement psalms played a part in leading imaginatively to the narrative of the ascension. So for centuries Christians have sung Psalm 47 on Ascension Day, not pretending to be ancient Israelites who are celebrating the ark of the covenant, an Israelite king, or a tribal deity, but as Christians, lauding the risen Christ and triune God.

An interesting (indeed, preferred) alternate for Ascension Day is Psalm 93. This choice is less focused on a three-tier universe. Instead, God is enthroned "in majesty," "more majestic than the waves of the sea" (Ps. 93:1, 4). In this psalm, God is the creator who tamed the waters and now rules over the waters. Always scriptural passages are referring to other scriptural passages; so Psalm 93 asks us to recall the watery chaos before creation, the waters of the flood, and the waters of the exodus. God as creator said to these, and to all waters, "Thus far you come, and no farther" (Job 38:11). For Christians, all these waters are channeled into the water in our font, through which we have been led by the resurrection of Jesus Christ to the safe side of the sea. Thanks to our baptism, we too can join in praise of the God above all waters. A documentary about floods that was shown on public television stated that "water wins." By faith, on Ascension Day we proclaim that Christ is there at our font, no longer dead, but reigning forevermore in majesty, calming the floods of death and the grave through the water of our baptism.

GAIL RAMSHAW

Ephesians 1:15–23

¹⁵I have heard of your faith in the Lord Jesus and your love toward all the saints, and for this reason ¹⁶I do not cease to give thanks for you as I remember you in my prayers. ¹⁷I pray that the God of our Lord Jesus Christ, the Father of glory, may give you a spirit of wisdom and revelation as you come to know him, ¹⁸so that, with the eyes of your heart enlightened, you may know what is the hope to which he has called you, what are the riches of his glorious inheritance among the saints, ¹⁹and what is the immeasurable greatness of his power for us who believe, according to the working of his great power. ²⁰God put this power to work in Christ when he raised him from the dead and seated him at his right hand in the heavenly places, ²¹far above all rule and authority and power and dominion, and above every name that is named, not only in this age but also in the age to come. ²²And he has put all things under his feet and has made him the head over all things for the church, ²³which is his body, the fullness of him who fills all in all.

Commentary 1: Connecting the Reading with Scripture

This is the epistle reading for Ascension Day, which has the same four readings every year. In addition to Ephesians 1:15–23, the readings are Acts 1:1–11, Psalm 47 or 93, and Luke 24:44–53. As is often the case in Eastertide, the OT reading is replaced by a reading from Acts.

Ephesians 1:15–23 is the thanksgiving section of the document. In letters from the Pauline tradition, the thanksgiving comes near the beginning of the letter and signals to the audience the main themes to be addressed. In the case of Ephesians, the thanksgiving follows a lengthy section of blessings of the triune God for the benefits of salvation. This form of prayer is distinctively Jewish in origin; by combining it with the thanksgiving typical of a Hellenistic letter, the author demonstrates the gospel reconciliation of Jew and Gentile in the literary form of the document as well as in its theological content.

The thanksgiving is linked to what precedes it by the phrase "on this account" ("for this reason," NRSV Eph. 1:15). The author's thankfulness is occasioned by God's saving action and by the positive response of the Ephesian believers.

Their response has been "faith in the Lord Jesus and love toward all the saints." The writer, whom the letter identifies as Paul, seems not to have visited the church in person, writing that the thankful prayer is a response to having heard (1:15) about their faith and love.

In addition to giving thanks for the Ephesians' faithfulness, the author requests for them God's gift of "a spirit of wisdom and revelation as you come to know" the "God and Father of our Lord Jesus Christ" (vv. 17, 3). God is known through Jesus, who was identified with wisdom in 1:9.[1] The result of God's gift will be the enlightenment of the "eyes of [the believers'] hearts" (v. 18), and the purpose of this enlightenment is that they will know three things. These are listed in parallel clauses beginning with the same pronoun: the hope the Ephesians have because God has called them; the fact that they are now part of the "riches" that constitute Christ's inheritance; and the greatness of God's power toward believers. At this point the writer employs hyperbole, piling up nouns for power, energy, might, and strength (v. 19). This power at work for believers is the same power that

---

1. Bonnie Bowman Thurston, *Reading Colossians, Ephesians, and 2 Thessalonians: A Literary and Theological Commentary* (New York: Crossroad, 1995), 99.

raised Christ from the dead and exalted him to God's right hand, above any and all other powers that the Ephesians may have been inclined to fear or to respect. Just as the Davidic monarch was promised that God would make his enemies his footstool (Ps. 110:1), our author assures the Ephesian believers that "all things" are ultimately submitted to Christ for his body, the church (Eph. 1:20–23).

The final four verses of the passage are what make it a reading for Ascension Day. God not only raised the Messiah from the dead, but also "seated him at [God's] right hand in the heavenly places" and subordinated to him all other powers and "every name that is named, not only in this age but also in the age to come" (vv. 20–21). The allusion, either to Philippians 2:9 or to a similar hymn that emphasized the power of the "name above every name," reminds the audience of the exaltation of the Messiah following his humble obedience.

The psalms appointed for the day stress the majestic reign of God (Ps. 93), who has "gone up with a shout" and "sits on [God's] holy throne" (Ps. 47:5, 8). The two New Testament narratives of the ascension (Luke 24:51; Acts 1:9) and this reading from Ephesians all point to the activity and sovereignty of God. Jesus is not said to have risen from the dead, but to have been raised by the God who "seated" Christ in the "heavenly places" and "put all things under his feet" (Eph. 1:20–22). Nor does Jesus ascend into heaven (as the creeds would later put it), but Jesus "was carried up into heaven" (Luke 24:51). Similarly, in Acts, Jesus "was lifted up" (Acts 1:9) and the "two men in white robes" who promise Jesus' return repeat the passive: "This Jesus, who has been taken up from you into heaven" (v. 11).

The narratives of the ascension, Luke 24:44–53 and Acts 1:1–11, account for the bodily absence of the risen Lord in the church's present and prepare for the compensatory presence and power of the Holy Spirit promised in Luke 24:49 and Acts 1:4–5, 8. The same promise is said to have been fulfilled in Ephesians 1:13, where it is the Holy Spirit whose seal marks the Ephesian believers and functions as the first installment of all Christians' inheritance. The

pronouns change from "we who first hoped in Christ" and "you [Gentiles] also" (Eph. 1:12–13) to "our" common inheritance (1:14). The passages from Luke–Acts stress the continuity with Jesus' Jewish followers, whose witness stands behind the narratives of his ministry, death, resurrection, and ascension. Ephesians celebrates the inclusion of Gentiles in the community of those who have been sealed by the Holy Spirit. Here, by contrast with Paul's undisputed letters, the church (*ekklēsia*) is not only a local group of believers, but includes all Christians in all times and places who constitute the body of which God has made Christ the head.[2]

Many themes of the Ephesian thanksgiving are picked up later in the letter. The prayer that closes out the first half of the letter (Eph. 3:14–21) repeats many of the ideas found in 1:15–23: riches, glory, power, strength, faith, and love. Again the author prays that they may understand (3:18) and know (3:19) what God has done for them and the depth of God's love for them.

The spiritual enlightenment that the author asks God to give the Ephesian believers stands in contrast with the darkness that engulfs their neighbors (called "Gentiles") who do not yet believe (4:18). The powers and authorities over whom Christ rules in the thanksgiving are shown to be the powers of death and disobedience that once ruled not only the Ephesians but all humanity (2:1–3). The God who raised Jesus from the dead and seated him "in the heavenly places" (1:20) has done the same for those who are "in Christ" (2:5–6). That this enlightenment and rescue are the gift of God is clear in the thanksgiving and elaborated on at length in 2:4–9. The hope that the author prays for God to make known to the Ephesians is a hope to which they had no access before God intervened (2:12). In the extended metaphor of the "armor of God" in 6:10–17, the Ephesian Christians are encouraged to make use of the power and strength available to them and mentioned in the thanksgiving. As the author gives thanks for their faith and love in the thanksgiving, they are to give thanks in their own prayers (5:20).

2. Thurston, 101.

Ephesians also echoes characterizations of God and God's people found throughout Scripture. People do not choose God but are chosen and called by God, not for their own merits, but because of God's unimaginable love. Christ is exalted and seated in the heavenly places, not in spite of his human vulnerability and suffering, but because of them. His ascension does not signal divine absence, but the abundant provision promised by the biblical witness.

SHARYN DOWD

Commentary 2: Connecting the Reading to the World

The church celebrates the ascension of the Lord Jesus to his heavenly throne, which Paul depicts here as a victory. In verse 22, God "has put all things under [Christ's] feet," a citation of Psalm 110:1, in which God installs his earthly king and grants him rule. This psalm was commonly cited by the early church as it proclaimed the triumph of Christ and the reality of his lordship. God acted powerfully not only to raise Jesus from the dead, but to make him ruler of all creation. This is an awesome reality in itself, worthy of celebration, but Paul sees this also as having great implications for the church's imagination and its practice.

God exalted Jesus Christ "far above all rule and authority and power and dominion" (Eph. 1:21), which indicates these entities are God's enemies that God defeated in the death and resurrection of Jesus. They are malignant powers that account for corruptions and perversions of human life, resulting in hostility between groups, oppression of some over others, and feelings of hopelessness and despair. Among these are racist ideologies that divide communities and the greed that drives people to mistreat others in their quest for more money and possessions. Everyone feels the effects of evil in the world, either in particular suffering or in general feelings of meaninglessness. Paul's message to the church is that the resurrection and ascension of Jesus Christ are good news for precisely these conditions of the world. He begins his letter by praying that God would enlighten "the eyes of your heart" (v. 18) so that they would truly see the great hope they have and the glorious calling of being "saints."

This text suggests an initial connection with the life and mission of the church regarding prayer. We often think of prayer as the time when we ask God for things, and we may even conceive of coming to church as a mere duty. Gathering as church, however, is a time of reorientation. We reset our lives and our minds toward God and remind ourselves of God's posture of love toward us and God's calling of us to love, bless, and offer hospitality to others. Gathering as church is for the purpose of imagination renovation. Our imagination, our capacity to conceptualize the world and our place within it, affects how we think and feel about ourselves and others. Our imaginations are naturally shaped by our culture's hopes, fears, and prejudices, and when we gather as church, we are helped to see God, ourselves, and the world as God does.

Prayer has the crucial function of calling upon God to help in this process of transforming our imaginations. We can pay special attention to each prayer during the service and ask how that prayer might redirect our minds and hearts. We might also pray short but meaningful prayers during the Eucharist or at other times during the service. Short prayers are often meaningful as they focus our thoughts and feelings. During the Eucharist, we might pray, "Lord, thank you for your love," or "Lord, this week, open my eyes to your wonder." Short prayers like these are memorable, reminding us throughout the week to notice the many blessings in our lives and the goodness in the world.

A second connection involves the ascension of Jesus Christ and the life of the church. God has appointed Jesus Christ as "head over all things for the church" (v. 22), and the church is the body of Christ on earth, the place where the spirit of Christ dwells (v. 23). Paul connects the exaltation of Christ with the church, which for some raises the ethical problem of the church's triumphal stance in culture over the last few centuries. The Western church has needed to come to terms with its exploitative posture toward the developing world in its colonial practices. Parts of Africa and Asia encountered a Christianity with exploitative business practices and oppressive politics. Christian faith for many was an experience of the malignant powers and rulers, not at all good news of hope and liberation.

Paul, however, is unembarrassed about the triumphant and militant language he deploys throughout this letter (see 6:10–18). This is because his exhortations are to a subversive way of life that is anything but triumphant. God triumphs over the evil powers corrupting God's good world in the death of Christ, which is paradoxical: God wins by losing. Paul experiences Christ's triumph by preaching as a shamed prisoner (3:2–13).

The church likewise enjoys the victorious presence of Christ by pursuing unity, humility, and becoming a community of ongoing, restorative justice. While the world enjoys triumph as triumphalism, the church embodies God's triumph in humility and service. God calls the church to adopt counterintuitive practices of love and service in order to experience God's victory in Christ. If we inhabit wealthier parts of town, we might consider how we can learn about ways the church has been an active participant in oppressive practices, such as neglecting the poor and dividing communities along racial and socioeconomic lines in the United States. We can name these realities and confess them as a church in prayer. Forgiveness follows confession, so we can celebrate God's grace, even as we become aware of the real dimensions of structural sin in our wider culture.

We can learn about ongoing dynamics of racism and how this takes place locally, so that we can name it and strategize regarding ways to counteract it. We can discuss as a church how to serve the least fortunate among us. We all have elderly people among us and those who have difficulty getting around. God's triumph is seen in a community prioritizing the least among us and making them the focus of day-to-day efforts of service and care.

A third connection comes in the personal realm. Paul prays for his audiences to have their eyes open to "the hope to which he has called you" (v. 18). This hope is the constant experience of God's presence among us in Christ, and the reality that when creation is renewed, we will inhabit a new world where the pain of physical and emotional wounds is healed. We are aware of the realities of how people hurt one another and how the vulnerable are mistreated. Such wounds leave lasting scars and hamper ongoing relationships and the ability of individuals to function fruitfully in the world. This is to say nothing of physical limitations.

We can invite one another to identify dynamics in their lives that generate despair and hopelessness. What messages does the world send that make us feel discouraged or hopeless? How do I feel about my identity when taking in social media, watching television, or just walking through my day? There are so many subtle but false identity-forming dynamics that affect us throughout the course of our lives.

The church is the institution in the world that is supposed to be a place of hope and relief, for it is the presence of Jesus Christ on earth. How might we speak to one another in ways that generate hope? We truly do participate together as a community that enjoys the presence of Christ on earth. How can this reality inform our identities in ways that give us life and open up vistas of promise and hopeful expectation? This should not at all be a sentimental or shallow practice. It may even come through the practice of prayerfully naming discouraging or painful aspects of our lives and expressing our longing that God would hasten the day when this pain or that grief is taken away, when God returns in Christ to make all things new.

TIMOTHY GOMBIS

Luke 24:44–53

[44]Then he said to them, "These are my words that I spoke to you while I was still with you—that everything written about me in the law of Moses, the prophets, and the psalms must be fulfilled." [45]Then he opened their minds to understand the scriptures, [46]and he said to them, "Thus it is written, that the Messiah is to suffer and to rise from the dead on the third day, [47]and that repentance and forgiveness of sins is to be proclaimed in his name to all nations, beginning from Jerusalem. [48]You are witnesses of these things. [49]And see, I am sending upon you what my Father promised; so stay here in the city until you have been clothed with power from on high."

[50]Then he led them out as far as Bethany, and, lifting up his hands, he blessed them. [51]While he was blessing them, he withdrew from them and was carried up into heaven. [52]And they worshiped him, and returned to Jerusalem with great joy; [53]and they were continually in the temple blessing God.

Commentary 1: Connecting the Reading with Scripture

Only Luke among the NT writers narrates the event of Jesus' heavenly ascension, and he does so twice: first, at the end of his Gospel (Luke 24:50–51), and then, with extra details, at the beginning of the book of Acts (Acts 1:9–11). In this two-volume framework, the ascension marks the critical hinge-point in God's mission of restoring a broken world through Christ, both consummating Jesus' earthly saving ministry and commencing an expanded phase of that mission to all nations through his Spirit-infused followers (Luke 24:47–49; Acts 1:8–11).

More immediately, Jesus' ascension culminates a breathtaking series of postresurrection encounters in Luke 24 involving various groups: (1) Mary Magdalene, Joanna, and other women disciples with "two men in dazzling clothes" (angelic messengers?) at Jesus' empty tomb (24:1–10); (2) Cleopas and companion (his wife?) with the risen Jesus himself on the Emmaus road, though they do not recognize him until he breaks bread with them in their home (24:13–32); and (3) the eleven apostles, Cleopas and associate, and other companions, likely including Mary Magdalene and the other women, with Jesus in a Jerusalem residence (24:33–49).

All these scenes negotiate tensions between Jesus' absence/presence and his followers' awareness/ignorance of his risen state and its significance. The living Lord pops in and out of rooms in startling fashion (24:31, 36–37). In the final visit, however, Jesus lingers to demonstrate his identity more clearly in word and deed and to delegate his mission to his coterie of disciples. Though opening with the conventional "Peace be with you," the risen Jesus' sudden appearance, as the group buzzes about the amazing report from Cleopas and his friend, fills them with anything but peaceful feelings. Taken utterly by surprise, they seize up with fear and doubt: are they hallucinating now, seeing some eerie ghostly apparition of Jesus? (vv. 36–38).

Jesus then offers not simply reasonable proof of life and identity, but tangible proof of his very own embodied life and identity: "It is I myself," he says emphatically, "in the flesh—real skin, blood, and bones, the whole human bit. Look, see for yourself; and go ahead, touch my hands and feet, if you like" (paraphrase of vv. 39–40). No ghostly, gnostic spook or spirit; this is the risen Jesus incarnate, the same Jesus who walked, talked, ate, and drank with them these past few years. Speaking of eating, Jesus reinforces his revealing demonstration with the remarkably ordinary act of requesting and consuming "a piece of broiled fish . . . in their presence" (vv. 41–43).

To be sure, the risen Jesus manifests some added powers of teleportation, to say nothing of conquering death! But he remains fully human, raised up in a human body, with the expressed purpose of continued dynamic relationship with other embodied persons, the terms of which he proceeds to outline to his now more joyful, but still "wondering" disciples (v. 41).

Jesus utters his final words to his disciples in Luke 24:44–49. Amid their wide-eyed mesmerism with his postcrucifixion/resurrection bodily presence, Jesus calls his confidants to attention and "opens their minds to understand" his words, focused on both seminal past instruction (review) and tantalizing future action (preview). In terms of past teaching that he communicated "while I was still with you [all]," Jesus homes in on its comprehensive scriptural foundation—spanning "Moses, the prophets, and the psalms" (representing the three parts of the Hebrew Bible: Torah, Nevi'im, and Kethuvim)—and personal fulfillment. Throughout his life Jesus sought not only to explain, but also to exhibit, to incarnate, to live out, to "fill full"/"fill out"/"fill up"[1] the Jewish Scriptures in his experience, reminding them of "everything written about me" (vv. 44–45).

Jesus does not, however, nostalgically reminisce about this Scripture-based experience, but rather proclaims it as completed reality with present and future effects: "It is written." It stands written now and forever (Greek perfect tense); and as the word of God for the people of God, it is also written for and about Jesus' followers. A triad of infinitive complements stresses the Messiah's scripted purpose "[1] to suffer and [2] to rise from the dead on the third day, and that [3] repentance and forgiveness of sins is to be proclaimed in his name to all nations" (vv. 46–47). The good news of Christ's restorative, reconciling death and resurrection is not for private, elite, or ethnocentric consumption, but rather for the whole world. It is

intentionally collaborative, in active partnership with the living Lord. Accordingly, Christ commissions his followers to proclaim God's saving word throughout the world from their own Scripture-rooted experience: "You [all] are witnesses of these things" (v. 48). Jesus' ambassadors can speak with authority, authenticity, and compassion only concerning what they know themselves from God's inscribed and incarnate word fulfilled in the suffering and living Christ.

But even then, they cannot hope to succeed by themselves, without continuing divine accompaniment and empowerment. Jesus has already hinted that his availability will be changing; the phrase "while I was still with you" (v. 44) implies impending absence. But the divine-human, heaven-earth connection that Jesus has solidified will by no means diminish if he is not "with" his disciples in the same way they have known to this point. Jesus promises to equip his witnesses with "power from on high [the heavenly sphere]." By all means they must wait in Jerusalem until they receive this dynamic endowment, this fresh "clothing" with divine energy before setting out from the Holy City to the "ends of the earth" (v. 47; Acts 1:8). As the book of Acts reports, they will not have to wait long for this high-voltage surge—in the person of the Holy Spirit, no less—not some amorphous special effect. Pentecost looms on the near horizon (Acts 1:4–5, 8; 2:1–4).

In Jesus' farewell acts, however, in Luke 24:50–53, his disciples get hit with another jolt before receiving the supercharged gift of the Spirit. Jesus' own imbuement with God's Spirit has been evident throughout his life and ministry (Luke 1:35; 3:22; 4:1, 18–19). He has already promised that the "heavenly Father" is "much more" than willing "to give the Holy Spirit to those who ask him" (11:13). Now the crucified-and-risen Jesus takes another monumental leap, solidifying his command of all the resources of heaven to equip his earthly witnesses for their evangelical mission. Nothing and no one stand still long in Luke's story: God's redemptive project moves persistently forward, outward, and upward.

---

1. John Goldingay, *Do We Need the New Testament? Letting the Old Testament Speak for Itself* (Downers Grove, IL: InterVarsity Press, 2015), 30–31.

In his last movements in this Gospel, Jesus leads his followers out of town to nearby Bethany, from where he "is carried up into heaven" (Luke 24:51; Acts 1:2, 9–11). Yet both before and while Jesus ascends, he blesses his disciples with uplifted hands, prompting their worship of Jesus, their return to Jerusalem, and their "continual blessing [of] God in the temple" (Luke 24:50–52). Note well the mutual blessing between God/Jesus and God's people. Though Jesus physically withdraws from his followers (24:51), these dramatic actions attending his ascension certify a persisting spiritual connection between Lord and disciples, God and people, heaven and earth, rooted in practices of joyous worship and gracious blessing.

The companion lectionary text in Acts 1:1–11, which opens Luke's second volume, adds the further promise from two attending divine messengers, perhaps the same pair as at the empty tomb, that Jesus "will come [again] in the same way as you saw him go into heaven" (Acts 1:11). In the meantime, however, Jesus' followers—then and now—need not fret or fear: their renewed fellowship with the living God—Father, Son, and Spirit—remains strong and vibrant on earth as it is in heaven.

F. SCOTT SPENCER

Commentary 2: Connecting the Reading to the World

This passage occurs at the end of Luke and serves as a preview to the book of Acts. At the ascension of the Lord, the community was facing a profound transition. What was the meaning of their Lord's death, and how did it fit into God's plan for the future? These questions shaped their identity for years to come and continue to shape our own witness.

In Luke 24:48, the assembly is described as "witnesses" to what Jesus had endured. They were called to witness to something they could barely understand: the death and resurrection of their Lord. Through witnessing, they engaged the trauma they faced at betraying him, their scriptural tradition that foretold his death, and forgiveness from sins as they shared with him at table. They witnessed an event but also witnessed to its meaning.

One important, though not exclusive, way to explore the text is in conversation with trauma studies, since this field offers new possibilities for interpreting this passage at this time in the liturgical year. The primary point is that, after betraying and abandoning their Lord, the church needed to make sense of trauma and begin to forgive themselves for betraying him, in order to witness to his resurrection. In her book *Spirit and Trauma*, Shelly Rambo explores how trauma interferes with the capacity to talk about experience afterward. Profound trauma disrupts memory and attention, and interferes with the ability to put experience into a story. This raises the question of how to witness to that which erases memory. Trauma is the fragmentation left behind by profound harm, threatening to disrupt witness.

Betrayal trauma is one of the most severe forms of trauma, since it ruptures interpersonal bonds. This is the kind of trauma Jesus and the disciples may have faced. Healing betrayal trauma often requires a long process that involves reestablishing trust and connection. As perpetrators of betrayal trauma, the disciples had to begin to feel forgiven before they could witness to the resurrection. In this context, part of the blessing offered to the disciples is an invitation to begin to forgive themselves for betraying their Lord. Experiencing self-forgiveness, an immediate pastoral concern at the heart of the good news, makes it possible for them to experience joy.

When Jesus commissions them to witness to his story, he instills in them hope by inviting them to proclaim the forgiveness of sins, and this constitutes a broadening of mission. As a pastoral concern, sin includes individual failing to live into God's promise, a falling short of the mark, but also a structural failing to meet the demands of God's justice. The preaching of the forgiveness of sins starts with the church, which always needs to repent. Because the church is forgiven, it has a reason to witness to the good news. In Luke's context, this means that the good news of the gospel is not the possession of only one people or spoken in only one language, but belongs to all people. By insisting that God forgives the world, the disciples share in a hope that God forgives them as well.

At the ascension, Jesus is taken from them. We might wonder if they experience a second loss after a recent tragedy. Yet their joy speaks to the fact that Jesus has been with them and helped them understand their loss. He blesses them, forgives them, and helps them move toward the future. They feel joy because they have been able to make sense of their trauma. Building on what they have already known, Jesus establishes an identity for this community beyond its trauma through giving them a blessing that makes witnessing possible. Taking them as far as Bethany—near the home of Mary and Martha, where he had been a frequent guest—he ascends and takes his wounds into the very heart of God, leaving the church behind to pray, worship, and proclaim.

The profound trauma of his death was not meaningless, but folded into a much larger meaning. Indeed, it fulfilled the Law, Prophets, and Psalms, the entire Hebrew Scripture. God's steadfast love for the Hebrew people is the larger frame in which Jesus' death can be understood. The witness of Scripture confirms that God is broader than human imagination, that people are part of a broader creation with purposeful significance, and that we are meant to live in relationships of justice that reflect God's mercy. The continuity with tradition paves the way for innovation. Luke starts with what is familiar—Jerusalem as the locus of God's action and God's Scripture as a testimony to covenant faithfulness—and then expands the vision to include repentance for all nations.

When God raises Jesus bodily from the dead, with the wounds of torture and crucifixion still in his flesh, God facilitates the disciples' meeting with Jesus in the flesh. Against the docetic notion that Jesus only appears to be raised, he is fully embodied but still bears scars, which helps the disciples seriously grapple with the suffering they have seen. It helps them both name what they have endured and also realize that, because God raised Jesus from the dead, there is hope in the midst of such death. The disciples have seen their Lord tortured and crucified, and now he stands before them, eating and drinking. It is important they experience their flesh-and-bones Lord at table.

When Jesus appears bodily with them and eats, it evokes the night of his betrayal, memorialized in the Lord's Supper, as it helps the disciples to experience grace. The connection with the sacrament can be highlighted if this text is preached along with communion. The one who was host at the Lord's Supper is now the guest when the disciples share food with their Lord and eat with him; through sharing this act of hospitality, their eyes are opened. As in the Lord's Supper the sign and seal of God's covenant with the church is made real, Jesus' broader purpose is made known through feasting. Eating what they feed him, he reincorporates into the body of believers the disciples who have betrayed him. In Luke's Gospel it is the disciples' faithful care for the risen Christ, feeding him meals, that helps them experience his presence fully.

According to Luke's Gospel, the ascension both confirms that Jesus Christ was resurrected by God and points to what this means for the church in a new liturgical season. The ascension creates the shape of the church, as Jesus' return to God grants the disciples a mandate to continue his mission, enabled by the Holy Spirit. The Eastern Orthodox celebrate the Feast of Ascension by exchanging the paschal greeting one final time. Ancient English churches beat the boundary rocks of the church during the Feast of Ascension, thereby marking its parameters and giving it shape in which to move into the future. These festivals indicate that the church gets a new opportunity with the ascension of their Lord, deeply wounded but nevertheless called to witness. The shape of the church that is initiated through the ascension helps make sense of the Law, Prophets, and Psalms, and helps the church to be forgiven of its sins, and thus to forgive the sins of others.

The ascension marks out the shape of the church that is called and equipped to act as witnesses. Through forgiveness of sins, sharing at Table, and calling to repentance, the risen Lord prepares the church for its key activities, fostering joy even in the midst of trauma.

PHILIP BROWNING HELSEL

Seventh Sunday of Easter

Acts 16:16–34
Psalm 97

Revelation 22:12–14, 16–17, 20–21
John 17:20–26

Acts 16:16–34

[16]One day, as we were going to the place of prayer, we met a slave-girl who had a spirit of divination and brought her owners a great deal of money by fortune-telling. [17]While she followed Paul and us, she would cry out, "These men are slaves of the Most High God, who proclaim to you a way of salvation." [18]She kept doing this for many days. But Paul, very much annoyed, turned and said to the spirit, "I order you in the name of Jesus Christ to come out of her." And it came out that very hour.

[19]But when her owners saw that their hope of making money was gone, they seized Paul and Silas and dragged them into the marketplace before the authorities. [20]When they had brought them before the magistrates, they said, "These men are disturbing our city; they are Jews [21]and are advocating customs that are not lawful for us as Romans to adopt or observe." [22]The crowd joined in attacking them, and the magistrates had them stripped of their clothing and ordered them to be beaten with rods. [23]After they had given them a severe flogging, they threw them into prison and ordered the jailer to keep them securely. [24]Following these instructions, he put them in the innermost cell and fastened their feet in the stocks.

[25]About midnight Paul and Silas were praying and singing hymns to God, and the prisoners were listening to them. [26]Suddenly there was an earthquake, so violent that the foundations of the prison were shaken; and immediately all the doors were opened and everyone's chains were unfastened. [27]When the jailer woke up and saw the prison doors wide open, he drew his sword and was about to kill himself, since he supposed that the prisoners had escaped. [28]But Paul shouted in a loud voice, "Do not harm yourself, for we are all here." [29]The jailer called for lights, and rushing in, he fell down trembling before Paul and Silas. [30]Then he brought them outside and said, "Sirs, what must I do to be saved?" [31]They answered, "Believe on the Lord Jesus, and you will be saved, you and your household." [32]They spoke the word of the Lord to him and to all who were in his house. [33]At the same hour of the night he took them and washed their wounds; then he and his entire family were baptized without delay. [34]He brought them up into the house and set food before them; and he and his entire household rejoiced that he had become a believer in God.

Commentary 1: Connecting the Reading with Scripture

At points, Acts has turned into an action movie. Prison breaks! Shipwrecks! Escapes! A snake leaping from a fire! Here, Acts brings us to the colonial city of Philippi and tells a rollicking account of healing, persecution, and liberation. Part of the challenge of preaching texts like these is emulating or at least communicating the lively feel of these texts. This story embraces delight as a mode of edification.[1] We can learn *and* be entertained. We can be shaped as a

---

1. See Richard L. Pervo, *Profit with Delight: The Literary Genre of the Acts of the Apostles* (Philadelphia: Fortress Press, 1987).

community even as our senses and imaginations are engaged.

The public reading of this text might prove vital to preaching it. Sometimes we assume that the reading of Scripture has to be intensely serious—and it is. However, the Bible is also comfortable with humor, familiar with spectacle, and unafraid to entertain. To what end? Where does this lively tale take us?

The lectionary drops us into the middle of the action in Acts 16:16. In verse 9, "a man of Macedonia" beckons the Pauline retinue, which arrives in Philippi, a city characterized in verse 12 by its importance and its colonial status. Both are important in understanding a dispute whose roots start in verse 16.

After Paul finds success at a place of prayer outside the city (vv. 13–15), the economics and politics of the city intercede. On their way out of the city, there is "a slave-girl who had a spirit of divination and brought her owners a great deal of money by fortune-telling" (v. 16). In this description, this unnamed woman is but a commodity, a profitable product. Though Paul heals her, he seems to do so more out of annoyance and frustration than compassion (v. 18). She correctly names who they are ("slaves of the Most High God," v. 17), but Paul, for whatever reason, cannot stand her statements. Is he simply frustrated at her presence? Is he offended by her use and even abuse in this profit making? Is it her association with fortune-telling that precipitates this reaction? Acts simply does not tell us. She disappears from the narrative as quickly as she emerges in it. In some ways, the narrative uses her only as long as she is "profitable" in advancing the story.

We might expect that her owners would bring a complaint against Paul's ending of a profitable business. She could be the lead witness, having lost her ability to soothsay. Instead, their motives for profit and their loss lead to a very different kind of accusation: "These men are disturbing our city; they are Jews and are advocating customs that are not lawful for us as Romans to adopt or observe" (v. 21). Notice the absence of any mention of the slave girl or the loss of a lucrative business. Instead, these slave owners accuse Paul and Silas of being Jews who

are disrupting the city's Roman identity. The accusation has shifted from finances to identity, from profitability to ethnocentrism.

An agitated crowd joins in the flogging and imprisonment of Paul and Silas. Despite their priding themselves as the best of Rome, this mob in its mentality belies the charges. This colonial extension of Roman power falls short of its own ideals.

God's verdict against this miscarriage of justice becomes quickly evident. Paul and Silas sing deep into the night, a faithful display of resistance in chains. We may recall the closing words of Acts, when Paul finds himself in prison yet "unencumbered" or "without hindrance" (28:31). Paul and Silas will momentarily find themselves wholly unencumbered. An earthquake rattles the prison, opening wide the doors and loosening the chains of all the prisoners. The prison guard fears this breach will be seen as his deadly dereliction of duty. About to sentence himself to death, Paul intercedes, stopping his hand, but also sharing the good news with the guard and *his house*. This detail is a vivid reminder that our notions about salvation are often too narrowly circumscribed; the power of Jesus' presence is such that entire households are drawn into God's grace by the Spirit. Faith in Luke–Acts is far more communal and collective than it is individualistic. Thanks to an earthquake and the God to whom Paul and Silas sang while in chains, the power of the Philippian mob is muted.

The lectionary closes with this triumph of God and God's servants over an unruly crowd and Roman injustice, but the story continues through the end of chapter 16. The next day the local officials, seeking to sweep away quietly the previous day's events, command the release of Paul and Silas (v. 37). Paul will have none of it and pulls a trump card. Both he and Silas are not just innocent of the charges brought by a hostile crowd. They cannot simply be demonized by the crowd's appealing to their ethnic identity as Jews. No. In a narrative surprise, Paul declares that they are Romans. They cannot be charged with being anti-Roman, for they are Romans themselves![2]

2. See Eric D. Barreto, *Ethnic Negotiations: The Function of Race and Ethnicity in Acts 16* (Tübingen: Mohr Siebeck, 2010), 139–80.

On Your Mercy Alone Rests My Hope

Late have I loved you, O Beauty so old and so new: late have I loved you! And look! You were within me, and I was outside myself: and it was there that I searched for you. In my unloveliness I plunged into the lovely things which you created: you were with me, but I was not with you. Those created things kept me far away from you: yet if they had not been in you, they would have not been at all. You called and shouted: and broke through my deafness. You flamed and shone: and banished my blindness. You breathed your fragrance on me: and I drew in my breath and I pant for you. I have tasted you: and now I hunger and thirst for more. You have touched me: and I have burned for your peace.

When I cleave to you with all that I am, I shall experience no more pain and toil, and my whole life will be alive, because it is filled with you. But now (given that anyone you fill, you raise up) I am a burden to myself, because I am not filled with you. Joys I ought to weep over are at war with sorrows that I should rejoice in: and which side will gain the victory I have no idea. But sorrows that are corrupt are also at war in me with joys that are good: and which side will gain the victory I have no idea. Me, Lord!—have mercy upon me!—pity me! Look, I cannot conceal my wounds. You are the doctor, I am the patient: you are full of pity, I am pitiful. Surely human life on earth is a time of trial? Who would long for troubles and difficulties? You tell us to endure them, not to enjoy them. No one loves the thing they must endure, even if they love the act of enduring. Even though they are glad that they can endure, they would prefer that there was no need for such endurance. When I am in adversity I long for prosperity; when I enjoy prosperity I fear adversity. What is the mean between these two extremes, where human life need not be a trial? To hell with worldly prosperity, once and for all, with its fear of adversity and corruption of delight! To hell with worldly adversity once, and again, and for all, with its longing for prosperity, both because adversity is harsh in itself, and to prevent its breaking down endurance! Surely human life on earth is a time of interminable trial?

On your exceedingly great mercy alone rests my entire hope. Give what you command, and command what you will.

Augustine, ed. and trans. Carolyn J.-B. Hammond, *Confessions, Book 10, 27–29,* Loeb Classical Library, vol. 27 (Cambridge, MA: Harvard University Press, 2016), 135–37.

For many scholars, Acts was written, at least in part, to prove that Christians were not a threat to Rome or perhaps that Rome was no threat to Christians. This narrative suggests that such accommodations to Roman power are not in the purview of this particular pericope. The gospel is a disruptive force but not in the way the merchants forward and the mob embraces. The disruptive effect of the gospel is more subtle but no less powerful. The gospel reveals injustice. The gospel makes clear the folly of imperial systems. The gospel does not tear down empires; it merely shows how empires are already teetering at the edge of destruction.

This story is told by delighting us with thrilling scenes. Acts entertains, to shape the identity of its readers. Perhaps the jailer can help us understand the dynamics of empire in his life and ours. That he has failed his duties marks an end to his life as he knows it. Empire has so shaped his identity that his very being is tied into the completion of his duties. Empire has taught him that his very worth depends on his function in the machinery of Rome. We no longer live under an empire akin to Rome, yet we have not escaped the clutches of imperial forces. As I have argued elsewhere,

> it may be more helpful to imagine the central meaning of empire not in its symbolic representations or its most explicit manifestations. Empires are more ideological than they are physical. Or better yet, the manifestation of empire is deeply rooted in all-encompassing ideologies. And so, we might define "empire" as an external system of identity and belonging that predetermines our way of life so much so that the system seems natural and inherent but is actually constructed

and ultimately destructive to human life. In short, empire is not defined by thrones, emperors, and armies but by the many ways in which empire shapes how we view the world and how we live in it.[3]

This is serious business taken up in this narrative of imaginative delights. What empires hold us still? What all-encompassing ideologies seek to define our identities over against a God who has created us? Perhaps these stories of annoyed healings, unjust punishment, escape, and restitution are not just a delightful distraction but a glimpse into the transformative power of the gospel.

ERIC D. BARRETO

Commentary 2: Connecting the Reading with the World

Philippi was a thriving Roman city, a trading center at the intersection of culture, religion, and economics. Paul's "healing" of a slave girl disrupted commerce, depriving the slave girl's owners of their profits, leading to the imprisonment of Paul and Silas. To describe Paul's action as healing might be a stretch, since it is not clear that the "spirit of divination" troubles the girl. The spirit seems to give her the ability to recognize truth when she sees it: "these men are slaves of the Most High God, who proclaim to you a way of salvation" (Acts 16:17). This spirit might better be classified as a gift, since it seems to enhance the slave girl's abilities rather than make her life more miserable.

Paul rids the slave girl of her spirit, but not out of compassion or concern for her well-being. He is "very much" annoyed by the irritating vocalizations that follow him around Philippi (v. 18). So he orders the spirit to "come out." It is remarkable that the church's ministry here is marked by less than pure motivations. The power that Jesus has granted to the church is not wielded by "holier-than-thou gurus" always looking out for what is best for others. It is wielded by apostles who get annoyed and use their power in their own self-interest.

Paul's impulsive act is troubling and exciting. It is troubling to concede the church can be rash in its exercise of power with less than pure motivations. It is also exciting to see what God seems to do with this kind of power, even when unleashed in less than strategic ways. When our motives are mixed, God can still use our actions to disrupt and transform. It can be helpful to review a congregation's history to see the times when impetuous decisions, even those driven by impure motivations, generated unexpected blessing for the church or the people it serves.

Paul's decision leads to trouble. It lands Silas and him in jail, a place most of us would not describe as "blessing." Most of us are trained to avoid trouble, but the church in Acts thrives on it. Public conflict is the arena where the gospel thrives the most, where powers and principalities are exposed for their malicious intent or hypocrisy, thereby setting the stage for God's alternative. The church that gets itself in trouble with powerful forces finds the gospel message much easier to preach.

Those powerful forces in Philippi counted on free-flowing trade and the ability of those with wealth to pursue more of it. We are reminded that the gospel cannot be limited to private spheres. It has social, political, and economic ramifications. Sometimes the healing that the church brings is a threat to the status quo.

A pastor in Dundalk, MD, landed herself in trouble on the front page of the newspaper for the congregation's decision allowing homeless men and women to camp on church grounds. Local business owners and the neighborhood association pressured the local government to act. A $12,000 fine was levied against the small church. The pastor told a reporter, "I'm not trying to be adversarial with anyone. We're just trying to do what a church is called to do, and that's to love people. In Scripture, it

3. Eric D. Barreto, ed. Adam Winn, *An Introduction to Empire in the New Testament* (Atlanta: Society of Biblical Literature, 2016), 109.

talks about feeding the hungry, clothing the naked, visiting the sick. Whatever we've done to the least of these, it's as if we've done it to Christ himself."[4] This one spontaneous sermon preached on a news site reached into thousands of homes that day with unusual clarity and conviction.

The gospel's best pulpits are created in public conflict, where God's power confronts competing powers and offers a compelling alternative. The gospel does not need to be dressed up or marketed or better translated to our Philippian audiences. It needs to be proclaimed fearlessly in a world of powerful interests. Brett McCracken, an author and millennial, wrote a *Washington Post* article warning Christians not to go down their hipster road of trying to make the church cool. "As a twenty-something, I can say with confidence that when it comes to church, we don't want cool as much as we want real."[5]

This is the central argument of Acts. The church thrives when it comes into conflict with the world around it. This fearlessness is rooted in a resurrection faith whose adherents no longer worry about death. Faith here is not so much an idea as it is fuel to live confidently in an insecure world. That faith is tested in Acts as apostles suffer because of their actions. Paul and Silas are "attacked," given a "severe" flogging with rods, and thrown in jail (vv. 22–23). Yet in every situation they find another opportunity to preach.

Such a word challenges congregations to spend less time managing internal structures and more time wielding gospel power in the world. Paul's reckless exercise of that power underscores how deeply God wants the church to engage the world. We are encouraged to get in trouble with the world, trusting that God will magnify our imperfect actions toward more perfect ends. In fact, every time disciples in the book of Acts challenge powers and suffer as a result, the church seems to add to its numbers.

The jailer and his household are perfect examples. The jailer first learns of the good news of Jesus Christ not from a pew, but from observing the power of God accompany brave disciples. The good news is preached not from a stationary pulpit but on the go, from disciples living their faith under pressure, under threat. Conversion is not a program or a strategy but the natural outcome of the fearless proclamation of the gospel. An inventory of the percentage of time today's church leaders spend maintaining internal structures versus the percentage spent getting in trouble with the gospel may help a congregation rediscover the joy of our evangelical faith.

In Philippi, Paul's action interferes with the profits of the slave girl's handlers. It is important to notice that the slave girl, the one who has harbored or endured this spirit, is silent in the text. We do not know whether she is upset over Paul's action, or freed from a repressive situation. Her voice is silent, while those profiting from her now-departed gift have agency and voice. Those who profit off another's gift now slander Paul and Silas, manipulating ethnic and religious prejudices ("They are Jews and are advocating customs that are not lawful for us as Romans to adopt or observe," vv. 20–21) to serve their own ends. This is how powerful interests often operate in our world. They find ways to silence the voices of those on the bottom rungs of society most affected by economic injustice. Meanwhile, divisions between peoples are exacerbated in order to distract those peoples from recognizing their common connections and unifying for the common good.

Fear is the main tool of powers and principalities—the fear of suffering and the fear of death. This is why resurrection proclamation is so threatening to empire. When death no longer holds sway over our actions, disciples are free to confront and challenge powers opposed to God. The witness of Acts is that such confrontations lead to conversions and strengthen the church to engage the world even more deeply. The prisons that hold us with fear crumble, God wins new converts, and the church is given new disciples and new life.

ANDREW FOSTER CONNORS

4. "Maryland Church Ordered to Evict Homeless or Pay Fine," Brandon Abrosino, *Yahoo News Service*, December 18, 2016; https://www.yahoo.com/news/maryland-church-ordered-to-evict-homeless-or-pay-12000–fine-101323402.html.

5. Brett McCracken, "Can Hipster Christianity Save Churches from Decline?" *Washington Post*, July 27, 2015.

Seventh Sunday of Easter

Psalm 97

¹The LORD is king! Let the earth rejoice;
  let the many coastlands be glad!
²Clouds and thick darkness are all around him;
  righteousness and justice are the foundation of his throne.
³Fire goes before him,
  and consumes his adversaries on every side.
⁴His lightnings light up the world;
  the earth sees and trembles.
⁵The mountains melt like wax before the LORD,
  before the Lord of all the earth.

⁶The heavens proclaim his righteousness;
  and all the peoples behold his glory.
⁷All worshipers of images are put to shame,
  those who make their boast in worthless idols;
  all gods bow down before him.
⁸Zion hears and is glad,
  and the towns of Judah rejoice,
  because of your judgments, O God.
⁹For you, O LORD, are most high over all the earth;
  you are exalted far above all gods.

¹⁰The LORD loves those who hate evil;
  he guards the lives of his faithful;
  he rescues them from the hand of the wicked.
¹¹Light dawns for the righteous,
  and joy for the upright in heart.
¹²Rejoice in the LORD, O you righteous,
  and give thanks to his holy name!

Connecting the Psalm with Scripture and Worship

In the first reading appointed for this Sunday, Acts 16, Paul and Silas exorcize a pagan sibyl, suffer a beating from the civil authorities, are imprisoned for spreading the word, and, in the aftermath of an earthquake, convert and baptize their jailer. Psalm 97 provides a most appropriate response to this set of adventures.

Some worshipers may recall that Psalm 97 is appointed also for Christmas dawn (Christmas Proper II). On that day, especially verse 11, "light dawns for the righteous," gives us a song for the early morning of the birth of Jesus, who comes to reign as God among us. On the Seventh Sunday of Easter, the Sunday after the Ascension, our joining in one of the enthronement psalms gives us words to praise Christ, who after the resurrection and his ascension to the right hand of God is enthroned as king over all the earth.

In the reading from Acts, Paul and Silas exorcize a pagan sibyl, thus lessening the livelihood of the woman's owners. Verse 7 of Psalm 97 responds to this part of the narrative: "All worshipers of images," "worthless idols," are silenced by the word of the risen Christ issuing from the preaching of the apostles. Although Paul and Silas are beaten and imprisoned, God "rescues them from the hand of the wicked" (Ps. 97:10) by sending an earthquake that overpowers the might of the Roman prison system. Gathered together at Sunday worship, we acknowledge God's supreme authority over the cosmos in the words of the theophany in Psalm 97:2–6: God is manifest in clouds, darkness, fire that "consumes his adversaries on every side," lightnings, and mountains that "melt like wax." Paul and Silas convert and baptize the jailer, and our psalm concludes with "joy for the upright in heart" (v. 11), and together with Paul, Silas, the jailer, and his family, we "give thanks" to God's holy name, made known to all the world through our testimony to Christ's resurrection. When we hear that the jailer "called for lights," we might smile to think of the light of Christ shining forth from the empty tomb and lighting our way to life in God, from the vigil of Easter to the candles on the table of the Lord.

Perhaps some worshipers are interested less in the surprising similarity of details in Acts 16 and Psalm 97 and more in the underlying themes of Psalm 97 at this time before Pentecost. To find words to proclaim the sovereignty of Christ, the church came to apply the ancient Israelite enthronement psalms to the birth, resurrection, and ascension of Christ. This is one thing that is meant by referring to the New Testament as a gloss on the Old. The ancient Jews praised their chieftain, and also their God, as king, and Christians borrow that language to praise Christ as sovereign over all. As we experienced in singing Psalm 47 on Ascension Day, the throne room of this king is "far above all gods," on a level of existence far above our own.

A second example of such Christian borrowing of ancient Jewish imagery is the pattern in the New Testament concerning divine theophany. Throughout the Hebrew Scriptures, God's presence is revealed in the overwhelming manifestations of nature—volcano, lightning, thunder, rainstorm, rainbow—and these same natural phenomena are hidden in the stories about Jesus: the heavens that opened at his baptism, the earthquakes that Matthew records at his death and resurrection, the cloud into which Jesus ascends. Thus, when as Christians we sing in Psalm 97:2 of thick darkness around the king, we are, it seems to me, to think of Golgotha and the darkness that the Synoptics say covered all the land at the time of Jesus' death. Such scriptural theophanies must raise questions in the minds of contemporary believers, schooled in scientific explanations for nature. So, do we continue to believe that God sends floods, or ever did, as punishment? Is this idea central to our faith, or merely a reminder of how different was the spirituality of our forebears in the faith?

Another example from Psalm 97 of Christian use of Hebrew phraseology has to do with "all gods." Ancient Israelites maintained a religious belief now termed henotheism. According to henotheism, all nations and lands have, of course, their own gods, who are appropriate to the specific weather patterns and food production of those areas. Yet in henotheistic understanding, our god is better than all those other gods, and in our area of the world, only our god is to be honored. So, in Psalm 97, "all gods bow down before him." Recall the first commandment: "you shall have no other gods before me."

Christian theology built not upon henotheism, but rather upon the later monotheism of the exilic prophets, according to which the God of the Hebrews was the only god that existed. According to monotheism, it is not so much lack of loyalty to one's own but, rather, stupidity that would impel a person to worship some other deity who was said by outsiders to hold divine might.

Ancient henotheism is present in Psalm 97, and in our time provides basis for thoughtful conversation. In our time, is the church now inserted back into henotheism? Despite our theological claim of monotheism, many Christians find themselves willing to grant that other deities, or at least other names of the unknowable divine, are quite alive, but that as Christians, we are called to proclaim the triune God as the one God over all. What is the meaning in our mouths in Sunday worship of the psalmist's talk of "other gods"? Do we think of these gods as genuine objects of devotion, or merely as "worthless idols" (v. 7)?

So much to reflect upon in this one psalm.

GAIL RAMSHAW

Seventh Sunday of Easter

Revelation 22:12–14, 16–17, 20–21

¹²"See, I am coming soon; my reward is with me, to repay according to everyone's work. ¹³I am the Alpha and the Omega, the first and the last, the beginning and the end."

¹⁴Blessed are those who wash their robes, so that they will have the right to the tree of life and may enter the city by the gates. . . .
¹⁶"It is I, Jesus, who sent my angel to you with this testimony for the churches. I am the root and the descendant of David, the bright morning star."

¹⁷The Spirit and the bride say, "Come."
And let everyone who hears say, "Come."
And let everyone who is thirsty come.
Let anyone who wishes take the water of life as a gift. . . .

²⁰The one who testifies to these things says, "Surely I am coming soon."
Amen. Come, Lord Jesus!
²¹The grace of the Lord Jesus be with all the saints. Amen.

Commentary 1: Connecting the Reading with Scripture

These verses from the Revelation of John form the epistolary reading for the Seventh Sunday of Easter in Year C. The other readings are Acts 16:16–34; Psalm 97; and John 17:20–26. The Seventh Sunday of Easter is the final Sunday before Pentecost. In this position, it looks back to the resurrection of Christ and forward to the gift of the Spirit to the church.

The readings from Revelation are selected from 22:6–21, sometimes called by commentators the book's epilogue. This epilogue or summary of the apocalypse-within-a-letter is composed of a series of sayings and exhortations that point to some of the main themes of Revelation as a whole. Since the lectionary reading has been created by selecting some verses from 22:6–21 and leaving out others, it cannot be examined as a literary whole. This commentary will focus, then, on the included sayings and exhortations and the way they echo earlier parts of Revelation and relate to the other readings for the day.

Revelation 22:12–14 begins with an announcement and a promise (v. 12) followed

by the basis for the promise (v. 13). The words "I am coming soon" appear in Revelation 3:11; 22:7; 22:12; and 22:20. The promise in verse 12b is the promise of judgment and reward. The claim of the risen Christ to be "the Alpha and the Omega" echoes Revelation 1:8 and 1:17; it appears again in 21:6. The claim in Revelation 1:8 makes clear that this is a claim to divinity, since it is followed by "says the Lord God, who is and who was and who is to come, the Almighty." Thus "Christ will judge because he is divine."[1] The psalm appointed for the day praises YHWH the king for the "righteousness and justice" on which God's rule is based.

"Those who wash their robes" (v. 14) is a reference to Revelation 7:9–14, where the visionary learns that the "great multitude that no one could count, from every nation, from all tribes and peoples and languages, standing before the throne and before the Lamb, robed in white, with palm branches in their hands" are "they who have come out of the great ordeal; they have washed their robes and made them

1. Charles H. Talbert, *The Apocalypse: A Reading of the Revelation of John* (Louisville, KY: Westminster John Knox Press, 1994), 107.

white in the blood of the Lamb." The reading from Acts 16:16–34 records the conversion of the Philippian jailer after Paul and Silas have undergone, not "the great ordeal," but a foretaste of that final persecution. Their suffering is followed by the addition of an entire family to the multinational throng of worshipers before the throne of the slaughtered and risen Lamb. This innumerable multitude of the redeemed gain access to the tree of life—the access that humanity forfeited by the idolatry of the self (Gen. 3:22–24).

This lectionary reading omits Revelation 22:15, which balances the promise of entry into the new Jerusalem for the redeemed with the promise of exclusion of idolaters and covenant-breakers. This is the warning issued in the letters to the churches against assimilation to the idolatrous culture of the Roman Empire.[2] The same promise of judgment is found in Psalm 97:7: "All worshipers of images are put to shame, those who make their boast in worthless idols."

Revelation 22:16–17 refers again to the beginning of the document, where the title is "Jesus Messiah" (Rev. 1:1). In verse 16 Jesus' messiahship is indicated by the phrase "descendant of David." By adding "I am the root" before "descendant of David," the visionary makes a claim similar to that of "Alpha and Omega." Jesus was before David ("root") and has the qualifications to rule as one from the Davidic line. Again Jesus is the one who has sent his angel with a message in 1:1. The message is to John and through him to "the churches" (22:16); here the angel brings "this testimony" "to you" (plural), probably indicating the churches.

The "bright morning star" in verse 16 is used only here as an appellation for God or Jesus, and it is not the single word *phōsphoros* (in Latin, *lucifer*) or *eosphoros*, both used in secular Greek for the planet Venus rising in the morning. Rather, John uses an entire phrase: "the star, the shining one, the dawn." This appears to be a different usage from that of 2 Peter 1:19, where "when the day dawns" is parallel to "the morning star [*phōsphoros*] rises in your hearts" and seems to refer to the *parousia*, or the return of Christ. The *parousia* may also be what is

promised to the faithful in the church at Thyatira in Revelation 2:28, who will be given "the morning star" (*ton astera ton prōinon*). In Isaiah 14:12 LXX the "morning star" (*eosphoros*) that falls from heaven is likely Babylon; of course, this passage becomes in later church teaching a reference to Satan's (Lucifer's) expulsion from the presence of God.

The return of Christ is prayed for in 22:17, where the Spirit and the bride (the church), as well as all who hear the message, read aloud in worship and cry out, "Come" (singular imperative, addressed to Jesus). The third invitation in verse 17, to "everyone who is thirsty" or who "wishes [to] take the water of life as a gift," echoes a theme heard in the lament of Jeremiah. The people have forsaken God, "the fountain of living water" (Jer. 17:13), and "dug out cisterns for themselves, cracked cisterns that can hold no water" (Jer. 2:13).

Passages like Revelation 22:17 are the evidence that some interpreters regard as proof of a connection between this document and the Fourth Gospel. In John 7:37–39 Jesus cries out at the Festival of Booths, "Let anyone who is thirsty come to me, and let the one who believes in me drink. As the scripture has said, 'Out of the believer's heart shall flow rivers of living water.'" This echoes John 4:10 and 4:14 and recalls Isaiah 12:3; 44:3; and especially 55:1, where the thirsty are invited to come and drink "without money and without price," just as in Revelation 22:17, where the water of life is "a gift."

The final promise and benediction of Revelation and, indeed, of the Christian Scripture as a whole, is found in Revelation 22:20–21. The promise of 3:11; 22:7; and 22:12 is repeated: "I am coming soon." The author, and presumably the audience, respond, "Amen. Come, Lord Jesus!" Finally, the author pronounces the benediction: "The grace of the Lord Jesus be with all the saints. Amen."

The expectation of the imminent return of Christ is characteristic of most of the New Testament writings, particularly the Gospels and the letters of Paul. That is because the resurrection of Christ is, by definition, an apocalyptic event.

2. Talbert, 11–12, 17, 19, 20, 25.

These readings from Revelation are appropriate for Eastertide because the resurrection changed everything. It marked the defeat of death and made possible access to the tree of life. It meant that the power of sin was broken as surely as the chains of Paul and Silas in the Philippian jail were broken (Acts 16:16–34). The resurrection guaranteed that the prayer of Jesus in John 17:20–26 would be answered and that those who came to trust the good news through the witness of the apostles would ultimately be united with each other, with the Father, and with the Son. It meant that Caesar was not Lord and that the Roman culture of excess, domination, and idolatry was doomed and, therefore, was not to be imitated by the churches but, on the contrary, was to be resisted.

SHARYN DOWD

Commentary 2: Connecting the Reading to the World

It is the Easter season, the time of the Christian year when the church lives in the shadow of God's victory in Christ over death. We continue to celebrate this victory by looking back on that day of triumph, and looking ahead to the day when God completes this victory by making all things new at the return of Christ. This text at the end of Revelation closes the Christian canon with a note of hopeful anticipation.

A first connection comes between this text and the liturgical calendar. It reminds us that the orientation of Christian life is toward hope, since God has struck a devastating blow to the powers of sin and death in the death and resurrection of Christ. The ongoing life of the church takes place in light of an overpowering victory, one that God accomplished over the powers that have devastated God's world. Though they continue to cause immense damage to creation and to humanity, God has opened up a horizon of hope that fires our hearts with eager expectation of that coming day of final triumph when God makes all things new.

Living after Easter and before the consummation of all things is a liberating experience. We do not have to deny our pains and the tragic suffering and loss that many of us experience. We are welcome to freely name our pains, tragedies, and suffering as those aspects of our sojourn through this world that God has known in the incarnation of Jesus Christ. These are the very parts of human experience that God has triumphed over and will one day completely overcome in the renewal of all things. God's action took place in the cross of Jesus Christ, a gritty, unjust, and awful reality.

That was the means of giving birth to the hope that animates the church. So too Jesus' suffering and victory dignify our suffering and give us hope of fully and finally participating in the triumph of God.

The words of Jesus in the beginning of this passage suggest a second connection: "See, I am coming soon; my reward is with me, to repay according to everyone's work" (Rev. 22:12). At the coming day of God's renewal of creation, there will indeed be a judgment when God rewards everyone according to their work—that is, according to the life they have lived. This might immediately cause anxiety in the hearts of many, causing them to wonder if they have indeed done enough or been good enough, so that when they are judged, they will pass the test of God's examination of their lives.

It is helpful to remind people that God is not looking for high performers or exceptionally heroic acts. Genuine Christian conduct consists in confessing sin, giving thanks to God for all things in Christ, and participating in the church in ways that take advantage of opportunities to serve and offer hospitality to the needy. Pastors can point to the prayer of confession in the liturgy as one opportunity to do a significant Christian "work." When we say the prayer of confession together, pay attention to what we are saying with an open heart to areas of our life where we have left something undone that we ought to have done, or where we have done something that we ought not to have done. Open this area up to God in prayer, silently agreeing with God about it and giving thanks for God's forgiveness and cleansing. An important part of this is to think about small ways to bring about change in this area.

Another important "work" that God rewards is giving thanks, naming the areas of our lives as gifts from God. A Christian sees her life differently from someone who is not a Christian. It is not that she is morally superior or better than anyone else; rather, what sets her apart is that she is grateful to God in Christ for the good things in her life and sees them as gifts. Again, this is a small way we can remind people that doing things that are Christian and that count as works are not beyond us, but are basic and simple, though crucial, components of Christian identity.

Revelation also reminds us of some other aspects of social and ethical living. Throughout this important, though often mystifying, biblical book, warnings are sounded about the economic injustices of the world and the social inequalities that result in the oppression of marginalized groups. Down the years of the church's history, the book of Revelation has inspired and comforted the victims of injustice. This is one of the main targets of the judgment that God in Christ will bring about at his coming. This is very good news, as it is a relief to so many who are crushed by the economic hardships in our world. It also should serve as a warning to those of us who are comfortable or who have enjoyed privileges denied to others.

It would be helpful to read the works of both Christians and non-Christians who are working on issues of social justice, such as refugee resettlement, care for immigrants, racial justice, and gender discrimination. How do some of our mundane practices—where we buy groceries and clothes—help to produce unsafe or inhospitable working conditions and contribute to the suffering of others? How can we begin to make small changes in our daily habits that will lead to the flourishing of creation and of other people? Again, the warning that Jesus Christ will repay according to everyone's work is meant to provoke us to think about how we can make small changes that stem from our Christian confession.

A third connection is an ecclesial one, considering the mission of the church as a people who express the longing for renewal, on behalf of creation itself, ourselves, and the rest of humanity. In the middle of this text, the Spirit and the bride—the church—say, "Come" (v. 17). That is, the church's task is to pray for the coming of Jesus Christ. The Spirit of God is also praying this. This is a striking window into the very heart of God, into the emotional drama going on inside the Trinity. God will one day send Jesus Christ to judge, save, and renew creation. God the Spirit is also longing for this to take place!

We can assure our churches that as we live with this future focus on the day when creation will be made new, we are participating with God in God's own longing for creation to be set right. We do not have to cajole or manipulate God to do this, as this flows from God's own desires for creation's flourishing. We might consider portraying this great hope for our people and then inviting them to share their sorrows, pains, and frustrations. As they mention or share specifics, we can pause to affirm and celebrate that this specific pain or sorrow will be reversed so that those affected can enjoy renewal and relief. These are all aspects of our experience that God is longing to heal, to restore, and to renew. We can draw comfort and assurance that God is indeed with us as we live in light of the victory of Easter and in hope of God's coming ultimate and consummating triumph.

TIMOTHY GOMBIS

John 17:20–26

²⁰"I ask not only on behalf of these, but also on behalf of those who will believe in me through their word, ²¹that they may all be one. As you, Father, are in me and I am in you, may they also be in us, so that the world may believe that you have sent me. ²²The glory that you have given me I have given them, so that they may be one, as we are one, ²³I in them and you in me, that they may become completely one, so that the world may know that you have sent me and have loved them even as you have loved me. ²⁴Father, I desire that those also, whom you have given me, may be with me where I am, to see my glory, which you have given me because you loved me before the foundation of the world.

²⁵"Righteous Father, the world does not know you, but I know you; and these know that you have sent me. ²⁶I made your name known to them, and I will make it known, so that the love with which you have loved me may be in them, and I in them."

Commentary 1: Connecting the Reading with Scripture

In the Christian tradition, the Lord's Prayer in Matthew 6:9–13, with a shorter version in Luke 11:2–4, has overshadowed the more personal and extended Lord's prayer in John 17:1–26. Apart from its greater length, the comparative neglect of John's version may owe to its focus on what Jesus prays for himself and his followers, rather than on how his followers should pray with him, though, of course, as their Lord, Jesus' prayer still serves as a model for disciples. This fullest recording of Jesus' passionate supplication to his Father in the Gospels requires careful attention.

Jesus utters his distinctive prayer in John 17 in private Jerusalem quarters as the climax of his extended final instructions to his closest disciples (John 13–17). Immediately afterward, he heads out to a garden site where he is arrested (18:1–14), but offers no further prayer that the "cup" or "hour" of death might pass from him, as we find in the Synoptic Gospels (Matt. 26:36–42; Mark 14:32–36; Luke 22:39–42). Indeed, earlier in the Fourth Gospel Jesus resists such a plea: "Now my soul is troubled. And what should I say—'Father, save me from this hour'? No, it is for this reason that I have come to this hour" (John 12:27). Nonetheless, though the prayer of the Johannine Jesus preceding his arrest is not

as desperate and plaintive as the "let this cup pass" cry in the other Gospels, it remains in its own way just as intense and reflective of Jesus' commitment to do his Father's will.

The concluding segment in John 17:20–26 caps off the entire prayer, reinforcing three key elements: the primary theme of unity, with supporting points of familiarity and glory.

As he faces imminent death, physical separation from his followers, and a new state of being in the world ("cosmos"), Jesus is consumed with desire for intimate connection, for "complete unity" (v. 23 NIV). Such passion partly reacts to the all-too-raw memory of Judas's defection and loss from the believing community, despite Jesus' faithful guarding of his flock. Although Jesus justifies Judas's loss as preordained, "so that the scripture might be fulfilled," a touch of lament remains (v. 12).

The breathtaking scope of Jesus' prayer for unity stretches in concentric circles as wide as the universe and as long as eternity, with the Father-Son bond of love forming both the dynamic core and the holistic circumference of this cosmic community. Everything generates and holds together by the interpenetrating and openhearted relationship between God and Jesus: "as we are one [*hen*], I in [*en*] them and you in [*en*] me, that they may become completely one [*hen*]" (vv. 22–23). Notice the play on words in Greek between *en* ("in") and *hen* ("one"). They actually have the same two letters, distinguished only by a rough breathing mark in *hen*. "Oneness" begins with and is sustained through "in-ness"—mutual, intimate intercourse, way beyond superficial association—the very oneness of Father-and-Son, which remarkably "they" are invited "in" on, to share together "in" the perfect (complete) divine love communion.

Who exactly are these additional "they" in this cosmic fellowship? Flowing out as well as in, the unifying love that Jesus seeks in this prayer concentrically reaches from the Father-Son to the immediate company of first disciples, to "those who will believe in me through their [the disciples'] word" (v. 20), to the entire "world" (vv. 23–24), and back to the Father-Son again as the overarching creator and sustainer (cf. 1:1–4).

Familiarity, the second element in this text, relies on unity. As John likes double meanings, I use this term in the double sense of becoming "familiar" with someone and getting to know them. The final two verses of this Lord's prayer (vv. 25–26) stress the loving knowledge and/or knowing love that prevails between Jesus and his "righteous Father," whom Jesus has faithfully made known to his disciples, not simply in an informational mode as a theological datum, but in an invitational posture, welcoming, incorporating, "adopting" his believing "friends" (see 15:12–15) into the divine family circle, where their loving familiarity with the Father, Son, and one another may grow fuller and deeper.

Although intimate, this familial fellowship is by no means insular. Jesus' main mission, according to the Fourth Gospel, for which God expressly sent him into the world (v. 25), is to make known God's name—which is Love (1 John 4:8)—and to keep making it known ("and I will make it known") through his followers, in whom he eternally abides (v. 26; cf. 1:18; 15:1–17). The world, now alienated from God's

original good purpose in creation and ignorant of God's loving way (v. 25), far from being abandoned by God, is the target of God's gracious sending of the loving Son and his emissaries. The extended family of God is ever extending, ever longing, ever praying for newly enlightened, beloved, and believing members. The companion lectionary text from Acts features a wonderful answer to Jesus' prayer in John, as Paul invites a jailer in the Roman colony of Philippi to "believe on the Lord Jesus . . . you and your household." The man and his entire family enthusiastically accept this invitation, sealing their new faith with baptism, hospitality toward Paul, and rejoicing that they "had become . . . believer[s] in God" (Acts 16:30–34).

As Jesus prays that the mutual eternal love binding Father and Son in perfect unity might encompass all who faithfully abide in Jesus, so he seeks a similar suffusion of divine glory, the third element in this text (17:22, 24). At first blush, this notion of glory may appear to overshadow the dark hour of Jesus' impending death, looking ahead to the restoration of his glorious state in God's heavenly presence that the Son enjoyed "before the foundation of the world" (v. 24; cf. 17:5; 1:1–5, 14). In turn, Jesus' beleaguered followers may take heart in this ultimate glorification, in which they participate.

That more triumphal perspective barely scratches the surface of John's message. The term for "glory/glorify," from which we get our word "doxology," appears frequently in this Gospel, carrying conventional notions of exalted majesty (often imagined as radiant light) and renowned honor, both ascribed and achieved. It is ascribed (inherited), in Jesus' case, by relationship with his divine Father; it is achieved (or vindicated) by his miraculous signs (2:11).[1] Of course, other powerful figures in the world, such as political rulers, wealthy patrons, and religious hierarchs, made their own claims to glory in the perpetual tug-of-war for public honor.[2] John maintains that Jesus does not simply receive from God and share with believers

---

1. Walter Bauer, et al., *A Greek-English Lexicon of the New Testament and Other Early Christian Literature*, 3rd ed., rev. and ed. Frederick William Danker (Chicago: University of Chicago Press, 2000), 256–58.

2. See the seminal chapter "Honor and Shame: Pivotal Values of the First-Century Mediterranean World," in Bruce J. Malina, *The New Testament World: Insights from Cultural Anthropology*, 3rd ed. (Louisville, KY: Westminster John Knox Press, 2001), 27–57.

a greater, bigger, brighter glory than anyone in the world, but has a glory that is qualitatively different: not self-sought, but God-given; not human- or worldly-touted, but God-affirmed (5:41, 44; 8:50, 54).

Most radically, however, this glory Jesus seeks in prayer and service is not self-advancing, but self-giving, self-emptying, self-sacrificing, even unto death. The hour of Jesus' greatest glorification is the hour of his death, wholly synchronous with the glory of creation and consummation. The cross upon which Jesus will be uplifted within hours of this final prayer is itself a glorious throne in God's economy, conveying the greatest love the Father could possibly show his beloved children in a suffering world (see 12:23–32; 13:31–35; 15:12–15; 17:2).[3]

F. SCOTT SPENCER

Commentary 2: Connecting the Reading with the World

This passage from John's Farewell Discourse is concerned with those who will come to believe in Jesus through John's testimony. The great vision of John's Gospel is incorporation with God through believing in Jesus. The glory of Jesus' ministry is the extent to which Jesus is loved by God. This love extends beyond the narrow circle of the first disciples to embrace all who have come to believe in Jesus through John's testimony. The primary point—that the church belongs to God because of God's love for Jesus—will be explained in connection with important issues in the church's life, psychological research, and spiritual practices.

The many denominations of the Christian church may look like a scandal to the unity of the faith. I was a child of missionary parents in Bangkok, Thailand. Our family often hosted ministers from across southeast Asia whose primary identity was as Christians. We shared this primary identity in spite of the many ways in which we were different from each other in nationalities and first languages. It was hard for Thai church leaders to understand how missionaries had disparate denominational identities. Similarly, when we reflect on this passage, the lack of visible unity in the church becomes scandalous.

Because of the richness of God's love for Jesus, the church should share in this love. One of the most important ways that the church expresses this is through loving others. John offers a vision of unity based on the knowledge and love shared between God and Jesus. To be incorporated into Jesus' love is to belong to him regardless of denominational affiliation. The primary purpose of ongoing fellowship is to incorporate outsiders into the orbit of this love.

Christians are saved by being incorporated into God's love, so that love is the central and operative force of faith. However, this faith also seems in John's eyes to separate Christians from society. John has separatist tendencies that can be understood through an exploration of acculturation drawn from migrant psychology. New Testament scholar Margaret Aymer Oget explains how Gospel writers either accepted or rejected their native Judaism in their attempts to fit into the Greco-Roman culture.[4] Borrowing from acculturation studies, she suggests that John goes even further, by rejecting both Judaism and Greco-Roman culture. She argues that John depicts a set-apart community traveling through this world with their eyes on Christ. God's love is what sets them apart from the "world," defined in John as those who do not yet recognize Jesus' connection with God.

If Jesus seems somewhat like a stranger in John's Gospel, it is because of the unique love he shares with God, a love in which we are invited to participate. Many people do not recognize

3. See Margaret Pamment, "The Meaning of *doxa* in the Fourth Gospel," *Zeitschrift für die neutestamentliche Wissenschaft und die Kunde der älteren Kirche* 74 (1983): 12–16.

4. Margaret Aymer, "The Migrant's God: World-Orientation and New Testament Theologies," *Insights* 132, no. 1 (Fall 2016): 3–10.

Jesus in John's Gospel and thus misunderstand him. Similarly, it can be hard to recognize the radical and inclusive love of Jesus today in an atmosphere of fear or discomfort. Jesus invites people to become strangers to their accustomed way of operating, in order to recognize him and understand him as the Son of God.

If church unity is rooted in God's love for Jesus, what does this mean in a situation of ecclesial conflict? John's Gospel casts this problem of fragmentation and conflict theologically. The church's unity is based on the intimate communion and organic knowledge shared between God and Jesus. God's gift expands this knowledge to include outsiders. Just as we as Gentiles were outsiders to God's activity, we might again imagine ourselves as outsiders rather than ones who are familiar with God's mercy. Since, in ecclesial conflict, members often set up a barrier between "us" and "them," one that is reinforced by theological arguments, imagining oneself as outsider can give intellectual humility. When Christians attempt to place others outside the bounds of God's grace, they misunderstand the situation. Christian identity cannot be bestowed or removed by human beings.

There is some indication the early church stood apart from its culture because of the love Christians showed one another. Indeed, this may have been the early church's evangelistic strategy. God has given a people to Jesus. The early church's evangelism rests on God's organic unity with Christ rather than human effort. In John's Gospel, God's love and freedom set the stage. By emphasizing this love and freedom, John shows the tendency of people not to recognize God's love or respond to it, thereby becoming estranged from this source of joy. The church increasingly seems like a mirror of a fragmented society. People often worship with similar people, making it difficult to see how God is including all people in God's love. Since the church is given to God by Jesus in an act of ongoing love, the passage reminds us that we are not meant to place a fence around the church to establish outsiders and insiders.

What does it mean to root ecclesial identity in God's indwelling love in Jesus? The intimacy between God and Jesus in this chapter echoes the close relationship between a young child and his or her caregiver. Research from attachment psychology offers a correlation to help us understand the tenderness of such a relationship and its importance. The self is based on attachment relationships with early caregivers. When a child between one-and-a-half and five years old feels safely mirrored by caregivers, the child feels remembered and can develop empathy as a result. Even those who did not experience early attachment can find it in later life through caregivers who provide a safe base from which to explore their world.

Perhaps the lesson from attachment psychology can be broadened beyond its individualism to pertain to the community. Jesus' mutual indwelling in God sounds like a secure haven in which bold, curious, and adventuresome community can be formed. Jesus tells us that this is a two-way relationship between God and himself: the love that is established in this relationship overflows to the disciples. With a secure base, it is easier to have empathy for others. Those who are securely attached more easily manage the boundaries of insiders and outsiders. At times God can substitute for harmful attachments to early caregivers, creating a new safe haven through faith.

What does it mean practically to experience the indwelling communion between God and Jesus? The passage invites us into a lived experience of the tenderness of God and deeper communion with the church that rests in the mutual knowledge and love between God and Jesus. Through contemplative practices, such as centering prayer taught by Thomas Keating, believers might imagine the profundity of God's love for Jesus and how this extends to the disciples. Centering prayer involves silencing the mind and becoming receptive for twenty minutes of quiet, dwelling on a sacred word, to which one returns despite the continual stream of thoughts. Centering prayer is one example of the lived experiential side of a relationship with God that involves listening in silence instead of speaking petitions. Rather than offering conceptual knowledge, such practices prepare us to be formed by God's love, helping us to discover peace and joy in the midst of conflict.

They create the conditions from which we are able more authentically to fulfill the calling of helping others believe in Jesus. As a practice of resting in the love of God, centering prayer is not self-serving or escapist, but is rather a manner in which believers can see the depth and glory of Christian community by glimpsing the indwelling love between God and Christ. John's Gospel reminds us that God's love is always pointed toward the future for the sake of those who believe.

PHILIP BROWNING HELSEL

Day of Pentecost

Genesis 11:1–9
Psalm 104:24–34, 35b
Acts 2:1–21

John 14:8–17 (25–27)
Romans 8:14–17

Genesis 11:1–9

¹Now the whole earth had one language and the same words. ²And as they migrated from the east, they came upon a plain in the land of Shinar and settled there. ³And they said to one another, "Come, let us make bricks, and burn them thoroughly." And they had brick for stone, and bitumen for mortar. ⁴Then they said, "Come, let us build ourselves a city, and a tower with its top in the heavens, and let us make a name for ourselves; otherwise we shall be scattered abroad upon the face of the whole earth." ⁵The LORD came down to see the city and the tower, which mortals had built. ⁶And the LORD said, "Look, they are one people, and they have all one language; and this is only the beginning of what they will do; nothing that they propose to do will now be impossible for them. ⁷Come, let us go down, and confuse their language there, so that they will not understand one another's speech." ⁸So the LORD scattered them abroad from there over the face of all the earth, and they left off building the city. ⁹Therefore it was called Babel, because there the LORD confused the language of all the earth; and from there the LORD scattered them abroad over the face of all the earth.

Commentary 1: Connecting the Reading with Scripture

As lectionary texts go, the tower of Babel story appears at first glance to be remarkably self-contained. Rather than plucked from a lengthier narrative, as some lections necessarily are, Genesis 11:1–9 gives us a complete, albeit brief, story. A monolingual humankind decides to build a city and an extraordinarily high tower; God observes the construction with concern; God decides to confuse the people's speech and scatter them throughout the earth. The story is tightly structured, indicating that it probably was composed all at once, rather than undergoing the layers of editing characteristic of many Pentateuchal texts.[1] As an etiology—an origin story—the prescientific tale of the tower of Babel explains how the peoples of the earth came to speak many languages, as well as, more incidentally, providing an account of how Babylon (*bavel*) got its name. Despite its seemingly

stand-alone nature, this story holds deep connections throughout the Bible, from the material surrounding it in Genesis all the way into the story of Pentecost in the New Testament book of Acts.

The tower of Babel account in Genesis 1–11, the portion of Genesis commonly referred to as the Primeval History, numbers among the many stories reflecting on the earliest days of earth. Like the creation and flood stories, it contains many elements that recall Mesopotamian culture. Unlike those other narratives, there is no particular Mesopotamian myth that serves as a clear parallel. YHWH's first-person-plural address in verse 7, "Come, let us go down," recalls a similarly jarring plural form for the Divine in the first creation story: "Let us make humankind in our image" (Gen. 1:26), and probably reflects an older tradition

---

1. See Terence Fretheim, "The Book of Genesis," in *The New Interpreter's Bible* (Nashville: Abingdon Press, 1994), 1:411.

of a "divine council" in ancient Near Eastern literature. Alternately, the formulation of God's speech here may be less of a reflection of ancient theological assumptions and more of a literary device, serving to echo the same grammatical construction used twice by the people in 11:3–4, "Come, let us make bricks" and "Come, let us build."

Throughout the Primeval History, genealogical formulas serve as organizational elements. Sandwiched as it is between genealogies, the Babel story offers some respite from its surrounding "begats." At the same time, however, the genealogical material tracing the lineages of Noah's sons provides a significant framework for this narrative. After all, genealogies by their nature contemplate unity and difference among human families, tracing the expansion of a family from a single pair of ancestors through a multitude of descendants. Genesis 10 undertakes this process with Noah and his three sons. The dispersion and division of humankind by family, language, and nation (10:5, 20, 31) features prominently in the genealogical material of chapter 10, which maps out not only family lineage but also national territory, concluding with the observation that "from these the nations spread abroad on the earth after the flood" (10:32b). Thus the opening sentences of the tower of Babel narrative ostensibly backtrack in the biblical chronology, imagining a time before this widespread dispersal. At Genesis 11:10 the genealogies recommence, tracing the line of Shem all the way down to Abram, thus linking the Primeval History with the ancestral narratives in the rest of Genesis.

As many commentators like to point out, the tower itself is mentioned in only two of the nine verses in this story. What is so bad about being scattered, anyway? Anxiety motivates this building project: specifically, a fear of being "scattered over the face of the whole earth" (11:4). The Hebrew verb for "scatter" (*puts*) used here is overwhelmingly associated with war. The survivors of Saul's defeat of the Ammonites are scattered, signifying that the Ammonite threat has been successfully quelled (1 Sam. 11:11). Psalmists pray that enemies will be scattered

in battle (Pss. 68:1; 144:6). Perhaps most significantly, in Deuteronomy, in 1 and 2 Kings, and throughout Jeremiah and Ezekiel, the verb refers to the scattering of the people of Judah in the Babylonian exile. Thus this verb connects accounts of the earliest origins of the world, however implicitly, with the sixth-century Israelite experience of Diaspora. To be together, not scattered, signals triumph, a victory in the face of a threat, a desire born out of the experience of fear, trauma, and defeat.

The people's effort not to be scattered yields precisely the effect they dread: God scatters them "over the face of the whole earth" (Gen. 11:8), in language essentially identical to the fear articulated in verse 4. Why? Unlike Eve's eating of the fruit in Genesis 3, there has been no divine admonition given, no regulation established, no law made to break. There has been no indication within this story that the people's work thus far has been out of order in any way. The text offers instead that God, alarmed by their collective efforts, decides that "this is only the beginning of what they will do; nothing that they propose to do will now be impossible for them" (v. 6b). Perhaps this means that the people have overstepped the bounds of their humanity; said another way, perhaps God is threatened by the people's power. Perhaps the people have invested their energy in service to self, making a name (i.e., a monument) for themselves (v. 4) in a case of primeval idolatry. Perhaps the text attempts to endorse a nomadic or rural lifestyle over an urban one. Perhaps, as Terence Fretheim asserts, the tower is in fact an affront to commandments from God, directives from the creation stories both to fill the earth and to care for creation.[2] Perhaps God is simply sovereign—or capricious—and sets limits according to God's freedom.

This sparse text provides little data by which to evaluate God's rationale, but two observations about humanity come to the fore. The first is that language is powerful. God does not observe a great mass of weaponry in this story, nor is God alarmed by a great cache of wealth. Rather, the people's possession of one language drives their accomplishments and elicits God's intervention. Effective communication has a power that can be harnessed for good or for ill, something as true today as in the ancient world.

The second observation is that difference is not a punishment in the tower of Babel story; rather, God thwarts a unity that has been forged by fear and gained at the expense of difference. In Year C, the tower of Babel narrative is paired with the story of Pentecost (Acts 2:1–21). When these two stories are juxtaposed, the temptation can arise to see Pentecost as an undoing of Babel. However, as New Testament scholar Eric Barreto emphasizes, Pentecost does not reverse the consequences of the tower, retreating to some imagined monolingual, monocultural ideal. Rather, ethnic, linguistic, and cultural differences are preserved, while the Holy Spirit serves, in Barreto's words, as a "binding agent," enabling each person to be understood in his or her own native tongue.[3] In the Babel account, fear is the binding agent that drives the building projects: fear of dispersal, of loss, of living with otherness. Both the Babel and the Pentecost accounts emphasize the power of human unity, without expecting human sameness, sending people out into the world to forge connections with those who are different from themselves.

CAMERON B. R. HOWARD

Commentary 2: Connecting the Reading with the World

A wide array of interpretations cluster around this biblical story. A challenge of interpretation, in any context, includes the sheer abundance of approaches. One familiar traditional understanding, captured perhaps by children's Bible story books of a generation or two ago, portrays the tower as an act of foolish pride by an arrogant community. The sixteenth-century Dutch painter Pieter Bruegel depicts this interpretation in his familiar renderings of the tower, a tall spiral structure that pierces the clouds, with smoking brick furnaces in the background and exhausted workers in the foreground. The paintings clearly assume that the overlords and the slaves are in their proper social places.

This interpretation suggests social and ethical assumptions of monocultural dominance. Such an interpretation was clearly at work in the context of apartheid South Africa in the twentieth century. In 1976, the Dutch Reformed Church in South Africa issued a document, *Human Relations and the South African Scene in the Light of Scripture*, that interpreted the Babel story as a divine command for separation of people based on racial identities.[4] Desmond Tutu refuted this interpretation: "The apologists of apartheid have sometimes used the story of the Tower of Babel as divine sanction for their ideology of 'separate development' and ethnic identity." He then went on to insist that "God's intention for humankind and for His entire universe is harmony, peace, justice, wholeness, fellowship."[5] Since the fall of apartheid in the early 1990s, the Dutch Reformed Church has, like Desmond Tutu, refuted that earlier interpretation. However, it serves as a sobering reminder that biblical interpretation is sometimes used to further oppression, not to encourage flourishing. This general interpretive approach of the tower of Babel was also used by some in the context of the civil rights movement in the United States as an explanation of the origin of racial human difference. In this context, the story supported racist attitudes toward African Americans by assigning them a subservient social position.

More recent interpretations understand the tower of Babel as a celebration of diversity and cultural differentiation. A positive reading of the story is one in which God stands up against the proclaimed intentions of the people and issues the divine decree that cultural differences are not judgment; rather, God values not

---

3. Eric D. Barreto, "Negotiating Difference: Theology and Ethnicity in the Acts of the Apostles," *Word & World* 31, no. 2 (2011): 129–37.
4. Mark Rathbone, "Reframing the Tower of Babel Narrative for Economic Justice within the South African Context," *Hervormde Teologiese Studies* 72, no. 3 (2016): 1.
5. Desmond Tutu, "Christianity and Apartheid," in J. W. de Gruchy and C. Villan-Vicencio, eds., *Apartheid Is a Heresy* (Cape Town: David Philip, 1983), 39–47.

punishment but promise. Walter Brueggemann suggests a deeply dialectic dynamic in the story. The scattering of the peoples is an ambiguous reality; it has negative and positive connotations. From a positive perspective, the scattering indicates the fulfillment of creation and a correction to homogeneity of language and culture, but the scattering can also be exile and displacement, a loss of identity and home. This is a deeply distressing reality for many displaced and traumatized refugees throughout human history, including tragic displacements in our contemporary contexts. Likewise, unity is a dialectic dynamic in this story. It can be a positive portrayal of covenant relationship, a unity of promise and purpose. It can also be a negative portrayal of oppressive homogeneity.[6] Brueggemann highlights the lively dialectical energies in this text and thus reveals the multiple layers of meaning, including social, ethical, political, and cultural realities.

The story is not only a highly structured and compressed commentary on communal human behavior. It is also a vivid portrayal of divine action. The human instinct to self-preservation and rejection of others is met by God's action of scattering the people and thwarting their fearful instincts. In response to the human longing for connection and identity, God does not refute and deny that human longing. Rather, God's action calls human community to a deeper unity, one found in covenantal relationship with God, so that an openness to the other is possible. God's scattering, then, paradoxically calls people to commitments of connection and cooperation.

The dialectics of the tower of Babel suggests the complex dynamics of life-giving unity as well as life-crushing unity, of life-giving diversity as well as life-crushing diversity. These dialectical energies open pathways of insight and application for pastoral leaders in the challenges of contemporary culture. When this text is brought to bear on communities that have experienced radical displacement and loss, the text is a story of hope for future stability. When it is brought to bear on communities that are privileged and secure, it may well be a prophetic

call to risk for the sake of the other. As always, the preaching of the word is highly contextual, connecting the community of faith both at the point of its needs and longings, and at the points of its sin and brokenness.

At heart, the tower of Babel issues a protest against the kind of unity and independence attempted in human self-sufficiency. The story critiques the "us vs. them" rhetoric of our political culture; it critiques the power dynamics of hierarchy at the expense of community; it critiques autonomy disconnected from God. All these critiques profoundly resonate with deep currents in Christian theology. Christian theological reflection, across multiple centuries and contexts, points out the folly of a prideful autonomy, the delusion of a rejection of creaturely identity, and the blindness of a denial of vocation and call. Christian doctrines of creation, theological anthropology, redemption and salvation, sin and brokenness, new life and hope for fulfillment, all find their echo in the tower of Babel. Perceptive pastoral leaders will hear those echoes in the contexts of their ministry.

The deep biblical themes that spill out of this story into the multiple realities of human life touch not only on political and communal life but also personal and individual life. Some persons experience the scattering of personal identity in mental illness. Others cling desperately to a false identity and a false unity based on the shaky foundations of money or influence or clan. The opportunities for preaching pastoral care in this story are fruitful, precisely because the story is so evocative of the range of human failure and human opportunities. Here is the full and complicated array of life-crushing as well as life-giving possibilities.

Pentecost is the church year location for the story of the tower of Babel. The potential for mutual illumination and interpretation between the Old Testament reading of the tower of Babel and the New Testament reading of Pentecost is strong. Just as, in the tower of Babel, dialectical tensions are perceived of positive and negative renderings of both unity and diversity, so these same tensions are echoed in the story of

6. Walter Brueggemann, *Genesis*, Interpretation (Atlanta: John Knox Press, 1982), 101–2.

Pentecost. Pentecost is not a story of diversity without difficulty. The differentiation of tongues is both a gift and a challenge to the church. Pentecost is not a story of unity without deep dislocation. God promises, in Pentecost, a unity and a diversity that is both call and lavish gift.

Likewise, the tower of Babel is an elusive portrait of both call and gift. When it has been used to legitimate an oppressive uniformity, it does not live into its potential to portray God's delight in multiplicity and generosity. Pastoral leaders will find this story richly evocative for unmasking both false divisions and false unity, as well as evoking fruitful differences and faithful unity.

LEANNE VAN DYK

Psalm 104:24–34, 35b

[24]O LORD, how manifold are your works!
   In wisdom you have made them all;
   the earth is full of your creatures.
[25]Yonder is the sea, great and wide,
   creeping things innumerable are there,
   living things both small and great.
[26]There go the ships,
   and Leviathan that you formed to sport in it.

[27]These all look to you
   to give them their food in due season;
[28]when you give to them, they gather it up;
   when you open your hand, they are filled with good things.
[29]When you hide your face, they are dismayed;
   when you take away their breath, they die
   and return to their dust.
[30]When you send forth your spirit, they are created;
   and you renew the face of the ground.

[31]May the glory of the LORD endure forever;
   may the LORD rejoice in his works—
[32]who looks on the earth and it trembles,
   who touches the mountains and they smoke.
[33]I will sing to the LORD as long as I live;
   I will sing praise to my God while I have being.
[34]May my meditation be pleasing to him,
   for I rejoice in the LORD.
. . . .
[35b]Bless the LORD, O my soul.
Praise the LORD!

Connecting the Psalm with Scripture and Worship

On the Day of Pentecost, the Revised Common Lectionary offers two options for the first reading: Luke's narrative of the first Pentecost and the legend of the tower of Babel. In the reading from Acts 2, the Jewish festival commemorating the giving of the law on Mount Sinai has been Christianized: now the fire appears, not on top of a terrifying mountain that the people cannot approach, but as flickering tongues on the heads of the gathered community. Not merely the leader Moses, but now all the people are filled with words from the Spirit of God. These words are meant not only for the tribe of Israelites, but for the whole of the Roman Empire. If we choose to begin our readings with Acts 2, we introduce Pentecost as the presence of the Spirit of God given in Christ to the whole world, as we join with the early disciples to receive the Spirit poured out on all flesh.

In the alternative choice, the tale in Genesis 11, what scholars call an etiological myth, explains the multiplicity of human languages as

God's way of counteracting the human aggrandizement that erected the sky-high ziggurat. The societal confusion caused by language diversity is seen as a result of sin. If we select this option at the outset of our readings, our Pentecost celebrates the church's joy when in Christ we speak all the world's languages, not to "make a name for ourselves," but with the apostle Peter to call "upon the name of the Lord." By the mercy of God, the world's multiple languages have become vehicles for spreading the gospel.

Psalm 104 means to serve as a response for either of these options, not so much by specific correspondences to the first reading, but rather by leading us into the Spirit festival of the Day of Pentecost. Psalm 104 is one of the Psalter's creation psalms, appropriate to sing on this day, because we confess that the Spirit of God continually creates not merely the church, but the entire cosmos. Neither the earth nor the church was created on a single day long ago. Rather, the creation continues today, and the church is created as we sing this psalm.

Verse 24 speaks of wisdom, a divine quality manifest in the earth's creation that is sometimes personified in the Hebrew Scriptures as a goddess-like companion of God in the task of ordering the universe. Today's intercessions do well to beg God to continue the creation of an earth we have often disordered and to plead for the gift of wisdom as our communities make decisions about our use of lands and waters.

Verses 25–26 are good news, especially to the ancient landed Israelites, who thought of the uncontrollable sea as the symbol of chaos. However, in this song of praise, the sea is only one of God's many creations. Even the sea monster (see Isa. 27:1), that entity embodying all evil, is merely one of earth's creatures, formed by God just for the fun of it. One wonders whether the original poet of this verse was an early scientist, rejecting any fear of mythical beasts, and instead praising all the animal life of God's wondrous creation.

In verses 27–28 we acclaim God as the giver of food for all these creatures. Thus, on Pentecost, as believers praise the coming of Spirit into the church, this creation song extends our praise from this assembly, this denomination, this world religion, to include even the mythical sea monster as a recipient of God's bounty.

Verses 29–30 are central to a Christian spirituality that takes with seriousness both our species and the earth God created, by acknowledging God's role in all of life. The Hebrew word of note here is *ruah*, which can be rendered in English as "spirit," "breath," or "wind." Recall that in Genesis 1:2, God's *ruah* swept over the waters of chaos: your Bible translation may cast this as spirit, or wind, or breath. Also, in this psalm, contemporary translations differ: God both takes away and sends forth either the divine spirit or breath. However, current linguistic discrepancies notwithstanding, the Christian tradition saw in this verse a reference to the Holy Spirit, and thus arose the practice of assigning this psalm to Pentecost and, in the English language, of capitalizing the noun "Spirit."

God gives breath to all (v. 29), and when that breath is taken away, we revert to dust. As Christian funeral rites say it: "earth to earth, dust to dust." We are not little angels running around, but dust creatures of God's handiwork. In most translations of this psalm, verse 30 states that God sends forth the divine Spirit, and so all creatures are created. We in the church are to think of even the church as one of those creations, by which the very face of the ground is to be renewed. Yet we are not to forget that this benevolent Creator also sends earthquakes and volcanoes (v. 32). As they say in Narnia, Aslan is not a tame lion. When we imagine God as only a kind uncle, we have quite underestimated the breadth of power of the Creator of the universe.

The lectionary stipulates that verse 35a be omitted. Contemporary sensibilities tend to see the imprecatory psalms as cruel, vindictive, unfitting for Christian use. I would suggest that you follow the advice of the lectionary design in this. However, in the worldview of the psalmist, God created a good and perfect earth, and at the end of time—that eschatological climax of this earth that in Acts 2:19–20 Peter preaches, quoting the prophet Joel—on that "great and glorious day" (Acts 2:20b; Joel 2:31 "great and terrible day"), God will do away with evil. God's holiness will consume all that is wicked. The Christian tradition applied this idea to an afterlife of a perfect heaven and a fiery hell. Such a description of divine justice is a distasteful notion to some contemporary Christians and a fervent article of faith for others, but it does indicate the ancient belief in God's utter righteousness, the divine victory over sin that Christians see as enacted in the resurrection of Jesus Christ.

GAIL RAMSHAW

Acts 2:1–21

[1]When the day of Pentecost had come, they were all together in one place. [2]And suddenly from heaven there came a sound like the rush of a violent wind, and it filled the entire house where they were sitting. [3]Divided tongues, as of fire, appeared among them, and a tongue rested on each of them. [4]All of them were filled with the Holy Spirit and began to speak in other languages, as the Spirit gave them ability.

[5]Now there were devout Jews from every nation under heaven living in Jerusalem. [6]And at this sound the crowd gathered and was bewildered, because each one heard them speaking in the native language of each. [7]Amazed and astonished, they asked, "Are not all these who are speaking Galileans? [8]And how is it that we hear, each of us, in our own native language? [9]Parthians, Medes, Elamites, and residents of Mesopotamia, Judea and Cappadocia, Pontus and Asia, [10]Phrygia and Pamphylia, Egypt and the parts of Libya belonging to Cyrene, and visitors from Rome, both Jews and proselytes, [11]Cretans and Arabs—in our own languages we hear them speaking about God's deeds of power." [12]All were amazed and perplexed, saying to one another, "What does this mean?" [13]But others sneered and said, "They are filled with new wine."

[14]But Peter, standing with the eleven, raised his voice and addressed them, "Men of Judea and all who live in Jerusalem, let this be known to you, and listen to what I say. [15]Indeed, these are not drunk, as you suppose, for it is only nine o'clock in the morning. [16]No, this is what was spoken through the prophet Joel:

[17]'In the last days it will be, God declares,
that I will pour out my Spirit upon all flesh,
   and your sons and your daughters shall prophesy,
and your young men shall see visions,
   and your old men shall dream dreams.
[18]Even upon my slaves, both men and women,
   in those days I will pour out my Spirit;
      and they shall prophesy.
[19]And I will show portents in the heaven above
   and signs on the earth below,
      blood, and fire, and smoky mist.
[20]The sun shall be turned to darkness
   and the moon to blood,
      before the coming of the Lord's great and glorious day.
[21]Then everyone who calls on the name of the Lord shall be saved.'"

Commentary 1: Connecting the Reading with Scripture

The lectionary texts for Pentecost are, not surprisingly, connected by their references to the Spirit. Perhaps surprisingly, they say very different things about the character and work of the Spirit. The preacher who might become frustrated by the lack of commonality can opt instead to revel in the variety of ways these biblical witnesses reveal glimpses of the many-faceted Spirit of God.

The story of Pentecost as told in Acts 2 is itself a commentary of sorts on the Joel 2 passage that Peter adapts: "In the last days . . . they shall prophesy" (Acts 2:17–18; cf. Joel 2:28–29). God pours out the divine Spirit on "all of them" in the form of a violent wind and tongues of fire distributed among them, and they all speak, in various languages, "about God's deeds of power" (Acts 2:11).

Attending to the inclusivity of the Joel passage, which speaks of sons and daughters, young men and old men, and slave men and women, we note that "the eleven" apostles are not specified in the Acts text until verse 14. "They" and "all of them" in the previous verses should be understood as the entire group of believers, which Acts 1:15 says "numbered about one hundred twenty persons." The Acts 1 text names eleven men, the twelve apostles of Luke 6:14–16 minus Judas Iscariot; one woman, Mary the mother of Jesus; "certain women"; and Jesus' "brothers." While no age or economic data are supplied, from what we know of Jesus' ministry it is reasonable to assume that there were also old and young members of the group, as well as both slaves and free people. Jesus' ministry was wide-ranging and inclusive, as Luke's Gospel makes particularly clear with its attention to shepherds, foreigners, and even Roman soldiers who recognize Jesus' importance and power. Now those socially and economically disparate folk will come together to proclaim Christ crucified and risen.

The list of ethnic identities represented in the crowd—the terror of every lay liturgist, and even clergy readers—reflects the widespread Diaspora of Jews in the first century. The list begins with Persian peoples, Jews who remained after the Babylonian captivity rather than return to Palestine. It moves generally westward to Asia Minor, North Africa, and distant islands (the exceptions are "Judea" and "visitors from Rome," which are out of order). The purpose of listing these nationalities, in this order, is debated by scholars, and relatively insignificant to the overall story. It may or may not be significant that twelve regions are named. What matters more is that the reality of the Jewish Diaspora and the traditions that brought Jews from all over the world to Jerusalem on certain occasions work together to make the church's initial proclamation of the gospel a word that simultaneously reaches people from many lands. The program set forth in Acts 1:8—that through the Spirit's power the gospel will be proclaimed "in Jerusalem, in all Judea and Samaria, and to the ends of the earth"—is both inaugurated and anticipated in its fullness.

The crowd's identification of the believers as "Galileans" (v. 7) is subtle, and perhaps comical, social commentary. Galilee was a rural backwater in the minds of Jerusalemites and, presumably, the Diaspora Jews whose means allowed them to travel to Jerusalem for the Feast of Shavuot (Festival of Weeks; Pentecost). Galileans spoke with a distinctive accent that this cosmopolitan crowd would notice and likely scorn. One wonders whether the Parthians, Medes, Elamites, and so forth heard their own languages spoken with a Galilean drawl.

In the Last Days . . . The text tells us that the question voiced by those who heard the variety of languages is "What does this mean?" (v. 12). Peter is quick to clarify that these are, indeed, the "last days" of which Joel and other prophets spoke: a time of judgment, with accompanying apocalyptic portents, during which people are called to make decisions regarding their allegiance. The time of God's salvation has arrived. The advent of the Spirit brings wind and fire, and the people who hear the gospel message are challenged to call upon the name of the Lord and be saved.

The event of Pentecost is also an inversion of the story of Babel (Gen. 11:1–9), a reordering of the chaos that began there when God confused human language so that people could not build a "tower with its top in the heavens" (11:4). The word the Septuagint uses to translate the Hebrew root *bll*, "confuse," is the same word Acts uses of the crowds who initially "were bewildered" (*synechythē*, Acts 2:6), but were enabled to understand the apostles' message. Continuing to read the Babel story backwards, Pentecost may also be understood as inverting God's concern regarding the ancient peoples into a divine promise for the newborn church: "This is only the beginning of what they will do; nothing that they propose to do will now be impossible for them" (Gen. 11:6).

Printed on My Heart

When called of God, on a particular occasion, to a definite work, I said, "No, Lord, not me." Day by day I was more impressed that God would have me work in his vineyard. I thought it could not be that I was called to preach—I, so weak and ignorant. Still, I knew all things were possible with God, even to confounding the wise by the foolish things of this earth. Yet in me there was a shrinking.

I took all my doubts and fears to the Lord in prayer, when, what seemed to be an angel, made his appearance. In his hand was a scroll, on which were these words: "Thee have I chosen to preach my Gospel without delay." The moment my eyes saw it, it appeared to be printed on my heart. The angel was gone in an instant, and I, in agony, cried out, "Lord, I cannot do it!" It was eleven o'clock in the morning, yet everything grew dark as night. The darkness was so great that I feared to stir. . . .

One night, as I lay weeping and beseeching my dear Lord to remove this burden from me, there appeared the same angel that came to me before, and on his breast were these words: "You are lost unless you obey God's righteous commands." I saw the writing and awoke my husband, who had returned a few days before. He asked me why I trembled so, but I had not power to answer him. I remained in that condition until morning, when I tried to arise and go about my usual duties, but was too ill. Then my husband called a physician, who prescribed medicine, but it did me no good.

Julia Foote, *A Brand Plucked from the Fire. An Autobiographical Sketch by Mrs. Julia A. J. Foote* (Cleveland: W. F. Schneider, 1879), 65–67.

. . . I Will Pour Out My Spirit . . . The gift of the Spirit, according to Peter's sermon the fulfillment of Joel's prophetic vision, is also the fulfillment of John's prediction, near the beginning of the Gospel of Luke, that Jesus "will baptize you with the Holy Spirit and fire" (Luke 3:16). In Luke, the Holy Spirit descends upon Jesus at his baptism (3:22) and he is thereafter said to be "full of the Holy Spirit" (4:1; cf. 4:14). At Nazareth Jesus proclaims that God's Spirit is on him, identifying himself with the divine messenger in Isaiah (4:18–21). Pentecost is the second outpouring of the Spirit, this time not on Jesus alone but on his followers, the newly constituted church. Once again Scripture announces God's work in bestowing the Spirit, as Peter cites the prophet Joel.

. . . Your Sons and Your Daughters Shall Prophesy. While the common understanding of prophecy tends toward the notion of telling the future, in the biblical record the prophet is not so much one who foretells coming events as one who interprets current events, who makes the present times meaningful, including as appropriate how the present is likely to unfold

into the future. God's new community in Jesus Christ, the ones who have just received the Holy Spirit, are a community of prophets, proclaiming the good news and interpreting to the Pentecost crowd what the strange happenings among them mean. It is important, therefore, to understand the reference to "all of them" who received the Spirit as meaning the entire congregation, not just the twelve male apostles, even though Peter's is the only voice we hear.

The Pentecost event is thus both an occasion of prophecy and a fulfillment of prophecy. The Servant text from Isaiah that Jesus reads in Nazareth at the beginning of his public ministry is preceded, a few chapters earlier, by God's promise to Israel, "I will pour out my spirit on your descendants, and my blessing on your offspring" (Isa. 44:3). Ezekiel records the divine promise, "A new heart I will give you, and a new spirit I will put within you; . . . I will put my spirit within you" (Ezek. 36:26–27a). The birth of the church is, Acts affirms, both a completely new thing *and* entirely in keeping with God's promises to God's people throughout their shared history.

SANDRA HACK POLASKI

Commentary 2: Connecting the Reading with the World

This text is so familiar it is easy to underestimate. We get so comfortable rehearsing it that we often overlook its capacity to shine a light on what it means to spread the news of God's deeds.

As the disciples gathered to celebrate the Feast of Weeks with other Jews from the Diaspora, a mighty wind came through. Tongues of fire appeared over them and gave them the power to speak about God in multiple languages. People who spoke these languages heard accents and words in syntaxes that were familiar. As a result, they did not have to nudge the person next to them and ask, "What are they saying? What is that word? What do they mean?" Nor did they have to take on the shame that often comes with having to confess, "I do not understand." They could hear the good news of God for themselves. No one had to abandon the culture that gave them an identity in order to hear from God. God's word came that day in a way that expressed God's deep affirmation of diversity as a key ingredient in unity.

For some, this level of diversity was so foreign that it had to be the work of too much wine. Peter, however, is clear: This was *that* day—the one prophets foretold about how God's spirit would one day pour out on female and male, young and old, free and enslaved. This was it! In this moment it is diversity, not homogeneity, that brings this community of believers together. Difference is no longer an excuse for division or a justification for disparity.

In reading Peter's response to the cynical crowd, we are reminded that God's Spirit chooses whom God wills regardless of age (young and old), gender (sons and daughters), or class (even the slaves). As the church considers its ecclesial practices, this text can provide an opportunity to grapple with how it practices the diversity God affirms. The text speaks of the Holy Spirit's coming as a new communal order reflecting egalitarianism rather than hierarchy, and diversity rather than homogeneity. This is the power of God at work in transforming institutions—including the institutionalized body of Christ. Do we elevate some to positions of privileged speech based on their gender, race, or class, at the expense of silencing others who Peter reminds us are equally valued in God's sight?

In the liturgical calendar, we celebrate Pentecost as a barrier-breaking moment when God spoke to, through, and in whatever language was necessary to communicate the good news. Peter invites us to think about what it means for the Holy Spirit to come into our own lives so that we too can be empowered to carry news of God's deeds in a way that makes the good news accessible in relevant and tangible ways.

This is significant for the contemporary church, given the sheer volume of humanitarian needs resulting from hurricanes, mudslides, earthquakes, and massive flooding, and the secondary disaster of governmental benign neglect and apathy that only exacerbate the struggle to survive. This was certainly the case in 2006 with Hurricane Katrina,[1] but a similar predicament presented itself in 2017 when the United States government was painfully slow in delivering aide to US territory Puerto Rico following Hurricanes Irma and Maria.[2] In both New Orleans and Puerto Rico, the condition of their infrastructures was a significant factor in the aftermath residents faced. Financial and public policy decisions that deprioritized long-term quality of life created infrastructure hurdles that deeply impacted quality of life before and after these catastrophic natural disasters.[3] Contemporary word of God's deeds sounds like the clamor between interpreters and churches coordinating delivery of the food, water, medical supplies, baby formula, underwear, toiletries, and sanitary products they have taken it upon themselves to collect and to ensure get delivered. This is a sort of "word in action" moment when congregations reach across the differences

---

1. "The Storm," *Frontline*, PBS, November 22, 2005, https://www.pbs.org/wgbh/pages/frontline/storm/.

2. Robinson Meyer, "What's Happening with the Relief Effort in Puerto Rico?," *Atlantic*, October 4, 2017, https://www.theatlantic.com/science/archive/2017/10/what-happened-in-puerto-rico-a-timeline-of-hurricane-maria/541956/.

3. Luis Ferré-Sadurní, "Irma Grazes Puerto Rico but Lays Bare an Infrastructure Problem," *New York Times*, September 10, 2017, https://www.nytimes.com/2017/09/10/us/irma-puerto-rico-infrastructure.html.

of language and culture to extend themselves in a way that lets people know they have a stake in the good news of the gospel. Aid in times of crisis *is* the living word of God's deeds.

When the Holy Spirit sets the disciples in motion with multiple languages, diversity is affirmed as a primary tool through which God's love is expressed. Recognition of this affirmation can be an important touchstone for congregations struggling with how to claim voice and agency in local and global conversations where difference often invokes suspicion. When we do not know the language, we often respond with intolerance. Rather than affirm diversity as reflective of God's will, assimilationist tactics that blot out distinctions while also reinforcing a culture of fear and suspicion are common responses to people who are unlike ourselves.

Even though scientific research from the National Human Genome Institute confirms that all human beings are 99 percent genetically identical (alike), differences in language, culture, hair texture, and skin and eye color are still interpreted as reasons for suspicion.

The body of Christ is called to disrupt suspicion of difference by centering the good news in a way that prompts us to extend toward, not retreat from, people who are unlike ourselves. This may look like taking the time to learn how to say, "You are welcome here," in the language of an immigrant or refugee family, so that the metal from the keys to their new home does not feel so cold as they find sanctuary from the struggles and love they had to leave behind when they fled Syria, Sierra Leone, Honduras, and other parts near and far.

The suspicion of cultural difference does not occur just between international communities; it is equally present in the relationships within communities, including the church. An older preacher who was deeply committed to his congregation's restoration of their cultural heritage dealt with this challenge nearly every time he preached or taught. He was deeply committed to supporting his community in reclaiming their ethnic heritage as a key facet in their Christian identity. Congregants often grew suspicious of what would happen (how they would be viewed, how would they view themselves) if they embraced their cultural legacy and traditions as distinctive assets in their Christian walk. When the fear of cultural suspicion creeped in on them, he would patiently affirm, "Different does not mean deficient." Contemporary word of God's deeds disrupts the fear of difference and the culture of suspicion.

A final connection between this ancient text and contemporary life is more personal. We can only imagine how the disciples felt when they noticed that they had been misunderstood. The languages were so different from what was expected that some suspiciously dismissed their holy work as the result of too much drinking. They could not even begin to think that God might be at work in it. Nevertheless, the disciples carried God's word forward, in spite of how it even made them different, and in spite of the inevitability of life that always put them at risk of being misunderstood. The good news is that they were not alone, in Spirit or in community. They were faithful to the vision of how God works through diversity to gather community. This is an important insight for everyday people of faith. This is the gift of the contemporary word of God's deeds at work in the world.

STEPHANIE M. CRUMPTON

John 14:8–17 (25–27)

[8]Philip said to him, "Lord, show us the Father, and we will be satisfied." [9]Jesus said to him, "Have I been with you all this time, Philip, and you still do not know me? Whoever has seen me has seen the Father. How can you say, 'Show us the Father'? [10]Do you not believe that I am in the Father and the Father is in me? The words that I say to you I do not speak on my own; but the Father who dwells in me does his works. [11]Believe me that I am in the Father and the Father is in me; but if you do not, then believe me because of the works themselves. [12]Very truly, I tell you, the one who believes in me will also do the works that I do and, in fact, will do greater works than these, because I am going to the Father. [13]I will do whatever you ask in my name, so that the Father may be glorified in the Son. [14]If in my name you ask me for anything, I will do it.

[15]"If you love me, you will keep my commandments. [16]And I will ask the Father, and he will give you another Advocate, to be with you forever. [17]This is the Spirit of truth, whom the world cannot receive, because it neither sees him nor knows him. You know him, because he abides with you, and he will be in you. . . .

[25]"I have said these things to you while I am still with you. [26]But the Advocate, the Holy Spirit, whom the Father will send in my name, will teach you everything, and remind you of all that I have said to you. [27]Peace I leave with you; my peace I give to you. I do not give to you as the world gives. Do not let your hearts be troubled, and do not let them be afraid."

Commentary 1: Connecting the Reading with Scripture

This passage, set in John's story just after Jesus washes the disciples' feet and dismisses Judas Iscariot, is part of the section known as Jesus' Farewell Address. This section contains many of the best-known passages in all of Scripture ("I am the way, and the truth, and the life" [14:6]; "I am the vine, you are the branches" [15:5]; "love one another as I have loved you" [15:12]; "I have conquered the world!" [16:33]; "so that they may be one, as we are one" [17:22]) as well as some of Jesus' most circular and inscrutable statements about himself and "my Father."

Thomas Tallis (1505–1585), a church musician who, during the reign of Edward VI, was mandated to use English rather than Latin texts, famously set the Geneva Bible's translation of John 14:15–17a as a hauntingly beautiful motet for four voices, "If ye love me, keep my commandments."

Our text picks up in the middle of a conversation that clearly has already confused and upset the disciples. As is typical in the Gospel of John, Jesus seems to be talking over the heads of his conversation partners. (Good examples are Jesus' conversations with Nicodemus and with the woman at the well.) They ask what they think are cogent questions, but Jesus answers to another level of reality. Jesus speaks of going away to a place that he will prepare for them, so Thomas asks how they are going to know how to get there. Jesus' answer, "I am the way, and the truth, and the life" (14:6), is a powerful statement, but hardly a road map.

Father, Son, and Spirit. Thomas picks up on another clue dropped by Jesus, and we can hear the frustration in his comment: "Lord, show us the Father, and we will be satisfied" (v. 8). Far from clarifying, though, Jesus' comment rebukes him for not already understanding. The lengthy section in which Jesus expounds on the relationship between the Father and the Son

(vv. 8–14) could lead into a theological discussion of the relationship of the Father and the Son, and then by extension to the Trinity; alternatively, it might cause the proclaimer to feel compelled to expound on alternative language for God and Jesus. Neither of these options is the best choice for this liturgical occasion, since the resonance of this text with the other two lectionary texts is clearly on the role of the Spirit.

John and Acts offer quite different accounts of the outpouring of the Spirit. The disciples in Acts wait for the advent of the Spirit, which, when it occurs, is apocalyptic. In John, Jesus promises the effects of the Spirit before he makes clear that he is speaking of the "Advocate" (*paraklētos*, v. 16b), the "Spirit of truth" (v. 17a). The Spirit's presence will make possible for those who believe the same works that Jesus accomplished while he was with them. Indeed, they will do "greater works than these" (v. 12); Jesus' earthly ministry has been geographically and temporally limited, but the growing community of believers will continue to have the guidance of the Holy Spirit.

Jesus makes clear that he must leave in order for the Spirit to be given to the disciples; the Spirit is a continuation of Jesus' own presence with them, superfluous while he is present, essential once he is gone. Jesus and the Spirit are separate but have the same task relative to believers. Also, as Jesus and the Father are both distinct and one in John, so too with God, Jesus, and the Spirit: when believers call on *God* in *Jesus'* name, they invoke the power of the *Spirit*.

The Spirit, Jesus promises, will abide with Jesus' followers. "Abide" (*menō*) is a favorite Johannine term; more than half the NT occurrences of the word come from the Gospel or Epistles of John. Sometimes it simply means "remain" in the geographical sense; but more often it has the additional sense of significant presence. Frequently Jesus speaks of his word "abiding" in his followers (5:38; 8:31). At Jesus' baptism, John declares that "the one who sent me to baptize with water said to me, 'He on whom you see the Spirit descend and remain [*menō*] is the one who baptizes with the Holy Spirit'"

(1:33). The same Spirit who abided with Jesus at his baptism now abides with his disciples.

The Role of the Paraclete. John's distinctive term for the Spirit is "Paraclete" (*paraklētos*), a word that does not appear elsewhere in the NT or in the Septuagint. The constellation of meanings found in Greek literature includes "intercessor," "mediator," "advocate," and "helper." John parallels "Paraclete" with the "Spirit of truth." In the Farewell Discourse the Paraclete has a teaching function, reminding the disciples of what Jesus has said to them. The familiar "comforter" translation of the KJV is less accurate than other options, but it emphasizes the sense of security that believers should experience by having such an effective advocate.

The Greek word translated as "Spirit" and transliterated as *pneuma* also means "wind" or "breath" and points toward the *nature* of the Spirit: omnipresent and uncontrollable; felt or sensed rather than seen; inextricably connected with life itself. (Ancient Greek did not use initial capitals to distinguish between "Spirit" and "spirit."[1]) Jesus' description of the Spirit as Paraclete points to a *functional* definition, what the Spirit *does*: teach, help, advocate, intercede, and so on. Because the Paraclete is the Spirit of truth, it empowers the disciples to speak and act truthfully, even in the midst of opposition, temptation, and suffering.

More often overlooked is Jesus' promise of "*another* Paraclete." That is, the disciples have already had a Paraclete, presumably Jesus himself (although Jesus is never identified as such). Since Jesus fulfilled the role(s) of the Paraclete, the Spirit will fulfill those same role(s); thus Jesus' promise not to leave the disciples alone is fulfilled.

Peace. Optional verses 25–27 strengthen the text's focus on the Spirit and, for the first time in our passage, use the phrase "Holy Spirit" (*to pneuma to hagion*). (The phrase appears elsewhere in John's Gospel in 1:33 and 20:22.) The Spirit's teaching function operates both forward, guiding the disciples in God's ways, and

---

1. During the time of composition of the New Testament, Greek was written in all capital letters (uncials), without punctuation or spaces (LIKETHIS). Around the end of the ninth century, scribes began using lowercase (minuscule) letters, and did not mark proper nouns with initial capitals.

backward, reminding them of what Jesus said when he was among them. Grounded in their life with Jesus and led by the unfailing instruction of the Spirit, the disciples are able to experience peace.

"Peace" is the translation of the common Hebrew greeting "Shalom," and the risen Jesus will greet his startled disciples with "Peace be with you" (20:19). Just as this proclamation is much more than a greeting, the peace that Jesus promises his followers is much more than simply a good and contented feeling. The Synoptic Gospels often associate the kingdom of God with peace, and Paul asserts that "the kingdom of God is . . . righteousness and peace and joy in the Holy Spirit" (Rom. 14:17). Hebrew Scriptures also affirm that the messianic age, the coming reign of God, will be characterized by peace: "there shall be endless peace for the throne of David and his kingdom" (Isa. 9:7). Indeed, this is not the peace of this world, but the peace of the coming kingdom of God, given in advance to the disciples through the Holy Spirit.

SANDRA HACK POLASKI

Commentary 2: Connecting the Reading to the World

In John, miracles and signs affirm Jesus' identity and purpose as the Christ. Without Jesus, there was pain and suffering, with few possibilities for release from Roman oppression. With Jesus, healing happened wherever and whenever it was prudent. These life-altering signs proved that he was the Christ—and now he was talking about leaving?

As the disciples went through the motions of trying to get their minds around what Jesus was saying, Jesus reinforced their faith by pointing them to the source of the miracles he performed. Even so, they could not help but fixate on the profound sense of separation that this news brought about, and perhaps the fear that things would go back to the way they were before he had come. He was their sign of hope. Where was he going? Would there be any more miracles after he left? How were they going to do what he was asking them to do? They became afraid, and acted as if they had forgotten everything Jesus had taught them.

Older people who have ventured through many seasons in their faith lives often say that "the only way out is back through." In this case, the only way to bring the disciples out of their anxiety is for Jesus to take them back through the foundation of their relationship and his ministry with the people of God.

Jesus first reminds them that his relationships, works of healing, and teaching are founded in love. This was the case concerning those whom he healed and on whose behalf he spoke truth to power. This would be the rule for his disciples. This love requires action. If they love him, the disciples have to take care of the people. If they love him, they should demonstrate the same care, compassion, and concern to the people of God that he first showed them. Even as he directs them to do this, he knows they are unable to do it on their own. He promises to send the Advocate who will give them the power to live out the faith with which they have been entrusted. What does this mean for us?

The liturgical calendar moves the church through ongoing cycles of anticipation, celebration, and action. While there is much overlap between these cycles, this text in John 14 is used here to introduce months of ordinary time between the celebration of Pentecost and the coming of Advent. This window of time allows us to settle into the lessons gleaned from the high holy seasons in the preceding months.

Ordinary time is a blend of reflection and action that makes dedicated room for prayer, meditation, and congregational reflection on Jesus' love. It is an opportunity for the contemporary church to remember, prepare, and venture forward in Jesus' name. Setting aside this kind of time in congregational life can powerfully impact how we demonstrate the inclusivity, diversity, accountability, and compassion that characterized Jesus' love of the people. Imagined from this perspective, worship is one of the places where the fruit of this dedicated time of focus can become evident. Loving the people can look like inviting persons in our congregations who are often marginalized in worship to play active, central roles in liturgy.

Imagine how different the gospel may sound when we hear its nuances from the mouth of someone whose cadence is particular because they are reading from a braille Bible. Consider what new meanings may emerge about the Eucharist when persons whose humanity defies gender binaries serve communion as ordained deacons, elders, and ministers of the good news. Envision the presence of a young person (not only on Youth Sunday) regularly joining the pulpit alongside of adults to preach the Sunday morning sermon. These shifts in worship honor tradition by making room for the new ways in which the Advocate breaks through with the truth of God's love.

Jesus' command to love compels us to work within congregational life, but congregational life prepares us to demonstrate beyond the comfort of our own brick and mortar. It can equip us with a counternarrative for conversations that are often underscored by violence, fear, and apathy. In an analysis of the connection between violent language and violent acts, pediatrician and ordained pastor Michael Traylor writes, "When you regularly use the language of violence and degradation, you soon become participants in its degradation and pain, whether as victim or perpetrator."[2] Love calls us to heal this.

Loving the people involves rejecting all death-dealing practices, including, and perhaps even beginning with, the words we use to communicate with one another. Toni Morrison's thoughts on the power of language are helpful here. For her, words are the vehicle through which ideas gain their efficacy. She describes language as a contested site in which the use of power to secure the authority to speak often results in various forms of personal, intellectual, and spiritual annihilation. For her, language can either open up or shut down life. Relative to Jesus' command, language is a primary resource

in the act of love. In her Nobel Prize acceptance speech for *Beloved,* Morrison wrote,

> A dead language is not only one no longer spoken or written, it is unyielding language content to admire its own paralysis. Like statist language, censored and censoring. Ruthless in its policing duties, it has no desire or purpose other than maintaining the free range of its own narcotic narcissism, its own exclusivity and dominance. However moribund, it is not with effect for it actively thwarts the intellect, stalls conscience, suppresses human potential. Unreceptive to interrogation, it cannot form or tolerate new ideas, shape other thoughts, tell another story, fill baffling silences.[3]

The annihilating language that she describes has physical, spiritual, intellectual, cultural, and psychological fallout. "When you regularly use the language of violence and degradation," Traylor says, "you soon become participants in its degradation and pain, whether as victim or perpetrator." The speech Morrison describes is neither compassionate nor just, and it is an insufficient resource for cultivating love. Instead, it is a better fit for the process in which language is a key resource in maintaining and sustaining violence. Traylor maps out how this works: (1) Calling a group of people or an individual a derogatory name first creates psychological violence. (2) Psychological violence leads to moral violence. (3) Moral violence leads to physical, emotional, and sexual violence. Further, sexist, racist, homo/transphobic, ageist, classist, and ableist words are the vehicles through which stereotypes come to life. Words are powerful.

Jesus' commands to love have deep ecclesial and social implications during this season of ordinary time. His words about peace, however, invite a more personal reflection. After taking the disciples back through his teachings, Jesus reminds them, "Peace I leave with you; my peace I give to you. I do not give to you as the world gives. Do not let your hearts be troubled, and do not let them be afraid" (John 14:27).

---

2. Michael Traylor, "Stop the Language of Violence," *Sojourners,* July 3, 2012, https://sojo.net/articles/stop-language-violence.
3. https://www.nobelprize.org/nobel_prizes/literature/laureates/1993/morrison-lecture.html.

This peace is powerful. It safely takes us back through memories in our own walks with Jesus to bring out memories of the care, compassion, and healing God has shown us. When peace is this steadfast, the love we are called to demonstrate to the people of God cannot be weak or sentimental. Rather, it is a strong, deep, and healing love that brings us into communion with God and one another. This love is the sort of miracle that reminds us daily of the ongoing power of Christ at work in this world.

STEPHANIE M. CRUMPTON

Romans 8:14–17

¹⁴For all who are led by the Spirit of God are children of God. ¹⁵For you did not receive a spirit of slavery to fall back into fear, but you have received a spirit of adoption. When we cry, "Abba! Father!" ¹⁶it is that very Spirit bearing witness with our spirit that we are children of God, ¹⁷and if children, then heirs, heirs of God and joint heirs with Christ—if, in fact, we suffer with him so that we may also be glorified with him.

Commentary 1: Connecting the Reading with Scripture

The lectionary passage comes near the end of the broad sweep of Romans 1–8, in which Paul first demonstrates that Gentiles and Jews alike need a Savior and then expounds on the nature of Jesus Christ as Savior of all: "There is therefore now no condemnation for those who are in Christ Jesus" (8:1). Human beings have been transformed from enemies of God to those who have been justified by God and reconciled to God; the presence of the Spirit is the proof of that transformation. In this chapter, Paul celebrates the life that those who are "in Christ Jesus" have "in the Spirit."

In the Spirit. While the passages in Acts and John focus on the source and gift of the Spirit, Paul understands life "in the Spirit" or "led by the Spirit of God" to be a state of human existence, contrasted to living "according to the flesh" or "under the law." Paul is not specific about the relationship of the Spirit to the believer; in a few lines, he tells his audience that "you are in the Spirit" (v. 9), that the Spirit "dwells in you" (v. 9), and that they are "led by the Spirit" (v. 14). The Spirit functions to assist the individual believer; for example, "the Spirit helps us in our weakness" by interceding for us (v. 26), but the primary role of the Spirit is the building up of the church, the body of Christ.

A Spirit of Adoption. When people speak of adoption today, attention is generally focused on

the desire of would-be parents to create a family unit, or on the need for children to grow up in a stable and loving home. In ancient Rome, however, and particularly among higher-class families, adoption was a way for a family with no surviving sons to choose and designate an heir, a person who would become the paterfamilias, the head of the household, after the death of the current head. Frequently such a person would not be an infant; he might even be a grown man at the time of his adoption. Adoption was not a secret matter and did not carry any onus of shame, and the adopted person might retain a connection to his birth family. The emperor Augustus, a figure of very recent history to Paul's readers, was a famous adoptee, born and raised outside Rome and then adopted by his great-uncle, Julius Caesar.

The legal process of adoption, then, was less about establishing a family than it was about establishing an heir. Being adopted meant you had something to gain. People of humble circumstances would not have practiced adoption in this legal sense, even if they took the children of others into their homes and raised them as their own. They might, however, spin fantasies about someday being adopted by a family of means. Being adopted by God meant being a member of the most important family of all.

Slaves and Heirs. Paul frequently identifies himself as a "slave of Christ" (*doulos christou*), and speaks metaphorically of taking on slave status for the sake of the gospel (1 Cor. 9:19: "I have made myself a slave to all"). However, Paul is flexible in his use of metaphor, and here he makes use of the negative connotations slavery carried in the minds of his audience. His language invites us to imagine two members of a Roman household, both subservient to the head of the household, who in Roman law and tradition controlled all the household property as well as the household's other members. One of those household members is a slave. He remains subservient and without property, subject to the fear of violence and threatened violence upon which slavery is based, dependent on the decision of the master not only relative to the work that he does and his freedom of movement; but even in his most intimate relationships, since a master can permit or prevent slave marriages, or break up families by selling them apart.

The other household member is a son—in this case, an adopted son. He too is responsible to the head of the household as long as he remains a member of the household; technically he owns no property on his own and must behave in accordance with the father's decisions. However, the son has a goal that the slave will never possess: he is the heir and will someday become the household's head, owner of all its property, and director of all its functions.

"Abba! Father!" The first word is Aramaic, transliterated into Greek; the second, the Greek *patēr*. Here is a rare reminder that earliest Christianity was bilingual: Jesus, his disciples, and those around them spoke Aramaic; most of those who spread Jesus' message and wrote down his story spoke and wrote in Greek. (Paul's own first language was almost certainly Greek, although there is evidence that he knew Hebrew and Aramaic as well.) Both times Paul uses this phrase (here and in Gal. 4:6), it is in reference to the adopted children of God being enabled to say, "Abba! Father!" by the Spirit of God. Perhaps only children adopted past infancy and their families understand the startling significance of addressing someone as "father" or "mother" for the first time. This naming points to the family-creating aspect of adoption rather than its legal and economic aspect, which may also be the reason believers are called, literally, "sons of God" (*huioi theou*) in verse 14,[1] emphasizing the legal aspect of sonship, and "children of God" (*tekna theou*) in verse 16, emphasizing the emotional connection between parent and child.

It is, of course, impossible to know with certainty whether Paul knew Mark's story of Jesus' Gethsemane prayer, in which he addresses God as "Abba, Father" (Mark 14:36), since Paul relates very little of the story of Jesus apart from his death and resurrection. On the other hand, it may be that Paul had access to traditions that identified "Abba, Father" as part of Jesus' prayer language, but that have been lost to us except in the single Markan prayer. If so, Paul's claim that the Spirit leads believers to call out, "Abba! Father!" connects us even more closely with Christ, who is named as essentially our brother ("joint heir") in verse 17.

If We Suffer with Him. Paul concludes this soaring passage on a solemn note. We are, indeed, adopted into God's family, joint heirs with Christ, justified and sanctified. We also know that God's kingdom has not yet come. Our personal struggles, our struggles with evil in the world, our susceptibility to pain and disease, even harmful divisions within the body of Christ—these do not vanish because we are "led by the Spirit of God" (v. 14). Indeed, since we continue to experience suffering and see suffering around us, it is important to know that this is not all that God intends for us. Christ suffered, and we will suffer: that is the truth of this world. However, Christ also was glorified, and we will, indeed, be glorified as well.

SANDRA HACK POLASKI

---

1. The NRSV and some other modern translations use "children of God" to translate *huioi theou* in verse 14, an appropriate choice since the ancient Roman context is not immediately available to contemporary readers, and the English translation "sons of God" inappropriately implies that maleness is valued for its own sake.

Commentary 2: Connecting the Reading to the World

Although the shortest distance between two points is a straight line, this epistle reminds us that faith is not about the short trip. It is about finding and following the Spirit as we wind through life. This may be at play in the eighth chapter of Romans. Paul wants the community to know they belong to God, and how to make it through when they suffer for the sake of their faith. This is his message, but he takes the long route to get there.

Verses 14–17 are the focus for this entry in the Pentecost commentary. However, to get the full meaning of these verses, it is helpful to examine them as part of a larger section within this Letter to the Romans. Verses 14–17 are the conclusion of Paul's effort to lay out the contours of a choice: stay captive to flesh, which puts distance between us and God, or receive God's adoption of us through fellowship with Christ.

A key to understanding the persuasive power of his arguments lies in his capacity to engage language and concepts that are familiar to his intended audience to talk about how Christ's death and resurrection mean an end to being enslaved to sin. This is significant, given Paul's focus on how sin (symbolized by the will of the flesh) separates humanity from God. However, in Christ, believers are set free from sin and brought into communion with God. They are reclaimed as God's own, and as God's own they now have a new context for relating to their Creator. Paul instructs them that this is not just your God; this is your *Abba*.

Abba is the Aramaic word for father, and it is the same word that Jesus used to call out to God in the Garden of Gethsemane. *Abba*. The intimate cry comes from a raw and tender space. It speaks to a familiar tension in our faith lives: the comfort of intimacy with God, and the awareness of how deeply painful it is to be in a situation that warrants such an intense cry. This is the word that Paul uses as he talks about what it means to live for Christ, to suffer in Christ's name, and stay in a sacred covenant with the Creator.

When Paul invokes Jesus' distressed cry to God, *Abba*, he lets this community know that the God to whom Jesus cried out will also hear and answer them in times of distress. Revisiting this text reminds contemporary believers that we are part of the legacy that includes those who have endured the angst of sinful acts and evil structures, yet who have found resilience in knowing that God hears them. This points to the profound importance of making space for the faithful to lament.

American artist Kehinde Wiley's *Lamentations* visually invites communities to see and cry out to God about the predicament of social injustice. For many people, the twelve-foot-tall stained-glass images of contemporary African American bodies depicting the Madonna and child and the passion of Christ highlight the irony of faith in the face of injustice. The massive installations in the Petit Palais, Paris Museum of Fine Arts present international audiences with an opportunity to examine powerfully rich portrayals of brown skin. The images are vivid, large, and full of texture. For some observers, in one breath they smile deep and wide at the sight of that much beauty in one place; and in the next breath their exhales are filled with the sound of grief (*Abba*) over how that same skin invokes intense hatred; *Abba* over the predicaments of mass incarceration, racialized violence, structural poverty, internalized oppression, and many other struggles. For others it is a place to examine what it meant to know that although their social location and historical trajectories were different, the same *Abba* to whom they call, hears, sees, and answers the people of faith depicted in these complex images. Wiley's particular use of modern black women, men, and children to engage classic Christian iconography can be engaged as a commentary on what is at stake and what it takes to remain faithful in the face of suffering and injustice.

Emilie M. Townes, dean of the School of Divinity at Vanderbilt University, writes about the integral role that lament plays in keeping Christian communities honest in their covenant with God: "The need to cry to God with all of one's heart was natural. Also natural was a God who was deeply concerned about the cries of distress. There was (and is) no boundary that forbids lamentation."[2] By including the word *Abba*, Paul communicates that adoption does not exempt them from suffering, and they do not have to anguish in silence over it. Lament is a time of communal truth-telling that is often ugly and intense, yet here Paul convincingly argues for rather than against it, as the act that brings succor in the face of unjust suffering. In this light, verses 8–17 can be engaged as an important discourse about being made whole, the strength of community in times of distress, and what it takes to sustain genuine and honest covenant with God.

The focus on Romans 8 for the season of Pentecost affirms the gift of being brought into God, but it is also about the power of lament to help communities recover from brokenness and suffering. Ecclesial focus on this text can create an opportunity for a ministry to consider moments when it has not taken time to heal itself as it exists for the sake of Christ.

This is the kind of internal housekeeping that the church must undertake, given reports that Christianity is declining. The reasons for this decline are numerous, and the implications of this decline are significant, when we consider the views of younger Christians on whose shoulders the church's future sits. A Pew Research report indicates a significant decline in millennials who espouse any kind of religious affiliation.[3] The decline is real, but it does not mean they have walked away from God. Many claim a sense of being spiritual, but not religious. What the report does not address is the crisis of faith that many millennials experience over believing, while confronting the immense brokenness that persists, even as they do God's work in the world. In this regard a millennial *Abba* emerges from their own pain that is often related to grief they carry over injustice others suffer in the world. Dean Townes writes,

> laments mark the *beginning* of the healing process
> and people need and want to be healed
> If we learn anything from Joel . . .
> It is to know that healing of brokenness and injustice
> the healing of social sin and degradation
> the healing of spiritual doubts and fears
> begins with an unrestrained lament
> one that starts from our toenails and is a shout by the time it gets to
> the ends of the strands of our hair
> it's a lament of faith
> to the God of faith
> that we need help
> that we can't do this ministry alone
> we can't witness to the world in isolation
> we can't fight off the hordes of wickedness and hatred with a big stick
> we can't do this by ourselves anymore, God
> we need some divine help.[4]

Lament allows us to reach out to God, and find that our *Abba* has not let go.

STEPHANIE M. CRUMPTON

2. Emilie M. Townes, *Breaking the Fine Rain of Death: African American Health Issues and a Womanist Ethic of Care* (Eugene, OR: Wipf & Stock, 2006), 16.
3. "America's Changing Religious Landscape," Pew Research Center, May 12, 2105, http://www.pewforum.org/2015/05/12/americas-changing-religious-landscape/.
4. Townes, 12.

Contributors

CHARLES L. AARON JR., Associate Director of the Intern Program, Perkins School of Theology, Dallas, TX

ERIC D. BARRETO, Weyerhaeuser Associate Professor of New Testament, Princeton Theological Seminary, Princeton, NJ

MICHAEL BATTLE, Herbert Thompson Professor of Church and Society, and Director of the Desmond Tutu Center, General Theological Seminary, New York, NY

MARIANNE BLICKENSTAFF, Managing Editor, *Interpretation: A Journal of Bible and Theology*, Union Presbyterian Seminary, Richmond, VA

WALTER BRUEGGEMANN, William Marcellus McPheeters Professor Emeritus of Old Testament, Columbia Theological Seminary, Cincinnati, OH

LEIGH CAMPBELL-TAYLOR, Interim Pastor, Oakhurst Presbyterian Church, Decatur, GA

GREG CAREY, Professor of New Testament, Lancaster Theological Seminary, Lancaster, PA

GARY W. CHARLES, Pastor, Cove Presbyterian Church, Covesville, VA

ANDREW FOSTER CONNORS, Pastor and Head of Staff, Brown Memorial Park Avenue Presbyterian Church, Baltimore, MD

ADAM J. COPELAND, Director of the Center for Stewardship Leaders, Luther Seminary, St. Paul, MN

STEPHANIE M. CRUMPTON, Assistant Professor of Practical Theology, McCormick Theological Seminary, Chicago, IL

DAVID A. DAVIS, Pastor, Nassau Presbyterian Church, Princeton, NJ

JOSEPH A. DONNELLA II, Chaplain Emeritus and Adjunct Professor of Religious Studies, Gettysburg College, and Pastor, St. Mark's Evangelical Lutheran Church, Baltimore, MD

SHARYN DOWD, Retired Pastor and Professor, Decatur, GA

DAVID G. GARBER JR., Associate Professor of Old Testament and Hebrew, McAfee School of Theology at Mercer University, Atlanta, GA

MARCI AULD GLASS, Pastor, Southminster Presbyterian Church, Boise, ID

TIMOTHY GOMBIS, Professor of New Testament, Grand Rapids Theological Seminary, Grand Rapids, MI

WILLIAM GREENWAY, Professor of Philosophical Theology, Austin Presbyterian Theological Seminary, Austin, TX

A. KATHERINE GRIEB, Professor of New Testament, Virginia Theological Seminary, Alexandria, VA

CAROLYN B. HELSEL, Assistant Professor of Homiletics, Austin Presbyterian Theological Seminary, Austin, TX

PHILIP BROWNING HELSEL, Assistant Professor of Pastoral Care, Austin Presbyterian Theological Seminary, Austin, TX

LUCY LIND HOGAN, Hugh Latimer Elderdice Professor of Preaching and Worship, Wesley Theological Seminary, Washington, DC

CATHY CALDWELL HOOP, Pastor, Grace Presbyterian Church, Tuscaloosa, AL

CAMERON B. R. HOWARD, Associate Professor of Old Testament, Luther Seminary, St. Paul, MN

JAMES C. HOWELL, Senior Pastor, Myers Park United Methodist Church, Charlotte, NC

PATRICK W. T. JOHNSON, Pastor, First Presbyterian Church, Asheville, NC

BARBARA K. LUNDBLAD, Joe R. Engle Professor of Preaching Emerita, Union Theological Seminary, New York, NY

J. CLINTON MCCANN JR., Evangelical Professor of Biblical Interpretation, Eden Theological Seminary, St. Louis, MO

IAN A. MCFARLAND, Regius Professor of Divinity, University of Cambridge, Cambridge, UK

MARTHA L. MOORE-KEISH, J. B. Green Associate Professor of Theology, Columbia Theological Seminary, Decatur, GA

D. CAMERON MURCHISON, Professor Emeritus, Columbia Theological Seminary, Black Mountain, NC

ANNA B. OLSON, Rector, St. Mary's Episcopal Church, Los Angeles, CA

PETER J. PARIS, Elmer C. Homrighausen Professor of Social Ethics Emeritus, Princeton Theological Seminary, Princeton, NJ

AMY PLANTINGA PAUW, Henry P. Mobley Jr. Professor of Doctrinal Theology, Louisville Presbyterian Theological Seminary, Louisville, KY

ZAIDA MALDONADO PÉREZ, Retired Professor of Church History and Theology, Asbury Theological Seminary, Clermont, FL

SANDRA HACK POLASKI, Executive Director, Southeastern Commission for the Study of Religion, Richmond, VA

MARK PRICE, Pastor for Congregational Life, Christ United Methodist Church, Franklin, TN

GAIL RAMSHAW, Professor Emerita of Religion, La Salle University, Arlington, VA

CYNTHIA L. RIGBY, W. C. Brown Professor of Theology, Austin Presbyterian Theological Seminary, Austin, TX

RUTH FAITH SANTANA-GRACE, Executive Presbyter, Presbytery of Philadelphia, Philadelphia, PA

CAROLYN J. SHARP, Professor of Homiletics, Yale Divinity School, New Haven, CT

JOSEPH D. SMALL, Retired, Office of Theology and Worship, Presbyterian Church (U.S.A.), Louisville, KY

DENNIS E. SMITH†, LaDonna Kramer Meinders Professor Emeritus of New Testament, Phillips Theological Seminary, Tulsa, OK

SHANELL T. SMITH, Associate Professor of New Testament and Christian Origins, and Director, Cooperative Master of Divinity Program, Hartford Seminary, Hartford, CT

SHIVELY T. J. SMITH, Assistant Professor of New Testament, Wesley Theological Seminary, Washington, DC

F. SCOTT SPENCER, Professor of New Testament and Biblical Interpretation, Baptist Theological Seminary at Richmond, Richmond, VA

MARIANNE MEYE THOMPSON, George Eldon Ladd Professor of New Testament, Fuller Theological Seminary, Pasadena, CA

PATRICIA K. TULL, A. B. Rhodes Professor Emerita of Old Testament, Louisville Presbyterian Theological Seminary, Jeffersonville, IN

LEANNE VAN DYK, President and Professor of Theology, Columbia Theological Seminary, Decatur, GA

ERIC WALL, Assistant Professor of Sacred Music, and Dean of the Chapel, Austin Presbyterian Theological Seminary, Austin, TX

RICHARD F. WARD, Fred B. Craddock Professor of Homiletics and Worship, Phillips Theological Seminary, Tulsa, OK

BEVERLY ZINK-SAWYER, Professor Emerita of Preaching and Worship, Union Presbyterian Seminary, Richmond, VA

Author Index

Abbreviations

C1	Commentary 1	NT	New Testament
C2	Commentary 2	OT	Old Testament
E	Epistle	PS	Psalm
FR	First Reading (when not from the Old Testament)	SR	Second Reading (when not from the Epistles)
G	Gospel		

Numerals indicate numbered Sundays of a season; for example, "Lent 1" represents the first Sunday of Lent, and "Easter 2" the Second Sunday of Easter.

Contributors and entries

Charles L. Aaron Jr.	Liturgy of Passion OT C1, Holy Thursday OT C1, Good Friday OT C1
Eric D. Barreto	Ascension FR C1, Easter 7 FR C1
Michael Battle	Easter Day FR C2, Easter 2 SR C2, Easter 3 SR C2
Marianne Blickenstaff	Easter 4 FR C2, Easter 5 FR C2, Easter 6 FR C2
Walter Brueggemann	Easter Day OT C1, Easter 2 FR C1, Easter 3 FR C1
Leigh Campbell-Taylor	Lent 4 PS, Lent 5 PS
Greg Carey	Easter 4 SR C1, Easter 5 SR C1, Easter 6 SR C1
Gary W. Charles	Easter 4 FR C1, Easter 5 FR C1, Easter 6 FR C1
Andrew Foster Connors	Ascension FR C2, Easter 7 FR C2
Adam J. Copeland	Lent 3 G C2, Lent 4 G C2, Lent 5 G C2
Stephanie M. Crumpton	Pentecost FR C2, Pentecost G C2, Pentecost E C2
David A. Davis	Lent 3 OT C2, Lent 4 OT C2, Lent 5 OT C2
Joseph A. Donnella II	Holy Thursday PS, Good Friday PS, Easter Day PS
Sharyn Dowd	Ascension E C1, Easter 7 SR C1
David G. Garber Jr.	Liturgy of Passion OT C2, Holy Thursday OT C2, Good Friday OT C2
Marci Auld Glass	Easter 2 PS, Easter 3 PS, Easter 4 PS, Easter 5 PS
Timothy Gombis	Ascension E C2, Easter 7 SR C2
William Greenway	Ash Wednesday OT C2, Lent 1 OT C2, Lent 2 OT C2, Lent 3 E C1, Lent 4 E C1, Lent 5 E C1

A. Katherine Grieb   Easter Day FR C1, Easter 2 SR C1, Easter 3 SR C1

Carolyn B. Helsel   Easter 4 G C1, Easter 5 G C1, Easter 6 G C1

Philip Browning Helsel   Easter 6 G C1, Ascension E C2, Easter 7 G C2

Lucy Lind Hogan   Liturgy of Palms G C2, Liturgy of Passion G C2, Liturgy of Passion G C2

Cathy Caldwell Hoop   Easter Day OT C2, Easter 2 FR C2, Easter 3 FR C2

Cameron B. R. Howard   Pentecost OT C1

James C. Howell   Ash Wednesday G C2, Lent 1 G C2, Lent 2 G C2

Patrick W. T. Johnson   Liturgy of Palms G C1, Liturgy of Passion G C1, Liturgy of Passion G C1

Barbara K. Lundblad   Ash Wednesday E C1, Lent 1 E C1, Lent 2 E C1

J. Clinton McCann Jr.   Ash Wednesday PS, Lent 1 PS, Lent 2 PS, Lent 3 PS

Ian A. McFarland   Holy Thursday G C2, Good Friday G C2

Martha L. Moore-Keish   Ash Wednesday OT C1, Lent 2 G C1

D. Cameron Murchison   Lent 4 G C1

Anna B. Olson   Ash Wednesday E C2, Lent 1 E C2, Lent 2 E C2

Peter J. Paris   Ash Wednesday OT C2, Lent 2 G C2

Amy Plantinga Pauw   Easter Day G C2, Easter 2 G C2, Easter 3 G C2

Zaida Maldonado Pérez   Holy Thursday G C1, Good Friday G C1

Sandra Hack Polaski   Pentecost FR C1, Pentecost G C1, Pentecost E C1

Mark Price   Easter 4 G C2, Easter 5 G C2, Easter 6 G C2

Gail Ramshaw   Easter 6 PS, Ascension PS, Easter 7 PS, Pentecost PS

Cynthia L. Rigby   Liturgy of Passion E C2, Holy Thursday E C2, Good Friday E C2

Ruth Faith Santana-Grace   Easter 4 SR C2, Easter 5 SR C2, Easter 6 SR C2

Carolyn J. Sharp   Ash Wednesday OT C1, Lent 1 OT C1, Lent 2 OT C1

Joseph D. Small   Easter Day E C2, Easter Day G C2

Dennis E. Smith†   Lent 3 G C1, Lent 5 G C1

Shanell T. Smith   Liturgy of Passion E C1, Holy Thursday E C1, Good Friday E C1

Shively T. J. Smith   Ash Wednesday G C1, Lent 1 G C1, Lent 2 G C1

F. Scott Spencer   Easter 6 G C1, Ascension G C1, Easter 7 G C1

Marianne Meye Thompson   Easter Day G C1, Easter 2 G C1, Easter 3 G C1

Patricia K. Tull   Lent 3 OT C1, Lent 4 OT C1, Lent 5 OT C1

Leanne Van Dyk   Pentecost OT C2

Eric Wall   Liturgy of Palms PS, Liturgy of Passion PS

Richard F. Ward   Lent 3 E C2, Lent 4 E C2 ,Lent 5 E C2

Beverly Zink-Sawyer   Easter Day E C1, Easter Day G C1

Scripture Index

Scripture citations that appear in boldface represent the assigned readings from the Revised Common Lectionary.

OLD TESTAMENT

Genesis

Genesis	25
1	141
1:1–2	282
1:2	324
1:6–10	282
1:9–10	259
1:20–23	282
1:26	318
2:7	195, 212
3	193, 272, 319
3:16	177
3:22–24	310
4	17
6–8	139
8:20–22	24
10	319
11:1–9	**318–23,** 327
11:10	319
11:31	26
12:1	289
12:1–3	43
12:1–4	46
12:2	41
12:2–3	194
12:3	139, 251
12:10–20	26, 40
13–14	40
14	166
14:17–24	165
15:1	250
15:1–2	**40–44,** 46–47
15:13–16	42
15:17–18	**40–44,** 46–47
15:17–19	47
16	41
17	222
17:15–16	194
17:17	41
18:11	41
20	40
21:8–14	41
22:1–18	46
22:18	251
24:4	26
24:10	26
26	40
28–31	26
32	222
37	97
37–50	201
46:27	26
47:29–49:33	262

Exodus

Exodus	76
1	5
2:23–25	138
3:7	131
3:8	26
3:8–10	22
3:12	131
3:13–14	172
3:17	26
4:13	117
7:5	139
12:1–14	**138–42,** 146
12:11	152
12:21–28	139
12:22	173
12:29–32	139
12:48	76
13:1	36
13:5	26
13:21	42, 59
14–15	94
14:11–12	36
15:2	182
15:24–26	16
16	79
16:1–3	36
16:3–4	16
16:4	77
16:9–10	36
16:11–17	36
16:18	77
16:23	36
16:25–26	36
16:29–30	36
16:35	76
19	275
19:1–6	138
19:5	158
19:6	139, 185, 208
19:9	59
19:10–25	24
19:16	3
19:19	3
20:1–17	8
20:18	3
20:8–11	5, 36, 77
22:21–24	5, 16
22:21–27	16
22:22	236
23:10–11	77
23:12	77
24:3	8
24:7	8
24:18–25:1	36
24:32–34	8
31:13–17	36
32–34	8
32:6	68
32:35	69
33:2–3	26
33:15	117
34:6–7	8, 67
34:9	67
34:28	36
40:30	94

Leviticus

Leviticus	76
1–7	8
16	158, 165
19:9–10	5, 77
19:18	263
19:33–34	5
23:9–10	193
25:4	77
25:10	77

Numbers 76
6:24–26 272
10:8 21
29:1 21

Deuteronomy 27, 76, 319
2:14 283
4:37 139
5:12–15 5, 77
5:15 94, 96
6:4 184
6:13 36
6:16 36
7:1 24
7:2 139
7:7–11 158
7:18–19 94
8:3 36
10:18–20 16
11:18 33
15:15 94
16:3 94
20:17 24
24:17–18 16
24:17–21 236
24:19–22 77
25:17–19 25
26:1–11 **24–30**
26:9 62
26:10 27
26:11 43
26:12 28
27:19 16
30 32
30:11–14 31
32 94
32:11 53

Joshua 25, 139
1:9 244
3:10 139
4 81
5:9 81
5:9–12 **76–79**, 85
5:10–12 81
6 81
22–24 262

Judges 139

1 Samuel 139
6 112
11:11 319
15:22 8

2 Samuel 139
3:33–34 52
11–12 8

13:1–22 159

1 Kings 139, 319
6 247
1:28–40 112
17:17–22 236
19:11–13 275

2 Kings 139, 319
2 278
4:1–37 201
4:32–35 236
5:10–14 201
9:13 112
17:20 157

1 Chronicles
16:12 96
28–29 262

2 Chronicles
3 247

Nehemiah
9:26 53

Job
24:21 236
38:11 293

Psalms 130, 275
2:12 29
3 52
5:7 67
5:11 29
7:1 29
11:1 29
13 52
13:5 67
22 52, 155, **161–64**, 172
22:3 225
22:7 135
22:17–18 135
23 233, 234–35, **237–39**, 245
27 40, **45–47**, 58
28 52
30 216, **221–23**
30:5 218
30:9 228
31 122, 135
31:5 30
31:9–16 115, 117–18, **120–21**
31:24 47
32 76, **80–82**, 85, 88
33:5 67

36:5 67
41:13 242
42–44 52
47 286, **291–95**
47:1 287
47:5 295
47:8 295
50:14 8
50:23 8
51 52, 158
51:1–17 2, **7–9**
51:19 8
63:1–8 61, **66–68**
67 266, 269, **271–72**, 274–75
67:2–3 269
67:5 269
68:5 236
69:1 66, 319
81:3 21
86:9 251
86:15 20
89:3 62
89:19–20 62
89:33 62
89:38 62
89:38–51 30
89:49 62
90–91 30
90:1 30
91:1–2 24, **29–30**
91:9 30
91:9–12 36
91:9–16 24, **29–30**
91:11–12 29–30, 32
93 286, **291–95**
97 302, **307–9**
97:7 310
100:5 67
103:8 20
104 324
104:24–35 318, **323–25**
105:10 63
106:48 242
110:1 130, 193, 295–96
116:1–2 137, **143–46**
116:3 144
116:12–19 137, **143–46**
117–18 151
118 110, 112, 121
118:1 190
118:1–2 **108–10**, 176–77, 181–82
118:1–4 67
118:14 193
118:14–24 176, **181–82**
118:14–29 200, **204–6**
118:15–16 201

118:17	193	42:1	3, 62
118:19–29	**108–10**	42:1–4	116, 156
118:22	213	42:1–9	117, 158
118:22–24	190	42:3	94
118:23	193	42:6	63
118:25–26	201	42:9	178
118:29	177	42:19	3, 62
126	93, **97–100**	43:9–10	202
126:5	105	43:9–20	99
133:1–2	239	**43:16–21**	**93–99**, 178
137	52	43:19	98, 105, 116
137:5–6	94	43:20	62, 99
144:6	319	43:21	98
145:8	20	43:25	63
148	249, 251, **254–56**,	44:1–2	3
	259, 263	44:3	62, 310, 328
150	200, **204–6**	44:8	202
		44:9–20	116
Proverbs		44:21	3, 62
9:5–6	62	44:22	63
17:2	41	45:4	3, 62
		46	94
Ecclesiastes	141	46:1–7	116
		46:8–9	94
Isaiah	20, 129, 275	46:9	96
1	177	48:6	178
1–39	61, 177	48:20	62
1:1	251	48:21	62
1:4–5	20	49:1–6	156
1:10	177	49:1–13	117, 158
1:10–20	8	49:3	3, 62
1:11	42	49:3–6	116
1:16	20	49:6	62–63
1:17	42, 236	49:10	62
2:2–4	63	50	122
2:3	251	50:1–3	116
6	208, 224	**50:4–9**	**115–20**, 130,
7:12	36		156, 158
9:2–7	178	50:6	117
9:7	332	50:7	111
12:3	310	50:7–8	130
14:12	310	50:10–11	116
20:3	3	52	156
26:19	193	52–54	157
27:1	324	52:7–10	178
28:16	31	52:13	3, 172
31:5	53	**52:13–53:12**	116–17,
37:33–38	177		**155–60**, 163–64
39:1–8	177	52:14–15	163
40–55	61, 93, 116	53:6	172
40–66	177	53:8	163
40:1–5	116	53:11	3, 163, 172
40:2	63	53:12	135
40:26	94	54	156–57
41:8–9	3	54:17	3
41:10	46	55:1	310
41:13–14	46	**55:1–9**	**61–68**, 116
41:17–18	62	56–66	3, 61

56:3–6	177		
58	3		
58:1–2	17		
58:1–12	**2–6**, 8–9, 30		
58:5–9	177		
58:13–14	8		
60:2–3	274		
60:3	63, 244		
60:6–11	177		
61:1	73		
61:2	177		
61:6	208		
61:8	63		
61:10	258, 273		
62:2	178		
62:4	177, 178		
62:5	258, 273		
62:6–12	178		
65	83, 193		
65:8	3		
65:13–14	3		
65:17	182, 190, 259		
65:17–25	**176–80**		
65:22	83		
65:25	84		
Jeremiah	319		
1:6	117		
1:4–10	208		
1:18	136		
2:2	258		
2:13	310		
4:23–26	52		
14:14	251		
16:14–15	94		
17:13	310		
20:7–18	117		
23:1–2	246		
23:7–8	94		
30:3	178		
30:18	178		
31:33	33		
32:40	63		
33:7	178		
33:11	178		
33:26	178		
34:18–20	42		
38:22	52		
50:5	63		
Lamentations	129		
2:9	251		
5:4	62		
5:20–22	94		
Ezekiel	319		
1	224		
1–2	208		

Ezekiel (*continued*)
9:4 — 141
12:7 — 141
16:60 — 63
34:1–6 — 246
34:16 — 178
36:26–27 — 328
36:28–32 — 178
37:1–14 — 178, 195
37:26 — 63
40–48 — 274
43–44 — 178
47:1–12 — 178

Daniel — 273
1 — 201
3 — 203
3:16–18 — 201
4:27 — 201
7:10 — 225
7:13 — 130, 208
11:33–35 — 117
12:2 — 117, 158, 193

Hosea
2:23 — 185
6:6 — 8
11:9 — 67
12:12 — 26

Joel
1:1–20 — 20
2:1–2 — 2, 17, **19–23**
2:12–17 — 2, 17, **19–23**
2:18–27 — 20
2:28 — 97
2:28–29 — 326–27
2:31 — 324–25
2:32 — 31, 185
3 — 20

Amos
5:1–3 — 53
5:16–20 — 53
5:21–24 — 3, 8
7:10–17 — 201
7:14–17 — 208

Jonah
4:2–3 — 20

Micah
1:2–16 — 53
2:6 — 4
3:11 — 4
4:1–2 — 251
4:2 — 244

6:6–7 — 4
6:6–8 — 8
6:8 — 123, 277

Habakkuk
2:11 — 112

Zechariah
9:9 — 112
12:10 — 208

Malachi — 20
4:5–6 — 20

NEW TESTAMENT

Matthew — 53
1 — 41
3:2 — 21
3:7 — 53
3:13 — 16
4:1–11 — 35
4:2 — 15
4:12–13 — 16
4:17 — 21
4:23 — 16
5–7 — 16, 275
5:1–2 — 16
5:3–12 — 275
5:9 — 279
5:13–16 — 151
5:43–44 — 84
6:1–6 — 2, **15–18**, 21
6:2–18 — 16
6:9–13 — 313
6:16–21 — 2, **15–18**, 21
9:13 — 226–27
10:34 — 279
12:10 — 283
15:21–28 — 252
16:18 — 231
17:1–13 — 275
21:8 — 112
23:26–27 — 53
25 — 6
25:31–46 — 160, 226, 227
25:34–36 — 210
25:36 — 235
26:17–30 — 141
26:36–38 — 151
26:36–42 — 313
26:38 — 151
26:39 — 172
27:46–48 — 173
27:50 — 173
27:57 — 174

28 — 196
28:16 — 275

Mark — 53
1:12–13 — 35
1:13 — 15
2:3–4 — 283
2:19–20 — 258
3:3 — 283
4:35–41 — 259
5:36 — 46
5:40–41 — 234
7:24–30 — 252
8:31–32 — 131
9:33 — 37
10:1 — 37
10:43–44 — 105
11:8 — 112
12:41–44 — 6, 26
12:42 — 236
14:3–9 — 104–5
14:12–25 — 141
14:32–36 — 313
14:34 — 151
14:36 — 172, 337
15:34–36 — 173
15:37 — 173
15:43 — 174
15:46 — 105
16 — 196
16:1 — 105

Luke — 36, 270
1–2 — 196
1:1–4 — 286
1:1–4:1 — 271
1:8 — 36
1:8–9 — 53
1:11 — 197
1:26 — 197
1:30 — 46
1:32 — 112
1:35 — 58, 299
1:37 — 252
1:48 — 267
1:53 — 267
1:55 — 287
1:80 — 36
2:7 — 136
2:9 — 197
2:10 — 46
2:21–24 — 52
2:22–38 — 36
2:25–38 — 130
2:34 — 111
2:38 — 111
3 — 57

3:1	134	9:20	113
3:1–20	53	9:20–21	58
3:2	36	9:22	53, 136–37,
3:4	36		197
3:16	328	9:23	30, 135–36
3:22	57, 136, 299, 328	9:23–24	58
4:1	299, 328	**9:28–36**	40, **57–60**, 197
4:1–13	24, 29, 32,	9:29–30	197
	35–39	9:33	186
4:2	15	9:34	287
4:10	287	**9:37–43**	40, **57–60**
4:10–11	29–30, 32	9:44	57
4:13	136	9:51	52, 57, 117, 129
4:14	328	9:51–19:27	111
4:15–17	52	9:51–19:28	37, 53
4:18	73	9:53	129
4:18–19	6, 299	9:58–62	52
4:18–21	328	10:1–12	52, 129
4:21	135	10:13–15	52
4:42	36	10:17–2	52
5:8	131	10:25–37	52
5:14–15	84	10:38–42	52, 105, 196
5:16	36	11–24	288
5:17	53	11:2–4	52, 313
5:29–30	250	11:13	271, 299
5:29–32	73	11:14–23	52
6:6	283	11:25–26	104
6:8	283	11:29	134
6:14–16	327	11:37	53
6:20	73	11:41	16
6:22	137	11:42–44	52
6:24	73	11:53	53
6:24–25	267	12:2–12	52
6:27	84	12:3	16
6:43–45	72	12:13	112
7:11–15	236	13	55
7:11–17	196	13:1	134
7:19	113	**13:1–9**	61, 68, **72–75**
7:22	73	13:10	52
7:24	36	13:10–17	52
7:34	73	13:18–21	52
7:36	53	13:22	53
7:36–50	105, 196, 270	13:31	53
7:37	191	13:31–33	134
7:46	105	**13:31–35**	40, **52–56**
8:1–3	196	14:1	53
8:3	134	14:13	73
8:40–42	196	14:15–24	73
8:41–42	236	14:27	135–36
8:43–48	196	**15:1–3**	76, 85, **87–92**
8:49–55	236	**15:11–32**	76, 85, **87–92**
8:49–56	196	15:17	81
9:1–3	129	16:14	53
9:7–9	53	16:19–31	73
9:9	134	16:27–31	73
9:16	131	16:29	58
9:18–23	57	16:31	58

17:11	53		
17:20	53		
18:10–14	53		
18:18–25	73		
18:33	53		
19	267		
19:1–10	73, 270		
19:28–40	**111–14**		
19:38	114		
19:39–40	105		
20:37	58		
21:1–4	6, 26		
22–23	122		
22:3	136		
22:8–13	114		
22:14–20	199		
22:14–23	141		
22:14–23:56	115, 118,		
	126–32		
22:20	263		
22:39–42	313		
22:41–45	151		
22:42	136, 172		
22:44	151		
22:53	135		
22:60	186		
22:61	249		
22:63	117		
22:65	117		
22:66–71	134		
23:1–49	115, **133–37**		
23:34	267		
23:46	30		
23:50–51	174		
23:53	136		
23:55	196, 199		
23:56	197		
24:1–10	298		
24:1–12	176, **196–99**		
24:4–5	58, 193		
24:5	136		
24:13–32	298		
24:27	58		
24:36–40	298		
24:44	58		
24:52	53		
24:52–53	37		
24:19	198		
24:21	198		
24:27	198		
24:30	198		
24:31	298		
24:33–49	298		
24:41–43	299		
24:44–53	286, 294–95,		
	298–301		
24:51	295		

John

1	222	7:37	282	12:25–26	151
1:1	151, 172, 212, 279	7:37–39	283, 310	12:27	152, 172, 313
1:1–4	314	8:12	284	12:27–34	140
1:1–5	314	8:28	173	12:28	152
1:4	152	8:31	332	12:31	152, 172
1:11	172–73	8:43	151	12:32	172–73
1:12	191	8:50	315	12:35	284
1:13	172	8:54	315	12:43	172
1:14	152, 172, 213, 314	9	246, 282	13–14	283
1:15	172	9:5	104	13–17	171, 313
1:17	172	9:6–7	283	13:1	282
1:18	151, 314	9:22	174	13:1–7	146
1:29	152, 212	9:35	247	13:1–11	105
1:32–33	278	9:35–38	189	**13:1–17**	137, 140, 146,
1:33	332	9:39	219		**150–54**
1:38	189	10	245	13:1–30	263–64
1:43	230	10:1–9	282	13:5–15	283
2:1–11	282	10:3	239	13:8	151
2:6	229	10:3–5	189	13:12–16	153
2:6–11	283	10:7	247	13:13	152
2:11	314	10:10	153	13:13–14	189
2:13	282	10:11	152	13:14–16	105
2:14	282	10:11–18	235	13:16	151, 154
2:17–22	190	10:11–21	247	13:17	151
2:23	282	10:14	247	13:21	151
3–4	331	10:16	232	13:21–30	152
3:1–21	263	10:17–18	173	13:27	262
3:5	283	10:18	172	13:29	282
3:14	173	10:19	172	**13:31–35**	138, 140, 146,
3:16	190, 231	10:22	282		**150–54**, 249, 259,
3:29	258	**10:22–30**	233, 234–35,		**262–65**, 315
4:1–42	263		**245–48**	13:32	152
4:4–15	283	10:31	247	13:34	145, 251
4:10	310	11	246	13:37	231
4:14	173, 310	11:1–44	236, 282	14	281
4:25–26	189	11:2	106	14–17	262, 280
4:26	152, 189	11:9–10	284	14:1	280
4:29	189, 283	11:16	211	14:5	211
4:45	282	11:23–27	189	14:5–6	331
4:46–54	282	11:25–27	189	14:6	172, 331
5:1–9	266, **282–85**	11:28	189	**14:8–17**	318, **331–36**
5:1–18	282	11:39–44	284	14:9	214
5:17	282	11:45–53	106	14:12	281
5:18	172	11:49–53	135	14:15	229, 281
5:38	332	11:55	282	14:17	211
5:41	315	12	151–52	14:18	281
5:44	315	12:1	282	14:21–24	229
6:1–15	104, 282	12:1–3	99	**14:23–29**	266, 274, **278–81**
6:4	282	**12:1–8**	93, **104–107**	**14:25–27**	318, **331–36**
6:13	229	12:11	172	14:26	211, 269
6:16–21	282–83	12:12	282	14:27	214, 334
6:22–59	104	12:12–19	105	14:30	172
6:39	229	12:16	190	14:31	172
6:51	131	12:19	172	15:1–17	314
7:1–14	282	12:20	282	15:5	331
7:13	174	12:23	152	15:12	145, 331
		12:23–32	315	15:12–15	314–15

15:13	152, 231	1:9	295	16:9	283, 303
15:14–15	151	1:9–11	299	16:9–10	266
15:26	211	1:10	197	**16:9–15**	**266–70**
16:11	172	1:11	299	16:12–15	303
16:13	211	1:15	129, 327	16:14–15	73
16:20	188	2	235	**16:16–34**	**302–11**, 314
16:22	214	2:1–4	299	16:35–40	303
16:33	211, 331	**2:1–21**	318, 320, 323,	16:40	73, 268
17:2	315		**326–30**, 336	17:2	269
17:5	314	2:6	284	18:7	267
17:12	229, 313	2:19–20	324	22	287
17:20–26	302, 309,	2:21	185	26	287
	311, **313–17**	2:44–47	73	26:20	72
17:22	331	3:6	287	28	287
18–19	155, 158,	3:11	245	28:31	303
	165, **169–75**	5	206		
18:1–14	313	5:12	205	**Romans**	
18:9	229	5:15	205	1–8	336
18:15–18	229	5:20	206	1:5–6	31
18:25–27	229, 231	**5:27–32**	**200–203**, 205–6	1:10	31
18:28	282	5:38–39	206	1:13	31
18:33–38	105	5:40	203	1:16	241
18:38	172	6:5–8	84	2:17–3:31	101
18:39	282	7:56	287	2:29	101
19:6	172	7:60	84	3	185
19:7	172	8:1–3	129	3–4	43
19:14	282	8:3	84	3:21–26	184
19:25	191	8:26	289	3:23	84
19:37	208	9	222, 287	4	41
20	196	9–10	183	4:3	46
20:1–18	176, **188–91**,	**9:1–20**	**216–20**, 229–30	4:9	43
	214, 230	9:17	271	4:16–17	44
20:3–10	230	9:18	267	4:21	46
20:18–19	213	9:36	239	5:8	69
20:19	332	9:36–40	269	6:4	194
20:19–31	200, **211–15**, 230	**9:36–43**	**233–36**, 239	8	339
20:22	279, 332	10	250, 263, 267	8:1	336
20:28	230	10–11	252	8:8–17	339
20:30–31	189, 231	10:1–33	186	8:9	336
20:31	172, 279	10:2	267	8:10	147
21	191, 219	10:10	266	**8:14–17**	318, **336–39**
21:1–19	216, **228–32**	10:34	190	8:23	194
21:7	218	**10:34–43**	176, **183–87**	8:26	336
21:15–19	235	10:40	193	8:35–39	69
21:20–22	231	10:41	186, 189–90	9–11	32
21:20–25	230	10:48	252	9:1	32
21:22	230	11	255, 263	9:3	32
21:24–25	231	**11:1–18**	**249–53**	10:6–7	31
21:25	231–32	11:12	256	**10:8–13**	24, **31–34**, 32n2
		12:1–5	129	11:1–15	32
Acts	36, 270, 332	13:9	222	11:2	32
1:1–11	**286–90**, 294–95, 300	15	217, 250, 266	11:16–19	241
1:2	299	15:23	129	11:36	32
1:4–5	299	15:32	129	14:17	332
1:6–11	197	16	279	15:13	218
1:8	266, 299, 327	16:6	267	15:23–24	31
1:8–11	298	16:6–7	266	16:1–16	269

1 Corinthians
1:11 — 192
1:11–17 — 147
1:12–13 — 10
1:13 — 147
1:18 — 103, 140
1:26–31 — 233
2:8 — 242
4:5 — 151
7:1 — 11
8:5 — 70
9:19 — 337
10:1–13 — 61, **68–72**
10:6 — 72
10:14 — 70
11:18–22 — 140
11:21 — 149
11:21–22 — 146
11:23–26 — 137, 140–42, **146–49**, 151, 199
11:25 — 178, 263
11:26 — 259
11:27–30 — 147
11:33 — 146
11:34 — 147
12:27 — 11
12 — 149
13 — 11, 68–69
14:1–25 — 147
15:1–6 — 199
15:1–11 — 192
15:12 — 194
15:12–18 — 192
15:17 — 193
15:19–26 — 176, **192–95**
15:22–23 — 190
15:24–27 — 194
15:26 — 177
15:35 — 195
15:54–55 — 177
15:57 — 194

2 Corinthians — 11
4:7 — 10
5:6–10 — 12
5:14–15 — 83
5:16 — 103
5:16–21 — 76, **83–86**, 90
5:18–19 — 10
5:19 — 21
5:20 — 86
5:20–6:10 — 2, **10–14**, 17, 20
5:21 — 20
6:4–5 — 48
11:2 — 258
11:3–6 — 12

11:23–28 — 12, 48
11:30 — 12
13:10 — 11–12

Galatians
1:12 — 147
1:13–16 — 32
2:1–3 — 295
2:1–14 — 251
2:11–14 — 252
3 — 41
3:6 — 46
3:27–28 — 250
3:27–29 — 267
3:28 — 31
4:5 — 44
4:6 — 337
5:20 — 295
6:4 — 147

Ephesians
1:3–14 — 294
1:5 — 44
1:9 — 294
1:13 — 295
1:15–23 — 286, **294–97**
1:20–23 — 295
2 — 185
2:4–9 — 295
2:11 — 185
2:12 — 185, 295
2:14 — 185
3:2–13 — 296
3:14–21 — 295
4:18 — 295
5:7–14 — 151
5:22–33 — 258
6:10–17 — 295
6:10–18 — 296

Philippians
1:3–4 — 123
1:5 — 123
1:11 — 123
1:12–13 — 48
1:15 — 48
1:18 — 48
1:19 — 123
1:27 — 48
2 — 38
2:2 — 48
2:2–3 — 123
2:3 — 101
2:4–5 — 83
2:5 — 48, 118
2:5–7 — 48

2:5–11 — 100, 115, 117, **122–25**, 130
2:6–11 — 69
2:8 — 83, 184
2:9 — 295
2:10 — 117
2:13 — 123
2:14 — 123
2:15 — 123
2:19–30 — 100
3:1 — 48, 100
3:2 — 48–49, 102
3:2–3 — 101
3:3 — 49, 123
3:4–14 — 93, **100–103**
3:5 — 44, 49
3:5–6 — 48, 99
3:9 — 49, 123
3:10 — 105
3:13–14 — 99, 124
3:15 — 48
3:17 — 123
3:17–4:1 — 40, **48–51**
3:18 — 50
3:20 — 51
4:2 — 48

Colossians
2:15 — 226

1 Timothy
1:17 — 242

Hebrews
2:14 — 226
2:17 — 165
4:2 — 166
4:14–16 — 155, 158, **164–68**
5:7–9 — 155, 158, **164–68**
5:9 — 173
5:11–12 — 165
5:14 — 165
6:1 — 166
6:12 — 166
7:13–17 — 166
8:8–12 — 178
10:16–25 — 155, 158, **164–68**
11 — 101, 166
11:1 — 47, 166
11:4–39 — 166
11:8–12 — 47
11:11 — 41
11:32–40 — 101
12:24 — 263

James
3:23 — 46

1 Peter
2:9–10 — 185

2 Peter
1:19 — 310
3:13 — 259
3:18 — 242

1 John
2:9–11 — 151
2:11 — 151
2:19 — 151
2:26 — 151
2:29 — 151
3 — 151
3:17 — 151
3:23 — 152
4:1–6 — 151
4:8 — 314
4:10 — 69

2 John
6 — 151

Revelation — 273, 275, 312
1:1 — 273, 310
1:1–3 — 207–8
1:4–8 — 200, 201, **207–10**
1:5 — 213, 257
1:8 — 309
1:8–9 — 209
1:11–12 — 208
1:16 — 208
1:17 — 309
1:20 — 208
2–3 — 208, 274
2:1 — 208
2:17 — 242
2:19–29 — 267
2:20–23 — 258
2:28 — 310
3:4–5 — 242
3:11 — 309–10
3:18 — 242
4–5 — 225
4:4 — 242
4:6 — 260
4:6–11 — 224
4:8–11 — 241
5:1 — 224–25
5:5 — 226

5:5–6 — 225
5:6 — 226
5:9 — 241
5:9–10 — 225
5:9–13 — 241
5:11–14 — 216, **224–27**
5:12–13 — 218, 230
6:1–8 — 227
6:9–11 — 241
6:12–17 — 240
6:16 — 240
7:1–17 — 240–41
7:9 — 235
7:9–14 — 309
7:9–17 — 233, 234–35, **240–44**
7:12 — 242
7:16–17 — 227
8:1 — 240
9:4 — 241
10:11 — 241
11:7 — 260
11:9 — 241
11:15–18 — 242
12:1–17 — 258
12:10–11 — 274
12:11 — 242, 257
13 — 273
13:1 — 260
13:4 — 242, 257
13:7 — 241, 257
13:11–18 — 242
13:16–17 — 241
14:1 — 241
14:6 — 241
14:9 — 241
14:9–11 — 242
15:3–4 — 242
16:5–7 — 242
17–18 — 258, 273
17:4–6 — 274
17:15 — 241
18:4 — 242
18:11–13 — 258–59
18:12–13 — 274
19:1–8 — 242
19:14 — 242
20:4 — 241
21:1 — 251
21:1–2 — 283
21:1–5 — 236
21:1–6 — 249, 251, **257–61**, 263
21:1–7 — 177
21:3–4 — 251

21:5 — 253
21:6 — 309
21:7 — 257
21:7–8 — 258
21:9 — 273
21:10 — 266, **273–77**
21:16 — 274
21:18 — 274
21:21 — 274
21:22–22:2 — 258
21:22–22:5 — 266, **273–77**
21:23–24 — 269
21:24 — 269
21:25–26 — 270
22:1–2 — 178
22:2 — 241
22:4 — 241
22:6–21 — 309
22:7 — 310
22:12 — 310
22:12–14 — 302, **309–12**
22:15 — 310
22:16–17 — 302, **309–12**
22:20–21 — 302, **309–12**
22:21 — 208

OT APOCRYPHA

Tobit
1:3 — 16
1:16 — 16
4:6–8 — 16
4:16–17 — 16
14:10–11 — 16

Sirach
12:3 — 16
35:3 — 16
40:17 — 16
40:24 — 16

1 Maccabees
4:52–59 — 245

OT PSEUDEPIGRAPHA

Jubilees
10 — 262
20–22 — 262
20:2 — 262
35–26 — 262
36:3–4 — 262